The Encyclopedia
of Edible Plants
of North America

Purchased with funds from the
Wyoming Community Foundation
McMurry Library Endowment.

"A PUBLIC LIBRARY IS THE NEVER FAILING
SPRING IN THE DESERT." ANDREW CARNEGIE

1910
1970

CARNEGIE LIBRARY

CASPER, WYOMING

The Encyclopedia of Edible Plants of North America

FRANÇOIS COUPLAN, PH.D.

KEATS PUBLISHING
NEW CANAAN, CONNECTICUT

This book is dedicated to the memory of Buzz Erikson.

THE ENCYCLOPEDIA OF EDIBLE PLANTS OF NORTH AMERICA

Copyright © 1998 by François Couplan

Printed in the United States of America

Library of Congress Cataloging-in-Publication Data

Couplan, François.
    The encyclopedia of edible plants of North America / François
Couplan.
        p.   cm.
    Includes bibliographical references and index.
    ISBN 0-87983-821-3
    1. Wild plants, Edible—North America—Encyclopedias.   I. Title.
OK98.5.N57C68   1998   98-23434
581.6'32'097—dc21   CIP

Keats Publishing, Inc.
27 Pine Street (Box 876)
New Canaan, Connecticut 06840-0876

Full catalog and ordering information: www.keats.com

    3 4 5 6 7 8 9 0   DSH/DSH   0 1 0 9 8 7 6 5 4

Contents 🌿

Acknowledgments 🌿

I would like to thank all the people who helped me with this book. They are by far too numerous to name all of them here, but some are particularly important to me.

My parents, who were the first to turn me on to the magic of gathering wild plants.

Zephyr, with whom I have shared for so long a deep, deep love for nature.

Jacques Poirier and Franz Boschiero, for our exciting walks up in the mountains and for our numerous wild dinners.

Jean-Marc Gambliel, with whom I have so much in common.

Sarah Murray, who put more energy than anybody else into making this book become a reality.

Diana Coogle, the lady of the woods.

Dan Barth, a real country boy.

Alfred Gormezzano, the crazy belly dancer.

Michael and Norissa Berardi, Bob and Jeanne-Elle Gover, who were game for many of my wild experiments.

Scott vanDenBergh, who showed me there is more than food about nature.

Marc Veyrat, my friend, who opened the door to a new world where all senses vibrate, combining plants and gastronomy in a truly spiritual experience.

Jean-Georges Vongerichten, who knows how to bridge the oceans and bring flavors to the top.

The thousands of people who attended my workshops and taught me so much.

The authors of the many plant books I read, with special thoughts to Richard Mabey, whose *Food for Free* was the first one I ever read on the subject, and to the memory of Euell Gibbons, whose *Stalking the . . .* were a lasting inspiration for me, as for so many people.

My fellow wild plants teachers, who do a great job, and from whom I learn a lot.

Last, but certainly not least, Norman Goldfind, my publisher, who allowed this book to be published after such a long time, and Susan E. Davis, my editor, who probably knows the manuscript by heart now, after all the time she spent on it.

Foreword

By James A. Duke, Ph.D.
Economic Botanist (USDA, ret.) and author of *The Green Pharmacy*

The French ethnobotanist François Couplan first showed me the manuscript for his ambitious *Encyclopedia of Edible Plants of North America* several years ago. Even then in the process of assembly, his first draft was obviously serious and scholarly. At the same time his enthusiasm for the plants and for how people might enjoy them made the draft fresh and exciting.

Now that François has completed his formidable task, I see he has ably fulfilled his labor of love. He has produced an exhaustive, well-researched work which will be with us for years to come. The book catalogs an impressive amount of basic information about more than 4,000 edible plants in North America, including, where known, the etymology, geographic distribution, cultivation, chemistry and many other uses, including medicinal uses, while flagging some endangered species that might be closely related. And François thoroughly enumerates their many edible parts and how to prepare them. Having all this information available in one book will immensely assist all who wish to enjoy nature's bounty.

What gives the book its unique personality is the original "grazing" research François conducted while living off the land in North America between 1974 and 1984. He survivied primarily on the plants he encountered as he walked around the country, belongings on his back. This experience provided highly useful, first-hand knowledge of many of the plants he writes about. François also lived for long stretches among various American Indian tribes, assimilating their historic knowledge of the uses of plants, which have been passed along for centuries from generation to generation. All these rich experiences he has distilled, based on extensive notes, supplemented with library research and continual learning, into this book. That makes his book a compendium of living lore – the kind of personal experience with plants that thrills an ethnobotanist like myself, who has indulged in many of the same culinary experiences.

I hope that publication of this book will inspire others to learn more about nature and become more intimately acquainted with edible and medicinal plants. And I hope it will also encourage Americans to take a new interest in the utilization and preservation of the myriad of useful plants around us. It's helpful to have a book that assembles so much useful information under one cover. In promoting an appreciation and awareness of our marvelous living environment, this volume can possibly help make the world an even better place in which to live.

Introduction 🌿

This book describes the edible properties of all the vascular plants growing wild on the North American continent that are known to have been used by humans as food.

Vascular plants comprise clubmosses, horsetails, ferns, conifers, all trees and shrubs, vines and herbaceous plants. Mushrooms, algae and mosses are excluded.

Purpose of This Book

The Encyclopedia of Edible Plants of North America is a reference for all people interested in learning about the numerous opportunities nature offers us in the form of healthful, intriguing, often delicious vegetables and fruits that we do not have to grow to enjoy. On this continent alone, there are no less than about 4,000 different wild plants that we can eat. Yet most of us, afraid or unaware, limit ourselves to the 60 or so vegetables, fruits, nuts and grains which are commonly cultivated in North America or imported from the tropics. These are often of low quality due to methods of cultivation and conservation which are detrimental to us and to the whole planet.

Many books have already been written on the subject of North American wild edible plants. Most of those published in English are listed in the Bibliography. They, as well as many more works in French, German, Italian and Spanish, have been used in preparing this book.

But *The Encyclopedia of Edible Plants of North America* is much more than a simple compilation of edible wild plants. It is based on my direct personal experience. I was introduced to the joys of eating wild plants about half a century ago, and for the past 30 years or so I have tasted and taken notes on hundreds of different species of plants worldwide, some of which had never been listed as edible before.

However, the subject of North American edible wild plants has certainly not been exhausted, even in this book. More than 25,000 different species of vascular plants grow wild on our continent. Listed here are approximately 4,000 of them. About 1,000 more are known to be toxic or at least nonedible. That leaves more than 20,000 plants whose edible and medicinal properties are as yet unknown to us. Much exploring remains to be done.

To aid the reader, I have organized the material so that the main body of the book is a detailed listing of the edible plants, both native and introduced, growing in a wild state within the geographical area. Then after a comprehensive glossary of botanical and medical terms, there is an extensive bibliography listing English works on edible plants found in North America, as well as books on toxic plants and other references used in preparing this text.

Where Our Plants and Their Uses Come From

The plants that grow wild on this continent can be divided into two main categories: native plants and introduced plants.

Native plants have evolved here for several millions of years. They are found in the woods, in the plains, in the mountains, in the deserts – mostly in places which have not been too drastically transformed by the encroachment of the white man.

Introduced plants have invaded all the areas where the ground has been disturbed: around dwellings, in cities, along roadsides, in fields and pastures. Some particularly adaptable ones can even be found high in the mountains or far into the deserts. The great majority came from Europe or Western Asia and have lived with people for centuries since the beginnings of agriculture. Many are commonly referred to as "weeds," although, to paraphrase Ralph Waldo Emerson, a weed is simply a plant, the uses and properties of which have been forgotten, or not yet discovered.

Many introduced plants crossed the Atlantic Ocean clandestinely, their seeds mixed with the cereals to be sown in the New Land, caught in the hairs of domestic animals or stuck in the mud under the soles of immigrants' shoes. Others were brought over by the settlers to be cultivated as vegetables or medicinal or forage plants but later fell into oblivion. Many more species of plants were grown in gardens and fields in the past than are cultivated today; examples will be found throughout this book. Most introduced plants were strong and adapted to living in disturbed ground; they escaped from cultivation and soon became naturalized, competing with, and often eliminating, native species.

It is easy to see now that the uses of our wild plants also come from two distinct sources. The Indigenous peoples, called Indians by the settlers, spent the totality of their lives within the heart of nature and had a use for almost all plants that surrounded them. Wild plants were sources of food, clothing, medicine, even transportation (like birch bark canoes). It is mostly through their knowledge that we have learned to use native plants.

As for the uses of introduced plants, we need to turn to the Old Continent where traditionally wild plants played an important role in daily life. Disdain for these "weeds" is a recent attitude. Less than 50 years ago, wild spring salads were still commonly gathered in southern France, and some are still sold in markets in Italy. To this day, Greek peasants have basically the same eating habits as their ancestors in the time of Pericles, 2,500 years ago. They grow cereals, olive and other fruit trees, but not much in their vegetable gardens, which they eat from during the summer months. From October until May, a lot of their salads and cooked greens are gathered from the wild. In other parts of Europe it is still commonplace to forage for food — greens in the spring, berries and mushrooms in the fall.

Humans have been eating wild plants ever since they appeared on earth four or five million years ago. When compared with the age of humanity, cultivation is a brand new phenomenon, dating a mere 10,000 years. Only recently has it been adopted by the majority of the human population. Now it is up to us to rediscover the myriad tastes and healthful effects that wild plants have offered humans since time immemorial.

Geographical Area Covered

This work encompasses Alaska, Canada, the contiguous United States and Northern Mexico. This area includes all the arctic, subarctic, temperate and subtropical zones found in America north of the Tropic of Cancer.

The southernmost tip of the Florida peninsula has also been taken into account, although the tropical flora found there has the strongest affinity with that of the West Indies, and is therefore a part of tropical America. However, Southern Florida is physically and politically contained within the United States and is included here for that reason. On the other hand, the flora of tropical Mexico has been excluded.

A map on page 14 shows the main geographical divisions referred to in this book.

Classification of the Plants

The plants are classified by botanical families. This is the most logical organization and has the advantage of emphasizing the fact that plants within the same family often have similar properties. Good examples of this are the Malvaceae, the Brassicaceae, the Lamiacae and the Poaceae.

The order of the families followed here is the one devised by Arthur Cronquist in his works, *Evolution and Classification of Flowering Plants* (1968) and *An Integrated System of Classification of Flowering Plants* (1981).

Within each family, the genus is, for our purposes, the fundamental unit of classification and therefore the basis for each article. In this book are listed 850 different genera.

Particular species are cited when they are definitely known to have been eaten as recorded. In a given genus, other species are very often (but not always) edible in the same manner and possess comparable chemical composition and similar medicinal properties.

Therefore, most of the time, a genus can be considered as a whole. However, this is not always true (see the section "What This Book Is Not" below). Known divergences in the edibility of different species are noted.

Outline of Each Article

The actual plants studied are the different edible species of each genus. In many articles, the main ones are treated at length individually. Other species are listed and discussed as a group. Some genera comprise only one species in our geographical range.

The 850 articles are composed as follows:

1. Botanical name of the genus in Latin.
Whenever necessary, name changes (former names which have been aban-

doned or synonyms accepted by some botanists) have been added in parentheses (preceded by =, in order to facilitate research, especially in ancient books). The same notation has been used as needed for the species mentioned in the text. If the generic name has been kept, it is simply abbreviated in the parenthesis: for example, *Eruca vesicaria* (= *E. sativa*). If the specific name has been kept, its initial is noted: for example, *Chamaedaphne calyculata* (= *Cassandra c.*).

2. Classification of the plant following the rating scale on pages 12–13. This scale indicates the plant's edible qualities (by letter) and its abundance (by number): for example, (G 4) for *Botrychium*.

The letter refers to the best edible species of the genus and is generally, but not always, a good indication of the quality of the genus as a whole.

The number refers to the most widely distributed edible species of the genus.

3. Etymology of the botanical name of the genus.

4. Geographical distribution of the genus in North America. If the plant has been introduced, its origin is mentioned before its area of distribution in North America.

5. When relevant, information that some species of the genus are cultivated for food, ornament or other purposes, such as fiber, oil, medicinal value or fodder.

6. Detailed discussion of the uses of the different edible parts of the plant in the following order: roots and underground parts (including bulbs, rhizomes and tubers, which are actually modified stems); stems; inner bark and sap (trees only); leaves; flower buds; flowers; fruits; seeds. The edible parts of the plants are <u>underlined</u> in the text.

When relevant, a brief history of these uses is also included.

The following are also indicated, when available, for each part of the plant:

7. Chemical composition. Chemical analysis has only been conducted on a small number of plants and is often incomplete. The more detailed composition of certain species does not necessarily imply that these plants are "richer" than others; it only signifies that they have been more thoroughly researched. This is especially true of common cultivated vegetables, fruits, nuts and grains which have been studied in detail.

On the other hand, although relatively few experiments have been conducted to determine the precise chemical composition of wild plants, all researchers concur that their nutritional value is superior to that of cultivated vegetables and fruits.

The chemical analysis provided is therefore only an approximation. In most cases, the presence but not the proportion of each element is entered. These proportions can vary considerably among individual plants of the same species, according to the soil, the quantity of rain received, the season and many other factors, including the part of the plant considered.

8. Medicinal properties. Internal uses are given in a first paragraph, external uses in a second.

9. Possible toxicity. In the event of toxicity, conditions of poisoning and average dangerous amounts are discussed.

10. Uses as dyes. Most, if not all, plants can be used for dyeing natural fibers, but the colors they yield are generally not fast and fade quickly. Some directions are provided for using some selected plants to dye wool with the help of various mordants (metallic salts allowing plant pigments to penetrate the fibers, thus making faster colors).

11. Other uses: for fiber, basketry, woodworking, soap and other industrial, craft or domestic uses.

12. Edible uses of exotic species of the same genus outside North America. Only the most important are listed because in some cases they are too numerous to mention. The names of species not found wild on our continent are in parenthesis.

13. Endangered species are always listed at the end of the discussion.

Conventions

The geographical distribution of the species listed in each article is given only when it differs from that of the genus listed at the beginning of each article. If no particular mention follows a specific name, the geographical distribution of that species in North America is the same as that of the genus.

Names in **bold type** indicate genera and species of edible plants found in a wild state (native, naturalized or escaped from cultivation) in North America.

Names in regular type are those of nonedible wild plants growing wild in North America, mentioned for their medicinal, tinctorial or other qualities, because of their toxicity or because they are endangered.

As noted above, the names of plants not growing wild in North America, whether edible or not, are in parentheses.

The Latin botanical names of all genera and species are in *italics*.

About Plant Names

Scientific names in Latin are used throughout this book. Their strange consonances make them usually more difficult to relate to than the more familiar common names in English.

Unfortunately, the latter generally lack precision. There are often several common names for the same plant according to the region. For example, *Tragopogon* species are known as oyster plant, salsify or goatsbeard. Conversely, the same name can designate totally different plants, creating confusions which could be dangerous. For example, the tree known as hemlock and the herbaceous poison hemlock have little in common: the latter is deadly, while the young foliage of the former, a conifer, is edible.

A common name often refers to a genus as a whole without differentiating the many species which it often comprises, making it impossible to accurately identify a particular species. This is not always critical, except in the case of a genus where some species are edible while others are toxic or if some species are endangered. These instances are not uncommon.

Many wild plants simply do not have common English names. Some people have therefore chosen to systematically translate specific Latin names into English in order to fashion common names for every species. This artificial practice, far from making things easier, is a source of confusion, creating names that never existed before. This only hinders those who are afraid of Latin names, preferring to use this crutch rather than slowly learning the scientific names universally employed by botanists. The advantages are doubtful. Is "Gooding's vervain" that much easier to remember or to pronounce than *Verbena goodingii*?

Scientific names are used throughout the world. If you travel abroad or if you read foreign books, you will notice that the same plant has a common name (sometimes more than one) in every language, and it is often much harder to pronounce than its Latin equivalent. It is easy to get confused about which plants are which. But by knowing the scientific name of a plant, you can easily find its local name(s) in a flora.

There is only one scientific name for every species of plant known, although some names are occasionally updated and equivalents may occur. The scientific name is used everywhere, independent of the local language; by international convention, all these names are Latinized.

The scientific name is composed of two parts: the first indicates the genus of the plant (all generic names are different); the second characterizes the species (but can be associated with different genera, for example: *Tilia americana, Fraxinus americana, Erythronium americanum*). The combination of the two defines one particular species without ambiguity.

It can be compared with the combination of last and first names that distinguishes a particular person. The great advantage of the bipartite scientific name is therefore, in addition to its precision, that it establishes the close relationship between different species of plants belonging to the same genus.

The major problem with scientific names is simply that we are not used to them: they seem forbidding and difficult to pronounce. This may be true, but in order to benefit from the information contained in books, don't we first have to learn how to read? The practice of driving a car isn't innate, either. Only by using the scientific names of plants will they become familiar to us, enabling us to fully appreciate both their efficiency and their slightly exotic charm. Botanical names often have an interesting meaning, usually drawn from the Greek or the Latin or commemorating a person. This can make them easier to remember. For this reason, the etymology of the names of each genus is given in the text.

Furthermore, many plants do not have common names and are known only by their Latin names, such as aster, begonia, fuchsia, geranium and zinnia.

However, it may be preferable to use the common name of the plant when there is no risk of confusion. In casual conversation it is definitely easier to talk about a dandelion than a *Taraxacum officinale*. Some common names are also of anecdotal interest. Dandelion, for instance, comes from the French "dent-de-lion," meaning lion's tooth, which refers to the deeply toothed leaves.

Picking Rules

Most of the following rules have to do with the conservation of our plants. It seems that the human race has often had a tendency to systematically destroy its natural environment. For the last century this has happened on an ever-larger scale at an increasingly alarming rate. It is true that the damage caused by an individual is slight compared with that of an army of bulldozers, but it is good to keep the following in mind:

Do not gather a plant if it belongs to an endangered species, or if it is uncommon wherever you are. The Indians, like other peoples living close to nature, never picked the first plant of a species they came upon: they waited to meet another one or more.

Do not uproot a plant unless you want to use its underground parts. Even so, do it only if the species is widespread and locally abundant. However, according to the circumstances, thinning out a patch of wild onions or dandelions, for instance, can possibly benefit the remaining plants.

As a rule, it is a good idea to pick only a few leaves from each plant (according to its size) in order to avoid killing it.
Do not take all the flowers or seeds from annual plants, as they are needed to produce a new generation.

Pick only what you need right away. There is no need to gather tons of plants only to store them for weeks in the refrigerator when your source of supplies is at your doorstep. Plants, wild and cultivated alike, are generally best eaten as fresh as possible.

Of course, fruits can be dried or frozen, acorns and nuts can be stored, and wild herbs and teas are often dried. But berries and nuts in season are also the principal foods of various wild animals, including birds. Do not forget to leave enough for them.

It is generally better to gather plants in cotton bags than in plastic bags, especially in warm weather. Never leave fresh plants unrefrigerated for too long, as they will soon spoil. They will keep in the refrigerator for a few days if wrapped in wet towels and stored in plastic bags.

Now a few rules for your own conservation:

Be wary of plants that may have been sprayed, intentionally or not, with pesticides, chemical fertilizers or herbicides – especially orchards, fields, vineyards, roadsides. Beware of plants growing in such heavily polluted areas as roadsides, factory sites and cities. Reject any plant that appears abnormal, sick or wilted. Gather only those that glow with health. Your intuition can guide you, but it's best to be informed of possible pollutants.

Wash carefully all the plants you have gathered and reexamine them one by one to avoid possible mistakes. For example, it is rather easy to pick two or three buttercup leaves or a small spurge with your chickweed salad. You'll find it preferable to become aware of this by sight rather than by taste.

It is always best to "pick clean": remove all foreign matter such as wilted leaves, grass leaves, dirt and twigs that you might inadvertently pick with the plants you are gathering. Pack each plant at harvesting time into a separate bag. You will thus save a lot of time in the kitchen.

What This Book Is Not

The Encyclopedia of Edible Plants of North America is not an identification manual. Because of space limitations, no description of the plants has been included. The drawings are in the text to enhance the visual appearance of the book and are not intended for indentification purposes. (They were drawn by the author for your enjoyment.) However, it is of utmost importance that the reader be able to recognize as precisely as possible the plants intended for use, preferably down to the specific level (the basic level for plant identification, as opposed to the family or the generic, less precise level). The reason for exerting so much care is to avoid gathering either poisonous plants or endangered species.

Numerous books can be found on plant identification. A local flora is definitely the best way to identify plants accurately down to the specific level. Although a flora does not usually have color pictures, it lists all the species growing in a particular geographical area and has keys to track them down precisely. (A flora is different from an identification manual, which is usually well-illustrated but presents a limited selection of plants.)

There are other good ways of getting acquainted with plants: picking samples in the field and having them identified by a botanist (at a university, college or botanical garden) or comparing them with herbarium specimens; attending local herb walks or workshops; or exploring the wilds with knowledgeable friends. It takes time, of course, and requires some work, but getting to know the plants can definitely be one of life's pleasures.

List of Abbreviations

Scientific Name of Plants

Composed of two parts, the first one indicates the genus, the second one, the species. Occasionally, a third name denotes a subspecies or variety.

sp. = species
spp. = species (plural)
subsp. = subspecies
var. = variety

Examples

Malva sp. stands for an undetermined species of the genus *Malva* (mallow).

Trifolium spp. stands for several undetermined species of the genus *Trifolium* (clover).

Hedysarum alpinum var. *americanum* stands for the variety *americanum* (the form growing in North America) of the species *Hedysarum alpinum*, which also grows in Europe and Asia.

Brassica oleracea var. *italica* stands for the variety *italica*, brocoli, of the species *Brassica oleracea*, cabbage. In many cases, varieties are obtained by cultivation, such as in this example, but natural varieties also occur.

An *x* placed in front of a specific name (*Fragaria x ananassa*) or between two specific names (*F. chiloensis x virginiana*) denotes a hybrid – in this example the cultivated strawberry, obtained by crossing the two species, *Fragaria chiloensis* and *F. virginiana*.

Geographical Distribution

Can. = Canada
E. = Eastern
E. N.Am. = Eastern North America
Eur. = Europe
Mex. = Mexico
N. = Northern
N. Mex. = Northern Mexico
N.W. Mex. = Northwestern Mexico
S. = Southern
S. Fla. = South Florida
S. U.S. = Southern United States
S.W. U.S. = Southwestern United States
W. = Western
W.I. = West Indies
W. N.Am. = Western North America

The various states are abbreviated in the usual manner – for example, Calif. – and not as in zip code addresses. (Note that N.M. is used to distinguish the abbreviation for the state of New Mexico from the abbreviation for Northern Mexico = N. Mex.) Canadian provinces (B.C. = British Columbia) and Mexican states (Son. = Sonora) are also abbreviated.

"Northern regions" refer to the areas located above the 45th parallel. (See map on page 14.)

"Mountains" include the Appalachians, the Rockies, the Cascades and the Sierras.

Others

(m.a.) = mentioned above

Rating Scale

The letter refers to the edibility of the genus.

The number designates how widely distributed the edible species is in North America.

Two letters are sometimes listed (for example, B–C) or two numbers (2–3); both must be taken into account.

If the genus includes a toxic species, that is indicated by the letter F, even if the plant is edible after preparation. The F generally follows another letter designating the edibility of the genus. If after preparation the toxic species becomes the most edible one of the genus, its edibility rating is then placed after the F rather than before.

Edibility

A   Plants of outstanding taste and edibility (not requiring any unusual preparation, of pleasant texture and having healthful, beneficial qualities), easy to gather.

B   Plants of good quality (not quite as pleasant to eat or less easy to gather).

C   Plants requiring long preparation or tedious to gather.

D   Plants of mediocre taste or texture.

E   Plants hardly edible (of bad taste, very tough or very small).

F   Plants that are toxic without special preparation mentioned in the text.

G   Plants of uncertain edibility (references not verifiable).

H   Genus includes at least one or more endangered species.

Abundance

1   Abundant over the whole North American continent.

2   Abundant only in parts of the continent.

3   Distributed throughout North America but rarely abundant.

4   Neither widely distributed nor abundant.

5   Very localized, more or less abundant.

6   Rare plants.

MAP OF THE MAIN GEOGRAPHICAL
DIVISIONS OF NORTH AMERICA USED IN THIS BOOK

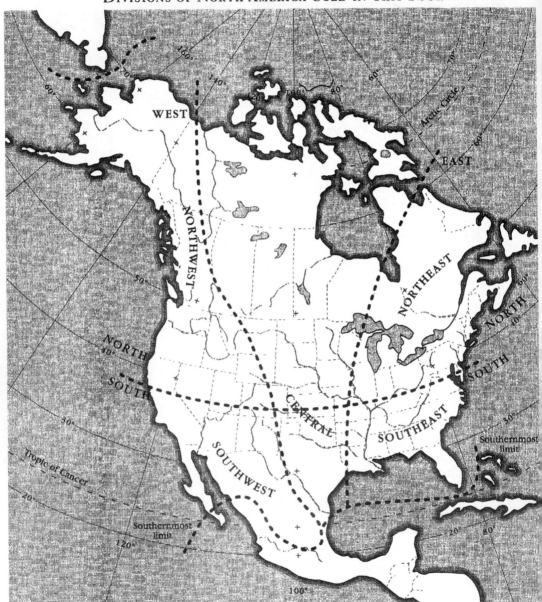

"Northern Regions" are mostly the areas above the 45th parallel. "Mountains"
include the Appalachian, Sierras, Cascades and Rocky Mountains.

Lycopods and Horsetails

(Lycopodiophyta and *Equistophyta)*

LYCOPODIACEAE

Lycopodium   (G-F 3)   Club Moss
From the Greek "lukos," wolf, and "podion," small foot: referring to the aspect of the plants.
Throughout.

The leafy aerial stems of *L. selago* have reportedly been eaten by Chippewa Indians after cooking.

However, most club mosses, including the two species mentioned above, are known to be somewhat toxic, due to the presence of several alkaloids (lycopodine, clavatine, clavotoxin).

Internally, club mosses can be somewhat diuretic and laxative. The active principles are not well-defined.

The spores contain sugar and a fixed oil (up to 50%) and are not toxic.

They constitute a very fine powder which has been used externally as a vulnerary, hemostatic and emollient, protecting the skin like talcum powder.

This powder also served to coat pills and was employed at the turn of the century as a flash powder for cameras.

Lycopodium clavatum

EQUISETACEAE

Equisetum   (D 1)   Horsetail
From the Latin "equus," horse, and "saeta," hair: referring to the aspect
of the plants.
Throughout.
Our native *E. hyemale* is sometimes planted as an ornamental.

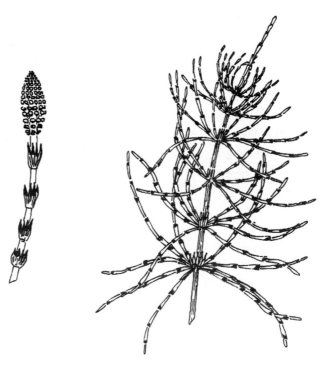

Equisetum pratense

The <u>starchy rhizomes</u> of *E. fluviatile* have reportedly been used as food in
Europe. It has been said that the "tuberous roots" of *E. pratense* – mostly N.
N.Am. – were eaten in Minnesota, but this statement is doubtful, as the plant
has a black creeping rhizome.

The <u>young shoots</u> of many species have been used as human food since Antiquity. Among these species, *E. arvense, fluvatile* (m.a.), *hyemale* (m.a.), *laevi-*
gatum and *pratense* (m.a.) are found in North America.

They are edible raw or cooked while they are still tender and juicy. Their taste is usually fairly mild. Later, they become impregnated with silicon and are too tough to eat. They have often been used at this stage for scouring cooking utensils, hence one of the names of the plant, "scouring rush."

Several species have two types of stems on the same plant. Fertile stems (light colored due to a lack of chlorophyll) appear first in the spring and are followed by sterile stems which are green and leafy. *E. arvense* (m.a.), *pratense* (m.a.), *sylvaticum* – mostly N. N.Am. – and *telmateia* (= *maximum*) – Pacific Coast and N. N.Am. – possess the two different kinds of stems.

In Japan, fertile horsetail stems are considered a delicacy. They are eaten raw in salads as vegetables (with soy sauce or ground-up sesame seeds) or pickled.

The sterile stems, picked until midsummer, are generally steamed, then sautéed. They can be pickled as well.

Horsetails are rich in minerals (15–20% cinders), particularly in silicon (SiO_2 is 5–10% of the dry weight). They also contain saponins, tannin, glucosides, organic acids, an alkaloid (equisetin), sterols, numerous flavonoids and a vitamin B1-destroying substance (thiaminase).

Medicinally, the green stems are diuretic and hemostatic and remineralize the body, especially in the case of tuberculosis.

Externally, the fresh plant is a vulnerary.

Horsetails should not be taken internally in excessive doses or regularly: mature plants can be toxic and have occasionally proven lethal to livestock, especially to horses, because of thiaminase.

The green stems dye wool, cotton and linen yellow with alum, green with copper sulfate and greenish-gray with ferrous sulfate.

Ferns
(Polypodiophyta)

The <u>rhizomes</u> of some species have been used as food or as medicine. They are generally rather thin, contain little starch, at least in our regions, and require long preparation. The rhizome of the male fern (*Dryopteris filix-mas*) has strong anthelminthic properties and can be toxic.

The <u>young unrolling fronds</u> (fiddlenecks) of many ferns are edible. They can sometimes be eaten raw, but in most cases it is necessary to boil them in a change of water or two to remove their acridity or bitterness and possible toxicity.

OPHIOGLOSSACEAE

Botrychium   (G 4)   Grape Fern
From the Greek "bunch": alluding to the aspect of the fructifications.
Almost throughout.

The cosmopolitan ***B. virginianum*** – mostly Northern Regions & Mountains – has reportedly been eaten in the Himalayas and New Zealand after cooking in water.

OSMUNDACEAE

Osmunda (D 4)   Cinnamon Fern
Name given by De l'Obel, possibly from Osmund, a germanic god (Thor);
or from L. "os," mouth, and "mundo," to purify; the plant has been credited with antiputrid properties.
E. & C. N.Am.
Our most common species is *O. cinnamomea*, cinnamon fern, which is
sometimes planted as an ornamental.

The young fronds are tender and edible but acrid. Those of *O. cinnamomea*
(m.a.) and *claytoniana*, interrupted fern – E. N.Am. – have been eaten in North
America.

In East Asia, the young fronds of *O. regalis*, royal fern – also native in E.
N.Am. – and of local species (*O. asiatica, japonica*) are boiled in water with wood
ashes to remove their acridity and then eaten as a vegetable or in soups (under
the name of "zen mai" in Japan). They are also dried or preserved in salt for later
use.
Starch was formerly obtained from the rhizome in Japan.
The rhizome of *O. regalis* (m.a.) contains mucilage.
It has occasionally been employed as an emollient, expectorant and tonic.
The leaf hairs of this fern were reportedly a source of fibers.

POLYPODIACEAE

Adiantum (B 2-3)   Maidenhair Fern
Greek name for a fern "a," without, and "diainaô," to wet: referring to the
foliage which repels raindrops.
Throughout.
Several species are planted as ornamentals.

The aerial parts of *A. capillus-veneris* and *pedatum*, five-finger fern, can be
prepared as a pleasant, aromatic tea. In 18th-century Europe, a popular drink
("bavaroise") was made by mixing with milk a syrup made with the European
maidenhair fern, *A. capillus-veneris* (m.a.).
The five-finger fern can be used in the same way.
In America it was often used to make cough syrup.

The fronds contain mucilage, tannin, an essential oil and bitter substances.
They are expectorant and emollient. The European maidenhair fern has been used similarly since Antiquity.
The stems are reported to be a source of fibers.

Matteucia struthiopteris (D 4) Ostrich Fern
(= *Pteretis pennsylvanica, P. nodulosa, Onoclea s.*)
After Carlo Matteuci (1800–1868), Italian physicist.
N. N.Am.
Occasionally planted for ornamentation.

The young fronds are edible cooked. They have been eaten in North America since the times of the first settlers.
In Japan, they are boiled and fried in batter as tempura or cooked slowly in shoyu (soy sauce). Their local name is "kusasotetsu." Another local species is used as well.
Recently, collective intoxications have occurred in some restaurants in New York State and Western Canada. The digestive troubles suffered by customers were linked to insufficient cooking of the fronds. It has therefore been recommended to boil them at least for 15 minutes in order to destroy a potential toxin.

Onoclea sensibilis (G 4) Sensitive Fern
Greek name of a plant, possibly of the bugloss (*Anchusa* sp.), "onokleia."
E. & C. N.Am. A monotypic genus.
Occasionally planted as an ornamental.

The rhizome has reportedly been used as food by Indians.
The young shoots of a local variety (var. *interrupta*) are eaten boiled in Northeastern Asia.
The mature fronds can be somewhat poisonous to horses.

Pellea (D 3) Cliff Brake
From the Greek "pellos," dark: referring to the color of the petioles.
Throughout.

Tea can be prepared from the dried fronds of *P. mucronata* and *ornithopus*.

Polypodium   (D 3)   Polypody
From the Greek "polys," many, and "pous," foot: referring to the branched rhizomes.
Throughout.
P. vulgare is planted as an ornamental in addition to another exotic species.

The rhizome of *P. glycyrrhiza*, licorice fern – Pacific Coast – tastes somewhat like licorice and can be chewed for its flavor in spite of its bitterness.
That of *P. vulgare* (m.a.) has a similar taste.
Its rhizome contains mucilage, sugars (including saccharose), glycyrrhizine (which gives a sweet taste), saponins, an essential oil and a bitter, resinous substance.
Polypody is anthelminthic, demulcent, expectorant, cholagogue and laxative, and has been used medicinally since Antiquity.
A local species is made into tea in Eastern Siberia.

Polystichum   (C-H 3)   Sword Fern, Holly Fern
From the Greek "polys," many, and "stichos," a row: referring to the regular rows of spore-containing sori.
Throughout.

The rhizome of *P. munitum* – W. N.Am. – was consumed by Indians who usually roasted it on embers.
A local species has reportedly been eaten in curries in India.
The rhizome of *Dryopteris filix-mas* (= *Polystichum f.-m.*), male fern, is a powerful anthelmintic (against taenias and nematodes) due to the filicine (a mixture of polyphenols) and the essential oil it contains. Too large doses can be toxic.
Endangered species: *P. aleuticum* – Alaska.

Pteridium aquilinum   (B-C 1)   Bracken Fern
Diminutive form of the Greek "pteris," fern, from "pteron," wing feather.
Throughout (cosmopolitan). A monotypic genus.

The rhizome of the bracken fern has been used as food in many parts of the world. It is reputed to be toxic raw and must therefore be cooked.
It can be chopped up, boiled and passed through a food mill to make a purée.

The Indians steamed the rhizome for hours in a fire pit and chewed the starch off the tough fibrous core.

In Europe, it was often dried, ground, sifted and mixed with cereal flour to make bread. Until the 19th century, bracken fern bread was a staple in some regions of France, especially in times of scarcity.

Up to World War II, the rhizome of bracken fern was dried and ground to make flour in the Canary Islands of La Palma and La Gomera. It was roasted before being ground, along with barley if available, to make "gofio," an instant food, easily digested, which dated back to the original inhabitants of the islands, the "Guanches."

In Siberia, the rhizomes were crushed and fermented in water with two thirds of their weight of malt (sprouted barley), producing a beerlike drink.

Pteridium aquilinum

In Japan, starch was extracted from them by a long process and used to make mochis (steamed cakes).

Thickness and starch content of the rhizomes vary, depending on the plant and its location. As mentioned above, they are generally thin and contain little starch in our regions.

The <u>very young fronds</u>, picked when still tender before they have started to unroll, have been eaten, cooked, in America, Europe and Asia.

They are mucilaginous, adding body to soups, and taste very good when properly prepared. When first boiled, they sometimes release a bitter almond smell, which disappears with further cooking.

The young fronds are frequently used in Japan. Their sometimes unpleasant taste is removed by boiling them in water to which wood ashes have been added. They are then eaten as vegetables, made into soups or preserved in salt, in lees of sake (rice wine) or in rice miso (fermented paste of rice and salt).

After soaking for 24 hours in water with wood ashes, the young fronds can be lightly steamed, or even eaten raw, in which case they are crisp.

They have reportedly been made into a fermented drink in Siberia and Scandinavia.

Raw young bracken fern fronds contain a carcinogenic substance, ptaquiloside. In Japan, a link has been made between esophagus cancers and the regular consumption of bracken fern. They also contain the enzyme thiaminase which destroys vitamin B1 in the body. Young bracken fern fronds must therefore be cooked (preferably in a change of water) and prepared as described above to eliminate the toxic principles.

The milk of cows grazing heavily on bracken fern is thought by some to be potentially toxic to humans due to the ptaquiloside.

Bracken fern fronds can also be toxic to livestock, who find them particularly palatable when young. When abusively eaten, either fresh or dried, they cause acute hemorrhages or chronic bleeding hematuria in cattle, depending upon the quantity ingested. This is due to ptaquiloside. With horses, thiaminase induces neurological disorders from the deficiency in vitamin B1.

It must be noted that members of the first scientific expedition to cross Australia from North to South (1860-61) died from beri-beri (vitamin B1 deficiency) after feeding on a thiaminase-rich fern, nardoo (*Marsilea drummondii*). This fern was commonly eaten by the aborigines, but only after soaking in water, which eliminates the heat-resistant thiaminase.

Bracken fern fronds contain potassium and make a good fertilizer for root crops. Ashes of the burnt plant, rich in potash, have been used in manufacturing glass.

Bracken fern rhizomes dye wool yellow with chromium. The fronds dye wool and silk greenish-yellow with alum or chromium, and they dye silk gray with ferrous sulfate.

Cycads and Conifers
(Pinophyta)

CYCADACEAE

Dioon   (B 5)
From the Greek "dis," twice, and "ôon," egg: the seeds are in pairs.
Mex.
D. edule and *spinulosum* are occasionally grown in greenhouses.

The large starchy <u>seeds</u> of *D. edule* (m.a.) have long been used as food locally after cooking.

Zamia   (F-H 4)   Coontie, Florida Arrowroot
Latin name used by Pliny meaning "pine cones" from the word for "loss" or "damage." The name was transferred to this genus because of the conelike fruits.
S.E. U.S., Mex.

In the following species, the <u>root</u> has been used as a source of starch: *Z. chigua, furfuracea* – both Mex. –, *integrifolia* (= *floridana*) – Fla., Ga. – and *pumila* – S. Fla.
If fresh, it is pounded or grated, if dried, ground or boiled until soft and mashed up, then washed with water in a container. The starch settles to the bottom and is gathered after draining off the water. It can be dried and ground into a flour or cooked as a mush with other foods.

The roots are considered toxic raw, but they are rendered consumable by the above preparation and cooking. The starch was an important food for local Indians.

Starch is also extracted from the roots of some tropical American species.

The starchy <u>seeds</u> of several West Indian species are eaten after cooking. They are usually boiled and mashed.

Roots, foliage and seeds of *Zamia* spp. are toxic raw. Dogs have died in Florida from ingesting *Zamia* seeds. However, as seen above, roots and seeds become edible after processing and/or cooking.

Endangered species: all our native *Zamia* spp.

PINACEAE

All members of this family are trees, many of which are sources of timber or are utilized in pulp production.

They are generally abused by humans: "virtus post nummos" (virtue after money). Clearcuts and the use of extremely toxic chemical defoliants threaten life, health and the ecological balance of the forest. Some of these chemical defoliants were devised during the Vietnam war to wipe out the dense cover of the jungle. Since then, they have been employed worldwide in forest farming to eliminate broad-leaved trees in favor of conifers, for higher yields, more profit and ease in management. One of the dangerous side effects of these chemicals is demonstrated by high statistics of miscarriage, deformity and infant mortality in women whose water sources are contaminated.

As a source of food, all members of this family yield similar products:

The <u>inner bark</u> (cambium) is edible raw but definitely better cooked. Indians steamed it in a fire pit, between layers of green leaves, and pressed it into cakes, sometimes adding dried berries. In Northern Europe, it was dried and ground into a bitter but nutritious meal, which was mixed with cereal flour to make bread in times of scarcity. Strips of inner bark can be boiled in water or cooked in soups, somewhat like resinous and chewy noodles.

The inner bark of trees should remain an emergency food, unless it can be gathered from already-cut specimens. Remember that girdling a tree will kill it.

The <u>resinous sap</u> of conifers is edible and nutritious, but its sticky texture and generally bitter taste make it a rather unpleasant food. However, in Europe, spruce and fir resin is sometimes made into a delicious cough candy by cooking it with sugar or honey. The sap of a few species is sweetish.

The best food obtained from the different members of this family is the new, light green <u>foliage</u> which appears in the spring. It is tender and has a very pleasant, lemony taste caused by an essential oil containing limonene, as in lemon oil.

The <u>young shoots</u>, rich in vitamin C, are excellent raw added to salads and other dishes.

After they have turned dark green, the <u>leaves</u> are too tough to eat but make a flavorful tea with expectorant and diaphoretic properties. Leaf buds of fir, spruce and pine trees are used in the same way.

Abies (B 2) Fir
Latin name of the tree.
N. N.Am. and Mountains.
Several native and Eurasian species are cultivated as ornamentals.

Fir trees have all the edible and medicinal uses described above.

The <u>inner bark</u> of *A. balsamea*, balsam fir – N.E. N.Am. – and *grandis* – N.W. N.Am. – was reportedly used as food by Indians.

The inner bark of the European fir (*A. alba*) was eaten by Lapps and Scandinavians who used to make "bark bread" with it.

"Canada balsam" is the resin obtained from the balsam fir (m.a.) and occasionally from other species as well.

Abies balsamea

It contains 24% essential oil, 60% of a resin soluble in alcohol and 16% of a resin soluble only in ether.

It is expectorant, balsamic and antiseptic.

The resin of the European fir (m.a.) is used similarly.

The seeds of a local species (*A. firma*) have reportedly been eaten in Northern Japan.

Larix (B 2)   Larch, Tamarack

Latin name of the tree derived from Greek name of an undetermined shrub.

Mostly N. N.Am.

Several native and Eurasian species are cultivated as ornamentals.

Larches are used in the same way as firs and other members of this family.

The young shoots of *L. laricina*, American larch – N.E. N.Am. – were eaten by some Indians.

Other tribes chewed the exudation of the trunk of *L. occidentalis* – W. N.Am.

The Yakuts of Siberia used to eat the inner bark of a local species (*L. russica*) boiled in a soup made from milk, flour and fish.

The inner bark of the European larch (*L. decidua*), occasionally planted for ornament, is diuretic and has been used externally as a vulnerary in powder form.

Its resin is known as "Venice turpentine." The oil obtained from distillation is anthelmintic, emmenagogue and vulnerary but must only be taken in very small amounts due to its strongly irritating qualities: it can cause kidney damage and blisters.

In Russia, the resin exuding from the trunks burned by forest fires was gathered and traded under the name of "Orenburg gum."

In autumn, larch leaves turn yellow and fall off the tree. At this stage, they dye wool brown.

Picea (B 2) Spruce

Latin name of the tree from "pix," pitch; "pissa" in Greek.
N. N.Am. & Mountains.
Several native and Eurasian species are planted as ornamentals.

Spruces have all the edible and medicinal uses described above.

<u>Inner bark</u> and <u>young shoots</u> of *P. mariana*, black spruce – N. N.Am. – and *rubens*, red spruce – N.E. N.Am. – have been eaten and the leaves made into tea.

The <u>young spray</u> of the black spruce has been used for flavoring beer in America.

The Norway spruce (*P. abies*) was employed similarly in Europe. Its young shoots have a very pleasant, sour, lemony flavor. They taste particularly good with fish and are used by some prominent chefs in France and Germany.

Picea rubens

Like those of other conifers, spruce leaves are expectorant and diaphoretic. They are also sedative when used in baths.

Spruce <u>gum</u> can be quite pleasant to chew.

The resin obtained from the Norway spruce (m.a.) is called "Burgundy pitch." It was formally used in medicinal plasters. The oil distilled from it is rubefacient.

Pinus (B-C 1) Pine

Latin name of the tree.
Throughout.
Many native, European and Asiatic species are planted as ornamentals, for timber or for their sap.

Pine trees have all the edible and medicinal uses already described.

The <u>inner bark</u> of some species is said to be quite palatable when gathered early in the year, especially that of *P. contorta, flexilis, ponderosa* – W. N.Am. – and *strobus* – E. N.Am. Indians ate it either fresh or dried, raw or cooked in a fire pit and pressed into cakes. Early settlers cut it into strips and boiled it like noodles.

Bark from the lower part of the tree is supposedly the best.

The inner bark of Scotch pine (*P. sylvestris*) was used as food in Europe, ground and boiled or mixed with cereal flour to make grilled cakes. Lapps and Scandinavians made "bark bread" with it.

This tree is occasionally planted for ornamentation.

The inner bark of pine trees is expectorant and vulnerary.

Pines are cultivated commercially for their sap (resin), which is known as turpentine, especially in the Southeastern United States and in Southern Europe.

Turpentine is antiseptic, stimulant, expectorant and diaphoretic, but in large doses or with susceptible individuals it can irritate the kidney.

It is distilled to yield oil of turpentine, which is used as a solvent in such products as paint, varnish and shoe polish.

This oil is antiseptic, anthelminthic, rubefacient and very irritating. It is not to be taken internally.

The solid residue left after distillation, "rosin" or "colophony," is used in the production of wax, varnish and soap. It is also employed in music (rubbed on the bow of certain instruments in order to make it catch on the strings) and in gymnastics (to prevent the gymnasts' hands and feet from slipping).

The <u>sap</u> of pine trees is often pleasant to chew. It can also be made into cough candy.

Pine resin is a good vulnerary: its stickiness makes it especially useful for foot wounds if one walks barefooted since it stays in place and prevents infection.

The sap exuding from a partially burnt trunk of *P. lambertiana*, sugar pine – W. N.Am. – is sweetish and has lost its turpentine flavor. It was used by the Indians both as a sweetener and as a laxative. The sugar pine is the tallest species of pine, reaching up to 230 ft (75 m) in height.

The sweet sap of a local species (*P. wallichiana*) is sometimes used as food in the Himalayas.

Young pine <u>shoots</u>, although pleasant tasting, are not always tender enough to be eaten like those of other conifers.

The leaves contain glucosides and a lemon-smelling essential oil, which can be extracted by distillation.

Pine leaf oil is balsamic and antiseptic and repels insects.

The young <u>male inflorescences</u> can be eaten raw or cooked, and have a nice flavor and a mealy texture.

Some Indians used to roast the center part of <u>green pine cones</u> in the fringes of their campfires and enjoy the syrupy results.

The best food product of pine trees is by far their <u>seeds</u>. They have a very delicate, sweet, piney taste. In several species they are large and easy to gather in quantity.

Pine seeds were often used as food by the Indians, especially in the Southwest, where "pinyons" (Spanish "piñon," pine nut) were a staple. Those of several local species are eaten in Europe and Asia, some of which are planted as ornamentals on our continent. Pine seeds have been commercialized on these two continents as well as in America where they are usually known as "pine nuts."

The seeds can be gathered from the ground where they have fallen, provided squirrels and other rodents have left some. It is often preferable to pick the cones before they open, make a large pile and build a fire around them so that the scales split apart; the seeds can then be easily removed.

Among the largest seeds are those produced by the small cones of the pinyon pines of Southwestern United States and Northern Mexico. They are thin-shelled and about 15 mm long.

There are four closely related species: *P. edulis*, pinyon pine; *P. monophylla*, single-leafed pinyon; *P. quadrifolia*, Parry pinyon; *P. cembroides*, Mexican pinyon.

Since pinyon pines are relatively small trees, their seeds can be gathered by placing a sheet under the tree and shaking it.

The seeds of *P. edulis* (m.a.) are an important source of revenue for the Indians of Northern Arizona and New Mexico: they form the bulk of the commercial "pine nuts" in America.

However, more and more pine nuts are imported from China where several local species have been used for a long time as food.

Pinyons are ripe in early September, but abundant crops usually occur every other year.

In Western North America, several species have seeds large enough to be worth gathering, which were eaten by Indians:

P. albicaulis, whitebark pine.

P. coulteri, bigcone pine. It has the largest cones of all pines; seeds are about 15 mm long.

P. flexilis (m.a.), limber pine. Seeds are about 10 mm long.

P. jeffreyi, Jeffrey pine. Seeds are about 10 mm long.

P. lambertiana (m.a.), sugar pine. It has the longest cones of all pines; seeds are about 10 mm long.

P. monticola, Western white pine.

P. ponderosa (m.a.), ponderosa pine, Western yellow pine. Seeds are about 7 mm long.

P. sabiniana, digger pine. Seeds are about 20 mm long.

P. torreyana, Torrey pine. This pine has the largest seeds of all North American pines, reaching up to 25 mm in length. Unfortunately, the Torrey pine is very rare. It is native only to a very small area north of San Diego to Santa Rosa Island, where it is planted locally as a street tree.

Among Eastern pines, *P. strobus* (m.a.), white pine, is the only one with seeds of usable size.

The different species listed above are occasionally planted as ornamentals or for timber.

Pine nuts are edible raw and used like almonds in cakes, desserts and other dishes.

The European stone pine (*P. pinea*) has some of the largest seeds (25 mm). They have been eaten in the Mediterranean region since Antiquity, and are still part of such traditional recipes as "pesto" or Provençal beet pie. In the Middle East and India, they are cooked with rice, meat or fish. They are also added to salads or simply crushed and mixed with honey.

In the mountains of Europe, the large seeds of the Alpine stone pine (*P. cembra*) were also used as food.

Pine seeds contain a fixed oil (40–50%), starch (30%), sugars (5–10%), proteins (10–15%), minerals and traces of essential oil.

They are very nutritious. But they turn rancid rapidly and must be stored in an airtight container.

The most important native pine species used for timber is *P. ponderosa* (m.a.).

Pseudotsuga (B 2) Douglas Fir

From the Greek "pseudos," false, and "tsuga"; Japanese name for the hemlocks, *Tsuga* spp.

W. N.Am. Mostly *P. menziesii*. This is the most important timber tree on the Pacific Coast; it is sometimes planted as an ornamental.

The tree has all the uses described in the introductory paragraph.
The <u>young shoots</u> are excellent.

Tsuga (B 2) Hemlock

Japanese name of a local species.
Mostly N. N.Am. & Mountains.
Some species of E. N.Am. and Asia are planted as ornamentals.

The tree has all the uses described in the introductory paragraph.

The <u>inner bark</u> of *T. heterophylla*, Western hemlock, and *mertensiana*, mountain hemlock – both W. Mountains – was pressed into cakes and baked by Indians.

The <u>foliage</u> has occasionally been used like that of spruce in beer making. That of *T. canadensis*, Eastern hemlock – N.E. N.Am. & Appalachians – was made into tea.

The <u>young shoots</u> of hemlocks have a pleasant, sour, lemony taste.

The inner bark and the young twigs are diuretic, diaphoretic and astringent.

The sap of *T. canadensis* (m.a.) is official under the name "pix canadensis."
The bark dyes wool brown.

Sequoia sempervirens (B 5) Redwood

After Sequoyah (1770–1843), Cherokee scholar.
N.W. Calif. & S.W. Ore. along the coast.

It is used locally for timber production, thus destroying forever some of the most magnificent forests of the world. This, the tallest of all trees, is often planted for ornament.

The <u>young foliage</u> is tender and lemony. It makes a pleasant addition raw to salads and other dishes.

The outer bark is extremely thick – an effective protection against fire – which makes it next to impossible to reach the inner bark.

CUPRESSACEAE

Juniperus   (B 2-3)   Juniper, "Cedar"
Latin name of the plant.
Throughout.
Several native, European and Asiatic spp. are planted as ornamentals.

The sweet, aromatic "<u>berries</u>" of *J. communis* – mostly N. N.Am. & W. Mountains – are a well-known condiment, especially in Europe. From a botanical standpoint, they are actually fleshy cones, not berries.

Their traditional use is for flavoring sauerkraut, "genévrette" (a beer obtained by fermenting a mixture of sprouted barley and juniper berries), "genièvre" or "genever" (a spirit made by distilling the berries with alcohol) and gin. To prepare gin, a distilled spirit is redistilled in the presence of juniper berries and other flavoring agents (including sweet flag, orris root, angelica, caraway, orange peel) through which the vapors pass as they rise.

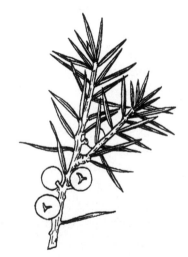

Juniperus communis

The cones can be used as a condiment in a variety of dishes.

Some Indians ate the "berries" by themselves or mashed them up into a paste which was mixed with food. A finer purée is obtained by passing them through a food mill or a sieve. However, this flavoring should be eaten in moderation as it can irritate the kidneys.

In some valleys of the southern Alps, a dark syrupy extract is still made from the berries. It is traditionally eaten as a dessert with cream or in hot milk.

Torrefied juniper berries have been used as a coffee substitute.

They contain an essential oil, sugars (30%), organic acids, a bitter principle and other substances.

They are diuretic, tonic, stomachic, carminative and antiseptic. But as mentioned above, too large a dose, or continuous use over a period of time, can irritate the kidneys.

The oil distilled from the berries has rubefacient and parasiticidal properties as well.

The cones of the common juniper dye wool a brownish color.

The "berries" of several native species were eaten by Western Indians fresh or dried, generally ground and mixed with seed flour to make a mush. These junipers are *J. californica, deppeana, monosperma, occidentalis, scopulurum, utahensis* – all W. N.Am. – and *tetragona* – Mex. In some species they are extremely sweet and pleasant; when dry, they make a natural candy.

The cones of various local species are used as food in the Bermudas (*J. bermudiana*), in Europe and the Middle East (*J. drupacea*) and in Asia (*J. chinensis, conferta, recurva* and *rigida*).

The young shoots of the common juniper can be added to salads when still fresh, young and tender. When dried, they make a pleasant tea.

The foliage of the common juniper is aromatic: it contains an essential oil and can be used medicinally in the same way as the cones.

However, the foliage of *J. virginiana*, red cedar – E. N.Am. – is toxic. It is known to cause digestive troubles in cattle when ingested in large amounts.

The oil distilled from the leaves has antiseptic properties and is emmenagogue.

Its wood has been used as an insect repellent, and the oil distilled from it is an insecticide.

The leaves of a Mediterranean species (*J. sabina*, occasionally planted in America as an ornamental) are very poisonous. They were formerly used as an abortive, but along with the expulsion of the fetus, they would often cause the mother to die as well.

The toxic principle, sabinol, irritates the mucous membranes and acts on the nervous system. It can cause convulsions.

Cade oil is distilled from the wood of a southern European juniper (*J. oxyce-*

drus). It is used externally for skin problems and loss of hair and as an antiseptic and insecticide.

Thuja (D 2)   Cedar, Arborvitae

Greek name "thuia" which designated both a fragrant tree from Africa, whose wood was highly prized, and an evergreen shrub from the mountains of Greece.

Mostly N. N.Am. & Mountains.

Our native *T. plicata*, giant cedar, Western red cedar – N.W. N.Am. – and an Asiatic species are planted as ornamentals.

The inner bark of the giant cedar was used as food by Northwestern Indians. It is also a source of fibers.

The young shoots of *T. canadensis* (= *T. occidentalis*), arborvitae – N.E. N.Am. – have reportedly been eaten by some Indian tribes, in particular the Ojibway. But they have a strong aromatic taste.

Shoots are occasionally used, as well as wood chips, for making an aromatic tea with diaphoretic, diuretic and emmenagogue properties.

However, the essential oil they contain is rich in thujone, a stimulant of the central nervous system, an overdose of which can cause convulsions, abortion and death. Thujone is also found in other plants such as wormwood (*Artemisia absinthium*) and tansy (*Tanacetum vulgare*).

The arborvitae also contains tannin and a glucoside.

The seeds of the cultivated Oriental thuja (*T. orientalis* = *Platycladus o.* – India to Japan) have been eaten in Asia after their bitterness has been removed.

TAXACEAE

Taxus (B-F-H 4)   Yew

Latin name of the tree from the Indo-European root "tecs," to work skillfully: the wood is easy to carve and was highly prized for bow-making.

N.E. & N.W. N.Am., Fla.

Our native *T. canadensis* – N.E. N.Am. – is planted for ornamentation, as well as some Eurasian species and hybrids.

In the various species, the <u>red aril</u> surrounding the seeds is fleshy and edible. It has a mucilaginous texture and a sweet, pleasant taste. It can be added to fruit salads and other desserts or eaten alone.

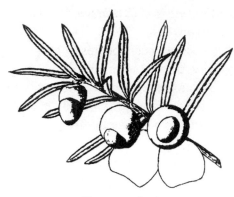

Taxus canadensis

The arils of our native *T. brevifolia*, Western yew – N.W. N.Am. – and *canadensis* (m.a.), American yew, were eaten by Indians.

Those of the cultivated European yew (*T. baccata*) and of the Japanese yew (*T. cuspidata*) were eaten in their countries of origin.

The seed, however, is very toxic, although not unpleasant tasting. Care must be taken not to ingest it with the aril, and especially not to chew it. Like the foliage, it contains a glucoside and several alkaloids, including taxine, a very dangerous heart depressant, and ephedrin.

Yew seeds and leaves, taken internally, produce digestive, nervous, respiratory and cardiovascular disorders, which can result in death. Those of the European yew (*T. baccata*) have occasionally been used as an expectorant, purgative and abortive; they have also been used to poison arrow points and people. Horses, cattle, sheep, goats and wild animals have been poisoned by browsing in the foliage of various species.

The bark of the trunk contains taxol, a substance active against certain forms of cancer.

Yew leaves can serve as an insect repellent.

It is important to be able to differentiate the young shoots of yew trees from those of the other conifers such as fir, larch, pine or spruce, which are edible. Yew leaves do not have the same lemony taste and smell, and are rather bitter and odorless.

Endangered species: *T. floridana* – Fla.

Torreya (B-H 5) Torreya
After J. Torrey (1796–1873), New York botanist.
Calif. & Fla.
Our two native species, *T. californica* – Calif. – and *taxifolia* – Fla., Ga. – as well as an Asiatic species are sometimes planted as ornamentals.

The <u>seeds</u> of *T. californica* (m.a.), California nutmeg, are edible raw. They are rich in oil.

Those of local species have been used in Japan (*T. fargesii, grandis, jacki* and *nacifera*; the last is cultivated for ornamentation in America).

Endangered species: *T. taxifolia* (m.a.).

EPHEDRACEAE

Ephedra (D 4)   Mormon Tea

Greek and Latin name of an undetermined plant, possibly horsetail (*Equisetum* sp.), from the Greek "epi," on top of, and "edra," seat. S.W. U.S. & Mexico.

The <u>twigs</u> were made into tea by the Indians long before the settlers learned to use the plant and gave it its common name. They are often roasted before being boiled or steeped.

The plants contain tannin and alkaloids such as pseudoephedrin but do not contain ephedrin. This well-known stimulant of the sympathetic nervous system (a composant of amphetamines) and powerful antiallergic comes from an East-Asian species (*E. sinica*, Ma-huang) which has been used medicinally for several thousands of years in China.

Southwestern Indians credited the decoction of our native Ephedras with beneficial digestive properties. It is also diuretic, febrifuge and tonic.

The <u>seeds</u> were roasted, ground and mixed with other flours to be eaten as a mush by Indians.

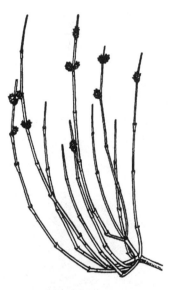

Ephedra trifurca

The species used most widely for both tea and seeds are *E. nevadensis* and *trifurca*.

A few Eurasian species (*E. distachya, major*) bear small red fruits which are sweetish and edible.

Flowering Plants
(Magnoliophyta)

I. DICOTYLEDONS
(Magnoliatae)

MAGNOLIACEAE

Liriodendron tulipifera (G 2)   Tulip tree, Yellow Poplar
From the Greek "lirion," lily, and "dendron," tree: referring to the showy flowers.
E. N.Am.
The tree is planted as an ornamental.

The root has reportedly been used as a flavoring for spruce beer.
The inner bark of the roots and trunk contain a heart-stimulating alkaloid.

Magnolia (B 4)   Magnolia
After Pierre Magnol (1638–1715), French botanist.
E. N.Am.
Several native and East Asian species are planted as ornamentals.

The leaves of *M. virginiana*, laurel magnolia, sweet bay – S.E. U.S. – are fragrant and have been used as a condiment. Those of *M. grandiflora*, bull bay – S.E. U.S. – can be used in the same way.
In Japan, the leaves of related species are wrapped around a handful of rice to preserve it and to give it a pleasant flavor.

Magnolia grandiflora

38

The young and tender leaves of some East Asian magnolias are boiled and eaten in their countries of origin (including *M. stellata*, planted in N.Am.).

In several species, mature leaves are also used as a spice.

The flower buds and flowers of *M. acuminata*, cucumber tree, are edible. Those of *M. grandiflora* (m.a.) were pickled in Devonshire, England, where the tree is planted for ornamentation.

Buds and flowers of local species are also eaten in Eastern Asia either boiled and pickled (after removing the calyx) or used in flavoring rice.

Magnolia bark is astringent, febrifuge and tonic.

ANNONACEAE

Annona   (B 5)   Annona
Latin "annona," year's harvest. This name was applied to these trees because "anon" was the Haitian name of a local species.
S. Fla.
Several tropical American species are cultivated for their fruits in S. Calif., S. Fla. and Mex. Some are naturalized in the last two regions.

A. glabra, pond apple, is native to Southern Florida. Its fruits are edible raw but are better cooked. They are made into jelly.

A. cherimolia, cherimoya – native to S. Am. – is cultivated in Southern California, Southern Florida and Mexico. It is found as an escape in Mexico.

The custard-like fruit pulp is sweet, aromatic and delicious raw. It is often made into cooling drinks and sherbets.

A. squamosa, sweet sop or sugar apple – native to W.I. – is cultivated in the areas previously mentioned and naturalized in Southern Florida.

Its fruit is excellent raw: the pulp is soft, sweet and aromatic. It is made into sherbets and preserves and fermented into an alcoholic drink.

The other species cultivated within our zone also bear edible fruits. Some of them might occasionally persist on cultivation sites.

The fruits of over 20 other trees of this genus are commonly eaten in the tropics. Most of them are native to Central and South America.

Asimina   (B-H 4)   Papaw, Custard Apple
From the French "asiminier," itself derived from a local Indian name of
the tree "assimin."
E. & C. N.Am.
Our species are occasionally grown as ornamentals.

The fruits of *A. grandiflora, speciosa* – both Ga. and Fla. – and *triloba* are
edible raw when ripe. Beneath the brown skin, the pulp is sweet, aromatic and
creamy. Papaws are up to about 4 inches (10 cm) long.
Some people develop allergic reactions when touching or eating the fruits.
The seeds contain an alkaloid which has a depressant effect on the brain.
Endangered species: *A. tetramera* – Fla.

CANELLACEAE

Canella alba   (B 5)   Wild Cinnamon
Latin diminutive form of "cana," tube. By analogy with *Cinnamomum*
spp., cinnamon, named "canella" because the bark is sold rolled up into
tubes.
S. Fla.

The bark and leaves are strongly but pleasantly aromatic. They are used as a
spice in the West Indies, where the tree is also native.

CALYCANTHACEAE

Calycanthus   (D 3)   "Allspice"
From the Greek "calyx," calyx, and "anthos," flower: referring to the col-
ored calyx.
E. N.Am. & Calif.
Our Eastern species, *C. floridus*, Carolina allspice, is sometimes culti-
vated as an ornamental.

The bark of *C. fertilis* – S.E. U.S. – *floridus* (m.a.) and *occidentalis*, Cali-
fornia allspice – Calif. – is used as a cinnamon substitute.
The leaves are fragrant as well.
The seeds of *C. fertilis* (m.a.) contain an alkaloid (calycanthine), similar to
strychnine.
They have occasionally poisoned cattle.

Lauraceae

The Lauraceae are aromatic trees and shrubs whose bark and/or leaves are often used as spices. The best known is the Mediterranean bay laurel (*Laurus nobilis*).

These plants grow mostly in tropical and subtropical regions, with some notable exceptions in our flora (sassafras, spice bush and California laurel).

Cassytha filiformis   (G 5)   Love Vine
Etymology unknown.
S. Fla. (seemingly native to tropical regions of both hemispheres).

The plant has reportedly been used in India to flavor buttermilk.
However, it contains an alkaloid, laurotetanine, which is toxic in large doses.
The fruits are supposedly edible.
An Australian species bears white drupes which are said to be edible.

Cinnamomum camphora   (B 5)   Camphor Tree
"Cinnamomum," "cinnamum" and "cinnamon" are the classical Latin names of the cinnamon tree, *C. zeylanicum*.
Originally from S. China, this tree is cultivated and locally naturalized in S. Fla. It is occasionally planted in S. Calif.
The cinnamon tree (*C. zeylanicum*) – Sri Lanka – is sometimes grown as an ornamental.

Young shoots and leaves of the camphor tree are eaten boiled in Southeastern Asia. The older, aromatic leaves are used as a spice.
Camphor is distilled from the wood of the tree.
This solid volatile oil has antispasmodic and rubefacient properties.
The bark of many *Cinnamomum* spp. is used as a spice; most of them (about 30) are in tropical Asia, where the trees are native. The most widely utilized species is the Ceylon cinnamon tree (m.a.), which yields our household cinnamon.

Lindera   (B-H 4)   Spice Bush
After Johan Linder (1676–1724), Swedish physician.
E. & C. U.S. (mostly *L. benzoin*).

Root and stem <u>bark</u>, <u>twigs</u> and <u>leaves</u> of the spice bush are very fragrant and make a pleasant, aromatic tea and an interesting flavoring.

The <u>fruits</u> are used as a spice. They can be dried and powdered.

The plant contains an essential oil.

<u>Twigs</u>, <u>leaves</u> and <u>fruits</u> of several East Asian species are used locally as a spice or as tea. Their young leaves are sometimes cooked and eaten.

Endangered species: *L. melissifolia* – S.E. U.S.

Persea   (A 5)   Persea
Classical name of some undetermined Egyptian tree.
P. borbonia, red bay, and *palustris* are native to S.E. U.S.

The aromatic <u>leaves</u> of the red bay are used fresh or dried for flavoring dishes and for making tea.

P. americana, avocado – tropical Am. – is cultivated on a large scale in Southern California, Southern Florida and Mexico. Avocado trees persist near old homesites and occasionally become naturalized.

The ripe <u>fruit</u>, yellowish-green inside, is delicious raw in salads or alone. It is also an excellent ingredient for salad dressings and dips due to its soft, oily texture.

Avocados can be picked long before maturity and ripen perfectly after a few days or weeks.

They contain 2% protein, 20% oil, 7% carbohydrates, vitamins B1, B2, C, niacin and some minerals. They are very easily digested.

Three main varieties – Mexican, Guatemalan and West Indian – differ mostly in size and thickness of the skin.

The fruits of other tropical American species are edible.

Sassafras albidum (B 2) Sassafras
From the Spanish vernacular name "salsafras."
E. N.Am.
Sometimes planted as an ornamental.

The <u>root bark</u> is thick, spongy and very aromatic. White at first, it turns red on contact with the air. It is often made into a delicious tea, a popular blood purifier and used for flavoring root beer (see *Smilax* spp.).

It can also be powdered and used as a spice or made into chutney.

The root bark contains an essential oil which is anodyne and antiseptic. It has been banned by the Food and Drug Administration (FDA) as being possibly carcinogenic due to its safrol content. This oil has been used for flavoring beverages, candies, chewing gum and tobacco.

Unfortunately, the sale of sassafras bark has also been prohibited, although its normal use can in no way be detrimental to health: pounds of it would have to be ingested to equal the amount of oil considered toxic. Sassafras tea is diaphoretic, diuretic and stimulant, and has been drunk for centuries without harmful effects. In the Appalachians and in the Ozarks, sassafras roots are sometimes sold in the produce sections of supermarkets for use as a spring tonic.

The young <u>leaves</u> can be eaten raw or cooked. They have a very pleasant, lemony flavor, a mucilaginous texture and make excellent additions to salads and various dishes. They are also easily dried and stored.

Older leaves should be dried, powdered and sifted to remove the hard parts. They are used in making "gumbo" or "filé," a flavorful Creole soup from Louisiana. Sassafras leaf powder can be employed as a thickener for sauces, soups and stews.

Umbellularia californica (B 4) California Laurel, Oregon myrtle
From the Latin "umbellula," a small umbel: referring to the shape of the inflorescence.
Pacific Coast of N. Calif. & S.W. Ore.
The tree is sometimes planted as an ornamental.

The <u>root bark</u> has reportedly been used for making tea.

The aromatic <u>leaves</u> are an excellent condiment: they are sold commercially in the United States (especially in the Pacific Northwest) in place of, and under the name of, bay laurel, a Mediterranean tree of the same family (*Laurus nobilis*). They can also be made into tea.

However, these leaves are very pungent, especially when fresh. If crushed and inhaled too strongly, they cause sneezing and burning of the eyes.

They were used for headaches by the Indians.

The <u>nut</u> is edible raw or roasted and has a pleasant taste.

Its <u>envelope</u> has an interesting, spicy flavor.

The hard wood of the Oregon myrtle (the local name of the tree.north of the California line) is often used in Southwestern Oregon for turning and for carving small objects.

ARISTOLOCHIACEAE

Asarum   (D 4)   Wild Ginger

"Asaron" in Greek and "asarum" in Latin designated an undetermined plant.

Almost throughout.

The <u>rootstock</u> of *A. canadense* – E. N.Am. – and *caudatum* – W. N.Am. – has been used as a spice either fresh (crushed) or dried (powdered). It is aromatic, its smell and taste vaguely reminiscent of ginger (*Zingiber officinale*, Zingiberaceae). It can also be candied.

It has been used as a carminative, diuretic and expectorant, and was reportedly made into a contraceptive tea for women by the Indians.

Externally, it is an irritant, provoking dermatitis in certain people.

The <u>leaves</u> can also be used fresh or dried as a condiment.

It is wise to use moderation with all parts of this plant as a related European species (*A. europaeum*) is known to have emetic properties.

NYMPHAEACEAE

In spite of their difficult underwater harvest, the rhizomes of water lilies (*Nuphar* and *Nymphaea*) and lotus (*Nelumbo*, Nelumbonaceae) have been eaten by humans since prehistoric times in various parts of the world.

Brasenia shreberi (C 3) Water Shield
Etymology unknown.
Throughout. A monotypic genus.

The tubers were boiled or ground into flour by Indians. Like most underground parts, they are richer in starch from fall until early spring.

The slimy young shoots, leaves and stems are eaten raw or cooked in Japan, where the plant is also native.

Nuphar (C 2-3) Water Lily
Derived from the Greek, Egyptian and Persian names of the plant.
Throughout.
Certain species are sometimes grown for ornamentation.

The thick, fleshy rhizome is edible after long cooking. That of *N. advena* – E. & C. U.S. – and *polysepalum* – W. N.Am. – was eaten by Indians. In Northern Europe people used to eat the rootstock and the leafstalks of *N. luteum*, yellow water lily, native both on our continent and in Europe.

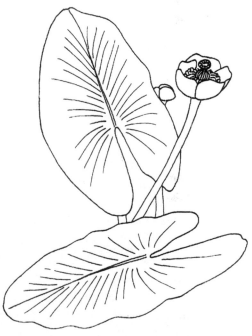

Nuphar luteum

The rhizomes grow in the mud, often many feet below the water surface, and are generally difficult to gather, especially since they are best gathered in winter.

Once boiled or roasted, they peel easily. The sweetish interiors are cut up into soups or stews. Indians also dried the rhizomes and ground them into flour.

The rhizomes of a local species were eaten in Japan.

In Turkey, the flowers of the yellow water lily (m.a.) are made into a refreshing drink.

The seeds of *N. advena, luteum* and *polysepalum* (all m.a.) were used as food by Indians. However, it is usually difficult to remove them from their pods. The Indians placed the whole pod in a hole in the ground to let them ferment and become mucilaginous, after which the seeds were easily freed by washing.

When heated, water lily seeds swell to some extent because of their water content. They can be heated in a frying pan, possibly with some oil, or in embers if wrapped in aluminum foil. They can also be boiled after cracking.

Indians roasted or ground the seeds and added the flour to stews and soups.

Seeds of the yellow water lily were also eaten in Europe after being cracked and boiled or dried and ground into flour. Those of local species were also used as food in Japan.

The seeds are rich in starch.

The yellow water lily contains alkaloids (nupharine) with antispasmodic and hypotensive properties. It can be used medicinally in the same way as *Nymphaea* spp.

Nymphaea (C 2)   Water Lily

Greek name of the plant "nymphaia" from "nymphê," nymph, goddess of water. Almost throughout.

Several native, exotic and hybrid species are cultivated as ornamentals.

The thick, fleshy rhizomes are edible after long cooking. Those of the following species have reportedly been eaten in North America: *N. elegans* – Fla., S. Tex., Mex. –, *mexicana* – Mex., naturalized in S. Fla. –, *odorata* – E. N.Am. –, *tetragona* – N. N.Am. – and *tuberosa* – N.E. & C. N.Am.

A fermented drink is said to have been made in France with the rhizome of the European water lily (*N. alba*). The rootstock was eaten in Scandinavia.

Water lilies are known to contain starch, sugars, mucilage, tannin, alcaloides (nupharine), a glucoside (nymphaline) and an estrogen.

They are anaphrodisiac, antispasmodic and astringent. Nymphaline is a heart tonic.

The rhizome of *N. odorata* (m.a.) is antiseptic, emollient and astringent.

But that of *N. tuberosa* (m.a.) contains acrid, more or less toxic substances, which can be eliminated by boiling in several changes of water. It is likely that other species contain similar acrid principles.

The rhizomes of several *Nymphaea* spp. are used as food in tropical America, Asia and Africa.

The flowers of a local species have been eaten in Asia.

The peduncle of the fruits of another species was eaten raw or roasted in tropical America.

In Ceylon, the unripe, tender fruits of a local nymphaea (*N. lotus*) are pickled or eaten in curries. The seeds of this species were eaten in ancient Egypt 5,000 years ago.

Nymphaea seeds are commonly used as food by peoples in Africa, Asia, Australia and Central America. They are boiled, ground into flour or sometimes even cooked whole in hot sand.

They contain protein, starch and some oil.

In Ireland and Scotland, the rhizome of the European water lily (*N. alba*) was used for dyeing wool blue-black.

NELUMBONACEAE

Nelumbo (C 2-3)   Lotus
(= *Nelumbium* spp.)
Ceylonese name of the sacred lotus, *N. nucifera*.
N. lutea, American lotus, is native to E. N.Am.
N. nucifera, sacred lotus – native to E. Asia and introduced into Egypt around 5,000 B.C. – is planted for ornament and occasionally escapes from cultivation, especially in Fla.

The starchy rhizomes of the American lotus were used as food by Indians after repeated boiling to remove their acrid taste. In Eastern Asia, those of the sacred lotus are prepared in the same way, then sliced and eaten (often in banquets) or fried, pickled or candied. A starch ("gaou-fun") is extracted from the rhizomes in China.

The stems, petioles, peduncles and young leaves of the American lotus were eaten by Indians.

The stems of the sacred lotus are used as food in Japan. They have a somewhat spicy aftertaste. The young leaves are eaten cooked.

Lotus flowers hold an important place in the Hindu and Buddhist religions. Their stamens are reportedly used for flavoring black tea in Indochina.

The seeds of the American lotus were eaten raw before they matured or roasted when ripe to loosen the inner kernels. The seeds were then cracked and winnowed to remove the hard coverings. The kernels have a pleasant taste.

The seeds of the sacred lotus are eaten in China and Japan raw, boiled or roasted; they are also exported to Western countries.

RANUNCULACEAE

Most members of this family are irritating when fresh: they contain an acrid and vesicant substance (protoanemonine), which disappears on drying.

Several genera also contain toxic principles (alkaloids, cardiotoxic glucosides), which are sometimes extremely dangerous. Some of these plants can be deadly.

Anemone (F-H 4) Anemone
Greek name of a poisonous plant, "anemos," wind: referring to the feathery seeds which are dispersed by the wind.
Throughout.
A Mediterranean species (*A. coronaria*) is planted as an ornamental.

The young growth of *A. narcissiflora* – Alaska – is eaten in early spring in the Aleutian Islands. But in general *Anemone* spp. are irritating when fresh.

The leaves of a few local species are eaten cooked as potherbs or in soups in Northeastern Asia.

A. patens, pasque flower – C. N.Am. – has been used medicinally as a diaphoretic, diuretic and rubefacient. It contains dangerous alkaloids, which act on the nervous and digestive systems, and has also poisoned sheep. Cases of cattle poisoned from grazing on anemone leaves have also been reported.

The natives of Kamtchatka in Northeastern Asia used to poison arrow points with the juice of local anemones.

Endangered species: *A. oregana* var. *felix* – Ore., Wash.

Anemonella thalictroides (F 4)   Rue Anemone
Diminutive form of "anemone."
E. N.Am. A monotypic genus.

The starchy <u>root</u> is edible after cooking.

Aquilegia (F-H 4)   Columbine
Name of doubtful origin: supposed to be derived from the Latin "aquila,"
eagle, because its spurs suggest claws, or "aquilegius," water-drawer, because some species grow in moist places.
Throughout.
A native columbine (*A. formosa*) and several European and Asian species
are planted as ornamentals.

Columbines are generally rather toxic. They contain alkaloids and have poi-
soned cattle in Western North America.
The <u>root</u> of **A. canadensis** – E. N.Am. – was reportedly eaten by Indians.
The crushed seeds have been used as an insecticide, especially for lice.
A few local species have been used as food or tea in Japan.
Endangered species: *A. barnebyi, coerulea* var. *daileyae* – both Colo. –, *cana-
densis* var. *australis* – Fla. –, *chaplinei* – Tex., N.M. –, *hinckleyana* – Tex. – and
micrantha var. *mancosana* and *samimontana* – both Colo.

Caltha (F 3)   Cowslip
Latin name of a yellow-flowered plant, probably a marigold (*Calendula* sp.,
Asteraceae).
Throughout. Mostly the cosmopolitan *C. palustris*, which is occasionally
cultivated as an ornamental.

The <u>roots</u> have been eaten after they have been boiled or cooked after drying in Alaska and Northeastern Asia.
The <u>leaves</u> have long been eaten as a vegetable in North America, Europe
and Asia.
When fresh, the mature plant contains protoanemonine (an acrid and vesicant substance), saponins, flavones and reportedly an alkaloid (jervine) and a
glucoside (helleborin). But while very young, its content in irritating principles

is so low that it can be eaten raw; often it is added to salads in moderate quantities. Later, it needs to be boiled in several changes of water.

The plant loses its acridity on drying, as the protoanemonine is transformed into anemonine, a nonirritating substance.

However, if eaten in too large a quantity, or by susceptible people, cowslip can be dangerous: gastrointestinal and nervous disorders have been reported in people who have ingested a fairly large amount of the raw leaves.

Cattle, sheep and horses have occasionally been poisoned by eating the fresh plant.

The <u>flower buds</u> have been pickled like capers, especially in the Southern United States after being boiled in two changes of water.

The whole plant has been used medicinally as a diuretic, diaphoretic, antispasmodic, sedative and rubefacient.

Caltha palustris

Clematis (F-H 2-3) Virgin's Bower
Greek name of a vine, possibly a local *Clematis* sp., from "klêma," a flexible piece of wood.
Throughout.
A Chinese and a Japanese species are commonly planted as ornamentals.

The <u>young shoots</u> are edible after boiling in several changes of water to eliminate their acridity. Those of several species (such as *C. flammula, recta* var. *mandschurica, vitalba*) were eaten as vegetables in Europe and Asia.

They can be pickled in vinegar.

The plants contain protoanemonine. The vesicant properties of European species were put to use by beggars, especially in the Middle Ages, who rubbed the acrid juice on their bodies to produce welts and thus attract the sympathy – and money – of passersby.

Virgin's Bower (especially *C. virginiana* – E. & C. U.S.) can cause dermatitis in susceptible individuals by simple contact.

It also contains saponin.

The plant is diuretic, diaphoretic and stimulant.

Externally, it is rubefacient and analgesic.

Endangered species: *C. addisonii* – Va. –, *galtingeri* – Ala., Tenn. –, *micrantha* – Fla. – and *viticaulis* – Va.

Coptis (C 4)   Goldthread
From the Greek "coptô," to cut: alluding to the divided leaves.
N. N.Am, especially *C. groenlandica* (= *C. trifolia*).

The bitter <u>roots</u> have been used for flavoring beer.

The plant has reportedly been eaten in Northern Asia where it is native as well (it grows naturally in the colder regions of the Northern hemisphere).

Goldthread is used as a bitter tonic, sedative and antiphlogistic.

Ranunculus (F-H 1)   Buttercup
One of the Latin names of the plant, a diminutive form of "rana," frog; the other name "batrachium," from the Greek "batrachion," from "batrachos," frog.

Throughout. Several species were introduced from Eur.

A few Eurasian species (especially *R. asiaticus*) are planted as ornamentals.

The <u>roots</u> of *R. bulbosus* – introduced from Eur. – have been eaten in early spring after boiling in several changes of water or drying to remove their acridity. They are then fairly bland but perfectly edible.

They contain starch and minerals.

Those of *R. inamoenus* were reportedly used as food by Indians in New Mexico.

The roots of a local species (*R. edulis*), known as "morchserdag," are eaten in the Middle East along with the young <u>stems</u> and the <u>leaves</u> of the plant.

The <u>young shoots</u> of *R. pallasii* have been eaten in Alaska.

The <u>young leaves</u> of *R. ficaria* (= *Ficaria verna*, = *F. ranunculoides*), pilewort – introduced from Eur. into N.E. U.S. – can be added to salads. They are usually not excessively acrid, but when eaten alone they sometimes leave a tingling sensation in the throat. Older leaves must be cooked. In Europe, people used to cover the plant with old leaves or sawdust in early spring; this prevented the formation of chlorophyll and of the caustic protoanemonine at the same time. The whitish leaves were harmless.

Ranunculus ficaria

Ranunculus sceleratus

Pilewort roots contain ficaric acid and ficarine. They have long been used to ease the pain of hemorrhoids.

The <u>leaves</u> of *R. repens* and *sceleratus* – both introduced from Eur.; the latter is native to N. N.Am. as well – have also been used as food after repeated boiling to remove the acrid principle, protoanemonine, which is also destroyed by drying.

The <u>flower buds</u> of buttercups can be pickled after boiling in a change of water.

The <u>seeds</u> of *R. californicus* – Calif., Baja, S. Ore. – and *occidentalis* (= *eisenii*) – Calif., S. Ore. – were reportedly parched and ground into a meal by Indians.

Buttercups have been used medicinally as a diaphoretic, antispasmodic, analgesic and rubefacient.

Some species such as *R. sceleratus* (m.a.) can produce blisters if rubbed on the skin. *R. acris* – introduced from Eur. into N. N.Am. – is also very irritating. These and other species are known to have poisoned cattle in the fresh stage, although hay containing dried buttercups is harmless.

The leaves of local species have been eaten as vegetables in Asia.

R. acris (m.a.) is said to dye wool a purplish color with soda bicarbonate as a mordant.

Endangered species: *R. fascicularis* var. *cunei-formis* – Tex. – and *inamoenus* var. *subaffinis* – Ariz.

Thalictrum (D-H 4)   Meadow Rue
From the ancient Greek name of the plant.
Throughout.

T. aquilegifolium – native to the cooler regions of the Northern Hemisphere – is used as food in Japan:
The roots are reportedly eaten raw or roasted.
The young leaves are used as a boiled vegetable.
The leaves of other species (such as *T. minus*) are also eaten in Asia.
Endangered species: *T. cooleyi* – N.C.

BERBERIDACEAE

Berberis (B-H 3)   Barberry, Oregon Grape
(Including *Mahonia* spp.)
Arabic name of the fruit of *B. vulgaris*.
Throughout (including *Mahonia* spp.).
Several native (especially *B. aquifolium*) and Eurasian species, as well as hybrids, are cultivated as ornamentals. The European barberry, *B. vulgaris*, is found as an escape in E. U.S.

The very young leaves of barberries are slightly acid and good raw as long as they are still tender. They can be added to salads.

Barberry fruits are edible raw when ripe, but they are usually better cooked because of their acidity. They were often made into jams and jellies. They can be added to blander fruits to enhance their flavor.

Those of the following species have been used, especially by Indians, in North America: *B. aquifolium* (= *Mahonia a.*), Oregon grape – N.W. N.Am. –, *canadensis* – E. N.Am. –, *fendleri* – N.M. –, *haematocarpa*, red hollygrape – S.W. U.S., Mex. –, *nervosa* (= *Mahonia n.*), Oregon grape – N.W. N.Am. –, *pinnata* – S.W. U.S., Mex. –, *repens* (= *Mahonia r.*), Western barberry – N.W. N.Am. –, *swaseri* – Tex. – and *trifoliata*, agrito – N.M., W. Tex., Mex. The fruits of *B. pinnata* are good raw.

The berries of the Oregon grapes (*Mahonia* spp.) are dark blue with a lighter bloom. They are laxative and said to help build blood. Those of the true barberries are generally red.

The fruits of *B. vulgaris* (m.a.) were often used in Europe. They were made into a sour sauce, preserves and sometimes pickled. A barberry jam was formerly sold in France.

Barberry fruits contain sugars, organic acids, pectin and vitamin C.

They are laxative and refrigerant.

The berries of various local species are eaten in Asia and in South America.

The roots of barberries and Oregon grapes contain several alkaloids, including berberin, which gives the inner root bark a bright yellow color.

The root is chologogue, laxative, diuretic, tonic and vasoconstrictor. It has a very bitter taste. Indians used it mostly as a tonic.

The root bark of our native species was utilized by Southwestern Indians for dyeing wool yellow. That of the European barberry (m.a.) was used similarly on the Old Continent.

The young leaves dye wool an orange-yellow color.

Crushed Oregon grape berries yield a deep purple juice with which Indians sometimes painted their skin and ceremonial objects.

Endangered species: *B. harrisoniana* – Ariz. – *nevinii* and *sonnei* – both Calif.

Caulophyllum thalictroides (E 4) Blue Cohosh

From the Greek "caulos," stem, and "phyllon," leaf: referring to the large leaves borne on the stem.
E. N.Am.

The seeds have been roasted and used as a coffee substitute.

The young leaves of a local species have been eaten as a boiled vegetable in Korea.

The root of blue cohosh contains an alkaloid (methylcytisine) and glucosides. It is used as a diuretic, emmenagogue and oxytoxic. However, it can be very irritating to mucous membranes and cause dermatitis.

The fruits, dark blue berries, have been reported to be poisonous.

Podophyllum peltatum   (B 2)   May Apple
From the Greek "pous," foot, and "phyllon," leaf; meaning obscure.
E. N.Am.

The berry is edible raw when ripe. It is pale yellow, soft, sweet and mildly sour at that stage. It can also be cooked into compotes or jams. The green fruit is unwholesome.

Leaves and fruits of a local species are eaten in the Himalayas.

All other parts of the May apple are toxic.

The rootstock contains a bitter resinous substance (podophyllin). It is a powerful cathartic, an overdose of which can be very dangerous, even fatal. It should never be used during pregnancy, as it can cause birth defects in the fetus. May apple roots have also been used for removing warts, but susceptible individuals may contract dermatitis from handling them.

LARDIZABALACEAE

Akebia quinata   (D 4)   Akebia
From "akebi," Japanese name of the plant.
Originally from China and Japan, this tree is cultivated as an ornamental and has become naturalized on our continent. Another Asian species (*A. lobata* = *A. trifoliata*) is planted for ornament.

The leaves are made into tea in Eastern Asia.

The ripe fruit has a rather insipid, sweet pulp with many black seeds. It is commonly eaten in Asia.

Other East Asian species have similar uses, including *A. lobata* – cultivated in N.Am.

PAPAVERACEAE

Eschscholtzia (G 2) California Poppy
After J. F. Eschscholtz (1793–1831), physician from Estonia, who accompanied the Russian explorer O. de Kotzebue to the Pacific Coast in 1816 and 1824.
W. N.Am.
Our native *E. californica* is often planted as an ornamental.

It has been reported that the <u>leaves</u> of this species were used as greens by Indians either boiled or roasted on hot stones. However, they are extremely bitter.

The plant contains a small quantity of alkaloids, especially in the root. It is said to be mildly narcotic and supposedly was used by Indians to alleviate toothaches.

Papaver (B 2-3) Poppy
Latin name of a European species.
Throughout. Some species are introduced from Eur.
A few species are planted for ornamentation, including *P. nudicaule*, arctic poppy – Arctic regions of Am., Eur. and Asia – and *P. somniferum*, opium poppy – from W. Asia and S.E. Eur.

The rosette of young basal <u>leaves</u> of several species formed before the plant has bloomed is excellent raw. Those of the *P. nudicaule* (m.a.) and of *P. rhoeas*, corn poppy – introduced from Eur. – have also been eaten.

The leaves of the arctic poppy helped members of polar expeditions (Kane, 1856) to fight scurvy.

Those of the corn poppy are highly esteemed in parts of the Mediterranean region such as Southern France. They have a very pleasant, nutty taste and make excellent salads or cooked greens.

The <u>petals</u> and the <u>unripe ovaries</u> ("heads") of the two species mentioned are edible raw. They taste good and make an interesting addition to salads.

Flowers of the corn poppy contain saccharose; as well as a coloring matter and an alkaloid with little toxicity (rhoeadine).

They are emollient, sedative, bechic and diaphoretic.

The seeds of both species have been used as a condiment, with a very nutty taste. They can be roasted and mixed with some salt, like the Japanese condiment "gomasio" made with sesame seeds.

An excellent oil can be extracted from them by cold-pressure.

Egyptians, Greeks and Romans held the seeds of the corn poppy in high esteem and considered them to be slightly laxative.

The large-scale cultivation of *P. somniferum* (m.a.) is forbidden or subject to license in many countries, including the United States and Canada, since the plant is the source of opium and its extracted alkaloids. However, some varieties known as "garden poppies" are planted in gardens and found as escapes in waste places. The opium poppy has been cultivated for millenia for its latex and its seeds.

Papaver rhoeas

The young leaves in the spring are delicious in salads. They were commonly used in Southwestern France and China.

In Central Europe, Western Asia and India, poppy *seeds* are still widely used. They are sprinkled over breads and pastries, in curries (India) or crushed and cooked in milk with honey as a filling for cakes.

They contain proteins, lecithin and over 50% of an excellent edible oil, which is also used for making paints. The seeds do not contain toxic alkaloids.

Opium is the air-dried latex of the opium poppy. It is obtained through an incision made on the green capsule just before maturity.

It contains rubber, resin, sugars, fats, organic acids, minerals and over twenty different alkaloids (such as morphine, papaverin, codeine, narcotin, thebain, heroin), some of which are toxic.

Opium has been used medicinally since Antiquity as an analgesic and a soporific with incomparable virtues. It is also antitussive and antidiarrheic. Various preparations were made with it, such as theriaque and laudanum.

The use of opium, morphine and heroin as narcotics is well-known. It has been said that "opium has been the source, by its judicious employment, of more happiness, and, by its abuse, of more misery than any other drug employed by mankind."

Other *Papaver* spp. are used as food. These include the Asian poppy (*P. orientale* – W. Asia – cultivated as an ornamental in N.Am.). The green unripe capsules, though rather acrid, are eaten as a condiment in Armenia.

Platystemon californicus (G 4)   Cream Cups
From the Greek "platys," broad, and "stemon," stamen.
S.W. U.S., Baja. A monotypic genus.

The leaves were reportedly eaten cooked by Indians in California.

FUMARIACEAE

Dicentra   (F-G-H 4)   Squirrel Corn
From the Greek "dis," two, and "kentron," spur: the name describes the shape of the corolla.
Throughout.
Some species are planted as ornamentals.

The tuberous roots of *D. canadensis* – N.E. N.Am. – were used as food by Indians in New York State.

However, *Dicentra* spp. (including the species mentioned) are known to contain toxic alkaloids and to be potentially dangerous. Some species are called "staggerweed" and have occasionally been fatal to cattle.

Endangered species: *D. ochroleuca* – Calif.

PLATANACEAE

Platanus   (C 3)   Sycamore, Plane Tree
Latin name of the tree.
Throughout.
Two native species (*P. occidentalis, racemosa*), an Asian species and a hybrid
(*P. x acerifolia*, London plane tree) are planted as ornamentals.

Chips of <u>bark</u> from the lower trunk and roots of *P. racemosa* (= *P. californica*),
California sycamore – S. Calif., Baja – are boiled in water as a coffee substitute.
   The <u>sap</u> of *Platanus* spp. can be drunk like water. It contains small quantities
of sugar. The sap of *P. occidentalis*, American sycamore – E. N.Am. – has been
boiled down into a syrup. But it takes large amounts of sap to yield even small
quantities of syrup.

HAMAMELIDACEAE

Hamamelis   (E 4)   Witch Hazel
From the Greek name of the medlar: *Mespilus germanica*, Rosaceae.
E. N.Am.
Two Asian species and a hybrid are cultivated as ornamentals.

The <u>leaves</u> of *H. virginiana* were made into a tea by the Iroquois, which was
sweetened with maple sugar.
   Leaves and bark contain tannin, saponin and other substances (flavones).
   They have astringent, hemostatic, vasoconstrictor, sedative and tonic proper-
ties. Witch hazel activates and regularizes the circulation of the blood.
   Externally it is made into a poultice for insect bites, burns and skin irrita-
tions, including those caused by poison ivy.
   The very small <u>seeds</u> have been reported to be edible.

Liquidambar styraciflua (E 4) Sweet Gum
From the Latin "liquidus," liquid, and the Arabic "ambar," amber: referring to the fragrant resin secreted by the plant.
E. N.Am.
This tree, as well as a Chinese species, is often planted for ornamentation.

The hardened sap, fragrant but bitter, makes an interesting chewing gum. It has antiseptic properties.

ULMACEAE

Celtis (D 3) Hackberry, Sugarberry
Latin name of the tree "celthis."
Throughout.
Several native (*C. laevigata, occidentalis*), European and Asian species are planted as ornamentals.

The fruits are edible raw. They are sweet but usually small with a thin, dry pulp and a large pit, the kernel of which is also edible and good tasting. Indians often dried and ground the fruit, pulp and pit together, thus obtaining a pleasant-tasting meal.
The fruits of the following species have been eaten in North America: *C. douglasii* – W. N.Am. –, *laevigata*, sugarberry – S.E. U.S. –, *occidentalis* – E. N.Am. –, *pallida* – S.W. U.S., N.W. Mex. –, *reticulata*, paloblanco – S.W. U.S., N.W. Mex. – and *tala* – Mex.
The fruits of many other local species have been used in a similar way in Europe, Asia, Africa and in South America. In some species, they are excellent raw.
The kernels of the European hackberry (*C. australis*) yield oil.
The leaves of some hackberries are eaten in Asia and Africa.
Among the species mentioned above, the Chinese hackberry (*C. sinensis*) and the European hackberry (*C. australis*) are planted for ornamentation in North America.

Ulmus (B 4) Elm
Latin name of the tree.
E. N.Am.
Several native (*U. americana*), Eurasian and Asian species are planted for ornament.

The inner bark of *U. fulva*, slippery elm, is dried and mixed with water as food for babies and invalids: it is nutritious and easily digested. Indians ate it raw or boiled with fat.

It contains much mucilage and thus has demulcent and emollient properties, both internally and externally.

In several exotic species, the inner bark, the young leaves (raw or cooked), the mature leaves (dried, powdered and sifted into a flour or made into tea) and the young fruits (raw or more often cooked into a sauce) are used as food. These are mostly Asian species and the Eurasian English elm.

Some of these trees (*U. campestris, parvifolia, pumila*) are planted as ornamentals in North America.

Our elms are susceptible to a serious disease introduced from Asia, called the "Dutch elm disease," which is causing them to slowly die off.

MORACEAE

Broussonettia papyrifera (B 4) Paper Mulberry
After P. Broussonet (1761–1807), botanist from Montpellier, France, and French consul in Teneriffe (Canary Islands).
Originally from E. Asia, it is cultivated for ornament and naturalized in S.E. U.S.

The leaves are edible.
The red fruit is fleshy, sweet and can be eaten raw.
In Asia, this small tree is planted for the fibers of its inner bark, which are used for making paper.

Young leaves, flowers and fruits of a local species are eaten in Eastern Asia. The fruits of another are eaten in Brazil.

Ficus (A 4) Fig Tree
Latin name of the Mediterranean fig tree (*F. carica*); in Greek "sykea" of
Phoenician origin.
A few species are native to Fla. and Mex.
Several tropical Asian species are planted for ornament in N.Am. Some of
these bear edible figs (*F. benghalensis, benjamina, elastica, pumila*). *F. carica*,
the common fig tree, originally from the Mediterranean region and W.
Asia, is cultivated for its fruit in S. U.S. and Mex. and is often found natu-
ralized.

The fruits of *F. aurea*, strangler fig – Fla. –, *laevigata*, wild banyan – S.
Fla. – and *palmeri* – Baja – are edible raw but of inferior quality. They were
eaten by local Indians.

Common figs have been used for ages in the Mediterranean area. They are
delicious when fresh but can easily be dried in the sun. Dried figs have long
been employed as a sweetener for all kinds of dishes and drinks. They can also
be preserved, used in filling for pastries, boiled into a naturally sweet drink or
fermented with water to make a wine.

There are many varieties of figs, which are purple or green at maturity.

The fig is a hollow, fleshy receptacle called a "sycone," the inner walls of
which are covered with many "seeds" (actually the true fruits) produced by
minute flowers. Their very particular fertilization is linked to specific insects as
the usual pollinators are too big to pass through the entrance.

They contain sugars, little protein, vitamins A, B1, B2, C, niacin and minerals.

Dried, they are very nutritious, emollient (both internally and externally),
pectoral and laxative.

The milky juice exuding from a cut in the twigs or in the skin of unripe figs
has been used for ages to curdle milk for making cheese. This method is still
current in Israel and some Jewish communities.

The dried latex is sometimes chewed like gum. The latex contains rubber
and protein-digesting enzymes.

Fresh, it is very caustic: it is used for removing corns and warts but is dangerously irritating to mucous membranes. Eating unripe figs with their skins can be
a very unpleasant experience.

The young branches are said to be laxative and diuretic.
The leaves have been used as an emmenagogue.

The <u>young shoots</u> of several tropical Asian and Australian species are eaten locally.

The <u>fruits</u> of more than 80 local fig trees are eaten in tropical Asia, Africa, America and Australia.

Morus (B 4) Mulberry
Latin name of the black mulberry, *M. nigra.*
Several species are native to E., C. & S. U.S. & Mex.
Two Asian species, *M. alba*, white mulberry, and *M. nigra*, black mulberry, have been introduced in E. and C. N.Am. to provide food for silkworm production and have escaped from cultivation. The fruitless mulberry, a cultivar of *M. alba* (m.a.), is often planted as an ornamental.

<u>Young shoots</u> and <u>leaves</u> of most mulberry trees are edible after cooking.

The ripe <u>fruits</u> are generally juicy, sweet and tasty. They are edible raw. They can also be dried, juiced or fermented into a wine.

Leaves and fruits of *M. microphylla*, Texas mulberry – S. U.S., Mex. – and *rubra*, red mulberry – E. N.Am. – have been eaten in North America.

The fruits of the red mulberry are delicious and wholesome when ripe. Before maturity, however, they contain a milky juice which can cause nervous and digestive disorders; it is also said to have mild hallucinogenic properties.

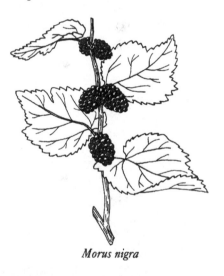

Morus nigra

The fruits of the Texas mulberry are not quite as sweet.

The bark of the tree is anthelmintic and laxative.

The leaves of the white mulberry (m.a.), originally from China and Japan, are the favorite food of the silkworm. The tree has been cultivated for thousands of years and was introduced to Europe in the 11th century.

The taste and texture of the <u>young shoots</u> are quite pleasant.

In Asia the <u>leaves</u> are eaten with rice or in stews.

The usually light-colored <u>fruits</u> (sometimes reddish or even black) are sweet but generally not as tasty as those of other species. They are commonly dried in India and Afghanistan.

The bark of the tree dyes wool yellow in the presence of alum.

The tougher leaves of the black mulberry (m.a.), originally from Central Asia, are also eaten by silkworms but not as avidly as those of the white mulberry.

Its black fruits, however, full of a purple heavily staining juice, are probably the best of all mulberries. They have a slightly acid, very aromatic flavor. The black mulberry is often cultivated as a fruit tree, especially in Asia and less commonly in Southern Europe.

The fruits contain sugars, organic acids, pectin, tannin, vitamins A and C, minerals and other substances.

They are depurative, laxative and refrigerant.

The bark of the tree is anthelmintic and laxative.

The leaves lower the blood sugar level.

Leaves and fruits of several species are eaten in tropical Asia and South America.

CANNABACEAE

Cannabis sativa   (C 4)   Hemp, Marijuana
Greek name of the plant.

Hemp was formerly much cultivated for the fibers obtained from the stem, which are used for making rope and cloth. It is now seldom grown for this purpose on our continent but rather illegally for the euphoric properties of its resin.

The young leaves are edible raw added to salads.

The resin of the female inflorescences contains tetrahydrocannabinol and similar substances and is strongly psychoactive.

It is also antispasmodic, analgesic and aperitive.

This resin is present in variable proportions depending on the cultivated strain and the climate: plants grown in temperate areas generally contain little resin, while those planted in warmer countries contain larger amounts of it.

Hemp has been cultivated for thousands of years in certain parts of Asia for its psychosoactive effects, and nowadays it is smoked or ingested in various ways (dried inflorescences – "buds" – hashish, oil, jam) on all continents of the

Cannabis sativa

world. Its use is frequently forbidden by law, although it is not physically addictive and is far less dangerous than coffee, alcohol or tobacco (each of which was prohibited at some point in history before becoming the source of a large, profitable industry).

Hemp <u>seeds</u> have been eaten since Antiquity. They are often roasted in Eastern Europe and Asia, but in America they are mainly used as birdfeed.

The seeds do not contain the active substances present in the resin, and thus do not have the same properties. They contain vitamin K and 30% of a drying oil, which is edible. This oil is used for culinary purposes in S. Russia and Asia. It is also employed in making soaps, varnishes and paints. It was formerly burned in oil lamps. Hemp is legally cultivated in fields in Switzerland for the oil extracted from the seeds.

Hemp fibers are used as an ecological building material.

Humulus (B 4) Hops

Name of the plant in the Middle Ages from the Latin "humus," soil, and "lupus," wolf: it was believed that the plant was stealing much substance from the earth.

Throughout

H. japonicus, Japanese hops, from N. Japan is sometimes planted as an ornamental. It is naturalized in E. U.S. *H. lupulus* (including *H. americanus*) is native almost throughout and often escapes from cultivation. The European form of this species is cultivated on a large scale for its female catkins or cones ("hops") that give beer its characteristic bitter, aromatic flavor. Hops have been used for brewing since the 9th century.

The native form of *H. lupulus* (m.a.) was used as food by the Indians. Its Apache name means "to make bread with it."

The young shoots of the European form have been eaten raw or cooked since

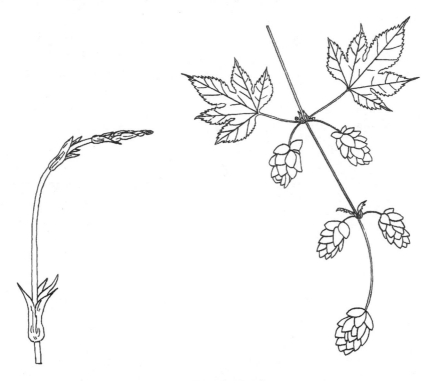

Humulus lupulus

Antiquity in Europe and Asia. They are still sold in some local markets and are used by creative chefs in high-class restaurants. Their taste is very aromatic with a touch of bitterness.

The female <u>cones</u> can also be used as a flavoring for drinks or to make tea, though in moderation because of their strong taste.

They are rich in a resinous substance (lupulin) which contains an essential oil, a crystalline principle (also called lupulin), estrogens and various other substances.

Hops are sedative, hypnotic, anaphrodisiac, tonic, stomachic and diuretic. They can be made into pillows and used to prevent insomnia.

Too large a dose can cause nervous disorders (headaches), often observed in people who manipulate important quantities of hops. Contact with the plant occasionally causes a skin eruption in some rare individuals.

The flexible stems of this vine have been used for basketry. They yield fibers which can be easily woven; hop weaving is an ancient industry in Sweden, for instance. The plant has many other uses: paper is made with its fibers; glass was made in Bohemia with the ashes; wax and a reddish-brown coloring are made with the tendrils.

The <u>young shoots</u> of *H. japonicus* (m.a.) are edible raw or cooked.

URTICACEAE

Laportea canadensis   (D 4)   Wood Nettle
After F. L. de Laporte (1810–1880), Comte de Castelnau, French entomologist.
E. & C. N.Am.

The fresh plant can sting painfully like nettles, although more subtly.

The <u>young shoots</u> and <u>leaves</u> are edible cooked as greens or in soups but are not very good. Raw, they are bitter.

Two local species are eaten similarly in China and Japan.

Parietaria (B 5) Pellitory
Latin name of a plant growing on a wall, possibly *P. officinalis*, from "paries," wall.
Throughout. Both native and species introduced from Eurasia.

P. officinalis – originally from Eurasia and collected as a ballast waif at Eastern seaports – is edible raw or cooked. The <u>leaves</u> and the tender top of the <u>stems</u> have a pleasant taste and have been used as food since Antiquity.
The plant contains mucilage and potassium nitrate.
It is diuretic, depurative and emollient.
Pellitory must be used fresh, as it loses its medicinal properties on drying. The juice extracted from the plant has been employed for the same medicinal purposes as well.

Pilea (G 4) Clearweed, Richweed
From the Latin "pileus," a kind of hat: referring to the enlarged sepal covering the achene in certain species.
E. & C. N. Am.
Some exotic species are planted for ornament.

P. pumila has been reported to be edible. It is somewhat succulent.
Similar species are commonly eaten in Asia.

Urtica (A-H 1) Nettle
Latin name of the plant from "uro," to burn.
Throughout. Both native and introduced species.

Nettles are a staple: the <u>young shoots</u> and <u>leaves</u> of some species are one of the best wild vegetables. Their taste is exquisite, they can be gathered in quantity, and the plant is easy to identify through touch alone.
Young leaves are edible raw added to salads. They must be chopped fine, mixed with other greens and coated with salad dressing or made into a spread with butter or tofu. They generally stop stinging a few hours after their harvest or when they are wet. Raw nettles have a very distinct, green beanlike flavor, which is very different from that of the cooked plant.
Nettle leaves are usually eaten cooked in soups, as greens or in all types of

dishes both savory and sweet in Europe, Asia and America. Nettle soup is one of the most popular wild dishes in Europe.

A concentrated decoction of nettle leaves saturated with salt has been used for curdling milk.

Whether eaten raw or cooked, it is always better to gather only the tops of the plants with the shoots and a few leaves. It is wise not to eat the old leaves raw in summer and fall, for their repeated use could produce lesions on the kidneys. Besides, their texture is rather unpleasant and they have a strong taste. Because of the stinging principles in the hollow hairs on the leaves and stems, ingestion of the plant has been known to cause skin and urinary disorders in susceptible individuals.

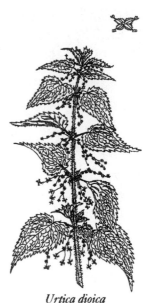

Urtica dioica

The leaves contain protein (7% fresh; over 40% dry), fats, vitamins A and C, minerals (a lot of iron), much chlorophyll, tannin, mucilage and organic acids (gallic, formic).

Their urticating effect is due to histamin and acetylcholin.

They are depurative, tonic, astringent, vasoconstrictor, hemostatic, diuretic, galactagogue and antianemic.

Applied in lotions, they tonify the scalp.

Nettle stings have a beneficial effect on arthritis and rheumatism.

Plantain (*Plantago* spp.) or dock (*Rumex* spp.) leaves rapidly alleviate the painful sensation caused by contact with nettles.

The rhizomes can be placed in a pot filled with earth and kept inside in winter: they will send up young shoots, a most welcome addition to the diet when few greens are to be found outside. During the growing season, nettles can be cut everytime they start sending up stems in order to obtain young shoots year-round.

The fibers of the stem have been employed from time immemorial for making ropes, fishing nets and cloth, especially in Northern Europe.

Nettles dye wool a yellowish-green in the presence of alum.

The following species have been commonly used as food on our continent: *U. californica* – Calif. –, *dioica* – both native and introduced from Eur. –, *holosericea* – W. N.Am. – and *urens* – introduced from Eur.

U. *dioica* and *urens* (m.a.), as well as many other species, are eaten in Europe and Asia. The former is probably the very best of all nettles.

Endangered species: U. *chamaedryoides* var. *runyonii* – Tex.

JUGLANDACEAE

Carya   (B 4)   Hickory

Greek name of the walnut tree, "karya."

E. N.Am.

C. illinoensis, pecan – S.C. U.S., Mex. – is planted in S. and E. U.S. both for its nuts, often in commercial orchards, and as an ornamental.

The sap of the various species contains some sugar and can be boiled down to a syrup.

The fragrant leaves of some hickories are traditionally used by the Cherokee Indians in North Carolina to wrap bean dumplings, to which they give a pleasant flavor. Those of *C. ovata*, shagbark hickory – E. N.Am. – have a citrus-like fragrance.

The ashes of hickory wood can be used as a salt substitute.

The nuts of these trees are edible raw, like walnuts, but their quality varies widely according to the species.

A favorite Indian drink was obtained by pounding whole nuts (shell and meat) in a mortar for a long period of time, after which water was added to form a milky liquid called "powcohiccora," hence the common name of the tree.

If the nuts are too hard to crack, they can be soaked in water and allowed to dry, which causes them to split.

Besides pecans, the nuts of the following species have been used as food in North America: *C. aquatica*, water hickory – S.E. U.S. –, *buckleyi* – E. U.S. –, *carolinae-septentrionalis*, Southern shagbark – S.E. U.S. –, *cordiformis*, bitternut – E. N.Am. –, *floridana* – Fla. –, *glabra*, pignut – E. & C. U.S. –, *laciniosa* – E. & C. U.S. –, *mexicana* – Mex. –, *myristicaeformis*, nutmeg hickory – S. U.S., Mex. –, *ovalis*, small pignut – E. U.S. –, *ovata* (m.a.), *pallida* – E. U.S. –, *texana* – S.C. U.S. – and *tomentosa*, mockernut – E. N.Am.

The best nuts are the pecans and the seeds of *C. laciniosa, ovalis* and *ovata* (all m.a.). Those of *C. aquatica* and *cordiformis* (m.a.) are small and bitter, while those of *C. glabra* (m.a.) are astringent; all three are of inferior quality.

Pecans are sold commercially throughout the United States to be eaten raw or used in cakes, pies and candies. They have a sweet and very delicate taste.

They contain an oil (68%), which can be extracted by cold-pressure, protein (13%), vitamin E and minerals.

The nuts of two local hickories are eaten in China and Indochina. Oil is also extracted from them.

Juglans (B-H 4) Walnut

Latin name of the walnut and of the walnut tree from "Jovis glans," Jupiter's acorn.

E., C. & S. N.Am.

The native *J. hindsii* – Calif. – and *nigra*, black walnut – E. & C. N.Am. – are planted as ornamentals (the former as a street tree in central Calif.) and occasionally for their nuts.

The English walnut (*J. regia*), originally from Southeastern Europe and Western Asia, is now cultivated throughout North America for its nuts, often, as in California, in large commercial orchards. In fact most of the commercially sold walnuts come from the English walnut (m.a.).

The sap of the tree contains some sugar and can be boiled down to a syrup. *J. cinerea*, butternut – E. N.Am. – has particularly been used for this purpose.

The kernels of the fruit of various species are edible raw. They are usually good-tasting but sometimes of small size and enclosed in a very hard shell.

Walnuts contain protein, vitamins, minerals and a large quantity of an excellent oil, which rapidly turns rancid even when refrigerated.

Indians often pounded whole nuts and boiled them in water. The oil was then skimmed off, and the meats were freed from the broken shells, mixed with meal and eaten or pressed into cakes, which were dried for later use; the cakes were then broken up and soaked in water to soften. The oil was used as a food seasoning.

Walnuts can be crushed into a nut butter.

The nuts of the three native species mentioned above – J. *cinerea*, *hindsii* and *nigra* – have been eaten in North America as well as those of *J. californica*, California walnut – Calif. – and *major*, Arizona walnut – S.W. U.S., N.W. Mex.

The best native nuts are the black walnuts and the butternuts. They are used in pies, cakes, candies and ice cream and are also popular as a simple raw snack.

The nuts of many other walnut trees are used as food in the West Indies, South America, Europe and Asia.

Walnuts and butternuts are rich in fat (60%), protein (21-24%), sugars (10-15%), vitamins and minerals.

The bark of the black walnut is astringent. That of the butternut is anthelmintic, laxative and tonic. The leaves can be used to make a cleansing wash for wounds.

The wood of these trees, especially that of the black walnut which is a beautiful chocolate-brown color, is highly prized for carving and furniture making.

The green husk of the fruit is used for dyeing wood or wool brown.

Endangered species: *J. hindsii* (m.a.) – Calif.

MYRICACEAE

Comptonia peregrina　(D 4)　Sweet Fern
(= *Myrica asplenifolia*)
After Henry Compton (d. 1713), bishop of London, patron of horticulture.
E. N.Am.
The shrub is sometimes planted as an ornamental.

The <u>leaves</u> of this species are fragrant and make a pleasant spicy tea with astringent and tonic properties.

They can also be used as a condiment.

The <u>nutlets</u> have reportedly been nibbled by children. They are somewhat aromatic.

Myrica   (B-F 4)   Bayberry, Wax Myrtle
Greek and Latin name of the tamarisk (*Tamarix* spp.) and of other shrubs
from the Greek "myrikê."
E. & N. N.Am., Pacific Coast.
M. pennsylvanica – E. N.Am. – is sometimes planted as an ornamental.

The <u>leaves</u> of various species are aromatic.
They are a good condiment, quite similar to bay
leaves, for soups and stews and can also be made
into tea.

Those of *M. gale*, sweet gale – N. N.Am. &
Eur. – were traditionally employed in Western
Europe for flavoring beer before hops came into
general use. They are still occasionally used for
this purpose in England.

Wax myrtle leaves are astringent and tonic.

Leaves and fruits of the following species
have been used in North America: *M. californica* – Pacific Coast –, *cerifera* – E. U.S. –, *gale*
(m.a.), *pennsylvanica* (m.a.) and *pusilla* – S.E.
U.S.

Myrica gale

The fruits of several Asian and African species are fleshy and are eaten locally.

The aromatic <u>resin</u> contained in the leaves and fruits of the sweet gale is reported to be emetic and purgative. An overdose could produce digestive and
nervous disorders. In moderate quantities, however, use of the plant as a condiment is perfectly safe.

The bluish, aromatic <u>nutlets</u> have also been used as a spice.

They are covered with a white wax which has been used for making candles
in America, Europe and Africa: the fruit is boiled in water and the wax skimmed
off the surface.

FAGACEAE

The starchy seeds of several members of this family are edible.

Castanea (B-H 4)   Chestnut, Chinquapin
Greek and Latin name of the Old World *C. sativa* and its fruit.
E. N.Am.

Two East Asian chestnuts are planted as ornamentals (*C. mollissima*, Chinese chestnut) or for fruit (*C. crenata*, Japanese chestnut, which is not susceptible to the blight).

Our most widespread species, *C. dentata*, American chestnut, was one of the most common trees of Eastern North America: it was both widely distributed and abundant. Yet it has been largely destroyed by a blight (*Endothia parasitica*) introduced from Asia. The blight girdles the trees and the aerial parts die, but the stumps continue to live and send up sprouts which usually die before they are old enough to bear fruit. Dead trunks are now found all over the forest floor; due to the high tannic acid content of the tree, they take dozens of years to decay.

Chestnuts are delicious raw, boiled (and possibly made into a purée) or roasted fresh or dried. They can be ground into a sweet and aromatic flour used to make breads, cakes or mush. Torrefied chestnuts are a good coffee substitute.

Castanea dentata

The seeds of our native species were an important food for Eastern Indians. Besides the American chestnut (m.a.), the following species were used: *C. ozarkensis* (= *C. pumila* var. *ozarkensis*), Ozark chinquapin – Ark., Mo., E. Okla. – and *pumila*, chinquapin. The Ozark chinquapin is not subject to the blight.

The seeds of the Spanish chestnut (*C. sativa*) have been eaten in Europe since Antiquity. They used to be a staple in siliceous mountains of Southern Europe and were often boiled with fennel twigs or seeds as flavoring. Nowadays, they are used mostly for making "marrons glacés," a well-known French confection, and "crème de marrons," chestnut cream. "Marrons" are large chestnuts whose seed is free from inner partitions.

Chestnut flour is used in Corsica to make a mush locally known as "pulenta" and in Italy to make cakes.

Several species yield edible seeds in East Asia, including the Chinese and Japanese chestnuts mentioned above (cultivated in North America).

Chestnuts contain protein (4%), starch (25%), sugars (15%), fats (3%), vitamins B1, B2 and C (as much as lemons) and minerals. They are very nutritious.

Bark, leaves and wood are astringent and extremely rich in tannin. Chestnut bark has been commercialized for tanning hides in both North America and Europe.

The beautiful wood is highly prized for furniture and paneling. "Wormy chestnut" (from the trunks of trees killed years ago) is sold in some parts of the Eastern United States.

Endangered species: *C. ozarkensis* (m.a.).

Castanopsis (D 4)   Chinquapin
From the Greek "kastanea," chestnut, and "opsis," appearance: the fruit resembles a small chestnut.
West Coast.

The <u>seeds</u> of *C. chrysophylla*, giant chinquapin – Pacific Coast – and *sempervirens*, bush chinquapin – N. Calif. & S. Ore. – were eaten by Indians.

They are small but have a pleasant taste and can be eaten raw or cooked like chestnuts.

The seeds of many local species are used as food in Asia.

Fagus grandifolia (C 4)   American Beech
Latin name of the tree; from the Greek "phagô," to eat. In Greek "phê-gos" used to designate oaks with edible acorns.
N.E. N.Am. (south to N. Ga. in the Appalachians).
The European beech (*F. sylvatica*) is planted as an ornamental.

The <u>inner bark</u> of the trunk is edible.

The <u>young leaves</u> can be eaten raw as long as they are tender. Their taste and texture are very pleasant, and they make delicious salads. But they do not remain soft very long, soon becoming rubbery.

The <u>seeds</u>, beechnuts, were eaten by Indians. They were also highly esteemed by the white settlers and in former centuries were sold in Eastern markets. Beechnuts have a sweet taste and can be crushed into a nut butter or torrefied to make a coffee substitute.

Besides protein, beechnuts contain a large proportion of an excellent edible oil.

The seeds of many local species and the oil extracted from them were used as food in Europe and Asia.

Those of the European beech (m.a., cultivated in N.Am.), however, although commonly eaten in the past, are known to contain a slightly toxic principle, fagin. Fagin is contained in the pericarp, the thin brown skin surrounding the kernel. Roasting the nuts makes the skin brittle and easy to remove. (Fagin is found in the nuts of our American beech as well.)

Ingestion of too many beechnuts can cause hepatic, renal and respiratory disorders.

The oil pressed from the seeds is harmless, though beechnut oil was highly esteemed in Northern Europe as a salad and cooking oil. It keeps for years if it is transferred to a different container every year so as to remove the mucilaginous deposit that forms.

In times of scarcity, sawdust from the <u>wood</u> of the European beech was sometimes mixed with flour and baked into bread by European peasants.

The distilled wood of the European beech yields a creosote, formerly used in the treatment of such pulmonary diseases as tuberculosis.

Beech wood is highly esteemed in furniture making and as firewood.

Beech bark is astringent and febrifuge.

Lithocarpus densiflora (E 5)   Tanoak

From the Greek "lithos," stone, and "karpos," fruit: referring to the hard acorn.
N.W. N.Am.

The <u>acorns</u> become edible after their tannin has been leached out (see *Quercus* spp. for the process). They measure approximately 1 inch in length.

Quercus (A-C-H 1) Oak
Latin name of the tree.
Throughout.
Many native oaks, as well as a few European (*Q. ilex, suber*) and Asian (*Q. acutissima*) species, are planted as ornamentals.

Acorns have been used as food by humans since prehistoric times in Europe, Asia and North Africa. They were the staple food of California Indians and were eaten all over our continent.

In several species, acorns are sweet and can be simply roasted or boiled or even eaten raw like chestnuts. Some Indians ground them into a meal which was often cooked with fat. They have occasionally been candied.

More often, however, they are bitter and astringent due to their high tannic acid content (up to 10%). Ingested in large quantities, tannin can cause digestive problems, by inhibiting digestive en-

Quercus sp.

zymes in the body, and headaches. Fortunately, tannin is soluble in water and can easily be eliminated: the acorns are chopped up and boiled in several changes of water until the bitterness has disappeared and the water remains clear.

After draining, the resulting mush can be mixed with various ingredients and eaten salty or sweet. If any bitterness persists, the mush can be mixed with milk, the proteins of which bind the remaining tannin and remove the unpleasant taste. The mush can be spread in a thin layer on a cookie sheet, dried in the oven, then ground to yield a meal which will keep for months. Mixed with cereal flour, the meal makes excellent breads and cakes.

California Indians often had a preference for bitter acorns, as they keep better (due to their tannin) and are more abundant than sweet ones. Acorns were ground between a stone ("mano") and a flat rock ("metate," or grinding rock). After a few generations of use, a depression was worn into the rock; many of these grinding rocks can still be seen in California. The coarse meal obtained was placed in a basket which was left for a few days in a stream, or it was packed in a hole dug on the sandy bank of a creek and water was poured over it until the tannin was leached out and the bitterness was gone. The resulting paste was boiled and eaten as a rather tasteless and often gritty gruel.

Another method was to bury whole acorns in wet ground and leave them for a year. They turned black and became sweet, and then they were simply roasted.

Torrefied acorns have been used as a coffee substitute.

Bitter acorns contain protein (4%), fats (4%), starch (30-35%), sugars (10%), minerals and tannins (5-10%).

They can be used medically as an astringent. The mold that develops on acorn meal has antibiotic properties.

Our oaks are basically divided as follows:

1. *Lepidobalanus*
The fruit matures at the end of the first season and the stigmas are sessile or nearly so. This group includes:

a. The white oaks, with deciduous leaves, the tips of which are not bristle-tipped.

b. The live oaks, with thick, persistent leaves resembling those of hollies (*Ilex* spp.).

White oak and live oak acorns are generally sweet and edible without much preparation.

2. *Erythrobalanus*
The fruit requires two seasons to mature and the stigmas are persistent. The involucral cups bear thin, closely imbricated scales. In most species, the leaf lobes are tipped with bristles. These are the red and black oaks. Their acorns are bitter and must be leached of their tannin as described above.

In each category, the following species have been used as food in North America:

1. a. White oaks

In E. N.Am:

Q. alba, white oak.

Q. bicolor, swamp white oak.

Q. macrocarpa, bur oak.

Q. muehlenbergii, yellow chestnut oak – E. U.S., N.E. Mex. It bears small, sweet acorns.

Q. nigra, water oak – S.E. U.S.

Q. phellos, willow oak – E. U.S.

Q. prinoides, chinquapin oak.

Q. prinus (= *montana*), chestnut or mountain oak – E. U.S. It is said to bear the sweetest acorns of all American oaks.

Q. stellata, post oak – E. U.S.

In W. N.Am:

Q. castanea, mexican chestnut oak – Mex.

Q. douglasii, blue oak – Calif.

Q. gambelli, shin oak – W. U.S.

Q. garryana, oregon oak – Calif. to B.C.

Q. lobata, California white oak, valley oak – Calif. The acorns were frequently used by Indians for meal.

Q. reticulata, netleaf oak.

Q. sadleriana, deer oak – Calif., S.W. Ore.

Q. utahensis – W. U.S.

b. Live oaks

In S.E. U.S.:

Q. virginiana, live oak. The tree bears very sweet acorns in large quantity. An edible oil was obtained by crushing and boiling the seeds in water: the oil was then easily skimmed from the surface.

In W. N.Am.:

Q. chrysolepis, canyon live oak – S.W. U.S., Ore.

Q. dumosa, scrub oak – Calif., Baja.

Q. engelmannii – Calif., Baja.

Q. undulata – S.W. U.S., N. Mex.

2. Red and black oaks

In E. N.Am.:

Q. ellipsoidalis, jack oak – S. Mich. to Minn. & Mo.

Q. marylandica, blackjack oak – E. U.S.

Q. velutina, black oak – E. U.S.

In W. N.Am.:

Q. agrifolia, coast live oak, encino – Calif., Baja

Q. kellogii, California black oak – Calif., Ore.

Q. wislizeni, interior live oak – Calif.

The acorns of many local species have been used as food in Europe and Asia. Some of these oaks are cultivated in North America as ornamentals, including the European *Q. robur*, English oak, reported as escaped in Eastern Massachusetts.

Sweet acorns, sometimes as pleasant tasting as hazelnuts, are eaten in the Mediterranean region, especially in Spain and North Africa. In Provence and Italy, a kind of bread was made with acorns and dried figs. In Arab countries, "racahout" made from a mixture of acorns, cocoa, sugar or honey and starch was used to fatten women.

During World War II, bitter acorns were roasted as a coffee substitute.

Ashes from the wood of *Q. alba*, white oak (m.a.), are said to be usable as baking powder.

Oak bark was reportedly pounded and eaten by the Digger Indians of California in times of famine, but this is doubtful as the bark contains up to 20% tannic acid and is therefore both bitter and unwholesome.

The bark of *Q. suber*, cork oak – W. Mediterranean – has been used since Antiquity as a source of cork for many applications: bottle stoppers, floats, insulation materials.

Bark, acorn cups and galls (growths caused by an insect) found on oak leaves have been used commercially for tanning hides.

They also dye wool brown.

Ink was made from them by mixing a strong decoction with a concentrated solution of iron salts (such as water in which nails have been left to rust for some time) and then filtering the black liquid. It is possible to dye cloth black with this ink.

Bark and leaves have been used medicinally for their astringent, tonic and antiseptic properties. However, they should only be used externally due to their irritating qualities of tannin.

The leaves contain glucosides (quercitrin, quercetol).

Oak leaves have been employed as fertilizer and a fairly nutritious cattle feed, but livestock may develop digestive and renal disorders from browsing exclusively on oak leaves because of their high tannic acid content.

The hard wood of oak trees is highly prized for building, furniture making and paneling.

The "oak scale" (*Cerococcus quercus*) is an insect that lives in colonies on twigs of the scrub oaks (*Q. turbinella* and others – S.W. U.S., N.W. Mex.), covering them with yellow warts of wax. This wax, although very bitter, was used by Southwestern Indians as a chewing gum.

Q. sebifera – Mex. – is also said to be a source of wax.

In Southeastern Europe and Western Asia, the leaves of a local species (*Q. calliprinos*), when bitten by an insect, yield a sweet exudation, which solidifies into small granules. In Kurdistan, nomads soaked the leaves in hot water, which dissolved this manna. The water was then boiled until it turned into a syrup, which was used to sweeten food.

Endangered species: *Q. graciliformis*, *hinckleyi* and *tardifolia* – all Tex.

BETULACEAE

Alnus   (E 3)   Alder
Latin name of the tree.
Throughout.
A native species (*A. Rhombifolia* – Pacific Coast) and a European species (*A. cordata*) are sometimes planted as ornamentals.

The <u>cambium layer</u> of *A. rubra*, red alder – W. N.Am. – was eaten by Western Indians. It was usually cooked with other food in a fire pit.

The fresh bark of this tree and of other alders is reported to be emetic. Dried, it has been used medicinally as an astringent and hemostatic. It contains about 7% tannin. A decoction in vinegar has parasiticidal properties.

It dyes wool a reddish color.

Alders are among the rare plants, besides the legumes (*Fabaceae*), that are able to directly utilize nitrogen from the atmosphere, thanks to bacteria living symbiotically in their root nodules.

Betula   (C-H 2)   Birch
Latin name of the tree from the Celtic "betul."
Almost throughout.
Our native *B. papyrifera*, paper birch – N. N.Am. – and the European birch (*B. pendula*) are planted as ornamentals.

The <u>cambium layer</u> of the various birches is edible, and was eaten fresh or dried, raw or cooked, by Indians.

That of the European birch was ground into a coarse meal in Lappland and Siberia and eaten mixed with sturgeon eggs (caviar).

The cambium of *B. lenta*, black birch, and *lutea*, yellow birch – both E. N.Am. – contains oil of wintergreen, which is commonly distilled from the <u>twigs</u> and <u>bark</u> of these trees and used as a flavoring for such things as toothpaste, medicines and chewing gum. This oil is very fragrant due to its methyl salicylate content (a substance closely related to aspirin: methyl acetylsalicylate). An overdose of it can be toxic, but the bark, the twigs and the leaves can be made into a wholesome, aromatic tea with diuretic and anthelmintic properties.

The scented <u>leaves</u> of *B. glandulosa*, shrub birch – N. N.Am. & Mountains – are also made into tea.

The very young leaves of various species, both aromatic and bitter, can be added to salads as a flavoring.

They contain resin, tannin, an essential oil and various substances.

The sap of all birches has often been gathered in the spring by drilling a small hole into the trunk and placing a hollow elder twig or a straw in it so the sap can thus be drained into a container. Care must be taken to stop the process after a few days so as not to exhaust the tree. The hole is then plugged up with a small wooden peg.

This sap can be drunk as is, but it can also be fermented. It is, however, often preferable to add a small quantity of honey to ensure a good fermentation. After about a month this pleasant-tasting birch beer can be bottled. If it is left in the open, it will soon sour and be transformed into vinegar by an acetic fermentation.

Birch sap is only about half as sweet as maple sap, but it can also be boiled down into a syrup.

Besides the three species mentioned above, paper, black and yellow birch (*B. papyrifera*, *lenta* and *lutea*), *B. nigra*, river birch – E. U.S. – and *populifolia*, gray birch – N.E. N.Am. – have been used for their sap in North America.

The sap is reputed to be diuretic and depurative.

Bark and sap of various European and Asian species, including the European birch (m.a.), have been used as described above.

Sawdust from the wood of this tree was sometimes mixed with flour in Scandinavia for making bread in times of scarcity.

Birch bark contains betulinol as well as a glucoside.

It is depurative, astringent and febrifuge.

The white bark of the paper birch (m.a.) was used by Indians to make containers and canoes, to cover their huts and as drawing material.

The inner bark dyes wool a light brown without mordant and a green with copper sulfate.

The roots of the black birch (m.a.) dye wool a reddish-brown color.

Endangered species: *B. uber* – Va.

Corylus   (B 3)   Hazelnut, Filbert
Latin name of the tree.
Throughout.
The European filbert (*C. avellana*) is cultivated for its fruit in N.Am.

The seeds of *C. americana*, American hazel (including var. *californica*, California hazel – Calif. to B.C.) – E. & C. N.Am – and *cornuta*, beaked hazelnut (including *C. rostrata* – E. N.Am.) – almost throughout – have been eaten on our continent.

Hazelnuts are delicious raw. They are also used for flavoring cakes and various desserts and can be crushed into a delicately flavored nut butter.

The thin skin surrounding the kernels can be easily rubbed off after drying the nuts in the oven at low temperature.

Hazelnuts contain protein (15%), 60% of an edible oil, vitamins and minerals.

They are the richest of all nuts in protein and fats. Hazelnuts are highly nutritious and at the same time very digestible.

The oil extracted by cold-pressure has anthelmintic properties.

The seeds of many species have been used as food by humans from time immemorial in Europe and Asia, including those of the European hazel (m.a., cultivated in N.Am.).

Hazelnut leaves are depurative and also act as a vasoconstrictor like witch hazel (*Hamamelis virginiana*, Hamamelidaceae), a well-known veinous tonic.

CASUARINACEAE

Casuarina equisetifolia   (E 5)   Horsetail Tree, She-Oak, Beefwood
Etymology unknown.
Originally from S.E. Asia and the islands of the Pacific, this tree is planted as an ornamental and naturalized in S. Fla. Another Australian species is also cultivated for ornament.

The sap of the tree can be drunk like water. It can be gathered by cutting a large branch and letting it drain, although this process is quite brutal.

It has been reported that in Australia the aborigines obtain water from the roots of the tree.

PHYTOLACCACEAE

Phytolacca   (B-F 2)   Pokeweed
From the Greek "phyton," plant, and Persian-Arabic "lakk," lacquer: the juice of the fruit has a deep purple color.
Throughout.
A few native or S.Am. species are planted as ornamentals.

Phytolacca americana

The <u>young shoots</u> of *P. americana* – native to E. N.Am. and introduced into W. N.Am. – are commonly picked in the spring in Eastern North America. They were sold in markets at the turn of the 20th century.

Various species, including this one, are used as food in tropical America, Asia, Hawaii and Africa. Plants are gathered from the wild, and pokeweed is sometimes cultivated as a vegetable in these regions, as it was formerly in Europe – especially an Asian species (*P. acinosa*).

To render them edible, the <u>young leaves</u> and <u>stems</u> must be boiled in a change of water. Their flavor is excellent and their texture pleasant although slightly mucilaginous. In the Appalachians, processed poke shoots are usually made into omelettes.

A substance contained in the leaves (pokeweed antiviral protein) might help to cure cancers and fight viruses.

The tender stems can be sliced, blanched, drained and pickled.

Pokeweed contains vitamin A, large quantities of vitamin C (three times more than lemons even after cooking) and minerals, especially P and Fe.

However, in the fresh state, the whole plant, especially the roots and the mature stems, is violently purgative and toxic. The roots contain the alkaloid phytolaccine and can produce general depression, respiratory difficulties and irritation of the intestinal tract. Humans have occasionally been poisoned by eating parts of the roots when cooked along with the young shoots as potherbs.

The root can be placed in a container filled with earth and brought inside during the winter months. It will send up shoots, which provide a welcome addition to meals when few edible plants are left outside.

The juice of the berries has a beautiful purple color. It was formerly used as a food coloring but is now forbidden in several countries, as the saponins it contains (phytohemagglutinins) can, in large quantities, cause digestive, cardiac and other disorders.

The juice of the berries dyes wool a beautiful purplish-pink but is not fast.

Children are sometimes poisoned by eating the berries. However, some birds, including chickens, can feed on them with impunity.

The seeds are said to be toxic as well.

NYCTAGINACEAE

Abronia (E-H 4)   Sand Verbena
From the Greek "abros," delicate, graceful: referring to the appearance of the involucre.
W. N.Am.
Some native species are occasionally cultivated for ornament.

The roots of the following species have been used as food by local Indian tribes: *A. fragrans* – W. N.Am. – and *latifolia* (= *arenia*) – S. Calif. to B.C. Those of the first species mentioned were said to be ground up and mixed with cornmeal.

Endangered species: *A. alpina* – Calif. – and *bigelovii* – N.M.

CACTACEAE

Except for one epiphytic species, all members of this large family are native to the New World. They are best developed in arid regions.

Most species of cactus have edible fruits. For many Indians of Southwestern United States and Mexico, they were, and in some cases still are, a staple food. Whole tribes walked many miles to gather them. Following the harvest, a large feast was held, which was an important event in the calendar of these people.

In Mexico, certain people revert seasonally to a cactus fruit diet to improve their health.

Cacti seeds were commonly eaten in Precolumbian Mexico, and are still sold in markets in some areas. Those of prickly pears, chollas, different *Cereus*-types and barrel cacti (including many species with dry fruits) are used most commonly. The seeds are put aside while preparing pastes and juices from the fleshy fruits. They are dried in the sun, beaten and winnowed to remove the dry pulp and foreign matter and often slightly roasted. They are then ground on the "metate" (a flat grinding stone) just before using. The resulting meal is eaten as a mush or used for thickening soups.

Opuntia, Nopalea, Pereskia, Lemairocereus and *Pachycereus* spp. are used for hedges.

Cacti have been classified by Indians, and to a large extent by scientists, according to their fruit and the general appearance of the plant.

1. *Opuntia*-type

Opuntia (B-H 2)   Prickly Pear, Cholla
Latin name of a fruit in Pliny; Opous was a city in Ancient Greece.
This is our most common genus of cacti, found throughout N.Am. north to Can.

a. Subgenus *Platyopuntia*, prickly pear
The stems are flat; the fruits are fleshy.

Several native, Central and Southern American species are planted for ornament. Some are cultivated for their fruits in Mexico and occasionally in Southwestern United States.

Known by the name of "nopales," the young joints of these cacti are commonly sold in markets and eaten in Mexico, boiled or fried as long as they are tender and spineless. They can also be pickled, candied or dried and stored for future use.

Their pleasant flavor is reminiscent of that of green beans, but their texture is very mucilaginous and requires getting used to. It is best to boil the chopped-up stems first and then sauté them in a frying pan.

Sliced in half, the stems make good poultices (acting as a pain killer, disinfectant and healing agent) for burns, abcesses or rheumatic pains.

The flowers are edible cooked and locally used as food.

The fruits, known as prickly pears, are highly esteemed in many parts of the

world. They are sold in markets in Mexico,
Central and South America, Northern Africa
and Asia. Their Mexican name is "tuna."

When ripe, they are fleshy, juicy and delicious to eat raw. Unfortunately they are very difficult to gather and to handle, since their surface
is covered with tiny barbed bristles, called
"glochids." These glochids (characteristic of
cacti in the genus *Opuntia*) readily penetrate the
skin and can cause painful and sometimes dangerous inflammations, especially if they come in
contact with the mucous membranes of the
mouth.

Tunas are gathered with three-pronged sticks,
and the glochids are removed by rubbing the
fruits in the sand with leafy branches or by scrub-
bing them with a brush in running water. They
can then be peeled and eaten as such. The numerous hard seeds can be removed or spat out.

This was the most important fruit for the Ancient Mexican peoples who devised many ways
of using and preserving the abundant crops.

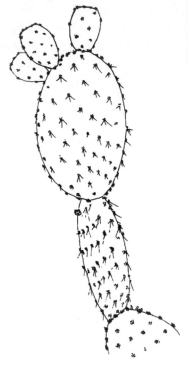

Opuntia ficus-indica

The pulp or the juice were made into "miel de tuna," "melcocha," "queso de
tuna" and "colonche."

The aspect and quality of prickly pears varies according to species and variety. They are usually large, purplish-red and delicious to eat raw (provided not a
single glochid remains).

If the skin is intact, they will keep fresh for over a month. They can also be
juiced, made into jams or dried in the sun after peeling (this preparation is called
"tunas passadas" in Mexico). Tuna fruit paste, drinks and ice-cream are sold in
Mexican markets.

Prickly pears contain 10-15% sugars (glucose, levulose), mucilage, pectin, organic acids (malic, tartric), tannin, vitamin C and minerals.

In Ancient Mexico, the <u>seeds</u> were carefully collected and dried, sometimes
lightly roasted, and ground. The resulting meal was used, as mentioned above,
as a thickener for soups or eaten as a mush.

The thick <u>mucilage</u> expressed from the <u>stems</u> of *Opuntia* spp. is sometimes chewed like gum or mixed with fat and made into candles. It can also be heated up and concentrated to be used as an adhesive.

In this subgenus, the following species have most commonly been used as food in North America:

O. azurea, nopalillo – Mex.

O. basilaris, beavertail cactus – S.W. N.Am. Often it is planted as an ornamental.

O. brasiliensis, figueira – from S. Am., naturalized in S. Fla.

O. chlorotica – S.W. U.S.

O. dillenii – S.E. U.S., Mex.

O. engelmanii – S.W. U.S., Mex.

O. ficus-indica, "indian fig" – Mex., naturalized in S. U.S.

O. fragilis – W. U.S.

O. laevis – Ariz. & N. Son.

O. leucotricha – Mex.

O. lindheimeri – La., Tex. & N. Mex.

O. macrocentra – Tex. to Ariz.

O. macrorhiza – S.C. U.S.

O. megacantha – Mex.

O. occidentalis – S. Calif., Baja.

O. phaeacantha – Tex. to Ariz., N. Mex.

O. polyacantha – W. U.S.

O. pottsii – N.M., Tex. & N. Mex.

The <u>fruits</u> may vary in size from ½ inch to over 3 inches (1 to 8 cm). The largest ones are yellowish of *O. megacantha* (m.a.).

O. basilaris, beavertail cactus (m.a.), is sometimes attacked by two cottony cochineal insects (*Dactylopius tomentosus* and *confusus*) of a bright red color. The scales feeding on *Nopalea coccinellifera* are used commercially for dye (see *Nopalea* spp.).

b. Subgenus *Cylindropuntia*, cholla

The stems are cylindrical, the spines are enclosed in a papery sheath and the fruits are generally dry.

Papago Indians used the young joints of *O. arbuscula*, pencil cholla – S.W. U.S., N.W. Mex. – and of similar species as food in times of scarcity.

The flower buds of *O. acanthocarpa* var. *ramosa* – S.W. U.S., Son. – were eaten by Pima Indians, often combined with piñole or wild greens.

The fruits of the following species have reportedly been used as food by Indians:

O. clavata (= *Corynopuntia c.*), club cholla – N.M.

O. fulgida – Ariz. & N. Mex.

O. grahamii, club cholla – W. Tex., N.M. & N. Mex.

O. imbricata – S. U.S., Mex.

O. versicolor – Ariz., N. Mex.

O. whipplei – Ariz., N.M.

The seeds of chollas were sometimes eaten like those of prickly pears and other cacti.

The wood is used as fuel.

Some *Opuntia* spp. have thick, tuberous roots, which, however, have not been reported as being edible.

Endangered species: *O. basilaris* var. *treleasei* – Calif., Ariz.

Nopalea (B) Nopal
After the Mexican name of various cacti, "nopal."
Mex.
N. coccinellifera (= *N. cochinellifera*), cochineal plant or nopal, is culti-
vated in Mexico for raising cochineal insects, which feed on this cactus.
They are used in the fabrication of a red dye, one the few natural sources
of this color. The importance of its culture has declined with the advent of
synthetic dyes.

The young joints of the nopal are edible like those of *Opuntia* spp. They are
often sold in markets as "nopales." Another commonly used species is *N. de-
jecta*, nopal chamacuero.
The fruits of the two cacti mentioned above and of other species are eaten
raw or processed like tunas (see *Opuntia* spp.).

Pereskia aculeata (B 5) Lemon Vine
Etymology unknown.
S. Fla., Mex.

The leaves of this cactus are edible raw. (Plants of this genus bear persistent
leaves which are not to be confused with the fleshy stems. Other cacti grow real
leaves on the young joints, but they rapidly fall off as the stems mature.)
The yellow fruit is edible and tasty. It is called "barbados gooseberry" in
some of the West Indies where it is native.
Fruits and leaves of other tropical American species are eaten both where the
plants are indigenous and where they have been introduced.

Pereskiopsis (B 5)
From *Pereskia*, name of a genus of cacti (see above), and the Greek "op-
sis," appearance, because the plant resembles some *Pereskia* spp.
Mex.

The fruits are aromatic and slightly acid. Their local name is "tunas de agua"
(water tunas), and they are used mostly for making cooling drinks. They can also be
boiled and eaten as vegetables or candied in honey syrup after being precooked.
The most commonly used species is *P. aquosa*.

2. *Cereus*-type

These cacti are divided primarily between "pitayos," which are tall, bear large fruits ("pitayas") and are sold commercially in Mexico, and "pitahayos," which are small in stature or creeping and bear smaller fruits ("pitahayas").

The fleshy fruits are sometimes covered with a spiny burr which falls off at maturity, but they do not bear glochids like prickly pears. They usually appear in the spring and are generally eaten fresh. Both pitayos and pitahayos are highly esteemed and often planted for their fruits in backyards and gardens of Mexico. In some areas, cacti are the only fruit "trees."

The small seeds contained in the fruits are generally eaten along with the pulp. In some species of this group, they are saved and ground into a paste.

Acanthocereus (B 5)
From the Greek "acantha," spine, and the Latin "cereus," candle.
Fla., Tex., Mex.

The ripe fruits are edible raw. One of the most commonly used species is *A. pentagonus* (= *A. tetragonus*), dildoe, naranjada – Tex., E. Mex.

Cephalocereus (B 5)   Tree Cactus
From the Greek "kephalê," head, and the Latin "cereus," candle. The long white fibers growing at the top of the stems make them resemble hairy heads.
Fla., Mex.

The ripe fruit is edible.

"Wool" from the top of the stems (the long, flexible fibers mentioned above) is woven into a cloth which dries rapidly when wet, does not become moldy and is not attacked by animals.

Cereus (B-H 5)
From the Latin "cereus," candle: the name describes the appearance of these cacti.
S. U.S., Mex.
A S.Am. species (*C. peruvianus*) is planted for ornament in S. U.S. and Mex. It is commercially cultivated for its large, luscious fruit, which is exported to N. Am. and Eur.
C. giganteus (= *Carnegia gigantea*), saguaro – S. Ariz., N. Son. – is often planted as an ornamental in Arizona.

The fruit of the saguaro (m.a.) was a staple for Papago and Pima Indians of Arizona and Sonora. Harvest time in July was an occasion for festivities which would last for weeks.

The pulp of the fruit is sweet and red, somewhat resembling that of a watermelon. The fruits are eaten fresh or made into syrup or preserves. They were often gathered after having fallen to the ground and naturally sundried; at this point they were simply pressed into cakes and stored.

Juice obtained from the fruits is thick and sweet. During the annual harvest, it was fermented into an alcoholic drink.

The seeds were mashed into a buttery paste. They are rich in oil.

The long, woody ribs from the skeleton of saguaros are used as building material.

Endangered species: *C. eriophorus* var. *fragrans*, *gracilis* var. *aboriginum* and *simpsonii* and *robinii* var. *robinii* and *deeringii* – all Fla.

Echinocereus (B-H 2)   Hedgehog Cactus
From the Greek "echinos," hedgehog, and the Latin "cereus" candle: the name describes the appearance of the plants.
S.W. U.S., Mex.
Some native species are planted as ornamentals.

The fleshy stems of **E. fendleri** – Ariz., N.M., N. Mex. – and **reichenbachii** – Tex., N.M. – have reportedly been eaten after roasting.

The fruits of many species are eaten fresh or made into preserves. They are juicy and generally good tasting, sometimes reminiscent of strawberries (as in *E. engelmanii*, *enneacanthus* and *stramineus*). The following species have been used as food:

E. coccineus – S. U.S.

E. conglomeratus, pitahaya de Agosto – Mex.

E. dasyacanthus – W. Tex., N.M., Chih.

E. dubius – S.E. Tex.

E. engelmanii – S. U.S., N. Mex.

E. enneacanthus – Tex., N.M., N. Mex.

E. fendleri (m.a.)

E. stramineus, Mexican strawberry – Tex., N.M., Chih.

E. triglochidiatus, clear-up cactus – S.W. U.S.

Endangered species: *E. blanchii* var. *angusticeps, chloranthus* var. *neocapillus* – both Tex. –, *engelmanii* var. *howei* – Calif. – and var. *purpureus* – Utah –, *fendleri* var. *kuenzleri* – N.M. –, *llyodii* – Tex., N.M. –, *reichenbachii* var. *albertii, russanthus* – both Tex. –, *triglochidiatus* var. *arizonicus* – Ariz. – and *viridiflorus* var. *davisii* – Tex.

Escontria chiotilla (B 5)   Chiotilla
Etymology unknown.
Mex.

The fruits, called "chiotillas," are purple and fleshy. They are sold fresh or dried in markets.

Harrisia (B 5)   Pricky Apple
After Wilson Harris, superintendent of public gardens and plantations in Jamaica.
Fla., Mex.
A tropical American species is cultivated as a house plant.

The fruits of several species are eaten, especially in the West Indies and in S.Am.

Heliocereus (B 5)   Pitahayo
From the Greek "hêlios," sun, and the Latin "cereus," candle.
Mex.

The flavorful spineless <u>fruits</u> are made into refreshing drinks. They are called "pitahayas de agua" (water pitahayas).

Hylocereus (B 5)   Night-blooming Cereus
From the Greek "hylê," thicket, and the Latin "cereus," candle: the plant forms dense thickets.
Mex.
Some species, including *H. undatus*, pitahaya (actual country of origin unknown but frequently naturalized in Mex.), are cultivated in S. U.S. for their large, white, scented flowers which bloom at night.

The spineless, good-tasting <u>fruits</u> are edible raw. In some species of the pitahaya group they attain a large size and are highly prized.
The fruits of *H. ocamponis* and *undatus* (m.a.) are eaten in Mexico.
Those of other species are used as food in tropical America.

Lemairocereus (B 5)   Pitayo
Etymology unknown.
Ariz., Mex.
Some native species are occasionally planted as ornamentals. *L. queretaroensis* – Mex. – and other species are cultivated for their fruits.

The <u>fruits</u> of the following species are eaten: *L. queretaroensis* (m.a.), *thurberi*, organ pipe cactus, pitayo dulce – S. Ariz., Son. – and *weberi* (= *Pachycereus w.*) – Mex.
Large and quite delicious, those of the organ pipe cactus were a staple for Papago Indians. They ripen in summer and, if the year has been neither too dry nor too wet, are extremely abundant. Gathering these fruits was a very important event for local Indians, who feasted on them fresh, fermented them into wine and dried the rest for later use. They are called "pitayas dulces" in Mex.
The <u>seeds</u> of the various species were commonly ground into a butterlike paste. They were such an important food source for some tribes that, after eat-

ing pitayas, the people would collect the seeds from their feces, dry them in the sun, clean them by beating and winnowing and use them for making flour.

The fruits of other species are eaten in Central and South America.

The pulp of the stems of the organ pipe cactus can be eaten, but it remains tough, even after long cooking.

Mucilage extracted from the stems of some species has reportedly been chewed like gum or used as an adhesive.

Lophocereus (B 5)   Senita, Cabeza de Viejo

From the Greek "lophos," tuft, and the Latin "cereus," candle. The stems are topped with long grayish spines, which also refers to the meaning of the Spanish name "old man's head."
S.W. Ariz., N.W. Mex.
L. shottii is occasionally planted for ornament.

The small fruits are edible raw and have a pleasant flavor. They are called "carambullos" in Mexico.

The stems contain a toxic principle. In Mexico they are chopped up and thrown into streams or lagoons as fish poison.

Machaerocereus (B 5)   Pitayo agrio

From the Greek "machaira," knife, and the Latin "cereus," candle. The name describes the appearance of the plant.
Baja.

The fruits ripen in summer. Those of *M. gummosus* have a pleasant taste and are sold in local markets under the name of "pitayas agrias" (sour pitayas).

Like those of *Lophocereus* spp., the stems contain a toxic principle and are used as fish poison.

Myrtillocactus (B 5)   Candelabra Cactus

From the Latin "myrtillus," the specific botanical name of *Vaccinum myrtillus*, the European blueberry, and "cactus," derived from the Greek "cactos," thistle or spine. The fruits of these cacti are thought to resemble blueberries.
Mex.

The flowers are edible. They are often sold in markets as "claveles de caram-bullos." They are cooked like *Agave* flowers.

The fruits are small, the size of grapes, but are extremely abundant and very good tasting. They are sold in markets fresh or dried under the name "caram-bullos" (like the fruits of *Lophocereus* spp). After their juice is expressed, it is al-lowed to slowly evaporate on a heated plate; the resulting dry extract is spread into sheets known as "tortilla de carambullo" or "dulce de carambullo."

M. cochal – Baja – and *geometrizans* – C. Mex. – are the most commonly used species.

Neovansia diguettii (B 5)

(= *Peniocereus d.*)
Etymology unknown.
S. Ariz., Son.

The fruits are edible and highly prized locally.

Nyctocereus (B 5)

From the Greek "nux, nuktos," night, and the Latin "cereus," candle: re-ferring to the fact that the flowers bloom at night.
Mex.

The fleshy fruits are edible.

Pachycereus (B 5)   Cardon

From the Greek "pachys," large, thick, strong, and the Latin "cereus," candle. These are the largest of all N.Am. cacti.
Mex.

The fruits of the following species have been used as food: *P. columna-trajani* (= *Cephalocereus c-t.*, = *Haseltonia c-t.*) – C. Mex. –, *pringlei* – N.W. Mex. – and *tetatzo* (= *Neonuxbaumia t.*), higos de tetatzo – C. Mex.

Fleshy but rather insipid, they are eaten fresh, dried or toasted. Spanish mis-sionaries made them into jams and jellies.

The seeds of *P. pecten-aboriginum*, cardon hecho hecho, and *pringlei* (m.a.)

are ground into a meal which is used for making a sort of "tamales" (steamed cakes).

The dry fruit of *P. pecten-aboriginum* (m.a.) is covered with long, flexible spines. It can be made into a comb (hence the specific name from the Latin "pecten," comb) by cutting the spines an equal length, putting them into hot water to soften and then shaping them.

The stems of cardon cacti contain a toxic substance that can cause spasms.
The wood of these "trees" has been used as building material.

Peniocereus   (C 4)   Night-blooming Cereus
From the Greek "penia," poverty, and the Latin "cereus," candle. When the plant is not blooming, its aerial parts are reduced to wiry, gray stems which are usually hidden under bushes.
S.W. U.S., Mex.

The huge <u>tuberous root</u> of *P. greggii* can weigh up to 85 pounds and grow to 2 feet long by 10 inches wide. Often eaten by Indians, it is said to taste somewhat like turnips. It is sometimes fed to cattle.

The scarlet <u>fruit</u> is edible.

The beautiful white flower (up to 6–8 inches [15–20 cm] long) blooms at night; its fragrance can be smelled from a distance of 200 feet.

Rathbunia   (B 5)
Etymology unknown.
N. Mex.

The <u>fruit</u> is edible and has a sweet taste.

Selenicereus   (B 5)
From the Greek "selenê," moon, and the Latin "cereus," candle: because it blooms at night.
Mex., one sp. naturalized in S. Fla.
S. grandiflorus, snake cactus – E. Mex., W. I. – is cultivated as an ornamental and naturalized in S. Fla. This cactus (along with several other genera, including *Hylocereus*, *Peniocereus*) is also sometimes called "night-blooming Cereus."

The large fruit (up to 3 inches) of snake cactus is edible and has a pleasant flavor.

The stem contains a substance (cactin) that has a strong action on the heart.

Wilcoxia (B 5)
Etymology unknown.
Ariz. to Tex., Mex.

The fruits are edible, with a sweet and pleasant flavor.
The plants have a thick, fascicled, tuberous root.

3. *Echinocactus* type
These are the barrel cacti, or "visnagas" (pronounced *bis-na-ga*). The pulp of the large stem has been used as food:

As a drink which has saved a few desert travellers from dehydration: The top of the cactus is chopped off with a machete, and the pulp is mashed inside the stem and strained through a piece of cloth to yield a rather bitter, mucilaginous liquid, which is unpleasant to drink even in an emergency.

As "cactus candy" or "dulce de visnaga": The top and the external spiny rind are cut off, and the pulp is divided into pieces of suitable size which are cooked for a long time in a thick, raw sugar syrup. After draining and cooling, the product, which is good but rather insipid, keeps very well if stored in a dry place. Cactus candy is commonly sold in Mexico and occasionally in Southwestern United States.

As a part of the regular diet of the nomadic tribes of Northern Mexico: the pulp was cooked in a fire pit.

As cattle feed.

Barrel cacti were sometimes used as cooking pots by Indians. They removed the pulp, filled the empty cactus with water and placed red-hot stones in it to cook meal.

All these uses are now discouraged, since it takes 50 to 100 years for a barrel cactus to reach maturity.

There is some controversy as to the taxonomical status of the following two genera.

Echinocactus (E-H 4)   Barrel Cactus, Visnaga

From the Greek "echinos," hedgehog, and "cactos," thistle, spine: the name describes the appearance of the plant.

S.W. U.S., Mex.

Two Mexican species are sometimes planted as ornamentals, especially *E. grusonii*, golden cactus.

The pulp has been used as described above.

The most generally used species are *E. grandis* – C. Mex. –, *horizonthalonius* – S. U.S., Mex. – and *visnaga* – Mex.

The fruits are generally dry and wooly, although fleshy, but rather tart in some species.

The seeds of *E. polycephalus*, niggerhead cactus – S.W. U.S., N.W. Mex. – were reportedly used as food by the Panamint Indians of California.

Endangered species: *E. horizonthalonius* var. *nicholii* – Ariz.

Ferocactus (D-H 4)   Barrel Cactus, Visnaga

(including some *Echinocactus* spp.)

Etymology unknown.

S.W. U.S., Mex.

The pulp of *F. acanthodes* – S.W. U.S., Baja – and *wislizeni* – Tex. to Ariz., N. Mex. – has been used as described above.

The fruits of several species have an acid pulp that tastes somewhat like lemons. They are used in cooking in Mex. and sold in markets under the name "lima de visnaga" (barrel cactus lime).

Those of the following species are eaten: *F. hamatacanthus* (= *Hamatocactus h.*) – Tex., N.M., N. Mex. –, *melocactiformis* (= *histrix*) – C. Mex. – and *viridescens* – Calif., Baja.

The fruits of *F. acanthodes* and *wislizeni* (m.a.) are also edible raw or cooked. They resemble mucilaginous green peppers and can be found on the plants throughout the winter.

The <u>seeds</u> of the last two species were reportedly ground into a meal by Indians.

Endangered species: *F. viridescens* (m.a.).

4. Small Cacti

Because of their small size, these cacti are of minor importance. However, many species yield pleasant-tasting berries in great abundance. They are gathered and sold in markets in Mexico as "chicotl" or "chilitos dulces" and are eaten raw.

Ancistrocactus (E 5)

From the Greek "agkistron," hook, and "cactos," thistle, spine: because the plant has hooked spines.

Tex., Mex.

The green <u>fruits</u> are juicy but thin-fleshed.

Ariocarpus (E 5)   Living Rock

From the Latin "aria," name of a tree with edible red fruit in the family Rosaceae, and "carpos," fruit. The fruit of this cactus is supposed to resemble that of the service tree, *Sorbus aria*.

Mex.

The <u>fruits</u> are fleshy but have a thin pulp.

The pulp of the stem of *A. fissuratus* (= *Roseocactus f.*) is reportedly chewed by Indians to produce a delirious intoxication. It contains anhalonin and pellotin, which have an action similar to that of strychnin and digitalin.

Cochemia   (E 5)

Etymology unknown.

Mex.

The <u>fruit</u> is an edible red berry.

Coloradoa mesae-verdae (E 5)
Named for its location: this cactus is found mostly in the state of Colorado.
S.W. Colo., N.W. N.M. A monotypic genus.

The naked fruit is juicy and edible.

Coryphantha (D-H 4)   Desert Pincushion
From the Greek "koryphê," cluster, and "anthos," flower. The flower
blooms in clusters at the top of the stem.
C. & W. N.Am.
Some species are cultivated as house plants.

The fruits are fleshy. Those of *C. vivipara* – C. U.S. & S.C. Can. – were
eaten by Indians.
Endangered species: *C. minima, ramillosa, scheeri* var. *uncinata* – all three
Tex. –, *sneedi* var. *leei* – N.M. –, *sneedi* var. *sneedi* – Tex., N.M. – and *strobiliformis*
var. *durispina* – Tex.

Epithelantha (E 4)
(including *Mammillaria* spp.)
Etymology unknown.
W. Tex., Mex.

The fruit is fleshy and edible but has a thin pulp.

Lophophora (E 5)   Peyote, Peyotl
From the Greek "lophos," tuft, and "pherô," to bear. The plant is topped
by a tuft of soft hairs.
Tex., Mex.

The fruit is a small, few-seeded berry.
The flesh of the stem of *L. williamsii* has well-known hallucinogenic properties, due to the alkaloid mescalin. It also contains other toxic principles, such as
anhalonin and pellotin (see *Ariocarpus* spp.).

Mammillaria (D 4)   Pincushion Cactus, Visnaguita
From the Latin "mammilla" (diminutive form of "mamma"), breast: re-
ferring to the shape of the tubercles covering the stem.
W. & C. N.Am.
Some species are cultivated for ornament, especially as house plants.

The small fruits, red or green when ripe, are edible. Those of *M. meicantha*
and *microcarpa* – both S.W. U.S., N. Mex. – among other species, are pleasant
tasting.
It has been reported that the whole stems of an undetermined species were
cooked and eaten by Indians after they burned off the spines.

Neobesseya (D 4)
Etymology unknown.
C. U.S., Mex.

The fruits of *N. missouriensis* – C. U.S. – have been eaten.

Neogomesia agavioides (H 6)
Etymology unknown.
Mex. (Tamaulipas). A monotypic genus.

The fruit is a small edible red berry.
This is a very rare cactus.

Neomammillaria (E 4)
(including *Mammillaria* spp.)
From *Mammillaria*, generic name of the pincushion cacti, discussed
above.
S.W. U.S., Mex.

The small fruits are edible like those of *Mammillaria* spp.

Obregonia denegrii (E 5)
Etymology unknown.
Mex. (Tamaulipas). A monotypic genus.

The fruits, white and juicy, are edible.

Pediocactus (E-H 4)
From the Greek "pedion," flat land, field, and "cactos," thistle, spine.
W. N.Am.

The fruit is a juicy, edible berry.
Endangered species: *P. bradyi* – Ariz. –, *knowltonii* – N.M., Colo. –, *peeble-sianus* – Ariz. – and *sileri* – Ariz., Utah.

Sclerocactus (E-H 4)
From the Greek "sclêros," hard, and "cactos," thistle, spine.
S.W. U.S.

The fruits are often dry but have occasionally been used as food.
Endangered species: *S. glaucus* – Utah, Colo. –, *mesae-verdae* – Colo., N.M. –
and *wrightiae* – Utah.

5. Epiphytic Cacti
These cacti grow as epiphytes on trees in tropical forests.
The only species to be found in our area is:

Rhipsalis baccifera (D 5)   Mistletoe Cactus
(= *R. cassutha*)
From the Greek "rhiptô," to throw.
Mex.

The red berries, sweet and mucilaginous, are edible.
Rhipsalis spp. are the only cacti to be native outside the American continent;
a few species are found in Africa.

AIZOACEAE

Generally fleshy plants, several members of this family are cultivated as ornamentals (ice plant) or as vegetables (New Zealand spinach). The main center of distribution for plants in this family is South Africa.

Mesembryanthemum   (B 2)   Ice Plant

From the Greek "mesêmbria," midday, and "anthemos," flower: it is said to open its petals towards noon.

The native *M. chilense* (= *M. aequilaterale* = *Carpobrotus chilensis*) – coasts of S. Ore., Calif. & Baja – is planted for ornament and as a soil-binder along roads and freeways in S. Calif.

M. edule (= *Carpobrotus edulis*), Hottentot fig, from South Africa is naturalized in California. It is planted for the same reasons as our native species.

The fleshy <u>leaves</u> of the two species mentioned above, triangular in section, are edible after cooking, but they are astringent. Their astringency makes them unpalatable raw, but they can be pickled.

The mucilaginous *fruit* can be eaten raw when ripe, but it is rather insipid. It is known by the name "Hottentot fig," as it was used for food by the Khoin (formerly named Hottentots) of South Africa.

Leaves and fruits of some local species are eaten by the natives of South Africa, and their <u>seeds</u> are reportedly ground into a meal.

The fleshy leaves and <u>stems</u> of *M. crystallinum* – naturalized from S. Africa along the coasts of S. Calif. & Baja –

*Mesembryanthemum
crystallinum*

are very good to eat raw in a salad or as a cooked vegetable in many parts of the world. They are extremely tender, slightly salty and sour. The surface of the plant seems to be covered with small particles of ice that reflect the light, hence the name "ice plant." The plant is cultivated and sold in markets in Europe.

The leaves can supposedly be used as soap.

Sesuvium (B 4)   Sea Purslane
Etymology unknown.
Atlantic & Gulf Coasts, Mex.

The fleshy and salty <u>leaves</u> and <u>stems</u> of **S. maritimum** – coasts of N.Y. to Tex. – and **portulacastrum** – coasts of S.E. U.S., Mex. – are edible raw. They are also eaten cooked as a vegetable or pickled.

The tiny <u>seeds</u> can also be gathered and used for food.

Tetragonia expansa (B 4)   New Zealand Spinach
(= *T. tetragonoides*)
From the Greek "tetra," four, and "gonu," knee: the fruit is four-pointed.
Originally from Australia and New Zealand (and also possibly from S.Am.), this plant has often been cultivated in gardens, especially in Eur. It is naturalized along the coasts of S. U.S. and Mex.

The <u>young shoots</u> are edible raw. Older <u>leaves</u> are better cooked. They are eaten in many parts of the world. The taste of the plant is definitely reminiscent of spinach, though it has a somewhat stronger flavor.

A few local species are used similarly as food in Australia, South Africa and South America.

Tetragonia expansa

Trianthema portulacastrum (B 4)
From the Greek "treis," three, and "anthemon," flower: referring to the clustered flowers.
S. U.S., Mex.

Young <u>leaves</u> and <u>stems</u> are eaten raw or cooked in tropical and subtropical parts of the world.

Those of related species are used as food in tropical Asia and Africa.

MOLLUGINACEAE

Mollugo (D 3)   Carpetweed
Name derived from *Galium mollugo* (Rubiaceae), a plant with similarly whorled leaves.
Throughout.

M. verticillata, originally from tropical America, is a common weed in gardens.
In spite of its small size, the young plant is eaten cooked in tropical and subtropical regions of the world.

CARYOPHYLLACEAE

Cerastium (D-H 1)   Mouse Ear Chickweed
From the Greek "keras," horn: referring to the hard capsule.
Throughout. Both native (few) and species introduced from Eur.
A European species (*C. tomentosum*) is planted for ornament.

These small hairy plants are edible when young. Picked before the plant blooms, the leaves and stems of *C. semidecandrum* – introduced from Eur. into E. N.Am. – have been eaten cooked.
Similar species have been used as food in Asia.
Endangered species: *C. arvense* var. *villosissimum* – Pa. – and *clawsonii* – Tex.

Honkenya peploides (B 4)   Sandwort, Sea Chickweed
(= *Arenaria p.*)
After G. H. Honkeny (1724–1805), botanist from Brandenburg, Germany.
Coasts of Northern circumpolar regions. A monotypic genus.

The whole plant is edible raw or cooked. It is fleshy but does not have a pleasant flavor.
Alaskan Inuits make a product resembling sauerkraut by chopping up the plant, boiling it and letting it ferment. They eat it with berries and fat.

Lychnis (D-F 3) Campion
From the Greek "lychnos," lamp. The dried leaves of a Mediterranean species (*L. coronaria*) were used as a wick.
Throughout. Introduced from Eur.
Two European species are sometimes planted as ornamentals.

The young <u>leaves</u> of various species are edible, preferably cooked, but in moderation only since they contain saponins.
Roots and leaves of *L. dioica* and probably of other species can be used as soap.
The seeds are said to be somewhat toxic.
The leaves of a local species are eaten in Northeastern Asia after parboiling and further cooking.

Silene (D-F-H 3) Catchfly, Campion
Etymology unknown; possibly from the Greek "sialon," saliva, referring to the sticky secretion on the stems of certain species, or from Silenus, foster father of Bacchus, supposedly covered with foam.
Throughout. Both native and introduced European species.

The <u>young leaves</u> of *S. cucubalus* (= *S. vulgaris*), bladder campion – introduced from Eur. – make a good potherb and were used traditionally as food in springtime in various parts of Europe, especially in Southern France. They have a definite sweet pea flavor. With age, they become bitter and, when eaten, can remove the perception of the sweet taste, a very unpleasant feeling.
The plant contains saponin, especially when it gets older.
The <u>leaves</u> of *S. alba* (= *S. latifolia* = *Lychnis a.* = *Melandrium album*), white campion, are slightly bitter but can be eaten raw as additions to salads.
Endangered species: *S. douglasii* var. *oraria* – Ore. –, *invisa*, *marmorensis* – both Calif. –, *plankii* – Tex., N.M. –, *polypetala* – Fla., Ga. –, *rectiramea* – Ariz. – and *spaldingii* – Ore., Wash., Idaho, Mont.

Spergula (E 3) Spurrey
From the Latin "spargere," to sprinkle, hence paintbrush: referring to the shape of the groups of leaves.
Throughout. Introduced from Eur.

S. arvensis, corn spurrey, has been used as food: the <u>young plant</u> is edible raw or cooked.

In Scandinavia, the tiny <u>seeds</u>, although they contain some saponin, have occasionally been gathered, ground up and mixed with flour to make bread.

Stellaria (A 1) Chickweed

From the Latin "stella," star: referring to the shape of the flower.
Throughout. Both native and introduced European species.

S. media – introduced from Eur. – is undoubtedly one of the best wild salads. <u>Leaves</u> and <u>stems</u> are tender and juicy with a delicate nutty flavor, and the plants are easy to gather in large quantities. Chickweed also makes an excellent potherb.

In Japan, it is traditionally eaten in the spring with rice and other wild plants. It is also used for making tea.

Chickweed is known to contain vitamin C, minerals, a fixed oil and some saponin.

It is tonic, diuretic, expectorant and slighty laxative.

The tiny <u>seeds</u> are also edible but are tedious to gather.

Stellaria media

Other species are edible but generally inferior in quality. *S. aquatica*, giant chickweed, is one of the best. Several *Stellaria* spp. are eaten cooked in Japan.

PORTULACACEAE

Many members of this family have fleshy, edible stems and leaves.

Calandrinia (B 4)   Red Maids
After J. L. Calandrini, Swiss botanist of the 18th century.
W. N.Am.

The fleshy <u>leaves</u> of *C. ciliata* are edible raw.
The <u>seeds</u> can also be used as food.
Other species have been eaten in South America and Australia.

Claytonia (B 2)   Spring Beauty
After John Clayton (1685–1773), early American botanist.
Almost throughout.
Some native species are cultivated for ornament.

The small <u>tubers</u> or the fleshy <u>taproots</u> of several species were eaten raw or cooked by Indians. Starchy, they have an excellent flavor when boiled or roasted that is reminiscent of choice potatoes, with overtones of cooked chestnut.

The following species have been eaten on our continent: *C. acutifolia* – Alaska –, *caroliniana* – E. U.S. –, *lanceolata* – W. N.Am. –, *megarrhiza* – Rocky Mountains –, *tuberosa* – Alaska – and *virginica* – E. N.Am.

The <u>leaves</u> of all the species mentioned above are good to eat raw.

Lewisia (D-H 4)   Bitterroot
After Meriwether Lewis (1774–1809), famous for his transcontinental expedition with Clark in 1806–07.
W. N.Am.

The fleshy <u>rootstocks</u> of several species were used as food by Western Indians. After they were cooked by boiling, roasting or steaming in a fire pit, the bitter outer rind was removed from the edible, mucilaginous core. The latter can be eaten as such or dried and ground into a meal. It is preferable to gather the roots before the plant blooms because otherwise they lose nutritious substance.

The following species were eaten in North America: *L. brachycalyx*, *columbiana*, *pygmaea* and *rediviva*.

Nowadays, it is wise not to disturb these plants as they are relatively rare.

Endangered species: *L. maguirei* – Nev.

Montia (A 2)   Miner's Lettuce
After G. Monti (1682–1760), botanist from Bologna, Italy.
W. & N. N.Am.

<u>Leaves</u> and <u>stems</u> of the various species are juicy and edible raw.

Tender, delicious and abundant, *M. perfoliata* (including *M. parviflora*) – W. N.Am. – is probably the very best wild salad plant to be found. It was a favorite of the Indians and also of the miners during the 1849 gold rush in California (hence the common name).

The plant has been cultivated since the 18th century in French and English vegetable gardens. It is still popular in France, where it is known under the name of "pourpier d'hiver" (winter purslane). It can also be found in U.S. markets.

Miner's lettuce, especially the pink base of the stems which is very juicy and sweet, is also a good thirst quencher while hiking.

Montia perfoliata

The following species have been used as salad plants in North America: *M. cordifolia* (= *M. asarifolia*) – W. N.Am. –, *fontana* – N.E. N.Am., also native in Eur. – and *sibirica* – N.W. N.Am.

M. fontana (m.a.) was eaten raw or cooked in Europe, but its leaves are quite small. *M. sibirica* (m.a.) was used as food by the Inuits in Alaska and Siberia.

The <u>seeds</u> have reportedly been eaten as well.

Portulaca (H 3)   Purslane

Latin name of the plant.

Throughout. Both native and introduced species.

A S.Am. species *P. grandiflora*, rose moss, is planted for ornament. It is occasionally found as an escape.

In the Andes the <u>roots</u> of this plant are used as food after cooking.

P. retusa – C. U.S. – was eaten as a vegetable by Indians.

P. oleracea, originally from the tropical and subtropical regions of the Old World, is a common weed in North America. It has been used as a vegetable for over 2,000 years in India and Persia. Purslane is cultivated as a salad plant or potherb in Asia, Europe and South America.

Portulaca oleracea

<u>Leaves</u> and <u>stems</u> are fleshy and slightly acid. They are edible raw, preferably mixed with other greens because of their mucilaginous texture. The plant can be used as a thickener for soups and stews. It is excellent in omelettes and can also be pickled.

Purslane contains vitamins A, B and C, minerals (much iron) and mucilage.

It is emollient, depurative, diuretic and refrigerant.

The tiny <u>seeds</u> have often been used as food either cooked whole or ground into a meal. They can be gathered by picking the plant before maturity and letting it dry out on a baking sheet for a week or so. The capsules ripen, and the seeds can be extracted by threshing and winnowing.

Other species are eaten in Asia, Australia, Polynesia and South America.

Endangered species: *P. smallii* – N.C., Ga.

Talinum (D-H 4)   Fame Flower

Name derived from the aboriginal name of an African species.

S. U.S., Mex. Both native and introduced from tropical American species.

Indians cooked and ate the <u>root</u> of *T. aurantiacum* – W. Tex. to Ariz., N. Mex. – which often reaches a large size but also becomes more or less woody.

The leaves of related species are eaten as greens in tropical America and Africa.

Endangered species: *T. appalachianum* – Ala.

BASELLACEAE

Basella rubra (= *alba*)   (B 5)   Malabar Spinach

From the Malabar name.

Originally from tropical Asia, the plant is cultivated as a vegetable or an ornamental in the warmer parts of N.Am. and is naturalized in Mex.

The fleshy leaves are good to eat raw or cooked.

The juice of the fruit is reportedly used for coloring edible agar (seaweed) in Japan.

Malabar spinach is a commonly cultivated vegetable in tropical Africa, America, Asia, Hawaii and even Southern Europe.

Boussingaultia baselloides   (B 5)   Madeira vine

After J. D. Boussingault (1802–1887), French chemist and agronomist.

Mex. & tropical Am.

The plant is sometimes cultivated as a vegetable and an ornamental in N.Am.

The tubers are edible cooked but have a rather unpleasant taste.

The leaves can be eaten raw or cooked.

CHENOPODIACEAE

The best-known members of this family are beet and spinach, but many others are edible. Their leaves are often fleshy.

Many of the Chenopodiaceae have the characteristic ability to grow on saline (halophytic) soils from which they derive a salty flavor.

In some cases, plants in this family can accumulate high amounts of nitrates, which, when ingested, are reduced to toxic nitrites. The latter cause the red blood cells' pigment, hemoglobin, to transform into methemoglobin, dark brown in color and unable to transport oxygen to the body tissues. This can provoke severe troubles, including abortion (by suffocation of the fetus) and death. The accumulation of nitrates is due to the high content of nitrogen and phosphorus in the soil, especially common with artificial fertilization, and to a slow rate of metabolism in the plant, which occurs when the amount of sunlight, available water or outside temperature is too low or the plant has been sprayed with herbicides. Among the Chenopodiaceae, beet (*Beta vulgaris*), lamb's quarter (*Chenopodium* spp.), summer cypress (*Kochia scoparia*) and tumbleweed (*Salsola kali*) are known to accumulate potentially toxic amounts of nitrates.

The same phenomenon occurs in other families, such as Amaranthaceae (*Amaranthus* spp.), Apiaceae (*Daucus carota*), Asteraceae (*Franseria* spp., *Helianthus annuus*) and Poaceae (*Avena sativa, Hordeum vulgare, Panicum* sp., *Sorghum vulgare, Triticum* spp., *Zea mays*).

Other plants in the Chenopodiaceae family can be toxic through the accumulation of selenium absorbed from the soil: they are known as "facultative selenium absorbers." The main ones are *Atriplex* spp. and *Eurotia lanata*.

Allenrolfea occidentalis (D 4)   Iodine bush, Pickleweed
(= *Halostachys o.*)
After Allen Rolfe, English botanist.
W. N.Am. A monotypic genus.

The young stems are edible raw, in moderation, because of their concentration of salts. They are more palatable and wholesome after cooking. The stems become fleshy and filled with a salty juice; the leaves are reduced to scales.

The seeds are also edible.

The abundant pollen is said to cause hay fever in susceptible people.

Atriplex (B-H 2–3)   Saltbush
Latin name of the plant.
Throughout. Both native and species introduced from Eurasia.
A. hortensis, orach, from Central Asia is sometimes cultivated as a vegetable and escapes locally in Calif., Ore. & E. N.Am. A few native and Mediterranean species (such as *A. halimus*, sea purslane) are occasionally planted for ornament.

The <u>leaves</u> of many species were eaten by Indians, especially in Western North America. They are very salty and tend to irritate the throat if eaten raw alone. But they are excellent after cooking, preferably in a change of water, which also eliminates the saponins they contain.

The <u>seeds</u> were generally parched and ground into piñole.

Leaves and/or seeds of the following species have been used as food in North America: *A. argentea* (including *A. expansa*) – W. & C. N.Am. –, *californica* – Calif., Baja –, *canescens* – W. N.Am. –, *confertifolia* – W. N. Am. –, *coronata* – Calif. –, *elegans* – S.W. U.S. –, *lentiformis* – S.W. U.S., N.W. Mex. –, *nuttalii* – W. N.Am. –, *patula* – throughout, also in Eurasia –, *serenana* (= *bracteosa*) – Calif., Baja – and *truncata* – W. N.Am.

Atriplex hortensis

The leaves of a few European and Asian species are eaten as vegetables, including orach and sea purslane (both m.a.). The former has very large leaves, which can be eaten raw or cooked like spinach. The latter has small, very salty, fleshy leaves, which are best after boiling in water.

Hopi Indians used the <u>ashes</u> from the leaves of *A. canescens* (m.a.) as baking powder.

The roots of *A. californica* (m.a.) can serve as a soap substitute.

Atriplex are facultative selenium absorbers.

Endangered species: *A. griffithsii* – Ariz., N.M. –, *klebergorum* – Tex. – and *pleiantha* – Colo.

Beta vulgaris (A 4) Beet

Latin name of the plant.

This well-known vegetable, originally from Eur., is commonly cultivated for its root (red beet var. *rapa*; sugar beet var. *altissima*), for the large, fleshy petioles (Swiss chard var. *flavescens*) or for the leaf blades (var. *cicla*). It is often found naturalized in N.Am.

The <u>root</u> is usually too thin to be of any use as food unless a very young plant growing in deep, rich soil is picked. It becomes woody with age. It is possible, however, if the outer part of the root is still somewhat tender, to peel it off, grate or chop it, boil it and pass it through a food mill to make a purée.

Red beet roots contain much sugar and vitamin A. Cultivated beets are delicious raw, grated or juiced, preferably in combination with other vegetables, as they can sometimes be irritating to the throat. Sliced, torrefied and ground, they make an excellent coffee substitute, said to improve with age. It can also be fermented into a kind of sauerkraut.

Sugar beet roots contain vanillin and a large amount of saccharose. White sugar, refined from this root or from the stem of the sugar cane, is chemically pure saccharose. This well-known sweetener has been extracted from the beet only since the end of the 18th century.

The <u>leaves</u> of the wild plant are edible raw or cooked and are as palatable as those of the cultivated vegetable.

They contain vitamins A, B1, B2, C, niacin, minerals (much iron), saponins, asparagin and other substances (such as betain).

The roots of several local species have been used as food in Europe.

The leaves of various other beets in different parts of the world are edible and often excellent.

If heavily fertilized, beets can occasionally accumulate toxic amounts of nitrates.

Chenopodium   (A 1)   Lamb's Quarter, Goosefoot
From the Greek "chên," goose, and "podion," small foot: referring to the web-footed shape of the leaves.
Throughout. Both native and introduced species.
A S.Am. species, quinoa (*C. quinoa*) is traditionally cultivated for its seeds in the Andes and is now also cultivated in N.Am. It is also planted for ornament.

C. album, lamb's quarter, a common weed introduced from Europe, is probably the best wild species of this genus.

When the plants are young, their <u>leaves</u> are delicious raw. When older, they are excellent cooked, with a very fine spinach flavor.

The <u>seeds</u> are edible as well, but they are rich in saponin, which must be leached out first by boiling in water.

This species has been eaten by humans at least since Neolithic times as the seeds are commonly found in archeological diggings. It was cultivated as a vegetable by the Romans and grown in European gardens up until the 18th century. It is still used as food in many parts of the world. The Japanese, for instance, eat the leaves fresh or preserve them in salt. Leaves and seeds of this plant were eaten by American Indians.

The leaves contain much protein, much vitamin A, vitamins B1, B2, C, niacin, saponins and large proportions of calcium, phosphorus and iron, which is better assimilated raw than cooked. They are also rich in soluble oxalates, which can be eliminated by boiling the plant in two changes of water. People with arthritis, gastric or intestinal inflammations, hepatic conditions or rheumatism should be particularly careful.

Chenopodium album

In heavily fertilized fields, where it occurs as a weed, or if sprayed with herbicides, the plant can accumulate toxic amounts of nitrates.

The plant is sedative and refrigerant.

C. bonus-henricus, Good King Henry, wild spinach, was also introduced from Europe: it was cultivated as a vegetable in our gardens until the turn of the 20th century and has become locally naturalized in parts of Eastern North America.

Its large leaves are excellent raw or cooked. In the mountains of Europe, where the plant forms large colonies, the tradition of picking wild spinach leaves to prepare alpine soup, green dumplings or other traditional dishes is still alive.

Their composition is similar to that of lamb's quarter.

The young flowering spikes are cooked and eaten like asparagus while still tender. They have a pleasant flavor, with a slight bitterness when the plant is older.

The seeds are edible as well, but they are rich in saponin, which must be leached out first by boiling in water.

Good King Henry is emollient, refrigerant and slightly laxative.

The leaves and/or seeds of the following species have been used as food on our continent: *C. californicum* – Calif., Baja –, *capitatum*, strawberry blite, strawberry spinach – locally naturalized from Eurasia –, *fremontii* – N.Am. –, *leptophyllum* – W. N.Am. –, *murale* – introduced from Eur. and naturalized throughout –, *rubrum* – occasionally naturalized from Eur. – and *urbicum* – introduced from Eur.

Chenopodium bonus-henricus

Indians ate the leaves raw or cooked of our native species and of introduced ones as well, when available. The small seeds, easy to gather in quantity, were ground into piñole and made into mush or cakes, sometimes mixed with cornmeal.

C. capitatum (m.a.) has small edible red <u>fruits</u>, formed by the fleshy calyx, which are juicy and sweetish but rather insipid. They stain the fingers a nice brick-red.

The roots of *C. californicum* (m.a.) were reportedly used as soap.

The <u>aromatic leaves</u> of *C. ambrosioides*, Mexican tea, epazote – originally from tropical Am. and naturalized almost throughout – are used as a condiment in Mexico and Guatemala, especially with beans. The plant aids digestion by preventing gas formation. It is preferable to use them with moderation because of their strong, camphorous flavor and their definite bitterness. They can also be made into a pleasant tea with tonic, stomachic and carminative properties or dried, powdered and used sparingly as a condiment.

The <u>seeds</u> are edible as well.

The leaves and flowering tops of var. *anthelminticum* are a powerful vermifuge. This is due to an essential oil, an overdose of which can produce vomiting, headaches and sometimes death. This variety must therefore be employed with moderation.

C. pueblense, cuahzontl – Mex. – is also used locally as a spice.

C. botrys, Jerusalem oak – naturalized from S. Eur. – is still another aromatic species. Tea made with the leaves is carminative, diuretic and antispasmodic.

Leaves and seeds of other species are eaten in various parts of the world.

Quinoa (m.a.) seeds were the main component in the diet of local Indians and are still widely used as food. They are now also known in North America and Europe, where they are commonly sold as a cereal in health food stores.

Cycloloma atriplicifolium   (D 4)   Winged Pigweed
From the Greek "cyclos," circle, and "lôma," fringe, border: referring to the winged fruiting calyx.
C. & S.W. N.Am. A monotypic genus.

The seeds were ground and made into mush or cakes by Indians.

Eurotia lanata   (D 4)   Winterfat
From the Greek "euros," mould: alluding to the hairy surface of the stems and leaves.
W. U.S.

The plant is edible cooked.
Indians applied the powdered root to burns and used to treat fevers with a decoction of the leaves.
The plant is a facultative selenium absorber.

Kochia   (C 2)   Summer Cypress
After W. D. Koch (1771–1849), German botanist.
W. N.Am. Both native and introduced species.
K. scoparia, originally from Eurasia, is planted as an ornamental under the name of burning bush or summer cypress. It is locally naturalized.

Young shoots and leaves of this species can be eaten raw in moderation or cooked. They have a pleasant but very salty taste.
The plant is cultivated for its edible seeds in China and Japan.
It was formerly grown for raising silkworms which form their cocoons on the

twigs. Brooms were made from the branches, hence the specific name "scoparia," from the Latin "scopae," broom.

The plant can accumulate toxic amounts of nitrates.

Monolepis (D 4) Patata

From the Greek "monos," one, and "lepis," scale: referring to the single sepal.

C. & W. U.S.

M. nuttalliana was used as food by Indians: the <u>roots</u> were cooked with fat; the <u>leaves</u> were eaten as greens; the <u>seeds</u> were ground into piñole.

Salicornia (B 2) Glasswort

Italian name of the plant from "sal," salt, and "cornu," horn: the stems have a salty taste.

Along the seashores and salt lakes of the interior.

The <u>fleshy stems</u>, filled with a salty juice, are delicious raw as long as they are tender. Later, they develop a woody core and are less pleasant to eat. They can also be cooked or pickled.

Glasswort contains vitamin C and various minerals.

The <u>seeds</u> are said to be edible as well.

The most commonly used species in North America are *S. bigelovii* – coasts of Calif., Mex. & E. N.Am. –, *europaea* – E. & W. Coasts –, *subterminalis* (= *Arthrocnemum subterminale*) – Calif., Mex. – and *virginica* (= *ambigua*) – E. & W. Coasts.

S. europaea (m.a.) is commercially gathered for pickling or eating raw with fish on the coasts of France.

Other species are eaten raw, cooked or pickled in Europe, Asia and Australia.

Salicornia europaea

Salsola (D 2) Tumbleweed

From the Latin "salsus," salty: referring to the taste of the plant.

Throughout. Introduced from Eurasia.

The very <u>young tops of the stems</u> of **S. kali**, Russian thistle, are tender, salty and edible raw.

The plant soon becomes woody and spiny and turns into well-known tumbleweeds ("desert balls") blown by the wind for miles.

The Russian thistle is rich in many minerals.

The <u>seeds</u> are said to be edible as well.

S. kali (m.a.) can occasionally accumulate toxic amounts of nitrates.

The *young shoots* of other species are used as food, generally cooked as greens, in Europe and Asia.

Due to their high sodium content, the ashes of a related species (*S. soda*) were used to make glass in the Middle Ages.

Salsola kali

Sarcobatus vermiculatus (D 2) Greasewood

From the Greek "sarx, sarcos," flesh, and "batos," spine, bramble. This thorny plant has thick, fleshy leaves.

W. N.Am. A monotypic genus.

The young fleshy <u>leaves</u> are edible raw in moderation. It is wise to cook them in a change of water because of oxalates of sodium and potassium in the plant.

Sheep and cattle eating this forage too freely are susceptible to bloating and even poisoning from the oxalates.

The <u>seeds</u> have reportedly been eaten as well.

Spinacia oleracea (B 5) Spinach

Name derived from the Persian or the Arabic: referring to the spiny seeds. Probably native to W. Asia, this well-known vegetable has only been cultivated for a relatively short period of time. It was introduced into Spain by the Moors in the 15th century.

Spinach sometimes escapes from gardens in the Southern United States and Mexico.

The leaves can be eaten raw or cooked.

They are known to contain vitamins and minerals, chlorophyll, mucilage, saponin (especially in the root) and other substances, including flavonoids. While the chemical analysis of spinach is very thorough, it must be realized that many wild vegetables have similar or superior virtues, though, unfortunately, their composition is only partially known.

The iron in the leaves is better assimilated if they are eaten raw. Moreover, if spinach is to be eaten cooked, it is preferable, especially in dry seasons, to boil the leaves in a change of water to eliminate the calcium and potassium oxalates which form during cooking. They are very irritating to the body and injurious to people with arthritis, asthma, gastric or intestinal inflammations, gout and rheumatism. Some very sensitive people get an allergic reaction from eating spinach, even in moderate amounts.

Cooked spinach should not be kept long as the nitrates (especially plentiful if the plant has been grown chemically) are transformed into toxic nitrites.

Spinach is emollient and slightly laxative.

A local wild species is used as food in Afghanistan.

Suaeda   (B-H 2–3)   Seepweed, Desert Blite, Sea Blite
Name derived from the Arabic "suwed mullah," name of *S. baccata*.
Throughout. Many native species (= *Dondia* spp.), especially in W. N.Am.

Western Indians used the following native species for food: *S. californica* – Calif., Baja – and *depressa* – W. & C. N.Am.

Young shoots and leaves were eaten as greens, sometimes with cactus fruits, by desert Indians such as Pimas. They have a pleasant salty flavor.

The seeds were ground into piñole.

Leaves and seeds of *S. linearis* (= *Dondia l.*), sea blite – coasts of S. Fla. & Mex. – are also edible.

The tender parts of *S. maritima*, sea blite – possibly introduced from Eurasia to the coasts of E. N.Am. – are eaten raw or cooked in Asia (especially in India), where other local species are also used as food. Sea blite is good tasting.

The Coahuila Indians extracted a black dye by soaking the leaves and stems of *S. torreyana*, inkweed – W. N.Am. – in water for use in artwork.

The plant contains tannin and is astringent, but it is also known to produce dysentery in animals consuming it.

Endangered species: *S. duripes* – Tex.

AMARANTHACEAE

Acanthochiton wrightii (D 4)   Greenstripe
From the Greek "acantha," spine, and "chitôn," envelope, tunic.
W. Tex. to Ariz., N.M.

Young shoots and leaves were eaten as greens by local Indians. They were also dried and stored.

Amaranthus (A 1)   Amaranth, Pigweed
From the Greek "amarantos," not wilting. This ancient Greek name refers to the scarious bracts and sepals. It was originally applied to a species of Celosia.
Throughout. Both native and species introduced from tropical regions.
Some tropical amaranths are planted as ornamentals, among them *A. caudatus*, love-lies-bleeding – tropical Am., native to Mex. and naturalized farther north.

A few species are currently being introduced into our vegetable gardens for their edible seeds (as "edible amaranth"). These plants have been cultivated from time immemorial for this purpose in Asia and America. For instance, the pink seeds of *A. caudatus* (m.a.) were a staple in the diet of the Aztecs and also held an important role in their religious life. Various species are or have been cultivated as a leaf vegetable in Europe and Asia.

Young shoots and leaves of the various species are good to eat raw. Older leaves are better cooked. They form an excellent vegetable, with a pleasant flavor. In most cases, the tops of the young stems, still tender, can be eaten as well.

Amaranth leaves are rich in proteins, vitamins A and C and minerals.

They have been used medicinally as an astringent.

The following species were used as food by North American Indians: *A. cruentus* (= *hybridus*), *graecizans* (= *blitoides*) – W. & C. N.Am. –, *lividus* –

E. & C. N.Am. –, *palmeri* – W. & C. N.Am. –, *powelli* – W. N.Am. – and *retro-flexus* – naturalized throughout from tropical Am.

The leaves were eaten as greens. The seeds, ground into piñole, were often mixed with cornmeal for making mush or cakes. The Hopis used the crushed seeds of *A. cruentus* (m.a.) to give their cornbread a light pink color.

When grown on heavily fertilized soil or under drought conditions, amaranths can accumulate toxic amounts of nitrates.

Leaves and seeds of tropical species naturalized in North America, such as *A. caudatus* (m.a.) or *spinosus*, can be used in the same manner.

Those of other species are commonly eaten in Central and South America, Africa and Asia. Some of these plants are in cultivation as ornamentals in North America.

The pollen of amaranths is a possible cause of hay fever.

Philoxerus vermicularis (D 5) Samphire
From the Greek "philos," loving, and "xêros," dry: a drought-loving plant.
S. Fla., Mex.

Leaves and stems are edible cooked.

BATACEAE

Batis maritima (B 5) Saltwort
Greek name of some seashore plants.
Coasts of S.E. U.S. & Mex., from N.C. south.

The plant is fleshy and edible raw. It has a pleasant, salty flavor.

POLYGONACEAE

Many members of this family are considered weeds, although most of them are endowed with edible properties. The best-known cultivated plants among the Polygonaceae are buckwheat and rhubarb.

Antigonon leptopus (C 5)   Coral Vine, San Miguel
Etymology unknown.
Mex.
This native of Mex. is planted for ornament. It is naturalized in S. Fla,

Edible cooked, the tuberous <u>root</u> is said to possess a pleasant, nutty flavor. It can reach a large size and weigh up to 15 pounds.

In some parts of Mexico, the <u>seeds</u>, harvested in the fall, are toasted by stirring them in a container with live coals until they crack open. They are then ground into a meal.

Coccoloba (B 5)   Seagrape
From the Greek "coccos," seed, and "lobos," lobe: referring to the end of the fruit.
Coasts of southernmost U.S. & Mex.
Three native species are sometimes planted as ornamentals, including *C. diversifolia* (= *floridana*), pigeon plum, and *uvifera*, seagrape.

The ripe <u>fruit</u> of those species is very good to eat raw, having a slightly sweet and sour flavor; *C. uvifera* is somewhat reminiscent of yogurt. The fruits ripen a few at a time and are quite astringent before maturity.

Those of *C. uvifera* (m.a.) are sold in markets in tropical America. They are often juiced, made into jellies or fermented into a kind of wine.

A few local species yield edible fruits in Central and South America.

Eriogonum (E-H 2)   Wild Buckwheat
From the Greek "erion," wool, and "gonu," knee or joint. Some species are hairy at the nodes.
Throughout, but especially in W. N.Am.

The <u>root</u> of *E. longifolium*, Indian turnip – S.C. U.S. – was reportedly used as food by Kiowa Indians.

The <u>young leaves</u> of two western species were eaten by Indians: those of *E. inflatum*, desert trumpet – S.W. U.S., Mex. – are palatable raw; those of *E. latifolium* – Calif., Ore. – require cooking.

Wild buckwheat leaves, often quite small, are usually very astringent.

Endangered   species: *E.   alpinum* – Calif. –, *ammophilum* – Utah –, *anem-*

ophilum – Nev. –, *apricum* – Calif. –, *aretioides* – Utah –, *argophyllum* – Nev. –, *breedlovei, butterworthianum, caninum* – all Calif. –, *capillare* – Ariz. –, *chrysops* – Ore. –, *corymbosum* – Utah –, *crocatum* – Calif. –, *cronquistii* – Utah –, *darrovii* – Ariz., Nev. –, *diclinum* – Calif., Ore. –, *ephedroides* – Colo., Utah –, *ericifolium* – Ariz., Calif. –, *flavum* var. *aquilinum* – Alaska –, *giganteum* var. *compactum, gilmanii, grande* var. *timorum* – all Calif. –, *gypsophilum* – N.M. –, *hirtellum* – Calif. –, *humivagans, hylophilum, intermontanum* – Utah –, *intrafractum, kennedyi* var. *pinicola* – both Calif. –, *lemmonii* – Nev. –, *loganum* – Utah –, *longifolium* var. *harperi* –Ala., Tenn. –, *microthecum* var. *johnstonii* – Calif. –, *mortonianum* – Ariz. –, *nealleyi* – Tex. –, *nudum* var. *murinum, ovalifolium* var. *vineum, parvifolium* var. *lucidum* – all Calif. –, *pelinophilum* – Colo. –, *smithii* – Utah –, *suffruticosum* – Tex. –, *thompsonae* var. *atwoodii* – Ariz. –, *truncatum, umbellatum* – both Calif. –, *viscidulum* – Nev. –, *wrightii* var. *olanchense* – Calif. – and *zionis* – Ariz., Utah.

Fagopyrum   (B–C 5)   Buckwheat

From the Greek "phêgos," name of an oak with edible acorns or the beech tree, and "pyros," wheat: translation of a Germanic name.
Almost throughout.

Two species from Central Eastern Asia are cultivated for their edible seeds in North America, as well as other temperate parts of the world: *F. esculentum* (= *F. sagitattum*) often escapes from cultivation but does not usually persist; *F. tataricum* is naturalized in Alberta, Manitoba, and locally in Northeastern North America. Buckwheat thrives on poor, acidic soil.

The leaves are edible.

A local species is cultivated for its leaves in the Himalayas.

But in our regions, the part of the plant most generally utilized is the seeds. They are hulled and boiled whole, sometimes after roasting as in an Eastern European dish called "kasha." They are also ground into the grayish, distinctively flavored buckwheat flour used in making "galettes" (flat, thin pancakes) in Brittany, noodles in Japan or a nutritious mush. Buckwheat seeds can also be sprouted.

The seeds are rich in proteins and carbohydrates. They also contain vitamins A and rutin and minerals.

However, some people are allergic to buckwheat and develop a rash from eating foods made with buckwheat flour.

The green plant contains a photosensitizing substance (a fluorescent red pigment), fagopyrin, which is not found in the seeds. Unpigmented animals exposed to sunlight after eating buckwheat hay may develop a skin inflammation.

Buckwheat is the only common cereal not belonging to Poaceae (Graminae).

Oxyria digyna (B 4)   Mountain Sorrel
From the Greek "oxys," sour: referring to the taste of the plant.
Circumpolar Arctic regions and high Mountains.

The leaves are edible raw or cooked. Their sourness is similar to that of sorrel.

In Alaska and Siberia, Inuits ferment them into a kind of sauerkraut, often adding other plants in the process.

However, they contain oxalic acid and should be avoided by people with arthritis, asthma, gastric or intestinal inflammation, gout and rheumatism. Oxalic acid can be eliminated by boiling the plant in a change of water.

Polygonum (B-H 1)   Knotweed, Smartweed
From the Greek "polys," many, and "gonu," knee: referring to the knotty stem. Greek name of an undetermined plant.
Throughout. Both native and species introduced from Eurasia. Many of these are common weeds growing in lawns, gardens and along roadsides. Some E. Asian species are cultivated as ornamentals.

P. bistorta, bistort, originally from Eurasia, is occasionally planted or sometimes found as an escape from cultivation.

Its fleshy rhizomes have been eaten in Alaska, Northern Eurasia, Russia and Siberia. They are often first soaked in water, then cooked on embers. As it is bitter and astringent because of its tannin, the rhizome should be chopped up and boiled in several changes of water until all bitterness is gone. It can then be passed through a food mill to make a purée.

It contains much starch, 15 to 20% of a nonirritating tannin and oxalic acid (also removed by cooking in water).

The rhizome of *P. viviparum* - N. N.Am. & Mountains, also Eurasia – and the small bulbils on the stem were eaten raw in the spring by Siberian Inuits. Hardly astringent, the latter have a nutty flavor, making them a pleasant nibble.

Young shoots and leaves of most knotweeds are edible. A few species are even cultivated as vegetables in Asia.

The very young leaves of *P. bistorta*, bistort (m.a.), can be eaten raw. They were traditionally used in the south of England to make a spring "dock pudding." Even when older, they can be cooked as greens or in soups.

The leaves of the native *P. coccineum* (= *P. muhlenbergii*) have been eaten on our continent. Those of the introduced *P. aviculare*, both native and introduced *lapathifolium* and *persicaria*, "red leg," were cooked as greens in Europe and still are in parts of Asia.

P. aviculare (m.a.) contains tannin, mucilage, silicon and other substances, including flavonoids.

It is astringent, diuretic, depurative, hemostatic and vulnerary.

Some smartweeds, such as *P. hydropiper*, water pepper – naturalized from Eur. – and to a lesser extent *P. persicaria* (m.a.), contain an acrid essential oil which renders them pungent: they can be used as a peppery condiment in moderation. However, if they are eaten fresh in too large a quantity, they are irritating and have occasionally poisoned domestic animals in Europe.

Water pepper is a vasoconstrictor.

It gives wool, cotton and linen a yellow color with alum or chromium.

In Asia the leaves of many local species are eaten as greens or sometimes used as a spice.

The seeds of some knotweeds are edible. On our continent, those of *P. douglasii* – mostly N. N.Am. – were parched and ground into meal by Indians.

In Europe, the seeds of a local species (*P. convolvulus*) have been used as food since neolithic times. They were usually eaten as a mush.

Polygonum bistorta

Polygonum persicaria

Endangered species: *P. pensylvanicum* var. *eglandulosum* – Ohio – and *texense* – Tex.

Reynoutria   (D 2)   Reynoutria, Knotweed
(= *Polygonum* spp., subgenus *Pleuropterus*)
Etymology unknown.
Throughout.
Originally from E. Asia, **R. japonica** (= *Polygonum cuspidatum*) and **sakkha-linensis** (= *P. sacchalinense*) have been cultivated as ornamentals and forage plants. They are naturalized on our continent, especially the former.

The <u>roots</u> of these two species, after soaking in water and cooking, are reportedly eaten in the areas where the plants are native.

The young <u>stems</u> shooting out of the ground can be peeled and used like rhubarb petioles (rhubarb belongs to the same family). They are very tender and have a sour taste, though not as pronounced as that of rhubarb, and can also be eaten raw. They are hollow and can be filled and baked to make desserts or other dishes.

In Japan, the stems are often preserved in salt: they are peeled, sliced, placed in a container, covered with salt and pressed under a heavy stone. The <u>young shoots</u> are often blanched during their growth by covering them with leaves. They are eaten cooked in a wide variety of ways.

Rumex   (B-H 1)   Dock, Sorrel
Latin name of the plant.
Throughout. Both native and species introduced from Eurasia; the latter are ubiquitous "weeds."

1. Subgenus *Eu-Rumex*
The following native species were used as food by Indians: **R. hymenosepa-lus**, canaigre – W. N.Am. –, **mexicanus, occidentalis** – W. N.Am. –, **venosus** – W. & C. N.Am. – and **violascens** (= *berlandieri*) – S.W. U.S., Mex.

The <u>leaves</u> of all the species are edible. When very young, they can be eaten raw in salads, but in most cases they rapidly become bitter and astringent with age. Then it is necessary to boil them in one or several changes of water, after which they are drained and used in various ways. The leaves can also be cooked in milk, whose proteins attenuate their astringency due to tannins. The Papago Indians roasted rather than boiled them, as they would other greens which were succulent, because of the scarcity of water.

They contain important quantities of vitamins A, B1, B2 and C, minerals (much iron), chlorophyll, tannins and oxalic acid.

The seeds can be ground into a meal, but the very astringent hulls must first be removed. This meal can be mixed with flour and made into bread. If not very palatable, it is at least nutritious.

Rumex crispus

Canaigre (m.a.) is an interesting species. This tall plant has very large, fleshy leaves with thick petioles.

The stems and petioles were eaten by Indians. They are sour and can be made into pies and compotes, like rhubarb, but first they must be boiled in a change of water.

The leaves make a good vegetable after their bitterness has been removed.

The roots of canaigre are an uncommonly rich source of tannin, as they contain up to 35% of this substance, which is widely used for tanning hides. The U.S. Department of Agriculture (USDA) has conducted experiments for the commercialization of canaigre roots, but so far, attempts to cultivate the plant have not been financially successful.

Navajos used to extract a brown dye from the roots.

The stems of *R. venosus* (m.a.) are used like those of canaigre.

Leaves and seeds of the following introduced species have been eaten in Europe, Asia and America: *R. crispus*, curly dock, *obtusifolius*, broad-leaved dock, *patientia*, yellow dock, *pulcher* and *sanguineus*.

R. patientia (m.a.) has been cultivated as a vegetable in Europe and used like spinach.

The roots of these docks are known to contain tannin and minerals, especially iron. Yellow dock root is used as an anti-anemic to increase the red blood cell count. As it is extremely bitter, it is pulverized and packed in capsules or macerated in wine.

Dock root is also astringent, depurative and tonic. It is used externally crushed as a vulnerary on wounds and ulcers.

The petioles of a European species (*R. alpinus*) are used like rhubarb. Its roots were formerly much in favor in Europe as a laxative.

2. Subgenus *acetosa* and *acetosella*

The species in this subgenus are known collectively as sorrel. They are very rich in oxalic acid, which gives them a characteristic sour taste, and low in tannin. They are neither bitter nor astringent, and can be eaten raw in salads or cooked in soups or purées.

However, it is necessary to partake of them with moderation, as oxalic acid is irritating to the body and can produce kidney stones. People with arthritis, asthma, gastric or intestinal inflammations, gout, rheumatism, tuberculosis or who are prone to stones should definitely avoid them (see *Spinacia, Oxyria, Polygonum*).

The following species can be used as food in North America:

R. acetosa, garden sorrel – introduced from Eurasia. This plant is commonly cultivated in gardens in North America, Europe and Asia and locally naturalized. It has been reported that the root was dried, powdered and made into noodles in Japan.

R. acetosella, sheep sorrel – introduced from Eur. This plant is very common as a weed. It can bear fairly large leaves, which are very tender and pleasant tasting.

R. articus – Arctic regions. The Inuits of Alaska eat the leaves fresh or boiled and ferment them into a kind of sauerkraut.

R. paucifolius, mountain sorrel – W. N.Am.

Rumex acetosa

Finely chopped sorrel leaves can also be mixed with flour for making bread or pancakes, added to eggs for omelettes, cooked with honey as pie filling or macerated in water with some honey for a refreshing drink.

The leaves have been used in Europe to curdle whey in the process of making ricotta cheese.

In moderation, sorrels are depurative, stomachic, diuretic and laxative. When cooked, they are emollient.

Endangered species: *R. orthoneurus* – Ariz.

PLUMBAGINACEAE

Armeria (G 4)   Thrift
Name supposedly of Celtic origin.
Almost throughout.
A. maritima – along cosmopolitan sea coasts – is planted for ornament.

The leaves of *A. labradorica* (= *A. maritima* subsp. *sibirica*) – Lab. & Iceland – have reportedly been eaten. In Iceland they were boiled in milk.

A. maritima (m.a.) contains various minerals and plumbagin, a very irritating and even vesicant substance in high doses, which also has antibiotic properties.

The plant has been used as a sedative, a weight reducer for obesity and in the treatment of epilepsy.

PAEONIACEAE

Paeonia (G 4)   Peony
After Paeon, mythological physician who used the plant to heal the wound that Hercules inflicted upon Pluto.
W. N.Am.
A Eurasian (*P. officinalis*) and a Chinese (*P. suffructicosa*) species are planted for ornament.

The roots of *P. brownii* have reportedly been eaten by California Indians. They are said to taste somewhat like licorice.

The roots of some Asian peonies are locally used as food.

The <u>flowers</u> of *P. suffruticosa*, tree peony (m.a.) – cultivated in N.Am. – are eaten in China.

P. officinalis, the Eurasian ornamental species (m.a.), is supposedly toxic.

GUTTIFERAE

Hypericum (D-H 1) St. John's Wort

From the Greek "hypo," almost, and "ereikê," heather. Greek name of the plant.

Throughout. Both native and species introduced from Eur.

A few Asian species, as well as hybrids, are cultivated as ornamentals.

The <u>leaves</u> of *H. perforatum* – introduced from Europe – are edible raw in small quantities. They are astringent and slightly aromatic with a fugitive lemony smell and make pleasant additions to salads. They can also be made into a pleasant tea.

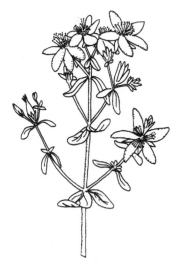

It has been reported that Indians dried and powdered the leaves to mix with their food.

They contain an essential oil, a red pigment, tannin, pectin and a glucoside.

The <u>flowers</u> have been used for flavoring fermented drinks.

A maceration of the flowering tops in olive oil is an excellent vulnerary (wounds, burns, ulcers) and anodyne (rheumatism pains). St. John's Wort oil has a deep red color.

Hypericum perforatum

The plant is astringent, calmative, stomachic and expectorant.

It also contains a fluorescent substance, hypericin, with photosensitizing properties which, in susceptible individuals, can produce skin inflammation upon exposure to strong sunlight. White-skinned cattle, horses and sheep grazing on the plant in large quantities are subject to loss of hair and blistering when exposed to the sun. It is not known whether native *Hypericum* species produce the same effect.

The flowering tops dye wool yellow with alum.

The young <u>leaves</u> and <u>flower buds</u> of *H. pyramidatum* (= *H. ascyrion*), great St. John's Wort – N.E. & N.C. N.Am. – have reportedly been eaten as a cooked vegetable.

St. John's Wort is now widely sold commercially as a supplement in health food stores. It is taken as a natural antidepressant.

The European St. John's Wort has been used since Antiquity. It was said to have magical virtues for keeping evil spirits away.

A few local species are eaten cooked in Northeastern Asia.

Endangered species: *H. cumulicola* – Fla.

Mammea americana (B 5)   Mamey Apple
From the West Indian name of the fruit, "mamey."
Originally from tropical Am. naturalized in S. Fla. & Mex.
The tree is cultivated for its fruit in the tropics of both hemispheres.

The large <u>fruit</u> has a sweet, aromatic, apricot-colored pulp which is edible raw.

In tropical America it is made into jam or fermented into wine.

The <u>flowers</u> are used for manufacturing a liqueur in the French Antilles known as "Eau de créole."

ELAEOCARPACEAE

Muntingia calabura (B 5)   Calabur, Capulin, Strawberry Tree
Etymology unknown.
Originally from tropical Am.
The plant is cultivated for its fruit and naturalized in S. Fla. & Mex.

The <u>fruit</u> is a red berry with a sweet pulp. It is edible raw and also made into jam.

The <u>leaves</u> are used as tea in Northern South America.

TILIACEAE

Corchorus (D 4) Jute
From the Greek "corchoros," name of a wild edible plant.
Some species are native to S. U.S. and Mex. In the same areas, a few species are naturalized from the tropics.

C. olitorius, Jew's mallow, jute – originally from India – is cultivated in tropical and subtropical regions of both hemispheres for the fibers of its stem (jute) or as a vegetable. It is naturalized in Southern North America.

The young <u>leaves</u> of this species have been used as food since Antiquity. They are eaten raw or cooked and are highly prized in many parts of the world. They form, for instance, the national dish of Egypt, a thick, mucilaginous soup called "molokhia."

The leaves are usually used fresh but they can also be dried and powdered. They can thus be kept for a long time, but they do not taste as good as the fresh leaves.

C. siliquosus, broomweed – southernmost U.S., Mex. & tropical Am. – is made into tea.

Other species are eaten as greens in tropical regions.

Tilia (B 4) Basswood, Linden
Latin name of the tree.
E. N.Am.
A native species, *T. americana*, American basswood, and a few European lindens are frequently planted for ornament.

All species can be used as food in a similar manner.
The <u>inner bark</u> (cambium) is edible.
It contains mucilage and various substances, and is emollient and cholagogue.

The <u>sap</u> of the trunk can be harvested and drunk. As it contains some sugar, it can be boiled down to a syrup; however, large quantities of sap, long cooking time and much fuel are required.

The sap of the American basswood (m.a.) was drunk by Indians.

The <u>leaves</u> of these trees, picked when very young, still translucent, make excellent salads. They are very tender, slightly mucilaginous and pleasant tasting. They can also be cooked to thicken soups and stews.

Older, tougher leaves can be dried, pulverized and sifted. The green meal obtained is mixed with cereal flour to make bread, cakes or mush. In France, where this nutritious meal was used during World War II as a food supplement, it was estimated that one pound of leaves yields approximately five ounces of a finely sifted product.

The leaves have also served as tea, but they do not have much flavor.

Linden and basswood leaves contain inverted sugars, easily assimilated even by diabetics.

The leaves of some Asian lindens are used locally as vegetables or tea.

The flowers of the European lindens make a fragrant tea which is still commonly drunk on the Old Continent as a nightcap. Those of our basswoods can also be used as tea, or added to salads for flavor.

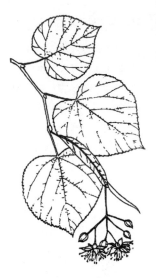

Tilia americana

Linden flowers contain an essential oil, mucilage, tannin, vitamin C, glucosides and various substances.

A light infusion of the flowers is sedative, antispasmodic and diaphoretic. It also thins the blood and enhances circulation. A stronger dose, however, acts as an excitant and can cause insomnia. Caution must therefore be used.

The fruits contain a small edible kernel, rich in oil. The French chemist Missa discovered in the 18th century that by grinding the fruits with linden flowers, he obtained a product having an aroma very close to that of chocolate. This process was tentatively commercialized in Prussia, but the project had to be abandoned, as this "linden chocolate" did not keep well. It is, however, possible to produce small quantities at home. The fruits and flowers of our native basswoods can be used for that purpose.

The torrefied fruits have also been used as a coffee substitute.

The European species cultivated as ornamentals on our continent have all the same uses described here.

The sapwood of a linden growing wild in the south of France (*T. cordata*) is used as a diuretic, choleretic, hypotensive and antispasmodic.

The cambium of these trees is a source of fibers, formerly much used by gardeners before the introduction of raffia.

MALVACEAE

Most of the plants in this family contain mucilage and therefore possess emollient properties.

Many of them are edible.

Among the Malvaceae are found a common vegetable (okra), well-known ornamentals (hibiscus, hollyhock) and an industrial textile plant (cotton).

Abelmoschus esculentus   (B 5)   Okra
(= *Hibiscus e.*)

Originally from tropical Africa, okra is cultivated in warm parts of our continent, as well as in tropical and subtropical regions of the world. It is naturalized in Fla. and Mex.

The young fruits are edible raw, but are generally cooked as vegetables or made into thick soups, which are somewhat laxative. They have a specific mucilaginous texture, relished by some but loathed by others. Okra is a favorite in the Southeast U.S., as in the West Indies, Egypt, tropical Africa and India.

The fruits can be pickled. In Japan, they are preserved in miso (fermented soybean paste). In Africa, they are dried for later use, powdered and made into mucilaginous sauces.

With the torrefied and ground ripe seeds, a good coffee substitute can be prepared.

The leaves are said to be edible.

Leaves and young fruits of a few other species are eaten in Asia.

Abutilon   (C 4)   Abutilon
Name given to *A. theophrasti* by Avicenna.

Several species are native to S. U.S. & Mex.

A. theophrasti, originally from S. Asia, is occasionally cultivated. It is established in various parts of N.Am.

In Asia the unripe seeds of this plant were eaten raw, while ripe ones were soaked in water to remove their bitterness, then dried, ground into a flour and made into noodles.

Other species are used as food in the tropics of both worlds.

Alcea rosea (B 4)   Hollyhock
(= *Althaea r.*)
Greek and Latin name of a mallow.
Scattered throughout.

Of unknown origin (probably from Asia), the plant is commonly used for ornamentation and locally escapes from cultivation.

The <u>leaves</u> are edible raw. They are tender, especially when young, and good flavored. The plant is still cultivated as a vegetable in Egypt.

The <u>flowers</u> can also be eaten raw. They have reportedly been used for coloring wine in Europe.

Leaves and flowers contain mucilage. They are emollient and demulcent.

The flowers dye wool a bluish color, but it is not permanent.

Althaea officinalis (B 4)   Marshmallow
Greek name of the plant, "althaia" from "althainô," to heal.
Originally from Eur., the plant is occasionally cultivated as an ornamental;
it is naturalized in E. U.S.

Marshmallow has been known since Antiquity for its emollient, demulcent and antitussive properties. It was frequently cultivated as a medicinal plant.

The <u>root</u> has been eaten cooked or candied in a honey syrup. The concentrated decoction of the root was formerly the main ingredient of the original "marshmallows" recipe. Nowadays, commercial marshmallows are made with gum, starch, sugar, artificial colorings and various additives.

A maceration in water of the pulverized root yields a much pleasanter drink than the decoction, with the same demulcent and laxative virtues.

Marshmallow roots contain about 10% mucilage, sugars, starch, a fixed oil, asparagin and other substances.

The <u>leaves</u> are edible, but their cottony texture is not the most pleasant. When young, they can be added raw to salads, soups or vegetables. Older leaves should be cooked.

They are emollient, demulcent and laxative, like the rest of the plant.

<u>Flower buds</u>, <u>flowers</u> and <u>young unripe fruits</u> can be eaten raw or cooked in the same manner. The young green fruits are an interesting substitute for okra, and they can also be pickled.

Callirhoe (D-H 4)   Poppy Mallow
Greek name of a nymph, to which a fountain was consecrated in Athens,
from "kallos," beauty and "rhoê," stream.
Mostly C. N.Am.

The large <u>roots</u> of *C. digitata* – S.C. U.S. – and *involucrata* – C. N.Am. – were
used as food by Indians.
The last species mentioned is occasionally cultivated in Europe as an ornamental.
Endangered species: *C. scabriuscula* – Tex.

Gossypium (C 4)   Cotton
Ancient name of a tree (from Pliny), the fruit of which contains a kind of
cotton.
Some species are native to S. U.S. & Mex.
G. hirsutum, native to Fla., Mex. & tropical Am., is cultivated for the
fibers surrounding its seeds and is found as an escape in S. U.S. Other
tropical species are cultivated on a large scale as a source of fibers.

Cotton <u>seeds</u> contain an edible oil.
Torrefied seeds were used in the South as a coffee substitute during the Civil
War.
Cottonseed meal, the ground cake left after cottonseed oil has been expressed, is a common animal feed. However, it contains a toxic substance, gossypol, and has caused poisoning in cattle, sheep and pigs. The gossypol content in
the meal varies with the process used for extracting the oil and with the locality
where the plant was grown: Seeds from the Atlantic coast are known to be more
toxic than those produced in the Southwest.
The flowers dye wool and cotton a brownish yellow.

Hibiscus (B-H 4)   Hibiscus
Ancient name of marshmallow from the Greek "hibiskos," and the Latin
"hibiscus."
S. U.S., Mex.
Our native H. *moscheutos* is cultivated as an ornamental. *H. rosa-sinensis*
and *syriacus*, originally from tropical E. Asia, are planted for the same pur-

pose and occasionally escape from cultivation. Roselle (*H. sabdariffa* – originally from N.E. Africa) is cultivated in S. Fla. and Mex. for the red, fleshy calyx of its flowers, commercialized as "hibiscus tea."

The <u>roots</u> of *H. tiliaceus*, mahoe – coasts of S.Fla. & Mex.; cosmopolitan in the tropics – were reportedly used as food by Australian Aborigines.

The <u>young leaves</u> are eaten in Southeast Asia, and the *cambium* in Polynesia. It contains mucilage and is emollient.

The cambium is also a source of fibers, which are still used in Hawaii for making rope.

The <u>flowers</u> of *H. rosa-sinensis* (m.a.) are used for coloring food in Asia.

Leaves and flowers of *H. syriacus* (m.a.) are eaten on the same continent.

Leaves, flowers and <u>seeds</u> of many *Hibiscus* spp. are used as food in all tropical parts of the world, especially in Asia.

The <u>fleshy calyx</u> of roselle (m.a.) is cooked as a vegetable in Africa or made into jams in various parts of the tropics. When dried and made into tea, they form the most common drink in Egypt and the Sudan, "karkadeh." Hibiscus tea, bright red, sour-tasting and rich in vitamin C, has spread from there all around the world.

The <u>leaves</u> and <u>seeds</u> are edible.

Endangered species: *H. californicus* – Calif. – and *dasycalyx* – Tex.

Malva   (A 1)   Mallow, Cheeseweed
Latin name of various Malvaceae.
Throughout. Very common weeds, introduced from Eur.

All species are edible in the same manner.

The <u>root</u> can be eaten when very young, before it becomes woody. It can be cooked and passed through a food mill or processor to make a purée.

<u>Young shoots</u> and <u>leaves</u> of various mallows have been eaten in Europe and Asia since Antiquity. They are tender, good-flavored and delicious raw in salads.

Malva sylvestris

Older leaves should be cooked, preferably with other greens, as they are very mucilaginous. They can be made into excellent soups, which have a laxative effect if eaten abundantly – a property already mentioned by Cicero – or into an interesting vegetable fondue.

The leaves contain mucilage, vitamins A, B1, B2 and C and minerals.

Mallows have been known since Antiquity for their emollient, demulcent, expectorant and laxative properties.

Flower buds, flowers and young, unripe fruits are edible raw or cooked, and can also be pickled. The latter can be used as a substitute for okra.

The best species in North America are *M. neglecta* (= *M. rotundifolia*), *parviflora*, *sylvestris* and *verticillata*.

M. neglecta (m.a.) is sometimes cultivated as a vegetable in Egypt.

After the introduction of these plants in North America, mallows became a part of the diet of Indians.

Malvastrum (D 3)   White Mallow
From "malva," mallow.
S. U.S., Mex.

M. exile – S.W. U.S. – was cooked and used as food by the Pima Indians of Central Arizona when little else was available. The plant is not very palatable.

Sidalcea (D-H 4)   Prairie Mallow
From "Sida" and "Alcea," two genera in the Malvaceae.
W. N.Am.

S. neomexicana and possibly other species were eaten as cooked vegetables by Indians.

Endangered species: *S. campestris, nelsoniana* – both Ore. – and *oregana* subsp. valida – Calif.

Sphaeralcea (G-H 2)   Globe Mallow
From the Greek "sphaira," globe, and "alcea," the Greek and Latin name of a mallow: referring to the shape of the inflorescence.
W. N.Am.

It has been reported that the mucilaginous <u>stèm</u> of *S. angustifolia* was used as chewing gum, which was called "kopona" by the Hopis of Northeast Arizona. They also used the plant for treating intestinal disorders.

Hairs on certain species – such as *S. ambigua* and *malvaefolia* – can cause allergic reactions in some people, and also can be irritating to the eyes, hence the common names "sore-eye poppies" or "plantas muy malas" (very bad plants) in Baja.

Endangered species: *S. fendleri* var. *albescens* – Ariz.

Thespesia populnea (B 5)   Seaside Mahoe
Etymology unknown.
Originally from the coasts of tropical Asia, the tree is naturalized in S. Fla. and Mex.

<u>Young leaves</u> and <u>flowers</u> are edible raw. They are also eaten boiled, made into soups or fried.

DROSERACEAE

Drosera (H 4)   Sundew
From the Greek "droseros," covered with dew: referring to the leaves, which are covered with a liquid used to digest trapped insects; sundews are carnivorous plants.
Almost throughout.

When added to lukewarm milk, the <u>juice</u> of *D. rotundifolia*, round-leaved sundew, makes it curdle in a day or two.

The plant contains resin, tannin, organic acids, glucose, minerals and plumbagon, a substance with antibiotic properties.

It is antispasmodic and expectorant.

Boiled with wool in ammonia, sundew gives the wool a yellow color, but the plant is too rare to be picked for any purpose.

FLACOURTIACEAE

Flacourtia indica (D 5) Governor's Plum, Ramontchi
Etymology unknown.
Originally from tropical Africa and Asia, it is cultivated and naturalized in
S. Fla. and Mex.

The sour fruits are edible raw. They are also made into jam.
The fruits of several species are used as food in Africa and Asia.

VIOLACEAE

Viola (B 1) Violet
Latin name of various plants.
Throughout.
A few Eurasian species and hybrids are frequently cultivated as ornamen-
tals including V. odorata, native of Eur. and frequently escaped from cul-
tivation.

The leaves of the various species are edible
raw. They can be added to salads or cooked as a
vegetable. Those of **V. palmata** – E. N.Am. –
were made into thick, mucilaginous soups by
black people in S. U.S.

The leaves of **V. pedunculata** – Calif., Baja –
were eaten by Western Indians.

Violet leaves contain vitamin A, much vitamin
C, minerals and saponins.

The leaves of several species of violets are
cooked as greens in Asia.

In all species, the flowers are edible as well.
They can be added raw to salads and desserts or
made into a surprising consommé.

Viola

Those of **V. cucullata** – E. N.Am. – have been used as food.

Violet flowers are emollient, expectorant, diaphoretic and laxative.

The flowers of *V. odorata* (m.a.) have a delicate fragrance and are used in perfumery and confectionery.

They contain an essential oil.

The roots of this violet are emetic.

The flowers of most violets are not fragrant. Apart from *V. odorata* (m.a.), only those of *V. blanda* – E. N.Am. –, *macloskeyi* – N. N.Am. – and a few others give off the sweet aroma so often linked with these plants.

PASSIFLORACEAE

Passiflora (B 4)   Passion Flower, Maypops

From the Latin "passio," passion (here, the Passion of Christ), and "flos, floris," flower: referring to the symbolism attached to the flower: the corona represents the crown of thorns and the stamens, hammers and styles the nails.

S.E. U.S., Mex.

A few tropical American species are planted as ornamentals and one of them (*P. edulis*) for its edible fruit.

The <u>fruits</u> of many species are commonly used as food in tropical regions. For instance, they are known as "granadillas" in Central America and "lilikoi" in Hawaii. They are filled with seeds surrounded by a juicy, acid, aromatic pulp. The acidity, sweetness and aroma of the pulp varies greatly according to the species.

The fruits are eaten raw or made into juices and sherbets.

They are diuretic and tonic.

Our best native species is probably *P. incarnata*, apricot vine or maypops, although its fruits are much smaller than those of some tropical species and not as flavorful.

Leaves, flowers and stems of this passion flower contain alkaloids and are used medicinally as an antispasmodic and sedative. At the same time calming and strengthening the nervous system without secondary effects, this plant is one of the very best natural tranquilizers.

The <u>fruits</u> of *P. lutea* and *pallens* – S. Fla. – have also been eaten in North America.

COCHLOSPERMACEAE

Amoreuxia (D 5)
Etymology unknown.
S. Ariz., N. Mex.

The <u>roots</u> of *A. gonzalezii* and ***palmatifida*** were cooked and eaten by local Indians. They are said to taste somewhat like parsnips.

The <u>fruits</u> are reportedly used occasionally as food in Sonora and Chihuahua, Mexico.

BIXACEAE

Bixa orellana (D 5) Lipstick Tree
Etymology unknown.
Originally from tropical Am., this shrub is naturalized in S. Fla. and Mex.

The lipstick tree is cultivated, mostly in C. and S.Am. for the scarlet waxy substance covering the <u>seeds</u> which is used commercially in many parts of the world, including the United States, for giving butter and cheese a yellow color (anatto dye). This is possibly the only widely used food coloring known to be completely safe.

In tropical America the <u>roots</u> were reportedly used as a condiment.

CISTACEAE

Cistus (G 5) Rockrose
From the Greek name of the plant "kisthos."
A few Mediterranean species, as well as hybrids, are planted for ornament.
C. salvifolius and *villosus* are naturalized locally in Calif.

The <u>leaves</u> of both species are sometimes made into tea in Algeria and in Greece, although they are only slightly aromatic.

TAMARICACEAE

Tamarix (G 4)   Tamarisk
Latin name of the tree.
Several European, Asian and African species are planted for ornament. A few of them have become naturalized in arid regions of W. and C. N.Am., where they often present serious problems by competing with the natural vegetation and plugging up irrigation ditches. Among these are *T. aphylla*, *gallica* and *pentandra*.

A sweet, gummy <u>exudation</u>, caused by the perforation of the stems by an insect, is gathered from some tamarisks, including the species mentioned above, in Western Asia. It is often harvested by stretching a sheet on the ground and shaking the tree. This manna is used locally as a sweetener and is mixed with flour and almonds for making cakes. It has medical applications as well.
It is probable that this manna does not occur in our regions.

FOUQUIERIACEAE

Fouquieria (D 2)   Ocotillo
After P. E. Fouquier, medical professor from Paris.
S.W. U.S., Mex.
F. splendens is sometimes planted in desert regions as an ornamental and as a living fence, since it propagates readily from cuttings.

The <u>young leaves</u> are edible raw in salads. They can often be gathered in large quantities: after strong rain showers, new leaves sprout from the shrub and are shed during the dry season. Since the appearance of the leaves depends upon the frequency of precipitation, there can be several sets of leaves each year.
Indians ate the <u>flowers</u>. The corolla imparts a sweet and pleasant flavor to fruit salads and other desserts. The calyx should be removed as it is astringent. The flowers can also be macerated for a few hours in cold water to make a refreshing drink.
The roots were used medicinally by Indians as a tonic and antiphlogistic.
The bark contains a resin, a gum and a wax. It burns with a bright flame, giving off an intensely black smoke.

CARICACEAE

Carica papaya   (B 5)   Papaya
Etymology unknown.
Native to S. Mex. and tropical Am., the papaya "tree" is cultivated for its luscious fruit throughout the tropics. It is naturalized in S. Fla. and Mex., the only areas in N.Am. warm enough for the tree to grow.

There are a few different varieties of papayas.
The <u>roots</u> are said to be edible cooked.
The <u>pith</u> inside the stem of this giant herb can be eaten raw.
<u>Young leaves</u> and <u>flowers</u> are edible after cooking. Older leaves must be boiled in several changes of water to remove the alkaloid carpain.
The milky juice of the plant contains papain, a protein-digesting enzyme similar to pepsin. It irritates the skin, especially the mucous membranes, and it can be used as a meat tenderizer.
Green, unripe <u>fruits</u> are eaten boiled, roasted or fried, as a vegetable. In the West Indies, they are used as a thickener for hot chili sauces. They can also be pickled.
The ripe fruit is definitely the best edible part of the plant. With their soft and fragrant apricot-colored pulp, raw papayas are exquisite – although some people dislike their smell and taste.
In the tropics, they are made into sherbets, pies, preserves or chutneys.
Papayas contain vitamin A, potassium and enzymes. They are easily digested.
The leaves can reportedly be used as soap.
The <u>fruits</u> of local species are eaten in Central and South America.

LOASACEAE

Mentzelia   (E-H 4)   Blazing Star, Stickleaf
After Christian Mentzel (1622–1701), German botanist.
W. & C. U.S., Mex.

The <u>seeds</u> of *M. albicaulis* were parched, ground into a meal and eaten as a mush by Indians. They contain a fixed oil.

M. decapetala is a facultative selenium absorbèr. The leaves of some species are known to cause dermatitis in susceptible individuals.

Endangered species: *M. leucophylla* – Calif., Nev. –, *nitens* var. *leptocaulis* – Ariz. – and *packardiae* – Ore.

BEGONIACEAE

Begonia (B-D 5)   Begonia
After M. Bégon, governor of Santo Domingo during the 17th century, patron of botany.
Several species from tropical America, Asia and S. Africa, as well as hybrids, are widely cultivated as ornamentals. A few of them are naturalized in S. Fla. and Mex., including *B. semperflorens*, an everflowering begonia, originally from S.Am.

The fleshy leaves and flowers of many species, including the one mentioned above, are edible raw. They have a pleasant acidy taste.
Some begonias are used as food in their native regions.

CUCURBITACEAE

This large family of vines provides humanity with such well-known vegetable-fruits as cucumber, gerkin, squash, zucchini, gourds, melon, cantaloupe, watermelon and pumpkin.

Citrullus vulgaris (B 5)   Watermelon
(= *C. lanatus*)
From the Latin diminutive form of "citrus," citron tree.
Originally from tropical Africa, this plant is commonly cultivated in warm areas for its large fruit which can weigh up to a hundred pounds. The watermelon is naturalized in S. U.S. and Mex. The var. *citroides*, citron melon, is found as an escape in Calif.

The watery red pulp of the <u>fruit</u>, often very sweet, is delicious to eat raw, especially on a hot summer day. Watermelons can be juiced or made into jam. Young green fruits are cooked as a vegetable in Asia, or they are pickled. In North America it is generally the rind of the ripe fruit that is pickled.

Watermelons have depurative and refrigerant properties.

The <u>seeds</u> can be eaten raw. The excellent flavor of their kernel is further improved with roasting.

The seeds of the Eurasian and African species *C. colocynthis* are consumed locally.

Cucumis   (B 4)
Latin name of the cucumber, *C. sativus*.
Fla. to Tex., Mex.

C. anguria, bur cucumber, gooseberry gourd – Fla. to Tex., Mex. – is sometimes cultivated for its edible <u>fruit</u>, which is boiled, cooked in stews or pickled.

C. melo, melon, cantaloupe – originally from Old World tropics – is widely cultivated for its luscious <u>fruit</u> and escapes from cultivation in Florida and Mexico. Many varieties are known.

Cantaloupes are best raw, but they can be dried, candied or made into preserves. The green, unripe fruits are sometimes pickled. In the United States, syrup and sugar were reportedly made from the ripe fruits during the Civil War.

The apricot-colored flesh of cantaloupes contains sugars, vitamins A, B and C and minerals.

It is refrigerant, laxative and diuretic.

The <u>seeds</u> are edible in spite of their small size. Their white kernel has a nutty flavor. A pleasant drink is made by blending the seeds with water and straining. An edible oil can be extracted from the seeds by simple pressure.

They are emollient, demulcent and expectorant.

The pulp of var. *agrestis* – reportedly naturalized in S. La. & Tex. – is bitterish and inedible, but the seeds can be eaten.

The cucumber (*C. sativus*) is another well-known garden vegetable that belongs to this genus.

The fruits of many other species are eaten in Asia and Africa.

Cucurbita   (B 4)

Latin name of the gourd, *Lagenaria siceraria*.

Scattered throughout.

Several species are native to S. U.S. and Mex. Three American species, *C. maxima, moschata* and *pepo* – exact origin unknown – are commonly cultivated in our gardens for their vegetable-fruits. They seldom escape from cultivation.

The small seeds of the fruits of *C. digitata* – Calif. to N.M., Son. –, *foetidissima*, buffalo gourd, calabazilla – S.C. & S.W. U.S. – and *palmata*, coyote melon – Ariz., Calif., Baja – were eaten by Western Indians, roasted and ground into a mush. Oil can be obtained by crushing the seeds and boiling them in water; it is then easily skimmed off.

Pulp of the fruits of these species is bitter and inedible. That of the buffalo gourd (m.a.) is purgative and can be used as soap, as it contains saponin. It has been reported, however, that the fruits of this species were eaten cooked by Arizona Indians.

The roots of the buffalo gourd were highly esteemed as soap, but care was taken to rinse the clothes thoroughly, as particles of the roots clinging to the fabric would irritate the skin.

The fruits of *C. okeechobeensis* – S. Fla. – were eaten by local Indians.

The three following species are better known:

C. maxima (m.a.), squash, is cultivated worldwide for its edible fruit which is eaten cooked: baked, boiled, fried, roasted and, in Asia, candied or processed into starch and maltose.

The seeds are edible as well. They contain an edible, dark green-colored oil which is extracted and used as a salad oil in Europe, especially in Southern Austria.

Many cultivated varieties of this plant are known. Some are occasionally found as escapes from gardens.

C. moschata (m.a.), crookneck, Seminole melon, was extensively cultivated by Indian tribes. The fruit was cooked in a fire pit or made into soup. It was also dried and sometimes ground. It can be fried, stewed or boiled. Green, unripe fruits are sometimes pickled.

Young shoots, leaves and flowers are edible cooked.

The seeds can be eaten raw.

This plant is now commonly cultivated throughout the world.

C. pepo (m.a.), pumpkin, is commonly grown for its large orange fruit, which can weigh up to 130 pounds. As everyone knows, the pulp is made into pies, but it is also eaten in soup, a French tradition, or as a vegetable.

Pumpkins contain sugars, starch, vitamin A and minerals, phosphorus in particular.

Cooked and mashed, the pulp is emollient, demulcent, laxative, diuretic and sedative. It is also nutritious and very digestible.

Pumpkin seeds are edible raw or roasted, and are sold on the street in various parts of the world (usually roasted and salted).

Pumpkin seed paste is sold in markets in Yucatan. It is used for thickening soups, and is also sprinkled with hard-boiled eggs on tostadas.

With simple pressure, the seeds yield an orange-colored edible oil that does not become rancid.

They are emollient, demulcent, slightly laxative, and above all anthelmintic (taenifuge in particular). Their action is neither irritating nor toxic.

C. pepo (m.a.) var. **ovifera**, yellow-flowered gourd, is native to Texas and Mexico. The fruit has very little pulp and is hardly edible.

The fruits of other species are used as food in tropical America.

Lagenaria vulgaris (D 5)   Bottle Gourd
(= L. siceraria)
From the Latin "lagoena," bottle: referring to the use of the fruits.
Originally from the Old World tropics, this vine is cultivated in warm parts of the world for its ornamental fruits which are made into containers when they are ripe and dry. It is naturalized in S. U.S. and Mex.

Unripe and still tender fruits are eaten cooked, especially in Asia, but they are often bitter. Small ones are pickled in Japan.

The seeds are said to contain saponin.

Young leaves have reportedly been eaten in China.

The ripe fruits have a woody rind and are used as containers after removing the dried flesh with the seeds.

Luffa cylindrica (B 5) Luffa
Arabic name of the plant, "luff."
Originally from India, the plant is cultivated for its fruits and is naturalized in Fla. and Mex.

In Asia, the unripe fruit is commonly eaten as a vegetable. In India it is cooked in curries.

Flower buds, flowers, young leaves and seed kernels are also used as food.

The seeds yield an edible oil, sometimes utilized in cooking.

When the fruit is ripe and dry, the outer skin and the seeds are removed while the inner fibers, naturally woven into a cylindrical network, are used like a sponge, hence the common name of "vegetable sponge" often attributed to the plant. Luffa or loofah sponges are commercialized in the United States and in many warm parts of the world.

The fruits of some varieties are bitter and inedible.

Those of another species, as well as buds, flowers, young leaves and seeds, are commonly used as food in tropical Asia.

Melothria (D 4) Creeping Cucumber, Melonette
Greek name of bryony (*Bryonia* sp.) "mêlothron," a European cucurbit.
S. U.S., Mex.

The small fruits of *M. pendula* and *scabra* – Mex. – have been used as food. They are said to be edible raw, but are more often cooked or pickled.

The seeds are reportedly purgative.

The fruits of a few local species are eaten in Asia.

Momordica charantia (D 4) Balsam Apple
From the Latin "momordi," I have bitten, the past tense of "mordeo," to bite: the seeds seem to have been gnawed at both ends.
Originally from the Old World tropics, the plant is cultivated in Am., Asia and Africa for its fruit. It is naturalized from Fla. to Tex. and Mex.

The leaves are parboiled and eaten as greens in Eastern Asia. Raw, they are said to be more or less toxic.

The unripe fruit is steeped in brine to remove its intensely bitter taste, then boiled, fried or roasted. When very young it can be pickled. It is especially used in India and in the West Indies.

The red arils surrounding the seeds in the ripe fruit are edible. They are sweet but rather insipid.

The seeds themselves, as well as the raw pulp of the fruit, are purgative.

A few other species are used as food in tropical Asia and Africa.

Sechium edule (B 5)   Chayote
Etymology unknown.
Mex.
This vine is often cultivated for its edible fruit in tropical Am., including Mex., and occasionally in southernmost U.S.

The starchy roots are eaten boiled.

The young shoots make a good cooked vegetable. They are a favorite food on Reunion Island in the Indian Ocean, under the local name of "brèdes chou-chou."

The fruit is used while still green. It can be steamed, boiled, baked, sliced and fried, made into purées and so on. The large single seed softens with cooking and is eaten along with the pulp. Chayotes have an excellent flavor. They are commonly sold already cooked by street vendors in Mexico. In the French West Indies, they are commonly made into gratins.

Sicyos angulatus (D 2)   Bur Cucumber
Greek name of the cucumber "sikys."
E. & C. U.S.

The fruit has reportedly been eaten as a cooked vegetable.

SALICACEAE

Populus   (D-H 3)   Cottonwood, Poplar
Latin name of the tree.
Throughout.
A few native and European species, and especially cultivars and hybrids, are planted as windbreaks and for ornament.

The cambium of poplars is edible raw. It was much used as food by Indians and that of local species was eaten by the inhabitants of Europe and Asia. This inner bark was also cut into strips and boiled or dried, ground and mixed with flour to make bread or mush.
It is antiscorbutic.
The sap can be collected and drunk. As it contains some sugar, it is possible to boil it down to a syrup, but the quantities of sap and fuel required make it impractical.
Indians used to eat raw catkins of certain poplars.
The young shoots are edible as well.
The following species have been used as food by Indians in North America: *P. angustifolia*, narrow-leaved cottonwood – C. & W. N.Am. –, *deltoides*, cottonwood – E. N.Am. –, *fremontii*, Fremont cottonwood – S.W. U.S. –, *grandidentata*, large-toothed aspen – E. & C. N.Am. –, *sargentii*, Sargent cottonwood – C. N.Am. – and *tremuloides*, aspen.
P. alba, white poplar – introduced from Eur. and occasionally escaped from cultivation – has similar uses on the Old Continent.
The young leaves of two local species are eaten in China and Japan.
The resinous, aromatic buds of P. *balsamifera,* tacahamac – N. N.Am. –, *candicans* (= *giladensis*), balm of Gilead – N. N.Am. – and *tremuloides* (m.a.) are used medicinally as a balsamic, expectorant and stimulant.
A salve used externally to soothe burns and heal wounds is made by boiling them slowly in oil.
The buds contain an essential oil, tannin and two glucosides, populin and salicin. The latter is transformed by a ferment in the body into glucose and salicylic acid.
Their balsamic odor is found in the propolis of beehives. Propolis is a substance secreted by bees that has antibiotic properties, and it generally contains resin from poplar buds.

The bark of *P. tremuloides* (m.a.) has been used as a febrifuge and stomachic.

Carbonized poplar wood ("carbum ligni") is antiseptic for the intestinal tract.

Poplar pollen has been found to be responsible in some cases of hayfever.

Poplar twigs were used in basketry by Indians.

The bark of poplars and willows is the main food of beavers.

Endangered species: *P. hinckleyana* – Tex.

Salix (D-H 1)   Willow

Latin name of the tree.

Throughout.

A few European and Asian species, and cultivars, are planted as ornamentals. These include *S. alba*, white willow, and *fragilis*, introduced from the Old World in Colonial times for shade and gunpowder charcoal.

The inner bark of willows is edible, but it is usually bitter raw. It could possibly be boiled in several changes of water.

The cambium of *S. alba* (m.a.) was dried, pulverized and mixed with flour to make bread in Scandinavia.

The young shoots and leaves are in most cases also very bitter. In some species, however, they are good to eat raw. Those of *S. alba* (m.a.) and of some Alaskan species, as well as their catkins, have been used as food. They are edible raw.

Willow leaves contain vitamin C.

Leaves and catkins of the various species are anaphrodisiac, antispasmodic and sedative.

The bark is a febrifuge and an anodyne, with tonic properties.

Bark and leaves contain tannin and a glucoside, salicin, which is transformed in the body into salicylic acid (and glucose) by the action of a ferment.

It has been reported that in Iran, a sweet exudation from *S. fragilis* (m.a.) was used locally as food.

In Asia, the leaves of a few other willows are sometimes eaten, including those of the weeping willow (*S. babylonica*), planted for ornament in North America.

Twigs from willows were used in basketry by Indians.

Endangered species: *S. floridana* – Fla., Ga.

CAPPARIDACEAE

Cleome (D-H 4) Bee Plant
Latin name of some crucifer.
Several species are native to W. N.Am.
A few tropical American species are planted for ornament and some of them escape from cultivation in S. U.S. and Mex.

The leaves of *C. serrulata* were used as food by Indians. They must be boiled to remove their strong taste and pungent odor, which is responsible for the other common name of the plant, skunkweed. Indians would often dry the boiled leaves and store them for later use.
The flowers are edible as well. They are rich in nectar, and this species has been cultivated to provide food for domestic bees.
The seeds make a good spice. They are relished by doves.
The plant was boiled by Indians to produce a black dye.
Other species are eaten in the tropics of America, Asia and Polynesia.
Endangered species: *C. multicaulis* – Ariz., N.M., Colo., Tex.

Cleomella (D 4) Stinkweed
Diminutive form of "Cleome."
W. N.Am.

The leaves of some species, such as *C. plocasperma* – Calif. to Utah – are edible.

Forchammeria watsonii (G 5) Palo San Juan
Etymology unknown.
N.W. Mex.

The thin flesh of the mature fruit is reportedly edible.

Isomeris arborea (D 5) Bladder Pod
From the Greek "isos," equal, and "meris," part.
S. Calif., Baja. A monotypic genus.

The pods are edible cooked.
The leaves have a strong odor.

Polanisia   (D 3)   Clammyweed
From the Greek "polys," many, and "anisos," unequal: referring to the
stamens.
Throughout.

The leaves of *P. trachysperma* – W. N.Am. – were eaten, cooked, by Indians.

Wislizenia   (D 4)   Jackass Clover
After A. Wislizenius, early botanical collector in the Southwest.
S.W. U.S., N.W. Mex.

The leaves of *W. refracta* are edible after cooking.

BRASSICACEAE (CRUCIFERAE)

Leaves and inflorescences (flower buds and flowers) of most of the crucifers
are edible.

The seeds are often used as a spice, as are the leaves of numerous species.
Their hot, pungent taste is due to essential oils formed by the action of ferments
upon sulfured glucosides. They are contained in the cells of the living plant and
are freed when the plant tissues are crushed. Lukewarm water activates the ferments, and by hydrolysis the glucoside is split into essential oil and glucose. The
optimum level of temperature and moisture is achieved, for example, when
mustard seeds are macerated in vinegar (to make mustard) or by simple masti-
cation (as with watercress and other leafy crucifers). However, if the ferments
are not activated because of too low or too high a temperature, toxic compounds
can form.

In moderate amounts, the essential oils of crucifers stimulate the appetite
and activate digestion. But in large doses they strongly irritate the mucous membranes and can cause digestive or urinary disorders. They are used externally as
a rubefacient, but care must be exerted as they can also produce skin inflamma-

tion. Thanks to their sulfur content, the essential oils of crucifers have antiseptic, and often antibiotic, properties.

These plants contain much vitamin C and are an excellent antiscorbutic. Some, such as *Coclearia* spp., have been used specifically to fight scurvy.

The properties mentioned here are relevant for almost all the members of the family and will not be repeated in the particular study of each genus.

Among the crucifers are found such well-known vegetables as cabbage and its relatives (cauliflower, kohlrabi, Brussel sprouts, broccoli), mustards (black, white, Indian), radish, turnip, horseradish, watercress, various cresses, rocket and more.

Honesty, dame's rocket and wallflower are commonly planted as ornamentals.

Alliaria petiolata (B 4)   Hedge Garlic, Garlic Mustard
(= *A. officinalis*, = *Sisymbrium alliaria*)
From the Latin "allium," garlic: referring to the odor of the plant.
Naturalized from Eur. in N.E. N.Am.

The <u>leaves</u> have a very definite smell and taste of garlic. They are slightly bitter, with a sweetish aftertaste and make an excellent addition to salads. With cooking, they lose their aroma while retaining mostly their bitterness and are therefore better raw.

The <u>plant</u> was formerly much eaten in Europe.

It contains a glucoside (sinigrin) and essential oils.

Hedge garlic is diuretic, vulnerary and antiputrefactive.

The <u>seeds</u> can be used as a spice, but they are bitter as well as pungent.

Alliaria petiolata

Alyssum   (B 4)   Alyssum
From the Greek "a," without, and "lyssa," rabies: ancient name of a plant
supposed to cure rabies.
Almost throughout. Introduced from Eur.
A few European species are planted as ornamentals.

The small <u>leaves</u> of *A. alyssoides* are mild tasting and can be eaten raw.

Arabis   (B-H 3)   Rockcress
From the Latin "arabus," Arabic: possibly the ancient name of a crucifer.
Throughout. Both native and species introduced from Europe.
Our native *A. alpina*, alpine cress – E. Can. & Eurasia – is sometimes
planted for ornament, along with another Eurasian species.

A. glabra (= *Turritis g.*), tower mustard – N. N.Am. – and *hirsuta* – almost
throughout – have been eaten raw or cooked. They have a pleasant, rather pungent taste. The leaves were sometimes preserved in salt, especially in Northern
Asia where the plants are native as well.

Other species are used as food in Europe and Asia, including *A. alpina* (m.a.).

Endangered species: *A. breweri* var. *pecuniaria* – Calif. –, *crandallii* – Colo. –,
fruticosa – Wyo. –, *gunnisoniana* – Colo. –, *koehleri* var. *koehleri* – Ore. –, *macdonal-
diana* – Calif. –, *oxylobula* – Colo. –, *perstellata* var. *ampla* – Tenn. – and var. *perstellata* – Ala., Ky.

Armoracia (B 3)   Horseradish

Latin name of the plant, from "Aremorica," Brittany.
A. aquatica is native to E. N.Am.
The European *A. rusticana* (= *Cochlearia armoracia*),
originally from Southern Russia and Ukraine, is naturalized throughout N.Am. It has been cultivated in
vegetable gardens since the Middle Ages for its root,
which was used both medicinally and as a spice.

The fresh root of the European horseradish yields the
well-known garnish: it is grated and mixed with vinegar,
salt and a touch of honey. In Alsace, horseradish root is
made into a warm sauce with fresh cream.

Besides a mustard oil glucoside and a ferment, the
root contains a large quantity of vitamin C and various
minerals.

It is stomachic, diuretic, expectorant and antiscorbutic. It is an even stronger rubefacient than mustard
seeds. The very pungent essential oil it
contains is vesicant and toxic, even is
moderate amounts.

Frequent handling of the root can
cause serious irritation.

The large leaves of horseradish are
edible raw or cooked. They have a flavor
reminiscent of that of cabbage, but are
pungent and bitter.

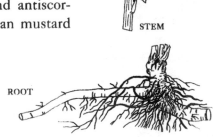

STEM

ROOT

Armoracia rusticana

Athysanus perpusillus (G 4)   Sandweed

From the Greek "a," without, and "thysanos," fringe: alluding to the wing-
less fruit.
W. N.Am. A monotypic genus.

The small seeds have reportedly been used as food.

Barbarea (D 3)   Winter Cress
The plant is dedicated to Saint Barbara.
Throughout. Introduced from Eurasia.
B. verna (= *B. praecox*) is occasionally grown in vegetable gardens of Eur. and N.Am. for its slightly pungent <u>leaves,</u> which are not bitter. The plant is
naturalized throughout.

The very young <u>leaves</u> of ***B. vulgaris*** are edible raw in
the spring, but they soon become bitter. Older leaves usually require cooking in a change of water. The young
flower heads, which look like small broccoli, can also be
eaten after their bitterness is removed by boiling.
Winter cress contains much vitamin A and C.

Barbarea vulgaris

Brassica (A 1)   Cabbage, Mustard
(including *Sinapis* spp.)
Latin name for cabbage, from its Celtic
name, "brassic."
Throughout. Introduced from Eurasia.
Several of the various species mentioned are commonly cultivated in
vegetable gardens throughout the
world. Some often escape from cultivation. Other *Brassica* species are
ubiquitous "weeds."

B. campestris, field mustard, is one of
these. For its uses, see *B. nigra*.

B. hirta (= *Sinapis alba*), white mustard, has long been cultivated as a source of
the well-known condiment and frequently
naturalized in North America as a weed.

Brassica campestris

Young shoots and leaves are edible raw or cooked. They have a pleasant, rather pungent taste.

The seeds are prepared like those of black mustard (see *B. nigra*).

They contain a fixed oil, mucilage and a glucoside (sinalboside) which yields an essential oil by hydrolysis with a ferment (myronase).

B. juncea, Indian mustard – from S. & E. Asia – is occasionally naturalized.

The pungent leaves known as "mustard greens" are very good raw, added to salads, or cooked. It is cultivated as a vegetable in North America, Europe and especially in East Asia where several varieties are known. In some, the swollen bases of the stem are peeled and eaten raw or pickled.

The seeds are used as a condiment. In Southern Russia, the plant is cultivated on a large scale for the edible oil which is extracted from them.

B. kaber (= *B. arvensis*, = *Sinapis arvensis*), charlock, is a frequent weed.

Young shoots and leaves are edible raw in salads or cooked.

The seeds have been used as a condiment since Antiquity. Their composition and medicinal properties are the same as those of black mustard (see *B. nigra*).

The plant is much cultivated for its seeds in Southern Russia.

B. napobrassica (= *B. oleracea* x *napus*), rutabaga, Swedish turnip, escapes from cultivation.

The plant is cultivated for its large root with a yellow flesh which is edible raw (grated) or, more commonly, cooked. The root can be made into sauerkraut. It is often used as fodder.

It contains starch, traces of an essential oil and many minerals.

B. napus var. oleifera, rape, temporarily persists after cultivation.

The plant is cultivated for its seeds which yield about 40% of an edible oil, much used as salad and cooking oil in Europe and Asia.

Rape oil contains erucic acid, which was shown to potentially cause heart damage. Varieties with a very low erucic acid content have subsequently been developed.

Leaves and inflorescences are edible.

B. nigra, black mustard, is a very common weed in North America.

This species has been used as food since Antiquity. Young shoots and leaves are edible raw or cooked. The latter make a very good vegetable.

The young flowering tops, still in buds, look like broccoli and are still commonly gathered in the Mediterranean region, along with those of other crucifers. They are generally cooked in water and eaten with olive oil, lemon juice and salt.

The flowers are edible as well.

Black mustard is cultivated as a source of mustard seeds, which are generally mixed with those of *B. hirta* and *B. juncea* to yield the well-known condiment.

Mustard seeds, as well as the condiment, are aperitive and digestive.

A poultice made by mixing mustard seed flour (freshly ground, if possible) with water is used as a rubefacient. Only lukewarm water should be used, as the essential oil responsible for the activity of the poultice is destroyed by temperatures above 125° F.

Brassica nigra

After being soaked in water, whole seeds have a mechanical laxative effect, but they can produce irritating or toxic compounds within the intestinal tract.

The seeds contain a glucoside (sinigroside), an alkaloid (sinapin) and about 30% of a fixed oil.

The composition of the leaves of black mustard is similar to that of cabbage leaves (see *B. oleracea*).

Hippocrates already knew of the medicinal properties of black mustard in 450 B.C.

B. oleracea, cabbage, is originally from the coasts of Europe. Various forms have been cultivated since Antiquity; the plants temporarily persist after cultivation.

The following varieties are common in North America:

Var. *acephala*, kale, collard. The <u>leaves</u>, and sometimes the <u>pith of the stem</u>, are eaten as a vegetable. Some cultivars with colored leaves are occasionally planted for ornament. The plant is also used as fodder.

Var. *botrytis*, cauliflower. The part eaten is the white mass composed of a close aggregation of abortive <u>flowers</u> with thickened peduncles. It is eaten raw or cooked. The large <u>leaves</u> are edible as well.

Var. *capitata*, head cabbage. This is the common cabbage of which the closely imbricated young <u>leaves</u> are eaten raw or cooked. Cabbage leaves are often fermented into sauerkraut. The <u>pith of the stem</u> is sweet and edible. The young <u>flowering tops</u>, still in buds, are commonly eaten like broccoli in the Mediterranean region. The red cabbage is forma *rubra*, so named because of the deep purple color of the leaves.

Var. *caulorapa* (= *B. caulorapa*), kohlrabi. The part eaten is the swollen, fleshy <u>base of the stem</u>.

Var. *gemmifera*, Brussel sprouts. The <u>axillary buds</u> looking like small cabbage heads borne on the stem at the base of each leaf are usually eaten cooked. The <u>leaves</u> are edible as well.

Var. *italica*, broccoli. The young <u>inflorescences</u>, with thickened peduncles, are a common vegetable. The <u>leaves</u> are edible as well.

Cabbages (mostly var. *capitata*) used to be one of the most important food and medicinal plants in Europe. They are still commonly eaten in temperate countries. They are sometimes considered to be more digestible raw than cooked.

The leaves contain proteins, carbohydrates, vitamins A, B1, B2, C, niacin and minerals.

They are very beneficial for the human body, both internally (balancing its various functions, such as antiscorbutic) and externally (vulnerary, detergent, anodyne, antibiotic).

Sauerkraut can easily be made at home with cabbage leaves and salt. It is better to eat it raw in order to fully benefit from the favorable action of its ferments upon digestion and the intestinal flora. This preparation can actually be made with many different kinds of plants, wild or cultivated – the name in German means "acid herb." It is a traditional way of preserving leaves, sometimes roots, young shoots or other plant parts, known at least since Neolithic times. This process fell into disuse in Western Europe (except in Germanic countries with cabbages) but retains its importance to this day in Eastern Europe and especially in the Far East, where many vegetables are still commonly preserved in salt (with a much saltier result than European sauerkraut, which is more sour than salty).

B. rapa, turnip, temporarily persists after cultivation. Turnips have been eaten since the days of the Celts and the Romans, at least 2,500 years ago.

The root is excellent raw, grated. It is traditionally made into sauerkraut in Switzerland ("compote de raves"), but it is more commonly cooked in soups or as a vegetable.

It contains carbohydrates, vitamins A, B and C, minerals, an essential oil and a glucoside.

It is emollient (cooked), diuretic and expectorant.

The leaves are also very good to eat raw or cooked. They are especially rich in provitamin A, vitamin C and iron. At the turn of the century, an outbreak of pellagra (a serious niacin deficiency) in the Southern United States was promptly checked by feeding people cooked turnip leaves.

The seeds yield an edible oil, known as "canola oil."

Many other species are used as food in Asia, some of which have been used for millenia. Among these, two are occasionally cultivated in North America: headed Chinese cabbage "pe-tsai" (*B. pekinensis* = *B. rapa* var. *pekinensis*) and Chinese celery cabbage "pak-choi" (*B. chinensis* = *B. rapa* var. *chinensis*).

Bunias orientalis   (B 4)   Turkish Rocket

From the Greek "bounias," a large turnip, from "bounos," hill, derived from a Cyrenean word.

Scattered throughout.

Introduced from S.E. Eur. & W. Asia. Naturalized locally.

The plant has been cultivated as a vegetable (especially in France) and as fodder.

The young leaves are edible raw or cooked.

Cakile (D 2)   Sea Rocket
From the Arabic name of the plant, "kakeleh."
Along the coasts of E. & W. N.Am.

The <u>roots</u> of *C. edentula* – native – and possibly of *C. maritima* – introduced from Eur. – were eaten in times of scarcity in Canada. The outer fleshy part was removed from the woody core, crushed and mixed with flour to make bread.

The fleshy <u>leaves</u> are salty and rather bitter with a rather unpleasant ether flavor. They are edible raw, as well as the young shoots, the <u>flowers</u> and the tender, unripe <u>fruits</u>.

Camelina (C 4)   False Flax, Gold-of-Pleasure
From the Greek "chamai," close to the ground, dwarf, and "linon," flax: dwarf flax.
Introduced from Eurasia into N.E. N.Am.
C. sativa has been cultivated since the Neolithic Age, especially in N. Eur. for the fibers of its stem and the edible oil contained in the <u>seeds</u>.

Capsella bursa-pàstoris (B 1)   Shepherd's Purse
From the Latin "capsella," small box (diminutive form of "capsa," box): referring to the shape of the fruit, a silicle.
Throughout. Common weed introduced from Eur.
The plant has been used as food since Antiquity.

When the plant is very young, the <u>roots</u> are still tender and can be eaten. Later on, they become too woody.

The <u>young leaves</u> which form a basal rosette are edible raw or cooked in late winter and spring. They provide one of the earliest – and the best – wild salads. After the stem has appeared they become tougher and soon disappear.

Shepherd's purse is eaten in Eastern Asia. In Japan it is one of the seven herbs of spring, traditionally cooked with rice and other wild plants.

Capsella bursa-pastoris

The pungent <u>seeds</u> can be employed as a spice.

The leaves contain tannins, organic acids, an alkaloid (bursin), minerals and various substances (such as flavonoids and acetylcholine).

The whole plant is hemostatic, tonic and diuretic. It is preferable to use it fresh. The juice expressed from it can be employed medicinally.

Cardamine (B-H 2-3)   Bitter Cress
(including *Dentaria* spp.)
Greek and Latin name of a cress – "kardamon" – probably the garden cress, *Lepidium sativum*.
Throughout. Both native and introduced species.

The <u>leaves</u> of these plants are edible raw or cooked, and several species are used as food in America, Europe and Asia.

The most commonly eaten species in North America are *C. hirsuta* – naturalized from Eur. in E. U.S. –, *pennsylvanica* – E. N.Am. – and *pratensis* – both native throughout and introduced from Eur. They are commonly called "creasy greens" on the East Coast.

The leaves of *C. pratensis* (m.a.) are pungent and bitter. They are mostly used as a condiment.

They contain much vitamin C and a glucoside, and are tonic, stomachic, expectorant and antiscorbutic.

The leaves of *C. hirsuta* (m.a.) are milder.

The tuberous <u>rhizome</u> of *C. rhomboidea* (= *C. bulbosa*) – E. N.Am. – was used as a spice by Indians.

The elongated, fleshy <u>rhizome</u> of *C. diphylla* (= *Dentaria d.*), pepper root, toothwort – E. N.Am. – is pungent and was used as a spice by Indians. It tastes somewhat like horseradish and can be made into a condiment.

The <u>leaves</u> are edible raw or cooked.

Endangered species: *C. constancei* – Idaho –, *incisa* (= *Dentaria i.*) – Tenn. –, *micranthera* – N. C. – and *pattersonii* – Ore.

Cardaria draba (D 4)   Hoary Cress
(= *Lepidium d.*)
From the Greek "kardia," heart: alluding to the shape
of the fruit.
Throughout. Introduced from S. Eur. & W. Asia. A
monotypic genus.

The <u>leaves</u> are eaten raw or cooked in Western Asia.
They have a pleasant taste, with a pungent flavor when
raw.
The <u>young inflorescences</u> resemble small broccolis (*Brassica oleracea* var. *italica*) and are edible as such.
They are very good raw or cooked, although sometimes slightly bitter. As the plant grows in colonies, it is
easy to gather large quantities of these miniature broccolis.
The <u>seeds</u> can be used as a spice.

Cardaria draba

Caulanthus (D 4)   Squaw Cabbage
From the Greek "kaulos," stem, and "anthos," flower: referring to cauli-
flower, as some species can be used in a similar manner.
W. N.Am.

The inflated <u>stems</u> of *C. crassicaulis* – S.W. U.S. – and *inflatus* – S. Calif. –
were used while young and fleshy as food by Indians.
They would also eat the <u>leaves</u> and <u>seeds</u> of these two species, as well as
those of *C. glaucus* – S. Calif., Nev.

Cochlearia (B 4)   Scurvy Grass
From the Latin "cochlear," spoon: referring to the shape of the leaves.
Coasts of N. N.Am.
C. danica and *officinalis* – native to the colder regions of the hemi-
sphere – were occasionally cultivated.

The <u>leaves</u> are edible raw. They were eaten by sailors as a remedy for scurvy,
hence the common name. They are tender, sweet, slightly salty and quite pungent.

The plant is rich in vitamin C and minerals, especially iodine. It also contains tannin, glucosides and various other substances.

It has tonic, stomachic, diuretic and antiscorbutic properties.

Conringia orientalis (B 4)   Hare's Mustard
After Herman Conring (1606–1681), German physician.
Introduced from Eurasia into W. N.Am.

The leaves are edible raw or cooked.
The seeds yield an edible, yellow oil.

Coronopus (D 3)   Wart Cress
(= *Senebiera* spp.)
Greek and Latin name of the plant from "koronê," raven, and "pous," foot.
Throughout. Introduced from S.Am. & Eur.

The leaves of *C. didymus* – probably introduced from S.Am. – and *procumbens* – introduced from Eur. – have been used as food. Those of the first species are acrid, pungent and rather ill-smelling: they require cooking in at least one change of water.

A few local species are eaten in Asia and North Africa.

Crambe maritima (B 5)   Sea Kale
From the Greek "krambê," cabbage, crucifer.
Established along the Ore. coast, originally from Eur.

The wild plant has been used as food in Europe since Antiquity. It was preserved in barrels by the Romans for their long sea travels.

Since the 17th century, sea kale has been cultivated in Western Europe and in North America for its fleshy stems and petioles, which are blanched by heaping dirt around them. They are eaten raw or cooked. After about sixty years of oblivion, this delicate vegetable is making a comeback in France.

The leaves are edible as well. When raw, they are quite tough and have a pleasant cabbage flavor with both a sweet and salty taste. They can be made into very good soups and cooked vegetables.

Descurainia (B 2-3) Tansy Mustard
(= *Sophia* species)
After F. Descourain (1658–1740), French botanist.
Throughout.
Many native species, especially in W. & C. N.Am., plus ***D. sophia*** (= *Sisymbrium s.*) – naturalized from Eurasia.

Our native ***D. pinnata*** (including *D. halictorum*, = *Sisymbrium canescens*) and ***richardsonii*** (= *incisa*) – W. & C. N.Am. – were used as food by Indians.

The <u>leaves</u> were eaten cooked and the <u>seeds</u> made into piñole.

It has been reported that in Mexico, a poultice of the seeds of some species is applied to wounds.

If *D. pinnata* (m.a.) grows on soils rich in selenium, it can poison livestock which graze on it, as it tends to concentrate this element. However, very large doses of the plant must be ingested over a long period of time before the toxicity will manifest. Symptoms include paralysis of the throat accompanied by blindness.

The <u>leaves</u> of the Eurasian species *D. sophia* (m.a.) have been eaten cooked in America, Europe and Asia.

The <u>seeds</u> can be used as a spice.

Draba (E-H 3) Whitlow Grass
Name used by Dioscorides for a certain cress.
Throughout. Both native and species introduced from Eur.

Although tiny, the <u>leaves</u> and <u>flower heads</u> of ***D. verna*** (= *Eriophila v.*) – introduced from Eur. – are edible.

Endangered species: *D. aprica* – S.E. U.S. –, *arida* – Nev. –, *asprella* – Ariz. – and *paucifructa* – Nev.

Eruca vesicaria (D-F 4) Rocket
(= *E. sativa*)
Latin name of the plant.
Introduced from Eur. into N.Am.

Ezuca vesicaria

Rocket is cultivated as a vegetable in Europe and North America. It is known in the U.S. under its Spanish name, "arrugula." Its young shoots and leaves have a strong smell, somewhat reminiscent of roasted hazelnuts or of burnt rubber and a more or less pungent taste (rather mild in varieties sold in markets).

The plant contains erucic acid, which is toxic in large quantities. In the raw stage, rocket should be eaten only in moderation, as a condiment in salads, for instance. But after cooking in a change of water, it can be partaken of freely – although it has lost most of its interest.

It is tonic, stomachic, diuretic and reputedly aphrodisiac.

The seeds can be made into a mustard-like condiment, and when pressed yield an edible oil.

Hesperis matronalis (B 4) Dame's Rocket
Greek name of a Southern European species from "hesperos," evening: the flowers become fragrant in the evening. This characteristic is also found with the large purple or white flowers of our species.
Originally from Eur., the plant is often cultivated for ornament and is locally naturalized in N.Am.

Leaves, flower buds and flowers are good to eat raw in salads.
They have diaphoretic and diuretic properties.

Isatis tinctoria (D-F 4) Woad
Greek and Latin name of the
plant from "isazô," to equalize.
Scattered throughout.
Introduced from S. Eur. & W.
Asia; formerly much cultivated for
dye and locally naturalized.

Isatis tinctoria

The young plant has been eaten in
Europe and Asia. Excessive amounts
of it can prove to be somewhat toxic.
It is preferable to cook the leaves in
several changes of water.

Woad has been grown for centuries
as a dye plant. To obtain a light blue
dye, the flowering stems are cut,
partially dried in the sun and then
ground into a paste which is left out-
side to ferment in a place protected from the rain. The paste is then pressed into
cakes, left to ferment once again, and finally dried. For dyeing, a piece of the
product is dissolved in warm lime-water and the cloth is soaked in this bath.

The leaves of a local species are eaten in China.

Lepidium (B-H 2-3) Pepper Grass
Greek and Latin name of a plant in this genus from "lepis," shell, scale:
referring to the shape of the fruits.
Throughout. Both native and species introduced from Eurasia.

In most species, the leaves are pungent and can be added raw to salads, as a
condiment, or cooked as a vegetable.

The seeds have been used as a spice. Western Indians used to mix them with
other seeds in their piñole.

The following native species have been used as food on our continent: ***L. dif-
fusum*** – S.E. U.S. –, ***flavum*** – S.W. U.S., N.W. Mex. –, ***fremontii*** – S.W. U.S. –,
nitidum – W. N.Am. – and ***virginicum*** (including *L. intermedium*) – throughout.

L. sativum, garden cress, originally from Western Asia and Egypt, has been cultivated as a vegetable since Antiquity. It is locally found as an escape in North America.

The spicy <u>leaves</u> are added to salads and various other dishes as a condiment.

They contain an essential oil and the same glucoside (glucotropaeolin) as nasturtium (*Tropaeolum majus*). By hydrolysis, this glucoside yields glucose and antibiotic compounds (benzyle isothiocyanate). But if the ferment (see Brassicaceae) is not activated by lukewarm water, a toxic substance (benzyle cyanate) is formed as well. It might therefore be a good idea to chop up the plant and let it macerate for a few minutes in lukewarm water (or vinegar for salads) before using it.

The medicinal properties of garden cress are similar to those of watercress (*Nasturtium officinale*). It was used externally for sciatica in ancient times.

The <u>roots</u> of *L. latifolium* – naturalized from Eur. – were used like horseradish in Great Britain, and the plant was formerly cultivated for this purpose.

The <u>leaves</u> are also edible.

In the spring, the <u>young inflorescences</u> of *L. campestre* – naturalized from Eur. – resemble small broccolis (*Brassica oleracea* var. *italica*) and can be used as such, either raw or cooked.

The <u>seeds</u> of various species are a good condiment. Those of *L. latifolium* (m.a.) were commonly called "poor man's pepper" in England.

Local species are eaten throughout the world.

Endangered species: *L. barnebyanum* – Utah – and *davisii* – Idaho.

Lesquerella   (H 4)   Bladder Pod
After L. Lesquereux (1805–1889), American botanist.
W. & C. N.Am.

The <u>plants</u> are edible in spite of their small size.

L. intermedia (S.W. U.S.) was reportedly used by Hopi Indians as a snakebite remedy.

Endangered species: *L. aurea* – N.M. –, *densipila* – Tenn., Ala. –, *filiformis* – Mo. –, *fremontii* – Wyo. –, *lata* – N.M. –, *lyrata* – Ala. –, *perforata* – Tenn. –, *pruinosa* – Colo. –, *stonensis* – Tenn. –, *tumulosa* – Utah – and *valida* – Tex., N.M.

Lobularia maritima (B 2) Sweet Alyssum
(= *Alyssum maritimum*)

From the Latin "lobula," small lobe: referring to the shape of the fruit.

Throughout.

Originally from Eur., it is frequently planted for its white, honey-smelling flowers, and escapes from cultivation.

The small leaves are edible raw. They are quite pungent.

Besides being fragrant, the flowers have a sweet taste; the inflorescences make delicious additions to salads.

Lobularia maritima

Lunaria annua (B 4) Honesty

From the Latin "luna," moon: referring to the appearance of the septum of the fruits.

Originally from Eur., the plant is cultivated for the decorative value of the paper-thin septum of the silicle. It is locally naturalized in N.Am.

Roots and seeds have occasionally been used as food in Europe.

Leaves, flowers and green, unripe fruits are edible raw or cooked, but they are rather bitter.

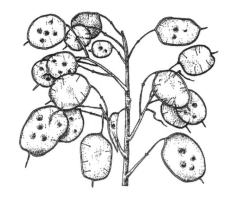

Lunaria annua

Matthiola incana　(D 4)　Stock
After P. A. Mattioli (1500–1577), Italian author.
Originally from S. Eur., the plant is occasionally cultivated as an ornamental, and it is naturalized locally on our continent.

<u>Leaves</u>, <u>flowers</u> and <u>young fruits</u> are edible but they are not very good. They were used as food in times of scarcity in Southern Europe.
Another species has reportedly been eaten in Arabia and in Egypt.

Nasturtium　(A 3)　Watercress
Latin name of the garden cress (*Lepidium sativum*) from "nasus," nose, and "torqueo," to twist: referring to the strong smell and taste of the plant.
Throughout. Naturalized from Eur.
N. officinale, the most common watercress, has been cultivated as a vegetable since the 16th century in Eur., and later in Am. and Asia. It is naturalized in running water throughout our continent.

Watercress has been used as food since Antiquity. The <u>whole plant</u> is eaten raw in salads (where it is then pungent), or cooked in soups or as greens (where it becomes much milder). Its characteristic taste is very pleasant. It can also be fermented into sauerkraut.

Beware: eating excessive amounts of raw watercress can lead to urinary troubles (cystitis).

If it is to be drunk, watercress juice must always be diluted with water as it is very irritating.

The plant must never be picked in streams running through pastures, as it may be contaminated by the liver fluke (*Fasciola hepatica*), a common parasite of livestock (especially sheep) which is very dangerous for humans. Watercress leaves must always be thoroughly washed, but this is not enough to get rid of the fluke larvae

Nasturtium officinale

which stick to the plant. In case of any doubt, they should be cooked, which solves the problem by killing the parasite.

Watercress contains vitamins A, B, C, E, rutin and niacin, many minerals (much iodine), a bitter principle and a sulfured oil (from a glucoside).

The plant is tonic, aperitive, stomachic, depurative, diuretic, antiscorbutic, and expectorant.

N. microphyllum – occasionally naturalized from Eur. – is edible as well.

A local species is eaten in Southeast Asia.

Parrya nudicaulis (D 4)   Parry's Wallflower
Etymology unknown.
Alaska.

Roots and leaves of the plant are edible raw.

Phoenicaulis (D 4)   Dagger Pod
From the Greek "phainô," to show, and "kaulos," stem: alluding to the aspect of the plant.
W. N.Am.

On various species, such as *P. cheiranthoides* – Calif. to Idaho –, the leaves, the flower buds, the flowers and the long siliques, while unripe and still tender, can be eaten raw.

Raphanus (A 1)   Radish
Greek and Latin name of the plant or of horseradish, *Armoracia rusticana*.
Throughout.
Two species have been introduced from Eur. and are commonly found as weeds.

R. sativus, the exact origin of which is unknown, was already cultivated by the ancient Egyptians over 4,000 years ago. Its culture has now spread to all parts of the world.

Besides the common red and white rooted radish, a black variety with a very large root (var. *niger*) is also grown in gardens.

Seldom are the roots of the wild plants as plump as those of the cultivated radishes. In order to be tender and fleshy, they must be gathered early in the spring before the flowering stems appear. Later, the outer part of the root can be

removed from the woody core and grated raw, or cooked
and passed through a food mill or processor to make a purée.

Radish roots contain vitamins B, C and rutin, minerals
and a glucoside (yielding an essential oil by hydrolysis).

They are aperitive, antiscorbutic and expectorant.

Those of var. *niger* (m.a.) are diuretic, choleretic and
sedative as well.

The leaves of *R. sativus* (m.a.) and of *R. raphanistrum*
are edible. They are large, fleshy and tender, with a mild,
pleasant taste. They are very good raw in salads, and excellent cooked in soups or as greens. They are used as food
in Europe and Asia.

The flower buds and the tender tips of the stems resemble broccoli (*Brassica oleracea* var. *italica*) and can be
eaten as such, raw or cooked.

*Raphanus
raphanistrum*

The flowers themselves add a decorative and tasty
touch to salads.

The unripe fruits are delicious raw. When very young, they are tender, with a
fine flavor reminiscent of that of the root, but less pungent. In Asia they are pickled, or a green sauce is made from their extracted juice. On the same continent,
some radish varieties are cultivated specifically for their fruits, which can reach
up to three feet in length.

Radish seeds are pungent and make a good condiment; they can be ground
up like mustard seeds.

Those of *R. raphanistrum* (m.a.) contain the same glucoside (sinalboside) as
white mustard (*Brassica hirta*), which is transformed by hydrolysis into mustard oil.

Some radish varieties without fleshy roots are cultivated in the Orient for the
edible oil extracted from their seeds.

Rorippa   (B 3)   Yellow Cress
Name without significance, created by Scopoli, who named the genus.
Throughout. Both native and species introduced from Eurasia.

Young shoots and leaves of *R. amphibia* – introduced from Eur. in N.E.
N.Am. – and *islandica* – N.E. N.Am. – were eaten by Indians. They are also
used as food, raw or cooked, in Europe and Asia, along with other species. They
have a pleasant taste.

Sisymbrium   (D-H 3)   Hedge Mustard, Tumble Mustard
Greek name of a cress and some aromatic plants.
Throughout. Naturalized from Eurasia.
In Eur., *S. officinale* has been cultivated in vegetable gardens.

The <u>leaves</u> of *S. officinale* were eaten raw or cooked in Europe; they have a good flavor when young.
Like most crucifers, the whole plant contains an essential oil.
It is diuretic, stomachic and expectorant. Fresh, it was reputed to act against irritations of the throat.
The seeds contain cardioactive substances.

Sisymbrium
officinale

The <u>leaves</u> of two introduced European species, *S. irio*,
London rocket, and *orientale* – naturalized in W. N.Am. – are edible as well.
A few local species are used as food in the Mediterranean area.
Endangered species: *S. kearneyi* – Ariz.

Stanleya   (D 2)   Prince's Plume, Desert Plume
After Lord Edward Stanley, English ornithologist of the 19th century.
W. U.S.

The tender <u>stems</u> and <u>leaves</u> of *S. elata* – S.W. U.S. – and *pinnata* – W. & C. N.Am. – were eaten by Western Indians.
These plants have the capacity to accumulate selenium, an element toxic in high doses: large amounts of the leaves are poisonous unless properly prepared. The fact was well-known by the Indians, who would always boil the plant in two changes of water to remove the harmful principles.
Stanleya spp. have caused livestock poisoning.
Indians made piñole with the <u>seeds</u>.

Thelypodium (D 4)

From the Greek "thelys," female, and "pous," foot: referring to the shape of the ovary.

W. N.Am.

California Indians ate the leaves and seeds of *T. flavescens* (= *Caulanthus procerus*) – Calif.

Endangered species: *T. repandum* – Idaho – and *texanum* – Tex.

Thlaspi (B 2-3)   Penny Cress

From the Greek "thlaô," to crush: alluding to the flattened fruit, or possibly referring to a plant the seed of which was crushed, as to yield oil.

Native species in W. N.Am.; some species introduced from Eurasia are naturalized throughout.

The leaves of several of these plants are edible raw, but they are pungent and often bitter. It is usually preferable to use them as a condiment or to cook them, possibly in a change of water. The very young leaves are best. Those of the Eurasian *T. arvense* have a pleasant, although somewhat bitter taste. They were widely utilized, and this species has been cultivated as a vegetable, especially in Asia.

Its seeds can be used as a mustard-like condiment.

They contain the same glucoside (sinigroside) as black mustard (*Brassica nigra*), as well as a fixed oil which was used for burning in lamps.

Thlaspi arvense

The pungent leaves and seeds of *T. perfoliatum* – naturalized from Eurasia – are edible as well.

Thysanocarpus (D 4)   Lace Pod
From the Greek "thysanos," fringe, and "karpos," fruit: referring to the
aspect of the fruits.
W. N.Am.

The seeds of *T. curvipes* (including var. *elegans*) were made into piñole by
California Indians.

RESEDACEAE

Reseda (D 3)   Mignonette
Latin name of the plant from "resedare," to soothe, to heal.
Scattered throughout. Naturalized from the Mediterranean region.

An Egyptian species, mignonette (*R. odorata*) is sometimes cultivated for its
sweet-scented flowers; it is one of the most fragrant of all plants. It rarely escapes from cultivation.

Young shoots and leaves of *R. lutea* are edible raw. Their spicy flavor is reminiscent of that of crucifers, with a slight bitterness.

Two other species (*R. alba* and *phyteuma*) were eaten in the Mediterranean area.

R. luteola, dyer's rocket, was frequently cultivated as a dye plant; it contains
luteolin (a flavonoid) and gives wool, cotton and silk a yellow color. This plant
was highly esteemed before the advent of synthetic dyes. It is locally naturalized in North America.

ERICACEAE

This large family, especially widespread in northern regions, includes shrubs
with delicious fruits such as blueberries or huckleberries, as well as toxic ornamentals such as rhododendrons and kalmias. The most important cultivated
fruit crop in this family is the cranberry.

Andromeda polifolia (F 4)   Bog Rosemary
From Andromeda, a character in Greek mythology.
Can. A monotypic genus.

A cold water maceration of the plant was drunk as tea by the Ojibway Indians.

Steeped in hot water, a toxic glucoside (andromedotoxin) contained in the leaves and flowers is extracted and the brew can cause digestive, nervous and respiratory disorders. Andromedotoxin also acts as a hypotensor.

The plant grows in Europe as well. There, cases of poisoning with honey from bog rosemary flowers have been reported since ancient times.

It is said that a decoction of the fruits has inebriating effects.

Arbutus (D 2)   Madrone
Latin name of the Mediterranean *A. unedo*.
W. N.Am.
Our native *A. menziesii* and the European strawberry tree (*A. unedo*) are planted for ornament.

The fruits of *A. arizonica*, Arizona madrone – Ariz. –, *menziesii*, Pacific madrone (m.a.) – Pacific Coast – and *xalapensis*, Texas madrone – W. Tex., N.M., Mex. – can be eaten when ripe. They are red, rather small and astringent, and although edible raw, they are better cooked. They can be boiled, stewed, or dried and ground into a meal.

A few local species are used as food in Europe and North Africa, especially the strawberry tree (m.a.), planted as an ornamental in North America. Its fruits are definitely better than those of our native trees. They are eaten raw in the Mediterranean area and often made into jam or distilled into alcohol.

Arctostaphylos (D-H 2)   Bearberry, Manzanita
From the Greek "arktos," bear, and "staphylê," bunch of ripe grapes:
bearberry, the fruits of *A. uva-ursi*, as many others, were eaten by bears
in Eur.

This genus can be subdivided into two groups: bearberries and manzanitas
(Spanish, meaning "little apple").

1. Bearberries

The <u>fruits</u> of *A. alpina*, black bearberry – N.
N.Am. – and *ruber* – N.W. N.Am. – are juicy and
edible raw or in jams. They are rather insipid.
Those of *A. alpina* are black, of *A. ruber*, red.

A. uva-ursi, a common ground cover in northern regions and mountains, also present in Europe, is cultivated as an ornamental.

A bitter tea known as "koutai" was made in
Russia with the <u>leaves</u> of this plant. They were
smoked by American Indians under the name
"kinnikinnick."

Arctostaphylos uva-ursi

They contain tannin, two glucosides (arbuto-
side and methylarbutoside) and other substances.

They are also astringent, diuretic and antiseptic to the urinary tract (provided
the urine is alkaline). Their medicinal uses date back to the Middle Ages.

But the high tannin content of bearberry leaves can, over a period of time,
cause digestive troubles; therefore they must be used in moderation only. For
therapeutic uses, it has been recommended to eliminate the tannins by agitating
an infusion of the leaves with charcoal powder.

High doses of the tea can be emetic.

The small red <u>fruits</u> are edible raw. They are dry, mealy with a sour, pleasant
flavor, although sometimes bitter. They can be cooked and sweetened. Jam was
sometimes made from bearberries. They can also be crushed and mixed with
flour to make breads and cakes.

Bearberry dyes wool gray-green without mordant, bluish-green with copper
sulfate.

2. Manzanitas

These are shrubs of Western North America; they are one of the main constituents of the vegetation type known as "chaparral" in Southwestern United States and Northwestern Mexico.

Some native species are cultivated as ornamentals.

The <u>flowers</u> are edible raw.

The reddish, dry <u>fruits</u> of many manzanitas were used as food by Western Indians, although their pulp is scant and their seeds are very large. The whole fruits, including the seeds, were ground up and the resulting meal sifted and mixed with other flours for making a mush.

In some species, the pulp has a pleasantly acid taste: pulverized and mixed with water, it makes a refreshing drink. With some honey or sugar added, it can be fermented into a cider.

The fruits can simply be nibbled on.

Among the best species are *A. glauca* – Calif., Baja –, *manzanita* – Calif. –, *nevadensis* – W. N.Am. –, *parryana* – Calif. –, *patula* – S.W. U.S., Mex. –, *pungens* – S.W. U.S., Mex. – and *tomentosa* – Calif.

Endangered species: *A. auriculata, bakeri, densiflora, edmundsii* var. *parvifolia, glandulosa* subsp. *crassifolia, glutinosa, hookeri, imbricata, myrtifolia, pacifica, pallida, pumila* and *refugioensis* – all Calif.

Calluna vulgaris (E 4)   Heather
From the Greek "kallunô," to clean up: the plant was used as a broom.
Introduced from Eur. into N.E. N.Am. A monotypic genus.
The plant is sometimes cultivated for ornament.

In ancient Europe, the various Celtic tribes used to prepare and ingest large quantities of heather mead, a decoction of the flowering tops of this plant (or of *Erica* spp.) mixed with honey and left to ferment. A similar beverage was still recently enjoyed in the Hebrides, but the honey was replaced by malt extracted from barley (see *Hordeum vulgare*, Poaceae).

Calluna vulgaris

Heather contains tannin, a resin, an oil and glucosides (quercitrin, myricitrin, arbutin).

It is astringent, depurative, diuretic and antiseptic to the urinary tract, like bearberry (*Arctostaphylos uva-ursi*).

The plant dyes wool green with alum, and the flowering tops give it a purplish color (which is not fast) with the same mordant. Without mordant, the flowering plant dyes wool a brownish yellow.

Chamaedaphne calyculata (F 4)   Leatherleaf
(= *Andromeda glaucophylla*, = *A. calyculata*, = *Cassandra c.*)
From the Greek "chamai," close to the ground, dwarf, and "daphnê," laurel: dwarf laurel.
N.E. N.Am. A monotypic genus.

The leaves were macerated in cold water and drunk as tea by Ojibway Indians, like those of bog rosemary (see *Andromeda polifolia*).

They contain andromedotoxin and are somewhat toxic.

Epigaea repens (E 4)   Trailing Arbutus
From the Greek "epi," upon, and "gaia," earth: referring to its prostrate habit.
E. N.Am.
The plant is sometimes grown for ornament.

The fragrant corollas are sweet and have a pleasant taste. They can be eaten raw.

The fruits of a local species are eaten in Japan.

Gaultheria (B 2-3)   Wintergreen, Salal
After Jean François Gaulthier (1708–1756), physician in Quebec.
Throughout.
Our native *G. procumbens*, wintergreen – E. N.Am. – and *shallon*, salal – N. Pacific Coast – are planted for ornament, along with a Chinese species.

The leaves of *G. hispidula* (= *Chiogenes h.*), creeping snowberry – N. N.Am. –, *humifusa*, Western wintergreen – W. Mountains – and *procumbens* (m.a.) are very aromatic due to the presence of an essential oil, oil of wintergreen, which contains methylsalicylate, a substance closely related to aspirin. The commercial source of this fragrant oil, however, is *Betula lenta*, black birch (see Betulaceae). *G. procumbens* (m.a.) was formerly used before black birch. Oil of wintergreen, obtained by distillation, is used for flavoring such items as toothpastes and medicines. The pure oil is irritating and toxic, and must be used with caution.

An infusion of the leaves is carminative, diuretic, stimulant and analgesic.

A method for obtaining the best wintergreen drink was devised by Euell Gibbons: the infusion is fermented for a few days in a glass container until bubbles appear. The liquid then acquires a transluscent pink color and a delicious taste.

The leaves can also be chewed for their fragrance, or they can be used for flavoring desserts. When very young and tender, they can be added to salads.

The red, aromatic berries of *G. humifusa* and *procumbens* (both m.a.) are edible raw. Those of the latter species were sold in Boston markets up until the turn of the century. They were sometimes made into pies and jam.

The white berries of *G. hispidula* (m.a.) are juicy, aromatic and slightly acid; they can be eaten raw. Those of a local variety are often used as food in Japan.

The leaves of salal, *G. shallon* (m.a.) are not fragrant like those of wintergreen. However, the ripe fruits, dark blue in color, are juicy, sweet and aromatic. They are delicious raw, and are found in quantity on the tall shrubs. Pacific Coast Indians used to eat huge amounts of salal berries in the fall and dry them for later use.

The fruits of several species are used as food in East Asia.

Gaylussacia (B 2)   Huckleberry
After J. L. Gay-Lussac (1778–1850), French chemist.
Throughout.

The fruits of the various species are edible raw. They are usually sweet and flavorful. The berries are also made into jams, pies and so on.

They resemble blueberries (*Vaccinium* spp.) with their dark blue or black fruits, differing from them by their few, relatively large seeds; blueberries have many tiny seeds. However, some *Vaccinium* spp. are also known by the name of huckleberry.

Among the most commonly eaten species are *G. baccata*, black huckleberry, *brachycera*, box huckleberry – E. U.S. – and *dumosa*, dwarf huckleberry, *frondosa*, dangleberry and *ursina*, bear huckleberry – all in E. N.Am.

Ledum (D-F 4)   Labrador Tea
From the Greek "lêdos," name of a rockrose (*Cistus ladaniferus*) producing ladanum, an aromatic resin.
N. N.Am.

In northern North America, Europe and Asia, the <u>leaves</u> of *L. palustre* (including subsp. *groenlandicum*) have been used to make an aromatic tea.

They contain tannin, a glucoside (arbutin), an essential oil and other substances.

In moderation, the tea is astringent, diaphoretic, diuretic and expectorant. But overdoses can irritate the digestive and nervous systems.

The leaves of *L. palustre* (m.a.) have been used as a parasiticide (for lice, scabies, ringworm, and so on) and even as an abortive.

Ledum palustre

L. glandulosum – N.W. U.S. – is known to be toxic and has poisoned sheep. It has a bitter taste.

Oxydendrum arboreum (D 4)   Sourwood
From the Greek "oxys," sharp, sour, and "dendron," tree: the leaves of this tree have a sour taste.
E. N.Am. A monotypic genus.
The tree is sometimes planted for ornament.

The <u>leaves</u> are slightly acid. When young and tender they make a good addition to salads. It is also pleasant to nibble on them while hiking.

The <u>flowers</u> are the source of sourwood honey, which is white when crystallized. This honey is prized for its delicate flavor.

Rhododendron (G-F-H 2)   Rhododendron, Azalea

From the Greek "rhodon," rose, and "dendron," tree: Greek name of the oleander, *Nerium oleander*.

Almost throughout.

Several native and Asian species, along with garden hybrids, are commonly cultivated as ornamentals.

The <u>leaves</u> and <u>flowering tops</u> of *R. lapponicum*, Lapland rosebay – N. N.Am. – were used as tea during Richardson's arctic expedition in 1851.

<u>A juicy growth</u> (a gall) found on the leaves and twigs of *R. nudiflorum* – E. U.S. – has reportedly been eaten raw in salads or pickled.

However, many *Rhododendron* spp. are known to cause serious digestive, nervous, respiratory and cardiac disorders. *R. albiflorum* – N.W. N.Am. –, *occidentalis*, Western azalea – Calif. –, *catawbiense*, rose bay – mountains of Va. to Ga. – and *maximum*, great laurel – Appalachians – have poisoned sheep.

<u>Leaves</u> and <u>flowers</u> of several local species are used as food in East Asia.

Endangered species: *R. minus* var. *chapmanii* – Fla.

Vaccinium   (A 2-3)   Blueberry, Huckleberry, Bilberry, Cranberry
Latin name of the plant.
Throughout.
A few native (*V. angustifolium* – N.E. N.Am. – and *ovatum*, California huckleberry – W. N.Am.) and Asian species are planted for ornament. *V. corymbosum* – N.E. N.Am. – and *macrocarpon*, cranberry – N. N.Am. – are cultivated for their fruits, both in individual gardens and in commercial orchards. *V. angustifolium* (m.a.) is also grown for this purpose: it is the most important commercial blueberry of the northern states.

Vaccinium myrtillus   *Vaccinium uliginosum*

1. Subgenus *Vaccinium*, blueberries, huckleberries (most huckleberries are *Gaylussacia* spp.) and bilberries

The fruits are usually juicy, sweet and aromatic. They are edible raw and are also commonly made into jams, jellies, pies, muffins and so on. A delicious juice can be extracted from them, which can be fermented into wine. They can also be dried and used like raisins. Indians would often grind and mix them with meal from various seeds to make a mush.

The fruits contain vitamins A, C and rutin, minerals (they are rich in iron), organic acids (malic, citric, tartric, benzoic), tannin, pectin, sugars and glucosides.

They are also astringent, tonic, antiseptic and refrigerant, and are reputed to improve night vision due to their vitamin A content.

All species yield edible fruits, but the following are the most widely utilized

in North America (the color of
the fruit is in parenthesis): *V. angus-*
tifolium (m.a.), including several -
varieties (blue); ***arboreum***, far-
kleberry – E. N.Am. – (black);
arbuscula – W. N.Am. – and
atrococcum – E. U.S. – (black);
australe – E. U.S. – (blue);
brittonii – N.E. N.Am. – (black,
about one-half inch in diameter);
caesariense – E. coast – (blue);
caespitosum, dwarf bilberry (blue);
constablaei – C.E. U.S. – (blue,
about one-half inch in diameter);
corymbosum (m.a.), ***crassifolium*** –
S.E. U.S. – (purple, black); ***elliottii***,

Vaccinium vitis-idaea

mayberry – S.E. U.S. – (black), ***marianum*** (= *virgatum*) – E. Coast – (black, about
one-half inch in diameter); ***membranaceum*** – N. N.Am. – (black); ***myrsinites***,
shiny blueberry – S.E. U.S. – (blue-black); ***myrtilloides*** (= *canadense*) – N.
N.Am. – (blue); ***myrtillus*** – N.W. N.Am., also in Eurasia – (blue); ***occidentale***,
Western blueberry – W.N.Am. – (blue-black); ***ovalifolium*** – N. N.Am. – (black,
about one-half inch in diameter); *ovatum* (m.a.), ***parvi-***
folium, red huckleberry – N. N.Am. – (red); ***scoparium***,
grouseberry, little-leaf huckleberry – W. N.Am. – (red); ***sim-***
ulatum – S.E. U.S. – (black); ***tenellum*** – S.E. U.S. – (black);
uliginosum, bog bilberry – N. N.Am. & Rocky Mountains,
also in Eurasia – and ***vacillans*** – E. N.A. – (blue); ***vitis-***
idaea, cowberry – N. N.Am., also in Eurasia – (red).

   The <u>fruits</u> of V. vitis-idaea (m.a.) are red and sour-
tasting. Their flavor improves with the first frost and
they are made into a sauce, like cranberries. Cowberries
are still used this way (the sauce being eaten with game)
in Europe, where the plant is native as well. They
were formerly sold in markets in London.

   Blueberries are eaten locally in Europe, including the
fruits of V. *myrtillus*, *uliginosum* and *vitis-idaea* (m.a.), in
Asia and in Polynesia.

Vaccinium oxycoccos

2. Subgenus *Oxycoccus* (= *Oxycoccus* spp.), Cranberries
The fruits are red and sour-tasting. They are usually eaten cooked.

V. macrocarpon (m.a.) is cultivated on inundated fields in Northeastern North America, from which cranberries are delivered throughout the country. The fruits are made into cranberry sauce, which is traditionally served with turkey for Thanksgiving dinner. An acidy juice (sweetened for drinking) is extracted from them. They can also be made into jam, pies, and so on.

The fruits of *V. erythrocarpum* – C.E. U.S. – (the fruits are red to purple), *microcarpum* – N. N.Am. – and *oxycoccos* (= *Oxycoccus palustris*, = *O. quadripetalus*) – N. N.Am. – have been made into sauces, jams or jellies.

V. oxycoccos (m.a.) was occasionally cultivated in England, where its fruits were considered superior to those of *V. macrocarpon* (m.a.). A juice was also extracted from them. The plant is native to Europe as well.

The leaves of several Vaccinium spp. included in both subgenera *V. myrtillus*, *oxycoccos*, *vitis-idaea* (m.a.) contain glucosides, arbutine in particular.

They act as an antiseptic in the urinary tract and help reduce the blood sugar level. But if they are used over a long period of time, they can produce unpleasant symptoms.

V. vitis-idaea dyes wool and cotton yellow with alum.

EMPETRACEAE

Empetrum (D 4)   Crowberry
Greek name of a plant growing on rocks, probably a kind of saxifrage.
Northern regions.

The berries of *E. nigrum* – N. N.Am. & W. Mountains. – and *rubrum* (including var. *atropurpureum* and *eamsii*) – N.E. N.Am. – are edible raw. They are juicy but generally insipid and rather bitter, although their flavor improves with the first frost. A juice can be extracted from them. In Iceland the juice is mixed with sour milk to make a beverage.

As the Latin specific names suggest, the fruits of *E. nigrum* (m.a.) are black and those of *E. rubrum* var. *atropurpureum* (m.a.) are dark purple.

Crowberries were formerly preserved by native people: Northwestern Indians used to dry them, while Inuits used to freeze them.

The berries of *E. nigrum* (m.a.) were also eaten in Northern Europe and Asia, and those of *E. rubrum* (var. *rubrum*) were used as food in southernmost South America.

PYROLACEAE

Chimaphila (E 4)   Pipsissewa
From the Greek "cheima," winter, and "philos," friend: the evergreen leaves persist throughout the winter.
Throughout.

Although the leaves of *C. umbellata* – N. N.Am. – and *maculata* – E. N.Am. – are very bitter, they have been made into a tea with astringent, diaphoretic and diuretic properties. In the Appalachians, the leaves are chewed to relieve heartburn.
Pipsissewa is one of the ingredients of root beer.

Moneses uniflora (G 4)   Woodnymph, Single Delight
From the Greek "monos," one, and "hesis," delight: referring to the solitary flower.
Almost throughout.

It has been reported that the fruits were edible and that Alaskan Inuits used them as food. They are seldom found in abundance, as each plant bears only one fruit.
In Europe where it is native as well, the whole plant is said to be somewhat toxic.

Pyrola (G 4)   Shinleaf
(= *Pirola*)
From the Latin diminutive form of "pirus," pear tree: the leaves look somewhat like those of the pear tree.
Almost throughout.

The young leaves of *P. rotundifolia* – N.E. N.Am. – have reportedly been eaten.

The leaves contain tannin, a glucoside (arbutin) and flavonoids.

They are astringent, diuretic and have an antiseptic action on the urinary tract.

Overdoses can be emetic.

Externally, shinleaf is used as a vulnerary.

MONOTROPACEAE

Monotropa (D 3)   Indian Pipe

From the Greek "monos," one, and "trepô," to turn: on *M. hypopythis*, the flowers are borne only on one side of the stem.

Throughout.

M. uniflora has been used as food. The whole plant can be roasted or boiled. It is rather tasteless by itself.

The roots have antispasmodic, sedative and tonic properties.

M. hypopythis is reported to be edible raw or cooked.

It contains two glucosides, one of which yields by hydrolysis an essential oil containing methyl salicylate.

The plant is antispasmodic and expectorant.

Sarcodes sanguinea (F-H 5)   Snow Plant

From the Greek "sarx," flesh, and "eidô," to look like: referring to the red color of this leafless plant, which is especially striking against the snow.

California, S. Ore.

The plant is poisonous raw, but it can be eaten after boiling in several changes of water or roasting in embers for hours until it loses all traces of bitterness.

This beautiful bright red plant must be considered as an emergency food only. At any rate, it is not very good.

SAPOTACEAE

Achras (B 5)
(= *Manilkara* spp.)
Etymology unknown.
A. emarginata (= *Manilkara bahamensis*, = *Mimusops emarginata*), wild dilly,
is native to S. Fla.

Its ripe fruit is edible after all the latex has gone.
A. zapota (= *Manilkara z.*), sapodilla, zapote blanco, originally from tropical
America, is cultivated for its fruits in Mexico, where it is naturalized.

The ripe fruit is edible raw and commonly sold in markets in Mexico and
Central America. It is also made into jams. Its juice is extracted and boiled down
to a syrup.

The young leafy shoots are usually eaten, cooked with other vegetables, in
Indonesia where the tree has been introduced.

The latex obtained from the trunk is known as "chicle," and is a base for
commercial chewing gums.

Bumelia (B-H 4)   False Buckthorn, Southern Buckthorn
Ancient Greek name of a tree from "bous," ox, and "melia," ash tree.
S. U.S., Mex.

The fruits of *B. celastrina*, saffron plum – Fla. to Tex., Mex. –, *laetevirens* –
Mex. –, *lanuginosa* – S.E. & S.C. U.S., N. Mex. –, *lycioides* – S.E. U.S. – and
reclinata – Fla., Ga. – are edible raw when ripe.

The bark of *B. lanuginosa* (m.a.) and the fruits of *B. laetevirens* (m.a.) are a
source of "chicle," a chewing gum.

The fruits of a local species are eaten in Brazil.

Endangered species: *B. thornei* – Ga.

Chrysophyllum oliviforme (B 5) Satinleaf
From the Greek "chrysos," gold, golden, and "phyllon," leaf: alluding to the color of the leaves.
S. Fla.
The star apple (*C. cainito*) – W.I. – is cultivated in S. Fla. for its large, delicious fruit, which is eaten raw or preserved.

The ripe fruit of *C. oliviforme* (m.a.) is edible raw. Its skin is used as chewing gum in the West Indies.
The fruits of many local species are eaten in the tropics of both hemispheres.

Mimusops sieberii (B 4) Naseberry
(= *Manilkara s.*)
Etymology unknown.
S.E. U.S., Mex.

The ripe fruit is edible raw. It has a pleasant flavor.
The fruits of many other species are eaten in tropical regions of both hemispheres.
A gum, "balata," is obtained from some of these trees.

Pouteria (B 5)
Etymology unknown.
P. domingensis, originally from the W.I., is naturalized in S. Fla.

Its fruit is eaten raw.
P. campechiana (= *Lucuma c.*), eggfruit, canistel – from S.Am. – is cultivated for its luscious fruit, edible raw, in Southern Florida and Mexico. The tree is occasionally naturalized in these areas.
The canistel, and a few other South American species, are cultivated in tropical regions of the world.

Sideroxylon (B 5)
(= *Mastichodendron* spp.)

From the Greek "sidêros," iron, and "xylon," wood: alluding to the weight of the wood.
S. Fla., Mex.

The ripe fruits of *S. capiri*, capiro – Mex. – and *foetidissimum* – S. Fla. – are edible raw. Those of the latter species, however, are acid and contain a bitter latex.

The bark of *S. angustifolium* – Mex. – is locally used for curdling milk.

The fruits of a few other species are used as food in tropical America, Asia and Australia.

EBENACEAE

Diospyros (B 4)   Persimmon
Greek name of the fruits of a W. Asian species *D. lotus* from "dios," pertaining to Zeus, and "pyros," wheat.
S.E. U.S., Mex.

Our native *D. virginiana* – E. N.Am. – and the Japanese persimmon, *D. kaki* – E. Asia – and hybrids are often cultivated for their fruits in the U.S.

D. ebenaster, sapote negro, originally from the W.I., is cultivated for its dark fruit in Mex., where the tree is naturalized.

Two other exotic species are occasionally planted in the U.S.

The fruits of *D. conzatti*, ozxaca – Mex. –, *ebenaster* (m.a.), *texana* – Tex., Mex. – and *virginiana* (m.a.) are edible raw when they are thoroughly ripe; immature persimmons are notoriously astringent and inedible.

The fruits of *D. virginiana* (m.a.), our most widespread species, are much improved by the first frost. They become soft, orange in color and extremely sweet and rich. Raw persimmons must be eaten in moderate quantities only, as they are hard to digest.

Fortunately, the often large supply of persimmons gathered can be used in various ways. The fruits can be dried whole (as was customary among Eastern Indians) or crushed, spread and dried to make persimmon leather; cooked into jam or made into persimmon bread; fermented into a wine which can be distilled or transformed into vinegar.

Persimmons contain large quantities of vitamin C, potassium and iron.

The torrefied seeds have been used as a coffee substitute.

The leaves are also rich in vitamin C and make a pleasant tea.

The fruits of many other species are eaten in various parts of the world, including those species planted on our continent – *D. discolor, tessellata, kaki*. The last was traditionally the most important fruit tree in Japan; the fruit of some varieties can be eaten while still hard.

STYRACACEAE

Halesia   (E 4)   Silver Bell
After Stephen Hales (1677–1761), English physiologist.
S.E. U.S.

The acid fruit of *H. carolina* can be chewed for its refreshing quality. It could possibly be pickled.

SYMPLOCACEAE

Symplocos   (D 4)   Sweet Leaf, Horse Sugar
From the Greek "symplokos," connected: referring to the united stamens.
S.E. U.S., Mex.

The leaves of *S. tinctoria* – S.E. U.S. – are both sweet and sour. They are chewed for their pleasant taste.

The leaves of a few local species are eaten in tropical Asia or used as tea in South America.

MYRSINACEAE

Ardisia   (B 5)
Etymology unknown.
A. escallionioides, marlberry, is native to S. Fla.

Its <u>fruit</u> is edible, but not outstanding.

A. solanacea (= *A. humilis*), originally from Southeastern Asia, is planted and naturalized in Southern Florida.

Young <u>leaves</u> and ripe <u>fruits</u> are edible raw.

The <u>fruits</u> of many other species are eaten in tropical America and Asia.

PRIMULACEAE

Anagallis arvensis (D-F 3)   Red Pimpernel
Greek and Latin name of the plant.
Throughout.
Originally from Eur., it is naturalized as a weed in gardens.
A few European species are occasionally planted for ornament.

The <u>plant</u> has been added raw to salads in moderate quantities in France and in Germany and eaten cooked in the Middle East. It is still sometimes eaten as a green vegetable in parts of Asia.

But red pimpernel contains saponins, and in high doses it can be slightly toxic. Sensitive individuals sometimes develop dermatitis from contact with the fresh leaves.

The plant is expectorant, diuretic, cholagogue and laxative. Externally it is used as a detergent.

The root contains a saponin particularly toxic to fish (cyclamin); in India, it is occasionally used as a fish poison.

Dodecatheon (B 2-3)   Shooting Star
From the Greek "dodeka," twelve, and "theos," god: the flowers, sometimes in an umbel of twelve, were said to represent the twelve Olympian gods.
Throughout. Mostly W. N.Am.
A few native species are planted for ornament.

The <u>roots</u> of *D. hendersonii* – W. Coast – were reportedly eaten roasted in embers by California Indians. But they are small and rather tough, and it would not be worth killing the plant for them.

The <u>leaves</u> of most species, however, such as those of *D. hendersonii* (m.a.)

and *jeffreyi* – W. Coast – are one of the best salad ingredients to be found in the mountains. They are tender and pleasant-tasting.

The <u>flowers</u> are also edible raw.

Glaux maritima (D 4)   Sea Milkwort

Greek name of a sea plant from "glaukos," bluish-green.
Almost throughout (also in Eurasia) coasts and salty soils in the interior. A monotypic genus.

The <u>young shoots</u> are said to be edible raw.
The fleshy <u>leaves</u> and <u>stems</u> can be pickled.

Lysimachia (E 4)   Loosestrife

From the Greek "lysimachion," name of a plant formed from "lysis," loosening, and "machê," strife.
E. N.Am.
A few European species are grown for ornament.

The <u>leaves</u> of *L. nummularia*, moneywort – introduced from Eur. – and *quadrifolia*, whorled loosestrife – E. N. Am. – have occasionally been used as tea.
Local species are eaten as pot herbs in Asia.

Primula (D-H 4)   Primrose

From the Latin "primulus," very first (diminutive form of "primus," first): the plant blooms in early spring.
Both native (N. N.Am. & Mountains) and species introduced from Eur. Many primroses from Eur. and Asia, as well as garden hybrids, are cultivated for ornament. Among the European species, *P. veris* (= *P. officinalis*) is found as an escape in N.E. N.Am.

The <u>leaves</u> of *P. veris* (m.a.) are edible raw in salads. They have a pleasant, somewhat spicy taste, with a slight anise smell, and can also be eaten cooked.

They contain vitamin C and minerals. The whole plant, but especially the root, contains saponins (up to 10% in the root), glucosides, a ferment and various substances.

The root is used as an expectorant, diuretic, antispasmodic and analgesic. Externally it has antiecchymotic properties.

The fresh root has the same anise odor as the leaves. With time, this is replaced by the characteristic smell of methyl salicylate (oil of wintergreen), as one of the glucosides of the plant contains salicylic esters.

Primula veris

The <u>flowers</u> have a delicate sweet smell and can be added to fruit salads or made into primrose mousse or other desserts.

They are made into a soothing tea.

<u>Leaves</u> and <u>flowers</u> of other species are used as food in Europe and Asia, including those of some cultivated primroses (*P. denticulata, vulgaris*).

The leaves of some exotic species can cause dermatitis in susceptible individuals.

Endangered species: *P. capillaris* – Nev. –, *cusickiana* – Idaho, Ore. – and *nevadensis* – Nev.

Trientalis (G 4)   Starflower

From the Latin "triens," one-third: the pedicel is said to be often one-third the height of the plant; "trientalis," meaning one-third of a foot, might also suggest the average height of the plant.
N. N.Am.

T. latifolia – Pacific Coast – is said to have edible starchy <u>tubers</u>.

HYDRANGEACEAE

Philadelphus (G 4)   Mock Orange, Syringia
After King Ptolemy Philadelphus of ancient Egypt.
Throughout.
Some native and Asian species, as well as hybrids, are planted as ornamentals.

The <u>fruit</u> of *P. microphyllus* – S.W. U.S., N.W. Mex. – has reportedly been eaten in New Mexico.

GROSSULARIACEAE

Ribes (B-H 3)   Gooseberry, Currant
Name of Scandinavian origin.
Throughout.
Three European species are commonly cultivated for their edible fruits: *R. grossularia* (= *R. uva-crispa*), European gooseberry, *nigrum*, black currant and *sativum*, red currant. All three occasionally escape from cultivation. A fourth one (*R. alpinum*) is planted as an ornamental. Our native *R. sanguineum*, red flowering currant – N.W. N.Am. – is commonly planted for ornament in Eur.

Wild gooseberries and currants are edible raw when ripe. In the best cases they are sweet and flavorful, although some species bear fruits with a bitter or otherwise unpleasant taste.

The <u>fruits</u> are often made into jellies and pies. A juice can be extracted from them, which is sometimes made into syrup. In Japan, the unripe berries of various species are preserved in a mixture of water, salt and sugar.

Gooseberries and currants were an important food for the American Indians who would eat them raw or cooked, and also dry and mix them with fat to make pemmican.

Ribes spp. can be divided into three categories:

Ribes

1. Gooseberries

These are spiny shrubs with relatively large fruits (which are also sometimes covered with spines). The berries are sweet and tasty when ripe; unripe, they are very sour and astringent.

Our most commonly eaten gooseberries are (the color of the fruit is in parenthesis): *R. californicum*, hillside g. – Calif. – (red); *cynobasti* – E. & C. U.S. – and *divaricatum*, coast g. – W. N.Am. – (dark); *hirtellum*, wedgleaf g. – N.E. & N.C. N.Am. – and *inerme* (sometimes included in *R. divaricatum*) – W. N.Am. – (black); *irriguum* – N.W. N.Am. –, *lobbii*, gummy g. – N.W. N.Am. –, *missouriense* – C. U.S. –, *niveum* – N.W. U.S. –, *quercetorum* (= leptanthum*)* – Calif., Baja – (black); *roezzlii*, Sierra g. – Calif., Ore. – (purple); *rotundifolium* – E. U.S. – (pale purple); and *setosum* – N.C. N.Am. – (greenish purple).

The European gooseberry, *R. grossularia* (m.a.) has been cultivated on the Old Continent since the 16th century.

The <u>fruits</u> are eaten raw when thoroughly ripe, or made into jam. They are sweet and aromatic. Unripe fruits are acid and astringent. They were formerly cooked as a sauce to be served with fish, especially mackerel.

Ripe gooseberries contain vitamins A, B, and C, minerals, sugars, pectin and organic acids (malic, citric and tartric).

They are aperitive, digestive, laxative, diuretic, depurative and they supposedly relieve congestion of the liver.

The European gooseberry is the alternate host of the wheat rust, and in some areas of our continent the plant has been eradicated from private gardens.

Wild gooseberries are alternate hosts to the white pine blister rust.

2. Black Currants

These are nonspiny shrubs with aromatic leaves and black berries having a musky flavor.

The most frequently used native black currants are *R. americanum*, wild black c. – N.E. & N.C. N.Am. –, *bracteosum*, stink c. – N.W. N.Am. –, *hudsonianum* – N.C. & N.W. N.Am. –, *lacustre*, swamp c. – N. N.Am. & W. Mountains –, *laxiflorum* – W. Coast –, *petiolare* – N.W. U.S. –, *sanguineum* (m.a.) and *viscosissimum*, sticky c. – W. N.Am.

R. nigrum (m.a.) has been cultivated in American and European gardens since the 18th century.

The <u>fruits</u> have a strong musky flavor. They are sweet when ripe, acid before.

They are sometimes eaten raw but more commonly are made into jams, jellies, juice, syrup, a liquor (very popular in France) and, fermented with sugar, a wine.

Black currants are extremely rich in vitamin C (four to eight times as much as oranges). They also contain the vitamin rutin, minerals, sugars, pectin, organic acids, pigments and an essential oil. Their vitamin C is more resistant to heat and oxidation than that of other plants: it is therefore preserved, for the most part, in the syrup.

The leaves are very aromatic and are often used to make a pleasant tea with digestive properties.

They contain tannin, an essential oil and vitamin C, as do the fruits.

The leaves and berries are diuretic, diaphoretic, antiscorbutic, tonic and vermifuge. They are known to ameliorate vision and to prevent vascular troubles.

3. Other Currants

These are nonspiny shrubs, usually having nonaromatic leaves and red, white, yellow or occasionally black fruits.

The best known species on our continent are (the color of the fruit is in parenthesis): *R. aureum*, golden c. – W. N.Am. – (red or black); *cereum*, squaw or wax c. – W. N.Am. – (with sticky, fragrant leaves and red fruit); *glandulosum*, skunk c. – N. N.Am. & E. Mountains – (dark red); *inebrians* – W. N.Am. – *laxiflorum* – W. N.Am. – and *montigenum* – W. Mountains – (red); *odoratum*, golden c. – C. U.S. – (yellow or black); *triste*, drooping c. – N.E. & N.C. N.Am. – (red); and *viburnifolium* – S. Calif., Baja – (red).

The fruits of *R. inebrians* (m.a.) were made into a fermented drink, and the leaves were reportedly eaten with deer fat by Indians.

The leaves of *R. cereum* (m.a.) were used by Hopi Indians for stomachaches.

R. sativum (m.a.) has been cultivated in Europe since the 16th century and was introduced in New England gardens in the 17th century. Many horticultural forms are known, with either red or white fruits.

The fruits remain acid when ripe, less so with white varieties. They are sometimes eaten raw but more often made into jelly.

The composition of the fruits is similar to that of the gooseberry, *R. uva-crispa* (m.a.), but they are richer in vitamin C. The red ones are richer in vitamin A. They are also tonic and refrigerant.

The juice of the fruits is rather astringent, while the mucilaginous seeds are laxative.

The <u>fruits</u> of many species are eaten in Europe, Asia and southern South America. Several of these shrubs are cultivated.

Endangered species: *R. echinellum* – Fla. to S.C.

CRASSULACEAE

Dudleya (B-H 4) Live Forever
(= *Echeveria* spp., = *Cotyledon* spp.)
After W. R. Dudley, early professor of botany at Stanford University.
S.W. U.S., Mex.
A few Californian and Mexican species are cultivated for ornament, known by the name "hen and chicks."

The succulent <u>leaves</u> have a very pleasant, acid taste, with a touch of astringency in some species. They are edible raw in salads, but only a few leaves should be picked on each plant, so as not to kill it. *Dudleya* spp. are not very common.

The best species are *D. collomae* – C. Ariz. – and *edulis, lanceolata* and *pulverulenta* – all three Calif. & Baja.

Endangered species: *D. bettinae, candelabrum* – both Calif. –, *collomae* (m.a.), *cymosa* subsp. *marcescens, multicaulis, nesiotica, stolonifera* and *traskae* – all five Calif.

Sedum (D-H 1) Stonecrop
Latin name of the plant.
Throughout.
Several Mexican, European and Asian species are planted as ornamentals, especially *S. acre* and *telephium* (including var. *purpureum*, = *S. purpureum*), live forever, both originally from Eurasia and escaped in E. N.Am.

The fleshy <u>roots</u> of *S. roseum* (= *Rhodiola rosea*), roseroot – N. N.Am. & Mountains, also in Eurasia – and *telephium* var. *purpureum* (m.a.) have been used as food after cooking. They are best gathered when the vegetation is at rest (dormant) from late fall to early spring. The roots of the latter species are sometimes pickled in Japan, where the plant is also native.

The <u>leaves</u> of various stonecrops, including the two species mentioned above, are edible raw. They are tender, juicy, more or less astringent and in most cases have a pleasant sour flavor.

S. acre (m.a.) has a pungent taste. It can be used in small amounts as a condiment.

The plant contains tannins, organic acids, an alkaloid (semadine), a glucoside and an irritating substance.

It has been used in cases of epilepsy and occasionally as an abortive. Externally it is said to remove corns. But large doses can cause blisters, and if taken internally, vomiting.

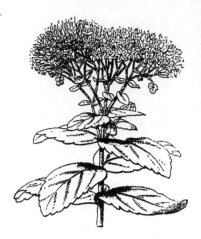

Sedum telephium

Many species are eaten in Europe and Asia. Some were formerly cultivated as vegetables. *S. telephium* var. *telephium* was grown as a salad plant in Europe. Its large fleshy <u>leaves</u>, tender and juicy with a slight acid taste, are delicious raw.

Endangered species: *S. moranii* – Ore. –, *nevii* – Ala., Tenn. -- and *radiatum* subsp. *depauperatum* – Calif., Ore.

SAXIFRAGACEAE

Chrysosplenium   (D 3)   Golden saxifrage
From the Greek "chrysos," gold, and "splên," spleen: referring to the color of the flowers and to an ancient medicinal usage.
Throughout.

The <u>leaves</u> of *C. americanum* – N.E. N.Am. – have been eaten raw in salads.

Those of two local species (*C. alternifolium* and *oppositifolium*) were eaten raw or cooked in Europe.

Heuchera   (E-H 2)   Alum root
After J. H. von Heucher, German medical botanist.
Throughout.
Our native *H. sanguinea*, coral bells, is sometimes planted as an orna-
mental.

The <u>young leaves</u> of various species, including *H. sanguinea* (m.a.) are edible.
But they usually require cooking in one or two changes of water, since they are
very astringent.
The roots are even more astringent than the leaves, and have been used to
treat diarrhea caused by alkaline water – hence the common name of the plant;
alum is a powerful astringent.
Endangered species: *H. missouriensis* – Mo.

Peltiphyllum peltatum   (D 5)   Indian Rhubarb
(= *Saxifraga peltata*)
From the Greek "peltê," small round shield, and "phyllon," leaf: alluding
to the shape of the leaf.
Calif. & S. Ore. A monotypic genus.

The fleshy <u>leaf stalk</u> is edible raw or cooked after peeling.

Saxifraga   (D 3)   Saxifrage
Latin name of various plants growing in rock crevices from "saxum," rock,
and "frango," to break.
Throughout.
An E. Asian species (*S. stolonifera*), known as "strawberry geranium," is
planted for ornament.

The <u>leaves</u> of *S. micranthidifolia*, lettuce saxifrage – C.E. U.S. – and *penn-*
sylvanica, swamp saxifrage – N.E. U.S. – are eaten raw in salads where the
plants are native.
Those of *S. punctata* – N.W. N.Am. – are edible raw as well. They are
sometimes kept in oil by Alaskan Inuits.
Those of *S. virginiensis* – E. N.Am. – were used as a cooked vegetable by
Cherokee Indians.
The <u>leaves</u> of local species are made into tea in Central Asia or into "tempura" (fritters) in Japan.

ROSACEAE

This large family includes most of the fruits commonly eaten in temperate regions of the world: strawberries, raspberries, blackberries, apples, pears, quince, almonds, peaches, nectarines, apricots, cherries, plums and so on.

Several Rosaceae are ornamental shrubs (roses, cotoneaster, pyracantha, spirea) or trees (hawthorn, flowering apples and cherries).

Many members of this family contain cyanogenetic glucosides in their leaves and flowers, and especially in the kernels of their fruits. These glucosides are transformed into hydrocyanic acid (HCN) and glucose through hydrolysis, under the action of a ferment present in the plant. Bitter almond oil (benzoic aldehyde), which has a characteristic odor, is often liberated in the process. In large quantities, hydrocyanic acid is extremely toxic: it has a depressant effect on the respiratory and cardiac centers of the brain, sometimes resulting in death, especially in children, who are more sensitive than adults. However, if this substance is present only in small quantities, the body can easily eliminate it, and even benefit from the favorable action it can have on the organism. In small amounts it is antispasmodic and sedative and helps both respiration and digestion.

Hydrocyanic acid can be eliminated by processing such as drying or boiling in water, which must be thrown away.

Agrimonia (D 3)   Agrimony
From the Greek "argemonê," name of a kind of poppy, and "argema," a spot on the white of the eye.
Throughout. Both native and species introduced from Eurasia.

The leaves of *A. eupatoria* – naturalized from Eurasia in N.E. U.S. – are somewhat aromatic. They are sometimes made into a pleasant tea in Europe, where the plant is also native.

They contain an essential oil and tannin.

The plant is astringent and vulnerary. It helps to reduce the blood sugar level, and has been used medicinally since Antiquity.

It dyes wool yellow with alum or chromium.

The leaves of a local species were eaten in Asia in times of scarcity.

Alchemilla (B 4)   Lady's Mantle
The dew drops which gather in the center of the leaves, known by European alchemists as "celestial water," were used in alchemy.
Throughout. Both native and species introduced from Eur.

The young <u>leaves</u> of *A. vulgaris* – native in Lab. and naturalized from Eur. in E. N.Am. – can be added raw to salads. They are astringent.
They contain tannin and various substances.
The plant is astringent, tonic, stomachic and diuretic. Externally it is detergent and vulnerary. It has been used medicinally since Antiquity.
Lady's mantle gives wool a green color.

Amelanchier (B 3)   Serviceberry, Juneberry, Shad bush, Shadberry
Provençal name of the European tree.
Throughout.
A. canadensis – E. N.Am. – and hybrids are cultivated for their fruits. *A. alnifolia*, saskatoon – N.W. N.Am. – and *laevis* – E. N.Am. – are planted as ornamentals, for their large white flowers.

Serviceberries are edible raw when ripe. They are often quite large, juicy, flavorful and very sweet. They were an important food for Indians who would mash up the fruits and shape them into cakes which were dried and stored. They would also mix them with fat to make pemmican. Serviceberries make good jams, jellies and pies.
The <u>fruits</u> of the following species have been used as food on our continent: *A. alnifolia* (m.a.), *bartramiana* – N.E. N.Am. –, *canadensis* (m.a.), *florida* – W. N.Am. –, *intermedia*, *laevis* (m.a.), *pallida* – S.W. U.S. –, *sanguinea* – E. N.Am. –, *spicata* – E. N.Am. – and *utahensis* – W. N.Am.
The <u>fruits</u> of local species are eaten in Asia and occasionally in Europe.

Amelanchier canadensis

Aronia (D 4)   Chokeberry
Name derived from "aria," ancient name of the European *Sorbus aria,* a
fruit tree of the same family.
E. N.Am.
A. arbutifolia and a few other native species are planted for ornament.

The <u>fruits</u> of *A. arbutifolia* (m.a.) and *melanocarpa* were used as food by Indians. They are often unpleasant to eat raw because of their astringency and are
better cooked.

Cercocarpus (E-H 4)   Mountain Mahogany
From the Greek "kerkos," tail, and "karpos," fruit: alluding to the long,
hairy styles persistent on the fruit.
W. N.Am.

Scraps of the <u>bark</u> of *C. ledifolius,* and possibly that of other species, have
been used as tea in the West, often added to Mormon tea (*Ephedra* spp.).
But *C. betuloides* (= *C. montanus*) – Calif., Ore., Baja – is known to contain po-
tentially dangerous amounts of cyanogenetic glucosides.
Hopi Indians used one species to give leather a reddish-brown color.
Endangered species: *C. traskiae* – Calif.

Cowania (E 4)   Cliffrose
After J. Cowan, British botanist.
S.W. N.Am.

The resinous, strong-smelling <u>leaves</u> of *C. mexicana* were made into tea.
Hopi Indians used the plant medicinally, as an emetic and a wash for wounds.
Branches were used for making arrows, and strips of the inner bark were
braided together and made into sandals, ropes and mats.
The flowers are fragrant.
Endangered species: *C. subintegra* – Ariz.

Chaenomeles speciosa (D 5) Japanese Quince
(= *Cydonia japonica*)
From the Greek "chainô," to open up, and "mêlon," apple: the fruit was
thought to split open at maturity.
Scattered throughout.
Originally from China, this shrub is widely cultivated for ornament; it is
occasionally found as an escape.

The small fruit is edible when ripe; it is astringent and better cooked than
raw. It makes good jams and jellies.

Crataegus (B 3) Hawthorn
From the Greek name of the Mediterranean *C. azarolus*.
Throughout.
Our native *C. crus-galli*, cockspur thorn – E. N.Am. – and several
Eurasian species are frequently planted for ornament, including *C.
monogyna* and *oxycantha*, occasionally escaping from cultivation.

The very young leaves of the various species
are edible raw. They are tender and have a
pleasant taste. They can be added to salads or
simply nibbled on, as was customary with children in Europe.

The white flowers have a peculiar smell.
They can be added to salads, desserts, drinks,
etc.

Hawthorn fruits were an important food for
American Indians. They would dry and grind
them into a meal which was mixed with flour to
make a mush or with animal fat to make pemmican.

The fruits of some species are large, juicy
and good enough to eat raw. In most cases, however, they are mealy and rather insipid. Cooking

Crataegus crus-galli

as compotes or jams improves them. The large seeds can be removed by passing
the fruits through a food mill. The fruits can be dried, ground, sifted and mixed
with flour to make breads and cakes as was formerly done in Europe.

The following species have been used as food in North America: *C. aestivalis*, may haws – S. U.S. –, *anomala* – N.E. N.Am. –, *arnoldiana* – E. Mass., Conn. –, *calpodendron* – E. N.Am. –, *canadensis* – Que. –, *chrysocarpa* (including var. *phoenicea*) – E. & C. N.Am. –, *coccinoides* – C. U.S. –, *columbiana* – N.W. N.Am. –, *crus-galli* (m.a.), *dispessa* – S. Mo. –, *douglasii* – W. & C. N.Am. –, *flava* – S.E. U.S. – (long cultivated in Eur. for ornament), *intricata* – E. U.S. –, *mollis* – E. N.Am. –, *pringlei* – N.E. N.Am. –, *pruinosa* – E. N.Am. –, *pubescens* – Mex. –, *rivularis*, Western black haw – W. N.Am. –, *submollis* – N.E. N.Am. –, *succulenta* – N.E. N.Am. – and *uniflora* – E. U.S.

Leaves and fruits of *C. monogyna* and *oxycantha* (m.a.) are edible as well.

The fruits of many other species are eaten in Europe and Asia. The azarole tree (*C. azarolus*) – originally from the Eastern Mediterranean area – has long been cultivated as a fruit tree in Europe and Western Asia for its relatively large, fleshy fruits.

Dryas octopetala   (D 4)   Mountain Avens

From the Greek "dryas," dryad, a nymph whose life was linked to that of a tree, from "drys," tree, especially the oak.
N. N.Am. & Mountains.
The plant is sometimes grown for ornament.

The leaves of this small plant have been used to make tea (Alpine tea, Swiss tea) in Europe, where it is native as well.
They contain much tannin.
The plant is astringent and stomachic.

Duchesnea indica   (D 2)   Indian Strawberry

After A. N. Duchesne (1747–1827), French botanist, author of works on cultivated plants.
Originally from Asia, this plant is occasionally cultivated for ornament and naturalized in E. U.S., Mex. and the Pacific Coast.

The fruit is edible, but it is dry and insipid. It looks deceitfully like a strawberry.

Filipendula   (E-H 4)   Queen-of-the-Meadow
(= *Spiraea* spp.)
From the Latin "filum," thread, and "pendulus," hanging: in a European
species *F. hexapetala*, planted in N.Am., the tubers are borne on wiry underground stems.
Almost throughout. Both native and species introduced from Eurasia.
The Eurasian *F. hexapetala* (= *F. vulgaris*), dropwort, and *ulmaria* (= *Spiraea u.*), queen-of-the-meadow, are occasionally planted for ornament;
they escape from cultivation in N.E. N.Am.

The small <u>tubers</u> of dropwort, *F. hexapetala* (m.a.), were eaten in Europe in
times of famine, according to Linnaeus.
The white, fragrant <u>flowers</u> of the queen-of-the-meadow, *F. ulmaria* (m.a.)
are used for flavoring desserts (especially ice cream) and drinks. They can be
made into a pleasant tea.
The fresh leaves are very aromatic when crushed: The plant contains a glucoside which is transformed into methyl salicylate through hydrolysis under the
action of a ferment present in the leaves. The dry plant contains salicylic acid; it
is from this substance that acetylsalicylic acid, aspirin, was derived.
The leaves also contain tannin, minerals and other elements.
Flowers and leaves are used as a diuretic, diaphoretic, febrifuge, antispas-
modic and anodyne (to relieve rheumatism pains, in a similar manner as aspirin).
The leaves are also astringent.
The root is employed as a vulnerary and as a detergent.
The flowering tops dye wool a greenish-yellow color with alum. The roots
give wool a black color without mordant.
Endangered species: *F. occidentalis* – Ore.

Fragaria   (A 2-3)   Strawberry
Name created in the 15th century by M. Sylvaticus from the Latin
"fraga," strawberry.
Throughout.
The common garden strawberry is *F. x ananassa*, an artificial hybrid between the Chilean form of *F. chiloensis* (also found wild on the W. Coast
of N.Am.) and *virginiana* – E. N.Am. It is cultivated throughout the

world for its fruit and is occasionally naturalized. Its culture dates back to the 16th century and many varieties are known. *F. chiloensis* (m.a.), beach strawberry, is also planted as a ground cover.

Young strawberry <u>leaves</u> are edible raw or cooked, but they are astringent. Older ones can be made into a pleasant tea.

They contain much vitamin C, tannin, minerals and various substances.

They are astringent, tonic, diuretic and help relieve rheumatism. The rhizome can be used medicinally in the same way as the leaves.

It is possible that strawberry leaves (like blackberry leaves – see *Rubus* spp.) might be toxic while in the process of drying due to a high hydrocyanic acid content. But they become innocuous once thoroughly dry.

The <u>flowers</u> can be eaten as well, but if they remain on the plant, chances are that they will produce luscious strawberries, juicy, sweet and aromatic. It is well worth waiting for them.

The <u>fruits</u> of all wild strawberries are edible raw, but their quality differs widely between the various species; some are among the most flavorful of all fruits while others are rather insipid.

The following species have been used as food in North America: *F. californica* – Calif., Baja –, *chiloensis* (m.a.), *mexicana* – Mex. –, *platypetala* (= *virginiana* var. *illinoensis*) – Calif. to B.C. –, *vesca* var. *americana* – E. & C. N.Am. – var. *vesca* – both native in E. Can. and introduced from Eur. in E. N.Am. – and *virginiana* (m.a.).

Garden strawberries are also made into jams and pies; juice is extracted from them and sometimes cooked into a syrup or fermented into a wine which can be distilled.

They contain vitamins A, B, C, E and K, minerals, sugar (mostly levulose, which is easily assimilated even by diabetics), traces of salicylic acid and mucilage.

Strawberries are tonic, depurative, diuretic and refrigerant.

The achenes dotting the surface of strawberries are mildly laxative. These "grains" are the actual fruits of the plant, as the strawberry itself is a false fruit, the enlarged receptacle of the flower.

Some sensitive individuals have allergic reactions after eating strawberries.

Externally, they are beneficial to the skin, thanks to their astringent and revitalizing properties.

The <u>fruits</u> of local species are eaten in Europe and Asia.

Geum   (D-H 3)   Avens
Latin name of the plant.
Throughout. Both native and species introduced from Eurasia.

The aromatic <u>roots</u> of **G. ciliatum**, prairie smoke – W. N.Am. –, *rivale*, purple avens – N.E. to W. N.Am. – and *trifolium* – N.E. to W. N.Am. – are boiled to make a beverage. The drink obtained with *G. rivale* (m.a.) is said to taste somewhat like chocolate, but the connection is actually rather far-fetched.

The <u>roots</u> of **G. urbanum**, herb-bennet – originally from Eurasia, rarely adventive in E. N.Am. – has a very definite scent of cloves. It can be used as a spice, but a larger quantity than cloves is necessary to flavor a dish. Boiled into tea, to which some milk can be added to remove all astringency, it yields a nicely flavored beverage reminiscent of the spiced tea, "chai," drunk in India.

The roots contain an essential oil rich in eugenol, which is the main constituent of clove oil, the essential oil distilled from cloves (dried flower buds of *Eugenia caryophyllata*, Myrtaceae).

Geum urbanum

They also contain tannin and a bitter substance.

They are tonic, stomachic, astringent and febrifuge.

Externally, they are used as a vulnerary.

The <u>young leaves</u> of herb-bennet can be added raw to salads in small quantities. They have a slight clove flavor but are astringent.

The <u>young leaves</u> of **G. aleppicum** – N.E. & C. N.Am. – are used as cooked greens in parts of Asia, where the plant is also native.

Endangered species: *G. geniculatum* – N.C., Tenn. –, *peckii* – N.H. – and *radiatum* – N.C., Tenn.

Heteromeles arbutifolia   (D 4)   Toyon

From the Greek "heteros," different, and "mêlon," apple: this genus is unlike closely related genera.

Calif. & Baja. A monotypic genus.

Sometimes planted as an ornamental for the contrast in winter of the scarlet berries with the dark green foliage.

The <u>fruits</u> are edible, but they are sour, astringent and rather bitter raw; they require cooking in order to be palatable. In Baja, they are sometimes roasted in a pan over hot coals. They can be dried and ground into a meal, or mashed up with some honey and water and fermented into cider.

The leaves contain a cyanogenetic glucoside and have occasionally poisoned livestock.

Horkelia   (G-H 4)

(including *Potentilla* spp.)

After J. Horkel (1769–1846), German physiologist.

W. N.Am.

The <u>root</u> of *H. parryi* (= *Potentilla p.*) has reportedly been used as food. Endangered species: *H. wilderae* – Calif.

Malus   (B 4)   Apple, Crabapple

(= *Pyrus* in part)

Latin name of the tree.

Throughout.

The Eurasian *M. domestica* (= *Pyrus malus*) of hybrid origin is cultivated throughout the world except in tropical regions for its well-known fruit. Innumerable cultivars have been listed. This tree is naturalized on our continent.

Our native *M. angustifolia* – E. U.S. – and several European and Asian species (including varieties of *M. domestica*) are planted for ornament. A favorite is the Japanese flowering crabapple (*M. floribunda*).

Apples, mostly the <u>fruits</u> of *M. domestica* (m.a.), are one of the most popular fruits. Many cultivated forms are edible raw, with notable differences in shape, color, texture and flavor. Apples are also eaten cooked, in pies, applesauce, apple butter and jellies, or baked, candied or made into chutney. They are often sliced and dried. A delicious, nutritious juice can be extracted by pressure from different varieties. Sour apples are crushed and fermented into hard cider. In Europe, the mash (or the cider itself) is distilled to yield alcohol ("Calvados" in Normandy, France), or left in contact with the air to produce apple cider vinegar (also in America). Green apples can be pickled.

Apples contain B vitamins (B1, B2, B5, niacin), small quantities of vitamin C (variable according to the variety – the 'Golden delicious,' for example, is one of the poorest in this vitamin) and rutin, a large number of minerals, sugars, pectin (apples are a commercial source of pectin), organic acids (malic, citric), tannin, enzymes and various substances.

They are tonic, refrigerant and depurative. Grated raw and eaten, they regulate peristalsis.

Apple <u>peel</u> tea is excellent, provided the fruits have been grown organically. It is diuretic and antirheumatic.

The kernel of the pips contains cyanogenetic glucosides, and their ingestion in excessive amounts has been known to be lethal to children.

Apple <u>blossoms</u> are edible and can be added to salads.

They have bechic properties.

Most wild apples are rather small and too sour and astringent for eating raw. They can, however, be cooked, pickled or made into cider. Several species yield aromatic fruits which are delicious when properly prepared. The Iroquois used to make applesauce with wild, unpeeled apples and maple syrup.

The following species have been used as food on our continent: *M. angustifolia* (m.a.), *coronaria* – E. N.Am. –, *fusca* (= *rivularis*), Oregon crab – Calif. to Alaska –, *ioensis*, Prairie crab – C. U.S. –, *pumila* – naturalized from Eurasia –, x *soulardii* (= *ionensis* x *sylvestris*, a natural hybrid) – C. U.S. – and *sylvestris*, crab apple – naturalized from Eur.

The <u>fruits</u> of many local species are eaten in Europe and Asia as well.

Apple trees have been in cultivation since prehistoric times.

The bark of the tree dyes wool yellow.

Osmaronia cerasiformis (D 4)   Oso Berry
From the Greek "osmê," smell, perfume, and "aronia," name of a genus
in the Rosaceae: alluding to the smell of the flowers.
Calif. to B.C. A monotypic genus.

The <u>fruit</u>, a black drupe, is edible raw but has a bitter pulp. Cooking improves its palatability.

Peraphyllum ramosissimum (D 4)   Squaw Apple
From the Greek "pera," beyond, and "phyllon," leaf: the tree is very leafy.
S.W. U.S. A monotypic genus.

The bitter <u>fruit</u> is edible.

Potentilla (D-H 1)   Cinquefoil, Silverweed, Tormentil
From the Latin diminutive form of "potens," powerful: name given to
P. erecta, tormentil, during the Middle Ages because of its medicinal prop-
erties.
Throughout. Both native and species introduced from Eur.
Some Eurasian species are cultivated as ornamentals.

The thickened <u>rootstock</u> of *P. anserina,* silverweed – N. N.Am. & W. Mountains, also in Eurasia – was eaten raw or cooked by Indians. It was also used as
food in Northern Europe, where the plant is native as well. It is quite palatable
when parboiled to remove its astringency, and roasted.
   The rootstock contains tannin, starch, resin, flavonoids and various other sub-
stances.
   The whole plant is used as an astringent, tonic and antispasmodic.
   The thin <u>rhizome</u> of *P. erecta* (= *P. tormentilla*), tormentil – introduced from
Eurasia in E. N.Am. – has been used as a famine food in Europe.
   However, it contains up to 20% tannin and is extremely astringent and bitter.
It must be boiled in several changes of water before it becomes somewhat palat-
able.
   It also contains a glucoside (tormentillin), a bitter principle and other sub-
stances.
   It is used as an astringent, tonic and hemostatic.

The leaves of *P. fruticosa*, shrubby cinquefoil – N. N.Am. & W. Mountains, also in Eurasia – were used as a tea known as "kuril chai" (kuril tea) in
Siberia.

P. glandulosa – W. Coast – has been used for making tea on our continent.

The very young leaves of various *Potentilla* spp. are edible, but they soon become astringent and bitter.

Roots and leaves of a few local species are used as food in Asia.

Endangered species: *P. hickmanii* – Calif. –, *robbinsiana* – N.H. –, *rupicola* –
Colo. – and *sierra-blancae* – N.M.

Prunus   (A-H 3)   Cherry, Plum and so on
Latin name of *P. domestica*, plum tree.
Throughout.
Several European and Asian species are commonly cultivated for their ed-
ible fruits. Some are naturalized on our continent; others occasionally es-
cape from cultivation and persist on old sites.

Our native *P. caroliniana*, American cherry-laurel – S.E. U.S., escaped in W.
U.S. –, *ilicifolia*, holly-leaved cherry, islay – Calif., Baja –, *lyonii*, Catalina
cherry – Channel Islands of S. Calif., occasional escape in Calif. – and *serotina*,
black cherry – E. & C. N.Am. – along with many European and Asian species
are planted as ornamentals. A favorite is the Japanese flowering cherry (*P. serrulata*). A few of these are found locally as escapes.

Prunus spp. can be classified in four categories:

Subgenus *Amygdalus*, peaches and almonds. The fruit is occasionally large
and fleshy (cultivated peach), but more often the pulp is thin and dry, and
only the kernel is edible.

Subgenus *Prunus*, plums. The fruit is relatively large (15 to 30 mm) and of
various colors – yellow, red, blue, purple.

Subgenus *Cerasus*, cherries. The fruit is small (6 to 15 mm), red or black.

Subgenus *Laurocerasus*, cherry laurels. The fruits are small, black and
tasteless. The glossy leaves can reach a large size and give these shrubs

value as ornamentals. They have a strong bitter-almond odor when crushed and are rich in hydrocyanic acid.

1. Our <u>native species</u> can be divided as follows:

a. Subgenus *Amygdalus* (= *Amygdalus* spp.)

P. andersonii, desert peach – Calif., W. Nev.

P. fasciculata (= *Emplectocladus f.*), desert almond – S.W. U.S.

P. fremontii (= *P. eriogyna*), desert apricot – Calif., Baja.

The <u>kernels</u> of the fruits were eaten by Indians. The pulp is too thin and dry to be of any use as food, except possibly in the case of *P. fremontii* (m.a.).

b. Subgenus *Prunus*, Wild Plums

In many species, the <u>fruits</u> are edible raw when ripe. They are juicy, sweet and aromatic. They can also be cooked into jams and pies, or fermented into wine. Unripe plums can be pickled or preserved in salt, as is done in some parts of Asia.

From the best varieties, a rich, thick juice can be extracted. These fruits can also be dried to yield prunes.

Wild plums were an important fruit for Indians and settlers, and several species are still commonly gathered for jam making in the fall.

Our best known native species are (the color of the fruit is mentioned in parenthesis):

P. alleghaniensis, Allegheny plum – N.E. U.S. – (dark purple). The fruit is better cooked.

P. americana, American plum – E. & C. N.Am. – (red). The ripe fruit is good to eat raw. The tree was sometimes planted by Indians and settlers.

P. angustifolia, Chickasaw plum – E. U.S. The fruit is good raw when ripe.

P. capollin, capulin – Mex. The fruit is eaten raw or cooked. The juice extracted from it is mixed with cornmeal to make cakes.

P. hortulana, wild plum – C. U.S. – (red to yellow).

P. maritima (including *P. gravesii*), beach plum – coast of N.E. N.Am. &
C. Mich. – (purplish black). The fruits are gathered every fall, particularly
in Massachusetts, on a large scale for making jam. They also make good
pies and jelly.

P. mexicana, big-tree plum – S.C. U.S., Mex. – (purplish red, 30 mm
long).

P. munsoniana, wild goose plum – S.C. U.S. – (red).

P. nigra, Canada plum – N.E. & N.C. N.Am. – (red to yellow, 30 mm
long).

P. subcordata, Sierra plum – Calif., Ore. – (usually dark red). Some varieties have a yellow fruit with a sweet, juicy pulp. Others are bitter and dry.

c. Subgenus *Cerasus*, Wild Cherries

In a few species, the ripe <u>fruits</u> are edible raw. But in many cases they must
be cooked in order to be palatable. Wild cherries are made into pies, jams, jellies
and syrup; they can be dried or crushed and fermented into wine.

They were an important food for Indians who used to dry the fruits, pound
them whole (pits and all) and press them into cakes which were cooked in a fire
pit. Cooking reduces the quantity of hydrocyanic acid contained in the kernels.
Dried cherries were also mixed with animal fat to make pemmican.

Our most common wild cherries are (the color of the fruit is in parenthesis):

P. emarginata, bitter cherry – W. N.Am. – (red). The bitter fruit requires
cooking.

P. ilicifolia (m.a.) (red to yellow). The pulp is thin and sweetish. Local Indians used to remove the kernel from the stone, crush it, leach out the
cyanide in running water and eat the result as a mush, or dry it for later
use.

P. lyonii (m.a.) (almost black). The fruit has a pleasant flavor.

P. pennsylvanica, wild red cherry, pin cherry – E. & C. N.Am. – (red).
The juicy fruit is better cooked. The mucilaginous gum exuding from the
bark can be dissolved in the mouth and eaten.

P. pumila, sand cherry – E. & C. N.Am. – (nearly black). The fruit is sweet and edible raw when ripe.

P. serotina (m.a.), (dark purple or black). The small fruits are aromatic and slightly bitter. They are edible raw, but are more often made into jams or used to flavor liquors.

The bark contains a cyanogenetic glucoside and is used medicinally for its antispasmodic and sedative properties. A cough syrup is prepared from it.

The leaves of the black cherry, as of other wild cherries and cherry laurels (subgenera *Cerasus* and *Laurocerasus*) are potentially toxic to livestock especially while wilting, when their hydrocyanic acid content reaches a maximum. Leaves from young shoots are more poisonous than those of a mature tree.

P. virginiana (including many varieties), chokecherry – throughout – (dark red). The fruits differ widely in quality according to the variety and to the individual tree; some are dry and sour, others juicy and sweet.

Chokecherries were eaten in large quantities by Indians. Today they are still made into jellies and jams.

d. Subgenus *Laurocerasus*, Cherry Laurels

P. caroliniana (m.a.). The small fruit is edible but not very flavorful.

P. myrtifolia, myrtle-leaved cherry laurel, West Indian cherry – S. Fla. The seeds are used in tropical America, where the tree is also native, for flavoring wine.

They are rich in hydrocyanic acid.

2. The following species, introduced from Europe and Asia, are naturalized on our continent or found as escapes from cultivation. They also often persist on old sites.

a. Subgenus *Amygdalus*

P. amygdalus (= *P. dulcis*, = *Amygdalus communis*), almond. Originally from Central and Southwestern Asia and North Africa. Much cultivated for the kernel of its fruit in warmer regions and locally found as an escape, especially in California.

Sweet almonds are delicious raw. A very fine oil is extracted from them. Almond butter is obtained by crushing the kernels, and almond milk by mixing this paste with water.

An excellent syrup, used as a demulcent, is made with almonds. It is known in France as "sirop d'orgeat."

Torrefied almonds have been used as a coffee substitute. Slightly roasted, they improve the flavor of cakes, desserts, etc.

Ripe almonds contain much vitamin A, some vitamin B, vitamin E, minerals, proteins (15%), fats (60%), sugars and a ferment.

They are very nutritious. Roasting increases their digestibility.

Almond milk is emollient, demulcent and expectorant.

The oil is laxative.

A variety has fruits with bitter kernels that contain a large proportion (4%) of a cyanogenetic glucoside (amygdalin), transformed by the action of a ferment (amygdalase or emulsin) and water into glucose, benzoic aldehyde (bitter almond oil, very aromatic) and hydrocyanic acid, a toxic substance.

Bitter almonds and their essential oil have been used to flavor desserts. However, this practice can be dangerous as thirty to fifty kernels can kill an adult if they are ingested at one time. The human organism can eliminate hydrocyanic acid but only below a certain quantity, and over a long period of time.

The distilling water of bitter almonds (the water obtained from distilling for the essential oil) also contains hydrocyanic acid, but in relatively small quantities. It is sedative and analgesic, as is a poultice of crushed bitter almonds applied externally.

The leaves, flowers and green husks of the fruits are emollient, demulcent, febrifuge, calmative, diuretic and laxative.

The leaves dye wool a golden yellow with alum.

Both the sweet and bitter forms of this tree have been cultivated since Antiquity.

P. persica, peach – originally from China. The tree is much cultivated for its <u>fruit</u> and escapes occasionally from cultivation.

Peaches are delicious raw – when fully ripened on the tree.

They yield large quantities of juice which has diuretic properties.

Peaches contain vitamin A (in the skin, and also in the pulp of yellow-fleshed varieties), some vitamins B1, B2, niacin, minerals, sugars and other substances.

They are diuretic and slightly laxative.

The kernel of the stone contains a large amount of amygdalin (about 2%), the same cyanogenetic glucoside as in bitter almonds, and can be toxic.

Leaves and flowers (they also contain some amygdalin) are antispasmodic, sedative, laxative and expectorant.

The <u>leaves</u> are used in France to make a liquor, "vin de pêche."

They give wool a yellow color with alum.

The tree was introduced in the 17th century into North America.

Nectarines are the fruits of var. *nucipersica*. They differ from peaches in that they have a thick, smooth skin.

b. Subgenus *Prunus*

P. armeniaca, apricot – from C. Asia and China. The tree occasionally escapes from cultivation.

The well-ripened <u>fruit</u> is delicious raw. It is often dried. A thick, orange juice, a veritable nectar, can be extracted from the pulp.

Apricots contain much vitamin A, some vitamins B, C, niacin, minerals, malic acid, sugars, etc.

Fresh, they are refrigerant and rather astringent; they are laxative when dried. Ripe apricots are very digestible. Commercial fruits, picked while still green, do not possess the taste, digestibility nor the beneficial properties of tree-ripened apricots.

The <u>kernel</u> of the fruit is generally bitter, but in some varieties it is sweet and edible like almonds.

It contains laetrile, which supposedly can be used for curing certain cancers. Although harmless, its medicinal use is banned in the United States.

The tree has been in cultivation in the Mediterranean area since Antiquity. It was introduced into North America in the early 18th century.

P. domestica, plum – originally from the Caucasus, it is cultivated throughout the world for its delicious <u>fruit</u>. Many varieties are known. The tree escapes from cultivation on our continent.

Plums are eaten raw or cooked in sauces or pies. Prunes are the dried fruits of certain varieties.

After fermentation, plums are commonly distilled in Europe to yield alcohol.

Freshly extracted from the pulp, the juice is excellent.

Plums contain vitamins A, B and C (in medium quantities), minerals, sugars (4%) and organic acids.

They stimulate the nervous system and help eliminate toxins.

Prunes, the dried plums of a few particular varieties, contain 45 to 60% sugars. After soaking in warm water for one night and cooking in a change of water to reduce their sugar content, they act as an efficacious laxative and also as a cholagogue. To take advantage of this remedy, chew five to fifteen prunes before a meal.

A thick, sweet juice can be extracted from soaked prunes.

Plum leaves are said to be diuretic, laxative, febrifuge and anthelmintic.

Plum kernels contain about 1% amygdalin.

The bark of the tree dyes wool black with ferrous sulfate.

The tree has been cultivated since Antiquity. It was introduced into North America in the 17th century.

P. insititia, bullace, damson plum – originally from W. Asia and S.E. Eur. Sometimes cultivated for its large, dark blue <u>fruit</u>, edible raw, the tree is found as an occasional escape in Eastern North America.

P. spinosa, European sloe – naturalized from Eur.

The black <u>fruit</u>, covered with a bluish bloom, is extremely tart and astringent before the first frosts. After the frosts it can be eaten, preferably after cooking.

Prunus spinosa

In Northern Europe, it is fermented and distilled into an alcohol known as "sloe gin." It also yields an excellent vinegar.

In France, the fruit used to be pickled in vinegar or preserved in brine like green olives. The latter process yields pink, salty and sour plums, which look and can be used like "umebosis" (Japanese apricots, fermented and employed as a sour, salty and aromatic condiment).

Sloes contain vitamin C, organic acids and tannin.

They are tonic and astringent.

The flowers contain glucosides when fresh.

They are diuretic, depurative and slightly laxative.

The <u>leaves</u> have been used to adulterate black tea.

Leaves and bark tend to reduce the blood sugar level.

The bark of this spiny shrub gives wool a reddish brown color without mordant.

c. Subgenus *Cerasus*

P. avium, sweet cherry – originally from Eurasia. The tree is widely cultivated for its <u>fruits</u>, and locally escaped.

Many varieties are in cultivation. The fruits of some are sweet and very good to eat raw. Others are sour and destined to be cooked in compotes, pies, jams or jellies, or fermented into cherry cider. The brew is distilled into the liquor "kirsch" in certain parts of Europe.

Sweet cherries can be dried or squeezed to obtain a delicious juice.

Prunus avium

Cherries contain much vitamin A, little of vitamins B and C, minerals and sugars (especially levulose, which is easily assimilated).

They are refrigerant, depurative, diuretic and laxative.

The kernel of the pit contains small amounts of cyanogenetic glucosides.

The peduncles contain tannin, potassium and flavonoids.

They are astringent and diuretic.

The leaves are sometimes used as a pectoral remedy.

The transluscent, mucilaginous <u>gum</u> exuding from the trunk is edible. It is said that a hundred people resisted a two-month long siege with this gum as their only food.

P. cerasus (= *Cerasus vulgaris*), sour cherry – from S.W. Asia – cultivated throughout the world for its edible <u>fruit</u> and sometimes found as an escape in N.Am.

Many varieties are known, some with sweet, juicy fruits which are edible raw. Most sour cherries, however, are cooked or fermented into wine. The fruits of this species have the same uses, composition and medicinal properties as those of *P. avium* (m.a.).

The kernels of the pits yield an edible oil when pressed, which is recommended for urinary stones and rheumatic pains.

The tree has been in cultivation since Antiquity.

P. mahaleb, Saint Lucie cherry, mahaleb cherry – originally from Eur. This small tree is cultivated as a grafting stock and occasionally escapes.

The black fruit has little pulp and is rather bitter, but not unpleasant. It can be good when cooked.

In Western Asia, the kernels were used in confectionary and the leaves for flavoring milk like bitter almonds (see *Prunus amygdalus*). Both are aromatic due to benzoic aldehyde derived, along with hydrocyanic acid, from cyanogenetic glucosides.

The wood of the tree has a pleasant smell.

P. padus, European bird cherry – from Eurasia – occasionally naturalized in N.E. N.Am.

The small fruit is black with a thin, sour and bitter pulp. It is sometimes used to make jam in Europe and Asia. In Northern Europe it is fermented and distilled into alcohol.

The bark contains a cyanogenetic glucoside (isoamygdalin) and has sedative properties.

d. Subgenus *Laurocerasus*

P. laurocerasus, cherry laurel – from S.E. Eur. This shrub (which can grow into a large tree if given the chance) is often planted as an ornamental hedge and rarely escapes from cultivation.

The leaves are sometimes used to flavor milk and beverages, to which they add a pleasant bitter almond smell. This odor is due to the presence of benzoic aldehyde, formed by hydrolysis of a glucoside (prulaurasin) contained in the leaves. However, hydrocyanic acid is also produced in the process. Three or four leaves in a quart of milk have been known to cause serious cases of poisoning, especially in young children. Cherry laurel leaves must be used with much caution – or not used at all.

They are antispasmodic and sedative and stimulate respiration.

The rather large, black <u>fruit</u> is insipid, but not toxic.

It has laxative properties.

The kernels contain the same cyanogenetic glucoside as bitter almonds (amygdalin). They have also been used as a flavoring.

P. lusitanica, Portugal laurel – from Portugal and Spain. The tree is planted for ornament and occasionally found as an escape.

The <u>fruits</u> are edible but tasteless.

The leaves contain a glucoside yielding benzoic aldehyde and hydrocyanic acid.

The fruits of many other species are used as food in Europe and Asia.

Endangered species: *P. geniculata* – Fla. – and *gravesii* (m.a.).

Pyrus (B 3)   Pear
(This genus is sometimes united with *Aronia, Malus* and *Sorbus* spp. under the name *Pyrus*.)
Latin name of the tree.
Throughout.
A few E. Asian species are cultivated as ornamentals.

P. communis, the pear tree from hybrid origin, is commonly cultivated for its fruit and sometimes escapes from cultivation. Many varieties are known, some of which are planted for ornament.
　　The <u>fruits</u> of the wild trees are usually small and remain hard and astringent even when ripe. This is also true with those of some cultivated varieties.
　　If they are inedible raw, pears can be cooked into sauces, pies or jams, or fermented into "perry," which is still popular in some parts of Europe, where an alcohol is also distilled from the fruits.
　　Left in contact with the air, perry will turn to vinegar.
　　Whole pears can be canned. The fruits of the best varieties are often juiced or sliced and dried.
　　Pears contain vitamins A, B1, B2, C, niacin and small quantities of minerals.

They also contain tannins, pectin, organic acids and sugars (especially levulose, which is easily assimilated).

They are refrigerant, diuretic, depurative and astringent.

The leaves contain the same glucoside (arbutin) as bearberry (*Arctostaphylos uva-ursi*) and other Ericaceae. They have similar diuretic properties.

The pear tree has been cultivated since time immemorial.

The fruits of local species are used as food in Europe and Asia. Some are excellent when overripe, like medlars (*Mespilus germanica*).

Rosa (B 1) Wild Rose

Latin name of the plant from the Indo-European root "vrod," flexible.
Throughout. Both native and species introduced from Eurasia.
Many roses are planted for ornament – mostly Asian species and garden hybrids. The following escape from cultivation: **R. canina**, dog rose – from Eur. –, *cinnamomea*, cinnamon rose – from Eurasia –, *gallica*, French rose – from Eur. – and *rugosa* – from E. Asia.

Rosa canina

The very young shoots of various species are edible but very astringent. Indians used to eat those of *R. cinnamomea* (m.a.), *fraxinellaefolia* and *virginiana* – N.E. N.Am.

The petals can be added raw to salads, fruit salads, desserts or beverages. In the Middle East, the fragrant petals of certain species are made into rose jam. In China, they flavor black tea. The Romans used to macerate rose petals in their wine and included them in pastries and various desserts. The tradition was kept throughout the Middle Ages. The petals of *R. gallica* (m.a.) were used to make rose preserves, rose honey and rose vinegar; the last was used both as food and as medicine.

Some of our wild species have fragrant flowers and can be used as mentioned above.

Rose oil is distilled in Southern France and Bulgary from two Asian species: (*R. x alba* and *x bifera* (= *damascena*). It is one of the most expensive of all essential oils, as one ton of fresh petals yields only one-half pint of oil. It is used in perfumery, usually adulterated with geranium oil.

Rose water, the aromatic water obtained as a byproduct of distillation, is used in the Eastern Mediterranean area for making confections, mixed with honey, almonds, etc.

It is slightly astringent, and has medicinal uses as an eyewash and a skin tonic.

The <u>false fruits</u> (rosehips) of all roses are edible, but they differ greatly in size and flavor (some taste like raspberries, others are bitter). They become soft with the frosts and generally acquire a pleasant sweet, acid and aromatic taste. They can be eaten as such, pressing the hips delicately between the fingers in order to let the pulp out at the base, like a natural jam out of a tube.

Rosehips can be gathered in quantity and often remain on the bushes throughout the winter. But the stiff hairs surrounding the "seeds" are unpleasant to swallow.

When rosehips are soft, they can be passed through a food mill or processor to remove the hairs and the seeds. The remainder can be mixed with some water and passed again. If the rosehips are ripe (red) but still hard, they must be boiled in water until they become soft. They can then be passed through the mill.

The purée obtained is dark red and flavorful. It can be eaten with yogurt or made into sauces for fruit salads. It is traditionally cooked into syrup and jam which is commonly sold in Europe. It can also be made into chutney or a "tomato sauce" which can be eaten with noodles or spread on pizzas.

Rosehips are often dried for making a fruity tea. In late winter and spring, they are sometimes found dried naturally on the bushes. In this state, rosehips can be ground – seeds and all – and finely sifted to yield a powder which, mixed with flour, makes delicious breads, porridges, cakes, cookies and other delights. It can also be used as a flavoring.

Rosehips are extremely rich in vitamin C, up to fifty times as much as lemons. They are one of the richest of all fruits in this vitamin. This property was utilized in England during World War II, when tons of rosehips were gathered to make a syrup which was distributed among the population.

They also contain vitamins A, E, K and niacin, minerals, organic acids (citric, malic), pectin, sugars, tannin and other substances.

They are tonic, astringent and depurative.

The seeds are rich in vitamin E and contain a glucoside. They have diuretic and sedative properties.

These are the actual fruits, as rosehips are a false fruit, formed by the enlarged, fleshy receptacle of the flower.

The following species have had edible uses in North America: *R. acicularis* – N. N.Am. –, *californica* – Calif., S. Ore., Baja –, *canina* (m.a.), *cinnamomea* (m.a.), *gymnocarpa*, wood rose – W. N.Am. –, *nutkana*, Nootka rose – N.W. N.Am. –, *rugosa* (m.a.), *suffulta* (= *arkansana*) – C. N.Am. –, *virginiana* – N.E. N.Am. – and *woodsii* – W. N.Am.

Rosehips were highly esteemed as food by Indians.

Leaves, flowers and fruits of many species are eaten in Europe and Asia.

Rubus (A 1)   Blackberry, Raspberry, Dewberry
Latin name of the plant.
Throughout.
The following native and Eurasian species, as well as garden hybrids, are cultivated for their fruits or for ornament:

Native Species

R. ursinus, California dewberry – Calif., Ore., Baja – and *vitifolius var. titanus*, a form of the California blackberry having fruits up to 6 cm (2⅓ in.) long; the latter shrub escapes from gardens in California.

Rubus sp.

Introduced Species

R. idaeus – originally from Eur. – is the most common species in cultivation; it is found as an escape in N.E. U.S.

R. illecebrosus, strawberry-raspberry – from Japan – is occasionally planted for its fruits and sometimes escapes.

R. phoenicaulasius, wineberry – from E. Asia – is cultivated for its fruit and naturalized in E. N.Am.

Hybrids

One of the most famous is *R. x loganobaccus* (= *R. strigosus x vitifolius*), Loganberry, created in the United States in 1881. Youngberries were derived from *R. ursinus* (m.a.).

Ornamental Species

R. caesius, European dewberry – originally from Eur. – is cultivated for ornament and sometimes escapes in E. N.Am. It has occasionally been cultivated for its fruits.

R. laciniatus, cut-leaf blackberry – exact origin unknown, probably from Asia – is planted as an ornamental and naturalized in N.W. N.Am.

Our native *R. odoratus*, flowering raspberry – E. N.Am. – and *spectabilis*, salmon berry – coast of N.W. N.Am. – are much appreciated as ornamentals in Eur., but little cultivated in Am.

Thousands of species belong to this worldwide genus. They are all basically edible in the same manner:

The very young shoots can be eaten after peeling and boiling in one or two changes of water to remove their astringency. Indians would frequently use them as food.

They give wool a light gray color with alum.

Tea is often made with blackberry and raspberry leaves. If they are allowed to ferment for a while, the flavor of the brew will be much improved. (This is the process which is used for developing the aroma of black tea.)

It has been reported, however, that wilting leaves could be slightly toxic when ingested in large quantities, probably because they develop a relatively high hydrocyanic acid content, which disappears on drying. Once thoroughly dried, they are definitely safe.

Blackberry leaves contain vitamin C, organic acids (malic, oxalic), tannin and various substances.

They are astringent and reduce the blood sugar level. Their medicinal uses date back to Antiquity.

The fruits of all species are edible, but their quality as well as their color varies widely.

Blackberries, raspberries, dewberries and salmon berries were an important food for the American Indians and for people in Europe and Asia. They rank first among the few wild fruits still commonly gathered, as they are easy to identify and pick in quantity.

In many cases the fruits are juicy, sweet and fragrant. They are usually so abundant that there is too much to eat fresh, so the rest of the crop is cooked or preserved in various ways: pies, jams, jellies, syrups and so on. The fruits are also fermented into wine and vinegar, and distilled to make an alcohol, especially in Europe.

A delicious juice can be extracted from the fresh fruits. It can be fermented into a wine. Blackberry juice was sometimes used to color grape wine in Europe.

The Indians used to dry blackberries and raspberries to preserve them, but the result is not as successful as with more fleshy fruits: little remains but the numerous seeds.

Inuits used to simply freeze the fruits to keep them through the winter. This is a common way of preserving the fruits nowadays.

Raspberries and blackberries contain vitamins A and C, sugars (mostly levulose, easily assimilated), pectin, organic acids (citric, malic), essential oils and other substances.

They are refrigerant, diuretic and depurative. Ingested in large quantities, they are laxative.

The seeds contain a fixed oil (up to 25%) which can be extracted by pressure.

A blackberry is actually not one fruit, but the agglomeration of many small drupelets; it is known as an aggregate fruit.

The genus *Rubus* is taxonomically difficult. It can be divided into five subgenera:

1. Subgenus *Chamaemorus*
Stems annual (herbaceous or nearly so), spineless; yellow fruit.

R. chamaemorus, cloudberry – circumpolar N. N.Am.

The fruits are juicy and sweet, good to eat raw. They are often cooked into jams or pies. A wine is brewed from them in Sweden; left in contact with the air, it turns to vinegar.

Inuits (in America) and Laplanders (in Northern Europe) preserve the fruits by freezing them in the snow.

Cloudberries were formerly sold in markets in Nova Scotia.

2. Subgenus *Cyclactis*
Stems annual, often spineless; red fruit.

R. arcticus (= *R. acaulis*), Arctic bramble, nagoonberry – N. N.Am.

The fruits are generally flavorful.

Inuits preserve them by freezing.

The leaves are used as tea in parts of Norway.

R. pedatus, five-leaved bramble – N.W. N.Am.

R. pubescens (= *R. saxatilis* var. *canadensis*), dwarf blackberry, stone bramble – N. N.Am.

The acid fruit is eaten raw or cooked.

In Russia it is fermented and distilled into alcohol.

3. Subgenus *Anoplobatus*, Flowering Raspberries
Glandular stems; large, showy flowers; red fruit.

R. deliciosus, Rocky Mountain flowering raspberry – W. N.Am.

R. odoratus (m.a.)

The ripe <u>fruit</u> has a pleasant flavor. As noted above, the plant is cultivated in Europe because of its ornamental flowers.

R. parviflorus, thimbleberry – W. & C. N.Am.

4. Subgenus *Idaeobatus*, Raspberries

Biennial stems, spiny (often with weak spines); red, black or yellow fruit, separating from the receptacle at maturity (the color of the fruit is in parenthesis):

R. idaeus (m.a.) is the most widely cultivated species.

Raspberry leaves are commercially sold for making a tea that has astringent, diuretic, emmenagogue and laxative properties.

The <u>fruits</u> have a rich aromatic flavor. Raspberries are eaten raw and are made into jams, jellies, pies and syrup. Raspberry syrup is used as a harmless food coloring, and to flavor ice cream and sherbets.

Alcohol is distilled from the fruits in Eastern France.

R. illecebrosus (m.a.).

The <u>fruits</u> are pleasant to eat.

R. leucodermis, Western raspberry, blackcap – W. N.Am. – (dark purple to black or yellow-red).

R. nigerrimus, Western raspberry – N.W. U.S.

R. occidentalis, black raspberry, blackcap – E. & C. N.Am. – (black, rarely yellowish).

The delicious <u>fruits</u> are eaten raw, in jams, jellies, sherbet and ice creams, canned and made into wine and vinegar.

R. phoenicaulasius, wine raspberry (m.a.)

The <u>fruit</u> is brewed into wine in Asia. It can be made into jam and jelly.

R. spectabilis, salmon berry (m.a.) (red to yellow).

<u>Young shoots</u> and <u>fruits</u> were used as food by Indians. The fruits are rather insipid and were often eaten cooked with fish.

R. strigosus (= *R. idaeus* var. *strigosus*), American red raspberry – N. N.Am. & Mountains – (red).

The <u>fruit</u> is eaten raw, made into jams, jellies, pies, drinks or sherbets and fermented into wine.

This shrub, along with *R. vitifolius,* is one of the parents of the Loganberry.

5. Subgenus *Rubus*, Blackberries, Dewberries

Biennial stems, armed with stout spines; black or red fruit, adherent to the receptacle at maturity.

The limits between the different species are often ill-defined: over 1,000 species have been described in this subgenus, and natural hybrids commonly occur. The species named in this section must be considered as collective species.

<u>Young shoots</u>, <u>leaves</u> and <u>fruits</u> of the species noted here have all the edible uses described above.

R. allegheniensis, common blackberry – E. N.Am.

R. argutus, highbush blackberry – S.E. U.S.

R. caesius (m.a.).

The fruits are composed of a few large, bluish druplets, with a whitish bloom. They are sour but aromatic and good to eat when thoroughly ripe.

R. canadensis, dewberry – N.E. N.Am. & Appalachians.

R. cuneifolius, sand blackberry – E. Coast of U.S.

R. enslenii – E. U.S.

R. flagellaris (= *R. baileyanus*), Northern dewberry – E. N.Am.

The <u>fruits</u> are eaten fresh, cooked into jams and pies, pressed to yield juice and fermented into wine.

R. hispidus, dewberry – E. N.Am.

R. laciniatus (m.a.).

R. nivalis (= *R. pacificus*), snow dewberry – N.W. N.Am.

R. orarius – N.E. N.Am.

R. ostryifolius (= *R. laudatus*) – mostly N.E. N.Am.

R. pensilvanicus (= *R. frondosus*) – N.E. N.Am.

R. procerus, Himalaya berry – naturalized from Asia in Calif., Ore. & Wash.

R. setosus – N.E. N.Am.

R. trivialis, Southern dewberry – S.E. U.S.

R. ursinus (m.a.).

The plant is cultivated for its fruits, which are pleasant to eat raw. This shrub has given birth to boysenberries and youngberries.

R. vitifolius (= *R. lemurum*), California blackberry – coast of C. Calif. var. *titanum* (m.a.) is cultivated for its very large fruits.

Sanguisorba (B 3) Burnet
From the Latin "sanguis," blood, and "sorbeo," to absorb: the plant has hemostatic properties.
Throughout. Both native and species introduced from Eurasia.

Sanguisorba minor

The leaves of *S. minor* (= *Poterium sanguisorba*) and *officinalis*, great burnet – both naturalized from Eurasia – have a very fresh taste, slightly astringent, reminiscent of cucumber or of green walnut.

They are excellent raw in salads. The tender young leaves growing in the center of the rosette are the best.

The plants have been cultivated in vegetable gardens since the 16th century, but have now fallen into oblivion. *S. officinalis* (m.a.) is still occasionally culti-vated and found as an escape.

In Eastern Asia, the leaves are often cooked or preserved in salt.

Burnets contain tannin, an essential oil, a saponin and flavonoids.

The leaves are astringent, carminative and hemostatic. Externally, they are used fresh for healing burns and cuts.

Sorbus   (B 4)   Mountain Ash
Latin name of the tree.

N. N.Am. & Mountains. Both native and introduced European species.

S. aucuparia, rowan, originally from Eur., is planted as an ornamental and occasionally escapes in N. N.Am. An Asian species is also grown for orna-ment.

The <u>fruits</u> of *S. americana* – N.E. N.Am. & Appalachians – and *aucuparia* (m.a.) and *decora* – N.E. N.Am. – have been used as food on our continent.

They are usually too astringent and bitter to eat raw, even when thoroughly ripe, although much im-proved by frosts. They are cooked

Sorbus aucuparia

into compotes and jams. Syrup can be made by extracting the juice and cooking it with sugar or honey. The Indians used to dry them and grind them into a meal.

The fruits of the European rowan, *S. aucuparia* (m.a.), have been dried, ground and mixed with flour to make bread in times of scarcity. They are also fermented and distilled into alcohol.

They contain vitamins A and C, sugars, pectin, malic acid, tannin and other substances.

The seeds contain a cyanogenetic glucoside.

The bark of the tree gives wool a gray color, without mordant.

Other species are used as food in Europe and Asia. Some of them are culti-vated as fruit trees.

CHRYSOBALANACEAE

Chrysobalanus (B 5)
From the Greek "chrysos," gold, and "balanos," acorn.
S. Fla., Mex.

The <u>fruit</u> of *C. icaco*, coco plum, as well as its kernel are eaten raw or cooked in tropical America.

Another species is used as food in tropical Africa, and an edible oil is extracted from the <u>kernel</u> of the fruit.

Licania (D 4)
(= *Chrysobalanus* spp.)
Etymology unknown.
S.E. U.S., Mex.

The <u>ripe</u> fruit of *L. michauxii*, gopher apple, is edible raw.
The <u>fruits</u> of several species are eaten in tropical America.

FABACEAE (LEGUMINOSAE)

This is probably the third largest family among the flowering plants, with 600 genera and more than 13,000 species distributed throughout the world.

It is divided into three subfamilies:

Mimosoidae, mostly tropical and subtropical trees, many of which are planted as ornamentals.

Caesalpinioidae, which include trees such as honey locust, redbud, palo verde, as well as small shrubs and several ornamentals of warm regions.

Papilionoidae, numerically and economically the most important division, to which belong those of our common vegetables generally known as legumes: beans, peas, lentils, cowpeas, fava beans, garbanzo beans, peanuts and soybeans; as well as some of our most frequently planted fodder plants: clover, alfalfa, sweet clover and vetch.

The ripe seeds of various members of this family are good protein sources, especially when mixed with cereals (caryopses of *Poaceae*) as is traditional throughout the world. The amino acids of their respective proteins combine, which increases their nutritional efficiency markedly. Legumes are also rich in carbohydrates.

But legumes must always be thoroughly cooked, since the raw seeds contain trypsin inhibitors which prevent digestive enzymes from doing their work. Traditionally, they are usually boiled until they partly dissolve in the cooking water and made into a sauce. Legumes should also be eaten in moderation as they can be hard to digest.

Some legume seeds, such as those of vetches and lima beans, contain hydrocyanic acid, which is toxic.

In this subfamily, numerous plants contain alkaloids which can cause nervous, hepatic or cardiac disorders.

I. MIMOSOIDAE

Acacia (D-H 4)   Acacia
Greek name of an Egyptian species.
S. U.S., Mex.
Our native *A. farnesiana*, sweet acacia, huisache, is sometimes planted for its fragrant flowers. The tree was possibly introduced from S.Am. in mission times. Many species from Australia, tropical Asia and Africa are cultivated for ornament.

The pods of *A. angustissima*, Prairie acacia, were eaten cooked in Mexico.
Southwestern Indians used to dry and grind the pods of *A. greggii*, catclaw acacia – S.W. U.S., Mex. – to prepare a meal used for making mush and cakes.

A gum much like gum arabic exudes from the bark of this small tree, and is used locally in Mexico. It is demulcent.

The flowers are one of the most important sources of honey for desert bees.
The flowers of *A. farnesiana* (m.a.) are used for making perfume in France.
The leaves and the gum exuding from the trunk are used as food in tropical Asia.

Gum, pods and seeds of many *Acacia* spp. are eaten in the tropics. Some of these species are planted as ornamentals on our continent.

Several of these trees yield gum arabic.
Endangered species: *A. emoryana* – Tex.

Albizzia julibrissim   (C-H 4)   Silk Tree
(= *Albizia j.*)
After Albizzi, Italian naturalist.
Native to Asia and Africa, the tree is planted as an ornamental and escapes
from cultivation in S.E. U.S. and Mex.

The <u>young leaves</u> are reportedly eaten in tropical Asia.
<u>Leaves</u>, <u>pods</u> and <u>seeds</u> of various species are eaten in the same regions.
Endangered species: *A. emoryana* – Tex.

Leucaena   (D 5)   Lead Tree
Etymology unknown.
S. Fla., Mex.

The <u>seeds</u> of *L. esculenta* – Mex. – are eaten cooked in that country, in spite
of their rather unpleasant taste. They are supposed to be an aphrodisiac.
  <u>Leaves</u>, <u>flower buds</u>, <u>young pods</u> and <u>seeds</u> of *L. leucocephala* (= *L. glauca*),
wild tamarind, jumbie bean, are eaten (after cooking) in Southeastern Asia,
where the plant is common. The roasted seeds are used as a coffee substitute.
  The raw plant is said to be toxic for horses and pigs, but harmless for cows,
sheep and goats.

Mimosa   (D 4)   Mimosa
Etymology unknown.
S.W. U.S., Mex.

The <u>seeds</u> of some species were eaten cooked by Indians. The whole <u>pods</u> of
M. biuncifera were ground into a meal.
  The flowers of these small trees are often fragrant and are a good source of
honey.

Pithecellobium   (D 5)   Blackhead
Etymology unknown.

A few species are native to S. Fla. & Mex.

P. dulce, Manila tamarind, guamachil, originally from tropical America, is naturalized in S. Fla. & Mex.

In the species mentioned above, the very young pod is occasionally boiled and eaten.

The white pulp surrounding the seeds is sweet and juicy. It is often made into refreshing drinks in Mexico and tropical America.

Young pods and parched seeds of *P. flexicaule*, ebony – Tex., Mex. – are said to be edible cooked.

The red seeds are used for making beads, and the reddish heartwood is used for carving.

Young shoots, pods and seeds of local species are eaten in tropical Asia.

Prosopis   (C 2)   Mesquite
"Prosôpis," ancient Greek name for burdock or mullein.

S. Calif. to Tex., Mex.

The pods of *P. juliflora* (including var. *torreyana* and *velutina*) were a staple for desert Indians.

When ripe, they contain a sweet pulp which can be scraped off and eaten raw. Generally the whole pod was ground into a nutritious meal which was moistened with water, shaped into cakes and baked in the sun or buried in hot sand. This sweet meal was also mixed with water and fermented into an alcoholic drink.

The young pods are tender and edible raw or cooked.

Prosopis juliflora

The seeds were sometimes removed from the pod and ground up separately.

A sweet gum exuding from the branches was eaten as candy by Indians, and also used to mend pottery. This gum yields a black dye.

The flowers are a most valuable source of honey.

The inner bark of the trunk was used in basketry and for weaving a coarse cloth.

The <u>pods</u> of *P. pubescens*, screw bean, tornillo, were used as food in the same manner. They are very sweet and can be boiled down to a light syrup.

<u>Pods</u> and <u>seeds</u> of other species are eaten in South America, tropical Africa and Asia.

II. CAESALPINIOIDAE

Cassia (D-H 4)   Wild Senna
From the Greek "kasia" or "kassia," name of the tropical Asian tree yielding a well-known purgative, from the Hebrew "ketzioth."
E. & S. U.S., Mex.
An Australian species is planted for ornament. Our native *C. marilandica*, wild senna – E. U.S. – is occasionally cultivated as an ornamental in Eur.

<u>Young shoots</u>, <u>leaves</u> and <u>unripe pods</u> of *C. marilandica* (m.a.), *occidentalis*, coffee senna – S. U.S., Mex. – and *tora* (= *obtusifolia*), sickle-pod – S.E. U.S. – are edible after cooking, preferably after boiling in a change of water to remove their strong smell.

These species and many others are eaten as cooked greens in tropical Asia.

The torrefied <u>seeds</u> are used as a coffee substitute.

The leaves, the ripe pods and the pulp of several tropical species are used as a powerful purgative known by the name of "senna."

The leaves of *C. marilandica* (m.a.) are purgative but irritating, diuretic and anthelmintic.

Endangered species: *C. keyensis* – Fla.

Cercidium (D 2)   Palo Verde
(= *Parkinsonia* spp.)
From the Greek "kerkidion," weaver's shuttle: referring to the shape of the fruit; same etymology as *Cercis*.
S.W. U.S., Mex.

The ripe <u>seeds</u> of *C. floridum*, *microphyllum* and *torreyanum* were parched and ground into a meal by Southwestern Indians.

If not thoroughly ripe, the seeds are reportedly cathartic.

The flowers are a good source of honey.

The Spanish name "palo verde" means "green stick": the bark of these trees is green and carries on photosynthesis as the leaves fall off early to prevent excessive transpiration.

A wax obtained from *C. praecox*, palo brea – N.W. Mex. – is used locally as a glue after heating.

Cercis   (B 4)   Redbud

Ancient Greek name of the tree, from "kerkis," weaver's shuttle: referring to the shape of the pods; same etymology as *Cercidium*.

Almost throughout.

Our native *C. canadensis* – E. N.Am. – and *occidentalis* – W. N.Am. – are planted for ornament, along with a Mediterranean and a Chinese species.

<u>Flower buds</u>, <u>flowers</u> and <u>unripe pods</u> of our two species mentioned above have a pleasant acid taste and are edible raw. The flower buds are sometimes pickled, and the flowers made into fritters.

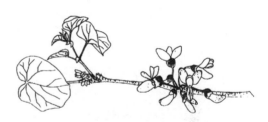

Cercis canadensis

The <u>seeds</u> of *C. occidentalis* (m.a.) were reportedly eaten cooked by Navajo Indians.

The bark of these trees is astringent.

The ornamental Mediterranean species (*C. siliquastrum*) planted in North America is used as food in the same manner as our native redbuds, especially in Greece and Turkey.

Gleditschia triacanthos (C-F 4)   Honey Locust

After J. C. Gleditsch (1714–1786), botanist from Berlin.
E. & C. U.S.
The tree is frequently planted for ornament.

The pods become quite large. The seeds are surrounded by a sticky pulp which is sweet and aromatic. If this pulp is eaten raw by itself, however, it tends to irritate the throat. The whole pods should be dried (possibly toasted first), ground and sifted. The resulting powder can be used as a sweetener or mixed with flour to make bread and cakes. But it must be used with moderation; the pulp of the fruits has been reported to be more or less toxic.

A slightly alcoholic beverage can be obtained by crushing the pods and fermenting them with water.

The cooked seeds were sometimes eaten by Indians.

Leaves and pods of other species are used as food in Asia.

Gymnocladus dioica (D 4)   Kentucky Coffee Tree

From the Greek "gymnos," naked, and "klados," branch: referring to the lack of small branches, especially conspicuous in the winter.
E. & C. U.S., S. Ont.
The tree is sometimes planted as an ornamental.

The roasted seeds were occasionally eaten by Indians, while the white settlers used them as a coffee substitute.

Foliage and pulp of fruits are toxic.

Hoffmanseggia (D-H 4)   Camote de Raton

After the Count of Hoffmansegg, co-author of a flora of Portugal.
S. Calif. to Tex., Mex.

The tuberous roots of *H. densiflora* (= *H. falcaria*) were cooked and eaten by desert Indians.

Endangered species: *H. tenella* – Tex.

Parkinsonia aculeata (D 4)   Horse Bean, Mexican Palo Verde

After John Parkinson (1567–1629), apothecary from London who wrote botanical works.
Ariz. to Fla., Mex.
P. aculeata (m.a.) is planted for ornament in the warmer parts of the U.S. and in Mex. Of the two species of this genus, this is our only native species; the other is native to Africa.

The seeds of this small tree were roasted and ground by Indians, like those of *Cercidium* spp.

Tamarindus indica (B 5)   Tamarind

After the Arabic name of the tree, "tamar hindi."
Originally from tropical Asia, the tree is cultivated in S. Fla. and Mex. for its edible pods. It is naturalized in the Florida Keys and Mex.

The pods are used as food throughout the world.
The sour pulp is eaten fresh out of the pod, after removing the outer skin and spitting out the large seeds. It is often pressed with the seeds and made into refreshing drinks which are occasionally fermented. Chutneys and curries are made from it in India, and in Africa tamarind is made into a fermented seasoning called "daudawa." The pulp is also made into preserves by boiling with raw sugar.
It contains pectin, sugars (especially levulose, easily digested) and organic acids (malic, tartric). Tamarinds are at the same time one of the most acid and one of the richest in sugar of all fruits.
The pulp is laxative and refrigerant.
The starchy seeds are eaten cooked in India, but they are very hard. They are said to contain an edible oil.
Flowers, young leaves, whole young pods and sprouted seeds are edible as well.
The leaves are said to have anthelmintic properties.

III. PAPILIONOIDAE

Amphicarpa bracteata   (C 2)   Hog Peanut

From the Greek "amphi," both, and "karpos," fruit: the plant bears two kinds of fruits, produced both above- (three-seeded pods from petaliferous flowers) and under- (one-seeded pods from apetalous flowers) ground. E. N.Am.

The brown seeds found in the one-seeded subterranean pods are very good cooked. They can be dug up at the base of the young plants in the spring.

Young pods and seeds of a related species are eaten after cooking in Eastern Asia.

Apios   (C-H 4)   Groundnut, Potato Bean

Greek name of the pear: referring to the shape of the tubers. E. & C. N.Am.
Our native A. americana (= A. tuberosa) is sometimes planted as an ornamental.

The tubers were an important food for Indians. They can be eaten raw, but leave a thin rubbery coating on the teeth. It is better to cook them and eat them hot to obtain maximum flavor. They are sometimes quite large, reaching up to 7 inches.

The plant was introduced in Europe in 1845 during the potato blight (which caused millions of deaths by starvation, especially in Ireland) as a possible potato substitute. But its cultivation was discontinued because of its extremely low yields.

The seeds are edible as well.

The flowers are fragrant.

Endangered species: A. princeana – Ill. to Miss.

Apios americana

Arachis hypogaea (B 5)   Peanut

From the Greek name of a vetch (*Lathyrus amphicarpus*), "arakos."
Originally from tropical America, widely cultivated for its seeds in S. U.S.
and Mex., and sometimes found as an escape.

The seeds are borne in a pod which buries itself in the ground before reaching maturity.

Peanuts are often eaten whole after roasting or, as in Southeastern United
States, after boiling. Like most legumes, they are very hard to digest in the raw
stage, as they contain substances which inhibit digestive enzymes. These substances are destroyed by thorough cooking.

Peanuts are commonly crushed into peanut butter, which is an excellent food
if pure and eaten in moderation, a poison if full of sugar and additives, and eaten
daily in quantity, especially with bread and jam.

The seeds yield an edible oil which has a pleasant taste and healthful qualities if unrefined and extracted by cold pressure, without heat and chemical solvents.

Innumerable ways of using peanuts have been devised.

In Asia, the seeds are sometimes fermented into a kind of "miso," or manufactured into a sort of "tofu," like soybean curd. They are also eaten after
sprouting. In Africa, they are made into a sauce ("mafé"), which is eaten with
chicken.

Peanuts contain proteins (25%), oil (50%), starch (15%), vitamins B6, E and
niacin, minerals and other elements.

Young leaves and stems are edible raw or cooked.

Astragalus (D-F-H 2-3)   Milk Vetch

Greek name of a plant from "astragalos," ankle bone or dice: applied to
some leguminous plant early on from the rattling of the seeds in the inflated pod.
Throughout. Several hundred species in W. N.Am.

The roots of *A. aboriginum* – N. N.Am. – were used as food by Indians.

The fleshy pods and the seeds of *A. crassicarpus* (= *A. caryocarpus*) – C.
N.Am. – and *mexicanus* – S.W. U.S., Mex. – were eaten raw or cooked by both
Indians and white settlers. Mature seeds were boiled. These species are known
collectively as "ground plums" or "buffalo beans."

Several milk vetches absorb selenium and other elements from the soil and concentrate them in harmful amounts. They are also known to contain cumulative poisons (including locoine) and cause the often fatal disease of livestock (especially horses) known as "loco" (meaning "crazy" in Spanish). These species are known collectively as "locoweeds."

The following species are incriminated: *A. bisulcatus* – C. U.S. –, *convallarius* – W. N.Am. –, *diphysis* – S.W. U.S. –, *earlei* – W. Tex. –, *emoryanus* – W. Tex. –, *hylophilus* – Colo. –, *lentiginosus* – W. U.S. –, *mollissimus* – C. U.S., Mex. –, *nothoxis* – Ariz. –, *scobinatulus* – Wyo. –, *tetrapeterus* – W. N.Am. – and *wootonii* – N.M. to Tex., N. Mex. They are sometimes separated into two groups, according to the symptoms of the disease that they produce.

Gum tragacanth is an <u>exudation</u> found on the stems of several Eurasian milk vetches. It is locally used as food. <u>Leaves</u>, <u>pods</u> and <u>seeds</u> of other species are eaten in Europe, North Africa and Asia.

Endangered species: *A. agnicidus* – Calif. –, *amnis-amissi* – Idaho –, *atratus* var. *inseptus* – Idaho –, *beathii* – Ariz. –, *beatleyae* – Nev. –, *castetteri* – N.M. –, *clarianus* – Calif. –, *columbianus* – Wash. –, *cremnophylax* – Ariz. –, *cronquistii* – Utah –, *desereticus* – Utah –, *deterior* – Colo. –, *funereus* – Calif., Nev. –, *hamiltonii* – Utah –, *harrisonii* – Utah –, *humillinus* – Colo. –, *iselyi* – Utah –, *jaegerianus* – Calif. –, *johannis-howellii* – Calif. –, *kentrophyta* var. *douglasii* – Wash., Ore. –, *lentiginosus* var. *maricopae* – Ariz. –, var. *micans* – Calif. –, var. *sesquimetralis* – Calif., Nev. –, var. *ursinus* – Utah –, *linifolius* – Colo. –, *lutosus* – Utah, Colo. –, *microcymbus* – Colo. –, *misellus* var. *pauper* – Wash. –, *moncensis* – Calif. –, *naturitensis* – Colo. –, *nyensis* – Nev. –, *oocalycis* – Colo., N.M. –, *osterhoutii* – Colo. –, *perianus* – Utah –, *phoenix* – Nev. –, *porrectus* – Nev. –, *proimanthus* – Wyo. –, *purshii* var. *ophiogenes* – Idaho, Ore. –, *pycnostachyus* subsp. *lanosissimus* – Calif. –, *ravenii* – Calif. –, *robbinsii* var. *alpiniformis* – Ore. –, var. *jesupi* – N.H., Vt. –, var. *occidentalis* – Nev. –, *schmollae* – Colo. –, *serenoi* var. *sordescens* – Nev. –, *siliceus* – N.M. –, *sinuatus* – Wash. –, *sterilis* – Ore., Idaho –, *tener* var. *titi* – Calif. –, *uncialis* – Nev. – and *xiphoides* – Ariz.

Baptisia (D-F-H 4) Wild Indigo
From the Greek "baptizô," to dye: referring to the use of some species as a substitute for indigo.
E. & C. N.Am.
Our native *B. australis*, blue wild indigo – S.E. U.S. – is sometimes planted for ornament.

The <u>young shoots</u> of *B. tinctoria* have been eaten cooked in New England. The plant contains a coloring matter similar to that of indigo.
It has been reported that cases of poisoning have occurred from taking large quantities of tincture of *Baptisia*.
The foliage of several species, eaten raw in large amounts, has reportedly poisoned cattle.
Endangered species: *B. arachnifera* – Ga.

Cajanus cajan (B 5) Pigeon Pea
Etymology unknown.
Originally from S.E. Asia, the plant is cultivated for its seeds. It is naturalized in S. Fla. and Mex.

The pigeon pea is one of the oldest cultivated plants. Its <u>young pods</u> and ripe <u>seeds</u> are eaten cooked. The sprouted seeds are also used as food. It is one of the most important legumes in tropical regions.

Canavalia (B-F 5)
Etymology unknown.
Several species are native to Mex. *C. maritima*, bay bean, is also indigenous to S. Fla.
C. ensiformis, jack bean, and *gladiata*, sword bean, are cultivated on our continent. The former species is naturalized in S. N.Am., the latter escapes from cultivation in S. Fla. and Mex. Both are originally from tropical America.

<u>Flowers</u>, <u>young pods</u> and ripe <u>seeds</u> of *C. ensiformis* and *gladiata* (both m.a.) are eaten cooked. The ripe seeds are sometimes used as a coffee substitute, but are reported to be potentially toxic, even after cooking.
The young pods of the sword bean are sometimes pickled in soy sauce in Japan.

Cicer arietinum   (B 5)   Chickpea, Garbánzo Bean

Latin name of the plant.

Scattered throughout.

Originally from W. Asia, the chickpea is cultivated almost throughout the world for its seeds. It sometimes escapes from cultivation in N. Am., but does not persist.

The seeds, usually dried, are cooked and eaten whole, or made into soups, "humus" (a thick purée, mixed with garlic and olive oil) in the Middle East or a sauce eaten with rice in India and Pakistan. They are roasted in hot sand and eaten as a snack in India.

They can also be ground and mixed with cereal flour for making bread or mush. This is a good way to ingest complete proteins, by the combination of a cereal and a legume, which together contain in balanced proportion all the essential amino acids.

Besides protein, chickpeas contain starch, sugars, fats, vitamins B and C, minerals and asparagin.

Like all dried legumes, they are extremely nutritious, but can be heavy and hard to digest by sedentary individuals, especially if not thoroughly cooked.

They are somewhat diuretic and anthelmintic.

However, it has been reported that if improperly cooked and eaten almost exclusively over a long period of time, chickpeas can produce the nervous disease known as lathyrism (see *Lathyrus* spp.).

The plant has been cultivated since ancient Egypt.

In India, the sour exudation of the leaves of a related species is gathered by covering the plant for the night with a sheet which is wrung out in the morning. The extracted liquid is rich in organic acids (malic, acetic and oxalic). It is used like vinegar and is made into refreshing drinks.

Young shoots and seeds of a few species are eaten raw or cooked in Asia.

Cytisus   (E-F 2)   Broom

Greek name of *Medicago arborea*.

Widely naturalized from Eur. & N. Africa.

Some species, including *C. scoparius* (= *Sarothamnus s.*), Scotch broom, and hybrids, are planted as ornamentals.

Scotch broom (m.a.) has been used as food in Europe.

The twigs were used to flavor beer before hops came into general use.

The flower buds were pickled in vinegar and eaten like capers, after they were macerated overnight in a strong brine and rinsed. However, the wilting flowers and the young pods are said to cause gastric ailments if ingested raw.

The torrefied seeds have been used as a coffee substitute in France, but they may be somewhat toxic.

Scotch broom contains several alkaloids (especially spartein) and various active substances. The flowers in particular contain a flavonoid with a diuretic action (scoparin).

The whole plant, including flowers and seeds, is diuretic, cardiotonic and vasoconstrictor. It also has antivenomous properties, due to the spartein it contains.

If ingested in large quantities, several *Cytisus* spp. – including Scotch broom – can produce nervous, hepatic and cardiac disorders, due to the alkaloids they contain.

The flowers of Scotch broom dye wool a pale green with alum.

The stems are a source of fibers.

Dalea (D 4)   Indigo Bush, Pea Bush
After T. Dale (1659–1739), early English botanist.
W. & C. N.Am.

The roots of *D. lasianthera* were chewed by children of Zuni Indians.

The roots of *D. terminalis* – S.W. U.S., Mex. – were eaten raw as a sweet by Hopi Indians.

The seeds of *D. emoryi* – S. Calif., S. Ariz., Baja, Son. – and *terminalis* (m.a.) were also used as food, after roasting and grinding.

A yellowish dye used for basketry was extracted from the twigs and flower heads of *D. emoryi* (m.a.) by Indians.

Dolichos lablab   (B 5)   Hyacinth Bean
Greek name of a bean.
S. U.S., Mex.
Originally from tropical Asia, the plant is cultivated on our continent, mostly for ornament, and is found as an escape in southern regions.

Young leaves, flowers and tender, immature pods are edible raw or cooked. The ripe seeds are eaten cooked, either boiled or roasted. In Asia, they are made into noodles.
The hyacinth bean is cultivated as a vegetable throughout the tropics.
Many local species are used as food in tropical Asia, Africa, America and Australia.

Erythrina   (D-F 5)   Coral Bean
From the Greek "erythros," red: referring to the color of the flower.
S. U.S., Mex.
A few tropical trees of this genus are planted as ornamentals in the warmest areas of our continent. These include *E. berteroana*, pito, and *rubinervia*, gallito – both from C.Am., naturalized in Mex.

Young shoots and leaves are eaten cooked in Central America.
The unopened flower buds and the flowers have a sour taste. They are used in salads, stews and various dishes in Mexico and Central America.
Other species are used as food in tropical America and Asia.
The scarlet seeds are often made into necklaces. They are extremely toxic and serve as rat, dog and fish poison in Mexico and Central America.

Genista tinctoria   (E-F 4)   Dyer's Greenweed
Latin name of a broom (*Cytisus* sp.), possibly from the Celtic "gen," a small bush.
Originally from Eur., this plant is sometimes cultivated as an ornamental; it is naturalized locally in N.E. N.Am.

The flower buds have been pickled in Europe, prepared like those of Scotch broom (*Cytisus scoparius*) – soaked overnight in brine and rinsed – and used like capers.

The plant contains alkaloids (cytisin, methylcytisin), a flavonoid (luteolin, a yellow coloring) and other active substances.

It is diuretic, laxative and vasoconstrictor.

As its name suggests, dyer's greenweed was formerly used as a source of dye: the flowering tops give wool and linen a beautiful yellow color with alum or chromium. They were often used to obtain green, by dyeing fibers already tinted with indigo.

Due to the alkaloids it contains, the plant can produce nervous, hepatic or cardiac disorders if ingested in large quantities.

Glycine max   (B 4)   Soybean

From the Greek "glykys," sweet.

Scattered throughout.

Originally from tropical Asia, the plant is widely cultivated for its seeds; it is often found as an escape and is naturalized locally in N.Am. The U.S. is the world's largest soybean producer; most of the crop is used as cattle feed.

Soybeans have been a staple for millenia in Eastern Asia.

The green, underlineunripe seeds are delicious steamed in the pod, as soon as possible after picking.

The ripe seeds can be boiled and eaten whole or mashed. In Asia they are often canned. They can also be ground into flour; however, commercial soybean flour is often chemically defatted, and the resulting oil sold separately. It is used by the food industry especially for meat substitutes and as a source of textured vegetable protein (T.V.P.).

In Asia, the ripe and dried seeds are made into soy milk, which can be used like cow's milk. It has a pleasant taste and is very nutritious and digestible.

It is used for making soy cheese or "tofu," curdled with "nigari," a natural magnesium and potassium sulfate extracted from unrefined sea salt.

Tofu is eaten in salads or cooked with vetetables and often fried. It is also dehydrated by quick-freezing in Japan and sold as "Kori-tofu." It can be aged like cheese, which it smells like. This is particularly popular in Viet Nam.

Soybeans are also fermented with cereals and salt, and aged to yield a thick, brown paste called "miso," and a dark-colored liquid called "shoyu" or "tamari," commonly used as condiments in Eastern Asia, especially in Japan. Commercial soy sauce differs from shoyu or tamari in that it is made industrially and is often colored with caramel.

Miso is commonly used in soups. Tamari is often used for pickling in East Asia.

Soy milk, tofu, miso and tamari are now commonly sold and utilized in North America and Europe. Soy milk is also dehydrated to yield soy milk powder.

Other soybean preparations include: "yuba," a yellowish thin film, eaten in Japan boiled and seasoned with shoyu; "nattô," made from whole beans fermented in a warm place with rice straw; and "tempeh," an Indonesian preparation in which cooked soybeans are inoculated with a white fungus. Tempeh is usually eaten fried. It can be found in health food stores on our continent.

Soybeans are also torrefied and used as a coffee substitute.

The seeds can be sprouted and eaten raw or cooked.

Soy oil is extracted chemically. It has a very strong taste and is usually refined and used industrially, especially for making margarine.

Lecithin is obtained from soybeans, also by chemical means. It is sold in health food stores for its supposedly beneficial properties, and is used commercially for emulsifying chocolate, mayonnaise and so on.

Soybeans contain 40% protein with all the essential amino acids in fairly good proportions, 20% oil, 15% starch, vitamins A, B1, B2, B6, D and E, minerals (including twice as much iron as spinach), lecithin, enzymes and other substances.

They are extremely nutritious and beneficial when properly prepared and eaten in moderation. But like other dried legumes, they cannot be digested raw and are too rich to be ingested in large amounts, especially by sedentary individuals.

Soybeans have been heralded as the potentially most useful plant in the world.

Glycyrrhiza (B 4) Licorice
From the Greek "glycys," sweet, and "rhiza," root: referring to the taste of the root.
C. & W. N.Am.

G. glabra, commercial licorice – from S. & E. Europe – is locally cultivated for its root; it escapes from cultivation in California.

G. lepidota, wild licorice – native to C. & W. N.Am. Its licorice-flavored roots were chewed raw by Indians, who also used to bake or roast them.

The particular sweet taste of licorice is well-known. A decoction or maceration of the pulverized root can be used for sweetening various dishes, and of course herb teas.

A thick, black extract is obtained by slowly boiling the filtered liquid. It is often sold commercially and used in confectionary, tobacco and brewing (it gives beer its "head" of foam).

When using licorice, it is a good idea to scrape off the grayish, external part of the root which is slightly bitter.

The root can simply be chewed for its pleasant taste, its thirst-quenching qualities and nutritious virtues.

The sweet taste of licorice is due to glycyrrhizin, a saponin fifty times as sweet as white sugar (saccharose). The root contains about 5% glycyrrhizin, sugars (3% saccharose and 3% glucose), starch (30%), a resinous oil (15%), flavonoids, asparagin, estrogen and various substances.

It is antispasmodic, expectorant, diuretic, antiphlogistic and refrigerant.

If used regularly over a long period of time, licorice can be a cause of hypertension.

The plant has been used medicinally since Antiquity.

Glycyrrhizin extracted from the roots is sometimes used as a sweetener in foods.

Our native *G. lepidota* (m.a.) contains in its roots practically as much glycyrrhizin as *G. glabra* (m.a.).

Roots and leaves of local species are used for their sweet taste in Asia.

Hedysarum   (E-F 4)   Sweet Vetch
From the Greek "hêdysaron," name of a leguminous plant.
N. N.Am. & W. Mountains.

The roots of *H. alpinum* subsp. *americanum* – N. N.Am. –, *boreale*, *hedysaroides* – Alaska & N.W. Can. –, *occidentale* – N.W. U.S. – and *sulphurescens* – N.W. U.S. & N. Can. – were eaten raw or cooked in the spring when sweet and tender by Inuits and other Indians of Northwestern North America. They have a pleasant taste.

The young shoots and stems of *H. alpinum* (m.a.) were eaten as well.

H. mackenzii – N. N.Am. – has been reported both to be edible and toxic by various authors.

Lathyrus (C-F-H 1)   Pea, Vetch
From the Greek "lathyros," name of a leguminous plant.
Throughout. Both native (mostly) and species introduced from Eurasia.
L. latifolius, everlasting pea – originally from S. Eur. – and *odoratus*, sweet pea – from the Mediterranean region – are planted for ornament and occasionally escape from cultivation.

Young shoots, inflorescences, pods and seeds of various *Lathyrus* spp. are edible cooked.

The following native species were used as food by American Indians: *L. japonicus* (= *L. maritimus*), beach pea – coasts of N.E. & N.W. N.Am. & Great Lakes –, *jepsonii* subsp. *californicus* (= *watsonii*) – Calif. –, *ochroleucus* – N. N.Am. –, *palustris* – N. N.Am. & Western Mountains – and *vestitus* – Calif., S.W. Ore.

The beach pea (m.a.) was also eaten in Europe and Asia, where the plant is native as well. The bitter seeds were sometimes ground into flour or torrefied as a coffee substitute. Immature seeds can be eaten like garden peas.

In Asia, the young shoots and pods of *L. latifolius* (m.a.) are eaten as greens after parboiling. The seeds are boiled and roasted.

The ripe seeds of *Lathyrus* spp. are not always wholesome, however, and some are known to cause a serious sickness called "lathyrism," characterized by lesions of the bones and of the nervous system. But in order for this disease to develop, the seeds must be eaten exclusively over a long period of time. This happens in areas where famine is chronic. Cases of it are still reported, many of which appeared in Northern India in 1979. *L. sativus*, chickling vetch – from S. Eur., occasional adventive about E. seaports – is the species usually incriminated, as it is often cultivated in arid countries of the Old Continent for its ability to withstand droughts.

If the seeds are eaten in moderation and the food intake is well-balanced, they are beneficial to the body, being, like all legumes, rich in vitamin B and protein.

The young and tender unripe seeds of *L. aphaca* – from S. Eur. and W. Asia, found as a waif around

Lathyrus tuberosus

E. seaports – have been used as food. But mature seeds are said to be narcotic and cause headaches.

L. tuberosus, earthnut – naturalized from Eur. in N.E. U.S. – has edible tubers with a sweet taste, reminiscent of chestnuts. The tubers were occasionally sold in markets in Europe, and the earthnut has been cultivated as a root vegetable in Holland.

Cases of motor paralysis in horses have been attributed to feeding on *L. incanus* – W. U.S. – but with no certainty.

Other species have been used as food since time immemorial in Europe and Asia.

Endangered species: *L. hitchcockianus* – Calif., Nev. – and *jepsonii* subsp. *jepsonii* – Calif.

Lens esculenta   (B 5)   Lentil
(= *L. culinaris*)
Latin name of the plant and of its seed.
Scattered throughout.
Originally from W. Asia and cultivated for its seeds since prehistoric times, lentils are found as occasional escapes in N.Am., but do not persist. Numerous varieties are in cultivation.

The seeds are eaten boiled, put into soups, or ground into flour for making bread and dumplings, especially in Western Asia.

They are rich in protein (23%) and carbohydrates (60%), vitamins B and C and minerals.

Lentils are very nutritious and are said to be galactagogue. Like all legumes, they must be eaten cooked or sprouted. Sprouted lentils are very good to eat raw when the tiny leaves turn green and are rich in chlorophyll.

This is one of the first plants to have been cultivated by humans as food. Lentils were highly esteemed by the ancient Egyptians, Jews and Greeks.

Lotus   (G-H 4)   Lotus, Trefoil
Greek name of a Mediterranean species and of various other plants.
Throughout.
A species from the W. African Islands is sometimes planted for ornament.

The <u>leaves</u> of *L. strigosus* – Calif., Baja – were reportedly eaten cooked as greens by Indians.

A decoction of the leaves of *L. rigidus* – S.W. U.S., Mex. – was used as a tonic by the early settlers under the name of "hills tea."

The <u>pods</u> of local species have been used as food in the Mediterranean area.

Endangered species: *L. scoparius* subsp. *traskiae* – Calif.

Lupinus (C-F-H 2-3)   Lupine

Latin name of the plant probably from "lupus," wolf: due to an old, false idea that lupines rob the soil of nutrients.

Throughout. Mostly W. N.Am.

Our native *L. polyphyllus* – W. Coast – and several hybrids are planted as ornamentals.

The roots of *L. littoralis* – N.W. N.Am. – and ***nootkatensis*** – Alaska – were used raw or cooked as food by Indians and Inuits, after they scraped off the exterior part.

<u>Young leaves</u> and <u>tops</u> of *L. affinis* (= *L. carnosulus*) and ***luteolus*** – both Calif., Ore. – were eaten as greens in the spring by California Indians.

<u>Pods</u> and <u>seeds</u> of *L. perennis*, wild pea – E. U.S. – have also been used as food after cooking. But the seeds of this lupine contain toxic alkaloids which must be removed by boiling in water.

The same must be done with the bitter seeds of *L. albus*, ***hirsutus*** and ***luteus*** – originally from Eur. – in order to render them edible. They are cultivated as green manure and for fodder, and are naturalized in North America. Some nonbitter varieties have been developed, which can be eaten like other legumes.

The square, yellow seeds of *L. termis*, now included in *L. albus* (m.a.), are soaked in brine and eaten as an appetizer in North Africa (under the name "termis") and parts of Europe. In the Mediterranean area, lupine seeds used to be boiled whole, ground into flour or torrefied as a coffee substitute. In Corsica, they were placed in a canvas bag which was left in a stream for over a week to remove the poisonous principle.

In addition to those of the four species previously mentioned, the seeds of the following native species are known to contain toxic alkaloids: *L. argenteus*, *barbiger, caudatus, comatus, corymbosus, kingii, leucophyllus, laxiflorus, palmeri, poly-phylus, sparsiflorus, spathulatus,* and *cereceus* – all W. N.Am.

Lupine seeds can produce nervous disorders, as well as inflammation of the stomach and intestines. Several species, such as *L. argenteus,* are responsible for livestock mortality.

The seeds of a few other species are eaten in Southern Europe and South America.

Endangered species: *L. burkei* subsp. *caeruleomontanus* – Ore. –, *guadalupensis, ludovicianus, milo-bakeri, tidestromii* var. *layneae* and var. *tidestromii,* and *tracyi* – all six Calif.

Medicago (B 1)   Alfalfa

Latin name of the plant from "medica," native of Medea, the supposed country of origin of alfalfa.

Introduced from Eurasia and naturalized throughout N.Am. Several species are cultivated as green manure and for fodder, especially *M. lupulina,* black medick, and *sativa,* alfalfa.

Leaves and flowering tops of the various species are edible raw in salads, or cooked. Those of the two species mentioned above and of *M. hispida* have often been used as food in Asia, Europe and America.

The leaves of *M. sativa* (m.a.) have a definite, quite pleasant flavor. They contain vitamins A, C, D, E, K and minerals.

The plant is tonic and diuretic.

The leaves are a commercial source of chlorophyll and vitamin K.

California Indians used to eat the seeds of M. lupulina (m.a.) parched or ground into flour.

Alfalfa seeds of *M. sativa* (m.a.) are commonly sold for sprouting in North America and in Europe. Alfalfa sprouts are among the best of all salads because of their tender and juicy texture and delicate flavor.

The seeds can be gathered by beating the ripe inflorescences on top of a sheet spread out on the ground, and subsequently winnowing the result.

The seeds of other species can also be sprouted.

A few local species are used as food in Northeast Asia.

Melilotus (D 1)   Melilot, Sweet Clover
Greek name of the plant from "meli," honey, and "lôtos," a plant name.
Introduced from Eurasia and naturalized throughout N.Am. *M. alba, indica* and *officinalis* are cultivated as green manure and for fodder, especially for hay.

The young leaves of the various species mentioned are edible raw, preferably before the plant starts to bloom. They have a bitter and aromatic taste, and are best when added in small quantities to salads.

The whole plant dried, especially the flowers, gives off a fragrance reminiscent of vanilla. It can be made into a pleasant tea and used for flavoring desserts and drinks.

The seeds can be used as a spice. In Switzerland, a special cheese is flavored with the dried leaves, flowers and seeds of a related West Asian species cultivated in Europe since the Middle Ages.

The sweet smell of dried melilot is due to coumarin, formed by the hydrolysis of a glucoside (melilotoside) under the action of a ferment.

M. officinalis (m.a.) is antispasmodic, sedative, diuretic and antiseptic of the urinary tract. It lowers the blood's clotting ability. Dicoumarol, used to kill rats and mice by causing internal hemorrhages, is extracted from fermented melilot; its action is due to a coumarin-like substance. For this reason, improperly cured or spoiled sweet clover hay is known to be dangerous to livestock. If fermented or moldy, sweet clover should never be used as food; care must be taken to dry it properly.

Also, excessive doses of fresh melilot can be emetic and more or less toxic.

Sweet clover is an excellent honey plant.

A few other species are used as food in Europe and Asia.

Melilotus officinalis

Mucuna (D-F 5)   Velvet Bean
Etymology unknown.
One species is native to S. Fla.
M. deeringiana and *pruriens* – both originally from tropical Asia – are cultivated in S. Fla. and Mex.; they are locally naturalized.

Young pods and seeds of the two species mentioned are eaten after cooking in the tropics of both hemispheres. In Asia, the seeds of *M. pruriens* (m.a.), cultivated there as a vegetable, are occasionally used for manufacturing a type of "miso," a fermented paste (see soybean, *Glycine max*).

Pods and seeds of many other *Mucuna* spp. are used as food in tropical regions. In several species they are toxic unless properly prepared by soaking or boiling in water.

Olneya tesota (D 4)   Ironwood
After S. T. Olney, New England botanist during the 19th century.
S.W. U.S., N.W. Mex.

The seeds, ripe in late summer, are edible raw or roasted like peanuts, which they somewhat resemble in taste. They were an important food for desert Indians.

The heavy wood is the best firewood in the desert. It was used by Indians for making arrowheads and tool handles.

Oxytropis (E-F-H 4)   Oxytrope, Locoweed, Crazyweed
From the Greek "oxys," sharp, and "tropis," keel: referring to the beaked lower petals.
C., W. & N. N.Am.

The roots of *O. mertensiana* – Alaska, Siberia – and *nigrescens* – Alaska, N. B.C., Yukon, Siberia – were eaten raw by Alaskan and Siberian Inuits.

Those of *O. lambertii*, crazyweed – C. & W. N.Am. – , were reportedly used as food by certain Indians. However, this plant is toxic to livestock, causing the nervous disease known as "loco" (meaning "crazy" in Spanish) which is sometimes fatal. Crazyweed is eaten readily by livestock and it is habit-forming. The toxicity is probably due to the concentration by the plant of elements from the soil in harmful amounts.

Other toxic species are *O. macounii* and *saximontana* – both W. U.S.

Endangered species: *O. kobukensis* – Alaska.

Pachyrhizus   (B 4)   Jicama, Yam Bean
From the Greek "pachys," thick, and "rhiza," root: referring to the large size of the root.

Mex.

P. erosus (= *Dolichos e.*) is naturalized from tropical Am. in S. Fla. The plant is widely cultivated as a vegetable in the Tropics of both worlds.

The tuberous <u>roots</u> are crisp, sweet and edible raw. They can also be cooked or dried and ground into flour.

The <u>flowers</u> are eaten in Java.

Other species are used as food in tropical regions.

Petalostemon   (E-H 4)   Prairie Clover
(= *Petalostemum* spp.)

From the Greek "petalos," petal, and "stemon," stamen: alluding to the peculiar union of these parts.

C. & W. N.Am.

The sweetish <u>roots</u> of *P. candidum, oligophyllum* and *purpureum* were chewed or eaten raw by Indians.

The <u>young foliage</u> is reportedly edible, and is high in protein. Older leaves were made into tea.

P. candidum (m.a.) was used as an emetic by the Hopi Indians.

Endangered species: *P. foliosum* – Ill. to Alaska – and *reverchonii* and *sabinale* – both Tex.

Peteria   (E 4)   Camote de Monte
Etymology unknown.

W. Tex. to Ariz., N. Mex.

The small, tuberous <u>root</u> of *P. scoparia* was eaten by Indians.

Phaseolus (B-F 4)   Bean
From the Greek "phasêolos" (for "phasêlos"), name of the cowpea, *Vigna sinensis.*
Many species native to S. U.S. & Mex.

P. acutifolius, tepary bean – S.W. U.S., Mex. – has been cultivated for hundreds of years by desert Indians (the Papagos were nicknamed the "bean people"). It is cultivated by white farmers in the Southwest and is becoming increasingly popular, being well-adapted to arid conditions.

The following three species sometimes escape from cultivation but usually do not persist.

P. vulgaris, common or kidney bean – originally from tropical Am. – is widely cultivated for its young pods and seeds. Many varieties are known.

P. limensis (= *P. lunatus* in part), lima bean – from S.Am. – is grown for its seeds.

P. coccineus (= *P. multiflorus*), scarlet runner bean – from S. Mex. and tropical Am. – is planted as an ornamental and also as a vegetable.

Pods and seeds from several native species were used as food by the Indians, who sometimes cultivated the plants. The best-known species are *P. metcalfei* – N.M., Ariz., N.W. Mex. – and *polystachios*, thicket bean – E. U.S.

Green and tender young pods are good to eat raw or cooked, preferably steamed to retain their flavor.

Those of the common bean contain vitamins A, B1, B2, C and niacin, minerals, and various substances, including inosite (especially in the fibers), which is said to be a cardiotonic.

Bean pods are diuretic and depurative.

The seeds are commonly eaten after long boiling. The Mexican staple known as "frijoles refritos" or "refried beans" consists of beans that have been boiled, mashed and then cooked in fat.

Bean seeds can also be ground into flour – sometimes used commercially in confectionary – or sprouted. Most commonly used for sprouts in the United States are the small green mung beans (seeds of *P. aureus*, from Asia). In Eastern Asia, mung beans and other species are made into noodles (ground up, mixed with water and passed through a sieve), jam (especially in Japan, with seaweed gelatin "kan-ten" and sugar added), wine (highly esteemed in China) or a "miso"-like fermented paste.

Raw beans contain a toxin, phasine, which causes serious digestive disorders (occasionally lethal) by inhibiting digestive enzymes and destroying red blood cells. Prolonged cooking (but not simple drying) will eliminate this toxin. For the same reason, bean sprouts must not be eaten raw until the leaves are green and well-developed. In East Asia, for instance, mung sprouts are always cooked.

Beans are rich in proteins and carbohydrates. They also contain vitamins A, B, C (small amounts) and E and minerals, with a particularly large amount of iron (more than lentils, known to be a good source of this mineral).

In some species such as the lima bean (m.a.), the seeds contain cyanogenetic glucosides which yield by hydrolysis toxic hydrocyanic acid. Cases of poisoning from eating improperly cooked lima beans are quite frequent. Fortunately, the hydrocyanic acid can be eliminated by boiling the seeds in water for a long time, but it is not destroyed; it is simply transferred to the water, which should be discarded.

In Indonesia, lima beans are ground into a meal which is washed repeatedly to remove the hydrocyanic acid, and cooked with rice.

Dried seed pods of the common bean are used as a diuretic. They help to reduce the blood sugar level of diabetics.

The roots of the scarlet runner bean (*P. coccineus* (m.a.)) are said to be poisonous.

Lima bean leaves are sometimes eaten cooked in Indonesia, but they are bitter.

Tubers, young pods, unripe and ripe seeds of various species are eaten in Central and South America, Asia and Africa.

Pisum sativum (B 4)   Pea
Greek and Latin name of the plant.
Scattered throughout.
Originally from S. Eur. & W. Asia, peas are widely cultivated for their young pods and their seeds. The plant is found as an occasional escape from cultivation, which does not persist.

Young pods and unripe seeds are sweet, with a delicate flavor. They can be eaten raw, but are most often cooked, and also canned or frozen.

The ripe seeds must be cooked. They are often made into "split pea" soup. The ripe seeds are rich in proteins and carbohydrates.

Peas contain sugars, vitamins A, B1, B6, C, folic acid and niacin and minerals.

In warm countries, the excessive use of fresh peas is occasionally responsible for cases of lathyrism (a serious disease of the nervous system and the bones; see *Lathyrus* spp.) caused by toxins (aminonitriles) they contain.

Peas have been cultivated since prehistoric times.

A few local species are used as food in Asia and North Africa.

Psoralea (C-H 4)   Breadroot, Indian Turnip
From the Greek "psoraleos," rough, scruffy: referring to the texture of the surface of the plant.
S., C. & W. N.Am.

The starchy, tuberous roots of several species were eaten raw or cooked by the Indians. They could also be dried and stored for future use, or ground into flour. Where the plants grew in abundance, they were an important food source for local tribes. The roots generally have a good flavor.

The following species have been used in North America: *P. argophylla* – C. N.Am. –, *californica* – Calif., Baja –, *canescens* – S.E. U.S. –, *castorea* – S.W. U.S. –, *cuspidata* – C. U.S. –, *epipsila* – S. Utah, Ariz. –, *esculenta* – C. N.Am. –, *lanceolata* – W & C. U.S. –, *macrostachya* – Calif., Baja –, *mephitica* – S. Utah, Ariz. – and *tenuiflora*, scurf pea – C. U.S.

The cooked leaves of *P. orbicularis* – Calif. – were reportedly eaten as greens by California Indians.

The foliage of *P. tenuiflora* (m.a.) is known to be toxic to cattle and horses.

Children have been poisoned by eating large quantities of the seeds of *P. argophylla* (m.a.).

The seeds of a local species are eaten in W. Asia.

Endangered species: *P. epipsila* (m.a.).

Pueraria lobata (C 2) Kudzu
After M. N. Puerari (1766–1845), botanist of Denmark and Switzerland.
S.E. U.S.
Introduced from Japan and China as a forage plant and ground cover, this aggressive vine has spread over the S.E. U.S.

Kudzu <u>roots</u> have been eaten in Japan for thousands of years. The starch they yield is highly valued for its nutritive properties and its great digestibility. It is made into a mush for invalids and also used as a soup thickener, for making sauces, steamed cakes, "mochis," noodles, among other things.

The roots are gathered in the fall or winter, and the starch is extracted by a long process: grating, soaking in water, filtering, letting the water settle, carefully pouring out the water, recovering the starch, drying it and crushing it into powder.

Kudzu starch is imported from Japan and sold in health food stores in the United States and in Europe. Impressive quantities of this plant are readily available in the Southeastern states and the commercialization of our naturalized kudzu would be a beneficial operation for the producer, the local rural people, and the native plants oppressed by this aggressive invader.

<u>Young leaves, flowers</u> and <u>unripe pods</u> are edible raw or cooked. Older leaves are sometimes used as tea in Japan.

After long processing, the inner bark of the stems yields fibers which were once woven into highly prized cloth in East Asia. The stems were cut, boiled, left in running water, removed, fermented, put back into running water, and crushed by stamping with the feet. The bark was then removed, scraped in water and dried in the sun. The fibers were separated by hand and spun.

The tuberous <u>roots</u> of other species are used as food in East Asia.

Robinia (B-F 2) Locust
After the Robins, Jean (1550–1629) and Vespasien (1579–1662), gardeners for Kings Louis XIII and Louis XIV of France, who cultivated the first locust tree in Eur.
Almost throughout.
Our native *R. pseudoacacia*, black locust – E. U.S. – is often planted as an ornamental. Two other species, native to S.E. U.S., are cultivated for the same purpose in our gardens.

In Japan, where the black locust was introduced at the end of the 19th century, the <u>leaf</u> <u>buds</u> are boiled and eaten with shoyu (soy sauce).

The fragrant white <u>flowers</u> are often made into fritters in America, Europe and Asia. They are sweet, containing much nectar, and can be added raw to salads, fruit salads or desserts.

They can also be made into a fragrant tea.

The tender <u>young pods</u> are edible after cooking.

The <u>seeds</u> were eaten boiled by Indians. The ripe seeds have been reported to yield an edible oil by pressure. Torrefied, they were sometimes used as a coffee substitute.

Raw seeds, however, contain substances that destroy red blood cells, phytohemagglutinins (closely related to those in castor bean seeds, *Ricinus communis*). Fortunately, these are eliminated by cooking. Similar substances are found in raw lentils and beans (see *Lens esculenta* and *Phaseolus* spp.).

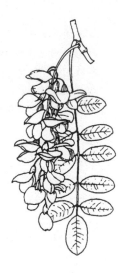

Robinia pseudoacacia

The roots and inner bark of the black locust have a slight but definite licorice taste, but they are somewhat toxic, causing nausea and dizziness. A group of children who had enjoyed chewing on black locust bark ended up in the hospital.

Animals and children have been poisoned by eating the leaves. Except for the flowers, all parts of the black locust, and of other species as well, are to be considered dangerous in the raw stage.

The pink <u>flowers</u> of *R. neomexicana* – N.M., Ariz., Mex. – were eaten raw by Indians in New Mexico.

All other parts of this small tree are toxic.

The Hopi Indians reportedly used the plant as an emetic.

The <u>roots</u> of a Chinese species are said to have been used as food locally in times of scarcity.

Sesbania (B-F 4) Coffee Weed

From the Arabic name of one species, "sesaban."
S. U.S., Mex.
S. grandifolia, Australian corkwood tree, from S.E. Asia & Australia, is sometimes planted for ornament; it is naturalized in S. Fla. & Mex.

Young leaves, buds, flowers and unripe pods are commonly eaten after cooking in tropical Asia. The very large flowers are sometimes added to salads.

Mature seeds are regarded as toxic.

The tree is cultivated in India for its edible parts.

The seeds of some of our native coffee weeds, such as *S. cavanillesii* (= *Daubentonia longifolia*) – Mex. – have been roasted and used as a coffee substitute.

Leaves and raw seeds are toxic and have poisoned sheep and goats.

Sophora (C-F 4) Mescal Bean

Etymology unknown.
S. U.S., Mex.
Our native *S. secundiflora* – Tex., N.M. & N. Mex. – and an E. Asian species (*S. japonica*) are planted for ornament.

The sweet roots of *S. sericea* were chewed as a delicacy by the Pueblo Indians of New Mexico.

The red seeds of *S. secundiflora* (m.a.) were made into a narcotic tea.

Leaves and seeds of these two species contain a toxic alkaloid, sophorine, and are poisonous.

Leaves and flowers of two local species (including *S. Japonica* (m.a.)), planted in North America) are eaten in East Asia.

Strophostyles (C 2) Wild Bean

From the Greek "strophê," turning, and "stylos," style: referring to the curved style.
E. N.Am.

Pods and seeds of *S. helvola* (= *Phaseolus helvolus*) – E. & C. N.Am. – have been eaten. The pods measure up to 10 cm (4 inches) long, and the seeds up to 1 cm long (1/2 inch).

Trifolium (B-H 1)   Clover

Latin name of the plant from "tres," three, and "folium," leaf.
Throughout. Both native and species introduced from Eurasia. Several introduced species are cultivated as green manure and for fodder.

Clover was highly esteemed as food by Indians. Certain tribes used to semi-cultivate patches of wild clover by favoring their growth through cultivation.

Some Indians used to steam the rather thin rootstock and eat it dipped in fat (often the oil of a small fish). The whole plant, with the roots, was sometimes smoked over a fire or soaked in brine for several hours.

Leaves and inflorescences were also eaten raw or boiled, and the small seeds gathered and ground into "piñole."

The following native species were used: *T. amabile*, Aztec clover – Mex. –, *bifidum, ciliolatum* (= *ciliatum*) – both Calif. to Wash. –, *cyathiferum* – N.W. N.Am. –, *dichotomum* – Calif. –, *furcatum* – Calif., Ore. –, *gracilentum, microcephalum* – both W. Coast –, *obtusifolium* – Calif., Ore. –, *variegatum* – Calif. – and *wormskioldii* (= *fimbriatum, involucratum*) – W. N.Am.

To this list must be added *T. pratense*, red clover, and *repens*, white clover, both from Eurasia and the most widespread species in North America today.

The leaves of these two clovers are also edible raw or cooked. They have a definite, not unpleasant taste. Large quantities are known to cause bloating in cattle; it is therefore probably better not to overindulge with leaves in the raw state, or to cook them instead.

The flowers are sweet and are commonly nibbled on by children. They make beautiful and pleasant additions to salads. They contain a delicious, sweet nectar: clover is an excellent source of honey.

In Ireland and Scotland, the inflorescences were dried, pulverized and mixed with flour to make bread in times of dearth. A decoction of red clover tops has depurative and diuretic properties.

The small seeds can be used as food, especially for sprouting, but they are difficult to gather. The best method is to beat the ripe heads over a sheet spread on the ground, and winnow the resulting debris.

T. hybridum, alsike clover – originally from Eur. – may produce dermatitis in a few susceptible individuals.

Endangered species: *T. amoenum* – Calif. –, *andersonii* spp. *beatleyae* – Nev. –, *lemmonii* – Calif., Nev. –, *polyodon* – Calif. –, *thompsonii* – Wash. – and *trichocalyx* – Calif.

Ulex europaeus   (E 4)   Gorse
Latin name of an undetermined shrub.
Originally from Eur., this prickly shrub is naturalized along the Pacific & N. Atlantic coasts.

The flower buds can be pickled and eaten like capers.
The plant contains slightly toxic alkaloids, and large quantities of it could cause nervous, hepatic and cardiac disorders.

Vicia   (B-F-H 1)   Vetch
Latin name of the plant.
Throughout. Both native and species introduced mostly from Eurasia.

V. faba, fava bean, horse bean, originally from W. Asia and N. Africa, is cultivated for its seeds; it occasionally escapes from cultivation in N.Am. but does not persist.

Its seeds are edible raw while still green, but require long cooking when ripe (dry).

Fava beans are a staple in Middle Eastern countries. They can be dried and ground into flour but are more often cooked into a sauce. In East Asia, they are fermented into a shoyu-like (soy) sauce or sprouted.

They are rich in protein and carbohydrates, and also contain vitamins A, B and C, minerals and other substances.

But fava beans can cause a dangerous anemia in certain people who eat them in large quantities over long periods of time, especially when eaten raw. They are toxic only to persons who hereditarily lack a digestive enzyme which normally destroys the hemolytic principles contained in the seeds. This happens mostly with people of Mediterranean origin.

Flowers and green pods are diuretic and sedative for the urinary tract.
The leaves are edible cooked.

Several Eurasian species are cultivated as green manure and for fodder. Of these, the following are widely naturalized in North America: *V. angustifolia*, *cracca*, *hirsuta*, *narbonensis* – naturalized near Washington, D.C. –, *sativa*, spring vetch, and *villosa*, winter vetch.

The young shoots, leaves, pods and seeds are edible after cooking.

Unripe seeds look like small sweet peas, but they contain some hydrocyanic acid, which is removed by boiling in water. They are not unpleasant to eat. Ripe seeds require a long cooking time and are not very good, but are nutritious.

The seeds can also be sprouted.

With the exception of V. angustifolia (m.a.), all these species have been cultivated for their seeds in Europe.

Of our native species, two are known to have been used as food by Indians: the young shoots of *V. americana* were cooked as greens, and the young seeds of *V. gigantea* – Calif. to Alaska – were also eaten.

Vicia angustifolia

Leaves and seeds of other species are used as food in Europe, North Africa and Asia.

Endangered species: *V. ocalensis* – Fla. – and *reverchonii* – Tex., Okla.

Vigna (B 4) Cow Pea
Etymology unknown.
S. U.S., Mex.
V. luteola (= *V. repens*) is native to Fla., Tex. & Mex. The young pods are edible.

V. sinensis (= *V. unguiculata*), cow pea, black-eyed pea, originally from East Asia, is widely cultivated for its seeds; the plant is occasionally found as an escape from cultivation in Southern regions.

The seeds are commonly eaten boiled in North America.

In East Asia, the immature pods are cooked as a vegetable.

Several other species are cultivated and used as food in the tropics.

Wisteria (B 4)
After Caspar Wister (1761–1818), Philadelphia anatomist.
E. U.S. Both native and species introduced from Japan.
Two E. Asian species are grown for ornament. One of these, *W. floribunda*
– from Japan – is found as an escape in S.E. U.S.

In Japan, the young leaves are eaten boiled.
The flowers are blanched in boiling water, strained and made into salads with
vinegar or shoyu (soy) sauce. They can also be dipped in batter (made with
starch rather than flour in order to be lighter) and fried, like black locust flowers.
The seeds are roasted.
But *Wisteria* spp. contain toxic principles (phytohemagglutinines and glucosides), at least in the raw stage. Children have been poisoned from eating raw
pods or seeds, which may produce digestive and nervous disorders.
Other species are used as food in East Asia, including *W. sinensis,* planted for
ornament in North America.

HIPPURIDACEAE

Hippuris vulgaris (D 4)   Marestail
Greek name of horsetail (*Equisetum* spp.) from "hippos," horse, and
"oura," tail: referring to the aspect of the plant.
Mostly Northern regions. A monotypic genus.

Alaskan Inuits cook the plant in soups. It can even be gathered in cold
weather, as it often sticks out of the ice after the ponds where it grows have
frozen.

LYTHRACEAE

Peplis portula (D 4)   Water Purslane
(= *Lythrum p.*)
Name used by Pliny.
Originally from Eur.; naturalized in Calif. (Placer County).
The plant has been eaten raw in Eur. since Antiquity. It was occasionally
cultivated as a vegetable.

TRAPACEAE

Trapa natans (B 4) Water Chestnut
(= *T. bicornis*)
Word first used by De l'Obel, formed from the French "chausse-trape," caltrop, a spiked iron ball used in warfare for maiming horses: referring to the appearance of the fruit.
Originally from Eurasia, naturalized in streams and lakes of E. N.Am.

The seeds have been eaten since Antiquity in Europe and Asia. They are boiled, roasted, fried, dried and ground into flour, or used in confectionary.
The plant is cultivated for its seeds in East Asia.
The seeds of a few other species used to be a staple for people in various parts of Asia.

MYRTACEAE

Eucalyptus (D 2) Eucalyptus, Gum Tree
From the Greek "eu," well, and "kalyptos," covered: stamens and pistil are covered in the bud by a woody "opercule" falling at anthesis.
Calif.
Originally from Australia, many of these tall trees are cultivated in southern regions for ornament, wood, essential oil and for drying off marshy land. Three species are naturalized in Calif., including *E. globulus*, blue gum.

The very young leaves are reddish, very tender and aromatic. They can be added to salads as a condiment.
Eucalyptus leaves contain essential oil, tannin and bitter substances.
They are antiseptic, expectorant, stimulant, and help to reduce blood sugar levels.
They can be used as an insect repellent.
The essential oil distilled from the leaves has an antibiotic action. It contains a camphor-like substance, eucalyptol.
Just before pollination, the flowers exude a sweet nectar that can be gathered with the tongue, as an insect or bird would do.

In Australia, the <u>sap</u> of the trunk of the blue gum and of other species (some of which are cultivated in North America) is used as a beverage.

A <u>manna</u> exuding from the leaves and trunk of several eucalyptus trees was eaten by Australian Aborigines.

Eugenia (B 5)   Stopper, Ironwood
(including *Syzygium* spp.)
S. Fla., Mex.
E. uniflora, Surinam cherry, pitanga, originally from Brazil, is planted as an ornamental and naturalized in S. Fla. and Mex.

Its large, ribbed <u>fruit</u> is bright red when ripe. It is juicy, aromatic and delicious raw. In the tropics, it is made into drinks, sherbets and jams.

Other species native to Southeast Asia and Australia are planted as street trees in Southern U.S. and Mexico. Among these, *E. cumini* (= *Syzygium cuminii*), jambolan, and *jambos* (= *Syzygium j.*), rose apple, both from tropical Asia, escape from cultivation in South Florida and Mexico.

Their <u>fruits</u> are good to eat raw. They are also made into juices, wine, vinegar, sherbets and jams.

<u>Flowers</u> and <u>fruits</u> of the rose apple are candied.

These two trees are sometimes cultivated for their fruits.

The <u>fruits</u> of our native *E. dichotoma* are edible raw when ripe.

The fruits of many other species are eaten in tropical regions of both hemispheres.

Myrcianthes fragrans (B 5)   Nakedwood
(= *Eugenia f.*)
Etymology unknown.
S. Fla.

The ripe <u>fruit</u> is edible raw.

Myrtus (B 4)
(= *Eugenia* spp.)
Greek name of the Mediterranean *M. communis.*
Fla.
A Mediterranean and a Chilean species are planted for ornament.

The ripe fruit of our native *M. verrucosa* (= *Eugenia longipes*), stopper, is edible when ripe.

Fruits and leaves of several species are used as food, as a condiment or for tea in various parts of the world (including those of *M. communis* and *ungi*, planted as ornamentals in North America).

Psidium guajava (B 5)   Guava
Etymology unknown.
Originally from tropical Am., the tree is cultivated in the warmer parts of N.Am. It is naturalized in S. Fla. & Mex.

The ripe fruit is good to eat raw. It is yellow with a pink or white pulp, very fragrant but usually filled with numerous hard seeds, although there are some almost seedless varieties. Guavas are also made into juices and jams. The fruits are ground up with the roasted seeds to make "guava cheese."

Guavas are very rich in vitamin C.

The leaves are sometimes made into tea.

A Brazilian species, the strawberry guava (*P. cattleianum*) is planted as an ornamental. Its red fruits are edible as well.

The fruits of many tropical American species are used as food.

PUNICACEAE

Punica granatum (B 5)   Pomegranate
Latin name of the tree "punica arbos": Carthaginian tree.
S. U.S.
Originally from W. Asia, this small tree is planted in S. regions for its fruit and as an ornamental. It occasionally persists on old homesites. Several varieties are known.

The sweet, juicy <u>pulp</u> surrounding the seeds is aromatic and delicious to eat raw. Pomegranate is made into a juice and a syrup, but the latter has been commercially replaced by an artificially colored and flavored substitute.

The <u>young leaves</u> have been reported to be edible after boiling, but they are astringent.

The bark, especially that of the root, contains alkaloids including pelletierine, which is dangerous and can produce digestive and nervous disorders.

Pomegranate bark and seeds are used medicinally as an anthelmintic and an astringent. They are rich in tannin.

The bark of the fruit dyes cloth yellow with alum, and dark brown with water in which nails have been placed to rust (iron salts plus tannin yields ink – see *Quercus* spp., Fagaceae).

OENOTHERACEAE

Boisduvallia (E 4)
After J. A. Boisduval, a French naturalist and physician.
W. N.Am.

The small <u>seeds</u> of *B. densiflora* were ground into piñole by California Indians.

Clarkia (B-H 4)
(including *Godetia* spp.)
After Captain William Clark, explorer of the N.W. U. S. with Meriwether Lewis in 1806–07.
W. N.Am.
Our native *C. unguiculata* – Calif. – is planted for ornament.

The small <u>seeds</u> of some species were ground into piñole by Western Indians.

Endangered species: *C. borealis* subsp. *arida, franciscana, imbricata, lingulata, mosquinii* subsp. *mosquinii* and *speciosa* subsp. *immaculata* – all Calif.

Epilobium   (D 2-3)   Fireweed
From the Greek "epi," upon, and "lobion," small pod: the petals, sepals, stamens and style are inserted on top of a long, thin ovary, which becomes a dry fruit splitting at maturity.
Throughout.

The <u>roots</u> of *E. angustifolium* (= *Chamaenerion a.*) were reportedly eaten by Inuits.

They contain mucilage, pectin and tannin, and have been used medicinally as an astringent.

The sweet and gelatinous <u>pith of the stem</u> is edible raw. It is easily obtained by cutting the stem into small lengths and peeling off the woody part.

It has been reported that in the 18th century, the inhabitants of Kamchatka (Northeast Asia) made a fermented drink from this pith.

The <u>young plant</u> shooting out of the ground makes a good vegetable.

The <u>leaves</u> were made into "Kurile tea" (Kurilski chai) in Russia, while in England, they were used for adulterating black tea.

An infusion of the <u>flowers</u> makes a pleasant beverage.

Epilobium angustifolium

The <u>young shoots</u> of various species are edible raw. The <u>leaves</u> have been cooked as greens in North America, Europe and Asia.

The species generally used on our continent are *E. angustifolium* (m.a.), *coloratum* – Ariz., Utah, Nev. –, *latifolium* (= *Chamaenerion l.*) – N. N.Am. – and *palustre* – N. N.Am. *E. angustifolium*, *latifolium* and *palustre* (all m.a.) are also native to Eurasia.

The <u>leaves</u> of *E. hirsutum* – introduced from Eurasia in Wash. – were made into tea in Russia.

Oenothera (D-H 1)   Evening Primrose
Greek name of a plant, possibly an *Epilobium* sp., from "oinos," wine, and "thêra," wild animal hunt: the roots were reportedly used (after infusing in wine) for taming wild animals.
Throughout.
Several native species, including *O. biennis* – E. & C. N.Am. – are planted for ornament, as well as *O. x erythrosepala* (= *O. lamarckiana*) – of garden origin – found as an escape on the W. Coast.

The roots of *O. biennis* (m.a.) are edible at the end of the first year of growth of the plant. They can be eaten raw (grated if too fibrous) or cooked. Their flavor is quite pleasant, reminiscent of parsnips or salsify. However, they often tend to irritate the throat when they are eaten alone, even cooked.

The following year, the flowering stem develops and the roots become woody and acquire a pungent taste. The fleshy part can still be removed from the core, boiled in a change of water and passed through a food mill to make a purée.

This species has been cultivated for its roots and young shoots in Europe. It was known in France as "jambon du jardinier" (gardener's ham).

Oenothera biennis

O. biennis (m.a.) contains, especially in its root, mucilage, tannin, sugars and various substances.

It is antispasmodic and antiphlogistic.

The roots of *O. hookeri* – W. N.Am. – have also been used as food.

The young shoots of *O. biennis, hookeri* and *x erythrosepala* (all m.a.) are edible raw. Older leaves must be cooked, preferably in a change of water to remove their sometimes unpleasant taste. Evening primrose's leaves have a rather mucilaginous texture.

The young fruits of *O. californica* – Calif., Baja – and *nuttallii* (= *albicaulis*) – N. N.Am. – and the seeds of *O. brevipes* – S.W. U.S. – were reportedly eaten by Indians.

Endangered species: *O. avita* subsp. *eurekensis, deltoides* var. *howellii* – both Calif. –, *psammophila* – Idaho – and *sessilis* – Ark.

MELASTOMATACEAE

Rhexia (D-H 2)   Meadow Beauty
Classical name of a plant, possibly a species of *Echium*, Boraginaceae.
E. N.Am.

A few species, such as *R. aristosa* and *virginica*, have tuberous-thickened rootstocks which could be eaten raw.
The young leaves of *R. virginica* (m.a.) are sweetish and slightly sour. Raw, they make a good addition to salads.
Endangered species: *R. parviflora* – Fla., Ga.

COMBRETACEAE

Terminalia catappa (C 5)   Indian Almond
Etymology unknown.
Originally from tropical Asia, the tree is planted as an ornamental and becomes naturalized in S. Fla. and Mex.

The pulp of the fruit has a pleasant flavor when it is thoroughly ripe, but it is still astringent and bitter.
The kernel inside the fruit is delicious raw and has a very delicate flavor reminiscent of that of almonds. Unfortunately, the thick shell protecting it is extremely hard to break.
An edible oil can be expressed from the seed.
Fruits and kernels of various species are eaten in the tropics of both worlds.

ELAEAGNACEAE

Elaeagnus (D 4)   Silverberry
Greek name of an undetermined shrub from "elaia," olive tree, and "agnos," sacred; also the name of the chaste-tree, *Vitex agnus-castus*.
E. commutata is native to N.W. N.Am.

Its rather dry and mealy fruit was eaten by Indians. Alaskan Inuits used to cook it in moosefat. The fruit is densely covered with silvery hairs.

E. angustifolia, Russian olive, oleaster, originally from North Asia, is much planted as an ornamental and to supply food for birds and wild animals. It often escapes from cultivation.

The <u>fruits</u> are mealy, sweet and acid, quite pleasant to eat raw or cooked. They were used as food in Europe, and in Asia are still sold in markets.

An alcohol was reportedly distilled from them in Western China (Yarkand).

Two East Asian species (*E. multiflora, pungens*) are planted as ornamentals in North America. Their <u>fruits</u> are edible as well.

Many other *Elaeagnus* spp. are used as food in Asia.

Elaeagnus angustifolia

Shepherdia (D 4)   Buffalo Berry
After John Shepherd (1764–1836), English botanist and horticulturalist, curator of Liverpool Botanical Garden.
W. N.Am.
Our native *S. canadensis*, russet buffalo berry, is sometimes planted as an ornamental.

The <u>fruits</u> of *S. argentea*, silver buffalo berry, and *canadensis* (m.a.) were an important food for Indians who would eat them raw or cooked, or dry them for future use. Early settlers made them into sauces, jams, jellies and occasionally into a fermented drink.

They contain pectin and saponin, a foaming agent. They can be mixed with water and honey, then beaten into a foam somewhat like whipped cream.

The fruits of *S. argentea* (m.a.) are sour and quite good raw. Those of *S. canadensis* (m.a.) are insipid and rather bitter. They are improved by frosts.

RHIZOPHORACEAE

Rhizophora mangle   (E 5)   Red Mangrove

From the Greek "rhiza," root, and "phora," bearing, from "pherô," to bear: referring to the ability of the seeds to germinate and start bearing roots before falling into the saline mud where the tree grows; also, aerial roots grow from the tree trunk.

Tropical shores of S. Fla. & Mex.

The inside part of the green sprouts or radicles can be eaten, but it is bitter.
The leaves can be made into tea. They contain tannin.
The fruits have reportedly been fermented into an alcoholic drink.
Another tropical species has been used as food.

NYSSACEAE

Nyssa   (D 2)   Gum, Tupelo

Name of a water nymph, applied to these plants because of the aquatic habitat of certain species.

E. N.Am.

Our native *N. sylvatica*, black gum, sour gum, is planted for ornament.

The fruits of the following species have been eaten in North America. They were mostly made into preserves and jams:

N. aquatica, water or swamp tupelo – S.E. U.S. – (bitter fruit), *ogeche*, Ogeechee lime – S.E. U.S. – (large, sour fruit) and *sylvatica* (m.a.) (fruit with thin, acid pulp).

The best species is *N. ogeche* (m.a.); its fruits were formerly sold in Southern markets.

The fruits of a local species are used as food in Southeast Asia.

CORNACEAE

Cornus (B 4)   Dogwood, Bunchberry, Cornel
(including *Chamaepericlymenum* spp.)
Latin name of the tree.
Throughout.
Our native *C. florida*, flowering dogwood – C. & E. U.S. – and *canadensis*
(= *Chamaepericlymenum canadense*), bunchberry, dwarf cornel – N. N.Am. –
are planted for ornament, as well as a few Asian species.

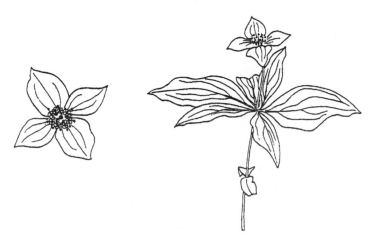

Cornus canadensis

Among our native species, the best fruits are obtained from the herbaceous
C. canadensis (m.a.) and *suecica* (= *Chamaepericlymenum suecicum*), Swedish cornel – N. N.Am.

The berries are juicy, sweetish but rather insipid and edible raw. Inuits used
to freeze them in wooden crates for winter use.

A natural hybrid between these two species occurs in Alaska.

The bitter fruits of the following species were reportedly eaten by Indians, in
spite of their unpleasant taste (the color of the drupes is mentioned in parentheses): *C. amomum* – C. N.Am. – (blue), *occidentalis* (= *pubescens*) – W. Coast –
(white) and *stolonifera*, red osier, American dogwood – N. & W. N.Am. –
(white).

The fruits of various *Cornus* spp. are used as food in Europe and Asia. Those
of the cornelian cherry (*C. mas*), formerly planted as a fruit tree, are delicious

when ripe, with a flavor combining that of raspberries, cherries and red currants.

The bark of the flowering dogwood is astringent, febrifuge, stimulant and tonic.

Ximenia americana (D 5)   Tallowwood Plum
Etymology unknown.
S. Fla., Mex.

The young leaves are edible after cooking.

The fruits can be eaten raw and have a pleasant taste. They are sometimes pickled while still unripe.

The kernel is edible raw or roasted, but large quantities are purgative. It yields by pressure an edible oil, sometimes used for cooking in the tropics.

Two other species are used similarly in South Africa and New Caledonia.

SANTALACEAE

Comandra (D 4)   Bastard Toadflax
From the Greek "komê," hair, and ."anêr, andros," man: referring to the tufts of hair attached to the stamens.
Mostly N. regions & Mountains.

The fruits of *C. pallida* – W. N.Am. –, *richardsiana* – N. N.Am. – and *umbellata* – E. N.Am. – were used as food by Indians. They are best while still slightly green. The seeds are sweet and oily.

C. pallida (m.a.) is known to be a facultative selenium absorber. Its foliage could therefore be toxic.

Geocaulon lividum (G 4)
(= *Comandra livida*)
From the Greek "gaia," the earth, and "kaulos," stem.
N. regions.

The fruit is said to be edible, but of rather unpleasant flavor.

Pyrularia pubera   (G-F 4)   Buffalo Nut
Diminutive of "pyrus," pear: alluding to the shape of the fruit.
E. N.Am.

The <u>fruit</u> has been reported to be edible, but it is bitter and known to be strongly cathartic.
The endosperm contains much oil, which can be extracted by pressure.
The <u>fruits</u> of a local species are eaten in the Himalayas.

LORANTHACEAE

Phoradendron   (E-F 2)   Mistletoe
From the Greek "phor," thief, and "dendron," tree: referring to the parasitic habit of the plant.
Throughout.

Some species are popular as Christmas decorations because of their white, pearl-like berries (similar to those of the European Mistletoe, *Viscum album*), especially *P. flavescens* – S.W. U.S., Mex.

The reddish <u>fruits</u> of *P. californicum*, mesquite mistletoe – S. Calif., Ariz., Baja, Son. – were used as food by Southwestern Indians. The Pimas used to boil the fruit-bearing stems in water and then strip the berries into their mouths; the Papagos simply dried the fruits and stored them. The berries are sweetish, but also bitter, mucilaginous and hardly edible, although much appreciated by birds who transport them to other host trees.

The <u>fruits</u> of *P. juniperinum* – S.W. U.S., Mex. – have reportedly been made into a coffee substitute.

The plant was chewed by Indians as a toothache remedy. A decoction of the leaves can be abortive.

Some species are known to be toxic. The berries of *P. flavescens* (m.a.) are responsible for several children's deaths. Its leaves are emetic and have been used as a nervine and an abortive.

CELASTRACEAE

Celastrus (D-F 4)   Bittersweet

Ancient Greek name of *Phillyrea latifolia*, Oleaceae, from "kelastros."
E. N.Am.
C. scandens, American bittersweet, is native to E. N.Am.

Tender twigs and sweetish inner bark of this shrub were used as food by
some Indian tribes, especially the Chippewas. But the plant is toxic and is
known to have poisoned horses: it contains saponin and euonymin. Long boiling
is therefore indispensable to dispel the poisonous substances.

Two East Asian species are planted for ornament, of which *C. orbiculatus* escapes from cultivation in Eastern North America

The young leaves are eaten boiled in the spring in regions of the Far East
where this shrub is native.

Crossopetalum (D 5)   Christmas Berry

(= *Rhacoma* spp.)
From the Greek "krossos," fringe, border, and "petalon," leaf, petal: re-
ferring to the fringed petals.
S. Fla.

The ripe fruit of *C. ilicifolium* (= *Rhacoma ilicifolia*) and *rhacoma* (= *Rhacoma
crossopetalum*) is said to be edible raw.

AQUIFOLIACEAE

Ilex (E 2)   Holly

Latin name of the Mediterranean live oak (*Quercus ilex*): referring to the
resemblance of the spiny leaves.
E. U.S.
The following native hollies are planted for ornament: *I. cassine*, cassine,
dahoon – S.E. U.S. –, *glabra*, inkberry – E. Coast of N.Am. –, *opaca*,
American holly – E. U.S. –, *verticillata*, black alder, winterberry – E.
N.Am. – and *vomitoria*, yaupon – S.E. U.S. – as well as a few European
and Asian species.

The leaves of the five species mentioned above have been used as tea on our continent.

A light infusion made by roasting the leaves and steeping them in hot water is pleasant to drink and can have diuretic and slightly stimulating effects.

Southeastern Indians used *I. cassine* and *vomitoria* (m.a.) in their purification rituals: a strong infusion of the leaves acts as an emetic (purifying the body by vomiting) and a stimulant. This latter effect is due to the caffeine contained in important amounts in the leaves of dahoon and yaupon. Our other native hollies do not contain caffeine. This

Ilex opaca

well-known alkaloid is present in coffee seeds, tea shoots and maté leaves – the latter is a South American holly (*Ilex paraguariensis*), closely related to dahoon and yaupon. Maté is a stimulant, stomachic and diuretic. It is the principal beverage in parts of South America.

The bark of *I. verticillata* (m.a.) is astringent, febrifuge and tonic.

The berries of several hollies, including *I. opaca* and *verticillata* (m.a.), are cathartic and toxic.

The fruits of a few local species are eaten in East Asia. The young leaves of others are used as food in the same regions.

The leaves of several hollies are made into tea in Brazil. The best known is, as mentioned above, yerba maté.

Nemopanthus   (G 4)   Mountain Holly
From the Greek "nema," thread, "pous," foot, and "anthos," flower: referring to the very slender pedicels.
N.E. N.Am. A monotypic genus.

The fruit of *N. mucronatus* was reportedly used as food by Indians.

BUXACEAE

Simmondsia chinensis (D 2-5)   Jojoba
(= *S. californica*)
After F. W. Simmonds, English naturalist.
Calif., Ariz., Baja, Son. A monotypic genus.
The shrub is cultivated in Ariz. & Calif., as well as in other dry and hot regions of the world (Africa, Australia) for its seeds, which are used commercially.

The reddish-brown <u>seeds</u> are edible raw in moderation. They have a slightly bitter taste which improves after roasting.

Jojoba <u>nuts</u> were an important food for desert Indians, as they are large and the shrubs are prolific.

They have been used as a coffee substitute. In Mexico they are made into a thick drink or confections.

An oil (actually, a liquid wax) can be expressed from the seeds. Jojoba oil is extremely resistant to hard-working industrial conditions such as high temperatures and pressure. It can replace sperm oil, obtained from the brain of the sperm whale; unfortunately, whales are still being destroyed for this ridiculously small portion of their body. Jojoba (the whale-saving plant) is now being cultivated as a substitute for sperm oil, but although the shrub is very drought-resistant, its cultivation is difficult because of its sensitivity to cold temperatures.

Jojoba oil is also commercialized for its beneficial properties for the hair and skin. It has been used instead of beeswax in electrical insulation, varnishes and so on.

EUPHORBIACEAE

Most members of this family contain an acrid, irritating juice, and are generally purgative. Some of them, such as the castor bean, contain extremely toxic substances and are deadly even in small amounts.

Cnidoscolus   (G 4)   Tread Softly, Spurge Nettle
From the Greek "knidê," nettle, and "skolos," thorn: referring to the
stinging hairs of the plant.
S. U.S., Mex.

The <u>tubers</u> of *C. stimulosus* – S.E. U.S. – are edible after cooking. However,
they grow deep in the ground and are difficult to gather.

The plants are called "mala mujer" (bad woman) in Mexico because of the
stinging hairs which can cause a painful inflammation.

The leaves of a related species are eaten cooked in Central America.

Croton   (D-F-H 4)
From the Greek "kroton," tick: ancient name of the castor bean, *Ricinus
communis,* an allusion to the appearance of the seeds.
S. U.S., Mex.
An Asian species (*C. tiglium*) is occasionally planted for ornament in S.
Calif.

The <u>flowering tops</u> of *C. corymbulosus,* chapparal tea, were made into a bitter tea by Indians. They are still sometimes used for this purpose in Mexico.
The plant has a strong odor, like most *Croton* species.

Some species are known to be toxic, especially *C. capitatus* – E. N.Am. – and
texensis – S.W. U.S., Mex. – which have caused cattle poisoning. The hairs of *C.
ciliatoglandulifer* – Tex. – may cause contact dermatitis and conjunctivitis.

A few *Croton* species were used medicinally by Indians, such as *C. californicus* – Calif., Ariz., Baja –, the leaves of which were applied externally to alleviate
rheumatismal pains.

Oil of Croton is extracted from the Asian species mentioned above (*C.
tiglium*). It is a powerful cathartic, and a poison if more than a few drops are ingested. It also strongly irritates the skin, and especially the mucous membranes.

The <u>leaves</u> of a local species are used as tea in tropical Asia.

Endangered species: *C. alabamensis* – Ala., Tenn. –, *elliottii* – Fla., Ala., Ga. –,
glandulosus var. *simpsonii* – Fla. – and *wigginsii* – Calif., Nev.

Euphorbia (E-F-H 1)   Spurge
(including *Poinsettia* spp.)
Ancient Greek and Latin name of the plant, after Euphorbus, physician of
Numidia.
Throughout. Both native and species introduced from Eurasia.
A few native species are cultivated as ornamentals, especially *E. pulcher-
rima* (= *Poinsettia p.*), poinsettia – Mex. – and *marginata,* snow-on-the-
mountain – C. N.Am.

The young tops and leaves of poinsettia are reportedly eaten after being
boiled in Indonesia, where the plant has been introduced.
E. serpyllifolia – C. & W. N.Am. – was chewed and mixed with cornmeal to
flavor it by some Indian tribes.
Among the spurges introduced from Eurasia, the following have been used as
food:

E. helioscopia – naturalized in N.E. N.Am. In Japan, the plant has reportedly been eaten after cooking, or used as tea, but
it is very acrid in the raw stage.

E. lathyris, mole plant – naturalized mostly in E.
N.Am. The unripe fruits are pickled after macerating in brine for several days to remove their acrid
taste. But if improperly prepared, they can be
toxic. People can develop serious dermatitis from
handling the fruits when gathering and preparing
them.

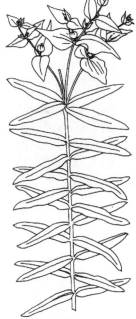

The seeds contain 50% oil. They are emetic.
The young plant was reported to be eaten occasionally in Europe, but it is very acrid.
It has depurative, laxative and expectorant properties.
Its latex contains a caustic substance (euphor-
bone), resin, etc.
The plant is sometimes grown in gardens for its
presumed mole-repelling ability.

Euphorbia lathyris

But most species are vesicant: they contain an acrid milky sap and cause dermatitis in susceptible individuals. The juice of *E. marginata* (m.a.) was used for branding cattle in Texas! If the sap of *E. esula* – introduced from Eur. – and *helioscopia* (m.a.) comes in contact with the eyes, blindness can result.

When taken internally, spurges are irritant, emetic and purgative, and some species cause nervous, hepatic or cardiac disorders as well. Dried in hay, the plants have sometimes proven fatal to cattle, which will usually not eat the fresh plants.

Several spurges have been used medicinally for their purgative effects, and *E. hirta* – S.E. U.S., Mex. – was an officinal drug used for asthma and bronchitis. However, an overdose is almost always toxic for humans.

A few species known as "rattlesnake weed" and "golondrina," including *E. albimarginata* – W. N.Am. –, were employed as a snakebite cure by Southwestern Indians.

Various species are used as food in Asia and in Africa.

Endangered species: *E. fendleri* var. *triligulata* and *golondrina* – both Tex.

Manihot   (C-F-H 5)
Etymology unknown.
A few species are native to S. Ariz., Tex., Mex.
M. esculenta, manioc, originally from Brazil, is naturalized in Fla. & Mex.

The plant is widely cultivated in the tropics for its large root, which is a staple for various populations.

In some varieties, mostly cultivated in Central and South America (where manioc is known as "yuca") and in the West Indies, the root is bitter and toxic in the raw stage. It must be grated and pressed in order to remove the hydrocyanic acid contained in the juice. The remaining solids, known as "cassava," are cooked and dried. They can be eaten by simply mixing with water or milk. The juice left in a container yields a starch which settles at the bottom. This starch is processed into what we know as tapioca, used in soups, puddings and so on.

In other varieties, largely cultivated in Asia and Africa, the root is sweet and edible without processing. It can be eaten raw but is usually cooked, boiled by itself or into a sauce. It has a mild, pleasant flavor.

The root is also dried and ground into flour, sliced and fried into chips or made into an alcoholic beverage by being masticated and then spit into a container (the enzymes in the saliva, ptyalin, allow the starch to become simple sugars which can be transformed into alcohol by yeasts).

Young shoots and leaves of manioc are eaten cooked. They are an important vegetable in Africa, where they are made into sauces to accompany local cereals or rice.

The tubers of a few other tropical American species are used as food.

Endangered species: *M. walkerae* – Tex.

Mercurialis annua (D 4)   Mercury

Latin name of the plant, dedicated to the god Mercury.

Naturalized in E. U.S. from Eurasia.

The plant has been eaten, boiled, in Germany, but toxic effects have occasionally been reported. The fresh plant has an unpleasant smell and taste, but these disappear on cooking.

It contains saponin, a bitter principle, and various substances.

Mercury is diuretic, purgative and possibly emetic. Cooked, it is still slightly laxative, but it loses its action upon drying.

Livestock has reportedly been poisoned by the raw plant, but animals do not usually eat it.

After long boiling, mercury gives wool a greenish-yellow color with blue overtones. It is said to contain a blue coloring matter close to that of indigo (*Indigofera* spp., Fabaceae).

Reverchonia arenaria (G-F 4)

Etymology unknown.

Ariz. to Tex., N. Mex.

The fruit was reportedly eaten by Indians.

The seeds were used by the Hopis for treating hemorrhages and for oiling stone griddles.

The plant is toxic.

Sapium sebiferum   (E 5)   Chinese Tallow Tree
Etymology unknown.
S. U.S., Mex.
Originally from tropical Asia, the tree is planted as an ornamental in the warmest parts of N.Am.; it occasionally escapes from cultivation in S.E. Tex.

Under pressure, the seeds yield an oil which is used for cooking in Asia. This oil is solid at room temperature.
A whitish wax is extracted from the seed coats by boiling in water.
The seeds of a few other species are used as food in Eastern Asia.

RHAMNACEAE

Ceanothus   (D-H 2-3)   Wild Lilac
Greek name used by Dioscorides for some spiny plant, "keanothos."
Throughout.
Several Californian species and hybrids are planted for ornament.

The leaves of *C. americanus*, New Jersey tea – E. N.Am. – have much been used in the United States as a substitute for black tea, which they resemble in taste after a process of slow drying with slight fermentation. A method for curing the leaves was to immerse them in a decoction of leaves and twigs of the shrub, and let them dry in the shade.
The rootbark has been used as an astringent, expectorant and sedative.
C. ovatus – E. & C. N.Am. –, *sanguineus*, Oregon tea tree – N.C. & N.W. N.Am. – and *velutinus*, tobacco brush – W. N.Am. – were also made into tea. Twigs and leaves of *C. sanguineus* (m.a.) have a fragrance reminiscent of wintergreen (*Gaultheria procumbens*, Ericaceae).
The small seeds of *C. fendleri* – S.W. U.S. – and *integerrimus*, deer brush – Calif. to Wash. – were ground into piñole by local Indians.
An infusion of deer brush bark was used as a tonic.
The flowers of wild lilacs are deliciously scented. They contain much nectar: *Ceanothus* spp. are good honey plants.
The flowers foam into a lather when crushed in water.
Endangered species: *C. ferrisae, hearstiorum, maritimus* and *masonii* – all Calif.

Colubrina (D-H 4)   Sankebark
From the Latin "coluber," serpent: of uncertain application.
S.W. U.S., S. Fla., Mex.

The <u>bark</u> of *C. elliptica* (= *C. reclinata*) – S. Fla to Tex., Mex. – is macerated
in water to make a drink which is sold on the streets in the West Indies.
It has astringent, digestive and tonic properties.
The <u>leaves</u> of a tropical species are reportedly eaten raw.
Endangered species: *C. stricta* – Tex.

Condalia (D-H 4)   Crucillo
(including *Ziziphus* spp.)
After A. Condal, Spanish physician.
S. U.S., Mex.

The small <u>fruits</u> of *C. mexicana* – Mex. –, *obovata* – Tex., Nuevo Leon –,
parryi, parry abrojo – S. Calif., Baja – and *spathulata* – Tex., N.M., Mex. – were
used as food by Indians.
The fruits of *C. parryi* (m.a.) are bitter. Coahuila Indians used to pound them
into a meal.
The fruits of *C. mexicana* and *obovata* (m.a.) are slightly acid. They have reportedly been made into jams.
The roots of *C. lycioides* (= *Zizphus l.*) were used as soap. A decoction was employed by Pima Indians to treat sore eyes.
The <u>fruits</u> of a local species are eaten in S. South America.
Endangered species: *C. hookeri* var. *edwardsiana* – Tex.

Gouania lupuloides (E 5)   Chew Stick
(= *G. domingensis*)
Etymology unknown.
S. Fla., Mex.

The bitter and aromatic <u>stems</u> are used for flavoring drinks.
Pieces of the stem are chewed to cleanse the teeth and to harden and heal the
gums.
The <u>young leaves</u> of a local species are eaten in India.

Karwinskia humboldtiana (G-F 5) Coyotillo
Etymology unknown.
W. & S. Tex., Mex.

The pulp of the <u>fruit</u> is reportedly edible.
But the seeds and foliage are toxic and children have been poisoned after eating the berries with the seeds.

Reynosia septentrionalis (B 5) Darling Plum
Etymology unknown.
Fla.

The ripe <u>fruit</u> is edible raw. It is sweet and has a pleasant flavor.

Rhamnus (D 3) Buckthorn
Greek name of a local species, "rhamnos."
Throughout.
Two European species are sometimes planted as ornamentals: *R. cathartica*, formerly much used for hedges and naturalized in E. U.S., and *frangula* (= *Frangula alnus*), alder buckthorn, locally escaped from cultivation.

The <u>fruits</u> of *R. carolinianus* – S.E. U.S. – and *crocea*, redberry – Calif., Baja – were eaten raw or cooked by Indians.

Those of *R. californica*, coffeeberry – Ore., Calif., Ariz., N.M. – have been used, roasted, as a coffee substitute.

However, the fresh fruits of several species, such as *R. cathartica* (m.a.) are emetic and cathartic. When dried, they are purgative, depurative and diuretic, and were used medicinally.

They contain glucosides and other substances.

The bark of *R. purshiana* – W. Coast – is called "cascara sagrada" (sacred bark in Spanish). It is often used medicinally for its gentle laxative action, but only after preparation: the bark must be dried for a year at room temperature, or for an hour in an oven above 210°F. The fresh bark is emetic and cathartic.

It contains glucosides, mucilage, enzymes and other substances, including cyanogenetic glucosides which have a sedative effect.

Though cascara sagrada is not irritating, it must not be employed too frequently, lest intestinal disorders and muscular weakness should occur. This is true with the prolonged use of any laxative.

The European *R. frangula* (m.a.) is used like cascara sagrada.

Its fruits, as well as those of *R. cathartica* (m.a.), are violently purgative and emetic in the fresh stage. Dried fruits of the latter species were used in Europe as a laxative, diuretic and depurative.

Leaves and fruits of a few local species are used as food in Asia.

R. crocea (m.a.) is the alternate host of the crown-rust disease of oats.

Ziziphus (B 5)
From the Arabic "zizuf," name of a Mediterranean species, *Z. lotus*.
S.C. U.S., Mex.
Z. jujuba, jujube – from temperate Asia – is planted as an ornamental and for its fruits in S. U.S. & Mex. It is naturalized, especially in Tex. Several varieties are known.

The reddish-brown fruits are rather acid when fresh and are commonly dried. Dried jujubes are sweet and flavorful. They are sometimes roasted or cooked in honey.

An edible oil is extracted from their kernel in S. India.

Jujubes contain sugars, mucilage, pectin and organic acids.

When dried, they are emollient, demulcent and pectoral.

The young leaves of a variety are eaten boiled in E. Asia.

Among our native species, the fruits of *Z. endlichii* – Mex. – and *obtusifolia* – Okla., Tex., N.M., Ariz. & Mex. – are eaten locally in Mexico.

Those of *Z. lycioides* (= *Condalia l.*) – Ariz. to Tex., Mex. – were reportedly used as food by Indians.

The fruits of many *Ziziphus* spp. are eaten in Europe, Africa and Asia.

Vitaceae

Parthenocissus quinquefolia   (G 2)   Virginia Creeper

From the Greek "parthenos," virgin, and "kissos," ivy: free translation of "Virginia creeper."

E. N.Am.

The plant is cultivated as an ornamental.

The <u>young shoots</u> have reportedly been eaten cooked, and the <u>fruits</u> raw. But the plant is considered by some to be toxic, especially the fruits.

The twigs have been used as an astringent, tonic and expectorant. They were sometimes made into a cough syrup.

The fruits are said to give wool a pink color.

An East Asian species, Boston ivy (*P. tricuspidata*) is sometimes planted for ornament.

The <u>sap</u> of this vine was used in Japan as a sweetener before the introduction of sugar.

The <u>berries</u> of a local species are used as food in the Himalayas.

Vitis   (B 1)   Grape

Latin name of the plant.

Throughout.

A few native and Asian species are planted as ornamentals.

Our native *V. aestivalis*, summer grape – E. N.Am. –, *berlandieri* – Tex., N.M. –, *rotundifolia*, muscadine grape – E. U.S. –, *rupestris* – C. U.S. –, *vulpina* (= *cordifolia*), frost or chicken grape – E. & C. U.S. – and especially *labruscana* are grown for their fruits on our continent. Improved by cultivation, they yield excellent table grapes. *V. labruscana* (m.a.) is the group of cultivated strains, including many hybrids, originating from *V. labrusca*, fox grape – E. U.S. Several varieties are known, including the Concord, Catawba, Niagara, Chautauqua and Worden grapes. They are sometimes found as escapes. *V. rotundifolia* (m.a.) is the ancestor of the cultivated Scuppernong variety, the best known of the muscadine grapes.

The native species mentioned have been used in Europe as grafting stocks since the epidemic of phylloxera, which wiped out most of the French vineyard at the end of the 19th century. They are immune to the disease.

Most commercial wines are made from varieties of the Eurasian Grape, *V. vinifera* – occasionally established locally in wine-producing areas (Calif., Ore., Wash., N.Y.). One of the oldest cultivated plants, more than 3,000 varieties are known.

Young shoots and leaves of all species are edible raw or cooked. They generally have a pleasant, acid flavor, but are usually astringent and in some cases rather bitter.

The leaves are sometimes preserved in brine. Stuffed with rice, they are a common dish in Greece, Turkey and the Middle East.

The red-colored leaves of a variety of *V. vinifera* are used medicinally as a venous tonic.

The sap of grapevines can be drunk. It is obtained by cutting part of the stem and draining it into a container, but this brutal process can kill the plant. Small quantities of sap exude from the tips of the vines in the spring, but it is hard to gather on wild plants that climb to the tops of surrounding trees.

It is diuretic and depurative.

Wild grapes were an important food for Indians. In many cases, the ripe fruits are sweet, aromatic, and excellent raw, although often thick skinned. They can be juiced and have a beneficial depurative effect on the body. In some species, they are sour at first and become sweeter with the coming of the frosts. Others are never very palatable raw. Wild grapes are often made into jelly.

Grapes can be crushed and left to ferment into wine. But to get good results, specific varieties and a definite know-how are required.

Acetic fermentation transforms wine into vinegar. The juice expressed from unripe grapes, verjuice, was much used instead of vinegar in Europe, up until the 18th century.

Grapes contain vitamins A, B1, B2, C, niacin and rutin, minerals, sugars (10-15%), pectin, and organic acids (malic, tartric). Black grapes also contain a glucosidic pigment (oenocyanine) with tonic properties.

Grapes are diuretic, laxative, refrigerant, and detoxicant.

Dried grapes, called "raisins" or "currants," are emollient, demulcent and pectoral.

Skins and seeds contain tannin.

The seeds also contain important amounts of an edible oil which must be heat extracted, but does not become rancid and can be used for cooking. It is rich in vitamin E and in polyunsaturated fatty acids, hence its ability to lower the blood cholesterol level. Grapeseed oil is produced commercially, using cultivated fruits.

The following species have been used as food on our continent (the color of the berries is in parentheses): *V. aestivalis* (m.a.) (dark purple or black); *arizonica* – Ariz. –, *baileyana* – S.E. U.S. – (black); *berlandieri* (m.a.), *californica* – Calif., S. Ore. – (purple); *caribaea* – Mex. –, *cinerea*, graybark grape – E. U.S. – (black); *girdiana* – Calif., Baja – (black); *labrusca* (m.a.) (dark red to black); *labruscana* (m.a.), *lincecumii* – Mo. to La., Tex. –, *riparia*, riverbank grape – E. & C. N.Am. – (black); *rotundifolia* (m.a.), *rupestris* (m.a.) (black); *shuttleworthii*, Calusa grape – S. Fla. – and *vulpina* (m.a.) (black).

V. riparia (m.a.) is sometimes planted as an ornamental because of the brilliance of its fall foliage.

The fruits of many local species are eaten in Asia and Africa, including those of an Asian species planted for ornament in North America (*V. coignetiae*).

STAPHYLEACEAE

Staphylea (D 4)   Bladder Nut
From the Greek "staphylê," bunch of ripe grapes: referring to the clustered flowers.
Almost throughout.

The oily seeds of *S. trifolia* – E. N.Am. – are edible.
Those of a European species (*S. pinnata*) have been used as food in Germany. They taste somewhat like pistachios.
The leaves of a local species were eaten cooked in N.E. Asia.

SAPINDACEAE

Cardiospermum (D 4)   Balloon Vine, Heartseed
From the Greek "kardia," heart, and "sperma," seed: the black seeds of *C. halicacabum* bear a white heart-shaped spot.
C. corindum is native to S. Fla.
C. halicacabum, originally from tropical regions, is cultivated as a curiosity for its inflated, bladder-like fruits; it is naturalized in S. & E. U.S. & Mex.

Young shoots and leaves are eaten cooked in Asia and Africa.
The seeds are made into necklaces.

Dodonea (E 4)   Hopbush
Etymology unknown.
S. U.S., Mex.

The winged <u>fruits</u> of *D. viscosa* have been used as a substitute for hops in beer making.

The sticky leaves were used medicinally by Indians. They contain saponin and are more or less toxic; the foliage was used as a fish poison in various countries (the plant is native to tropical and subtropical areas of both hemispheres).

A cultivar, *D. viscosa* "purpurea," is sometimes planted for ornament.

Sapindus (E 3)   Soapberry
Contraction from the Latin "sapo indicus," Indian soap: so named because the pulp of the fruit lathers in water.
S. U.S., Mex.

The <u>fruits</u> of *S. marginatus* were used as food by Indians. They were sometimes pounded into cakes.

Those of *S. saponaria,* Southern soapberry – Fla., Mex. – contain much saponin and are used as soap in tropical America. They are sold for this purpose in Central American markets; when mashed in water, the fruits yield abundant suds.

The fruits have also served as fish poison. Sensitive individuals can get dermatitis from handling them. The same is true with the fruits of *S. drumondii* – S.C. U.S., Mex.

The foliage of these trees is considered to be poisonous to livestock.

HIPPOCASTANACEAE

Aesculus (B-F 3)   Buckeye
Latin name of an oak.
Throughout.
Our native *A. parviflora* – S.E. U.S. – and the S.E. European horse chestnut, *A. hippocastanum*, are planted for ornament. The latter tends to escape from cultivation.

Buckeye seeds are rich in saponin. In large amounts, this substance is toxic as it destroys red blood cells (hemolysis). Fortunately, it is easily eliminated by boiling the seeds in water.

The seeds are therefore safe to eat after cooking in several changes of water, preferably chopped up or ground. They can be used after processing as a starchy, nutritious base for various dishes.

The seeds of *A. californica*, California buckeye – Calif. –, *octandra*, sweet buckeye – C.E. U.S. – and *parviflora* (m.a.) were eaten by Indians. They were baked in a fire pit until soft, then sliced and immersed in running water for several days.

Raw, they served as a fish poison.

Horse chestnuts, the seeds of *A. hippocastanum* (m.a.), can be used as food after processing (boiling in several changes of water) to remove the toxic principles.

Besides saponin, they contain a glucoside (esculoside), tannin and various substances. The bark of the tree has a similar composition.

Horse chestnuts are used medicinally to activate blood circulation. They also have astringent, diuretic and antiphlogistic properties.

The green husk of the fruit and the unprocessed seeds can produce digestive and nervous disorders.

Honey from the nectar of horse chestnut flowers can be toxic.

Leaves and seeds of various buckeyes have poisoned livestock.

The seeds of two local species have been used as food in Asia.

ACERACEAE

Acer (C 3)   Maple
Latin name of the tree.
Throughout.
Several native, European and Asian species are planted for ornament and as shade trees, especially, among our native species: *A. negundo*, box elder, *rubrum*, red maple – E. N.Am. –, *saccharinum*, silver maple – E. & C. N.Am. – and *saccharum*, sugar maple – E. & N.C. N.Am.

From the trunk of many of our species, it is possible to extract a sweet sap which can be concentrated into syrup and sugar by boiling. In early spring, warm, sunny days followed by very cold nights are required in order for the sap to rise at its best in quantity and quality (sugar content). New England and Eastern Canada, the main maple syrup producing areas, are typically endowed with such spring weather. The climate actually plays a larger part than does the species of the tree.

Most commonly used nowadays is *A. saccharum* (m.a.), although *A. negundo* (m.a.) is often considered to be superior as far as yield of sugar goes. The average yield is approximately 1 pound of sugar for 4 gallons of sap.

Indians used to also collect the sap of other species, such as *A. grandidentatum* – W. N.Am. –, *nigrum*, black maple – N.E. N.Am. –, *rubrum* (m.a.) and *saccharinum* (m.a.). They used maple syrup and sugar long before the coming of the Europeans. The sap was placed in a bark container and boiled by throwing red-hot stones into it. (This effective process was also used for making soups, mush and so on.)

Another totally different method was used: The sap was left to freeze overnight and the ice formed was removed every morning, thus reducing the water content of the sap. But above a certain sugar concentration, the liquid ceases to freeze and it cannot become a thick syrup, unless further reduced by boiling.

Left in contact with the air, the partly reduced sap ferments spontaneously into a pleasant drink. It is rapidly transformed into vinegar by acetic fermentation.

Maple syrup contains saccharose (like beet or cane sugar) and minerals, especially calcium, phosphorus and iron.

The inner bark of the trunk of the various maples is edible. That of A. saccharinum and saccharum (m.a.) was dried, ground and mixed with flour to make bread in Northeast North America.

The tender young leaves are good raw or cooked. They are rich in sugar.

The young fruits, typically winged, are sometimes pickled.

Their seeds are edible, but often bitter. They can be boiled in a change of water.

Those of local species were eaten in Asia.

The bark of maples dyes wool olive-green with alum and gray with ferrous sulfate.

Sap, leaves and seeds of several species have been used as food in Europe and Asia. Some of these are planted as ornamentals in North America.

BURSERACEAE

Bursera   (G 5)
After J. Burser, a 16th-century botanist.
S. Fla., Calif., Ariz. & Mex.

The leaves of *B. simaruba*, gumbo limbo – S. Fla., Mex. – are made into tea in the West Indies.

The twigs of *B. fragarioides* – S. Ariz., Mex. – and *microphylla*, elephant tree – S.E. Calif., S. Ariz., N.W. Mex. – yield a quantity of an essential oil with an odor close to that of tangerine. They are the source of a fragrant resin which is burned as incense in Mexico. That of other species, known as "copal," was burned in Aztec and Mayan temples and is still in use today in Central America.

The gum or resin of the elephant tree is also used to treat venereal diseases, as a cement, and for making a varnish.

The bark of this tree contains much tannin and was gathered in Sonora to be exported. Older bark can be removed in thin, transluscent sheets resembling parchment.

The foliage is aromatic.

Leaves and fruits of a few tropical American and Asian species are used as food.

ANACARDIACEAE

Cyrtocarpa edulis   (G 5)
From the Greek "kyrtos," curved, convex, and "karpos," fruit.
Mex.

The yellow fruit is said to be edible when ripe. The inside kernel can be eaten as well.

Mangifera indica   (B 5)   Mango
From the Tamil "mankay"(via the Portuguese "manga"), name of the fruit, and the Latin "fero," to bear.
Originally from tropical Asia, the tree is cultivated for its fruits in the warmest parts of our continent; it is naturalized locally in S. Fla & Mex. Many varieties are known.

Ripe mangoes have a juicy, aromatic, orange-colored pulp, which is delicious raw. They are also made into jams and chutneys.

The green fruits are cooked into sauces, curries in India or pickled. In Mexico they are peeled and eaten raw with cayenne pepper. They have a definite turpentine flavor.

Mangoes are rich in vitamins A and C.

The kernel is edible after cooking. It is often bitter, and in this case requires boiling in a change of water. In tropical Asia it is made into pudding or confectionary.

The fruits of many other species are eaten in Southeast Asia.

Pistacia (D 5)   Wild Pistachio
Greek and Latin name of a Mediterranean species.
Tex., Mex.
A Chinese species (*P. chinensis*) is sometimes planted for ornament.

In our native species *P. mexicana* – Mex. – and *texana* – Tex. –, the kernel of the small fruit is edible.

The commercial pistachio is the large kernel of a West Asian tree of the same genus (*P. vera*). Pistachios are eaten whole, roasted and used in confectionary, in making ice cream, etc. (although they are often replaced today by artificial coloring and flavoring). They are especially prized in the Middle East.

Pistachios are rich in protein and oil.

Leaves, gum and seeds of several species including the Chinese species mentioned above, are used as food in Southern Europe, Asia and Africa.

Rhus (D-F-H 3)   Sumac, Poison Ivy
Greek and Latin name of a Mediterranean species.
Throughout.
Our native *R. aromatica*, fragrant sumac – C. & S.E. U.S. –, *copallina*, dwarf sumac – E. U.S. –, *glabra*, smooth sumac, and *typhina*, staghorn sumac – N.E. N.Am. – are planted for ornament, as well as an African species.

The genus *Rhus* can be divided into two subgenera.

The species contained in the subgenus *Toxicodendron* must be, to some

people, the most obnoxious plants
in North America. Their toxicity is
due to a virulent but selective contact poison (urushiol).

These species are *R. diversiloba*,
Western poison oak – Baja to
Wash. –, *radicans*, poison ivy – almost
throughout –, *toxicodendron*, poison
oak – E. & C. N.Am. – and *vernix*,
poison sumac – E. N.Am.

But poison ivy and poison oak are
bothersome only to susceptible individuals. For others, the young leaves
are edible: California Indians would
sometimes mix poison oak leaves
with their acorn meal, and often lined
their fire pits with them. Not all Indi-

Rhus typhina

ans were naturally immune to the poison, but by eating tiny fragments of the
leaves in early spring and slowly increasing the doses, they would create an im-
munity in their bodies for the rest of the year. This method of immunization is
efficacious and can be practiced by most people, provided they are not dangerously allergic to these plants.

Species in this subgenus are easily recognized by their white fruits, when
present.

On the other hand, all species in the subgenus *Rhus* are harmless shrubs, generally known as sumac, and bear red fruits.

These small fruits are coated with red hairs filled with a sour liquid, rich in
malic acid.

They are often steeped in cold water to make a refreshing drink, hence one
of the common names of the shrub, "lemonade berry." If hot water is used however, some tannin will be extracted and the resulting beverage will be astringent
and rather bitter. The fruits should be gathered before they are too old and
tasteless.

The fruits were also used as food by Indians. They can be dried, ground,
sifted and mixed with flour.

The following species have been gathered on our continent: *R. aromatica* (m.a.), *choriophylla* – N.M., Ariz., Son. –, *copallina* (m.a.), *glabra* (m.a.), *integrifolia*, lemonade berry – S. Calif., Baja –, *kearneyi* – S.W. Ariz. –, *microphylla* – W. Tex. to Ariz., N. Mex. –, *ovata*, sugar bush – S. Calif., Ariz., Baja –, *trilobata*, squaw berry – W. N.Am. – and *typhina* (m.a.).

The waxy substance coating the leaves of the sugar bush might be of interest as food.

Southwestern Indians used to smoke the leaves of local species and use the twigs for weaving baskets. The stems of poison ivy and poison oak were also used for this purpose.

The bark of sumacs is astringent. The leaves are astringent and diuretic. The beverage made from the fruits is diuretic, refrigerant, febrifuge and tonic.

Leaves and fruits of local species are used as food in various parts of the world, especially in Asia. In the Middle East, the fruits of a Mediterranean species (*Rhus coriaria*) are crushed and mixed with salt to use as a condiment, known as "sumac," on meat and other dishes.

Japanese lacquer is produced by an East Asian tree of this genus (*R. verniciflua*). The tree has been introduced into the United States, but is rarely planted because of its poisonous properties which are due to urushiol, the same volatile oil as in poison ivy.

Endangered species: *R. kearneyi* (m.a.).

Schinus   (D-F 4)   Pepper Tree
Greek name of a Mediterranean shrub of the same family, *Pistacia lentiscus*, "schinos."

Originally from tropical America, these trees are planted for ornament in S. U.S. & Mex.; they are naturalized locally.

The small pink fruits of *S. molle* and *terebinthifolius* are sweetish, slightly pungent and aromatic. They can be used as a condiment, in moderation; they are often included in spice mixtures sold in supermarkets.

The seeds have been said to be possibly toxic.

In South America, an intoxicating beverage was reportedly made with the fruits by some Indian tribes.

The leaves can be chewed as a breath-freshener.

The fruits of a few local species have been used in South America.

Spondias purpurea   (D 5)   Hog Plum, Red Mombin
Etymology unknown.
Originally from tropical Am., the tree is planted and naturalized in S. Fla. & Mex.

The <u>fruit</u> is eaten raw or cooked. It is sometimes dried, or made into jelly or jam.
The <u>fruits</u> of several species are used as food in the tropics.

SIMARUBACEAE

Ailanthus altissima   (G-F 5)   Tree of Heaven
(= *A. glandulosa*)
From "ailanto," Moluccan name said to signify "tree of heaven."
Calif.
Originally from China, this tree is often planted for ornament and for shade; it is naturalized in Calif., where it was introduced by the Chinese in early mining days, and elsewhere in N.Am.

The <u>leaves</u> were reportedly eaten in times of famine in China. They have a characteristic smell of roasted almonds.
They were also used for growing silkworms. But the leaves cause dermatitis in some people and the sap of the tree is vesicant.

Simaruba glauca   (D 5)   Paradise Tree
Etymology unknown.
S. Fla., Mex.

The <u>kernels</u> yield an edible oil, used for cooking and manufactured into margarine in Central America.
The seed residue is toxic.

Rutaceae

Citrus (B 5)
Latin name of the citron tree – *C. medica* – and of a thuja.
S. Fla., Mex.
Originally from tropical Asia, several of these trees are cultivated in S. U.S.
& Mex. for their fruits and as ornamentals. The following are naturalized
in S. Fla. & Mex.:

C. aurantiifolia (= *C. limetta*), lime
The fruits are often used while still green. They turn yellow at maturity.
Limes have a very sour, acid pulp. Lime juice is used like lemon juice for drinks
and salad dressings.
An essential oil expressed from the rind is used as a flavoring. It is photody-
namic and can irritate the skin.

C. aurantium, sour orange
This is often planted as a street tree in Southern United States (rather than
the sweet orange, *C. sinensis*) since its fruits are inedible raw and will not com-
pete with commercially sold oranges.
The pulp of the fruit is sour and bitter. Although it cannot be eaten raw (ex-
cept for its juice in salad dressings), it makes excellent marmalades.
In Asia, immature fruits are pickled, fried or candied.
The rind is used for flavoring cakes, desserts and liquors, such as curaçao. It
can be dried and ground.
Sour oranges contain an essential oil, vitamin C, citric acid, a bitter principle
and various substances.
They are tonic, aperitive, stomachic and carminative, especially the bark.
The seeds are laxative.
Oil of orange is expressed from the rind.
Oil of petit grain is distilled from the leaves.
The leaves themselves give a fragrant tea, with sedative, antispasmodic and
stomachic properties.
Oil of neroli is distilled from the fragrant flowers. It is used in perfumery, es-
pecially for cologne water.
A byproduct of distillation is orange flower water, still commonly used in Eu-
rope as a sedative and antispasmodic. The flowers have the same properties.

This aromatic water can be used to flavor fruit salads, cakes, drinks, etc. It is commonly used in North Africa. The flowers themselves can be added to various desserts.

Crushed leaves and fruits of this tree have been used as soap and as shampoo.

C. limon (= C. limonia = C. limonium), lemon

Cultivars are planted for ornament. The yellow fruit with a sour pulp is well-known and used worldwide for making salad dressings, beverages (lemonade) and for flavoring various dishes. The juice is bottled and commercialized.

Lemons contain vitamins A, B1, B2, C and niacin, minerals, organic acids (citric, malic), glucides, an essential oil and other substances.

They are antiseptic, refrigerant, tonic, depurative, astringent and have an anti-venomous action. The seeds are anthelmintic. In large quantities, lemons demineralize the body due to their acidity.

They are a commercial source of citric acid.

The aromatic rind can be used for flavoring cakes and desserts, provided the tree has been grown organically and the fruits have not been treated with poisons for shipping. It can also be candied.

It is tonic, stomachic and carminative.

The essential oil extracted by pressure is used in perfumery and as a flavoring. When pure, it can irritate the skin of sensitive individuals.

In Asia, the dried leaves are sometimes mixed with black tea to enhance its flavor.

The leaves are said to repel insects.

C. medica, citron

The large fruits have an inedible, dry pulp. The thick, aromatic rind is candied or used for making liquors, especially in the Mediterranean region (such as cedratine, in Corsica).

C. sinensis, sweet orange

Also naturalized in Central Florida, this is one of the most popular fruits in the world and one of the most important crops of Florida and Southern California. Many varieties are in cultivation.

The generally sweet and aromatic pulp of the fruit is delicious raw. Fresh orange juice is an excellent drink, supposedly filled with vitamin C. This is only true if the juice has been freshly pressed, as vitamin C is highly sensitive to oxidation: Contact with the oxygen in the air destroys it rapidly. It is also very sensitive to heat. Lemons and oranges are held to be extremely high in vitamin C, but watercress (*Nasturtium officinale*) contains almost twice as much of this much needed vitamin, poke shoots (*Phytolacca americana*) three times as much, and roseships (*Rosa* spp.) up to fifty times more. However, among commercial fruits, *Citrus* spp. are the richest in vitamin C.

Orange juice is also used for flavoring sherbets, ice cream, jellies, confections and so on. It is commercially canned, packed and frozen.

Oranges contain vitamins A, B, C and niacin, minerals, organic acids (citric, malic, tartric), glucides, an essential oil and various substances.

They are tonic, stomachic and refrigerant.

The rind is used for flavoring desserts, or as tea – it is especially good after being lightly roasted. It is also candied or made into marmalade.

But oranges are usually treated with toxic products on and off the tree. In order to use the rind, care must be taken that the fruits were produced organically and shipped without having been sprayed.

Leaves and flowers can be used like those of the sour orange, and have similar properties. Once again, they can only be employed if the trees have not been treated. Orange flowers, although slightly bitter, are delightful in fruit salads.

The following species persist on old cultivation sites in the same areas:

C. grandis (= *C. decumana*), shaddock, pumelo

This is the largest of all our *Citrus*, resembling a huge grapefruit. Its rind, externally pale yellow, is very thick. The pulp is sweet and pleasant to eat raw.

In Asia, the peel is candied and a liqueur is made from the fruit.

C. paradisi, grapefruit

A cultivated hybrid; several varieties are known.

The large yellow fruits are very popular in the United States. Their bitterness is quite pleasant, but more recent varieties, often with a pink or red pulp, are not bitter at all. They are generally eaten as an appetizer before a meal or as a breakfast fruit.

Fresh grapefruit juice is an excellent drink. It is also commercially canned.

Grapefruits contain vitamins A, B, C and niacin, minerals, citric acid, an essential oil and various substances.

They are tonic, stomachic, depurative and refrigerant.

C. reticulata (= *C. nobilis*), mandarin
The cultivar 'Deliciosa' is known as "tangerine."
The small fruit, sweet and aromatic, is eaten raw.
It is slightly sedative.
Many other species are used for their edible fruits in East Asia.

Poncirus trifoliata (D 5) Trifoliate Orange
From the old French "poncire," a kind of citron.
Originally from Eastern Asia, this small tree is planted as a stock for grafting *Citrus* spp., and also as an ornamental; it escapes from cultivation in S. U.S. & Mex.

The small fruits are bitter and inedible, but their rind is used to flavor drinks and desserts.
The young leaves are reportedly boiled in a change of water and eaten in Asia.

Ptelea (D 3) Hop Tree, Wafer Ash
Greek name of a European elm (*Ulmus* sp.): the winged fruits of this tree resemble those of an elm.
Almost throughout.
The bitter, aromatic fruits of *P. trifoliata* – E. N.Am. – have been used to replace hops for flavoring beer.

They were sometimes ground, sifted and mixed with meal or flour to make bread.
The root bark is tonic and stomachic. It has occasionally been used as a quinine substitute.
The fruits of *P. angustifolia* (= *P. baldwinii*) and *pallida* – S.W. U.S., Mex. – can be used like those of *P. trifoliata* (m.a.).
However, some people suffer from dermatitis after contact with the leaves of *P. angustifolia* (m.a.).
It has been reported that the fruits of *P. tomentosa* – S.W. U.S., Mex. – were locally eaten by children.

Ruta (B-F 5) Rue
Greek and Latin name of the plant.
Scattered throughout.
Originally from the Eastern Mediterranean area, *R. graveolens* is sometimes cultivated in gardens and occasionally found as an escape here and there in N.Am.

The strongly scented <u>leaves</u> have been used as a condiment for centuries. They were formerly highly esteemed, especially in Roman times. Rue is excellent when added in moderation to salads; the flavor surpasses the odor. When dried, their smell and taste resemble somewhat that of tarragon. Fresh rue was mixed with garlic, olive oil, vinegar and aged goat cheese by the Romans to make one of their favorite condiments, "moretum."
The plant contains an essential oil and a glucoside, rutin.
It is emmenagogue, stomachic, carminative, antispasmodic, diaphoretic and anthelmintic. Large doses are abortive (rue was much used for this property in the past) and toxic.
The fresh leaves may cause dermatitis and photosensitization in certain individuals.
They also repel insects.
The <u>leaves</u> of *R. chalepensis* – native in the Mediterranean area, escaped from cultivation in Calif. – are used in the same manner as those of the previous species.

Triphasia trifolia (D 5) Limeberry
Etymology unknown.
Originally from S.E. Asia, the shrub is sometimes cultivated and naturalized in S. Fla. & Mex.

The small <u>fruit</u> is called the "miracle fruit" for a peculiar reason: It has the quality of communicating a strong, sweet taste to any food taken after the fruit was chewed raw. This effect lasts for several hours.
In Asia, it is made into jams or pickles.

ZYGOPHYLLACEAE

Larrea (E 2) Creosote Bush
After J. A. de Larrea, Spanish scientist.
S.W. U.S., Mex.

The flower buds of *L. mexicana* – Mex. – have reportedly been pickled and eaten like capers.

The twigs are sometimes chewed in Mexico to quench the thirst.

Beans cooked in the presence of creosote bush smoke – including that of *L. tridentata* (= *L. divaricata*), the most widespread species – acquire a special flavor.

The strong-smelling resinous leaves have often been used medicinally by Indians and Mexicans. Those of *L. tridentata* (m.a.) are sold in U.S. herb stores under the improper name of "chaparral" and are used as an antiseptic.

The gum exuded at the branch nodes contains a substance which prevents fats and oils from becoming rancid.

The small resinous incrustations caused by the lac scale insect (*Tachardiella larreae*) was gathered by Indians and utilized for fixing arrow points and for mending pottery.

Livestock do not usually eat the foliage, but sheep are reported to have been poisoned from grazing on it.

Tribulus (G 4) Puncture Vine
Latin name of the plant, from the Greek "tribolos," caltrop: referring to the aspect of the fruit.
T. cistoides, bur nut, is native to S.E. U.S. & Mex.
T. terrestris, originally from warm regions of the Old World, is naturalized in N.Am.

It has been reported that in Asia, the young leaves were eaten after boiling, while the capsules and their seeds were pounded and mixed with flour in times of scarcity.

Sheep have been poisoned by eating the raw plant, which has photosensitizing properties.

The spiny burs produce mechanical injury (both externally and internally) in livestock.

Another species is occasionally eaten in Asia and Northeast Africa.

OXALIDACEAE

Oxalis (B 1) Wood Sorrel

Greek name of sorrel (*Rumex acetosa*), from "oxys," sour, acid.
Throughout. Both native and species introduced from Eur., S. Africa &
S.Am.
A few *Oxalis* spp. are planted for ornament and some are naturalized.

The tuberous roots of *O. deppei*, *esculenta* and *tetraphylla* – all Mex. – have
been used as food for centuries in Mexico.

Their acidity is removed by parboiling, or drying in the sun for a week. The
tubers are then generally boiled or roasted.

O. deppei and *tetraphylla* (both m.a) have been cultivated as root vegetables in
Europe.

In Peru, the tubers of related species (*O. carnosa* and *crenata*), known as
"oca," are processed into "caui" (the tubers are dried and become sweet) and
"chuño de oca" (the tubers are frozen, then soaked in water where they ferment
and acquire a strong taste resembling that of some aged cheeses). Oca tubers
reach the size of an egg. They contain approximately 10% starch.

Other species, such as *O. cernua* (= *O. pes-caprae*) – naturalized from S. Africa
in S. U.S. & Mex. – have small, fleshy, sour-tasting roots which can be
eaten.

The aerial parts (leaves with their petioles, flowers, young fruits) of various
Oxalis spp. are edible raw, added to salads, to which their acidity brings a pleasant note.

The leaves have been fermented into a
kind of sauerkraut.

Macerated in water (they can first be boiled
for a few minutes), they make a refreshing
lemonade, to which sugar or honey can be
added.

The plant can also be made into a green
sauce to accompany various dishes.

The extracted juice can be used like vinegar.

The young fruits, still tender, can be added
raw to salads or other dishes for their crisp texture and pleasant sour taste.

Oxalis corniculata

The following species have been most commonly eaten on our continent: *O. acetosella* – N.E. & N.C. N.Am., Appalachians, also in Eurasia (American plants are sometimes separated as *O. montana*) –, *cernua* (m.a.), *corniculata* – naturalized from Eur. – *dillenii* – a cosmopolitan weed, S. U.S. & Mex. –, *oregana*, redwood sorrel – Calif. to Wash. –, *stricta* – E. & C. N.Am. – and *violacea* – E. & C. U.S.

All species contain oxalic acid and potassium oxalate.

In moderation, they are depurative, diuretic and stomachic. But in large amounts they are irritating, due to their oxalate content. They can produce renal and digestive disorders similar to those caused by sorrel (see *Rumex* spp., Polygonaceae), which contains the same substances.

People who are subject to arthritis, rheumatism, gout, asthma and kidney stones should abstain from eating wood sorrel.

Regular ingestion of the plant over a long period of time (several months) can inhibit the body's absorption of calcium.

A few species are used as food in South America and Asia.

GERANIACEAE

Erodium   (B 1)   Filaree, Storksbill
From the Greek "erôdios," heron: the fruits resemble a heron's beak.
Throughout. Introduced from Eurasia.

The leaves of *E. cicutarium* were eaten raw or cooked by Indians. They are astringent.
The plant contains tannin.
It is astringent and hemostatic.
The leaves of *E. moschatum* are edible as well but they are bitter.
A few local species are used as food in North Africa.

Geranium   (E 3)   Geranium, Cranesbill
Greek name of the plant, from "geranos," crane: the fruits resemble a crane's bill.
Throughout. Both native and species introduced from Eurasia.
Various native and exotic species are planted for ornament.

The <u>leaves</u> of several *Geranium* spp. are edible raw or cooked, but they are generally bitter and astringent.

G. robertianum, herb robert – N.E. & N.C. N.Am., also in Eurasia – contains tannin, an essential oil and a bitter substance (geranine). The plant is astringent and vulnerary.

Local species are used in East Asia, mostly for making tea.

Pelargonium   (B 5)   Geranium, Pelargonium

From the Greek "pelargos," stork: by analogy with the other members of the family.

S. Calif.

Several S. African species and garden hybrids are grown for ornament. The following occasionally escape from cultivation in S. Calif.:

P. peltatum, ivy geranium, and *zonale*, horseshoe geranium. The <u>leaves</u> of these two species are cooked and eaten as vegetables by natives in South Africa.

P. capitatum and *graveolens*, rose geranium, scented geranium. The <u>leaves</u> of these shrubs are very fragrant. Different varieties exist, as well as other species, each with a definite odor reminiscent of such things as rose, mint, lemon, apple and nutmeg.

They can be used for flavoring salads, desserts, jams and drinks and make excellent teas. Raisins placed in a metal box with layers of rose geranium leaves in between take on a delicious fragrance and can be used in fruit salads or cakes.

Rose geranium leaves contain an essential oil which is often distilled as a replacement for rose oil, since the latter is extremely expensive.

Geranium oil is tonic, astringent and antiseptic. It can be used as an insecticide.

A few South African *Geranium* spp. are edible, including some of our cultivated species.

LIMNANTHACEAE

Floerkea proserpinacoides   (B 3)   False Mermaid
After H. G. Flörke (1764–1835), German botanist.
Mostly N. N.Am. A monotypic genus.

The plant is tender and spicy. It is good to eat raw.

TROPAEOLACEAE

Tropaeolum majus   (B 4)   Nasturtium
Diminutive form of the Latin "tropaeum"; in Greek "tropaion," trophy:
the leaves have the form of a shield and the flowers are helmet shaped.
S. U.S., Mex.
Originally from the W. Coast of S.Am., the plant is widely cultivated for
ornament and often naturalized in warm areas. Another species, from
Mex. (*T. peregrinum*), is also planted as an ornamental.

The plant has an aromatic, pungent taste. It has occasionally been cultivated
as a vegetable in Europe. Leaves and flowers can be added raw to salads or used
as a condiment, while flower buds and young fruits, still tender, are pickled.

The flowers can be stuffed.

The taste of nasturtium is strongly reminiscent of that of garden cress (*Lepidium sativum*, Brassicaceae). The chemical composition of both plants is actually
very similar: They contain the same sulfur-containing glucoside (glucotropaeo-
line) which breaks down by hydrolysis into sugar (glucose) and substances with
antibiotic effects (benzyle isothiocyanate), under the action of a ferment (tro-
paeolase).

But if the ferment is not activated, due to a temperature too low or too high,
toxic compounds (benzyle cyanate) will form. It might therefore be worthwhile
to chop up the plant and let it steep in lukewarm water for a few minutes before
using it. But chewing well will also produce the desired result.

Nasturtium is rich in vitamin C and sulfur.

It is antiseptic, stimulant, expectorant, diuretic, emmenagogue and antiscorbutic.

The seeds have reportedly been eaten after roasting.

Other species are used as food in South America. Some are cultivated in the

Andes for their tubers, which are generally improved by cooking and freezing, or by drying in the sun for a few days. They can also be pickled.

BALSAMINACEAE

Impatiens (B-F 3)   Jewelweed, Touch-me-not
From the Latin "impatiens," impatient: referring to the fruits which explode at maturity.
Throughout. Both native and species introduced from Eurasia.
Some African and Asian species are commonly planted for ornament; some escape from cultivation.

Leaves and tender stems of different species are edible after boiling in a change of water (the cooking water must be discarded).
The raw plants are emetic.
I. biflora – E. & C. N.Am. –, *capensis* – E. N.Am. – and *noli-tangere* – naturalized from Eurasia in N.W. N.Am. – have been used as food on our continent.
The juice extracted from fresh jewelweed, or a strong decoction of the plant, makes an effective wash against poison ivy.
I. biflora (m.a.) is said to dye wool yellow.
Leaves and seeds of several species are used as food in Asia.

LINACEAE

Linum (E-F-H 3)   Flax, Linseed
Greek and Latin name of the plant.
Throughout. Both native and species introduced from Eurasia.
Two Old World species are sometimes planted as ornamentals.

The Eurasian *L. usitatissimum* (its exact origin is unknown) is one of the oldest cultivated plants. The fibers of its stem are made into linen, and the drying oil extracted from its seeds is used industrially for making paint and linoleum. The oil-cake is fed to cattle. On our continent, flax is cultivated mostly in the Northwestern United States and in Canada.

Linseed <u>oil</u> is edible, in moderation only because of its laxative properties. It is rich in polyunsaturated fatty acids (sometimes referred to as vitamin F) and was heralded by some European nutritionists as one of the best oils for human consumption. It must be cold-pressed, without chemical solvents, unlike the oil used for industrial purposes.

The <u>seeds</u> themselves have been used as food, cooked, since Antiquity. They are still eaten roasted in Northeast Africa.

They contain 30 to 40% of the drying oil mentioned, mucilage, pectin, a cyanogenetic glucoside (linamarin) and a ferment. Linamarin is similar to the glucoside found in the lima bean (phaseolunatin).

Macerated in water, flax seeds are employed as a mechanical laxative. Emollient poultices are made with freshly ground seeds.

The plant also contains a cyanogenetic glucoside yielding hydrocyanic acid. The unripe capsules are particularly dangerous and have been a cause of human poisoning. They are nonetheless reportedly used as a base for chutney in India.

Linseed oil-cake has sometimes proven to be toxic to livestock.

Cattle have been poisoned by grazing on a Southwestern species, *L. neomexicanum* – Ariz., N.M., Chih. Other *Linum* spp. are probably dangerous as well.

The <u>seeds</u> of *L. perenne* subsp. *lewisii* (= *L. lewisii*) were eaten by Indians. They were generally roasted and ground. Raw seeds contain small amounts of hydrocyanic acid, but they are safe to eat after cooking.

L. catharticum – naturalized from Eur. in N.E. N.Am. – is purgative and depurative. Large doses are emetic and can cause cardiac troubles.

The plant contains an essential oil, tannin and a bitter substance.

Endangered species: *L. arenicola, carteri* var. *carteri* and var. *smallii*, and *westii* – all Fla.

MALPIGHIACEAE

Byrsonima cuneata   (D 5)   Nance, Locust Berry
(= *B. lucida*)
Etymology unknown.
S. Fla.

The ripe <u>fruits</u> are edible raw, but they are small, sour, and have a rather unpleasant taste.

Malpighia   (B 5)   Acerola Cherry
Etymology unknown.
S. Tex., Mex.
M. glabra, acerola or Barbados cherry, is often cultivated in tropical and subtropical regions for its red, juicy fruit which is extremely rich in vitamin C. Pleasant to eat raw, it is also made into preserves and pies.

The fruit of *M. emarginata* – Mex. – is eaten in Mexico.
Other tropical American and African species bear edible *fruits*.

ARALIACEAE

Aralia   (B 2-3)   Spikenard, Wild Sarsaparilla
Name first used by Tournefort, who received the plant from French Canada, possibly after the Indian name of one of the species.
Throughout.
Our native *A. californica* – Calif., S. Ore. –, *racemosa*, spikenard – E. & C. N.Am. – and *spinosa*, Hercules club, devil's walking stick – E. U.S. – as well as several Asian species, are sometimes planted for ornament.

The aromatic roots of *A. nudicaulis*, wild sarsaparilla – N. N.Am., Appalachians & Rocky Mountains – and *racemosa* (m.a.) were reportedly eaten by Indians. They served in pioneer times to flavor root beer. They can also be made into a pleasant tea with diaphoretic, diuretic and stimulant properties.

Young shoots and leaves of all the species mentioned above are edible. They can either be used raw, as a condiment, or boiled in a change of water to lessen their strong aromatic taste.

Several Asian species are commonly cultivated and eaten in China and Japan, under the name of "udo." The roots are usually boiled. The young shoots and stems are fried, boiled, macerated overnight in vinegar, eaten in salads or preserved in salt.

The small fruits of *A. nudicaulis* (m.a.) have reportedly been used as food by Indians in British Columbia.

In some cases, handling the root or the bark of *A. spinosa* (m.a.) has been the cause of severe dermatitis.

Oplopanax horridum (D 4)   Devil's Club
(= *Echinopanax h.*)
From the Greek "hoplon," weapon, and "panax," botanical name of ginseng: referring to the stout prickles of the plant.
N.W. & N.C. N.Am.

The <u>roots</u> as well as the young, succulent <u>shoots</u> and <u>stems</u> were used as food by Indians and Inuits of Alaska.

Contact with the prickles of this outlandish plant can produce very painful wounds, which become easily infected and may cause severe swelling.

Panax (H 4)   Ginseng
From the Greek "pas, pan," all, and "akos," cure: referring to the medicinal uses of the E. Asian *P. ginseng*.
E. N.Am.

P. quinquefolium, American ginseng, is cultivated in Northern North America for its well-known fusiform root which is exported to China. The local Chinese ginseng (*P. ginseng* = *P. shinseng*) has been for thousands of years the most famous Chinese medicinal plant, bringing such high prices that almost all wild plants were uprooted. Only a few might be left in the mountains of Manchuria. When American ginseng was discovered in the 17th century in Canada, the Chinese were so eager to import it that overpicking became the rule to satisfy the demand. The trade was extremely profitable, but it caused the eradication of the wild plant over a large portion of its natural range. Ginseng is very slow-growing and takes many years to develop a root of suitable size.

Most ginseng on the market now comes from cultivated plants, although it is still occasionally picked in the wild, as is unlawfully done in Great Smoky Mountains National Park in the Southern Appalachians. Wild ginseng brings in a higher price than cultivated ginseng.

An interesting fact is that while the greatest part of our American ginseng crop still goes to China, we import tons of Korean ginseng yearly for our domestic use, to satisfy the ginseng craze which has recently reached America and Europe.

Ginseng is heralded as a panacea, a cure-all and, of course, an aphrodisiac. It might actually delay senility and it does regulate blood pressure. It also has demulcent, febrifuge, stimulating, stomachic and tonic properties, but certainly does not possess the universal powers it is sometimes thought to have. The fresh root seems to be more effective than the dried products (the best medicinal results are obtained by chewing it fresh), and the wild plant appears to be superior to the cultivated one. But cultivation is the only way to preserve wild ginseng.

Both American and Chinese ginseng have similar properties. They contain saponins, hormone-like substances and traces of essential oil.

The aromatic <u>roots</u> of *P. quinquefolium* (m.a.) can be eaten raw or cooked, but they are too infrequent to be used as food.

Its sweet and bitter <u>leaves</u> make a pleasant tea which is good for colds.

The small spherical <u>roots</u> of *P. trifolium*, dwarf ginseng – N.E. N.Am. & Appalachians – were often eaten boiled. They are also edible raw.

The <u>roots</u> of a Japanese species are used locally for flavoring teas and liqueurs.

APIACEAE (UMBELLIFERAE)

To this important family belong many of our common vegetables, herbs and spices: carrot, parsnip, celery, parsley, chervil, fennel, dill, coriander, caraway, cumin and angelica, among others.

On the other hand, extremely toxic plants are found here as well, such as poison hemlock, fool's parsley and water hemlock.

It is easy in most cases to determine whether a plant is a member of the Apiaceae but it is generally much more difficult to identify with any certainty a species, or even a genus within the family. The fruits are often essential to identification, as most of these plants have a similar appearance. Much care must therefore be exerted in order to avoid unpleasant or dangerous mistakes.

The essential oil extracted from the fruits of several Apiaceae causes nervous disorders in high doses. Excessive use of these fruits as a condiment should be avoided. The fruits of Umbellifers are generally referred to as "seeds." But although small and dry, they are botanically fruits, not seeds.

Aegopodium podagraria (D 4) Ground Ash, Goutweed

From the Greek "aix, aigos," goat, and "podion," foot: alluding to the shape of the leaflets.
Originally from Eur., the plant is occasionally cultivated and found as an escape in N.E. N.Am.

The young <u>leaves</u>, of a transluscent, shiny light green, are very tender and aromatic, excellent raw in salads. Older leaves, a dull green, are good cooked, especially in gratin, where their incense-like flavor is delicious. It is a very prolific vegetable as the plant spreads easily with its long rhizomes. They were formerly eaten as cooked greens in Europe, especially in Sweden and Switzerland.

The plant is stimulant, vulnerary and diuretic.

Aegopodium podagraria

Anethum graveolens (B 4) Dill

Greek and Latin name of the plant.
Scattered throughout.
Originally from India & S.W. Asia, dill has been cultivated as an herb since Antiquity. It is still common in our gardens, whence it occasionally escapes.

Dill is a popular condiment in America, especially for flavoring pickles.
<u>Leaves</u> and <u>flowers</u> make an aromatic addition to salads and soups.
The <u>fruits</u> (dill seeds) also make a good, although stronger, spice.
Dill contains an essential oil and is rich in sulfur.

Like fennel (*Foeniculum vulgare*) and anise (*Pimpinella anisum*), dill is stomachic, carminative, antispasmodic, diuretic and galactogogue.

Angelica (D-H 3) Angelica
From the Latin "angelus," angel: referring to the high esteem in which the medicinal properties of the plant were held during the Middle Ages. Throughout.

The Eurasian angelica (*A. archangelica*) has been cultivated in Eur. since the Middle Ages as a medicinal plant and for its tender stems which were candied and used as a stomachic flavoring in cakes. All parts of the plant give off an intense but delicious aroma. It is still occasionally grown in American gardens.

The roots of *A. atropurpurea*, purple angelica, have reportedly been candied. Its young stems and leaves were eaten in colonial days.

Young shoots, tender stems and leaves of *A. lucida* (= *Coelopleurum lucidum*), seacoast angelica, wild celery – N.E. & N.W. Coasts – and *venenosa* – E. U.S. – have also been used as food. The specific name of the latter means "poisonous," and the plant has been stated to be toxic, but it is more often considered harmless and edible.

Roots, stems and leaves of several East Asian species are locally used as food. The roots are cooked or pickled and the leaves are boiled and eaten as greens.

In very sensitive individuals, *Angelica* spp. have been known to cause skin inflammations.

Endangered species: *A. callii* – Calif.

Anthriscus (A 3)
Greek and Latin name of a wild chervil.
Throughout. Introduced from Eurasia.

A. cerefolium, chervil – originally from S. Eur. & W. Asia – has been cultivated in gardens since ancient days. It is occasionally found as an escape in E. N.Am.

Because of its very delicate aroma, it must only be used fresh; the leaves chopped finely are delicious in salads and soups. In France where it is still popular, it is, along with tarragon, parsley and sorrel, one of the "fines herbes," used in salads, soups, sauces and omelettes.

Chervil contains an essential oil, a glucoside (apiine), vitamins, minerals and various other substances.

It is stimulant, stomachic, diuretic and depurative.

Its <u>root</u> was possibly used as food. In the 17th century the English herbalist Gerarde mentions its edibility.

<u>Leaves</u> and <u>stems</u> of *A. scandicina* (= *A. caucalis*), wild chervil, beaked parsley – naturalized from Eur. – have a sweet and pleasant anise smell and taste. They are excellent raw.

The <u>young leaves</u> of *A. sylvestris*, cow parsley – locally naturalized from Eurasia – are also edible. They are cooked as greens or preserved in salt in N.E. Asia.

Besides an essential oil, however, the root contains toxic substances: It is abortive and potentially dangerous.

It is also wise to remember that *Anthriscus* spp. have often been confused with poisonous Umbellifers.

Apium   (A 3)

Latin name of celery, *Apium graveolens*.

Throughout. Both native and species introduced from Eur.

A. graveolens, celery – originally from the coasts of Eur. – is commonly grown for its petioles, leaves and fruits. It was anciently cultivated for its medicinal properties, but did not enter our vegetable gardens before the 17th century.

Celery is widely naturalized in N.Am. The wild plant has a much stronger smell and taste than its cultivated counterpart, often with some bitterness.

<u>Tender stems</u>, <u>petioles</u> and <u>leaves</u> are edible raw, preferably mixed with other vegetables, or cooked, especially in soups.

Celery contains an essential oil, particularly in the root, vitamins A, B and C, minerals, a glucoside and coumarins.

The fresh plant is diuretic, tonic, aperitive and digestive.

The aromatic <u>fruits</u> are used as a spice. They are generally ground, mixed with salt and sold as "celery salt."

They are rich in essential oil and have digestive and carminative properties.

Handling celery can occasionally cause dermatitis in very sensitive individuals.

If grown in overfertilized soils, the plant can accumulate potentially toxic quantities of nitrates.

A cultivar, celeriac, has a large fleshy <u>root</u> that is edible raw or cooked. It has been in cultivation since the end of the 16th century.

The root of wild celery, although thin and woody, can be used as well; it is strongly aromatic.

Celery root has all the medicinal properties mentioned, and was sometimes thought to be aphrodisiac.

A. leptophyllum, marsh parsley – S. U.S., Mex. – has reportedly been used as food.

Bupleurum (B 4) Thoroughwax

Greek name of an Umbellifer, "boupleuron," literally, oxen rib.
Introduced from Eurasia in E. U.S. & Calif.
The <u>young leaves</u> of *B. rotundifolium* – naturalized from Eur. in E. U.S. – were eaten in Ancient times.

The <u>young leaves</u> of a few local species are used as food in Europe and Asia.

Carum carvi (B 4) Caraway

Greek and Latin name of an aromatic Umbellifer. Originally from Eur., the plant is cultivated for its fruits (caraway seeds), commonly used as a condiment especially in breads (rye, pumpernickel) and cheese. Caraway is naturalized in N. N.Am.

In Northern Europe, the <u>fruits</u> are added to pastries and sauerkraut, besides being used in breads and cheeses. They also serve to flavor the spirit known as "kümmel." They are usually employed when ripe, but unripe fruits have a pleasant *Citrus* aroma and also make an interesting condiment.

They contain an essential oil and are stimulant, stomachic, carminative, antispasmodic, emmenagogue and galactagogue.

They have reportedly been used against parasites.

The essential oil distilled from the fruits is rubefacient and toxic in high doses, causing nervous disor-

Carum carvi

ders. This is also the case with many other essential oils, which must be used with caution.

Caraway fruits have been used as a spice since prehistoric times.

The roots are edible and were often eaten, cooked, in Northern Europe. They have a good flavor, reminiscent of that of carrots. Parkinson (1629) thought them to be superior to parsnips. They are at their best before the flowering stem starts developing.

The young leaves can be eaten raw or cooked. They are aromatic.

Roots, leaves and fruits of several local species are used as food in Europe, Asia and Africa.

Centella asiatica (3 4)   Coinworth, Gota Kola

(= *C. erecta*)
Etymology unknown.
Coasts of Del. to Fla., Tex. & Mex.

The leaves are edible raw and have a pleasant, carrot-like taste, slightly sharp. They are also cooked as greens in parts of Asia.

The plant is sometimes called "brain food" and has long been eaten or made into tea in India to promote intellectual activity.

It contains tannin, an essential oil and a saponoside (asiaticoside) with an antibiotic action.

Gota kola is also a diuretic and a vulnerary.

Chaerophyllum (D 4)   Wild Chervil

Greek and Latin name of chervil, *Anthriscus cerefolium*.
E. & C. U.S. Both native and species introduced from Eur. & N. Africa.

C. bulbosum, tuberous or parsnip chervil – originally from Eur. – has been cultivated in vegetable gardens since the 19th century for its large, fleshy, delicately flavored root. It has been reported as an escape from cultivation around Washington, D.C.

The sweetish roots of a local species are used as food in West Asia.

Various *Chaerophyllum* spp. can cause skin irritations in susceptible individuals.

C. temulum – from Eur. & N. Africa, adventive near E. seaports – has been suspected of being somewhat toxic, without certainty.

Coriandrum sativum (B 3)   Coriander

Latin name of the plant from the Greek "koris," stinkbug: referring to the strong odor of the fresh plant.

Originally from W. Asia & N. Africa, coriander, used as a condiment since Antiquity, is cultivated throughout the world for its fruits and leaves. The plant is naturalized and sometimes found as a weed, especially in S. U.S. & Mex.

The fresh <u>leaves</u> have a strong smell (which is actually that of a stinkbug) and a particular, somewhat oily taste. They are relished as an herb in Asia, Africa and Latin America, including Mexico, where "cilantro" is ubiquitous in markets. But Westerners do not usually share this taste. In the U.S. and Canada, the strongest demand comes from people of Spanish or Asiatic descent. Things are changing, however, and cilantro or "Chinese parsley" can now be bought in many American food stores.

Coriander leaves are delicious as a condiment in salads and soups.

They contain vitamin C, an essential oil and various other substances.

The juice extracted from the plant is known to have similar effects as alcohol: In small amounts it acts as a stimulant, then a depressant, and in larger doses it is inebriating. It was even considered dangerous by the ancients. Dried coriander no longer has these properties, as they are due to a particular oil contained only in the fresh plant.

Coriander seeds, actually the dried <u>fruits</u>, usually enjoy more favor than the fresh leaves as a condiment in Western countries, but they are even more popular in the Middle East, in India and in Greece.

Upon drying, the smell and properties of the fruits change: the flavor becomes sweeter and aromatic.

Dried coriander fruits are carminative, stomachic and antispasmodic. They contain an essential oil.

Besides their use as a spice, they also serve to flavor alcohols and liqueurs. The oil distilled from them is employed similarly with various foods.

Cryptotaenia canadensis (B 2)   Honewort

From the Greek "kryptos," hidden, and "tainia," band or stripe: referring to the hidden oil tubes.

E. & C. N.Am.

This species is also native in Japan, where the plant, along with Japanese honewort (*C. japonica*), is still grown in vegetable gardens and used as food, both in wild and cultivated forms.

The roots are generally boiled and served with oil. Those of the wild plant are rather thin and woody if the flowering stem has started developing.

Young leaves and stems are soaked in water to attenuate their strong taste and then cooked as greens or in soups.

They can also be added raw to various dishes as an aromatic herb.

Cuminum cyminum (B 5)   Cumin

Greek and Latin name of the plant.

Originally from N. Africa & W. Asia, cumin is sometimes cultivated for its fruits (cumin seeds) in S. U.S. & Mex.; it can be found as an escape in W. Tex. & Mex.

Cumin has been employed as a spice since Antiquity, but its use did not reach Northern Europe until the Middle Ages. It is used to flavor various dishes, breads, cheese and pickles. In India it is mixed with other spices to make curry powders.

The fruits contain an essential oil which can be distilled. In high doses, this oil can produce nervous disorders.

Cumin fruits are carminative, digestive and galactagogue.

Cumin and caraway are sometimes confused, although they are quite different in appearance, flavor and uses.

Cymopterus (C-H 4)   Corkwing, Gamote

(= *Phellopterus* spp.)

From the Greek "kuma," wave, and "pteron," wing: the fruits of some species bear undulate wings.

W. & C. N.Am.

The thickened <u>roots</u> of various species were often used as food by Indians. In the spring they are tender, sweet and mildly flavored, and can be eaten raw. Later, they are better cooked.

The following species were used: *C. acaulis* – N.C. N.Am. –, *bulbosus* – S.W. U.S., Mex. –, *fendleri* – Colo., Utah, N.M. –, *globosus* (= *montanus*) – Calif., Nev., Utah –, *multinervatus* – S.W. U.S., N. Mex. –, *newberryi* – Utah, Ariz., Colo. – and *purpurascens* (= *montanus*) – W. U.S., Mex.

The aromatic roots of *C. fendleri* (m.a.) were also used as a flavoring. Those of *C. purpurascens* (m.a.) are still eaten and relished in Mexico.

The <u>leaves</u> of the various species noted are edible raw or cooked, and were used as food by Indians.

Endangered species: *C. minimus* – Utah – and *nivalis* – Nev.

Daucus (D 1)   Wild Carrot

Greek and Latin name of the carrot, *Daucus carota*.
Throughout. Several native species in W. & S. N.Am. and the Eurasian *D. carota*, Queen Anne's lace, naturalized throughout N.Am.

The <u>roots</u> of this common weed are tender if gathered at the end of the first growing season before the flowering stem appears, as carrots are biennial. The second year, the plant goes to seed and its root becomes woody. Although white and not colored like those of the garden varieties, wild carrot roots have the same characteristic smell and taste, often somewhat more aromatic. They can be eaten raw but are not crisp and cannot easily be grated. They can be eaten cooked as well.

If the root has become woody, the thin outer layer can be removed from the core, chopped and eaten raw, or cooked and passed through a food mill.

It is quite easy to obtain plants with large, fleshy roots by cultivation in deep sandy soil and by selection of plants grown from seeds of the wild form. But they will remain white, often with a purple tinge. The direct ancestors of our garden carrots, cultivated since Antiquity, are forms coming from Western Asia.

Chopped and roasted, cultivated carrots were used as a coffee substitute in Germany. Sugar was even extracted from them, but the process was not found to be commercially profitable.

Both wild and cultivated carrots contain sugars, pectin, vitamins B1, B2, B6, C and niacin, minerals and an essential oil. The red forms contain much vitamin A.

Daucus carota

Carrots are an excellent regulator of intestinal function. They also have antiputrefactive, cholagogue and depurative properties.

The grated pulp can be used externally as a vulnerary.

The leaves are edible raw or cooked. They have a pleasant taste and are better when young.

The umbels of white flowers (with a dark red flower in the center) can be eaten as well.

The fruits are very fragrant, with a definite Williams pear aroma, and make an excellent spice, especially with yogurt or fruit salads. But they must be picked at the right stage: too early, they smell of turpentine; too late, they give off an unpleasant odor.

The fruits contain an essential oil and are stimulant, carminative and diuretic. Eating carrot "seeds" was reportedly an old Amish means of birth control for the day after.

The <u>roots</u> of *D. pusillus* – S. U.S., Mex. – were reportedly eaten raw or cooked by some Indian tribes (Navajo and Nez Percé).

Some very sensitive individuals contract dermatitis from handling Queen Anne's lace leaves. If cows are allowed to eat the plant too freely, their milk can have a bitter taste.

Erigenia bulbosa (B 4) Harbinger of Spring
From the Greek "erigineia," early born: the flowers bloom early in the spring.
E. U.S. A monotypic genus.

The small tuberous <u>root</u> is edible raw.

Eryngium (D-H 3) Eryngo
Greek name of a plant in this genus, "êryggion."
Throughout. Both native and species introduced from Eur.

The <u>roots</u> of *E. maritimum*, sea holly – originally from the coasts of Eur., reported as an adventive in New York City – are edible cooked. Their pleasant taste is said to resemble chestnuts. They were often candied in older days; Shakespeare mentions this use.

The roots contain an essential oil, saponins and minerals. They have been used as a diuretic.

The <u>young shoots</u> were occasionally eaten cooked, but they are rather bitter and are best boiled in a change of water.

<u>Roots</u> and <u>shoots</u> of a few local species were used as food in Europe and Asia.

The roots of *E. aquaticum*, water eryngo – E. N.Am. – are diaphoretic, diuretic, expectorant, stimulant and, in large doses, emetic.

Endangered species: *E. aristulatum* var. *pavishii* and *racemosum* – both Calif.

Foeniculum vulgare (A 2-3) Fennel

Latin name of the plant from "fenum," hay: alluding to the finely divided leaves.

Native to the Mediterranean region, fennel is widely naturalized in N.Am., especially on the coasts.

The plant has been cultivated since Antiquity for its aromatic foliage and its fruits (fennel seeds) commonly used as a spice.

In a cultivar (var. *dulce*) the enlarged petioles of the leaves overlap each other at the base of the stem to create a bulb-like structure: "finocchio" (the Italian name of this variety) is white, fleshy, sweet and aromatic. It is commonly eaten in Europe raw or cooked and sometimes pickled in vinegar.

Such a structure occasionally forms on a wild plant, but it is of course much smaller and tougher.

Fennel <u>roots</u> can be eaten raw or cooked while still tender. When the flower stalk appears, they become woody, with a thin, fleshy outer layer which can be eaten raw, chopped or grated, or cooked and passed through a food mill.

They have diuretic, emmenagogue and carminative properties.

Foeniculum vulgare

The young, tender <u>stems</u> were eaten raw in Naples under the name "carosellas." They are juicy, sweet and deliciously aromatic. The mature stem is hollow and has often been used as a straw for sipping wine, to which it communicates some of fennel's aromatic flavor.

One the best edible parts of the wild plant are the young feathery green <u>shoots</u>. They are juicy, sweet, aromatic and very tender. They can be gathered in quantity well into the summer months. The center of the plant makes delicious salads. Mature <u>leaves</u> are very good as well, raw or cooked, but they are somewhat tougher and it is better to remove the petiole.

They contain vitamins A, B and C, minerals and an essential oil.

Their properties are similar to those of the fruits (see below).

The umbels of yellow <u>flowers</u> make an excellent herb for salads, soups and greens. They are also the best part of the plant to be used for tea, fresh or dried, as they are very sweet and fragrant.

Fennel seeds, actually the <u>fruits</u>, are a well-known condiment that is highly prized in China and India. In Europe, they are especially enjoyed with fish.

They contain an essential oil which is extracted by distillation and used for flavoring alcoholic drinks. However, overdoses of this oil can lead to nervous disorders such as convulsions.

The fruits also contain 10% of a fixed oil.

They are stimulant, stomachic, carminative, diuretic, emmenagogue, galactagogue, expectorant and antispasmodic.

Heracleum   (B 2-3)   Cow Parsnip

Greek and Latin name of a plant first used by Hercules as medicine.

Throughout. Both native and species introduced from Eurasia.

Our native *H. lanatum* was used as food by the Indians.

The <u>roots</u>, preferably young and tender, were eaten cooked. They have a pleasant taste, although possibly too strongly aromatic for some.

They are stimulant and carminative.

<u>Young shoots</u> and <u>leaves</u> were eaten raw or cooked, along with their <u>petioles</u>, the still tender <u>stems</u> and the <u>unexpanded umbels</u>. Petioles and young stems were carefully peeled by Indians before eating. The flavor of the raw plant is quite strong and cooking reduces it.

The <u>leaves</u> were used by Indians as a salt substitute after being dried and burned; the ashes do

Heracleum lanatum

have a salty taste, although very different from that of sodium chloride. They contain mostly potassium chloride. It is therefore possible to season one's food with cow parsnip ashes while on a low-sodium diet. A few other plants are used similarly on our continent (see *Petasites, Tussilago,* Asteraceae).

Indians used to dry the petioles and stems of our cow parsnip and cook them as a flavoring with various foods.

In their view, the plant was not to be eaten by pregnant or lactating women, nor by infants.

The Eurasian *H. sphondylium*, European cow parsnip – adventive in N.E. N.Am. – was a common wild vegetable in Eastern Europe and parts of Asia.

The roots are strongly aromatic and can be used as a condiment.

The young stems are peeled and eaten raw, either whole as a treat or sliced in salads. They are sweet, aromatic (with a definite tangerine and coconut smell), tender and juicy. They contain an essential oil.

In Russia, stems and petioles were dried in the sun and tied in bundles; after they turned yellow, a sweet exudation could be gathered on their surface, which was a much appreciated delicacy. They were also fermented into a kind of beer, which was often distilled to yield alcohol.

Young shoots and leaves are edible raw or cooked. The aromatic leaves make excellent gratins. The European cow parsnip is much milder than the American and, when young, is pleasant to eat raw and excellent cooked.

In Eastern Europe, "bartsch" or "bortch" (in Polish, "barszcz") was prepared with the plant: leaves, stems and fruits were placed in a large pot or barrel and enough water was added to thoroughly cover them. After a few weeks, the mixture became sour due to lactic fermentation, and was then eaten as a soup. The plant could be preserved this way for several months throughout the winter.

The strongly aromatic fruits of both cow parsnips can be used in moderation as a condiment.

H. lanatum (m.a.) is antispasmodic, carminative and stimulant.

H. sphondylium (m.a.) is stimulant, digestive and hypotensive. It was thought by some to be somewhat aphrodisiac. It does contain a hormone-like substance analogous to testosterone.

Through skin contact, the foliage and the sap of both plants are known to cause dermatitis, or even burns in susceptible individuals, due to the photosensitizing furanocoumarins they contain.

A few local species are used as food in Southern Europe, Asia and South America.

Hydrocotyle (B 4)   Marsh Pennywort

From the Greek "hydor," water, and "cotylê," shallow cup: referring to the peltate leaves.
Native species throughout.
H. sibthorpioides is naturalized from tropical Asia in E. U.S.

The <u>leaves</u> of this species are eaten raw or cooked in Asia. They have a pleasant taste, somewhat reminiscent of carrots.

Imperatoria ostruthium (B 4)   Masterwort

From the Latin "imperator," emperor: referring to the reputed medicinal properties of the plant.
Originally from C. Eur., masterwort is sometimes cultivated as a vegetable; it is locally naturalized in N.E. U.S.

The <u>young leaves</u> can be used as a condiment. They could possibly be cooked, but they are strongly aromatic and rather bitter.
The roots contain an essential oil. They are used as a diuretic, emmenagogue, diaphoretic, stomachic and stimulant.

Levisticum officinale (B 4)   Lovage

Latin name of the plant; it was also called *"ligusticum."*
Originally from W. Asia, the plant is sometimes cultivated as an herb and occasionally escapes.

Lovage has been known since Antiquity. It has a strong aromatic smell and taste, reminiscent of celery (*Apium graveolens*). <u>Roots</u>, <u>stems</u>, <u>petioles</u>, <u>leaves</u> and <u>fruits</u> have been used raw as condiments for soups and various dishes, like those of celery. The <u>young shoots</u> can be eaten in salads, as well as the tender <u>petioles</u> and <u>stems</u> after peeling.
The plant contains an essential oil. It also contains sugars, resin and rubber.

Levisticum officinale

It is diuretic, emmenagogue, stimulant, stomachic, carminative and expectorant.

Ligusticum (D 3)   Lovage
Greek and Latin name of *Levisticum officinale* from the Greek "ligustikos,"
Ligurian.
Throughout.

Roots, young shoots, tender stems and leaves of *L. hultenii* (= *L. scoticum*
subsp. *hultenii*) – B.C. to Alaska –, *filicinum* – N.W. U.S. – and *scoticum* – N.E.
N.Am. – have been eaten, either raw or cooked, on our continent by Indians and
Inuits.
   L. hultenii (m.a.) was also used as food in Eastern Asia, where the plant is na-
tive as well. *L. scoticum* (m.a.) was also used as food in Northern Europe and Asia.
   The aromatic fruits of the species can be used as a spice.
   The roots of *L. porteri*, osha – S.W. U.S., N. Mex. – are used for colds. They
have a strong aromatic flavor. The leaves are said to be good forage for wild ani-
mals and livestock.

Lomatium (C-H 2)   Biscuit root, Cous
(= *Cogswellia*, *Leptotaenia* and *Peucedanum* spp.)
From the Greek "loma," border: referring to the wings on the fruits.
W. N.Am.

Several species have long, fleshy taproots and were an important food for
Western Indians. Edible raw or cooked, they were often dried, ground into flour
and made into cakes, which were dried in the sun and kept for later use (winter-
time and travels). Biscuit roots are whitish in color, starchy and tender. They
have a mild, pleasant taste.
   The roots of the following species have been used: *L. ambiguum*, breadroot –
N.W. N.Am. –, *canbyi* – C. N.W. U.S. –, *cous* (= *montanum*) – N.W. U.S. –, *dissectum* (= *Leptotaenia dissecta*) – W. U.S. –, *farinosum* – Wash., Idaho, Mont. –,
foeniculaceum – Ore. to Mont. –, *geyeri* – N.W. N.Am. –, *leptocarpum* – W.
U.S. –, *macrocarpum* – N.W. & N.C. N.Am. –, *nudicaule* – N.W. N.Am. – and
triternatum (= *platycarpum*) – N.W. N.Am.

Young shoots, leaves and fruits of *L. dissectum* (m.a.) var. **multifidum** (= *Leptotaenia multifida*) and **utriculatum**, Pomo celery – Calif. to B.C. – were also eaten by Indians. Shoots and leaves of all *Lomatium* spp. are actually edible raw or cooked. They are quite aromatic and pleasant. In some species the seeds have been dried and ground into flour.

Endangered species: *L. bradshawii, greenmanii* – both Ore. –, *laevigatum* – Wash., Ore. –, *ravenii* – Calif. –, *suksdorfii* – Wash., Ore. – and *tuberosum* – Wash.

Musineon   (C 4)
Ancient Greek name of some Umbellifer.
N.W. & C. N.Am.

The roots of *M. divaricatum* were eaten by Indians.

Oenanthe   (C-F 4)
Greek and Latin name of a Mediterranean species and of the flower of the grapevine, from "oinos," wine, and "anthos," flower.
W. N.Am.
Both native and species introduced from Eurasia.

The black tuberous roots of *O. sarmentosa*, water parsley – W. N.Am. – were boiled and eaten by Indians. They are said to have a pleasant taste.

Those of two local species (*O. peucedanifolia, pimpinelloides*) were used as food in Europe. The leaves of a third one (*O. stolonifera*) are eaten raw or cooked in Eastern Asia, especially in Japan ("seri") and Indonesia.

However, some Eurasian species are known to be extremely toxic; confusion of their roots with those of edible Umbellifers has been fatal. These plants were also used for poisoning people.

They contain oenanthotoxine, a virulent substance which fortunately is easily destroyed; the plant becomes almost harmless after drying. The symptoms caused by ingestion of the toxic species are respiratory, digestive, nervous and circulatory disorders, often resulting in a rapid death.

One of the toxic species, *O. aquatica* (= *Phellandrium aquaticum*), water fennel, has been found as an adventive near Washington, D.C.

The seeds of this plant were used medicinally in Europe as a carminative, diuretic, diaphoretic and expectorant.

Orogenia (C 4)   Indian Potato, Turkey Pea
From the Greek "oros," mountain, and "genos," race: referring to the habitat of the species.
N.W. U.S.

The enlarged fleshy roots of *O. fusiformis* and *linearifolia* were eaten raw or cooked by Indians.

Osmorhiza (B 3)   Sweet Cicely
From the Greek "osmê," odor, and "rhiza," root: referring to the pleasant anise smell of the root.
Throughout.

The roots of all species are aromatic and can be used for flavoring desserts and drinks or as tea: they contain an essential oil similar to that distilled from the fruits of anise (*Pimpinella anisum*).

Those of *O. longistylis* – E. & C. N.Am – are probably the most fragrant: they are almost pungent and very sweet and pleasant just to chew on.

The tender young stems make an excellent nibble while walking in the woods, and the young shoots and leaves can be eaten raw or cooked. The latter, like the rest of the plant, have a definite anise flavor but develop an unpleasant, bitter aftertaste.

Roots and foliage of *O. claytonii* – E. & C. N.Am. – were used as food by Indians. The leaves of *O. chilensis* and of other species are edible as well.

Roots and leaves of a local species are boiled as greens or in soups in Eastern Asia.

Pastinaca sativa (B 3)   Parsnip
Latin name of carrots and parsnips.
Widely naturalized in N.Am.
Originally from Eur., the plant has been cultivated since Antiquity.

Parsnips are grown for their white, fleshy <u>root</u> which becomes sweet over the winter months (when the root freezes, some of its starch is transformed into simple sugars).

The root of the wild plant is best when gathered at the end of the first growing season. It is then fleshy and tender but long rather than thick. When the flowering stem starts developing, the inner part of the root becomes woody. But the outer fleshy layer is still tender enough to be eaten raw, grated or chopped, or cooked and passed through a food mill to eliminate the fibers.

Pastinaca sativa

Like carrots, parsnips are biennial plants. The first year, they store energy in their root in the form of starch and sugars, to be used the following year for rapidly growing a stem and for making flowers and fruits. Then the plant dies.

Parsnips can be cooked in soups, stews, gratins or sauces. They have a soft texture and a sweet, aromatic flavor.

Parsnips contain proteins, starch, sugars, pectin, a fixed oil, vitamins in the B group and minerals.

They are very nutritious and have diuretic and emmenagogue properties.

The <u>young shoots</u> can be eaten raw. Older <u>leaves</u> are better cooked. They are quite strongly aromatic.

The <u>fruits</u> contain an essential oil. They have a particular aromatic smell and a rather pungent taste, like the fruits of cow parsnip. They can be used, fresh or dried, as a spice.

The fresh leaves also contain photosensitizing substances (furanocoumarins), especially in subsp. *urens,* and can severely irritate the skin of sensitive individuals, even causing severe burns.

According to certain legends, wild parsnips were believed to be toxic, but from what is known this was due to a confusion with some poisonous Umbellifers.

The <u>roots</u> of two local species are used as food in Asia.

Perideridia (C 2)   Yampa, Squawroot, Edible-Rooted Caraway
(= *Carum, Eulophus* spp.)
From the Greek "peri," around, and "derris," leather coat.
W. & C. N.Am.

The thick, fleshy <u>rootstock</u> (tuberous or fusiform) of several plants in this genus was an important article of food among Indians. It was usually cooked in the fire pit but was also eaten raw or dried and ground into flour. The roots are sweet and tasty.

The following species have been used: *P. bolanderi* – W. U.S. –, *californica* – Calif. –, *gairdneri* (= *Carum g.*) – W. N.Am. –, *howellii* – N. Calif., S. Ore. –, *kelloggii* (= *Carum k.*) – Calif. –, *oregana* (= *Carum oreganum*) – N. Calif. to Wash. –, *parishii* – Calif. – and *pringlei* – S. Calif.

Yampa <u>leaves</u> are edible as well.

The <u>fruits</u> were used as a seasoning by Indians.

Early settlers in the West also fed on some of these species, especially *P. gairdneri* (m.a.).

Petroselinum crispum (B 5)   Parsley
(= *P. hortense*, = *Carum petroselinum*)
Greek and Latin name of the plant.
Scattered throughout.
Originally from S.E. Eur. & W. Asia, parsley has been grown as an herb since Antiquity and is still a favorite in every garden. It occasionally escapes from cultivation.

Numerous varieties are known, one of which has a fleshy root, var. *tuberosum*, that is edible raw or cooked. This tuberous-rooted parsley was held in high esteem in Germany and Holland during the 16th and 17th centuries.

Parsley <u>leaves</u> must be eaten fresh, as they lose their delicate flavor upon drying.

They are rich in vitamins A, B1, B2, C, E, niacin and minerals, They also contain an essential oil, enzymes, chlorophyll and other substances.

Roots, leaves and fruits are diuretic, emmenagogue, depurative, stomachic, carminative and stimulant. But an overdose can irritate the kidneys, cause cardiac troubles and be abortive.

Externally, a poultice of the leaves is used to slow down the flow of mother's milk and as a vulnerary. The juice extracted from the plant is employed as an eyewash.

Handling parsley occasionally irritates the skin of very susceptible individuals.

Pimpinella (B 5)

This name, dating back to the Middle Ages, was used to designate plants in this genus, along with burnets or pimpernels, *Sanguisorba* spp., Rosaceae.

N. N.Am.

Introduced from Eur. & Asia.

P. anisum, anise, originally from Asia but unknown in the wild, has been grown since Antiquity for its sweet, aromatic fruits (anise seeds). Anise has been reported as a waif in Massachusetts and probably elsewhere.

The leaves can be added to salads.

The fruits are used almost universally for flavoring such things as breads, pastries and liqueurs. In ancient Rome, they were added to wines. They also make a delicious tea.

Anise fruits contain an essential oil (2-6%), 30% of a fixed oil, sugars and various other substances.

They are stimulant at first, then sedative, stomachic, carminative, antispasmodic, diuretic and galactogogue. Anise oil, distilled from the fruits, contains anethol and is narcotic in large amounts: an overdose can lead to nervous troubles.

A salve made with the fruits has been used externally for lice and scabies.

The leaves of *P. saxifraga*, burnet saxifrage – originally from Eur. and locally naturalized, mostly in N. N.Am. – are edible. The roots of the plant were also used medicinally.

They contain an essential oil, tannin, resin and other substances.

They are antispasmodic, diuretic, diaphoretic, carminative, stomachic and astringent.

The fruits of this species are galactagogue.

Pseudocymopterus (B 4)
(= *Cymopterus* spp.)
From the Greek "pseudês," false, from "pseudô," to cheat; "*Cymopterus,*" a genus in the same family.
W. N.Am.

The leaves of *P. aletifolius* (= *Cymopterus a.*) – N.M. – were cooked as a green by Indians.

Sanicula (G-H 4)   Snakeroot, Sanicle
Derived from the Latin "sanare," to heal: alluding to the supposed medicinal properties of the European *S. europaea.*
Throughout.

The roots of *S. tuberosa* – S.W. Ore., Calif., Baja – have reportedly been eaten cooked in California.
Those of *S. marilandica* – N., C. & E. N.Am. – contain saponins, tannin, a bitter principle and minerals.
They are used medicinally as an astringent and expectorant.
The leaves of a few local species are eaten in Eastern Asia.
Endangered species: *S. maritima, saxatilis* – both Calif. – and *tracyi* – Calif., Ore.

Scandix pecten-veneris (B 4)   Venus's Comb
Greek and Latin name of chervil, *Anthriscus cerefolium.*
Originally from S. Eur., the plant is naturalized over most of our continent.

The leaves are edible raw or cooked. They were used as food by the ancient Egyptians and the Greeks.
The leaves of another species are eaten in Greece.

Sium (G-F-H 3)
Greek and Latin name of an aquatic Umbellifer.
Throughout. Both native and species introduced from Eurasia.

Skirret (*S. sisarum* – originally from Eurasia) was formerly cultivated for its roots. It is rarely found in vegetable gardens nowadays.

The roots of *S. suave*, water parsnip, although rather fibrous, were used as food by Indians. They are at their best in winter, before new leaves appear, but one must be very careful to identify the plants properly at this stage, as they could easily be confused with poisonous water hemlocks (*Cicuta* spp.).

The aromatic leaves of the water parsnip are edible raw and were relished by some Indians.

In several parts of the United States and Canada, *S. suave* (m.a.) has been suspected of poisoning cattle, but those cases were not well-documented.

Roots and leaves of local forms of this species are eaten raw or cooked in Japan.

Endangered species: *S. floridanum* – Fla.

Torilis (D 3)   Hedge Parsley

Diminutive form of *Tordylium,* a closely related Eurasian genus in the same family.

Throughout. Naturalized from Eurasia.

The plant was reportedly eaten in Europe in ancient times.

The roots of *T. japonica* (= *Caucalis anthriscus*), hedge parsley, are peeled and eaten raw in Asia.

The young leaves are boiled as greens.

Zizia (G 4)   Golden Alexanders

After Johann Baptist Ziz (1779–1829), German botanist.

E. & C. N.Am.

The young umbels of flowers of *Z. aurea* and possibly of other species have reportedly been added to salads.

GENTIANACEAE

Frasera   (E-H 4)   Elk-weed, Green Gentian
After J. Fraser, English botanical collector.
W. N.Am.

The <u>root</u> of *F. speciosa* – W. U.S. – is fleshy but rather bitter. Mixed with greens, it was eaten raw or cooked by Western Indians.
Endangered species: *F. gypsicola* and *pahutensis* – both Nev.

APOCYNACEAE

Apocynum   (E-F 3)   Dogbane
Ancient Greek name of a local plant of the same family, "apokuon."
Throughout.
A few native species are occasionally planted for ornament.

The hardened <u>gum</u> exuding from the stems of several species, especially *A. angustifolium* – W. U.S. – were used as chewing gum by Indians.
The <u>seeds</u> of *A. cannabinum*, Indian hemp, have reportedly been eaten.
The stems of this species yield fibers.
But the leaves contain a toxic glucoside, cymarin (yielding cyanhydric acid upon hydrolysis) as well as a resin and other toxic substances, and are known to be extremely poisonous to livestock, both fresh and dried: 15 to 30 grams of green leaves can kill a horse or a cow. The leaves of all species must be considered dangerous.
A. androsaemifolium – N.Am. – has the same toxicity. Its leaves have also proved to be lethal to domestic animals.
However, the rootstock of this species was used medicinally in small amounts as a diaphoretic, expectorant and stimulant. Larger doses are emetic and cathartic.
The roots of *A. cannabinum* (m.a.) yield a cardiac stimulant.

ASCLEPIADACEAE

Asclepias   (B-F-H 2-3)   Milkweed
Greek name of the European *Vincetoxicum officinale*, commemorating Asclepias, the Greek god of medicine.
Throughout.
Various species are grown for ornament, especially in Eur., including *A. incarnata*, swamp milkweed, and *tuberosa*, butterfly weed, pleurisy root – both E. & C. N. Am.

The fleshy <u>root</u> of *A. tuberosa* (m.a.) was cooked and eaten by Indians.

Fresh, however, it is emetic. The dried root has been used as an expectorant and a diaphoretic.

The butterfly weed, with showy orange flowers, is the only species in this genus to have a clear juice rather than a milky latex.

Milkweed <u>shoots</u> and <u>leaves</u> are edible after cooking in a change of water as the raw plants are somewhat toxic. It is important to place the shoots and leaves in cold water before bringing to a boil; otherwise their bitterness is impossible to eliminate. When properly prepared, milkweeds are harmless and delicately flavored.

Asclepias sp.

The <u>flower buds</u> make an excellent cooked vegetable.

The opened <u>flowers</u> are edible as well. They contain a sweet nectar which can be extracted and concentrated by long boiling.

The tender <u>young fruits</u> can be cooked and eaten. They have a pleasant taste. But the downy seeds develop rapidly and the fruit soon becomes too tough to be used as food. At this stage, the fruits are sometimes used for decoration as they somewhat resemble green birds.

The hardened <u>sap</u> exuding from wounds on the stems and the leaves can be collected and chewed as gum. It is rather bitter but has an interesting flavor.

It contains rubber and asclepain, a protein-digesting enzyme (like papain of papaya leaves, *Carica papaya*, Caricaceae).

Indians knew of all the uses described above for milkweed shoots, leaves, flower buds, flowers, young fruits and sap.

The following species were used: *A. asperula* (= *Asclepiodora decumbens*) –
S.W. U.S. –, *A. californica, eriocarpa* – both Calif., Baja –, *galioides* – S.W.
U.S., Mex. –, *incarnata* (m.a.), *mexicana* – W. N.Am. –, *speciosa* – W. & C.
N.Am. –, *syriaca* – E. & C. N.Am. – and *tuberosa* (m.a.).

However, raw milkweeds contain a toxic resinous substance and several
species – especially *A. eriocarpa* and *galioides* (m.a.) – have caused death in livestock and particularly in sheep; 2 to 3 ounces of the fresh leaves of *A. galioides*
(m.a.) can kill a sheep. But the plants are distasteful to animals and are eaten
only exceptionally because of overgrazing.

The roots of *A. syriaca* (m.a.) are diuretic, emetic and purgative. An infusion
of them was used by some Indian tribes to produce temporary sterility, but large
doses are toxic.

The fresh juice was rubbed on warts to remove them.

Fibers from the stem were used as bowstrings.

Endangered species: *A. eastwoodiana* – Nev. – and *meadii* – N.C. U.S.

Marsdenia edulis   (D 4)
Etymology unknown.
Mex.

The tender green <u>fruit</u> is occasionally eaten cooked in Mexico.

Matelea   (G-H 4)   Spearleaf, Talayote
(incl. *Gonolobus* and *Vincetoxicum* spp.)
Etymology unknown.
W. N.Am.

The green <u>pods</u> of *M. pavifolia* (= *Gonolobus hastulatus*, = *Vincetoxicum hastu-
latum*) – S.W. U.S., Mex. – are said to be boiled in syrup and eaten as sweets.

The <u>fruits</u> of some species are reportedly eaten raw or cooked in Mexico.

Endangered species: *M. alabamensis* – Ala. –, *edwardensis, radiata* and
texensis – all three Tex.

Sarcostemma   (G 4)   Climbing Milkweed
(including *Philibertia* spp.)
From the Greek "sarx," flesh, and "stemma," crown: referring to the
fleshy inner corona.
S. U.S., Mex.

The leaves of *S. hirtellum* (= *Philibertia heterophylla*) were reportedly eaten
raw by California Indians.
The fruits of some species have reportedly been eaten.
Young shoots and sap of local species are used as food and beverage in tropical Asia.

SOLANACEAE

This important mostly tropical and subtropical family includes many poisonous plants, some of which can be deadly: jimsonweed, henbane, belladonna and
tobacco are probably the best known. Several of them also have hallucinogenic
properties.

Besides these dangerous plants, some of our most common vegetables are
found here: tomato, potato, eggplant and peppers (including green peppers,
chilis and cayenne).

But all Solanaceae contain more or less toxic alkaloids, at least in their green
parts (leaves, stems, shoots, immature fruits). The most prevalent is solanine,
which can produce digestive, nervous and cardiac disorders. Other alkaloids
(found in the four plants mentioned at the beginning of this chapter) are extremely dangerous, and even lethal in relatively small amounts; these are for the
most part: hyoscyamine, atropine (used medicinally as a mydriatic), scopolamine
and nicotine.

Capsicum (B 4)   Pepper

Etymology uncertain; possibly from the Latin "capsa," bookbox: alluding
to the shape of the fruits.

S. U.S., Mex.

Originally from tropical and subtropical America, *C. annuum*, bell pepper,
chili pepper, cayenne, paprika, and *baccatum* (= *C. frutescens* var. *baccatum*), bird pepper, are commonly cultivated for their fruits used as a vegetable or as a spice. The cultivated forms escape in S. U.S. & Mex. *C.
annuum* (m.a.) is also grown for ornament. *C. annuum* var. *minimum* is native from Ariz. to Tex., S. Fla. & Mex.; *C. baccatum* (m.a.) is native to Fla.,
S. Tex. to S. Ariz. & Mex.

More than a hundred different varieties of these species, mostly of *C. annuum*
(m.a.) are known. Their <u>fruits</u> come in a range of colors (red, yellow, deep purple, almost black and green before maturity) and pungency.

Peppers contain vitamin A (in the red and purple varieties) and large quantities of vitamin C, minerals, an essential oil and (in the pungent varieties) an extremely acrid substance, capsaicin.

In moderate amounts they are stimulant, aperitive and stomachic, but larger
doses are irritating and caustic, especially for the mucous membranes: they can
cause dermatitis and ulcers, as well as digestive and renal disorders.

Externally, peppers can be used as a rubefacient.

They have also been employed as an insect repellent.

Pungent varieties such as some chilis (or chiles) and cayenne are rich in cas-
paicin and must be used in moderation only as a condiment.

Mild ones, such as green or bell peppers or paprika, have a very low capsaicin
content; the former are commonly eaten raw or cooked as a vegetable. They are
sweeter and more aromatic after they have ripened and turned red or yellow, according to the variety.

Young pepper <u>leaves</u> are cooked and eaten in parts of Asia.

The <u>fruits</u> of local species are used as a condiment in tropical America, Africa
and Asia.

Chamaesaracha (D 4)

From the Greek "chamae," low, and "saracha," name of a S.Am. genus in the same family.

W. N.Am.

The <u>berries</u> of *C. coronopus* – S.W. U.S., Mex. – are eaten raw or cooked by the Navajos and Hopis. They are sometimes dried for later use.

Lycium (D 4) Box Thorn, Matrimony Vine

Greek name of a thorny shrub, "lykion."

U.S., Mex. Both native in S. U.S. & Mex. and species introduced from Eurasia.

L. chinense – originally from E. Asia – and *halimifolium* – from Eurasia –, both known as matrimony vine, are planted as ornamentals, along with a Mediterranean species (*L. europaeum*). They are naturalized in the U.S. & Mex.

The <u>young leaves</u> of *L. chinense* and *halimifolium* (m.a.) are eaten after cooking in Asia.

Those of the first species are also made into tea in Japan, under the name of "kuko."

Leaves and shoots of L. halimifolium (m.a.) contain an alkaloid similar to hyoscyamine; they are known to have poisoned cattle and sheep.

The <u>fruits</u> of *L. chinense* (m.a.) are eaten raw, cooked or dried. They have reportedly served for making a liqueur in the Far East.

On our continent, the ripe <u>fruits</u> of the following native species were eaten by Indians: *L. andersonii*, desert thorn – S.W. U.S., Mex. –, *fremontii* – S.W. U.S., N.W. Mex. –, *pallidum* and *torreyi* – both S.W. U.S., Mex.

When ripe the berries are red, juicy, sweetish, but generally rather insipid with a bitter aftertaste. They can be eaten raw or cooked, fresh or dried, and are not unpleasant. Indians used to make sauces with them.

They are known as "frutillos" in Mexico.

During famines, Indians of Northern Arizona ate a mixture of the dried berries of *L. pallidum* (m.a.) and saline clay.

The fruits of Eurasian species are known to contain some solanin and saponins: occasional cases of poisoning have been reported. The same probably applies to our species, so it is best to eat these berries in moderation only.

The leaves of our box thorns are fleshy, with a salty juice, and are pleasant to nibble on.

The fruits of local species are eaten in Europe, Asia, Northern Africa and Hawaii.

Lycopersicon esculentum (B-F 5)   Tomato

From the Greek "lykos," wolf, and "persikon," peach: wolf-peach.

Originally from W. S.Am., the plant is grown throughout the world for its fruits, most generally used as a vegetable and for making sauces. Some cultivars are planted for ornament. Tomato plants occasionally escape from cultivation but do not persist.

Ripe tomatos contain vitamins A and C in large quantities, vitamins B1, B2, B6, E, K and niacin, minerals, organic acids (malic, citric), pectins, saponins, histamine, a fixed oil, a coloring matter (lycopine), a substance with antibiotic properties (tomatine) and traces of solanine.

Tomato seeds contain an edible oil.

The fruits are diuretic, detoxicant, and refrigerant. They are generally more beneficial raw than cooked, as they become very acid with cooking. Certain persons are allergic to their histamine, saponin and solanine content.

Leaves and stems contain much solanine: large amounts of them can be dangerous and can cause digestive, nervous and cardiac disorders due to this toxic alkaloid.

The green fruits contain potentially harmful amounts of solanine, but are nonetheless commonly eaten in some parts of the world after cooking in sauces or in jams.

Tomato leaves have an aromatic odor: They repel insects and soothe the pain of their stings.

The fruits of a few local species are eaten in South America.

Physalis (B-F 3)   Ground Cherry, Tomatillo

Greek name of a plant with an inflated calyx, possibly of the Eurasian *P. alkekengi,* from "physaô," to swell up.

Throughout. Both native and species introduced from Eurasia & tropical Am.

P. ixocarpa   (= *P. philadelphica*),
tomatillo, Mexican ground cherry – Mex.,
naturalized in S. & E. U.S. – is commonly
cultivated in Mexico for its fruits which are
sold in markets. They are sometimes found
in U.S stores under the name of "husk
tomatoes."

P. peruviana, Cape gooseberry, Peru-
vian cherry – originally from S.Am. – is
planted now and then in North American
gardens for its fruits. It escapes from cultivation.

Physalis ixocarpa

Our native *P. pubescens* – S. U.S., Mex. – is occasionally grown for its fruits.
It escapes from cultivation up to Northern United States.

P. alkekengi, Chinese lantern plant – from S. & C. Eur. – is planted as an ornamental and sometimes escapes from cultivation.

The ripe fruits of the following native species have been eaten by Indians
and settlers: *P. fendleri* – S.W. U.S. –, *heterophylla* – E. & C. N.Am. –, *ixocarpa* (m.a.), *lanceolata* – C. U.S. –, *longifolia* – E. & C. N.Am., to Ariz. –, *neomexicana* – S.W. U.S. –, *pruinosa* – E. N.Am. & introduced elsewhere –,
pubescens (m.a.), *turbinata* (= *barbadensis* var. *obscura*) – S.E. U.S., Mex. –, *virginiana* – E. & C. U.S., to Ariz. – and *viscosa* – S.E. U.S., Mex.

They are generally sweet and pleasant to eat raw. In some cases, however,
there is a bitter aftertaste and the fruits are better cooked. They can be made
into jams, sauces or pies. In Southwestern United States and Mexico, "tomatil-
los," the green fruits of *P. ixocarpa* (m.a.), are made into a usually quite hot
"green sauce"; other species can be used as well.

Cape gooseberries, the orange-yellow fruits of *P. peruviana* (m.a.), have
a pleasant sweet, aromatic flavor. They are eaten raw, cooked as mentioned
above or dried. In Europe, they are sold in fancy food stores and high-class
restaurants.

Those of *P. alkekengi* (m.a.), a deep orange-red, are sweetish, sour and aromatic, but also bitter. They have been used as food since Antiquity in Europe,
generally after cooking.

They contain vitamin A, much vitamin C, minerals, a bitter principle (physaline), a fixed oil, tannin and mucilage.

They are diuretic, laxative and diaphoretic.

In the unripe stage, ground cherries should not be eaten raw in too large a quantity. They can be left to ripen in their husks.

Livestock has reportedly been poisoned from eating large amounts of the leaves and green fruits of *P. heterophylla* (m.a.) and *subglabrata* – E. & C. N.Am.

The <u>young leaves</u> of a tropical American species are eaten cooked in the Tropics.

The <u>fruits</u> of other species are used as food in various parts of the world.

Solanum (B-F 3)   Nightshade

Latin name of a species (possibly *S. nigrum*) from "sol," sun.

Throughout. Both native and introduced species.

Two tropical species (including *S. pseudocapsicum*, Jerusalem cherry) are planted for ornament.

The best-known member of this genus is undoubtedly *S. tuberosum*, potato – originally from the Andes. It is cultivated worldwide for its <u>tubers</u> and escapes locally on our continent, although not persistent. Its generalized use as food in Europe and North America dates back only to the 18th century, but potatoes rapidly became the staple of entire populations, to the point that the potato blight caused millions of the Irish to die or expatriate in the 1840s – a striking example of the dangers of monocultures and exclusive diets.

Hundreds of varieties have been developed and quite a few are in cultivation. Their edible uses are well-known. Moreover, alcohol (such as the Scandinavian aquavit) is distilled from potatoes. For this purpose, their starch must previously be transformed into simple sugars (as by the adjunction of malt; see *Hordeum vulgare*, Poaceae) to allow an alcoholic fermentation to take place.

The tubers contain starch, vitamins B (B1, B6, B9, niacin) and C in large quantities, vitamin K, minerals, tannins and so on.

Potatoes are nutritious and very digestible.

Externally, the tubers are emollient, either raw and grated or cooked and mashed. Slices of raw potato soothe the pain of burns and headaches.

The extracted juice is antispasmodic and reduces the hyperacidity of gastric secretions.

All green parts of the plant contain toxic alkaloids, especially solanine, including the young shoots and the green parts of tubers exposed to light during their growth or storage. Cases of human poisoning from eating green tubers are known. Animals have become seriously ill from feeding on potato sprouts.

However, potato <u>leaves</u> have been reported to be edible after boiling.

The small <u>tubers</u> of our native wild potatoes were much used as food by local Indians. These species are *S. cardiophyllum* – Mex. – and *S. fendleri* and *S. jamesii* – both Ariz. to Tex., Mex.

The tubers are good cooked, either boiled or roasted in embers. They were sometimes eaten with clay (it must be noted that Indians often used the beneficial properties of clay in their diet). It has

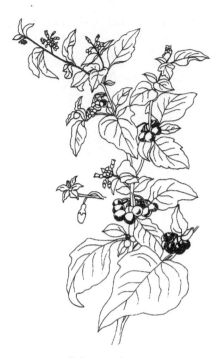

Solanum nigrum

been reported that the tubers of wild potatoes were occasionally eaten raw.

Following are some Indian uses of native species:

The <u>leaves</u> of *S. douglasii* – Calif., N.W. Mex. – were cooked and eaten as greens.

The <u>fruits</u> of *S. triflorum* – W. & C. N.Am., occasionally adventive in E. U.S. – were eaten raw or cooked with mush or with chili and salt.

Those of *S. piloferum* – Mex. – are fragrant. They were eaten locally in Mexico.

The <u>fruits</u> of *S. elaeagnifolium*, white horsenettle, silverleaf nettle – S.W. & S.C. U.S., Mex., introduced on Pacific Coast & in S.E. U.S. – and *xantii* – Calif. – (or their juice) were used for curdling milk. *S. elaeagnifolium* (m.a.) is known to contain a protein-digesting enzyme.

The <u>fruits</u> of *S. aculeatissimum*, soda apple – coast of S.E. U.S. & Mex. – are eaten after cooking in tropical America and Asia.

The <u>leaves</u> of *S. nigrum*, black nightshade (a cosmopolitan "weed," probably from Eurasia), have been used cooked as food in Southern Europe and Asia. Under the local name of "ana malaho," they are the most popular vegetable in

Madagascar, where they are cooked in sauces eaten with chicken and rice. They are also commonly used on the neighboring island of Réunion, under the name of "brède mafane." Even cooked, black nightshade leaves retain a definite bitterness, seemingly much appreciated in these areas.

In spite of these traditional uses, the leaves are generally considered poisonous in Western countries as they do contain solanine.

The black, ripe berries are eaten raw or cooked in parts of Southern Europe, Africa and Asia, as well as in Southern United States. A horticultural form is occasionally cultivated for its relatively large fruits and is known as "wonderberry." The fruits are generally made into pies.

Black nightshade is antispasmodic, analgesic and sedative.

Externally, the leaves are emollient.

S. melongena, eggplant – originally from India – is commonly cultivated for its large fruit. Wild plants occasionally appear from discarded seeds, but they do not persist.

Several varieties of all colors and sizes are known. The most frequent in North America is the large purple-fruited variety. The fruits are used as a vegetable, being generally fried, baked or pickled.

They contain vitamins A, B and C, niacin and minerals, all in relatively small proportions.

Leaves and green fruits contain solanine and are therefore toxic. However, in the Far East, the leaves are mixed with rice bran and salt, in which the root of a local radish (*Raphanus acanthiformis*) are pickled. They are also used externally as emollient poultices.

As with the potato and the eggplant, it must be noted that all green parts of *Solanum* spp. contain toxic alkaloids, especially solanine, and are potentially dangerous. Animals have been poisoned by eating leaves of *S. carolinense* – S. U.S., introduced northward –, *dulcamara* – introduced from Eur. –, *elaeagnifolium* (m.a.), *nigrum* (m.a.), *rostratum*, buffalo bur – C. U.S., Mex., introduced elsewhere – and *triflorum* (m.a.).

Cooked leaves are generally harmless, as boiling seems to destroy the toxic principle.

Unripe fruits are dangerous (they have caused animal poisoning) but their solanine content decreases upon ripening. The berries of *S. nigrum, piloferum* and *triflorum* (m.a.) become edible when ripe.

However, the fruits of some species such as *S. dulcamara*, bittersweet (m.a.) and *pseudocapsicum* (m.a.) are toxic, even when ripe.

Bittersweet berries contain solanine and saponins. The seeds are said to contain alkaloids close to those of the deadly nightshade, *Atropa belladona*, such as atropine.

They produce digestive, nervous, respiratory and cardiovascular disorders, occasionally resulting in death.

The stems of this plant contain saponins and have been employed as a depurative and diuretic, but they must be used in moderation.

Some species, such as *S. rostratum* (m.a.) and *sisymbryifolium* – introduced from S. Am. in S. U.S. & Mex. – are covered with sharp spines and can be mechanically injurious.

Roots, leaves and ripe fruits of local species are used as food in various parts of the world, mostly in the Tropics.

CONVOLVULACEAE

Convolvulus   (G 3)   Bindweed
(including *Calystegia* spp.)
From the Latin "convolvere," to roll together: referring to the twining stems.
Throughout. Both native and species introduced from Eur. & Asia.

Roots and young shoots of *C. sepium* (= *Calystegia s.*) – both native and forms introduced from Eur. into E. U.S – are said to have been used cooked as food in some parts of Asia.

The plant contains tannin and glucosides.

It is purgative and cholagogue.

The young shoots and the tender, fleshy stems of *C. soldanella* (= *Castylegia s.*), sea bindweed, beach morning glory – W. Coast of Mex. to Wash., also in the Old World – were reportedly pickled in vinegar in Europe, especially along the Southern coasts of England.

Ipomoea   (C-F-H 4)   Morning Glory
From the Greek "ips, ipos," worm, and "omoios," alike: referring to the
appearance of the rhizomes and stems of these plants.
E., C. & S. U.S., Mex. Both native and species introduced from trop-
ical Am.
A tropical American species (*I. purpurea*) is planted as an ornamental.

I. batatas, sweet potato – originally from tropical Am. – is cultivated in warm
regions of our continent and the rest of the world for its sweet and starchy
tubers. It is found locally as an escape in S. U.S. and Mex. Many cultivated
varieties are known.

Sweet potatoes are especially popular in Asia and on some islands of the Pacific. The tubers are boiled, steamed, baked, fried or roasted. They are sometimes ground into flour and a starch is extracted from them. They are also used
for brewing alcoholic drinks.

The tubers contain starch, sugars, vitamins B1 and niacin, plus vitamin A in
certain varieties, and minerals.

The leaves are edible raw or cooked. They are a common vegetable in some
parts of the Tropics.

They dye wool a yellowish-brown, with iron as a mordant.

Sweet potatoes are often the most productive crop of warm countries, in
terms of calories per weight.

The tuberous roots of the following native species were used as food by Indians: *I. leptophylla*, wild potato vine, bush morning glory, man root – W. U.S.,
Mex. –, *macrorhiza* – S.E. U.S. – and *pandurata* – E. N.Am.

The roots of *I. leptophylla* (m.a.) are said to be edible raw, but like the other
species mentioned, they were usually eaten boiled or roasted in embers. Those
of *I. pandurata* (m.a.) can reach up to two feet in length, but they are very hard
to dig out of the ground.

The roots of *I. plummerae* – Ariz., N.M. – are reported to be edible as
well.

Wild sweet potatoes vary much in taste according to locality and age.

It must be noted that some *Ipomoea* spp., including *I. pandurata* (m.a.) are
called "wild jalap" (jalap is the root of *I. jalapa* – Mex. – used medicinally as a
powerful cathartic) and are used when fresh as a strong purgative. It is therefore
important not to eat the tubers of this species in the raw stage (they are bitter as

such), but to boil them in a change of water. Care must be taken to properly identify the species.

Roots and stems of *I. cairica* – naturalized from Africa in S. Fla. – have been locally used as food in the Tropics.

Roots, stems and leaves of *I. pes-caprae* (var. *emarginata* is native from Ga. & Fla. to Tex. & Mex.) have been eaten as emergency food on Pacific islands. Large amounts are said to be toxic.

Young leaves and fleshy calyces and peduncles of *I. alba* (= *Calonyction aculeatum*), moon flower – S. Fla. & Tropics – are cooked in curries and soups in India.

The young seeds are said to be eaten in India.

The seeds of some species are known to have hallucinogenic properties.

Roots and leaves of many species are commonly used as food in the Tropics of both Worlds.

Endangered species: *I. egregia* and *lemmoni* – both Ariz.

CUSCUTACEAE

Cuscuta (G-H 4)   Dodder
Name possibly of Arabic derivation.
Throughout.

The seeds of *C. curta* and **umbellata** – both N.M. – were reportedly parched, ground and made into mush or soup by Indians.

Roots and vines of local species are used as food in Eastern Asia.

Dodders are parasitic to various plants.

Endangered species: *C. altenuata* – Okla. – and *howelliana* – Calif.

MENYANTHACEAE

Menyanthes trifoliata (E 4)   Bog Bean
Greek name of the plant from "minuthô," to diminish, and "anthos," flower: the flower does not last long.
N. N.Am. & Mountains. A monotypic genus.

The whole plant is strongly bitter. The <u>roots</u> were nonetheless used as food in Northern Europe (where the bog bean is also native), at least in times of dearth. They were dried, ground, washed several times to attenuate their bitterness, then dried and ground again. The meal obtained was mixed with cereal flours to make bread.

The <u>leaves</u>, also very bitter, have been used for flavoring beer.

The bog bean is a bitter tonic with stomachic, depurative and febrifuge properties.

POLEMONIACEAE

Gilia (G-H 4) Gilia
After Felipe Luis Gil, Spanish botanist.
W. N.Am.
Several native species are planted for ornament.

The <u>seeds</u> of *G. capitata* subsp. *staminea* (= *G. staminea*) were reportedly used as food by California Indians.
Endangered species: *G. caespitosa* – Utah – and *penstemonoides* – Colo.

Navarettia (G-H 4)
After Ferdinando Navarrette, Spanish physician.
Pacific Coast – Calif. to B.C.

The <u>seeds</u> of the strong-smelling *N. squarrosa*, skunkweed, have reportedly been used as food.
Endangered species: *N. pauciflora, pleiantha* and *setiloba* – all Calif.

HYDROPHYLLACEAE

Eriodyction (D-H 2) Yerba Santa
From the Greek "erion," wool, and "dictyon," net: referring to the undersurface of the leaves.
S.W. U.S. (to S. Ore.), Mex.

The leaves of various species are covered with a fragrant resin: Chewing on the fresh leaves alleviates thirst while hiking and imparts a sweet flavor to water which is drunk immediately afterwards. They also make an aromatic tea.

E. angustifolium – S. Nev., S. Utah, Ariz. – and *californicum* – Calif., S.W. Ore. – are especially pleasant to use.

The leaves of both species (but more generally the latter) are used medicinally as an expectorant, febrifuge, antispasmodic and tonic. *E. trichocalyx* – Calif. – was employed for similar purposes by Indians and settlers.

Endangered species: *E. altissimum* and *capitatum* – both Calif.

Hydrophyllum (D 3)   Waterleaf
From the Greek "hydor," water, and "phyllon," leaf; there is no known significance.
Throughout.

The fleshy roots of *H. canadense* – E. U.S. – and *occidentale* – W. U.S. – have reportedly been cooked and eaten by Indians.

Young shoots and leaves of *H. appendiculatum*, *canadense* (m.a.), *occidentale* (m.a.) and *virginianum* are edible raw or cooked. They were used as food by Indians, and, at least in the case of *H. appendiculatum* (m.a.), by early settlers. They have a pleasant flavor.

Phacelia (G-H 4)   Phacelia, Scorpionweed
From the Greek "phakelos," cluster: alluding to the crowded flowers.
Throughout, especially in W. N.Am.
A few native species are planted for ornament.

The leaves of *P. ramosissima* – W. U.S. – are said to have been used as cooked greens. Those of *P. dubia* – Appalachians – were cooked by Cherokee Indians.

Those of most species are small and hairy. Contact with the glandular hairs of some phacelias is known to cause dermatitis in susceptible individuals.

The species most commonly incriminated are: *P. brachyloba* – S. Calif., Baja –, *crenulata* – S.W. U.S. –, *grandiflora*, *minor*, wild canterbury bell – both S. Calif., Baja –, and *pedicellata* – S.W. U.S., Baja.

P. tanacetifolia is much planted, especially in Europe, as a bee plant, due to the quantity of nectar its flowers produce.

Endangered species: *P. argillacea* – Utah –, *beatleyae* – Nev. –, *capitata* – Ore. –, *cookei* – Calif. –, *filiformis* – Ariz. –, *formosula* – Colo. –, *indecora* – Utah –, *mammillariensis* – Utah –, *pallida* – Tex. –, *submutica* – Colo. – and *wilshii* – Ariz.

LENNOACEAE

Ammobroma sonorae (H 5) Sand Root
From the Greek "ammos," sand, and "brôma," food: a translation of the Papago name of the plant, "biatatk," sandfood.
S. Calif., S. Ariz., Baja & N.W. Son. A monotypic genus.

The long, fleshy underground <u>stems</u> were an important source of food for local Indians, especially the "sand Papagos." The stems were eaten raw or roasted, or occasionally dried and ground into a meal, often mixed with mesquite meal (*Prosopis juliflora*, Fabaceae). They are juicy and have a pleasant flavor.

The entire plant is found buried in the sand, with only the flowering tops lying upon the surface of the ground. Sand root is parasitic to *Coldenia* and *Eriogonum* spp.

The plant is endangered.

Pholisma arenarium (H 5)
From the Greek "pholis," fish scale: referring to the scalelike leaves.
S. Calif., Baja. A monotypic genus.

The fleshy underground <u>stem</u> was eaten by Indians like that of *Ammobroma sonorae*, which it resembles.

The plant, also buried in the sand, is parasitic to *Hymenoclea* and *Chrysothamnus* spp.

The plant is endangered.

BORAGINACEAE

Many plants in this family have traditionally been eaten by humans for centuries. Their leaves are generally tender and often have a pleasant taste.

These plants contain much mucilage, which gives them soothing properties.

But most, if not all, of them also contain pyrrolizidine alkaloids, which can cause severe liver diseases if ingested in quantity or, even in smaller amounts, regularly over a long period of time. Caution should therefore be used when using these plants.

Amsinckia (D-H 2)   Fiddleneck

After William Amsinck, patron of the Hamburg botanical garden during the 19th century.
W. N.Am.

The young shoots and leaves of *A. lycopsoides* – W. U.S. – were eaten by Indians in California. Those of other species, such as *A. intermedia* – W. N.Am., introduced eastward – are edible raw or cooked with no ill effects, at least in moderate quantities.

The small seeds of *A. tessellata* – W. N.Am. – were reportedly gathered and eaten by some Indian tribes in Utah.

It has been shown that horses, cattle and especially swine develop hepatic cirrhosis when fed wheat screenings containing seeds of *A. intermedia* (m.a.), due to the pyrrolizidine alkaloids they contain. *Amsinckia* spp. should therefore only be eaten sparingly.

Endangered species: *A. grandiflora* – Calif.

Anchusa (D 4   Alkanet, Bugloss

Greek name of a plant in this family, "agchousa" (possibly this plant): referring to its root from which was extracted a red dye used for cloth and as a cosmetic.
Introduced from Eur. in E. N.Am.
A few species are cultivated for ornament.

The young leaves of *A. officinalis* were cooked as greens in Southern France and in Germany.

A red coloring matter derived from the root has reportedly been used for coloring fats, oils and liqueurs.

Bugloss contains tannin, mucilage and alkaloids (cynoglossine, consolidine).

The plant is used medicinally like borage, *Borago officinalis,* as an expectorant, emollient and diaphoretic.

Borago officinalis (B 4) Borage

Name dating back to the Middle Ages from the Latin "burra," coarse woolen cloth: alluding to the rough texture of the leaves and stems.

Originally from S. Eur., borage is occasionally grown as a medicinal, ornamental, edible or bee plant. It escapes from cultivation in E. N.Am. Borage has been cultivated since the Middle Ages.

The young <u>leaves,</u> the top of the <u>stems</u> and the beautiful azure <u>flowers</u> can be eaten raw. The leaves have a refreshing cucumber taste, while the flowers have a definite oyster flavor.

Borago officinalis

Older <u>leaves</u> are better cooked, as they, along with the stems, are covered with stiff bristles that can irritate the skin. Raw, their texture is rather unpleasant. They are cooked as greens or as fritters in Southern Europe. In Greece, they are stuffed with rice to make "dolmades," as with grape leaves.

Borage leaves were pickled in Europe and in India.

The <u>flowers</u> have served to flavor drinks since the time of the Ancient Greeks who would call the plant "euphrosunon," meaning joy in a feast, as it was supposed to make one merry.

The plant contains mucilage, tannin, saponin, potassium and traces of essential oil.

Stems and leaves are diaphoretic and diuretic. The flowers are emollient, expectorant and slightly laxative.

Bourreria (D 5) Strongbark, Currant Tree

Etymology unknown.

S. Fla.

The small <u>fruits</u> of **B. obovata** are edible when ripe, but are of mediocre flavor.

The bark can be made into tea.

The <u>fruits</u> of other species are used as food in the West Indies.

Cordia   (D 4)   Cordia
Etymology unknown.
S. Ariz. to S. Fla., Mex.
C. sebestana, geiger tree – S. Fla., Mex., W.I. – is occasionally planted for ornament.

Its <u>fruits</u> are eaten raw or pickled.

Those of **C. alliodora** – Mex., C.Am. – are said to be used as food by Mexican Indians.

The <u>fruits</u> of various species are eaten raw or cooked throughout the Tropics.

Cynoglossum   (G 4)   Hound's Tongue, Wild Comfrey
Greek name of various plants, from "kyôn, kunos," dog, and "glôssa," tongue: alluding to the shape of the leaves in some species.
Throughout. Both native and species introduced from Eurasia.

The <u>roots</u> of **C. grande**, great hound's tongue – Calif. to Wash. – were reportedly cooked and eaten by some California Indians.

The <u>leaves</u> of **C. officinale** – naturalized from Eur. – are said to have been used raw in salads in Switzerland.

The roots of this species contain tannin, resin, an essential oil, inulin and alkaloids, including consolidine and cynoglossine. The latter is harmless for mammals, but is toxic for cold-blooded animals.

Externally, they are emollient and slightly astringent.

The leaves can irritate the skin of susceptible individuals. When ingested in large quantities, they are thought to be somewhat poisonous.

Ehretia (D 5)   Ehretia
Etymology unknown.
S. Tex., Mex.
Our native *E. anacua* (= *E. elliptica*) is planted for ornament in Tex. Its fruit is edible, but rather insipid, with a thin pulp.

The fruits of other species are used as food in various parts of the Tropics.

Lithospermum (G 4)   Gromwell
From the Greek "lithos," stone, and "sperma," seed: alluding to the appearance and the hardness of the seeds.
Throughout. Both native and species introduced from Eurasia.

The roots of *L. incisum* – W. N.Am. – were reportedly cooked (boiled or roasted) and eaten by some Indians.
The young leaves of *L. officinale* – naturalized from Eur. in N.E. N.Am. – are said to be edible, and also to have been made into "Croatian tea."
The plant contains minerals and hormone-like substances. It is also diuretic.
The seeds are coated with a mucilage layer and are used, after soaking in water, to remove foreign matter – to which they adhere – from the eyes.
A purple dye was obtained from the roots of some of these plants by Indians.

Mertensia (B 3)   Bluebell
After F. S. Mertens (1764–1831), German botanist.
Throughout.

The roots of *M. maritima*, oyster plant – coasts of Mass., north to Greenland & N. Can., west to Alaska & south to B.C.; also in Eur. – were reportedly eaten by the Inuits of Alaska.
The leaves were cooked as greens by various Indian tribes. They are also edible raw.

Plagiobotrys   (D 2)   Popcorn Flower
From the Greek "plagios," on the side, and "bothrys," pit: referring to the
caruncular scar of *P. fulvus*.
W. N.Am.

Young shoots and seeds of *P. fulvus* var. ***campestris*** (= *P. campestris*) – Calif.,
Ore. – have been used as food by California Indians.

Symphytum   (A 3)   Comfrey
Greek name of plants with healing properties, possibly that of comfrey,
from "symphô," to unite into a whole.
Scattered throughout.
Introduced from Eurasia.
S. officinale (as well as Russian comfrey, *S. x uplandicum*) is often grown in
gardens for its medicinal properties, as a vegetable, as green manure and
for its beneficial properties to the plants. It is locally naturalized on our
continent.

The young leaves are edible raw. Their texture and taste are pleasant. But they become
hairy and rough with age and need to be cooked.
They are mucilaginous and make good soups
and delectable fritters.

Young stems and petioles can be eaten raw,
but were formerly often blanched like asparagus.

Comfrey contains vitamins (including vitamin B12), minerals, tannin, mucilage, alkaloids
(including symphyto-cynoglossine), allantoin,
choline, etc. The root also contains starch, sugars, asparagine and traces of essential oil.

The pyrrolizidine alkaloids in comfrey are potentially toxic, but they are present in small
amounts and the occasional consumption of the
plant does not seem to be dangerous, according
to a survey conducted by the British Henry Dou-
bleday Research Association (an organization of

Symphytum officinale

organic gardeners). However, large quantities of comfrey or daily intake should be avoided.

Comfrey root is astringent, emollient and expectorant. It is grated raw for use in healing externally.

The leaves placed in vegetable waste will reduce the offensive odor.

The leaves of *S. asperum* (= *S. asperrimum*), rough comfrey – naturalized from Eurasia in N.Am. – are edible as well, as are those of the cultivated Russian comfrey (m.a.).

VERBENACEAE

Avicennia germinans (G-F 5)   Black Mangrove
After Abu Senna, an Arab physician in the Middle Ages.
(= *A. nitida*)
Gulf Coast – Fla. to Tex., Mex.

The sprouting seeds are said to be edible after thorough cooking. They are very bitter and toxic in the raw stage.

Salt can be gathered from the surface of the leaves.

The kernels of the fruits of another species are used as food in Southeast Asia.

Callicarpa (D 4)   Beauty Berry
From the Greek "kallos," beauty, and "karpos," fruit: beauty fruit.
E. U.S., Mex. Both native and species introduced from Eurasia.
Two Asian species are planted for ornament.

The small purple fruits of *C. americana* – S.E. U.S., Mex. – are edible raw. They are juicy, sweet at first, then pungent. It is preferable to partake of them in moderation only.

The fruits of a Northeast Asian species are eaten locally.

The bark of several other species is chewed like betel nut in tropical Asia.

The leaves of an East Asian beauty berry (*C. japonica*, planted for ornament in North America) are made into tea in China and Japan.

Citharexylum (G 5) Fiddlewood
From the Greek "kithara," zither, and "xylon," wood.
S. Fla., Tex., Mex.

The ripe fruit of *C. fruticosum* – Fla. – is said to be edible, but is unpleasant to eat.

Lantana (G 4) Lantana
Etymology unknown.
Introduced from tropical Am., *L. camara* is planted for ornament, as well as some S.Am. species; it is naturalized from Ga. to Tex. & Mex.

The fruit is sometimes eaten raw as a condiment or nibbled on by children. It is sweet and slightly aromatic.

However, cattle have been poisoned, sometimes fatally, by grazing on the leaves of this species and those of *L. involucrata*. A photosensitizing substance, lantanin, is found in their strongly odorous foliage.

The fruits of two other species are used as food in the Tropics.

Lippia (B 4)
After A. Lippi (1678–1704), botanist-physician from Paris, killed in Abyssina.
S. U.S., Mex.
L. alba, alfombrillo, oregano de burro – S. Tex., Mex. – is grown locally as an herb.
Lemon verbena (*L. triphylla* – W. S.Am.) is cultivated for its fragrant leaves, used as tea.
Varieties of *L. nodiflora* (= *Phyla n.*) – S.E. U.S. to S.Am. – are grown for ornament.

The following native species are aromatic and can be used as a condiment or made into tea: *L. alba* (m.a.), *geminata* – Key West, tropical Am. –, *graveolens*, hierba dulce – Tex., N.M., Mex. – and *wrightii* (= *Aloysia w.*), oreganillo – Calif. to Tex., N. Mex.

The leaves of *L. geminata* (m.a.) have a mint-like odor, and are reportedly eaten as a vegetable in India, where the plant was introduced.

Local species are used as tea or for flavoring food in various parts of the Tropics.

Livestock is thought to have been poisoned by grazing on *L. ligustrina*, white brush – Tex., Mex.

Stachytarpheta jamaicensis (G 5)   Blue Porterweed
(= *Valerianoides j.*)
From the Greek "stachys," flower spike, and "tarphys," dense, thick.
S. Fla., Mex.

The <u>leaves</u> are made into tea in the West Indies.
The <u>flowering tops</u> are said to be used for flavoring food in Java.

Verbena (C-H 4)   Vervain
Celtic "fer," to take away, and "faen," stone: alluding to the former use of the European *V. officinalis* in the treatment of bladder stones.
Scattered throughout. Both native and species introduced from Eurasia & S.Am.
A few S.Am. species are planted for ornament.

The <u>seeds</u> of *V. hastata*, blue vervain – almost throughout – were used as food by Indians. They were first soaked in several changes of cold water to remove their bitterness, then dried or roasted, and ground into flour.

The leaves have been made into a tea, which is diaphoretic, expectorant, sedative, vermifuge and vulnerary. Large doses are emetic.

The <u>leaves</u> of *V. officinalis*, European vervain – naturalized from Eurasia – although very bitter, are reportedly eaten in Japan after parboiling and seasoning.

The plant is used medicinally as an antispasmodic, sedative, galactagogue and expectorant.

Endangered species: *V. tampensis* – Fla.

Vitex (D 5)

Latin name of the Mediterranean *V. agnus-castus*, possibly from "vieo," to weave baskets: the flexible stems were used in ancient Greece for basket-making.

S.E. U.S., Mex.

Both native in Mex. and species introduced from Eur. & Asia.

V. agnus-castus, chaste tree – naturalized from S. Eur. into S.E. U.S. & Mex. – and *negundo* – from N.E. Asia, locally escaped – are planted for ornament.

The seeds of the chaste tree have been used as a spice, but they do not have much flavor. The shrub is sometimes known as "wild pepper" or "monk's pepper" in Europe.

The fruit, a small drupe, contains hormone-like substances.

It is said to have anaphrodisiac properties, hence the name "chaste tree."

The aromatic leaves contain an essential oil and glucosides. They are antispasmodic and sedative.

Roots and leaves of *V. negundo* (m.a.) are made into tea in East Asia.

The fruit of *V. mollis* – Mex. – is eaten raw.

The fruits of many species are used as food in the Tropics of both worlds.

LAMIACEAE (LABIATAE)

This family is comprised of more aromatic plants than any other: Many of its members contain essential oils and are used universally for flavoring food and making fragrant teas, with stomachic and antiseptic virtues. In most cases, both the flowering tops and the leaves can be employed.

The essential oils are contained in glands which can be observed on the leaves and flowers of numerous Lamiaceae. These oils are often extracted by distillation and many of these plants are cultivated on a large scale for this purpose. Essential oils are used in aromatherapy. In moderate quantities, they have beneficial effects, but large doses can be toxic.

Many plants in this family are cultivated for medicinal purposes or as ornamentals.

Acanthomintha (B-H 5) Thornmint
From the Greek "akantha," thorn, and "mintha," mint. This mint-smelling plant is spiny.
S. Calif., Baja.

The leaves of *A. ilicifolia, lanceolata* and *obovata* are aromatic.
Endangered species: *A. ilicifolia* (m.a.) and *obovata* (m.a.) subsp. *duttonii.*

Agastache (B 3) Giant Hyssop
From the Greek "agan," much, and "stachys," spike: alluding to the inflorescence.
Throughout, mostly W. N.Am.
A. foeniculum, lavender giant hyssop – C. N.Am. – is sometimes cultivated in gardens as an aromatic plant.

Leaves and flowering tops of the various species are aromatic and make pleasant additions to salads and other dishes.
Those of *A. foeniculum* (m.a.) and *neomexicana* – N.M. – were used as a flavoring by Indians.
They also made tea with the leaves of *A. anethiodora* – W. U.S.
The seeds of *A. urticifolia* – W. N.Am. – were eaten by some Indian tribes.
The young shoots of a local species are eaten cooked in E. Asia.

Ajuga (D 4) Bugle
Latin name of the plant.
Scattered throughout.
Introduced from Eur.
A few European species are planted for ornament; some of these, including *A. genevensis* and *reptans*, occasionally escape.

The leaves of the species mentioned are edible raw, but are quite bitter. They make little more than interesting additions to salads.
They contain tannin and are astringent.
Externally, the plant is used as a vulnerary.
In Japan, the leaves of a related species are boiled in several changes of water to lessen their bitterness, and are eaten with seasonings.

Blephilia (B 4)   Horse Mint
From the Greek "blepharis," eyelash: referring to the ciliate bracts.
E. & C. U.S.

The <u>leaves</u> of *B. hirsuta* smell like peppermint.

Cedronella (B 4)   Herb of Gilead
Diminutive of the Greek "kedros," cedar.
Both native in Ariz. & Mex. and species introduced from the Canary
Islands.
Our native *C. cana* – Mex. – and *mexicana* – S. Ariz., Mex. – are planted
for ornament, along with *C. canariensis* (= *Dracocephalum canariense*), herb
of Gilead – from the Canary Islands, occasionally escapes from gardens in
Calif.

These three species are aromatic. Their <u>leaves</u> are used occasionally for flavoring drinks or for making tea.

Conradina (H 5)
After S. W. Conrad (1779–1831), American botanist.
S. U.S.

The narrow <u>leaves</u> of *C. verticillata*, Cumberland rosemary – E. parts of Ky.
& Tenn. – resemble those of rosemary (*Rosmarinus officinalis*) in shape and odor.
Endangered species: *C. brevifolia, glabra, grandiflora* – all Fla. – and *verticil-
lata* (m.a.).

Cunila (B 4)   Dittany
Latin name of some species of Lamiaceae.
E. U.S. & Mex.

The <u>leaves</u> are aromatic. Those of *C. origanoides* – E. U.S. – and *longiflora* –
Mex. – have been used as an herb or for making tea.
The powdered leaves of the former species were used as an insecticide.

Glechoma hederacea (D 2)   Ground Ivy
(= *Glecoma h.*)

From the Greek "glêkhôn," pennyroyal (*Mentha pulegium*).
Originally from Eur., the plant is sometimes grown for ornament and is widely naturalized in N. N.Am.

The <u>leaves</u> have a peculiar, aromatic smell (reminiscent of mint, of lemon and of the back of the woods) and a slightly bitter taste.
They make a pleasant tea and were used to flavor beer in Europe up until the 17th century. They can be added raw to salads or made into aromatic sauces.
Ground ivy contains tannin, an essential oil, a bitter principle and vitamin C.
It is expectorant, tonic and astringent, and has been used medicinally since Antiquity.
Horses have occasionally been poisoned by eating very large quantities of the fresh or dried leaves.

Hedeoma (B-H 3)   Pennyroyal
From the Greek "hedyosmon," name of some fragrant species of mint, from "hedys," sweet, and "osmê," odor.
Throughout.
H. pulegioides – E. & C. N.Am. – is occasionally cultivated for the essential oil it contains, which is used as a mosquito repellent.

The <u>plant</u> has a strong mint-like odor, reminiscent of the European pennyroyal, *Mentha pulegium*.
It can be made into a tea with carminative, emmenagogue, diaphoretic and sedative properties. Large quantities may be abortive.
The <u>leaves</u> of *H. nana*, mock pennyroyal – W. U.S. – are said to be chewed in N.M.
The <u>flowering tops</u> of *H. drummondii* – C. N.Am. – are made into tea in Tex.
Endangered species: *H. graveolens* – Fla.

Hyptis (B 4) Desert Lavender
From the Greek "hyptios," turned back: referring to the lower lip of the flowers.
S. U.S., Mex.

The leaves of *H. albida* – Mex. – are used locally for flavoring food.
The seeds of *H. emoryi* – S. Ariz., S. Calif., N.M. – were reportedly gathered and used as food by Indians in the same manner as those of the chia sages (several *Salvia* spp.); they are also known as "chia."
Flowers and leaves of this species have a fragrant, lavender-like odor.
Leaves and seeds of other species are used as food in tropical Asia and Africa.

Hyssopus officinalis (B 4) Hyssop
Greek name of the plant, "hyssôpos."
Scattered throughout.
Originally from S. Eur., hyssop is cultivated as an herb and medicinal plant. It is occasionally found as an escape.

The leaves and flowering tops are an excellent condiment in salads and various dishes, although they are seldom used. They have also been employed for flavoring alcoholic beverages and for making perfume.
They contain an essential oil, tannins, a glucoside, saponin, minerals, and various other substances.
Hyssop is stimulant, expectorant, stomachic, carminative, antiseptic and emmenagogue. Externally it is used as a healing agent.
The essential oil distilled from the plant can, in large doses, lead to severe nervous disorders such as epilepsy.
Hyssop has been used by man since Antiquity.

Hyssopus officinalis

Lamium (B 2) Dead Nettle, Henbit
From the Greek and Latin "lamia," ogress, and "laimos," throat: alluding to the long, wide-open throat of the flower.
Throughout. Naturalized from Eurasia.

The <u>leaves</u> of *L. album* – naturalized in N.E. N.Am. – *amplexicaule* – naturalized throughout –, *maculatum* – naturalized in N.E. N.Am. – and *purpureum* – naturalized throughout – are eaten raw or cooked in Europe and Asia. They are not aromatic, but have a pleasant taste and make good salads and greens.

L. album (m.a.) contains tannin, mucilage, glucosides, potassium, sugars and histamine.

Leaves and flowering tops have been employed since the Middle Ages as an astringent, hemostatic and expectorant.

Lamium album

Lepechinia (G 5) Pitcher Sage
After Lepechin, Russian botanist and traveler.
Calif.

The <u>plants</u> are aromatic, especially *L. fragrans* – S.W. Calif.

Lycopus (C 4) Water Horehound
From the Greek "lykos," wolf, and "pous," foot.
Throughout.

The tuberous <u>rootstock</u> of *L. amplectens* – E. Coast of U.S. –, *asper* – C. & W. N.Am. – and *uniflorus* – N. N.Am. – was eaten raw or cooked by Indians. In these species, the rhizome is fleshy and has a mild, pleasant flavor.

That of *L. lucidus* – Calif. to Wash. – is eaten in E. Asia, where the plant is native as well.

The leaves of *L. virginicus* – E. N.Am. – and of related species have been used in cases of hyperthyreosis.

They contain tannin, a bitter glucoside (lysopine) and an essential oil.

Marrubium vulgare (D 3) Horehound
Latin name of the plant, possibly from the Hebrew "mar," bitter, and "rob," sap, juice.
Throughout. Naturalized from Eurasia.
The plant, formerly in cultivation for its medicinal virtues, was held in high esteem since Antiquity.

Horehound candy and syrup were made with the leaves.
The plant is said to have been used as a condiment, in spite of its strong bitterness and musky smell. It is occasionally used to flavor liquors.
Horehound contains an essential oil, a bitter substance (marrubine), mucilage, tannin, saponin, minerals, etc.
It is tonic, expectorant, stomachic, depurative, diuretic and stimulant for the heart and liver. Horehound is reportedly helpful in losing weight.

Melissa officinalis (A 3) Lemon Balm
Greek and Latin name of the plant, "melissaina," "melissophyllon," "meliteia" – from "melissa," bee: the flowers are much visited by bees.
Originally from S. Eur., lemon balm has been grown since Antiquity as an herb, for medicine and as a bee plant. It is locally naturalized on our continent.

Fresh leaves and flowering tops have a refreshing lemon odor and taste. They impart a delicious flavor to salads, desserts and drinks.
The plant contains an essential oil.
It is antispasmodic, sedative, stomachic, carminative and diaphoretic.
Along with other aromatic plants, lemon balm is distilled after macerating in alcohol to yield a spirit used as an antispasmodic and stomachic. Known as "eau des Carmes," it was first prepared in France in the 17th century.

Melissa officinalis

Mentha (A 2-3) Mint

Greek and Latin name of the plant, "minthê": classical Greek name. Throughout. One native and several species introduced from Eurasia. Several Eurasian species are planted as herbs or, on a large scale, for the essential oil distilled from the plants and used in flavoring drinks, toothpastes, chewing gum, candies and liquors. These mints are naturalized in N.Am. A Corsican species is planted as an ornamental.

Leaves and flowering tops of various mints have been used as a condiment since Antiquity. They are added fresh to salads, desserts and cold drinks, to which they impart their characteristic fragrance. Mint sauce is still a favorite in Anglo-Saxon countries, while mint tea is served in every French café.

American Indians often ate mint leaves after roasting them in a fire, or used them as a seasoning.

All *Mentha* spp. are aromatic. They contain essential oils, the composition of which varies according to the species: Each mint has its own particular odor.

Mints are stimulant, stomachic, carminative and antiseptic.

They are used to repel insects, and the essential oil distilled from the plant is an effective parasiticide.

The following species are used:

M. aquatica, water mint – introduced from Eurasia – has a refreshing odor due to the menthol it contains. The plant is used in Asia for flavoring food and liqueurs.

It contains tannins and an essential oil. It has stomachic, astringent, cholagogue and antispasmodic properties. Var. *crispa* is cultivated for ornament and rarely escapes.

M. arvensis (including *M. canadensis*), field mint – some forms are native to N.Am., others are introduced from Eurasia – has, when fresh, a very delicate smell. The plant is used as a condiment in Asia, and an oil is distilled from it. Our native varieties were much used by the Indians.

M. x citrata, bergamot mint – horticultural hybrid – has a definite smell of bergamot (*Citrus bergamia*, Rutaceae). An essential oil is distilled from the plant. Like lemon oil, this oil contains lemonene.

M. x gentilis = *M. arvensis* x *spicata* (= *M. cardiàca*), apple mint – introduced from Eur.

M. longifolia (= *M. sylvestris*) – from Eurasia and N. Africa. The leaves are made into tea. Their smell is not very pleasant, and the essential oil they contain is volatile. They are better made into sun tea (steeped in cold water and left for half a day in a glass jar in the sun) than infused in hot water.

M. x piperita = *M. aquatica* x *spicata,* peppermint – a natural hybrid introduced from Eur. – is cultivated commercially for its essential oil containing 40 to 80% menthol, a crystallizing substance with a cooling, aromatic odor.

Menthol is generally extracted from the Japanese mint (*M. arvensis* var. *piperascens*), whose oil contains over 90% menthol. Most mints do not contain menthol.

It is used medicinally as an analgesic and antiseptic, but if taken orally it tends to irritate the stomach.

Peppermint is an excellent condiment, especially in fruit salads, desserts and drinks.

The plant has the medicinal virtues mentioned above, and is also antispasmodic, but in high doses it acts as an excitant and supposedly as an aphrodisiac.

Peppermint oil is used as a flavoring, and besides all the medicinal uses already mentioned, as an antiemetic.

M. pulegium, pennyroyal – introduced from Eurasia – can also be used as a flavoring. It has a strong but pleasant smell.

The plant is stomachic, expectorant, emmenagogue and cholagogue.

It repels insects, including fleas: Pennyroyal oil is employed in the making of "flea collars" for domestic animals, and is also a mosquito repellent. It can be used as a parasiticide.

M. rotundifolia, round-leaved mint – introduced from Eur. – is not very fragrant.

M. spicata (= *M. viridis*), spearmint – introduced from Eurasia – is commonly planted in gardens and used as an herb. This species is generally the one used in making mint sauce. In the Middle East, it is used for flavoring tabouleh (a salad made out of cracked wheat and vegetables) and various dishes. A heavily sweetened infusion of spearmint and black tea leaves (*Thea sinensis*, Camelliaceae) is the "mint tea" of North Africa; often a pinch of wormwood (*Artemisia absinthium*, Asteraceae) is added for tang.

Spearmint is also cultivated for its essential oil, used in flavoring chewing gum, toothpaste, drinks, etc.

Other mints can be found on our continent, either native or introduced, including many hybrids. All can be used as described above.

Local species are used in various parts of the world.

Moldavica (C 4)
(= *Dracocephalum* spp.)
Name of the European country, "Moldavia."
Almost throughout. Both native and introduced species.

The seeds of *M. parviflora* (= *Dracocephalum parviflorum*), dragon head – N. N.Am. & W. Mountains – were ground into flour by the Havasupai Indians of N. Ariz.

Monarda (B 2)   Horsemint, Bee Balm
After Nicholas Monardes (1493–1588), Spanish physician and botanist.
Throughout.
M. didyma, Oswego tea – N.E. N.Am., Appalachians – is sometimes planted as an ornamental, especially in Eur.

Leaves and flowering tops of the various species are very aromatic. They were often used by Indians and white settlers as seasoning for stews and for making tea. They can also be added to salads and cooked vegetables.

The plants contain an essential oil rich in thymol.

They are carminative, stimulant and stomachic.

The following species were often used:
M. citriodora – N.M., Ariz., N. Mex. –, *didyma* (m.a.), *fistulosa* (= *menthaefolia*), wild bergamot – almost throughout – and *pectinata* – W. & C. U.S.

Monardella (B-H 2)   Western Pennyroyal
Diminutive form of Monarda, which it resembles.
W. N.Am.

The plants are very aromatic and can be used as an herb and as tea.
M. lanceolata – Calif., Baja –, **odoratissima** – Calif. to Wash. – and **villosa** subsp. **sheltonii** (= *sheltonii*) – Calif., S. Ore. – have been much used for this purpose.

Endangered species: *M. leucocephala, linoides* subsp. *viminea, macrantha* var. *hallii, pringlei* and *undulata* var. *frutescens* – all Calif.

Nepeta cataria (B 3)   Catnip
Latin name of a plant, possibly this one, from "Nepeta," a town in ancient Etruria.
Originally from S. Eur., catnip is cultivated in gardens for its aromatic leaves used as a condiment, and more often as tea. It is widely naturalized on our continent.

The plant has a peculiar smell which is especially attractive to cats.

Catnip contains an essential oil, vitamin C and other substances.

It is antispasmodic, stomachic and carminative.

Roots and leaves of local species are used as food in East Asia.

Catmint (*N. grandiflora*) and another exotic species are planted for ornament.

Nepeta cataria

Ocimum (B 4)   Basil
Greek name of *O. basilicum*: alluding to the aromatic smell of the plant.
Scattered throughout.
O. micranthum, wild basil, is native to S. Fla. & Mex. Other species introduced from the Tropics & Africa.

Var. 'Dark opal,' with deep purple leaves is sometimes planted for ornament.
O. basilicum – originally from tropical Asia & Africa – is often grown in veg-

etable gardens for its fragrant <u>leaves</u>. Fresh basil is one of the finest herbs to add to salads, vegetable dishes and soups. It goes especially well with tomatoes. The plant occasionally escapes, but it does not persist.

Basil contains an essential oil, which is distilled and used as a flavoring in some countries.

It is tonic, stomachic, carminative, antispasmodic and galactagogue.

The <u>seeds</u> have reportedly been used as food.

Basil has been known in Europe since ancient Rome.

Several other species are used as condiments in various parts of the Tropics.

Origanum vulgare (B 4)   Oregano

Greek name of some aromatic Lamiaceae, meaning "ornament of the mountains," from "oros," mountain, and "ganos," brightness.

Originally from S. Eur. & Asia, oregano is commonly cultivated as an herb; it is especially popular in Mex. The plant is naturalized on our continent.

Marjoram (*O. marjorana* – from N. Africa & S.W. Asia) is also often grown in gardens and used as a condiment.

The <u>leaves</u> and <u>flowering tops</u> of both oregano and marjoram impart an excellent, aromatic taste to salads and various cooked dishes. They also make pleasant teas. Oregano was reportedly used in Sweden for flavoring beer.

The plants contain an essential oil.

This oil is antispasmodic, stomachic, carminative, expectorant and tonic. Oregano oil has strong antiseptic properties.

Marjoram oil can be narcotic in high doses.

Both plants have been used as condiments since Antiquity.

A few local species are employed in Africa and Asia.

Origanum vulgare

Perilla frutescens (B 4)   Beefsteak Plant, Perilla, Shiso
East Indian name of this species.
Originally from E. Asia, the plant is grown for ornament in our countries. It
is naturalized locally in E. & C. N.Am.
In Asia, perilla is cultivated for its leaves and seeds.

The leaves have a purple color and a sweetish taste. In Japan, they are used
for flavoring salads, and a preparation of grated and beaten yams which is poured
over cooked rice. "Umeboshi" are the fruits of *Prunus mume,* dried and preserved in salt with perilla leaves. The leaves impart a pink color to the plums.
An infusion of perilla leaves is used for coloring food red or pink.
The leaves are also eaten raw with shoyu (soy sauce), or made into tempura
(fritters), macerated in salt for several hours or preserved in miso (fermented soy
and cereal paste) with other vegetables.
The young shoots are eaten with raw fish.
In Japan still perilla seeds, known as "egoma," are used like sesame seeds. It
is common to roll buckwheat and rice balls in a preparation of crushed egoma
and shoyu before roasting them on embers.
The seeds yield a drying oil which is edible. It is also used like linseed oil for
varnishes and paints.

Pogogyne (H 5)
From the Greek "pogon," beard, and "gynê," female: alluding to the
bearded style.
Calif.

The leaves of various species are aromatic and have been used as tea.
The seeds of *P. douglasii* subsp. *parviflora* (= *P. parviflora*) were ground and
eaten as piñole by Indians.
Endangered species: *P. abramsii, clareana, douglasii* subsp. *parviflora* (m.a.)
and *nudiuscula* – all Calif.

Poliomintha incana (B 4)   Rosemary Mint
(= *Hedeoma i.*)
From the Greek "polios," hoary, and "mentha," mint.
S.W. U.S., Mex.

The <u>leaves</u> were eaten by Indians, either raw or cooked with other greens, and the <u>flowering tops</u> were used to flavor food.

Prunella (D 3)   Self-heal
(= *Brunella*)
Etymology uncertain.
Throughout. Both native and species and varieties introduced from Eurasia.

The <u>leaves</u> of *P. vulgaris* (var. *lanceolata* and *hispida* are native; var. *vulgaris* is naturalized from Europe) are edible, but not excellent. They are astringent and rather bitter.
They contain traces of essential oil (though they are not aromatic), tannin, resin and a bitter substance.
The plant is astringent and hemostatic. Externally, self-heal is a good vulnerary.

Pycnanthemum (B-H 2)   Mountain Mint
From the Greek "pyknos," dense, and "anthemon," flower.
E. N.Am., Calif.

The various species are aromatic.
<u>Leaves</u> and <u>flowering tops</u> of *P. virginianum* (= *Koellia virginiana*) – E. & C. U.S. – were used as a flavoring by Indians.
Endangered species: *P. curvipes* – Ga., Ala., Tenn.

Salvia (B-C-H 2-3)   Sage
(including *Audibertia* and *Ramona* spp.)
Latin name of the Mediterranean *S. officinalis* from "salvo," to heal, to cure.
Throughout. Both native (mostly) and species introduced from Eur., S.Am. & N. Africa.
This genus, with 500 species, is numerically the most important of the Lamiaceae. A few species from S. U.S. (*S. coccinea, farinacea*), Mex. (*patens*) & S.Am. (*splendens,* scarlet sage) are commonly planted for ornament.
S. sclarea, clary sage – from S. Eur. – is also grown as an ornamental; it is occasionally found as an escape.

The <u>flowering tops</u> of clary sage, sticky to the touch, have a sweet, pervasive scent. They were formerly used in Europe for seasoning certain dishes and for imparting to wine the flavor of muscat grapes.

They contain a fragrant essential oil which is distilled and used in perfumery.

S. officinalis, garden sage – W. Mediterranean area – is often grown as an herb. It is naturalized in North America.

The <u>leaves</u> make a good condiment, especially in cooked dishes, and a pleasant tea. Their smell improves with drying. They are sometimes used for flavoring pickles in France.

In past centuries, the Chinese liked sage tea so much that they traded black tea for sage weight for weight with Europeans (especially the Dutch).

Garden sage leaves contain an essential oil extracted by distillation, tannin, niacin, sulfur and an estrogen-like substance.

Salvia officinalis

The plant is stimulant, stomachic, antisudoral, antiseptic and antiputrefactive, emmenagogue, astringent and antigalactic.

If ingested in large quantities over a long period of time, sage can be somewhat toxic.

Externally, the leaves help to heal wounds.

Fleshy <u>galls</u> growing on the leaves of the garden sage as a result of an insect bite (*Cynips* sp.) are eaten in the Mediterranean area. They were preserved in honey on the Greek island of Zante.

Sages can be divided into two main categories:

1. Shrubs with fairly small, aromatic leaves, containing much essential oil.

2. Herbaceous plants with large basal leaves (hardly aromatic) containing only traces of essential oils, although the inflorescences are often glandular and aromatic.

<u>Leaves</u> and <u>flowering tops</u> of the aromatic sages in the first group can be used as a condiment, like those of *S. officinalis* (m.a.), which they resemble.

Among our native shrubby species, the following deserve mention for their aromatic qualities: *S. apiana* (m.a.), *lemmonii* – S. Ariz., Mex. – (has a peppermint odor), *leucophylla*, purple sage – Calif. –, *mellifera*, black sage – Calif., Baja – and *mohavensis* – S.E. Calif. to Nev. & N.W. Son.

Indians used to burn the leaves of aromatic sages as a sacred incense in their religious ceremonies. The fumes are antiseptic.

The flowering tops of *S. ballotaeflora* – Tex., Mex. – have been locally made into tea.

Of the species in the second group, the flowers are probably the best part to use. Those of *S. spathacea*, hummingbird sage – Calif. – are large, dark red, and contain a large quantity of sweet nectar, hummingbird food, which can be sucked through the base of the flower tube.

The purplish-blue flowers of *S. pratensis*, meadow sage – naturalized from Eur. – can be added to salads.

A few herbaceous sages, such as *S. columbariae*, chia sage – S.W. U.S., Mex. – and other desert sages, have leaves which are aromatic enough to be used as an herb or as tea.

The seeds of several species from Southwestern United States and Mexico were commonly used as food by Indians. They are globally known as "chia" seeds. These small seeds are very nutritious and were often carried on long journeys: A handful was said to be enough to sustain a walking man for a day. Chia seeds were eaten whole, or roasted and ground into piñole. They were also made into a drink: When mixed, whole, with cold water, they swell up into a gelatinous mass which is very refreshing.

The seeds are obtained by gathering the mature heads into a pile, then threshing and winnowing them. It is possible to buy chia seeds in health food stores and coops in the United States and Canada.

The following species were often used for their seeds: *S. apiana*, white sage – S. Calif., Baja –, *carduacea*, thistle sage – Calif., Ariz., Baja –, *chia* – Mex. –, *columbariae* (m.a.), probably the most widely used, *dorrii* (= *carnosa*) – E. Calif., Nev. –, *pachyphylla* – S. Calif., Baja – and *tiliaefolia* – Mex., C. Am.

The leaves of *S. lyrata* – E. N.Am. – contain an acrid principle and should not be ingested. They have been used to remove warts.

All sages contain some essential oil, tannin and bitter substances.

S. reflexa – W. N.Am. – was used medicinally as a febrifuge, tonic and astringent.

S. lanceaefolia – C. U.S., Mex. – has occasionally poisoned livestock when mixed with hay.

Local species are used as food or spices in Europe and Asia.

Endangered species: *S. blodgettii* – Fla. – and *columbariae* (m.a.) var. *ziegleri* – Calif.

Satureja (B 2)   Savory

Latin name of *S. hortensis* of uncertain origin.

Almost throughout. Both native and species introduced from the Mediterranean area.

S. hortensis, summer savory – E. Mediterranean region – is commonly grown as an herb in gardens; it is occasionally found as an escape. Winter savory (*S. montana* – from the Mediterranean region) is also planted in herb gardens.

Savory has been used as a condiment since Antiquity. It is particularly helpful for digesting beans, hence its German name, "Bohnenkraut," bean herb.

The plant is very aromatic and has a pungent taste. It contains an essential oil.

Savory is stimulant, stomachic, carminative, antiseptic and antiputrefactive, expectorant, vermifuge and astringent.

It has also been used as an insect repellent, especially for fleas.

S. douglasii, yerba buena – W. Coast – is mildly aromatic and makes a pleasant tea.

S. rigida (= *Pycnothymus rigidus*), wild savory – endemic to S. Fla. – has aromatic leaves occasionally used as a spice.

Other native species are aromatic.

S. calamintha (= *Calamintha officinalis*), calamint – locally naturalized from Eurasia in E. N.Am – has a strong mint aroma. It is used as a condiment and for making tea.

The plant is stimulant, stomachic and carminative.

The essential oil distilled from calamint is an ingredient of an alcoholic preparation formerly used medicinally in France under the name of "eau d'arquebuse" (harquebus water). However, high doses of this oil can lead to nervous disorders.

Stachys   (C 2-3)   Hedge Nettle
Greek name of a plant in this genus from "stachys," spike: referring to its flower spikes.
Throughout. Both native (mostly) and species introduced from Eurasia.
S. olympica, lamb's ears – from the Mediterranean area – is sometimes planted for ornament and occasionally escapes.

The tuberous, fleshy rhizomes of *S. hyssopifolia* – Mass. to Ga. & around Lake Michigan – and *palustris* have been used as food on our continent. They have a crispy texture and a nutty flavor. They can be eaten raw, cooked or pickled. The rhizomes of the latter species were also used as food in Europe.

Young shoots and leaves of all *Stachys* spp. can be eaten raw or cooked. They have a fairly pleasant taste, in spite of their distinctive, musky smell; it may be preferable to mix them with other greens.

Those of *S. sylvatica* – introduced from Eur. in New York City – have been used as food in Europe. They have a definite taste of king boletus (after crushing the leaves between the fingers for a minute or two) and make very delicate consommés by themselves.

Hedge nettles contain some tannin.

The European betony (*S. officinalis*) has been used as an astringent, stomachic and expectorant, and externally as a vulnerary.

The seeds of our native *S. scopulorum* – W. U.S. – have reportedly been used as food by Indians.

The tuberous rhizomes of an East Asian species (*S. affinis*), known as "Chinese artichokes," are eaten in Japan, China, France and Belgium, where the plant is cultivated. They are white, crisp and have a very delicate flavor.

Teucrium   (D 5)   Germander
Greek and Latin name of a plant, possibly in this genus, from "Teukris," Troy.
Throughout. Both native and species introduced from Eur.
A few European species are grown for ornament.

The intensely bitter leaves of *T. scorodonia*, wood germander, wood sage – naturalized from Eur. in Ont. and Ohio – have been used instead of hops for flavoring beer on the Island of Jersey. They can be macerated in wine to give a tonic drink.

The plant contains tannin, resin, a bitter substance and an essential oil.

It is a bitter tonic with stomachic, cholagogue and antiseptic properties.

Other European species such as *T. botrys* – naturalized in Ohio & New England – and wood germander (*T. chamaedrys*), cultivated for ornament – are used similarly.

Thymus serpyllum (B 4)   Wild Thyme

Greek and Latin name of an aromatic plant of small size, from the ancient Egyptian "tham"; plant used for embalming.

Originally from Eurasia, the plant is grown as ground cover and as an herb; it is naturalized on our continent.

A few other European species are planted as ornamentals.

Thyme (*T. vulgaris* – from the Mediterranean region) is commonly cultivated in gardens as a culinary plant. Several varieties and hybrids, are known.

Thymus serpyllum

The small leaves and flowering tops of wild thyme make a good condiment, although they are not as strong as those of garden thyme. The plant can be used for flavoring salads, soups and various dishes. In Iceland, it was added to curdled milk.

Wild thyme contains a pungent essential oil (often distilled from the plant for medicinal purposes), tannin, as well as bitter and antibiotic substances.

It is stimulant, antiseptic and bactericide, stomachic, expectorant, antispasmodic and vermifuge. Externally, the plant can be used as a vulnerary and a parasiticide.

The essential oil contains thymol, a powerful antiseptic, but it is preferable not to use the oil externally, as it can strongly irritate the skin, especially the mucous membranes.

Other *Thymus* spp. are used as condiments in Europe and Asia.

PLANTAGINACEAE

Plantago (B 1)   Plantain
Latin name of the plant from "planta," sole of the foot, referring to the
shape of the leaves of some species.
Throughout. Both native and species introduced from Eurasia.

Several species have <u>leaves</u> that are large and tender enough to be used as
food. They can be eaten raw when young, and later cooked as greens or in soups.
In other species, the leaves are linear, tough and often hairy.
Plantain leaves generally have a pleasant taste.
Those of the following species have been eaten on our continent:

P. decipiens – N.E. N.Am.
The <u>leaves</u> were eaten raw or cooked by fishermen in Maine and Nova
Scotia.

P. lanceolata – a common weed, widely naturalized from Eurasia.
Uses and composition are similar to those of common plantain.

P. major, common plantain – a ubiquitous weed, widely naturalized from Eurasia
and probably native in N.Am. as well.
 Both *P. lanceolata* (m.a.) and *major* have
been frequently eaten raw or cooked in Europe, Asia and North America. Raw <u>leaves</u>
have a definite mushroom taste, with a slight
bitterness, and are excellent in salads when
young and tender. Older leaves make good
vegetables and soups.
 They contain mucilage, tannin, vitamin
C, minerals, a glucoside (aucubine) and other
substances.
 The plant is astringent, demulcent, emollient, expectorant, depurative and hemostatic.

Plantago major

It is used externally as an eyewash and as a vulnerary. It quickly soothes the pain of insect bites and stings (including those of wasps), as well as nettle stings.

Common plantain has been used medicinally since Antiquity.

The young flowering spikes, when still tender, can be eaten raw or cooked. They are delicious simply sauteed in butter.

P maritima (including subsp. *juncoides* and *oliganthos*), sea plantain – coasts of N.E. & N.W. N.Am.

The leaves were eaten raw, cooked or pickled.

P. coronopus, buckshorn plantain – introduced from Eurasia at E. seaports and on the Calif. Coast.

The plant was grown in European gardens from the 16th to the 19th century as a salad plant on account of its crisp, succulent leaves which have a pleasant taste and texture.

Plantain seeds can be finely ground, sifted and mixed with cereal flour for making bread and adding to soups, among other uses.

Those of *P. major* (m.a.) contain mucilage, pectin, vitamin B1 and choline. A decoction of plantain seeds is diuretic.

The seeds of some species, especially of *P. psyllium* – occasionally introduced from Eurasia into N.W. N.Am. – are used as a mechanical laxative, due to their mucilaginous outer layer: they are soaked in water, making them swell up, and then swallowed.

The seed mucilage of blond psyllium (*P. ovata* – Eurasia) is reportedly used as a stabilizer in ice cream and chocolate.

A few other *Plantago* spp. are eaten in Europe and Asia.

OLEACEAE

Fraxinus (C-H 4)   Ash
Latin name of the tree of unknown origin.
Throughout.
A few native and Eurasian species are planted for shade and ornament, including *F. pennsylvanica*, red ash – E. & C. N.Am.

The <u>cambium</u> layer of the red ash was reportedly cooked and eaten by Ojibway Indians. It can be boiled or dried, ground up and added to soups, or mixed with cereal flour.

The cambium of the European ash (*F. excelsior*) contains glucosides, sugars, resins, rutin and malic acid. It is tonic and febrifuge.

In the heat of summer, a gummy <u>sap</u> gathers on the leaves of the European ash, produced by the excretions of aphids feeding on the sap of the tree. It is thick and sweet and can be used as sugar if enough can be gathered. The leaves covered with this substance were soaked in water and fermented to make a refreshing drink, known as "frênette" in France (where the ash tree is called "frêne").

A sweet substance exuding from cuts in the trunk of certain Eurasian species (especially *F. ornus*) is gathered and used as food and medicine. It is known by the name of "manna."

The <u>fruits</u> of other species are pickled or used as a condiment in Europe and North Africa.

Endangered species: *F. gooddingii* – Ariz.

Jasminum sambac (B 5)   Arabian Jasmine
Arabic and Persian name of the plant "yâsimîn."
Originally from S. Asia, the plant is cultivated for its extremely fragrant flowers; it is naturalized in S. Fla.

The <u>flowers</u> can be infused into a delightful tea. They are commonly added to black tea to make jasmine tea.
Jasmine flowers are sedative.
Several other Asian species are planted in North America for their scented flowers and for ornament. White jasmine (*J. officinale*) is used like Arabian jasmine to perfume black tea. Other South Asian species are used similarly.

Osmanthus (D 4)   Wild Olive
From the Greek "osmê," odor, and "anthos," flower: referring to the fragrant flowers.
S.E. U.S., Mex.
A few native and Asian species, as well as a garden hybrid, are cultivated as ornamentals.

The flowers of *O. americanus* are used to scent black tea in Asia, where the tree is native as well.

The fruit is macerated in brine and eaten like green olives. It is somewhat bitter.

Flowers and fruits of another species (*O. fragrans* – from S.E. Asia, planted for ornament in N.Am.) are employed similarly.

SCROPHULARIACEAE

Castilleja   (D-H 3   Indian Paintbrush
After D. Castillejo, a Spanish botanist during the 13th century.
Throughout, especially in W. N.Am.

The flowering tops of various species are edible raw in small quantities.
They have a pleasant taste and their colorful bracts enliven a salad.

The flowering tops of *C. linariaefolia* – W. U.S. – were eaten by the Hopis and other tribes, who also used several species medicinally and in ceremonies.

However, on soils rich in selenium, the plants can accumulate high levels of this element, which can be toxic to grazing cattle when large amounts are ingested. *C. chromosa* – W. U.S. – has been particularly incriminated.

Endangered species: *C. aquariensis* – Utah –, *chlorotica* – Ore. –, *christii* – Idaho –, *ciliata* – Tex. –, *cruenta* – Ariz. –, *grisea*, *leschkeana* – both Calif. –, *ludoviciana* – La. –, *ownbeyana* – Ore. –, *revealii* – Utah –, *salsuginosa* – Nev. – and *uliginosa* – Calif.

Cymbalaria muralis   (G 3)   Kenilworth Ivy
(= *Linaria cymbalaria*)
Latin name of a plant in the Crassulaceae (*Umbilicus* sp.) from "cymba," skiff: alluding to the shape of the leaves.
Almost throughout.

The plant has reportedly been eaten raw in Southern Europe.

Mimulus (D-H 2-3)   Monkeyflower
From the Latin diminutive form of "mimus," mime, buffoon: referring to
the appearance of the flower.
Throughout, mostly in W. N.Am.
Several native species are planted as ornamentals.

The leaves of *M. glabratus* (= *M. geyeri*) – C. N.Am. – and *guttatus* – W.
N.Am., cultivated for ornament and escaped in E. N.Am. – are large and tender
and can be eaten raw. They are slightly aromatic and somewhat bitter.

Indians used to dry and burn them and use the ashes as a salt substitute.

Endangered species: *M. brandegei* – Calif. –, *gemmiparus* – Idaho –, *guttatus*
(m.a) subsp. *arenicola*, *pygmaeus* – both Calif. –, *ringens* var. *colpophilus* – Maine –,
traskiae and *whipplei* – both Calif.

Paulownia tomentosa (D-F 4)   Paulownia, Princess tree
After Anna Paulowna (1794–1865), Queen of the Netherlands.
Native to China and Korea, the tree is often planted for shade and orna-
ment. It is naturalized in E. U.S.

In times of scarcity in Eastern Asia, the leaves are boiled in a change of water
and eaten in small quantities, as large amounts are said to be somewhat toxic.

The flowers are eaten with miso (fermented soy paste).

Pedicularis (D-F-H 2)   Lousewort
Latin name of a plant used for treating lice, "herba pedicularis," from
"pediculus," louse.
N. N.Am. & Mountains.

The roots of *P. lanata* and *langsdorfii* – B.C. to Alaska – have reportedly
been eaten in Alaska, boiled or roasted.

The leaves of *P. canadensis* – E. & C. N.Am. – and *lanceolata* – N.E. &
N.C. N.Am. – were cooked and eaten as greens by some Indian tribes. Those of
P. langsdorfii (m.a.) were made into tea.

But sheep have been poisoned by grazing on *P. canadensis*, and other species,
especially in Europe, are also known to be toxic.

Louseworts contain a glucoside (aucubine).

In Europe, a decoction of certain species was used to kill parasites of humans and livestock, including lice.

The flowers of some louseworts – *P. densiflora, lanata* (m.a.) – yield a few drops of sweet nectar: one of the most delicious treats to be found in the wild.

The leaves of a few local species are cooked and eaten in Eastern Asia.

Endangered species: *P. duddleyi* – Calif. – and *furbishiae* – Maine.

Penstemon (G-H 4)   Penstemon

From the Greek "pente," five, and "stemon," thread, stamen: referring to the presence of a fifth stamen in the flowers.

Throughout.

A few native species are planted for ornament.

The leaves of *P. confertus*, yellow penstemon – N.W. U.S. – have reportedly been made into tea.

Endangered species: *P. barretiae* – Ore., Wash. –, *clutei* – Ariz. –, *concinnus* – Utah –, *decurvus* – Nev. –, *discolor* – Ariz. –, *garrettii* – Utah –, *glaucinus* – Ore. –, *grahamii* – Utah –, *keckii* – Nev. –, *lemhiensis* – Idaho, Mont. –, *nyeensis*, *pahutensis* – both Nev. –, *personatus* – Calif. –, *retrorsus* – Colo. –, *rubicundus* – Nev. – and *spatulatus* – Ore.

Veronica (B 3)   Speedwell

The flower is said to resemble the imprint of Christ's face (called "veronikon," true image) left on the Sindon, the cloth with which S. Veronica swabbed Jesus's face during the climb to Calvary.

Throughout. Both native and species introduced from Eurasia.

A few Eurasian species are planted for ornament.

The fleshy leaves and stems of *V. americàna*, American brooklime, **anagallis-aquatica**, water speedwell – almost throughout, also in Eurasia – and **beccabunga**, European brooklime – naturalized from Eur. in N.E. N.Am. – are edible raw. Their slightly pungent taste is reminiscent of watercress (*Nasturtium officinale*, Brassicaceae); they are bitter as well.

The plants contain vitamin C, a glucoside (aucubine) and various other substances.

They are stimulant, expectorant, diuretic and antiscorbutic.

These are tall species growing in or near water. The speedwells of dry places bear much smaller leaves and are not fleshy. Several of these are common weeds in gardens and lawns.

The leaves of *V. chamaedrys* – naturalized from Eur. in N.E. N.Am. – and *officinalis* – E. N.Am., also in Eur. – have been used as tea in Europe. The latter was sometimes called "European tea."

The leaves of *V. officinalis* (m.a.) contain tannin, aucubine and a bitter principle.

An infusion of the plant is tonic, stomachic, expectorant and diuretic.

The root of *V. virginica*, Culvers-root, Culvers-physic – E. U.S. – contains leptandrin, a violent emetic and cathartic.

Veronica beccabunga

OROBANCHACEAE

Members of this family are parasitic on the roots of various plants.

Boschniakia (D 4)   Poque
(including *Orobanche* spp.)
After Boschniaki, Russian botanist.
W. N.Am.

B. hookeri (= *Orobanche tuberosa*) was used as food by Indians. The whole plant was eaten after cooking.

Orobanche (D-H 3)   Broomrape
Greek name of a plant that is parasitic on the roots of *Vicia* spp.; "orobagchê" from "orobos," vetch, and "agchô," to smother).
Throughout.

O. californica – Calif. – and *fasciculata* and *ludoviciana* – both W. & C. N.Am. – were eaten by Indians after cooking. The plant, especially its underground part, is tender and fleshy.
Endangered species: *O. valida*–Calif.

BIGNONIACEAE

Tecoma stans (G 4) Trumpet Bush
Etymology unknown.
Ariz. to Tex., Mex.

The crushed roots have reportedly been fermented into a drink.

ACANTHACEAE

Beloperone (C 4)
From the Greek "belos," arrow, and "peronê," something pointed.
Calif., Ariz., Mex.

The shrimp plant (*B. guttata*) is planted as an ornamental.
The flowers of *B. californica*, chuparosa – S. Calif., S. Ariz., Son., Baja – are very good to eat raw. They were used as food by the Papagos.
Hummingbirds visit them to drink the nectar they secrete.

PEDALIACEAE

Sesamum indicum (B 5) Sesame
From the Arabic name of the plant, "semsem."
Probably from S.E. Asia (but unknown in its original wild state), sesame is grown in warm areas throughout the world for its seeds and the oil they yield; the plant is locally found as an escape in S. U.S. & Mex.

Sesame has been used for millenia in Asia and Africa. It was cultivated by the ancient Egyptians and Babylonians and is frequently mentioned by Greek and Roman authors.

The <u>seeds</u> are sprinkled on breads and pastries. They are crushed into "tahini," a paste commonly used in the Middle East for making dressings and candies. "Halva" is a mixture of tahini and honey. Sesame seeds, tahini and sesame oil are now used as well in the United States, Canada and Europe.

Sesame seeds are used as a condiment in Japan; they are roasted and mixed with salt. The local name of the seeds is "goma," and the mixture is called "gomasio."

Sesame seeds contain protein, glucides, the vitamin rutin, minerals and a semidrying edible oil (with a strong taste if the seeds have been roasted first, otherwise very delicate), much used for cooking in Asia.

The <u>leaves</u> of the plant are cooked and eaten in Asia and Africa.

<u>Leaves</u> and <u>seeds</u> of other species are used as food in tropical Africa.

MARTYNIACEAE

Proboscidea   (D 4)   Unicorn Plant, Devil's Claws
(= *Martynia* spp.)
From the Latin "proboscis," elephant's trunk: alluding to the shape of the fruit.
S.W. & S.C. U.S., Mex.

The <u>young pods</u> of the various species are tender and can be eaten cooked. Those of *P. fragrans* – Mex., adventive in the U.S. –, *louisianica* – S. U.S., escaped in Calif., & E. U.S. – and *parviflora* – Calif. to Tex., Mex. – are known to have been used as food by Indians.

P. louisianica (m.a.) was formerly grown in American gardens (and occasionally in England) for its young seed pods, which were pickled in vinegar.

This species, along with *P. fragrans* (m.a.) and a Brazilian species (*P. lutea*) is sometimes planted for ornament in Europe.

The mature pods of various species, including the ones noted above, were split and used by Indians to weave black designs into their baskets.

The <u>roots</u> of a South American species and the pods of a Brazilian species (*P. lutea*, m.a.) have reportedly been used as food.

LENTIBULARIACEAE

Pinguicula (E 4)   Butterwort
From the Latin "pinguiculus," chubby, diminutive of "pinguis," fat: referring to the texture and appearance of the leaves.
Almost throughout.

The Lapps of Northern Europe used to pour fresh, warm reindeer milk through a strainer lined with the leaves of *P. vulgaris* – N. N.Am., also native in Eur. In spite of the cold temperatures, the milk curdled in a day or two.
The leaves contain tannin, mucilage and other substances.
They have been used as an expectorant. Although the plant is protected in Europe, a Swiss medical laboratory used to carry on a profitable traffic, illegally importing hundreds of pounds of butterwort leaves from France, which it used to manufacture a cough syrup. Whole stations of this uncommon plant were destroyed in the process.

CAMPANULACEAE

Campanula (C 3)   Bellflower, Harebell
From the Latin "campana," bell: referring to the appearance of the flowers.
Throughout. Both native and species introduced from Eurasia.
Several European species are planted for ornament.

The fleshy rootstock of *C. rapunculoides* – naturalized from Eur. in N.E. N.Am. – was eaten in Europe. The plant has occasionally been cultivated as a vegetable both for its roots and its tender young leaves.
Roots and leaves have a pleasant, nutty taste and can be eaten raw or cooked.
Rampion (*C. rapunculus* – native from Eur.) was formerly abundantly grown in European vegetable gardens for its edible roots and young leaves, especially in the 16th and 17th centuries. It has now been totally forgotten.
Other species are used as food in Europe and Asia.

Specularia (D 2)

(= *Triodanis* spp., = *Legousia* spp.)

From the Latin "speculum," mirror: alluding to the appearance of the flowers.

Throughout. Both native and species introduced from Eur.

S. speculum-veneris (= *Triodanis s.-v.*), Venus's looking-glass – naturalized from S. & W. Eur. in E. N.Am. – is occasionally planted for ornament.

The <u>plant</u> was eaten raw in Europe.

RUBIACEAE

Asperula (D 4)

(= *Galium* spp.)

From the Latin "asper," rough: referring to the texture of the leaves of some species.

N.E. N.Am. Introduced from Eurasia & N. Africa.

A. odorata (= *Galium odoratum*), woodruff – sometimes planted for ornament and occasionally naturalized in N.E. N.Am. – has frequently been used for flavoring cold drinks. In Alsace (France), Eastern Belgium, Luxembourg and Germany, the <u>whole plant</u> is added to white wine: this scented beverage, known as "maitrank," is drunk both for pleasure and for its tonic, digestive and diuretic virtues.

Woodruff, preferably dried, can be infused in milk to make creams, puddings or other desserts. It can also be used to flavor sauces served with fish or poultry.

The plant contains a glucoside (asperuloside) which, under the action of a ferment, produces coumarin upon drying. Its sweet vanilla smell persists for several years (coumarin is also found in *Melilotus* spp. and in *Coumarouna odorata*, Fabaceae).

The fresh plant does not have this characteristic odor, but its small white flowers are fragrant.

Woodruff also contains tannin.

It is antispasmodic, sedative, diuretic and cholagogue.

Asperula odorata

An infusion of the dried plant makes a delicious beverage, which can be used for flavoring various desserts.

But in very high doses, woodruff occasionally causes headaches and digestive disorders. Also, improperly cured or spoiled woodruff can be dangerous due to dicoumarol, acting as a coumarin-like substance. If fermented or moldy, woodruff should never be used as food: care must be taken to dry it properly.

Casasia clusiifolia (D 5) Sevenyear Apple
Etymology unknown.
S. Fla.

The pulp of the ripe <u>fruit</u> is edible. It can be sucked out by piercing a hole in the skin.

Galium (D-H 1) Bedstraw
From the Greek name *G. verum*: "galion," from "gala," milk: the plant was used for curdling milk.
Throughout. Both native and species introduced from Eurasia.
The Eurasian *G. verum*, lady's bedstraw, is occasionally planted for ornament. It is naturalized in N.E. N.Am.

The <u>plant</u> contains a milk-curdling enzyme and its juice was formerly added to milk in cheese making. This is still sometimes done for Kosher cheese in Israel and in certain Jewish communities.

The <u>flowering tops</u>, yellow with a honey-like fragrance, were used for coloring and scenting cheese and butter, especially Cheshire cheese in England.

On drying, the plant exhales a faint vanilla smell.

Lady's bedstraw has medicinal properties similar to those of woodruff (*Asperula odorata*).

The roots impart a red color to wool with alum or chromium as a mordant. The flowering tops dye wool yellow with either of these two substances.

The <u>young shoots</u> of *G. aparine*, cleavers – throughout, also in Eurasia – are edible raw. Older leaves and stems become im-

Galium
aparine

pregnated with silicon and are too tough to be used as food. The long stems and the leaf margins are lined with hooked bristles and stick together. They were formerly used as a filter to strain milk and other liquids.

The fruits are one of the best coffee substitutes. They should be picked when their color turns from green to brown, and then torrefied. After roasting, they develop a distinctive aroma strongly reminiscent of coffee (*Coffea* spp.). It must be noted that coffee, like cleavers, also belongs to the Rubiaceae.

The plant contains a glucoside, asperuloside.

It is antispasmodic, antihypertensive, diuretic and diaphoretic. Externally, cleavers has been employed as a vulnerary.

G. triflorum, "sweet-scented bedstraw" -- throughout, also in Eurasia -- becomes very fragrant upon drying.

Local species are eaten in East Asia.

Endangered species: *G. angustifolium* subsp. *borregoense, californicum* subsp. *luciense,* subsp. *primum* and subsp. *sierrae, catalinense* subsp. *acrispum* – all Calif. –, *collomae* – Ariz. –, *glabrescens* subsp. *modocense, grande, hardhamae* – all three Calif. –, *hileniae* subsp. *kingstonense* – Calif., Nev. -- and *serpenticum* subsp. *scotticum* – Calif.

Hamelia patens   (D 5)   Fire Bush
Etymology unknown.
S. Fla., W.I.

The ripe fruit is edible raw.

Mitchella repens   (D 4)   Partridge Berry
After John Mitchell, early American botanist from Virginia and correspondent of Linnaeus.
E. N.Am.
The plant is sometimes grown as an ornamental ground cover.

The small red fruits are edible, but insipid.

Morinda (D 5)   Indian Mulberry
Etymology unknown.
S. Fla.

The young leaves of *M. citrifolia* – naturalized from S.E. Asia on the Florida Keys – are eaten cooked in tropical Asia.

The fruits are used as food in the same regions. When young, they are eaten raw or cooked. Ripe ones are mashed and made into a beverage which is sweetened. The ripe fruits have a gelatinous texture and a strong odor of blue cheese.

The fruits of other tropical Asian species are locally used as food, especially in curries.

CAPRIFOLIACEAE

Lonicera (B-F 1)   Honeysuckle
After A. Lonitzer (1528–1586), German physician and botanist.
Throughout. Both native and species introduced from Eurasia.
Several European and Asian species are planted as ornamentals. Among these, *L. japonica*, Japanese honeysuckle – introduced from E. Asia – has become a pest in E. U.S.

The young leaves of this honeysuckle are parboiled and used as a vegetable in Japan. In China, leaves, buds and flowers are made into tea. But the plant might not be totally exempt from toxicity.

The fruits of several of our native species are good to eat raw and can also be cooked. The following species have been used as food by Indians and settlers and are known to be wholesome (the color of the fruit is in parentheses): *L. ciliosa*, orange honeysuckle (red) – W. N.Am., *hispidula*, hairy honeysuckle (red) – Calif. to Wash. –, *involucrata*, twinberry, fly honeysuckle (black) – N. N.Am. & W. Mountains – and *villosa*, waterberry (blue) – N.E. & N.C. N.Am.

They contain pectin, sugars and various other substances.

However, the fruits of other species are bitter and inedible. Actually, in many honeysuckles, as with most European species, the fruits are toxic: they contain saponins and other poisonous principles. They can cause digestive, nervous and cardiac disorders, occasionally resulting in death. It is important to note that the

toxic fruits are not necessarily bitter, but can be sweet and pleasant to eat, pre-
senting thus a greater risk.

   L. caprifolium, woodbine – introduced from Eurasia, cultivated for ornament
and occasionally escaped – belongs to the category with toxic fruits. However,
its fragrant <u>flowers</u> can yield a few drops of a delicious nectar, a fact known by
many children. Nectar can be obtained from the flowers of other species.

   Leaves and bark of woodbine (m.a.) are diaphoretic, diuretic and emetic, but
the plant is thought to be rather toxic. The flowers are antispasmodic.

   The <u>fruits</u> of several East Asian species are eaten locally.

Sambucus (B-F 1)   Elder

Latin name of the tree.

Throughout. Both native and species introduced from Eurasia.

The Eurasian ***S. ebulus***, dwarf elder, is occasionally planted for ornament;
it is found as an escape in N.E. N.Am.

Its black <u>fruits</u> are bitter and generally considered to be toxic, at least in the
raw stage. However, they have reportedly been brewed into an alcoholic drink
and eaten after cooking.

   The <u>leaves</u> are said to have been used to make tea, but they are ill smelling.

   The very young leaves of ***S. canadensis***, American elder – E. & C. N.Am. –

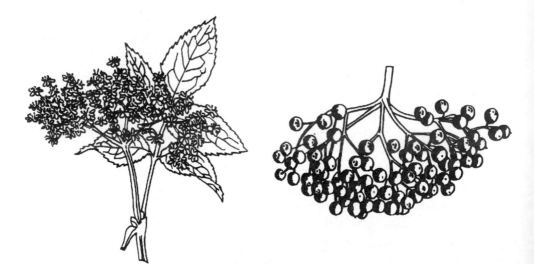

Sambucus canadensis

have been used as food after cooking. In Eastern Asia, those of a few local species are eaten with miso (fermented soy paste), tofu (soy curd) or crushed sesame seeds. But raw, American elder leaves are known to have poisoned people who juiced them along with the berries.

Elder leaves have a characteristic, rather unpleasant smell. They contain an essential oil and are diuretic and depurative.

The flowers are fragrant. They are made into fritters and can be added raw to salads and desserts. Those of the European black elder (*S. nigra*) have a much stronger but very pleasant, musky smell. They are used for flavoring wine (to which they impart a pleasant muscat flavor), cider and vinegar. They are also made into delicious pies and into an alcoholic drink.

The flowers of the black elder contain an essential oil, mucilage, tannins, a glucoside (quercitron) the vitamin rutin. They have been used medicinally since Antiquity as a diaphoretic and diuretic.

The black fruits of the American elder are edible raw or cooked. They must be eaten with moderation when fresh, as they can be emetic and purgative. They are cooked into jams, pies, jellies, chutneys, muffins, soups and were often dried by Indians.

A dark purple juice can be extracted from them. The juice of the European black elder (m.a.) was used for coloring red wines, especially port in Portugal.

The berries, or their juice, ferment readily and yield an excellent wine which sparkles naturally. Care must be taken to let the wine ferment long enough in the open before bottling, as the gas pressure could cause the bottles to blow up. Like champagne, elder wine must be served cold; otherwise, it may tend to run over because of its effervescent properties. Black elderberries used to be sold in London for making wine.

If left in contact with the air, elder wine slowly becomes sour and turns into vinegar.

Elderberry extract is now sold in health food stores as an antiviral medication.

Elderberries are very rich in vitamins A and C. They also contain minerals, organic acids (malic, tartric), sugars and an essential oil. They are slightly laxative.

Besides those of *S. canadensis* (m.a.), the black or blue fruits of the following species have been used as food by Indians and settlers: *S. coerulea*, blue elder, *melanocarpa* (= *pubens* var. *melanocarpa*), American black elder – both W. N.Am. – *mexicana*, Mexican elder – S.W. U.S., Mex. – and *neomexicana* – Ariz., N.M.

The fact that the red fruits of **S. callicarpa** (= S. pubens var. arborescens), coast red elder – Calif. to B.C. –, **microbotrys** (= pubens var. microbotrys), mountain red elder – W. U.S. – and **pubens** (= racemosa subsp. pubens), American red elder, red-berried elder – N. N.Am. & Appalachians – are edible or not is controversial. Some authors affirm their toxicity, but they are known to have been eaten, at least in small quantities, raw or cooked.

Red elderberries are very sour and unpleasant. They are definitely better cooked and can be passed through a food mill, a sieve or a cloth to remove the seeds. After cooking they are considered safe and can be made into sauces or jellies, as well as syrup, wine and vinegar. Red elder jelly is marketed commercially in Alaska.

The European red elder (*S. racemosa*) is known to be emetic when eaten raw. It is thought that only the seeds are toxic. The juice expressed from the berries is made into a translucent red jelly, which is both delicious and harmless.

The fruits of the European red and black elders are distilled in Eastern France into an alcohol with reputed stomachic properties.

The roots of *S. pubens* (m.a.) have reportedly been used for preparing a tea.

Roots and inner bark of various elders (such as *S. ebulus* and *nigra*) contain tannin, an alkaloid (sambucine), a glucoside (sambunigrine) yielding hydrocyanic acid, saponin and various other substances.

They are diuretic and slightly laxative but must be used in moderation only as all parts of elder (except for the flowers but including the raw berries) can be emetic and cathartic in high doses. All green parts should be considered toxic, at least when fresh and raw.

Elderberries give wool a purplish color with alum, and the leaves make a yellow tint.

Leaves and fruits of several species are used as food in Europe, Asia and Australia. Elderberries have been eaten since prehistoric times.

Symphoricarpos (G-F 2)   Snowberry
From the Greek "sympherô," to group together, and "karpos," fruit: referring to the disposition of the fruits.
Throughout.
Our native *S. albus* (= S. racemosus) – E. & N. N.Am – is sometimes planted for ornament.

The fruits of *S. albus* (m.a.), *occidentalis*, and *orbiculatus* have reportedly been eaten by Indians.

They are exceedingly bitter, however, and the fruits of some species are known to be emetic, at least in the raw stage. Those of *S. albus* (m.a.) have a rather high saponin content.

Snowberries are relished by various birds.

The leaves of these bushes contain saponin, but in small enough amounts to be browsed with impunity by deer and livestock.

Triosteum (D 4) Wild Coffee, Horse Gentian
From the Greek "treis," three, and "osteon," bone: referring to the hard seeds.
E. N.Am.

The ripe fruits of *T. perfoliatum* have long been used as a coffee substitute after roasting. They are most generally ground, placed in cold water which is brought to a boil and left to steep for a while. The resulting beverage is pleasant to drink.

Viburnum (B-H 2) Black Haw, Highbush Cranberry
Latin name of the shrub, possibly from "vieo," to braid, to tie: referring to the flexibility of the twigs.
Throughout, especially in E. N.Am. Two species occasionally found in the wild have been introduced from Eur.
Our native *V. alnifolium*, hobblebush – N.E. N.Am. & Appalachians –, *cassinoides*, Appalachian tea – E. N.Am. –, *prunifolium*, black haw –E. & C. U.S. –, *rufidulum*, Southern black haw – S.E. & S.C. U.S. – and *trilobum* (= *opulus* var. *americanum*), highbush cranberry – N. N.Am. – are sometimes planted as ornamentals, along with several Asian and European species, of which *V. lantana*, wayfaring tree and *opulus* var. *opulus*, Guelder rose – both originally from Eur. – occasionally escape from cultivation in N.E. N.Am.

The dried leaves of *V. cassinoides* (m.a.) have long been used for making tea.
The black fruits of the following species are sweet and good to eat raw: *V. alnifolium* (m.a.), *cassinoides* (m.a.), *lantana* (m.a.), *lentago*, nannyberry, sheep-

berry – E. & C. N.Am., – *nudum*,
withe rod, possum haw – E. U.S., –
prunifolium (m.a.) and *rufidulum*
(m.a.).

They are commonly known as
wild raisins, which they indeed resemble in taste, especially after drying. Like raisins, these fruits can be
eaten raw or used to sweeten and flavor various dishes.

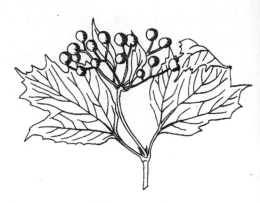

Viburnum opulus

The red <u>fruits</u> of **V. edule**, squash-
berry, (including *V. pauciflorum*,
mooseberry) – N. N.Am. & W. Mountains – and *trilobum* (m.a.) are edible as
well. They can reputedly be eaten raw, at least in small amounts, but they are
bitter and sour tasting. It is probably safer, however, to cook them as the fruits of
the related *V. opulus* (m.a.) are known to be purgative in the raw stage and to possibly cause serious digestive troubles (gastroenteritis). They contain a bitter
principle, viburnin.

The fruits of the Guelder rose, *V. opulus* (m.a.), although bitter and sour as
well, were cooked into jams and compotes (with honey and flour) in Europe, especially in Scandinavia, where they were also distilled into alcohol.

And, as the name suggests, the fruits of the highbush cranberry, *V. trilobum*
(m.a.) have been used on our continent to make a substitute for cranberry sauce.

The bark of the European *V. opulus* (m.a.) is used medicinally as a uterine
sedative.

The leaves contain viburnin, like the fruits.

Many Asian species, several of which are planted for ornament in North
America, also bear edible <u>fruits</u>.

Endangered species: *V. bracteatum* – Ala., Ga.

VALERIANACEAE

Centranthus ruber   (D 4)   Red Valerian
From the Greek "kentron," spur, and "anthos," flower:
alluding to the shape of the flower.
Originally from S. Eur., the plant is commonly cultivated for ornament, along with a few other European
species. It is locally naturalized on the W. Coast.

Leaves, flower buds and flowers are edible raw, but they
may be too bitter for some people and can be mixed with
blander vegetables. Red valerian is popular in Italy as a
salad plant.
Another species was cultivated in France for this purpose.
The roots have the same antispasmodic and sedative
properties as valerian (*Valeriana officinalis*).

Centranthus ruber

Valeriana   (C 3)   Valerian
Name dating back to the Middle Ages from the Latin "valeo," to be
healthy: alluding to the medicinal properties of *V. officinalis*.
Throughout. Both native and introduced species.
The European *V. officinalis* is sometimes planted for ornament under the
name of "garden heliotrope" and occasionally escapes from gardens.

The fleshy root of *V. edulis* (including *V. ciliata*), tobacco root, was used as
food by Indians after cooking in a fire pit for a whole day to remove its strong,
unpleasant taste and smell. It is then sweet and quite palatable. The roots can
reach a large size.
The leaves of *V. officinalis* (m.a.) are good to eat raw in salads, preferably
mixed with other greens as they are rather bitter.
The flowers are fragrant and can be used to flavor sauces and desserts.
The roots of the European valerian contain an essential oil, an alkaloid and a
glucoside.
They are antispasmodic, sedative and stomachic. Valerian is beneficial to the
nervous system, which it helps to strengthen. It is better to use the plant fresh.
However, very high doses can cause digestive, nervous and cardiac troubles.
Its frequent use over long periods of time can be dangerous as well.

The medicinal properties of valerian have been known since Antiquity, but the plant only became popular in the 17th century.

Valerian acts as an excitant for cats and puts them into a euphoric state.

Leaves, flowers and roots of a few local species have been eaten in Europe and Asia.

Dried valerian plants, especially the roots, have a strong odor which persists for years.

Valerianella (B-H 3)   Corn Salad
Diminutive form of *Valeriana*.
Throughout. Both native and species introduced from Europe.

The European *V. carinata* and *locusta* var. *oleracea* (= *V. olitoria*) are occasionally grown as salad plants in vegetable gardens; both are locally naturalized in N.Am. The Italian corn salad (*V. eriocarpa* – from S. Eur.) is also cultivated. The three species mentioned are very popular in Eur. *V. locusta* (m.a.) is commonly sold in French and Swiss markets. It is sold in the U.S. under the French name "mâche." The leaves of these plants are extremely tender and delicious raw.

The roots of our native *V. radiata* – S.E. U.S. – have reportedly been used as food.

The leaves of *V. chenopodifolia* – N.E. N.Am. – are eaten raw or cooked.

Endangered species: *V. texana* – Tex.

Valerianella locusta

ASTERACEAE (COMPOSITAE)

This is the second largest family of flowering plants (after the *Orchidaceae* in the number of species and after the *Poaceae* in the number of individual plants). About 250 genera occur in North America.

Many well-known food plants belong to this family, such as artichoke, chicory, endive, dandelion, Jerusalem artichoke, sunflower, safflower, salsify as well as aromatic and medicinal plants. Very few *Asteraceae* are toxic.

Species with wind-blown pollen – especially ragweed (*Ambrosia* spp.) and allies – are among the most important causes of hay fever.

Many *Asteraceae* contain a latex which is rich in rubber.

The seeds are contained in dry fruits called "achenes."

Achillea (D 1) Yarrow

From the Greek and Latin name of the plant, possibly after Achilles, the hero of Homer's *Iliad*.

Throughout. Both native and species introduced from Eurasia.

A few Eurasian species are planted for ornament, especially cultivars, including *A. millefolium* which is widely naturalized on our continent.

The bitter and aromatic <u>leaves</u> of this species have been used in Northern Europe for flavoring beer. They also serve as a condiment and if not too old can be eaten after boiling and seasoning. The young tender leaves in springtime make excellent, aromatic additions to salads.

The strongly aromatic <u>flowering tops</u> can also be used, sparingly, as a condiment.

In 16th century Germany, yarrow fruits were reportedly placed in wine barrels as a preservative.

The plant contains a bitter essential oil (containing achilleine), mucilage and potassium.

It is a bitter tonic, with antispasmodic, astringent, hemostatic, emmenagogue and cholagogue properties.

Externally, yarrow is a good vulnerary. However, used internally over a long period of time, it may cause photosensitization.

Achillea millefolium

If grazed too freely by cows, yarrow produce's an undesirable flavor in milk and milk products.

A decoction of the leaves and flowering tops of *A. lanulosa* – C. & W. N.Am. – was used as medicine by Western Indians.

The <u>leaves</u> of *A. ptarmica*, sneezeweed – from Eurasia, cultivated for ornament and naturalized in N.E. N.Am. – are said to be cooked and eaten in N.E. Asia.

A few related species are used similarly in these regions.

Achyrachaena mollis (C 4)   Blow Wives
From the Greek "achyron," chaff, and "achaenion," achene: referring to the very chaffy pappus.
Ore., Calif. & Baja. A monotypic genus.

The <u>achenes</u> were used as food, often after roasting, by California Indians.

Actinella (D 4)
Etymology unknown.
(= *Hymenoxys* spp.)
S.W. U.S., Mex.

The <u>root bark</u> of *A. biennis* (= *Hymenoxys cooperi*) was made into a chewing gum by Southwestern Indians.

A decoction of the <u>flowering tops</u> of *A. odorata* (= *Hymenoxys o.*) – S.W. & S.C. U.S., Mex. – was used as a beverage by local Indians.

Agoseris (D 4)   Mountain Dandelion
From the Greek "aix, aigos," goat, and "seris," chicory.
Throughout.

The <u>leaves</u> of *A. aurantiaca* – W. N.Am. – were eaten by Indians.

The <u>latex</u> of the stem of *A. villosa* – W. N.Am. – was reportedly used like chewing gum.

Ambrosia (G-H 2)   Ragweed
Classical name of several plants; in Greek mythology, the food of the gods.
Throughout.

The <u>achenes</u> contain about 20% of a semi-drying oil, which has been suggested for edible purposes. The oil is known as "oil of ragweed."
A Mediterranean species is used locally as a flavoring.
A. artemisiifolia, psilostachya – C. N.Am. – and *trifida* – E. & C. N.Am. – are the cause of most cases of hay fever in late summer and fall.
Endangered species: *A. cheirantifolia* – Tex.

Antennaria (E-H 3)   Pussytoes
From the Latin "antenna": alluding to the fancied resemblance of the pappus of the staminate flowers to insect antennae.
Throughout.

The <u>gum</u> exuding from the stalk has been used for chewing and was said to be nourishing.
Endangered species: *A. arcuata* – Idaho, Wyo.

Anthemis (D 4)
Ancient Greek and Latin name of some of the species in this genus.
E. N.Am. Introduced from Europe.

A. nobilis, Roman chamomile, and *tinctoria*, dyer's chamomile, are sometimes planted for ornament. The former species is also grown for its medicinal virtues. Both occasionally escape in E. N.Am.
The Roman chamomile is very fragrant as well as bitter. Its <u>flowering heads</u> have been used in Europe for flavoring beer.
The plant, especially the flowering heads, contains an essential oil having a beautiful blue color, which is used for flavoring certain liquors.
An infusion of chamomile is tonic, aperitive, antispasmodic, stomachic, carminative, emmenagogue, analgesic and febrifuge. Externally, it acts as a vulnerary and an antiphlogistic. It is also used as an eyewash.
A. tinctoria (m.a.) yields a yellow dye.

A. *cotula*, dog fennel or mayweed, has a strong, rather unpleasant smell. It has been suspected of being somewhat toxic and is known, along with A. *arvensis*, corn chamomile, to be a possible cause of dermatitis in susceptible individuals.

Arctium (C 2-3)   Burdock
Greek name of the plant "arktion," from "arktos," bear.
Throughout. Introduced from Eurasia.

Both **A. *lappa*** and ***minus*** can be used as food.

At the end of the first growing season of the plant, the <u>root</u> is fleshy and tender. It must be gathered between fall and the beginning of spring, before the flower stalk appears and uses up the reserves of the root. At the right stage, burdock roots are good to eat either raw or cooked. They have a pleasant artichoke taste and a sweet flavor due to inulin, an easily assimilated sugar (even by diabetics) commonly found in this family.

A. *lappa* (m.a.) is cultivated in Japan for its roots, which are cooked in water or in soy sauce after brushing and washing. They are also eaten raw. Burdock roots are sold in macrobiotic food stores and in New York City markets under the Japanese name "gobô" for quite a high price, considering the fact that the plant grows in nearby fields or empty lots and can be picked for free.

In order to preserve their white color, the cut-up roots must be soaked in vinegar water.

They have also been used, after chopping and roasting, as a coffee substitute.

Burdock roots contain an essential oil, minerals, tannin, a resin, an antibiotic substance and up to 45% inulin.

They are depurative, cholagogue, diuretic, diaphoretic, laxative and antidiabetic. It is best to use them fresh.

After peeling off the bitter outer layer, the inner part of the

Arctium lappa

stem is one of the very best vegetables to be found. It is tender, crunchy and sweet with a definite, delicate artichoke flavor. It can be eaten raw, steamed or cooked in other ways.

After peeling, the petioles can be cooked and eaten. When very young, they are quite palatable raw, and they can be pickled in vinegar or in brine.

The new, unfolding leaves are edible raw, but they very soon become exceedingly bitter and must then be cooked in several changes of water. Older leaves are inedible.

Burdock leaves have the same properties as the roots. They can be made into a poultice with healing, anti-infectious and antivenomous properties. They are popular for treating skin problems. A decoction of the roots can be used for the same purposes.

Burdock has been used medicinally at least since the Middle Ages.

The fruits contain a glucoside and a fixed oil which has reportedly been employed in medicine.

Artemisia (D-H 1)   Mugwort, Sagebrush

Greek and Latin name of *A. vulgaris* dedicated to Artemis, patroness of women and wild animals, because of its gynecological uses.
Throughout. Both native and species introduced from Eurasia.
Our native *A. ludoviciana* – C. & W. N.Am. – is sometimes planted for ornament.

A. dracunculus, tarragon – native both to N. Asia & C. & W. N.Am. (our plants are also known as *A. dracunculoides*) – is commonly grown in herb gardens. It is especially popular in France where the leaves are added fresh to salads, pickles, vinegar, dressings and various sauces. Tarragon is also used for flavoring liquors.

It is aromatic and slightly pungent – our plants range from almost odorless to very strong smelling – but tarragon is one of the few species in this genus not to be bitter.

It contains an essential oil and is stimulant, stomachic, antispasmodic and emmenagogue.

Foliage and flowering heads of all *Artemisia* spp. are odoriferous, from fragrant to strongly pungent, and many of these plants can be used as condiments.

Among our native species, the leaves of *A. frigida* – W. U.S., Can. – were roasted by the Hopis with corn to flavor it.

The leaves of *A. unalaskensis* – Aleutians – are used in Northeastern Asia to add flavor and green color to rice dumplings.

The achenes of the following species were ground and eaten as "piñole" by Western Indians: *A. biennis* – N.W. N.Am. & naturalized elsewhere in N.Am. –, *dracunculus* (m.a.), *ludoviciana* (m.a.), *michauxiana* (= *discolor*) – Rocky Mountains –, *tridentata*, big sagebrush – C. & W. N.Am. –, *tripartita*, threetip sagebrush – N.W. N.Am. – and *wrightii* – S.W. U.S.

This use was most prevalent in the Great Basin (Utah, Nev., E. Ore.) where sagebrushes of numerous species are omnipresent.

In New Mexico, the achenes of *A.wrightii* (m.a.) were ground with water, made into balls and steamed in a fire pit.

Among the introduced species:

A. absinthium, wormwood – from C. & S. Europe – has been cultivated in North America and is now established on our continent. In spite of their extreme bitterness, the leaves were formerly used in Europe for flavoring sauces. In Morocco, a tiny piece of leaf is added to mint tea (green tea with spearmint) to give it a tang. Wormwood has a very aromatic, penetrating odor.

The distilled liquor known as "absinth" is toxic in high doses. The essential oil contained in the plant, especially when mixed with alcohol, can give rise to dangerous nervous and mental disorders (hallucinations, convulsions), probably due to thujone, a substance found in other plants as well. The beverage, known to be particularly addictive, has caused the insanity and death of many individuals, but it was also the source of inspiration for more than one poet or painter. Very popular around the turn of the century, this beverage has been prohibited in many countries since World War I.

Besides its essential oil, the plant contains a bitter principle (absinthine) and a glucoside.

It is an excellent bitter tonic, with stomachic, aperitive, antiseptic, vermifuge, emmenagogue, diuretic and febrifuge properties.

However, very large amounts are abortive and toxic.

Externally, the plant is antiseptic and vulnerary. It repels insects.

The distilled essential oil acts as a local anesthetic, but it irritates the mucous membranes.

Artemisia absinthium

A. abrotanum, southernwood – from the Old World, cultivated & escaped in N.Am. The <u>leaves</u> have been used in Europe for flavoring certain beers.
It contains an essential oil.
The plant is tonic, stomachic, febrifuge and vermifuge.

A. annua – naturalized from Eurasia – is reportedly used in Kwangtung (China) as a medium for growing *Aspergillus* spp. (a yeast), which is used to brew wine. The plant is sweet scented.

A. stelleriana – from E. Asia, cultivated & escaped in N.E. N.Am. The <u>leaves</u> are put into rice dumplings to give them flavor and color.

A. vulgaris, European mugwort – naturalized from Eurasia in E. N.Am. The <u>young shoots</u> are edible raw if gathered while still tender with the tops of the stems. Their pleasant, aromatic taste is reminiscent of artichokes.

The <u>young stems</u> themselves are delicious raw after peeling. They can be added to salads or eaten as a delicacy.

In Japan, the leaves of this and other species (known as "yomogi") are eaten after cooking or used for flavoring rice cakes. The plant is preserved by dipping in boiling water and drying, first in the shade and then in the sun.

Mugwort was used in Europe as a condiment for various dishes and for flavoring beer before the introduction of hops in the Middle Ages. The mature plant is bitter.

Mugwort contains an essential oil and a bitter principle.

It is emmenagogue, cholagogue, digestive, antispasmodic and vermifuge. High doses can be toxic.

Many other species are used as food or condiments in Europe, Asia and South Africa.

Several of our native species have been used medicinally by both Indians and European settlers. A decoction of *A. ludoviciana* (m.a.), *douglasiana* – W. U.S., Mex. – and related species, all known as mugwort, is effective in cases of rashes due to poison ivy and poison oak (*Rhus* spp., Anacardiaceae). Crushed leaves can also be rubbed locally.

A tea from the leaves of *A. tridentata* (m.a.) was used as a cold remedy with tonic and antiseptic properties, and externally as a hair and eyewash.

Endangered species: *A. argilosa* – Colo.

Aster (D-H 2-3) Aster
Greek and Latin name of various plants with star-shaped flowerheads from the Greek "astêr," star.
Throughout.
A few native species and hybrids are planted for ornament.

The <u>leaves</u> of *A. ledophyllus* – Calif. to Wash. – and *macrophyllus* – N.E. N.Am. & Appalachians – are edible raw or cooked. Those of the latter were used as cooked vegetable by Cherokee Indians.

Those of several species are eaten, generally after boiling, in E. Asia. The flowers of some are also used as food.

A. *ascendens* – W. U.S., Can. –, *commutatus* – C. & W. N.Am. – and *xylorrhiza*, woody aster – Wyo., Utah, Nev. – can absorb enough selenium to become toxic to cattle. The latter species also contains a poisonous resinous substance.

Endangered species: *A. blepharophyllus* – N.M. –, *chilensis* var. *lentus* – Calif. –, *gormanii* – Ore. –, *pinifolius* – Fla. – and *vialis* – Ore.

Balsamorhiza   (C 2)   Balsam Root

From the Greek "balsamos," balsam, and "rhiza," root: alluding to the smell of the roots.
W. N.Am.

The thick roots were highly prized by Indians. They were generally cooked in a fire pit but can also be eaten raw. It is better to remove the brown outer rind and to use only the white inner portion, which has a sweet, pleasant taste.

The roots can also be cooked in various ways, or roasted and used as a coffee substitute.

The very young leaves, stems, flower stalks and flowers are tender and edible raw or cooked. When they become old they are tough and acquire a strong, aromatic taste. The leaves can still be eaten at this stage, but would require long cooking in several changes of water.

The achenes are quite large and the seeds they contain were much used as food by the Indians. They were generally parched and ground into a meal.

Roots, shoots and seeds of the following species were most commonly used: *B. deltoidea* – Calif. to B.C. –, *hookeri*, *incana* – both N.W. U.S. – and *sagittata* – W. N.Am.

Bellis perennis (D 2) Daisy

Latin name of the plant.

Throughout.

Originally from Eur., daisies are grown for ornament and are commonly naturalized on our continent.

The leaves are edible raw, in spite of a slightly acrid aftertaste. They are better when mixed in salads with other wild vegetables. They can also be cooked.

The flower buds can be pickled.

The flowers decorate salads and other dishes. They can be made into a pseudo-wine like those of dandelion (*Taraxacum* spp.).

They contain tannin, mucilage, saponin, an essential oil and a bitter substance.

Leaves and flowers are tonic, depurative and expectorant. Externally, they are antiecchymotic and antiphlogistic. The plant is a good vulnerary.

Bellis perennis

Berlandiera (D 4)

After Jean-Louis Berlandier (d. 1851), Swiss botanist.

S. U.S., Mex.

The flowers of **B. *lyrata*** have been used as a seasoning.

Bidens (D 4) Spanish Needles

From the Latin "bidens," with two teeth: referring to the two spines topping the achenes.

Throughout.

The young leaves of the cosmopolitan **B. *pinnata*** (= *B. pilosa* var. *radiata*) – E. & C. U.S., Mex. –, ***pilosa***, beggarticks – Mex. & tropical Am., naturalized in

S. U.S. – and *tripartita* – exact origin unknown – are cooked and eaten in tropical Asia.

The <u>leaves</u> of various other species are used as food in warm regions of the world.

A decoction of the <u>flowering tops</u> of *B. bigelovii* – S.W. U.S., Mex. – was used as a beverage by Texas Indians.

The spiny fruits of *Bidens* spp. can cause mechanical injury to animals.

Blennosperma (C-H 5)
From the Greek "blenna," mucus, and "sperma," seed.
Calif. (Two species in N.Am. and one in Chile.)

The <u>achenes</u> of *B. nanum* were parched and ground into meal by California Indians.

Endangered species: *B. bakeri* and *nanum* (m.a.) var. *robustum*.

Brickellia (D-H 4)
After D. Brickell, an early physician and botanist from Georgia.
Throughout.

The <u>leaves</u> of *B. californica* (= *Coleosanthus californicus*) – S.W. U.S., Mex. – were used for making tea by California Indians.

Endangered species: *B. biejensis* – Tex.

Calendula (C 4) Marigold
Name dating back to the Middle Ages from the Latin "calendae," calends, the first day of the month in the Roman calendar. Probably by analogy to the fact that the flowering heads open and close in relation to the appearance of the sun.
Scattered throughout.
Introduced from S. Eur.
C. officinalis, pot marigold, is planted for ornament and escapes locally from gardens. It has been cultivated in Eur. since the Middle Ages. Several varieties are in existence.

The <u>flower buds</u> have been pickled.

In Europe, especially in Britain and Holland, the deep orange <u>ray flowers</u> were added to butter as a coloring and to soups as a flavoring.

The flowers also make a very pretty and delectable addition to salads.

They contain an essential oil (rich in carotene), saponin, resin, a bitter principle, some salicylic acid and a relatively high phosphorus content.

The plant is emmenagogue, hypotensive, depurative, diaphoretic and cholagogue. It is an excellent vulnerary, known since Antiquity. Its physiological action can be compared with that of *Arnica* or *Hamamelis*.

C. arvensis – naturalized in Calif. – has the same edible and medicinal virtues and uses as the pot marigold.

Carduus (C 2-3) Thistle
Latin name of the plant.
Throughout. Introduced from Eurasia.

Generally, the various species of several genera of thistles (*Carduus, Carlina, Cirsium, Onopordum, Silybum,* among others) are all edible as described below.

The young, tender <u>stems</u> are delicious to eat raw after peeling. They are juicy and have a very pleasant flavor, both salty and sweet, somewhat reminiscent of artichokes. Each species has its own qualities, some being definitely better than others. The inner pith of older stems is potentially edible after removing the tough outer part, but it is usually not really worth it.

The <u>young leaves</u> can be eaten raw or cooked. If the marginal spines are too hard, they can be cut off with scissors.

The still tender, young <u>receptacles</u> are edible raw or

Carduus

cooked like artichokes – which actually are nothing other than large thistle heads (see *Cynara scolymus*) – after removing the spiny bracts.

The dried <u>flowers</u> of various thistles (including *Carduus* spp.) are still used in Europe, particularly in France, for curdling milk during the making of certain cheeses. The milk is heated to about 130°F (50°C), and water in which the flowers have macerated for five or six hours is added to it, or the flowers themselves are placed in a muslin bag directly in the milk. The milk curdles in about half an hour. Several hours are needed at colder temperatures.

The inner part of the young stem of *C. nutans*, musk thistle, has been eaten on our continent after boiling in salted water, and served with a dressing.

Carlina vulgaris   (D 2)   Carline Thistle

Italian name of the plant, probably from the Latin "cardus," thistle. Legend has it that *C. acaulis* was dedicated to the emperor Carolus Magnus, who supposedly acknowledged its medicinal virtues.
Naturalized from Eurasia in E. N.Am.

The young receptacles can be eaten like artichokes after removing the spiny bracts.
Two other species are occasionally used as food in Europe.

Carthamus   (C 5)   Safflower

Name of Semitic origin introduced during the 16th century
Originally from the Mediterranean region, it is occasionally found in Calif.
C. tinctorius – originally from Egypt – is cultivated throughout the world for the edible oil expressed from its seeds (safflower oil). The seeds are also eaten whole out of the achenes, like sunflower seeds.

The red and yellow flowers have been used for seasoning food, especially in Spain, the Middle East, South America and England during the 17th century. They are used nowadays for coloring confectionaries and cosmetics, and have a long history as the source of a yellow dye for cloth.
The flowers are diaphoretic and diuretic.
The leaves are reportedly cooked and eaten in Asia.
Oil is extracted from the seeds of two local species in Asia.

Centaurea (G 3)

Greek name of several medicinal plants "kentauriê," "kentaurion": dedicated to the Centaur Chiron.

Throughout. Both native and mostly species introduced from Eurasia.

Two European species, *C. cyanus*, cornflower, and *montana*, are planted for ornament; they occasionally escape from cultivation.

The young shoots of *C. calcitrapa*, caltrops, star thistle – naturalized from Eurasia & N. Africa – have reportedly been eaten raw in Egypt. Local species are used as food in Europe, in Africa and in Asia.

The flowers of *C. cyanus* and *montana* (both m.a.) contain a bitter substance (centaurin). Those of the cornflower also contain glucosides.

Leaves and flowers are tonic, digestive and diuretic.

The flowers are used as an eyewash.

Our native *C. americana* – S.C. & S.W. U.S., Mex. – is known to contain important amounts of hydrocyanic acid. The European *C. solstitialis*, Barnaby's thistle – widely naturalized in N.Am. – has caused animal poisoning.

Chondrilla juncea (D 4)   Skeleton Weed

Greek name of the plant "chondrilê" from "chondros," grain: as the latex becomes gritty upon drying.

Naturalized from S. Eur. & W. Asia in E. N.Am.

The leaves of skeleton weed have been eaten since Antiquity in the Mediterranean area, picked early in the spring when they form a rosette on the ground. They were commonly made into salads in Greece at the turn of the century and are still eaten as such in Southern France.

Another species is eaten in Southeastern Europe and Western Asia.

Chrysanthemum (D 3)

Greek name of a plant in this genus "chrysanthemon" from "chrysos," gold, and "anthemon," flower.

Throughout. Naturalized from Eurasia.

Several species native to Eur., Asia and North Africa, as well as hybrids, are planted for ornament. The following can be found in the wild on our continent:

C. balsamita (= *Balsamita major*), costmary – originally from S.W. Asia & locally escaped. The plant is strongly aromatic – its odor is reminiscent of spearmint (*Mentha spicata*, Lamiaceae) – and it used to be widely grown for this purpose.

The leaves have been used as a condiment in salads, as a flavoring for beer and for making tea. They are intensely bitter.

Costmary contains an essential oil.

It is tonic, carminative, antispasmodic, emmenagogue and diuretic.

C. coronarium, garland chrysanthemum – occasionally naturalized from S. Europe & W. Asia. Leaves and tender stems have long been eaten in Europe and are still used as food in China and Japan, where they are put into soups and boiled or fried as vegetables. They have a very pleasant, aromatic flavor, without any bitterness. The plant is commonly cultivated in the Far East and has found its place in European and American gardens.

C. parthenium (= *Tanacetum p.*), feverfew – originally from S. Eur. & W. Asia. The aromatic but bitter flower heads are made into tea and reportedly used as a flavoring for wines and pastries.

The plant contains an essential oil and a bitter principle.

It is stimulant, carminative, stomachic and emmenagogue. Feverfew is sometimes employed instead of chamomile.

The flowers have also been used as an insecticide like those of pyrethrum (*C. cinerariaefolium* = *Tanacetum cinerariifolium*).

C. segetum, corn chrysanthemum – naturalized from Eurasia. The young shoots and leaves have been eaten since Antiquity in Southern Europe and Asia. They are crisp, tender and aromatic, without any bitterness.

Leaves and flowers of various species are used as food in Eastern Asia.

Chrysothamnus (E 2) Rabbitbrush
From the Greek "chrysos," gold, and "thamnos," shrub: alluding to the showy golden inflorescences.
W. N.Am.

The roots of *C. viscidiflorus* were used like chewing gum by Indians.
The young flower heads of *C. confinis* were eaten by Indians.
C. nauseus is known to contain 5 to 6% rubber. Other species are likely to be rich in rubber as well.
Rabbitbrushes are strong smelling and commonly sticky with resin.
Some species have poisoned cattle.
Southwestern Indians used the wood for making arrows, for wickerwork and as fuel.
They obtained a yellow dye from the flowers and a green dye from the inner bark.

Cichorium intybus (B 1) Chicory
Greek and Latin name of the plant of Egyptian origin.
Throughout.

Originally from Southern Europe and Western Asia, chicory has been grown in gardens mostly in Europe since the 17th century. Its leaves are eaten in salads and as cooked vegetables (Brussel witloof), and its roots are commonly used in Europe as a coffee substitute after chopping and roasting. Chicory is widely naturalized on our continent.
The root of the wild plant can be picked before the flower stalk appears and torrefied to be used as a coffee substitute. Arabs used to eat chicory roots as a vegetable, after boiling in several changes of water to reduce its bitterness.
The very young leaves are edible raw in salads. Older leaves are bitter and are better cooked in a change of water or two. Chicory is one of the wild plants

most commonly gathered for food in Greece and Italy, where it is widely found in markets in the spring.

When the roots are transplanted in a dark cellar, the young leaves sprouting from the crown are whitish and hardly bitter at all; they will yield delicate salads even in winter. Young plants can also be left in place and blanched with earth to give white, tender leaves.

The flower buds can be pickled, and the beautiful light-blue ray flowers add a graceful touch to salads.

Chicory contains proteins, vitamins A, B, C, K and rutin, minerals, a latex and a bitter substance (intybine). The root is rich in starch and inulin (20 to 50%).

Chicory is a bitter tonic with stomachic, cholagogue, depurative and slightly laxative properties.

Cichorium intybus

Endive (*C. endivia* – from S. Eur. & W. Asia) has long been cultivated as a salad plant. It is especially popular in France where several varieties are known.

The leaves of several species are commonly eaten in Greece and in the Middle East.

Cirsium   (C-H 1)   Thistle

Greek name of a thistle used for healing varicose veins "kirsion," from "kirsos," varicose veins (Latin "varix").

Throughout. Both native and species introduced from Eur.

The roots of the following species were eaten raw or cooked by Indians: *C. drummondii* – W. N.Am. –, *eatoni* – S.W. U.S. –, *edule*, Indian thistle – Ore. to B.C. –, *foliosum* – W. N.Am. –, *hookerianum* – N.W. N.Am. –, *occidentale* – Calif. –, *ochrocentrum* – W. & C. U.S. –, *scopulorum* – Mont. –, *undulatum* – W. & C. N.Am. – and *virginianum* – coast of N.J. to Fla.

Those of *C. kamshaticum* – E. Aleutians – are used as food in Northeastern Asia.

The young tender stems of many species, including most of the *Cirsium* spp. described above, were eaten raw or cooked by Indians.

In fact, as mentioned for *Carduus* spp., the young shoots, stems, leaves and receptacles of basically all thistles (including *Cirsium* spp.) can be used as food either raw or cooked. The <u>pith</u> of older stems is edible after peeling off the outer part.

Those of the Eurasian *C. vulgare* – naturalized throughout – and *palustre* – naturalized in N.E. N.Am. – were eaten in Europe.

The <u>flowers</u> of *C. arvense*, Canada thistle – naturalized from Eurasia in N. N.Am. – have been used like those of *Carduus* spp. for curdling milk.

Its seeds, however, are said to contain toxic alkaloids.

The <u>seeds</u> of *C. pallidum* – S.W. U.S. – were eaten whole or parched and ground by the Chiricahua and Apache Indians.

Endangered species: *C. clokeyi* – Nev. – and *crassicaule, fontinale* var. *fontinale, obispoense, hydrophilum* var. *hydrophilum, loncholepis* and *rhothopilum* – all Calif.

Conyza (G 2-3)
Name used by Dioscorides and Pliny for some kinds of fleabane (*Erigeron* spp.), possibly from "konops," flea.
Throughout.

The young, leafy <u>seedlings</u> of *C. canadensis* (= *Erigeron c.*), horseweed, are reportedly eaten boiled in Japan where the plant has been introduced.

The <u>leaves</u> have a biting taste and an aromatic flavor reminiscent of tarragon.

<u>Shoots</u> and <u>leaves</u> of some other species are occasionally used as food in Eastern Asia.

Coreopsis (D-H 4)   Tickseed
From the Greek "koris," bug, and "opsis," resemblance: referring to the appearance of the achene.
Almost throughout.

The <u>leaves</u> of *C. cardaminafolia* – S.W. U.S. – were made into tea by Zuni Indians.

Endangered species: *C. intermedia* – La., Tex.

Cosmos (D 4)

From the Greek "kosmos," order, ornament: alluding to the beauty of the flowers.

S. U.S., Mex.

A few Mexican species are planted for ornament, including *C. sulphureus* – from Mex., cosmopolitan in the Tropics and occasionally found as an escape in S. U.S.

Young shoots and leaves of this species and of another one are eaten raw or cooked in Malaysia.

Crepis (B 1) Hawksbeard

Greek and Latin name of an undetermined plant from the Greek "krêpis," shoe.

Throughout. Both native and species introduced from Eurasia.

The leaves of various species can be eaten raw, but they are generally better cooked.

Those of *C. runcinata* subsp. *glauca* (= *C. glauca*) – Rocky Mountains & Great Basin – were used as food by Indians in Utah and Nevada.

Certain European species are thought to possibly produce nervous disorders.

Cynara (B 4)

Greek name of the plant "kinara," close to "kunara," wild rose, dog rose, from "kunos," dog.

Mostly Calif.

The following two species (mostly the latter) are grown as vegetables and are occasionally found as escapes from cultivation, especially in Calif.:

C. cardunculus, cardoon – originally from the Mediterranean area – has been grown since Antiquity for the petioles and the fleshy midribs of its leaves, but it has almost totally fallen into oblivion.

Cardoon is a thistle, and in its original state the leaves are extremely spiny, but spineless varieties have been selected, although these are considered to have less flavor.

The immature <u>receptacles</u> are edible raw and the <u>flowers</u> can be used for curdling milk. Up until this century, cardoon flowers were commonly used for making cheese, especially in Spain.

The <u>roots</u> are said to be edible as well.

C. scolymus, artichoke – unknown in its original wild state – is thought to have been derived from the cardoon. Its cultivation began in Southern Italy toward the turn of the 15th century. It is now a very popular vegetable. Artichokes are cultivated on a very large scale around Castroville, California. Many different varieties are known.

The immature <u>flower heads</u> can be eaten raw or cooked. The well-known artichoke "hearts" are actually the <u>receptacles</u> of the flowers, and the so-called "leaves" are the <u>bracts</u> of the involucre. Very young artichokes are sometimes eaten raw with salt in France, but they are most commonly steamed or boiled. They can also be pickled.

The flower heads contain about 12% sugars (especially inulin), 3% protein, vitamins A, B1, B2, and C, niacin, minerals and enzymes.

They are cholagogue, depurative and diuretic. But the very bitter leaves (not to be confused with the involucral bracts), stems and roots are the most medicinally active parts. In addition to the substances noted above, they contain tannin and a bitter principle (cynarine).

They are tonic, choleretic, cholagogue, diuretic, laxative and antigalactic.

In Europe, the leaves are made into an apéritif (Cynar), which is drunk as a bitter tonic.

Like those of cardoon and of other thistles, the flowers have been used for curdling milk. This property is due to an enzyme (cynarase) they contain; a dilution of 1 to 150,000 parts is sufficient to obtain the desired result.

The <u>receptacles</u> of a local species have been eaten in Spain.

Dahlia (C 4) Dahlia
After A. Dahl, Swedish botanist, student of Linnaeus.
Mex.
Several Mexican species and hybrids are commonly planted for ornament.

The tuberous <u>roots</u> of *D. pinnata* are eaten after cooking in some parts of Mexico. This tradition dates back to the days of the Aztecs and probably even earlier. Dahlia roots are sweet and quite aromatic, somewhat reminiscent of Jerusalem artichokes (*Helianthus tuberosus*).

They contain inulin, a sugar easily assimilated by diabetics, which is sometimes extracted from them.

The flowers can be added to salads.

Dicoria   (C 4)

From the Greek "dis," twice, and "koris," bug: from the aspect of the two achenes of the typical species.
W. U.S.

Flowers and seeds of *D. brandegei* – Colo., Utah, Ariz. – were used as food by Northern Arizona Indians.

Eclipta   (D 4)

From the Greek "ekleipein," to be deficient: referring to the absence of pappus.
E., C. & S. U.S., Mex. Introduced into W. N.Am.

The leaves of *E. alba* (= *E. prostrata*) are eaten cooked in Africa and Asia, where the plant is native as well.

Emilia   (B 4)   Emilia

Etymology unknown.
Naturalized in S. Fla. & Mex. from the Old World Tropics.

The leaves of *E. javanica* (= *E. coccinea*), tasselflower, and *sonchifolia*, Flora's paintbrush, are edible raw. They are made into salads or cooked as greens in Asia and Africa. Their taste is pleasant, although more or less bitter.

Encelia   (C 2)   Brittlebush

After Christopher Encel, who wrote about oak galls in 1577.
S.W. U.S., Mex.

The yellow resin exuding from the stems of *E. farinosa* makes a pleasant chewing gum and was often used for this purpose by Indians. The Spanish name of the plant, "incensio," denotes the use (still alive in Baja) of its resin as incense.

After being chewed and warmed, the resin was smeared on the body to relieve pain. When melted, it was used as a varnish for pottery, among other uses.

Contact with the leaves of *E. californica* – S. Calif. – can cause dermatitis in susceptible individuals.

Erechtites (G 2)   Fireweed
Name given by Dioscorides to a plant in this family.
Throughout.

Young tops, leaves and flower heads of *E. hieracifolia* – E. & C. N.Am. – are reportedly eaten raw or cooked in Eastern Asia where this species is native as well. The plant, however, has a very strong odor and flavor.

Erigeron (G 1)
From the Greek "eri," early, strongly, and "gerôn," old man: possibly referring to the early flowering and fruiting of most species.
Throughout.

The young leafy seedlings of *E. annuus* – N. N.Am. – are reportedly eaten boiled in Japan where the plant has been introduced.

The leaves of a few local species are occasionally used as a vegetable in Eastern Asia.

Endangered species: *E. basalticus* – Wash. –, *calvus* – Calif. –, *delicatus* – Ore., Calif. –, *eriophyllus* – Ariz. –, *flagellaris* var. *trilobatus* – Utah –, *foliosus* var. *blochmanae* – Calif. –, *geiseri* var. *calcicola* – Tex. –, *kachinensis* – Utah –, *kuschei* – Ariz. –, *latus* – Idaho –, *maguirei*, *religiosus* – Utah –, *rhizomatus* – N.M. – and *sionis* – Utah.

Eupatorium   (G-F-H 2-3)   Boneset
Commemorating Mithridates Eupator, king of Pontus in Antiquity.
Throughout.
A few native, European and Asian species are planted for ornament.

E. incarnatum – S.E. U.S., Mex. – and *purpureum*, Joe Pye weed – E. & C. U.S. – have a vanilla-like odor when dried and make a pleasant tea.

Another species (*E. dalea*) is used as a vanilla substitute in the West Indies and tropical America. Others are used as seasonings in tropical Asia and America. Still others are cooked and eaten as greens in Asia.

E. purpureum (m.a.) is sometimes called "queen-of-the-meadow" – the common name of the fragrant *Filipendula ulmaria* (= *Spiraea u.*), Rosaceae – to denote the pleasant smell of the plant.

Joe Pye weed contains tannin, a bitter principle and traces of essential oil. It has been used medicinally as a diuretic and tonic.

An infusion of *E. perfoliatum* – E. N.Am. – is tonic and mildly laxative when cold, diaphoretic and emetic when warm, and emetic and cathartic when hot.

E. rugosum, white snakeroot – E. N.Am. – is poisonous, due to tremetol, one of the higher alcohols. Especially when fresh, the plants produce the disease known as "trembles" in animals and "milk sickness" in humans (tremetol is soluble in milk fat); the milk of contaminated animals is thus dangerous. Milk sickness, known for about 150 years in Eastern United States, has at times reached epidemic proportions.

The botanical names of *E. aromaticum* – E. U.S. – and *odoratum* (= *Osmia odorata*) – S. Fla. – suggest that they might be used like *E. incarnatum, purpureum* (both m.a.).

Endangered species: *E. resinosum* var. *kentuckiense* – Ky.

Galinsoga   (D-H 1)   Quickweed
After Mariano Martinez Galinsoga, Spanish physician and botanist.
Some species are native to S. U.S. & Mex. Others from tropical Am. are naturalized throughout our continent as garden weeds.

When young, *G. parviflora* – naturalized from tropical Am. – is eaten as a cooked vegetable in Southeastern Asia where the plant has been introduced.

Named "guasca" in Quechua, it has been used as food in the Andes since the time of the Incas. It is cultivated along with corn and sold in markets. The whole plant is eaten and its flavor is very good. Cooked with chicken and potatoes, it forms the basis of the Bolivian national dish, "agiaco."

G. cilita is edible and has a pleasant flavor as well.

Endangered species: G. semicalva var. percalva – Ariz.

Galinsoga parviflora

Grindelia (D-H 4) Gumweed, Gum Plant
After David Hyeronymus Grindel (1776–1836), Russian botanist.
W. N.Am.

The resinous leaves of several species, including *G. squarrosa*, were chewed and made into tea by Indians, but they are rather bitter.

They contain an essential oil, resin, alkaloids and glucosides.

Grindelia tea is antispasmodic, expectorant and stomachic, and was used externally to relieve poison ivy rash.

On soils rich in selenium, the plant can accumulate potentially dangerous levels of this element.

Endangered species: G. fraxinopratensis – Nev., Calif. –, howellii – Idaho, Mont. – and oolepis – Tex.

Haplopappus (C-F-H 4)
(sometimes written *Aplopappus*)
From the Greek "haplous," simple, and "pappos," seed-down.
W. N.Am.

The achenes of *H. parishii* – Calif., Baja – were used as food by Indians.

The roots of *H. nuttallii* – W. U.S., Can. – were made into a cough-relieving tea by Hopi Indians.

H. heterophyllus – S.W. U.S., Mex. – and *fruticosus* – Ariz. to Tex., Mex. – contain the same toxic substance (tremetol) as *Eupatorium rugosum* and can poison cattle ("alkali disease," or "trembles") and humans ("milk sickness") in a similar manner. People are affected by drinking the milk of contaminated cows.

Endangered species: *H. canus, eastwoodiae* – both Calif. –, *fremontii* subsp. *monocephalus* – Colo. –, *salicinus* – Ariz. – and *spinulosus* subsp. *laevis* – N.M.

Helianthus (C-H 2-3)   Sunflower
From the Greek "helios," sun, and "anthos," flower: alluding to the aspect and color of the inflorescence.
Throughout.
Our native *H. annuus* and *tuberosus* are grown throughout the world – especially the former species – for their seeds and tubers. A few species are planted for ornament.

H. annuus (m.a.), sunflower – C. & W. U.S., naturalized elsewhere – is one of the most common oil crops in America, Europe (especially Russia) and Asia. It escapes from cultivation, but the varieties grown are unable to maintain themselves in the wild.

Sunflower seeds were an important food for certain Indian tribes. To remove their shells, Indians crushed the achenes and placed them in water; the shells, which are lighter, floated and were thus easily removed. The seeds themselves were then made into gruel or dried for later use.

Sunflower seeds are delicious whole, added to salads and various dishes, or crushed into a delicately flavored vegetable butter. They contain 30% of an excellent edible oil having a particular taste, which can be extracted by cold pressure. Indians would gather it by crushing the seeds, boiling them in water and skimming off the oil. Sunflower oil is rich in polyunsaturated fatty acids and has a favorable effect in cases of excess cholesterol and atherosclerosis.

Besides oil, the seeds contain vitamins B1 and B2, niacin, minerals, lecithin, choline, tannin and protein. The cake resulting from the extraction of the oil contains almost 50% protein.

The seeds have also been roasted and used, with or without their shells, as a coffee substitute.

The lower part of the <u>stem</u> was chewed like gum by Indians.

The stem yields fibers used for making paper.

The <u>leaves</u> are edible cooked. They have a pleasant flavor, reminiscent of artichoke.

The immature <u>receptacles</u> can be eaten like artichokes.

The bright-yellow <u>ray flowers</u> make a pretty and tasty addition to salads.

They contain a glucoside, resin and various substances. They have been used as a febrifuge.

The flowers give wool a light yellow color.

The <u>seeds</u> of *H. giganteus* – E. & C. N.Am. – and *petiolaris* – C. & W. N.Am., occasionally naturalized elsewhere – were also used as food by the Indians.

The Hopis used to extract purple and black dyes for decorating baskets and textiles and making body paint used in ceremonies from the seeds of *H. annuus* (m.a.) and other species.

H. tuberosus (m.a.), Jerusalem artichoke – C. N.Am., naturalized elsewhere – has been grown since pre-Columbian times for its <u>tuberous roots</u>. It is widely naturalized, as the plant propagates readily by its tubers and becomes sometimes almost impossible to eradicate long after its culture has been abandoned.

Jerusalem artichokes were first eaten by Indians long before the advent of the Europeans. They are delicious raw or cooked. Their sweet flavor is due to inulin, a sugar easily assimilated by diabetics. They can be pickled and have been chopped, roasted and used as a coffee substitute.

Jerusalem artichokes can be left in the ground during the winter.

They contain protein, vitamins A and C, minerals, mucilage, levulose and, as noted above, inulin.

The tuberous <u>roots</u> of *H. x doronicoides* (= *H. mollis* x *giganteus*) – N.J. to Ind. & Ill. –, *laetiflorus* – C. U.S., occasionally introduced eastward – and *maximiliani* – C. N.Am., occasionally introduced eastward – were also used as food by Indians.

Endangered species: *H. exilis, niveus* subsp. *tephrodes* – both Calif. –, *paradoxus* – Tex., N.M. – and *smithii* – Ala., Ga.

Hemizonia (D-H 4)   Tarweed
From the Greek "hemi," half, and "zonê," girdle: referring to the ray achenes, which are half enclosed by the bracts of the involucre.
Calif., Baja.

The seeds of *H. luzulaefolia* were ground into piñole and eaten by California Indians.

H. fasciculata was reportedly boiled down to a thick, tarry liquid and eaten in times of famine.

Endangered species: *H. conjugens, floribunda, minthornii* and *mohavensis* – all Calif.

Hieracium (E 4)   Hawkweed
Greek and Latin name of the Eurasian *H. pilosella*, from "hierax," hawk.
Throughout. Both native in N. N.Am and species introduced from Eurasia.

The coagulated milky latex of a native species was used like chewing gum by the Indians of British Columbia.

H. pilosella – naturalized from Eurasia in N. N.Am. – contains an antibiotic substance, an essential oil and tannin.

It is diuretic, cholagogue and astringent.

Hymenopappus (E 4)
From the Greek "hymen," membrane, and "pappos," seed down: referring to the texture of the pappus.
C. & W. N.Am.

The roots of *H. filifolius* – W. U.S. – were chewed like gum by certain Indians.

Those of *H. lugens* – S.W. U.S., Mex. – were used by Hopi Indians as an emetic and for treating toothaches.

Hymenoxys (D 4)   Rubberweed
(= *Actinea* spp.)
From the Greek "hymen," membrane, and "oxys," sharp: alluding to the
pointed pappus scales.
W. N.Am.

The root bark of *H. floribunda* (= *Actinea richardsonii*) was used like chewing
gum by Western Indians.
The flowering tops of *H. odorata* (= *Actinea o.*), fragrant bitterweed, were
made into tea.
But both species are known to be poisonous to livestock, especially to sheep.
The plants are eaten only when other forage is scarce. They are more toxic dur-
ing drought years.
The Hopis used to make a stimulating tea from *H. acaulis* var. *arizonica* –
S.W. U.S. – and would apply the bruised plant locally to alleviate pain, espe-
cially during pregnancy.
H. acaulis (m.a.) is cultivated in Europe as an ornamental.
The latex of several species contains rubber.

Hypochoeris (D 1)   Cat's Ear
Greek and Latin name of a kind of chicory, from "choiron," piglet.
Throughout. Naturalized from Eurasia as a weed.

The young leaves of *H. glabra* – naturalized almost throughout – can be
eaten raw. They are crisp and have a pleasant flavor, exempt of bitterness, and
make very good salads.
H. radicata – naturalized throughout – has been cultivated as a vegetable on
the Old Continent. Its leaves have the same characteristics as those of the previous species.
Other species are edible as well, but in some cases, the leaves are better
cooked.
Flower buds and heads, although much smaller, can be used like those of
dandelion (*Taraxacum* spp.).
Some species from Western South America have thick, edible roots.

Inula (C 4)   Elecampane
Latin name of the plant, possibly from "helenion," its Greek name.
Originally from S.E. Eur. & W. Asia, the plant was formerly grown in gardens for its aromatic root, which was used both medicinally and as a flavoring. It is naturalized throughout N. Am.

The <u>root</u>, which can reach a large size, is edible after boiling in several changes of water to eliminate its strong aromatic taste. It used to be candied in honey or sugar and was eaten to stimulate digestion.

It can be grated like ginger and added as a spice to cakes, fruits salads and various desserts. Elecampane root is used in Europe for flavoring liquors such as vermouth.

It contains an essential oil, much inulin, minerals, resin and various substances.

Elecampane is tonic, expectorant, cholagogue, stomachic, antiseptic, diuretic and vermifuge. It has been used medicinally since Antiquity.

The <u>young leaves</u> are edible after cooking, possibly in several changes of water.

The yellow <u>ray flowers</u> contain vitamin A. They can be added to various dishes as a flavorful decoration.

The <u>leaves</u> of some local species are used as food in Europe and Northeastern Asia.

Lactuca (D 1)   Wild Lettuce
Latin name of the plant, from "lac," milk: alluding to its milky sap.
Throughout. Both native and species introduced from Eurasia & S. Am.
L. sativa, garden lettuce – probably derived from the Eurasian *L. scariola* – is cultivated throughout the world in gardens and in fields. Many varieties are known. The plant occasionally escapes from cultivation but does not become established.

Lettuce contains vitamins A, B1, B2, C, D and E, minerals, a bitter principle and various substances, including a very large proportion of water for cultivated specimens: up to 96% in certain "iceberg" types, notwithstanding the chemical residues found in commercially grown plants.

The plant is soothing, emollient, laxative, depurative and refrigerant.

The latex of cultivated plants when they go to seed, or especially of wild lettuce (especially *L. virosa* – naturalized from Eurasia in Calif.), yields a dark brown, very bitter substance after drying known as "lactucarium," which has antispasmodic, sedative and hypnotic properties. It has been used medicinally like opium, the dried latex of the opium poppy (*Papaver somniferum*, Papaveraceae), with good results in certain cases. Moreover, lactucarium

Lactuca scariola

has no toxicity. It has even been used as a substitute to cure opium addiction.

The juicy <u>pith</u> within the stems of flowering lettuce is delicious to eat raw after peeling the outer rind of the stem. Some varieties, known as "celtuce," are now grown specifically for this purpose in North America.

Garden lettuce has been cultivated since Antiquity.

The very <u>young shoots</u> and <u>leaves</u>, light green and tender, of the various species of wild lettuce are delicious raw in salads. Older leaves may be cooked in several waters to eliminate their bitterness.

The <u>inflorescences</u> are edible as well.

On our continent, the following wild species have been eaten: *L. canadensis* – E. & C. N.Am. –, *intybacea* (= *Brachyrampus intybaceus*) – naturalized from S. Am. in S. Fla. & Mex. – and *scariola* (m.a.) – naturalized from Eurasia. The leaves of *L. canadensis* (m.a.) were eaten raw by Cherokee Indians.

The <u>leaves</u> of *L. muralis* (= *Mycelis m.*) – naturalized from Eur. in N.E. N.Am. – are tender and not too bitter, even when older. They make excellent salads.

The <u>gum</u> from the root of *L. pulchella* – C. & W. U.S., Can. – was used for chewing by Indians (as can be the latex of other species). However, the plant is reputed to be slightly toxic.

Lapsana communis   (D 3)   Nipplewort
Greek name of an undetermined edible plant "lap-
sanê," "lampsanê."
Throughout. Naturalized from Eurasia.

The very <u>young leaves</u>, forming a rosette on the
ground, are edible raw. Older ones are bitter and require
cooking.
    The plant is diuretic. Its juice has been used exter-
nally to heal chapped nipples, hence the common name
of the plant.
    The <u>leaves</u> of two local species are occasionally used
as food in N.E. Asia.

Lapsana communis

Lasthenia   (C-H 4)
Name of a Greek woman who was a student of Plato.
Calif., Ore.

The <u>seeds</u> of *L. glabrata* – Calif. – were ground into piñole and eaten by
California Indians.
    Endangered species: *L. burkei* and *conjungens* – both Calif.

Layia   (C-H 4)
(= *Blepharipappus* spp.)
After Thomas Lay, botanist on Beechey's journey in the "Blossom,"
which visited California in 1827.
W. U.S.
L. platyglossa – Calif. – is sometimes planted for ornament.

The seeds of *L. glandulosa* and *platyglossa* (m.a.) were ground into piñole and
eaten by Indians.
    Endangered species: *L. discoidea* – Calif.

Leontodon (D 1)   Hawkbit
From the Greek "leôn," lion, and "odous, odontos," tooth: alluding to the outline of the leaves.
Throughout. Naturalized from Eurasia as a weed.

The young <u>leaves</u> of the various species are edible raw. Older ones become bitter and should be cooked.
<u>Flower buds</u> and <u>heads</u> can be used like those of dandelion (*Taraxacum* spp.), although much smaller.
L. autumnalis, fall dandelion, was commonly eaten as a spring salad in Europe.

Leucanthemum vulgare (B 1)   Ox-eye Daisy
(= *Chrysanthemum leucanthemum*)
Greek name of Asteraceae with white ray flowers, "leukanthemon," from "leukos," white, and "anthemon," flower.
Almost throughout.
Some varieties of this plant are grown for ornament.

It has been reported that in the 17th century, the <u>roots</u> of the ox-eye daisy were eaten raw in salads in Spain.
The <u>leaves</u> have a pleasant, sweetish taste and are edible raw, added to salads.
The <u>young shoots</u>, including the <u>flower buds</u>, are best when slightly steamed. They have a very nice, aromatic flavor.
The plant is diaphoretic and diuretic. Externally, it is a good vulnerary, but the leaves are said to occasionally irritate the skin of susceptible individuals.
The <u>flower heads</u> decorate salads and other dishes. They have been made into a "wine," like those of dandelion (*Taraxacum* spp.).

Leucanthemum vulgare

Liatris (C-H 4) Blazing Star, Gayfeather
Etymology unknown.
Almost throughout.
Our native *L. scariosa* and *spicata* – both E. & C. N.Am. – are sometimes planted for ornament.

The <u>corms</u> of *L. punctata* – Mont. south to N.M. & Mex. – were eaten in early spring by local Indians.
The roots of *L. scariosa, spicata* (both m.a.) and *squarrosa* – E. & C. N.Am. – have been used medicinally as a diuretic.
Endangered species: *L. ohlingerae* – Fla.

Lygodesmia (D-H 4) Rush Pink
From the Greek "lygos," pliant twig, and "desmê," bundle: alluding to the habit of the plant.
C. & W. N.Am.

The <u>leaves</u> of *L. grandiflora* – W. N.Am. – were boiled with other foods by the Hopi Indians.
They were thought by this tribe to be galactagogue.
Indians obtained a <u>chewing gum</u> by cutting the stems of *L. juncea* – C. & W. N.Am. – and collecting the coagulated bitter latex.
The plant has been suspected of being somewhat toxic to cattle in Montana and Utah.
Endangered species: *L. grandiflora* (m.a.) var. *stricta* – Utah.

Madia (C 2) Tarweed
From "madi," Chilean name of *M. sativa*, the type species.
W. & C. N.Am. naturalized in E. N.Am.

The <u>seeds</u> of *M. elegans* (including subsp. *densiflora*) – Calif., Ore. –, *glomerata* – W. N.Am. –, *gracilis* (= *dissitiflora*), gumweed – W. N.Am. – and *sativa*, Chile tarweed – Calif. to B.C. & Chile – were eaten raw, roasted or ground into meal by various Indian tribes.
M. sativa (m.a.) is cultivated in Europe and in South America for its <u>seeds</u>,

which yield about 30% of a drying oil. This oil is edible and can be used in salads and for cooking. But it is more generally used for making soap.

The cultivated plant is native to Chile – although, as noted above, the same species is indigenous to W. N. America as well.

M. elegans (m.a.) is planted for ornament in Europe.

Malacothrix (C 4)
From the Greek "malakos," soft, and "thrix," hair: referring to the pappus.
W. N.Am.

The *achenes* of *M. californica* – Calif. – were used as food by California Indians.

Matricaria (B 1)
Name given by herbalists to plants of medicinal value, from the Latin "mater" or "matrix."
Throughout. Both native and species introduced from Eurasia.
A few Eurasian species are sometimes planted for ornament.

M. chamomilla (= *Chamomilla recutita*), German chamomile – originally from Eurasia – was formerly much cultivated in the medicinal garden and is naturalized throughout North America.

The plant, especially the flower heads, is aromatic and can be used as a seasoning. It makes a more pleasant tea than Roman chamomile (*Anthemis nobilis*).

The flower heads have been used for flavoring liquors and tobacco.

The plant contains an essential oil of a beautiful blue color. The flowers contain glucosides.

German chamomile is used medicinally in the same way as Roman chamomile, as a tonic, aperitive, antispasmodic, stomachic, carminative, emmenagogue, analgesic and febrifuge.

Externally, it is vulnerary and antiphlogistic, and can be made into an eyewash.

*Matricaria
matricarioides*

M. matricarioides, pineapple weed – native to W. N.Am. & naturalized in E. N.Am. – is aromatic as well, with a pleasant, fruity smell.

Its flower heads have a very clean, lemony taste and make delicious additions to salads.

Microseris   (C-H 4)
From the Greek "micros," small, and "seris," chicory.
W. N.Am.

The thick *roots* of *M. forsteri*, *laciniata* (= *procera*) – N. Calif. to Wash. – and *nutans* – N.W. N.Am. – were used as food by Indians.
The hardened latex of the plant can be chewed like gum.
Endangered species: *M. decipiens* – Calif.

Onopordum acanthium   (C 4)   Scotch Thistle
Greek name of a thistle, "onopordon," from "onos," donkey, and "pordê," fart: it was said to have this effect upon donkeys.
Almost throughout. Naturalized from Eurasia.

The roots were reportedly eaten after cooking.
Young tender stems and immature receptacles are edible like those of other thistles (*Carduus* spp.), but they are very bitter.
The flowers have been used to adulterate saffron (*Crocus sativus*, Iridaceae).
The achenes contain toxic alkaloids, but the oil extracted from the seeds is said to be edible.

Pectis   (D-H 4)   Chinchweed
From the Greek "pecteô," to comb: the leaves of most species are fringed with hairs arranged like the teeth of a comb.
W. N.Am.

·The leaves of *P. angustifolia* were eaten raw or cooked by Indians and were also used as a flavoring, either dried or fresh.
The ashes of the plant were mixed with blue corn meal by the Hopis when making "piki," a paper-thin stonecake. They were also rubbed on the body as a perfume.

A dye was extracted from this plant.

The aromatic <u>leaves</u> and <u>flower heads</u> of *P. papposa* – S.W. U.S., Mex. – were used for seasoning food by certain Indian tribes.

Endangered species: *P. rusbyi* – Ariz.

Petasites   (C 2)   Sweet Coltsfoot
From the Greek "petasos," large-brimmed hat: alluding to the shape of the leaves.

N. N.Am. & Mountains. Both native and species introduced from Eurasia.

<u>Ashes</u> from the leaves of *P. frigidus* (= *P. palmatus*, including *P. vitifolius*) were used as a salt substitute by Indians: the leaves were dried, then burned, and their ashes carefully gathered for seasoning various foods.

Leaves and flower <u>stalks</u> of *P. frigidus* (m.a.) were peeled and eaten raw.

The <u>young foliage</u>, the <u>petioles</u> and the <u>inflorescences</u> of *P. hybridus* – from Eurasia, escaped from cultivation in N.E. U.S. – have been used as food on the Old Continent after cooking. But they have a very strong, unpleasant smell and require cooking in several changes of water.

The plant is thought to be somewhat toxic.

In Northeastern Asia, especially in Japan, a local species (*P. japonicus*), known as "fuki" is sometimes cultivated as a vegetable. The <u>inflorescences</u>, the young <u>leaf shoots</u>, the <u>leaves</u> and the peeled <u>petioles</u> are cooked and eaten. Leaf shoots and stalks are preserved in salt or in shoyu (soy sauce). They are also candied.

The inflorescences of all the plants in this genus appear before the leaves in early spring, as soon as the snow has melted, hence their potential interest as one of the first wild foods of the year.

Picris   (D 1)   Ox Tongue, Bitterweed
Greek name of a bitter plant of this family, used in salads, from "pikros," bitter.

Throughout. Naturalized from Eurasia as weeds.

The very <u>young leaves</u> of *P. echioides* (= *Helminthia e.*), bristly ox tongue – naturalized in N.E. U.S. & Calif. – and *hieracioides* – naturalized in N.E. U.S. – are edible raw, although they are somewhat rough. Older ones become bitter and bristly, and require cooking in one or more changes of water. The former species is still commonly eaten in springtime in Greece.

Prenanthes (C 2)   Rattlesnake-root, White Lettuce
From the Greek, "prênês," nodding, and "anthos," flower.
E. N.Am.

The leaves of several species, such as *P. altissima* were eaten raw by Cherokee Indians.
Those of a European species (*P. purpurea*) are edible raw or cooked.

Ratibida (D 4)   Coneflower
Etymology unknown.
C. U.S., Mex.

Leaves and flower heads of *R. columnifera* (= *R. columnaris*) were made into tea by the Dakota Indians. The beverage obtained by infusion is quite pleasant to drink.
The plant has been suspected of being toxic to cattle, but it is rarely eaten by them.

Rudbeckia (D-F 2)   Black-eyed Susan, Coneflower
After Olaus Rudbeck (1660–1740), Swedish anatomist and botanist, professor at Uppsala, the first patron of Linnaeus.
Throughout.
Several native species are planted for ornament.

Young leaves and stems of *R. laciniata* – E. & C. U.S. – have been used as cooked vegetable by Indians.
However, the plant has been reported to be toxic to sheep and swine, although feeding experiments showed no definite results.

Santolina chamaecyparyssus (D 4)   Lavender Cotton
Italian name of the plant from "santo," saint: alluding to its medicinal properties.
Sometimes grown for ornament, the plant is naturalized from the Mediterranean region in Calif. & E. N.Am.

The aromatic <u>leaves</u> can be used as an herb in salads and various dishes, but in small quantity only, as they are very bitter.

They contain an essential oil and are stimulant, stomachic, antispasmodic, emmenagogue and vermifuge.

Scorzonera (C 4)   Black Salsify, Viper's Grass

Spanish name of *S. hispanica*, "escorzonera," and of a snake whose bite was said to be healed by the root of this plant.

Calif. Both native and species introduced from Eur.

Originally from S. & C. Europe, *S. hispanica*, black salsify, is occasionally cultivated for its long, fleshy taproot; the plant is found as an escape in California.

The black <u>roots</u> are often soaked in water before cooking as they are, to some people, slightly bitter. After this process, they are very pleasant to eat. They have also been torrefied and used as a coffee substitute.

The roots contain inulin.

The young <u>leaves</u> can be eaten raw in salads.

The plant was cultivated in 16th century Spain as a remedy for snakebites.

<u>Roots</u> and <u>leaves</u> of other species are used as food in Europe, Asia and Africa.

Senecio (G-F-H 1)   Groundsel, Ragwort

Latin name of the plant, which also means old man, from "senex," old, old man: when the flower heads are fruiting, their white egrets make them look like tiny heads covered with white hair.

Throughout. Both native and species introduced from Eur.

Several European, Asian and African species, as well as cultivars, are planted for ornament.

When very young, *S. vulgaris* – naturalized from Eur. – has reportedly been boiled and eaten as a potherb.

However, the plant is known to contain – like other species of this genus – hepato-toxic pyrrolizidinic alkaloids, and has caused cattle poisoning in South Africa where the plant is introduced.

It has been used as an emmenagogue in Europe, but large quantities are reputedly dangerous. The prolonged medicinal use of related species has caused human deaths in Jamaica.

Our native *S. aureus*, golden ragwort – E. N.Am. – has diaphoretic, diuretic and emmenagogue properties. It was used by Indians as an oxytocic and an abortive.

S. jacobea, European ragwort – widely naturalized from Eur. – is an important cause of livestock poisoning, often fatal, on our continent and elsewhere. It contains the dangerous hepato-toxic alkaloid, jacobin.

The following native species contain similar alkaloids and are known to be toxic: *S. aurea* (m.a.), *longilobus* – S.W. U.S., Mex. –, *retrorsus* and *riddellii* – C. U.S. – and *S. longilobus* and *riddellii* (both m.a.) have poisoned livestock.

Endangered species: *S. franciscanus* – Ariz. –, *hallii* var. *discoidea* – Colo. –, *layneae* – Calif. – and *porteri* – Colo., Ore.

Silphium   (E-H 4)   Compass Plant, Rosin Weed
Greek name "silphion" of an Umbellifer from Cyrenaica (North Africa), the latex of which was used as a condiment and a remedy, highly prized by the Romans.
E. & C. N.Am.

The fleshy <u>roots</u> of *S. laeve* have reportedly been used as food by Indians.

The hardened <u>sap</u> of *S. laciniatum* – E. N.Am. – was chewed like gum by Omaha Indians and possibly other tribes.

The plant is reputed to be alterative, tonic and emetic.

The <u>root</u> of *S. perfoliatum*, ragged cup, is diaphoretic and tonic. Its sap is antispasmodic and stimulant.

Endangered species: *S. brachiatum* and *integrifolium* var. *gattingeri*.

Silybum marianum   (B 2)   Milk Thistle
Greek name of an edible thistle "silybon."
Originally from the Mediterranean region, the plant is sometimes grown for ornament. It is naturalized, mostly in W. N.Am.

At the end of the first growing season, the <u>roots</u> are edible and were used in Europe like those of salsify (*Tragopogon* spp.).

<u>Young shoots</u>, <u>stems</u>, <u>leaves</u> and <u>receptacles</u> can be eaten raw or cooked like those of other thistles (see *Carduus* spp.).

If the stems are too bitter, they can be soaked in water after peeling to reduce their bitterness. The very young leaves are pleasant to eat raw and older ones are excellent when cooked. The receptacles reach a relatively large size.

The midribs of the leaves were eaten raw in salads by Arabs. They can be made into gratins, like cardoons or Swiss chards.

The wild plant was still commonly used as food in Greece in the first part of our century. Milk thistle has even been cultivated in vegetable gardens, especially in England.

The plant is a bitter tonic, with stomachic, cholagogue, depurative and diuretic properties.

Its achenes contain a fixed oil, flavonoids, a bitter principle and various other substances.

They have a hypertensive action by vasoconstriction, and are also choleretic and cholagogue.

Silybum marianum

It has been reported that milk thistle growing on heavily fertilized soils could accumulate important amounts of nitrates, potentially toxic to animals grazing the plants in large quantity.

Solidago (D-H 2)   Goldenrod

From the Latin "solidus" and "ago," to make solid: alluding to reputed medicinal properties of some of the species.
Almost throughout. Both native and species introduced from Eurasia.
A few native species are planted for ornament, including *S. canadensis* – N.E. N.Am. & Appalachians – especially popular in Eur. as an ornamental.

The young leaves of *S. missouriensis* – C. & W. U.S., Can. – were eaten raw or cooked by Indians.

Leaves and inflorescences of *S. odora* (= *S. suaveolens*), sweet goldenrod – E. U.S. – are fragrant and can be made into an anise-scented tea.

They contain an essential oil and are carminative, stimulant, diaphoretic, diuretic and astringent.

The flower heads of *S. uliginosa* – N.E. N.Am. & Appalachians – have reportedly been used as a spice.

The tiny achenes of *S. canadensis* (m.a.), *nana* – W. N.Am. – and *spectabilis* were used as food by certain Indian tribes.

Our native *S. nemoralis*, gray goldenrod – E. & C. N.Am. – has been used medicinally as a carminative and diaphoretic.

Several species of goldenrod are thought to be toxic to livestock, especially to sheep. Their poisonous properties might be due to a parasitic fungus (*Coleosporium* sp.) growing on the plant.

Endangered species: *S. albopilosa* – Ky. –, *porteri* – N.C., Ga. – and *shortii* – Ky.

Sonchus (A 1)   Sow Thistle
Greek and Latin name of the plant.
Throughout. Naturalized from Eurasia as
weeds.

S. arvensis, *asper* and *oleraceus* have been used as food for millenia on the Old Continent.

The roots of the young plants can be eaten: chopped up or grated when raw, or cooked and passed through a food mill or processor to eliminate the fibers.

The young shoots and leaves are delicious raw and yield one of the very best of all wild salads. And the plants are ubiquitous.

When they get older, the leaves may be better cooked. Those of *S. asper* (m.a.) become spiny and cannot be used anymore.

Flower buds and heads are edible as well.

Another species is used as food in Northeast Asia.

Sonchus oleraceus

Tagetes (D 4)   Marigold
From "tages,-etis," Etruscan name of the mythological inventor of divina-
tion; the name was given by early botanists to *T. erecta* and *patula*.
S.W. U.S., Mex.
Several Mexican and S. American species are commonly planted for ornament; some occasionally escape from cultivation and become naturalized,
including *T. erecta* and **minuta**, both from Mex.

The leaves of *T. lucida* and **multifida**, anisillo – both Mex. – are strongly aromatic and are used as an herb in Central America. Those of *T. lucida* (m.a.) were
used for the same purpose in England, where the plant is cultivated. Their flavor is reminiscent of that of tarragon (*Artemisia dracunculus*). *T. minuta* (m.a.) can
be used in a similar way, although its odor and taste are not as pleasant as those
of the previously mentioned species.

However, since marigolds can be somewhat toxic in large amounts, they must
be used only with moderation.

The essential oil extracted from the plants is used externally as a parasiticide.
It does not have any internal use due to its toxicity.

The flowers yield a yellow dye. The color obtained from those of *T. erecta*
(m.a.) is used like annato (*Bixa orellana*) in cheese and butter.

Tanacetum (D 3)   Tansy
(= *Chrysanthemum* spp.)
Etymology unknown.
Throughout. Both native and species introduced from Eurasia.
T. vulgare – from Eurasia – is grown for ornament, and because of its strongly aromatic
leaves; it escapes occasionally from cultivation.

In spite of its bitterness, tansy has been used
as a condiment, especially in 16th and 17th century England, where the <u>leaves</u> or the juice extracted from them were added to omelettes

Tanacetum vulgare

(named "tansies"), puddings and cheeses. The plant was cultivated at that time as a condimentary and medicinal herb.

Tansy contains an essential oil – containing about 70% thujone (see *Artemisia absinthium*) – and a bitter principle. The leaves, flowering tops and fruits are used as a tonic, emmenagogue and vermifuge.

Due to its thujone content, high doses of the plant are abortive and toxic. Tansy oil, distilled from the plant, is very dangerous: cases of poisoning have been recorded following its use as a vermifuge.

Tansy repels insects.

It can be used as an insecticide, but its action is not as powerful as that of pyrethrum (*T. cinerariifolium* = *Chrysanthemum cinerariaefolium* – from former Yugoslavia and Albania), used as an efficient insecticide, harmless to other animals and the earth.

Endangered species: *T. compactum* – Nev.

Taraxacum (A 1)   Dandelion
Name dating back to the end of the Middle Ages, probably from "tharakhchakon," the Arabic name of a similar plant.
Some circumboreal species are native to N. N.Am. The most frequently encountered ones, especially the ubiquitous *T. officinale*, have been introduced from Eurasia.

T. officinale (m.a.) has been used as a wild food since prehistoric times. It entered our vegetable gardens in the first part of the 19th century. Dandelions are still cultivated for salads in France and they are sold on New York markets. The leaves are often blanched like endives (*Cichorium endiva*) by piling up soil around the base of the plants.

The root is edible in spite of its bitterness. In Japan, it is cooked "nituke" style in soy sauce. Like chickory, it makes a good coffee substitute after roasting. Between late fall and early spring, the root is filled with starchy reserves.

The young leaves make a delicious salad. They are especially popular in the spring, but can be eaten all year long, as new tender leaves can be found within the heart of the rosette. Dandelions are still commonly picked in Europe for spring salads.

Older leaves are better cooked. Their bitterness varies according to the individual plant
and to the season. They can be made into
soups or cooked as a vegetable.

Dandelion roots can be planted in a cellar.
The leaves shooting from the crown, devoid of
chlorophyll, are whitish, tender and hardly bitter. On wild plants, the base of the leaves is
sometimes blanched naturally by growing below the surface of the ground.

The flower buds have frequently been
pickled. This is still a strong tradition in the
Czech Republic and Slovakia.

The yellow flower heads can be added to
salads. They are not only pretty, but tasty as
well. The peduncles, after the bitter latex has
drained, are sweet and can also be eaten.

Taraxacum officinale

A pleasant tea can be made with the flower
heads, as well as "dandelion wine," actually a kind of mead, and a jelly known
as "dandelion honey."

Dandelion roots contain proteins, starch, inulin, tannin and much latex, containing a bitter principle (lactupicrin) and rubber. A similar species was grown on
a large scale in Russia during World War II as a source of rubber.

The green leaves are very rich in vitamin A (700 times more than pears, 70
times more than oranges and twice as much as spinach). They also contain proteins, vitamins B1, B2, C and E, minerals and various other substances.

The plant is a bitter tonic, with stomachic, cholagogue, depurative and diuretic properties.

Other species such as *T. laevigatum* (= *T. erythospermum*) – naturalized from
Eurasia – have all the same edible and medicinal uses.

Various dandelions are eaten in Europe and in Asia.

Thelesperma (D 4)   Navajo tea, Greenthread
From the Greek "thelê," nipple, and "sperma," seed.
C. & W. N.Am.

Leaves and flower heads of *T. filifolium* (= *T. trifidum*) – S.C. U.S. –, *longipes*, gota – W. Tex. to S. Ariz., N. Mex. –, and *megapotamicum* (= *gracile*) – C. U.S., Mex. – were used as tea by Indians.

A reddish brown dye for baskets and textiles was derived from the plants by Hopi Indians.

Tragopogon (B 3)   Goatsbeard

Greek name of the plant, "tragopôgôn," from "tragos," billy goat and "pôgôn," beard.
Throughout. Naturalized from Eur.

T. porrifolius, salsify, oyster plant, is sometimes grown in vegetable gardens for its long, fleshy taproot. It is naturalized on our continent.

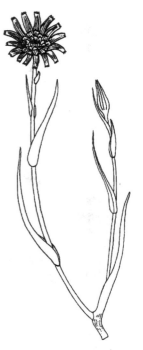

In France, where it is still a popular vegetable, the roots are dipped in batter and fried. They are excellent simply boiled or steamed, or even chopped raw and mixed with other vegetables in salads.

They can also be torrefied and used as a coffee substitute, like chicory.

The roots of *T. dubius* and *pratensis* can be used in the same ways as those of the oyster plant. Care must be taken to gather them before the flower stalk appears, as they then become woody.

They contain starch and inulin, and are stomachic, depurative and diuretic.

Young shoots and tender leaves of these plants are very good raw in salads. When the leaves get older they are too tough to be used.

T. pratensis (m.a.) has been cultivated in England for its roots and young leaves.

Tragopogon pratensis

The best part of the plant is the young flower buds, picked with the tender top of the stems before they start opening. They can be eaten raw or rapidly steamed, making sure they retain some crunchiness, and served with a sauce like asparagus. They are sweet and have a mild, pleasant flavor somewhat reminiscent of artichokes.

The hardened <u>latex</u> of some species has been chewed as a stomachic. That of *T. porrifolius* (m.a.) – gathered on naturalized plants – was chewed by Indians. The <u>roots</u> of other species are eaten in the Mediterranean area.

Trilisa (G 4)
Anagram of Liatris, a genus in the same family.
S.E. U.S.

The <u>leaves</u> of *T. odoratissima*, Carolina vanilla, have a pleasant vanilla smell. They can be made into a fragrant tea and have been used for flavoring tobacco.

Tussilago farfara (B 2)   Coltsfoot
Latin name of the plant from "tussis," cough, and "agere," to chase: alluding to its medicinal properties.
Naturalized from Eur. in N.E. N.Am.

The yellow <u>flower heads</u> which appear before the leaves in early spring, are very good raw in salads. Their peduncle is juicy, sweet and aromatic, and tastes

Tussilago farfara

even better than the flowers themselves. They are delicious simply sauteed in butter.

Coltsfoot flowers contain mucilage and a yellow coloring matter (xanthophyll).

The leaves are edible as well. When very young they can be eaten raw, especially the petiole which is juicy and pleasant tasting. The whitish down covering them can be removed, after which they are chopped up and added to salads.

When they get older, the rubbery leaves are better cooked. They make excellent fritters. In order to be used as a vegetable, they require long cooking and should preferably be boiled in a change of water.

Ashes made from the leaves can be used as a salt substitute. They are dried and burned in a dish so that the impalpable ashes can be easily gathered. (See *Heracleum lanatum*, Apiaceae and *Petasites* spp.)

Coltsfoot leaves contain mucilage, a resin, tannin, an essential oil, inulin, vitamin C, minerals and an antibiotic substance.

The plant also contains pyrrolizidin alkaloids, which have a detrimental effect upon the liver. It should therefore only be eaten in moderation.

Leaves and flowers are emollient, demulcent and expectorant.

Coltsfoot has been used medicinally in Europe since Antiquity. It has recently been banned in several European countries due to its alkaloid content.

The leaves dye wool yellowish green with alum and green with ferrous sulfate.

Viguiera (C-H 4)
After D. A. Viguier, physician and botanist from Montpellier, France.
S. U.S., Mex.

The seeds of *V. multiflora* – W. U.S. – have been used as food by Indians.

Some species, such as *V. annua* – W. Tex. to Ariz., N. Mex. – are good forage plants, especially for sheep.

Endangered species: *V. ludens* – Tex.

Wyethia (C 2)   Mule's Ears

After Nathaniel Wyeth (1802–1856), Western explorer, artist and the first collector of the plant.

W. N.Am.

The roots of *W. amplexicaulis* and ***helianthoides*** – both N.W. U.S. – were used as food by Indians. They were generally cooked and left to ferment on hot stones for a day or two.

Indians ate the young leaves and the seeds of *W. longicaulis* – Calif. – and *angustifolia* (= *robusta*) – Calif. to Wash.

The Hopis and the Navajos used *W. scabra* – S.W. U.S. – as an emetic, but the plant was considered dangerous.

Xanthium (F 2-3)   Cocklebur

Greek name of a plant which was used for dyeing hair blond, "xanthion" from "xanthos," yellow, blond.

Throughout.

The young shoots and leaves of *X. strumarium* – cosmopolitan weed, probably native in N.Am. – have reportedly been cooked and eaten in China, although they are rather unpalatable.

Its seeds were ground into meal.

On our continent, certain Indian tribes would grind the seeds of *X. commune* (= *X. orientale*) and mix them with corn meal and squash seeds. The mixture was then made into cakes or balls and steamed.

The germinating seeds and the very young plants still in the cotyledon stage contain a toxic glucoside (xanthostrumarin). Their toxicity decreases as the true leaves develop. Animals have been poisoned by eating the seedling plants in early spring. They generally do not eat older plants, as they are too bitter. The seeds themselves are considered dangerous.

The spiny burrs can occasionally cause the death of young animals by mechanically irritating or clogging their intestinal tract.

II. MONOCOTYLEDONS
(Liliatae)

BUTOMACEAE

Butomus umbellatus (C 4)   Flowering Rush
Greek name of the plant, or of a sedge, "boutomos" from "bous," ox, and "temnô," to cut: the leaves can cut the muzzle of oxen.
Naturalized from Eurasia at scattered locations in N. N.Am.

The fleshy rhizome is edible after cooking. Most of its acrid taste disappears on drying.
It was commonly used as food in Northern Europe and in Asia.
In Europe, the plant is sometimes grown for ornament.

ALISMATACEAE

Alisma (C 3)   Water Plantain
Greek and Latin name of the plant.
Throughout.

The rhizome of *A. plantago-aquatica* (including var. *geyeri* (= *A. gramineum*) and *triviale*) – N. & W. N.Am. – is rich in starch. It can be eaten after drying – to reduce its acridity – and cooking, and was commonly used as food by certain Asian tribes such as the Kalmuks.
The rhizomes should be dug from late fall to early spring, when their starch content is the highest.

Sagittaria (C-H 2–3)   Arrowhead, Wapato
From the Latin "sagitta," arrow: referring to the shape of the leaves.
Throughout.

The tubers produced at the end of the rhizomes are edible raw or cooked.
They are delicious after boiling, steaming or roasting. Their size and the quantity of starch they contain varies with the seasons. It is preferable to gather them
from late fall to early spring, which can be rather unpleasant, since they must be
dug up from the mud under several feet of ice cold water.

The tubers of *S. cuneata* and *latifolia*, Tule potato, were an important food
for Indians. Their traditional method of gathering the tubers was to dislodge
them with their toes, thus allowing them to float to the surface. Whenever possible, they would also be collected by raiding muskrat nests. The tubers of *S. latifolia* (m.a.) can reach a large size.

After cooking, the tubers were often sliced, strung and hung to dry for later
use. When thoroughly dried, they could be ground into flour.

Starch is obtained by crushing the fresh tubers, mixing them with water, filtering to eliminate the fibers and pouring the liquid into a container. After a
while, the starch settles to the bottom and is easily gathered by carefully pouring off the water. The starch can then be dried and ground, or cooked directly
into mush.

Several species are cultivated in Eastern Asia for their tubers which are commonly used as food and sold in markets. Chinese immigrants in California were
very fond of arrowhead tubers. Up until the first part of this century, an Old
World species (*Sagittaria sagittifolia*) was cultivated in California to supply the
Chinese markets in San Francisco.

The leaves and petioles of various species have also been used as food.
Endangered species: *S. fasciculata* – N.C., S.C.

POTAMOGETONACEAE

Potamogeton (D-H 2–3)   Pondweed
From the Greek "potamos," river, and "geiton," neighbor: referring to the
habitat of the plant.
Throughout. Both native and species introduced from Eurasia.

The small terminal <u>tubers</u> of *P. natans* and *pectinatus* – almost throughout, also in Eurasia – are rich in starch and are an important duck food.

<u>Leaves</u> and <u>stems</u> of *P. crispus* – naturalized from Eur. – and *pectinatus* (m.a.) are said to be edible. In Japan, the former species is pickled or eaten with miso (fermented soy paste).

Endangered species: *P. clystocarpus* – Tex.

JUNCAGINACEAE

Triglochin (E-F 4)   Arrow-Grass
From the Greek "treis," three, and "glôchis," point: referring to the shape of the fruit.
Almost throughout.

The <u>seeds</u> of *T. maritima* have been used as food. But they must be parched, as they may contain some hydrocyanic acid.

After torrefying, they can be made into a coffee substitute.

The <u>leaves</u> of this species and of *T. palustris* – N. N.Am. – are rich in hydrocyanic acid. Numerous cases of animal poisoning have been reported, mostly in Western North America, caused by eating fresh or dried leaves.

The <u>rhizomes</u> of a local species have reportedly been used as food in Australia.

ZOSTERACEAE

Zostera (D 2)   Eel-Grass
From the Greek "zôstêr," belt, stripe: referring to the shape of the leaves.
E. & W. Coasts along the seashore.

The <u>rhizome</u> and the <u>leaf bases</u> of *Z. marina* are juicy and sweetish. They are quite pleasant to chew.

COMMELINACEAE

Aneilma keisak   (D 4)

From the Greek "a," without, and "eilma," covering: referring to the lack of a spathe in the flower.

Thought to be native to S.E. Va.; found mostly in E. Asia.

The leaves are eaten cooked in China.

Tubers and leaves of local species are used as food in Southeast Asia.

Commelina   (B 2)   Dayflower

After the Commelijn brothers, Dutch botanists during the 17th century.

E. & C. U.S., Mex. Both native and species introduced from E. Asia.

The Mexican *C. coelestis* is sometimes grown as a house plant.

The fleshy roots of *C. coelestis* (m.a.), *erecta* (= *angustifolia*) – E. & C. U.S., Mex. –, *graminifolia* – Mex. – and *tuberosa* – Mex. – are edible.

The leaves of *C. communis* – introduced from E. Asia into E. & C. U.S. – and *virginica* – E. U.S. – have been used as food. They can be eaten raw when young, while older ones are better cooked.

The flowers make colorful additions to salads.

Other species are used as food in tropical Asia, Africa and Australia.

C. communis and *tuberosa* (both m.a.) are planted for ornament in Europe.

Tradescantia   (B 2)   Spiderwort

After John Tradescant (d. 1637), London botanist during the 17th century.

E. & C. N.Am. to Mont. & Ariz.

Our native *T. virginiana* is planted for ornament, along with the S.Am. *T. fluminensis*, and naturalized in Calif.

The tuberous <u>roots</u> of *T. pinetorum* – Ariz., N.M., N. Mex. – have reportedly been eaten after boiling or roasting.

The very young <u>leaves</u> of *T. occidentalis* – W.C. U.S. – *pinetorum* and *virginiana* (both m.a.) are edible raw. They were often cooked as greens by Indians. When the leaves get older, they quickly become too tough to be used.

The young <u>leaves</u> of *T. fluminensis* (m.a.) can be eaten as well.

Tradescantia virginiana

CYPERACEAE

Carex (D-H 1)   Sedge
Latin name of grasses with sharp leaves.
Throughout.

The tender, whitish <u>leaf base</u> of various species is edible raw. It has a very pleasant mild, nutty flavor, reminiscent of palm hearts.

That of *C. aquatilis* – N. N.Am. & Mountains – was eaten in Europe, where the plant is native as well.

The <u>grain</u> of a local species, *C. kobomugi* – introduced from E. Asia on the E. Coast from N.J. to Va. – was used as a famine food in Eastern Asia.

Endangered species: *C. aboriginum* – Idaho –, *albida* – Calif. –, *biltmoreana* – Va., N.C., Ga. –, *elachycarpa* – Maine –, *jacobi-peteri* – Alaska –, *latebracteata* – Okla. – and *specuicola* – Ariz.

Cladium jamaicense   (D 5)   Saw Grass
(= *Mariscus jamaicensis*)
Etymology unknown.
S. Fla. & Tex., Mex.

The overlapping <u>leaf bases</u> are tender and edible.

Cyperus   (C-H 2-3)
Greek name of the plant "kypeiros."
Throughout.
An Egyptian species, known as umbrella plant, is planted as an ornamental.

C. esculentus, chufa, galingale, is native to the warmer parts of the Northern Hemisphere, including North America. In the Mediterranean region, particularly in Spain and Italy, as well as in Africa, a variety (var. *sativus*) is cultivated for the corm-like thickenings on its rootstocks.

The <u>tubers</u> have been used as food at least since the ancient Egyptians. They reach the size of a hazelnut, and have a similar delicate flavor (they are often known as "earth almonds"). They are excellent raw and are also eaten boiled, roasted or candied.

Desserts are prepared with these tubers in Western Europe (especially Italy) and in the Middle East (especially Turkey). In Spain they are made into a delicious drink called "horchata."

A very fine edible oil can be expressed from the dried tubers. This is exceptional, as very few plants contain a fixed oil in their underground parts.

In Spain, an emulsion of chufa oil and fruit juice is drunk, chilled or frozen.

On wild plants of this species, the tubers are smaller and more widely spaced than on cultivated ones.

Chufa <u>seeds</u> have been used as a coffee substitute in Hungary.

As previously noted, one of the common names of the plant is "galingale." But the name actually refers to a Southeastern Asian plant (*Alpinia galanga*, Zingiberaceae) with an aromatic root which is used as a condiment or made into tea.

*Cyperus
esculentus*

On our continent, the rootstocks of *C. aristatus* – throughout, also in the Old World – were eaten by Indians.

The base of the stems and the stem pith of *C. utriculata* – W. U.S. – were eaten, or rather chewed, as they are fibrous.

The tubers of *C. rotundus* – S. U.S., Mex., also in the Old World – nutgrass, are edible raw, although inferior to those of chufa. When fresh, they have a strong odor due to an essential oil, which disappears on drying.

Fresh, they can be used as an insect repellent.

The roots of *C. flavus* – S. Ariz., Mex., to S.Am., and *pringlei* – S. Ariz., N. Mex. – are also strongly aromatic, with a camphor smell.

The seeds of *C. odoratus* were eaten by the Cocopah Indians.

Endangered species: *C. grayoides* – Ill.

Eriophorum (E 2)   Cotton Grass
From the Greek "erion," wool, and "pherô," to bear: alluding to the aspect of the inflorescences.
Mostly N. N.Am.

The base of the stem and the peeled rhizome of *E. angustifolium* (= *E. poly-stachion*) – N. N.Am. – were eaten raw by Alaskan Inuits.

They were often gathered in the tundra by raiding mice nests, as these animals hide them in significant quantities for their winter supplies. Raiding the caches of rodents was a frequent way for Indians to secure nuts and roots.

Scirpus (C-H 2-3)   Bulrush, Tule
Latin name of rushes *Juncus* spp.
Throughout. Mostly native species and one variety introduced from Eur.

The starchy rootstocks of *S. acutus* (= *lacustris* in part), *maritimus* (including var. *maritimus* – introduced from Europe on the E. Coast –, *paludosus* – native to W. & C. U.S. – and *fernaldi* – native on the E. Coast from N.S. to Va.), *nevaden-sis* – N.W. N.Am. – and *robustus* (= *paludosus* in part) – E. Coast of N.S. to Tex. – were used as food by Indians. They can be chewed raw, but are quite fibrous. They were generally dried, ground up and sifted to remove the fibers. They can also be cooked and passed through a food mill. These rhizomes are quite thin, but have a pleasant, sweetish taste.

The young shoots and the juicy base of the stems are edible raw.

The young stems of *S. fluviatilis* – almost throughout (except S.E. & N.W. N.Am.) – are peeled and eaten in Eastern Asia, where the plant is native as well.

The pollen of various species was gathered by Indians and mixed with different kinds of flours for making mush or cakes, like cattail pollen (see *Typha* spp., Typhaceae).

The small seeds of *S. lacustris* (m.a.) and *validus* (= *lacustris* in part), great bulrush, were also eaten.

Endangered species: *C. ancistrochaetus* – Vt., N.Y., Pa., Va.

POACEAE (GRAMINAE)

This is the most widespread family of all flowering plants. It is found over all continents – even in the Antarctic – and in practically all habitats, from tropical forests to the limits of perpetual snow.

The Poaceae come in first for the number of individual plants and second for the number of species (about 10,000) after the Orchidaceae (about 20,000).

This family is economically the most important of all plant families. For millenia, cereals have been the staple of most populations of the world (except for hunters, nomadic shepherds and, recently, the populations of Europe and North America) and have made possible the rise of numerous civilizations. They are cultivated throughout the world.

Cereals are an excellent source of proteins. However, the proteins they contain are incomplete, that is, they don't have all the essential amino acids. When cereals (lacking lysine but rich in methionine) and legumes (lacking methionine but rich in lysine) are eaten at the same meal, the amino acids present in legumes complement those found in cereals, thus providing the body with complete proteins.

This is why various peoples have always combined cereals and legumes in their food: wheat ("chapatis") and lentils or pigeon pea ("dahl") are eaten in India; wheat (bread, "pita") and chickpeas or fava beans in the Mediterranean area; wheat, rye, barley or oats (bread, mush) and beans, peas or lentils in Europe; rice and soybeans ("tofu," "miso," "shoyu") in Eastern Asia; corn ("tortillas," "tamales") and beans ("frijoles") in America; and millet and niebe or formerly wild legumes in Africa.

The grains of most Poaceae (actually their fruits, or caryopses) are edible, but they are often too small to be of much value. Patience and technique are required even with the largest ones, as the ripe ears must be gathered, threshed and winnowed.

They can be cooked whole or crushed, or ground into flour or meal, which can be made into breads, cakes and mush.

However, a leavened bread can only be obtained with wheat or rye, which contain gluten, a particular protein.

Slightly roasting the grains before cooking enhances their flavor and their digestibility. In the Canary Islands, "gofio" is prepared by roasting grains of various cereals and grinding them very finely. Gofio is sprinkled on food, especially soups, or mixed with water and made into balls. This tradition dates back to the first inhabitants of the islands, the Guanches. A similar instant food, "tsampa," is made with barley in Tibet, and mixed with yak butter and black tea.

A very good coffee substitute can be made with torrefied cereals.

The grains of cereals are edible raw but are hard to digest. In many cases they can be sprouted and then eaten raw.

Alcohol is commonly made by distilling the germinated and fermented grains of various cereals, especially barley, corn, rye and wheat.

The lower part of the stem, or "culm" of most Poaceae, tender and juicy, is edible raw. Children are fond of chewing on them.

The grains of some plants in this family can be toxic when they have been infested by parasitic fungi (rye, darnel, fescue). Those of darnel are also thought to contain a toxic alkaloid.

The leaves of sorghum and velvet-grass contain potentially toxic levels of hydrocyanic acid.

The family contains proportionally very few poisonous plants.

Numerous species are grown for forage.

Agropyron   (C 1)   Wheat Grass, Couch Grass
From the Greek "agrios," wild, and "pyros," wheat.
Throughout. Both native and species introduced from Eurasia.

The tender <u>new tips of the rhizomes</u> of *A. repens* (= *Elymus r.*) – naturalized from Eur. – are edible raw in the spring.

The whole rhizome can be dried, ground and sifted to remove the fibers. Cakes and breads have often been made with the resulting flour in times of famine.

The rhizome contains mucilage, minerals, starch, sugars (levulose) and a substance with an antibiotic action.

Since ancient times, it has been made into a tea with diuretic, emollient, depurative and refrigerant properties. It is best to boil the rhizome in a change of water, discarding the first decoction and using the second one.

The grains are edible.

Those of a local species are used as food in N.E. Asia.

Agrostis (C-H 1)   Bent Grass
Greek name of an undetermined grass, "agrôstis."
Throughout. Both native and species introduced from the Old World.

The grains of *A. perennans* – E. N.Am. – were eaten by Indians.
Those of other species are edible as well.
Endangered species: *A. blasdalei* var. *marinensis* – Calif. – and *hendersonii* – Calif., Ore.

Ammophila (C 2)   Beach Grass
From the Greek "ammos," sand, and "philos," friend: referring to the habitat of the plant.
One native species in N.E. N.Am. & *A. arenaria*, beach grass, naturalized from Eur. on the Pacific Coast.

The rhizome of the species mentioned has been used as food in Iceland. It can reach a length of 5 meters (16 ft).

Anthoxanthum (D 3)   Sweet Vernal Grass
From the Greek "anthos," flower, and "xanthos," yellow.
Throughout.

A. odoratum is much grown as forage.
On drying, the plant acquires a sweet vanilla fragrance, and can be made into a pleasant tea.

It contains coumarin, like woodruff (*Asperula odorata*, Rubiaceae and *Melilotus* spp., Fabaceae).

The grain is edible.

Arundinaria (C 2)   Cane
From the Latin "arundo," reed: the plant is reed-like.
Warm parts of E. & C. N.Am.
Some Asiatic species are planted for ornament.

The young shoots of *A. gigantea* (= *A. macrosperma*, including *A. tecta*), Southern cane – S.E. U.S. – are edible raw. They are whitish, tender, and have a nutty flavor.

Those of local species (bamboo shoots) are frequently used as food in Asia. They are eaten raw or cooked and preserved in vinegar or salt. In warm and humid regions, bamboos can grow up to 1 meter (3 ft) per day, the record rate of growth for the vegetable kingdom.

The outer envelopes of bamboo shoots are often covered with sharp bristles that can irritate the skin.

Our *Arundinaria* spp. actually belong to the bamboo group.

The grains of *A. gigantea* (m.a.) were eaten by Indians.

Those of local species are used as food in Eastern Asia, boiled whole or ground into flour, or made into fermented drinks.

Arundo donax (C 2)   Giant Reed
Latin name of the reed.
Originally from the Old World, the giant reed is often planted for ornament; it is naturalized in warm regions of our continent.

The grains have been used as food.

The culms are used for making musical instruments (including the reeds of clarinets and saxophones), windbreaks and framework for huts.

Avena (C 1) Oats

Latin name of the plant.

Throughout. Introduced from Eur.

A. *sativa*, cultivated oats, has been grown for millenia in Eur. and since the beginning of the 17th century on our continent. It commonly escapes from cultivation.

Oats were the staple food of populations in Northern and Central Europe, especially in Scandinavia and Scotland. Oatmeal or rolled oats (flattened between two steel cylinders) is still commonly eaten in Anglo-Saxon countries as "porridge," cakes, cookies and such. In some countries, beer is brewed from oats.

The grain contains proteins (15%), starch (55%), fat (5%), sugars (3%), vitamins B1, B2, niacin, minerals and other substances.

It is nutritious, being particularly rich in fat, and stimulant.

Oat straw has been used medicinally, especially in baths, for rheumatism and skin problems.

The grain of *A. fatua*, wild oats – widely naturalized in N.Am. – can be used like that of the former species.

The plant has occasionally been cultivated, mostly in Europe. It was introduced by the Spaniards to California, where it soon became naturalized, and was gathered and eaten by local Indians.

Bambusa (C 5) Feathery Bamboo

Etymology unknown.

Originally from tropical Asia, the plant is grown for ornament in the warmest parts of N.Am. and often persists on abandoned sites. Other Asian species (including cultivars) are cultivated as ornamentals.

The young shoots are often used as food in Asia. They are eaten raw or cooked and preserved in salt or vinegar.

The grains are boiled whole or ground into flour. They can also be made into fermented drinks.

Shoots and grains of local species are eaten in tropical Asia.

Beckmannia syzigachne   (C 3)   Slough Grass
After Johann Beckmann (1739–1811), professor at Göttingen, Germany.
Mostly C. & W. U.S. & Can.; also in E. Asia.

The grains have been used as food.

Bromus   (C 2-3)   Brome Grass
Greek name for wild oats, *Avena fatua*.
Throughout. Both native and species introduced from Eurasia.

The grains of *B. carinatus*, California brome, *marginatus* – both W. N.Am. –
and *rigidus* – naturalized from Eur. – were eaten by Indians.
Those of *B. japonicus* – naturalized from the Old World – were used as food
in Northeast Asia, where the plant is native as well.
The grains of a local species were eaten in Chile.

Calamagrostis   (C-H 4)   Reed Grass
Ancient Greek name of a plant resembling a reed from "calamos," reed,
and "agrôstis," name of a grass.
Throughout. Both native and species introduced from Eurasia.

The grain of *C. epigejos* – naturalized from Eurasia in N.E. U.S. – is used as
food in Asia.
Endangered species: *C. inexpansa* var. *novae-angliae* – Maine, Vt., N.H. –,
insperata – Ohio, Mo. – and *perplexa* – N.Y.

Cenchrus   (C 3)   Sandbur
Greek name of millet "kegchros."
Throughout. Both native and species introduced from the Old World.

The grains of *C. biflorus* have been used as food.
The spikes are protected with sharp spines which can be singed off to facilitate the removal of the grains. These spines, if stepped upon, can cause inflammation and infection in animals and humans.
The grains of several species are eaten in India and Africa.

Cinna (C 3)   Wood Reed
Ancient Greek name of an undetermined grass.
Throughout.

The grains of *C. latifolia* – W. U.S. – were eaten by Indians.

Coix lacryma-jobi (C 5)   Job's Tears
Greek and Latin name of an Egyptian palm tree.
Originally from tropical Asia and Africa, this tall grass is planted for orna-
ment in the warmest parts of N.Am.; it is naturalized in Mex.

The seeds reach a large size. Their envelope is very hard and porcelain-like;
necklaces are often made with the pearly-looking fruits of this grass. Unlike
those of most other members of the family, these fruits are achenes, and not
caryopses.
The fresh seeds are tender and have a pleasant, nutty flavor. They are edible
raw. In tropical Asia, they are dried and ground, or cooked into gruel or soup.
The seeds are made into tea, and a beer ("naga") is brewed from them.
The seeds of two other species are used as food in tropical Asia.

Cynodon (C 1)   Bermuda Grass
From the Greek "kynos," dog, and "odous," tooth: translation of the
French name "chiendent" (dog's tooth), alluding to the aspect of the tips
of the rhizomes.
Throughout. Naturalized from the Old World.

The rhizome can be dried, ground and sifted to obtain a kind of flour. It has
been torrefied and used as a coffee substitute.
It contains sugars and can be crushed fresh, mixed with water and left to ferment. A decoction of the rhizome makes a fairly good tea.

Dactyloctenium (C 4)   Crowfoot Grass
From the Greek "dactylon," finger, and "ktenion," comb: referring to the
digitate, comb-like spikes.
Introduced from the Old World Tropics into S. U.S. & Mex.

The grains of *D. aegyptiacum* have been used as food in Asia and Africa, especially by Arabs.

Deschampsia (C 3)
(including some *Aira* spp.)
After J. C. Deschamps (1774–1849), French physician, botanist and explorer.
Throughout. Mostly native and a variety introduced from Eurasia.

The grains of *D. caespitosa* (= *Aira c.*) – almost throughout, also in Eurasia (and the Eurasian var. *parviflora* is naturalized in N.E. U.S) – were eaten by Indians.

Digitaria (C 1) Crabgrass
From the Latin "digitus," finger: referring to the way the spikes are grouped together.
Throughout. Both native and species introduced from the Old World.

The grains of *D. sanguinalis* – naturalized from Eurasia – are edible and were highly prized by the Slavs. This crabgrass was at one point cultivated in Poland as a cereal plant.

Echinochloa (C 1) Barnyard Grass
From the Greek "echinos," hedgehog, and "chloê," young grass: referring to the awned scales of certain species.
Throughout. Both native and species introduced from the Old World.

The young shoots of *E. colonum* (= *E. colona*), jungle rice – naturalized from Old World Tropics in S. U.S. & Mex. – are eaten raw in Asia.
The grains of *E. colonum* (m.a.) and *crus-galli* – naturalized from Eurasia – are used as food, mostly in Asia. They are quite easy to gather and have a pleasant taste.
Other species are used as food in Asia, Africa and Australia, and some are even cultivated as cereal plants.
On soils too heavily fertilized, *E. crus-galli* (m.a.) can accumulate large amounts of nitrates in its leaves, which are potentially toxic to livestock.

Eleusine (C 1)   Goose Grass
After "Eleusis," city in Greece where Demeter (Ceres), goddess of harvests, was worshiped: alluding to the edible grains.
U.S., Mex. Introduced from the Old World tropics.

The grains of *E. indica*, wire grass, are used as food in the regions where the plant is native.

Those of another species (*E. coracana*, African millet), thought to be derived from the former, are made into flour or fermented drinks. The plant is cultivated in Asia and Africa.

The grains of local species are eaten in Ethiopia and Indochina.

Elymus (C 2–3)   Wild Rye
Greek name of a millet, "elymos."
Throughout. Both native and species introduced from Eurasia.

The grains of the following species were used as food by Indians: *E. canadensis* – throughout –, *condensatus, glaucus* – both C. & W. N.Am. –, *mollis* – E. & W. Coasts & Great Lakes – and *triticoides* – W. U.S., Baja.
The spikes bear long, awnlike glumes.

Eragrostis (C 1)   Love Grass
From the Greek "erôs," love, and "agrôstis," name of a grass. This name was created by Bauhin after the popular name of a similar plant *Briza media*, "amourette."
Throughout. Both native and species introduced from the Old World.

The grains of *E. caroliniana* – S.E. U.S. – were ground into flour by some Indian tribes.

Those of *E. cilianensis* (= *E. megastachya*), stink grass – naturalized from Eur. –, *ciliaris* – Fla. to Tex., Mex. – and *pilosa* – naturalized from Eur. in U.S. & Mex. – are edible as well.

Horses have reportedly been poisoned by eating *E. cilianensis* (m.a.) in large quantities or over a long period of time.

The grains of several species are used as food in Africa. One of them, "teff" (*E. tef*), is cultivated as a cereal plant.

Festuca   (C-H 1)   Fescue
From the Latin "festuca," straw; name used in the 16th century by Dodoens.
Throughout. Both native and species introduced from Eurasia.

A European variety (var. *glauca*) of *F. ovina* – native almost throughout, also in Eur. – known as "blue fescue," is planted for ornament.
The grains of *F. conferta* and *ovina* (m.a.) were used as food by Indians.
The grains of various species are occasionally infested by a toxic fungus (*Anguina agrostis*), which renders them inedible.
Endangered species: *F. dasyclada* – Utah, Colo.

Glyceria   (C-H 2–3)   Manna Grass
(including several *Panicularia* spp.)
From the Greek "glykeros," having a sweet flavor: referring to the edible grains of *G. fluitans*.
Throughout. Both native and species introduced from Eurasia.

The grains of *G. borealis* – N. N.Am. & Mountains –, *nervata* – W. U.S. –, *occidentalis* – W. N.Am. – and *septentrionalis* – E. N.Am. – were used as food by Indians.
Those of *G. acutiflora* – N.E. U.S. – were eaten in Northeastern Asia where the plant is native as well.
G. fluitans – possibly native in E. Can. & introduced from Eurasia in New York City – has long been grown as a cereal plant in Eastern Europe and is still occasionally cultivated in Poland. The grain was highly esteemed by the Slavs, who made gruel from it. It has a pleasant, mild flavor.
The spikes are sometimes covered with a sweet substance.
The leaves of *G. septentrionalis* (m.a.) and *striata*, fowl manna grass – almost throughout – are known to have a high cyanogenetic potential: they can be toxic to grazing animals.
Endangered species: *G. nubigena* – N.C., Tenn.

Hierochloë odorata (D 4) Sweet Grass
From the Greek "hieros," sacred, and "chloa" (or chloê: see *Echinochloa*), grass. The plant was highly esteemed by the Slavs for its fragrance and was used on certain saint's days.
N. N.Am. & W. Mountains.

In Eastern Europe (Poland, Russia) the whole <u>plant</u> is used for flavoring vodka and liquors. Sweet grass is native to Eurasia as well as North America.

Its fragrance is due to the coumarin it contains (like *Asperula odorata*, Rubiaceae, *Melilotus* spp., Fabaceae and *Anthoxanthum odoratum*).

The <u>grain</u> is said to be edible.

In North America, the culms were used by certain Indians for making fragrant baskets.

Hordeum (C 1) Barley
Latin name of the plant.
Both native and species introduced from Eurasia.
H. vulgare – probably native to the Middle East – has been cultivated since Antiquity. Today it is one of the most important cereal plants in the world after wheat, rice and corn. On our continent, this species is often found as a waif along roads and railways.

Barley has been eaten since prehistoric times. The <u>grain</u> is boiled whole (often after polishing, known as "pearled barley") in soups or alone as a grain or ground into flour which was formerly made into flat cakes and breads. Barley mush and cakes have been a staple among European populations for millenia.

Barley was often grown with wheat in the same fields, and the mixed grains, known as "maslin," were ground into flour and made into bread.

In the Far East, barley is steamed, inoculated with "kôji" fungi and added to cooked soybeans to ferment into the brown paste known as "miso."

Torrefied barley is often made into a coffee substitute.

The grain contains proteins, starch (75%), fats, vitamin B1, vitamin E in the germ and minerals.

Pearled barley is emollient and tonic. It is a good food for people whose digestive system is irritated (although, when the grain is polished, it is depleted of the most important part of its vitamins and minerals contained in the bran).

Barley is used most importantly as a source of malt. Malt is obtained by sprouting the grains, which are then dried or slightly roasted, and ground. The partial germination causes the internal composition of the grain to change: it becomes rich in sugars (maltose) and enzymes. It also contains an alkaloid, hordein, which is slightly toxic and acts as a vasoconstrictor. The enzymes can transform the starch of other plants, such as potatoes and corn, into sugars. By fermentation, these sugars are transformed into alcohol, which can be extracted and concentrated by distillation.

Sprouted barley contains proteins, vitamins and minerals, but most of the starch has turned into sugars.

The germination is stopped when the sprout has reached about three-quarters of the length of the grain. A low temperature (100 to 140°F) conserves the properties of the enzymes, while a higher temperature (roasting) destroys them, but enhances the aroma of the grains, which turn brown. The transformed barley grain is then ground into a meal and used for various food purposes: as a sweetener, for making a highly digestible mush or as an excellent coffee substitute.

A decoction of ground malt can be passed through a sieve and evaporated to yield malt extract in the form of powder or syrup.

Beer has been known for millenia. It was drunk by the ancient Egyptians ("zython") as well as by contemporary peoples in the Middle East. Beer is prepared by fermenting malt with water and yeast. In this process, hops are generally added as a bitter flavoring (see *Humulus lupulus*, Cannabaceae). Many other plants have been used throughout the ages for this purpose.

Well-prepared beer (i.e., without chemical additives – as is compulsory in Germany, for instance, following a law dating to the 17th century – and using quality products) is a nutritious and healthful drink, at least in moderate quantities, as it contains from 2 to 5% alcohol or more.

Whisky in Scotland or whiskey in Ireland is made by fermenting malt made from a mixture of barley (usually *H. distichon*, two-rowed barley), oats and rye. After it is sprouted and traditionally dried in the smoke of a peat fire, the resulting liquid is distilled.

The grains of the two following wild barleys were used as food by Indians: *H. jubatum*, squirrel tail grass, foxtail barley – native throughout – and *murinum* – naturalized from Eur. in C. & W. N.Am.

Those of the latter species have also been eaten in Europe, where the plant is native.

Several other species are cultivated as cereal plants in Africa, Asia and Europe.

The long awns of *H. jubatum* (m.a.) can be troublesome.

Koeleria (C 3) June Grass
After G. Wilhelm Koeler (1765–1807), German botanist.
Throughout. Both native and species introduced from Eurasia.

The seeds of *K. cristata* – almost throughout – were used as food by Indians.

Lolium (C–F 1) Rye Grass
Latin name of the plant.
Throughout. Naturalized from Eur.

The grains of *L. temulentum*, darnel, have been used as food by certain Indian tribes.

They are sometimes infested by a parasitic fungus (*Endocladium temulentum*) which is toxic and can produce mild nervous and digestive troubles.

Moreover, the ripe grains are thought to contain a dangerous alkaloid (temuline), which can cause nervous and respiratory disorders.

The grains of *L. perenne*, English rye grass – naturalized almost throughout – contain alkaloids (perloline, perlolidine) with little toxicity.

Milium effusum (C 2) Millet Grass
Latin name of the cultivated millet from "molô," to grind: referring to the alimentary uses of the grains.
N.E. N.Am.

Lolium temulentum

The grains are edible.

The cultivated millets are not related to this genus but rather to *Panicum* and *Setaria*.

The grains of local species are made into a drink ("ullpu") in Peru.

Muehlenbergia   (C-H 3)
(including some *Sporobolus* spp.)
After G. H. E. Muehlenberg (1753–1815), American botanist.
Throughout.

The grains of *M. asperifolia* (= *Sporobolus asperifolius*), scratch grass – almost throughout – were used as food by Indians.
Endangered species: *M. villosa* – Tex.

Oryza sativa   (C 4)   Rice
Greek name of the plant and of its grain of Indian origin.
Originally from tropical Asia, rice is cultivated in warm regions throughout the world. It occasionally escapes from cultivation in S. U.S. & Mex., but does not persist.

Rice is used as food by more human beings than any other plant. It has been grown in Southern Asia for millenia and was introduced into China about 5,000 years ago. Greeks and Romans knew of this grain but did not cultivate the plant. It was introduced into Sicily by the Arabs, was grown in Italy beginning in the 16th century, and was introduced into Virginia around the middle of the 17th century. Numerous varieties are known.

Rice is the staple food of about three-fifths of the world's population, and the remaining two-fifths eat it more or less frequently.

The grain is most generally boiled or steamed whole. It is also made into pudding and cakes. In the Far East, rice is fermented into wine and vinegar, distilled into alcohol ("sake"), or added to soybeans to make "miso" (see *Glycine max*, Fabaceae). It is also ground into flour. In Central America, a drink is prepared by cooking rice flour in water with raw sugar; this "atole de arroz" is commonly sold in markets. In Asia, cakes and noodles are made with starch extracted from the grain. Grains from a glutinous variety are cooked and pounded for making steam cakes ("mochis") and sweetmeats, or brewed into "mirin."

Whole rice contains proteins (7%), starch, vitamins A, B1, B2, B6, niacin and minerals.

Most of the vitamins and minerals are contained within the external layer (bran) of "brown rice," which is mechanically removed by polishing to obtain "white rice." Brown rice or "paddy" takes longer to cook and can be harder to digest if not properly chewed, but white rice lacks necessary vitamins. Used almost exclusively, it can cause beri-beri, a very serious disease due to a deficiency of vitamin B.

The traditional rice in Asia was simply semipolished. This preserved the greatest part of the vitamins and minerals, while at the same time making it easier to cook (thus saving precious fuel) and to digest brown rice. White rice is a fairly recent product of Western civilization. As a rule, refined products were for the nobles, while the peasants were left with "coarse," unrefined foods.

Various other species are used as food in Asia and Africa.

Oryzopsis (C 1)   Rice Grass
From the Greek "oryza," rice, and "opsis," like: referring to the aspect of the plant.
Throughout.

The grains of *O. aspera* – N. & C. N.Am. – and *hymenoides* were used as food by Indians. Those of the first species reach a large size.

Those of other species are good to eat as well but tend to fall off easily from the plant and thus are rather hard to gather.

Panicum (C-H 1)   Panic Grass
Latin name of the plant from "panis," bread, or "panus," panicle.
Throughout. Both native and species introduced from the Old World.

The grains of various species, including *P. capillare*, old-witch grass – almost throughout –, *obtusum* – S.C. U.S., Mex. – and *urvilleanum* – Calif., Ariz., Mex. – were used as food by Indians. They were often ground and mixed with cornmeal.

P. miliaceum, broomcorn millet – originally from C. Asia & naturalized in N.Am. – has been cultivated since Antiquity for its grain in Asia, Africa and Europe.

It was an important food in Europe for ages and is still a staple in parts of Africa. Several varieties are known.

The grain is boiled whole, ground into flour or fermented into a drink.

Millet contains proteins, starch, fats, vitamins and minerals.

Various species are used as food in Africa and Asia.

Our native *P. capillare* (m.a.) is sometimes planted for ornament in Europe.
Endangered species: *P. hirstii* – Ga., N.J. –, *mundum* – Va., N.C. – and *thermale* – Calif.

Paspalum   (C 1)   Knot Grass
From the Greek "paspalê," millet grain.
Throughout. Both native and species introduced from S.Am.

The grains of *P. ciliatum* – naturalized from S. Am. – and *scrobiculatum*, Kodo millet, are edible.
Those of other species are used as food in Asia, Africa and South America. Some of these plants are cultivated, and the name "millet" is used for plants of many different genera.

Pennisetum   (C 2)   Feathertop, Kikuyu Grass
From the Latin "penna," feather, and "seta," bristle: alluding to the feather-like bristles on the involucre.
Originally from the Old World, naturalized throughout.

P. glaucum, pearl millet, is cultivated for forage.
The grains are boiled whole, ground into flour or fermented into a drink in Asia and Africa, where the plant is grown as a cereal crop.
The grains of various species are used as food in tropical regions.

Phalaris   (B 2–3)
Greek name of an undetermined grass, possibly in this genus, from "phalaros," dotted with white.
Throughout. Both native and species introduced from the Mediterranean region.
P. arundinacea var. *picta* is planted for ornament under the name of "ribbon grass." The species is native to both N.Am. and Eurasia. The horticultural form rarely escapes from gardens.

P. canariensis, Canary grass – originally from N.W. Africa & the Canary Islands – is grown for the same purpose and also as birdfeed.

Its young shoots are edible raw or cooked.

The grains have been used as food by humans as well as birds.

Phragmites communis (B 1)   Common Reed
(= *P. australis*)
Greek and Latin name of a reed used for making fences from "phragma," fence.
Throughout. Cosmopolitan.

The rootstock was eaten by Indians. It can be crushed and washed in water to dissolve the starch. The water is then filtered and poured into a container, at the bottom of which the starch settles and can easily be gathered by carefully pouring off the clear water.

The very young shoots are tender and can be eaten raw. They have a strong, sweetish taste reminiscent of wheat grass. They have occasionally been pickled.

Before blooming, the stem is rich in sugars. It can be dried, ground into a sweetish powder and mixed with flour for making cakes and breads. The Indians used to moisten the powder, roast it and eat it as a delicacy.

A sweet gum exudes from the stems and was highly esteemed by Indians, who gathered it and rolled it into little balls eaten as sweets.

The nutritious seeds were also used as food by Indians.

Poa (C-H 1)   Bluegrass
From the Greek "poa," a grass.
Throughout. Both native and species introduced from Eurasia.

The grains of *P. fendleriana*, mutton grass – W. N.Am. – and *scabrella* – W. U.S., Baja – were used as food by Indians.

P. pratensis, Kentucky bluegrass – both native throughout and introduced from Eurasia – has reportedly been held as being edible in Eastern Asia.

The base of the culms of some species have been used as food in S. S.Am.

The grains of others were reportedly eaten in Eurasia.

Endangered species: *P. fibrata* – Calif. –, *involuta* – Tex. –, *napensis* – Calif. – and *pachypholis* – Wash.

Pseudosasa japonica (B 5)   Bamboo
(= *Bambusa metakae*)

From the Greek "pseudês," false, derived from "pseudô," to cheat, and "sasa," name of a bamboo genus.

Originally from Japan, it is cultivated for ornament in S. Fla. where it is occasionally found as an escape.

Young bamboo shoots are edible raw (see *Arundaria* spp.). The grains can also be used as food.

Puccinellia (C 2)   Alkali Grass
After B. Puccinelli, Italian botanist.
N. & W. N.Am.

The grains of *P. nuttalliana* – C. & W. N.Am. – were used as food by some Western Indians.

Saccharum officinarum (B 5)   Sugar Cane
From the Greek "sakcharon," cane sugar.
Originally from S.E. Asia, this giant grass is cultivated throughout the Tropics of both worlds. On our continent, it is grown in the southernmost U.S. & Mex., and is occasionally found as an escape.

Sugar was known to the ancient Greeks at least four centuries before Christ and had already been used for a long time in India. Sugar cane was introduced by the Arabs into Southernmost Europe. It reached the West Indies with Columbus and was first grown in Louisiana in about the middle of the 18th century.

In all regions where the plant is grown, the stem is cut into pieces and the hard envelope removed. The pith, filled with a sweet juice, is chewed mostly as a pastime. The juice itself is extracted by crushing the stem. Sugar cane juice is green and has an extremely sweet, slightly aromatic taste. It is commonly sold as a drink on the streets of tropical towns.

The juice is boiled to evaporate the excess water, and a dark-brown raw sugar is obtained. Raw cane sugar is used extensively for sweetening drinks in tropical America and in other parts of the world. In Egypt, it is made into candies and sold during religious festivities. Organically grown raw cane sugar has even found its way into the health food market in North America and Europe.

Raw cane sugar is refined into white sugar, which is practically pure saccharose, the eliminated "impurities" being vitamins (especially B6), minerals (including calcium and iron in important amounts) and various other substances. Refined white sugar has come into general use across the globe. The processing residue is known as "molasses." Often, what is sold commercially as "brown sugar" is actually nothing but crystallized white sugar mixed with some molasses.

In order to be assimilated by the body, pure saccharose like white sugar (also called sucrose) requires the vitamins and minerals necessary for enzymatic processes. But since the original ones found in brown sugar, concentrated in the molasses, have been eliminated, the body itself must provide for the lack of vitamins and minerals when ingesting white sugar. This process depletes the body's reserves, and if repeated often, it will eventually create a nutritional imbalance.

Morever, saccharose passes quickly into the bloodstream (contrary to starch, for instance, which takes longer to be broken down into simple sugars), increasing glycemia and thus giving an impression of having more energy, but at the same time overstimulating the pancreas to secrete insulin. Produced in large amounts as the result of too brutal a glycemia increase, the insulin lowers the blood sugar below its normal level and thus creates a need or a craving for sugar. This phenomenon is well-known by all candy bar and ice cream addicts, which form the majority of the United States and Canadian populations. It must be noted that white sugar is present as a "flavor enhancer" in virtually every processed food.

This overview also goes for refined beet sugar, which is pure saccharose as well.

Raw cane sugar and cane juice are not quite as harmful, as they contain all their vitamins and minerals. But the plant must be grown organically if one does not want to ingest a concentrated amount of the numerous chemicals used in growing sugar cane.

In some countries, cane wine is made by fermenting cane juice. Rum is obtained by distilling the wine or molasses fermented with water. Rum is normally colorless, but it is commonly dyed with caramel, which is sugar that has been partially burned. It can also be, but more rarely, naturally colored by aging it in wooden barrels.

Molasses is also used in manufacturing monosodium glutamate (MSG).

Sugar cane stems are covered with a layer of wax that has occasionally been recuperated for various uses.

Sugar cane is generally grown by large companies using cheap labor on soil heavily fertilized with chemicals, thus destroying the natural vegetation and in many cases reducing the native population to semi-slavery.

The young shoots of some tropical Asian species are eaten locally. Sugar is extracted from the stems of others in South America and Southeastern Asia.

Secale cereale (C 4)   Rye

Latin name of the plant from the root "sek," to cut.

The exact origin of rye is unknown (probably from N.W. Asia or E. Eur.). It has been cultivated as a cereal plant since time immemorial and does well on poor soil and in cold climates. Rye reached America in Canada at the turn of the 16th century. It often escapes from cultivation but seldom persists.

Rye has long been a staple food for the population of North and Central Europe and Asia. The grain is ground into flour and made into bread either alone for "black bread" in Northern and Central European countries or mixed with wheat for rye or pumpernickel bread. Rye and wheat were sometimes grown together in the same fields. The harvested mixed grain was known as "maslin" (see barley, *Hordeum vulgare*).

Torrefied rye has been used as a coffee substitute.

The grain is germinated (with or without barley and oats), fermented and distilled to yield certain kinds of whiskey.

Rye contains proteins, starch and minerals.

It fluidifies the blood. A decoction of the plant is emollient and laxative.

The ears are sometimes infested by a parasitic fungus, ergot (*Claviceps purpurea*), which takes the place of the grains.

This fungus contains several active substances, especially alkaloids. Its chemical composition is extremely complex.

Ergot is a vasoconstrictor, emmenagogue, abortive and stimulant. High doses produce gastric and nervous disorders.

In the Middle Ages, intoxications due to rye bread containing ergot at times reached epidemic proportions. This disease caused the arms and legs, contaminated by gangrene, to turn black, exude a fetid smell and fall off the body. This was accompanied by horrible pains and hallucinations.

LSD (lysergic acid diethylamide), the well-known hallucinogen with an extremely powerful action upon the cerebral functions, was synthesized from ergot in 1938 by Hofman in Switzerland.

The grains of a few local species have been used as food in temperate Asia.

Setaria (C 1)   Foxtail

From the Latin "seta," bristle: the spikelets are armed with stout bristles. Throughout. Both native and species introduced from the Old World.

S. italica, foxtail millet – from Eurasia – is grown mainly for forage and as birdfeed in N.Am. But its grains have been eaten since prehistoric times, and this millet is one of the oldest cultivated cereals. It is still highly esteemed in India. Several varieties are known.

The grains are eaten as porridge, cooked like rice, added to soups, made into cakes and syrup or brewed into wine.

The grains of *S. glauca*, cattail millet – naturalized from Eurasia –, *magna* (= *Chaetochloa m.*) – E. N.Am. – and *verticillata* and *viridis* – both naturalized from the Old World – have also been widely used as food.

The spores of a fungus parasitic on *S. glauca* (m.a.) have reportedly been eaten in tropical Africa.

A few related species are used as food in Asia and Africa.

Sorghum   (C 2–3)

Latin name of the plant, "sorgo," of unknown origin.
Introduced from the Old World.

S. halepense, Johnson grass – from the Mediterranean area – is cultivated as a forage plant. *S. vulgare* (= *S. bicolor*), sorghum, Sudan grass, broomcorn – from Old World Tropics – is grown for the sweet juice extracted from the stems, for the grains (used for feed in the U.S.) or as forage. Many varieties are in cultivation. Both species occasionally escape in the U.S. & Mex.

The juice of *S. vulgare* (m.a.) is boiled down to a golden-brown syrup, known as "sorghum molasses." It is still made locally in Appalachia and commercialized on a small scale. The stems can be chewed raw, like those of sugar cane.

The grain of both species is edible. It is used extensively like millet as human food in various parts of the world, especially in tropical Africa and Asia. The grains of *S. halepense* (m.a.) were reportedly eaten by Pima Indians of Arizona after the plant was introduced by the Spaniards. Most commonly in developed countries, the grain is used as cattle feed.

The leaves of both species are rich in hydrocyanic acid (hydrolyzed from the glucoside dhurrine) and have poisoned livestock. The HCN content varies greatly according to diverse factors such as soil quality, available water quantity and age of the plant. It is generally believed that thoroughly dried sorghum hay is no longer toxic. Older plants, as well as the stems of younger ones, are relatively free of HCN.

Grains and stems of many other species are used as food, mostly in tropical Africa and Asia.

A few of these are grown for forage in North America.

*Sorghum
halepense*

Sporobolus (C-H 2–3) Dropseed
From the Greek "spora," seed, and "ballô," to throw: referring to the free grains.
Throughout.

The grains of the following species were eaten by Western Indians: *S. airoides*, alkali sacaton – C. & W. U.S., Mex. –, *cryptandrus* – almost throughout –, *contractus* – S.W. U.S., Son. – and *flexuosus* – S.W. U.S., N. Mex.

Like other grains and seeds, they were generally parched, ground and made into mush. They are small, but easily removed from their husks.

Endangered species: *S. patens* – Ariz.

Tripsacum (C-H 2) Gama Grass
From the Greek "tribô," to rub, to grind: of uncertain application.
E. & C. U.S., Mex.

The grains of *T. dactyloides* have been used as food.
Endangered species: *T. floridanum* – Fla.

Trisetum (C-H 2–3)
From the Latin "tres," three, and "seta," hair, awn: each glume is tipped
with three awns.
Throughout. Both native and introduced species.

The grains of *T. spicatum* – N. N.Am. & W. Mountains, Mex., also in Eurasia – have been used as food.
Endangered species: *T. orthochaetum* – Mont.

Triticum aestivum (C 3)   Wheat
Latin name of the plant from "tritum," participle of "tero," to thresh,
grind.
Originally from W. Asia, wheat is now grown throughout the world where
soils, temperature and water permit. It often escapes from cultivation in
N.Am., but does not truly persist.

This exceptional cereal plant has been cultivated since Antiquity and its
grain has allowed the rise of the various civilizations of Western Asia, the
Mediterranean regions and Western Europe where whole wheat bread has long
been the staple food. Wheat has progressively eliminated several other traditional cereals such as oats, barley and rye.

Bread was originally made with whole wheat flour (flour containing all the
cortex of the grain, called bran) or slightly bolted flour (partially sifted to remove
some of the bran).

The whole grain, whole wheat flour and whole wheat bread contain proteins
(known as gluten), starch, vitamins A, B1, B2, B6, K and niacin, minerals, enzymes and a fixed oil very rich in vitamin E contained in the germ. Both
the germ and its oil are sometimes extracted and sold separately, but commercially sold wheat germs are best avoided, as they are dead and rapidly become
rancid.

However, the bread most generally eaten in Western countries today is made
with white flour (heavily bolted flour from which all the bran and the germ have
been removed). As most of the vitamins, minerals and enzymes are concen-

trated in the bran (as well as the many chemicals in nonorganically grown wheat) and in the germ, all that remains in white flour is basically starch and gluten.

The bran is rich in cellulose (35%) and is therefore a good mechanical laxative, but in high doses or in sensitive people, it can irritate the intestinal tract.

One of the most interesting constituents of wheat is gluten (wheat proteins), which distinguishes it from most other cereals. Gluten is what enables bread to rise, thus making it so digestible and nutritious. It can be isolated by washing wheat flour under a trickle of water; the remaining elastic mass is pure protein. In Japan this is· known as "sei-tan," and it is made into patties and fried. This use has also spread to our continent. The water used for washing the flour can be made into soups or sauces. Gluten is also used as a source of monosodium glutamate (MSG).

Wheat grain is cooked whole or after crushing (cracked wheat). "Bulgur" is made by sprouting the grain, boiling it, drying it in the sun and then crushing it. "Falafel," a traditional Middle Eastern food, is a mixture of bulgur, fava-bean flour, garlic and herbs, which is made into balls that are deep-fried. "Hishk" is made in the same regions from fermented bulgur. In the Far East, cooked wheat is mixed with steamed soybeans for making "miso" and "shoyu" (see *Glycine max*, Fabaceae).

Coarsely ground flour is cooked into gruel. When finely ground, it is made into sauces, unleavened breads ("chapatis" in India, "matzos" in Israel and Jewish communities, flour tortillas in Mexico and Navajo fried bread), half-leavened breads ("pita" in the Middle East) or thoroughly leavened breads of all kinds (sometimes with the addition of other cereal flours), as well as pie crusts, biscuits, cakes, dumplings and innumerable other preparations.

Noodles and "couscous" are made from hard wheat (*T. durum* – cultivated in N.Am.), which has an especially high gluten content.

Sprouted wheat is an interesting food. The internal composition of the grain is modified (see *Hordeum vulgare*) as the starch is partially transformed into sugars, the enzymes develop and the vitamin and mineral content increases.

Sprouted wheat is particularly digestible, energizing and stimulant. Home-grown wheat sprouts can be eaten frequently but in moderation.

Other wheat species (*T. compactum*, *dicoccon*, *monococcum*, *polonicum*, *spelta* and *turgidum*) are occasionally cultivated as cereal plants in Europe, Asia and North Africa. Some of these are grown in North America (including *T. polonicum* (m.a.)), named "kamut" after the Egyptian word for wheat and falsely described, for commercial reasons, as the oldest kind of wheat).

Uniola (C 2)   Spike Grass
From the Latin "unus," one: the glumes are united.
E. & C. N.Am.

A local species was an important cereal in Northern Mexico.
The grains of others are edible and of good flavor.

Zea mays (B 3)   Corn, Maize
Greek name of spelt (*Triticum spelta*) "zea" or "zeia."
Of hybrid origin – probably a cross between two or three Mexican grasses, including a *Tripsacum* sp. – corn is now grown throughout the world, due to its productivity and adaptability, both as human food and, mostly in developed countries, as animal feed. It sometimes escapes from cultivation.

Corn had been cultivated for centuries by Indians when Columbus reached America. It is still the most important food in Mexico, Central America and Western South America. Corn is also a major grain in parts of Africa and Asia.

Many varieties are known, the kernels of which are yellow, white, red, blue, black, variegated, hard ("flint corn," var. *indurata*), dented ("dent corn," var. *indentata*), sweet ("sweet corn," var. *amylea-saccharata*), popping readily when heated ("popcorn," var. *evata*) or enclosed separately in a husk ("pod corn," var. *tunicata*). A species with variegated leaves is sometimes planted for ornament.

Corn was considered a god by pre-Columbian populations, and numerous legends were built around it. It served as the basis of innumerable food preparations, some of which are still in use.

Immature grains, still tender and filled with water, were dried and sometimes parched, causing them to pop.

The ripe kernels are cooked in water to which wood ashes or lime has been added in order to soften the cuticle (outer envelope of the grain), at the same time freeing the niacin contained in the grain (see below). The kernels are then washed in cold water – the cuticle is removed by rubbing – and ground to yield "masa," the basic ingredient in the following preparations, in which it is generally used fresh. Dried masa is known as "masa harina."

"Tortillas" are still the staple food of millions of people in Mexico and in

Central and South America. They are commonly commercialized in the United States, but the plastic-packaged products found in American supermarkets don't have much in common with fresh, homemade Mexican tortillas. Tortillas are best eaten freshly cooked and still hot.

Masa is flattened into thick disks of variable size and cooked on a dry plate, traditionally a flat or concave stone, heated from below. In pre-Columbian times, various ingredients were added to masa in tortilla making such as orchid flowers for the rich (red corn was then generally used for preparing masa) and honey for dessert tortillas.

"Tamales" are made by including vegetables, beans, fruits and fish in the masa, which is then made into little cakes, wrapped in corn husks and steamed or roasted.

"Attoli," or "atole" in Spanish is a mixture of masa and water to which various ingredients were added: peppers (chiles), spices (chia seeds – see *Salvia* spp., Lamiacae), crushed beans, popped corn, fermented masa and honey. "Atole de maiz" is still commonly sold in Central American markets; it is made with masa, water and raw sugar and served hot.

"Pozole" is a drink made by emulsifying a caramelized mixture of corn meal and raw sugar in water. A wooden implement rotated between both hands was used for keeping the solids in suspension in the water. While travelling, certain Indian tribes would eat nothing but pozole. Pozoles (or "pozatl") were also made with other substances: "chocoatl," for instance, was prepared with cocoa seeds, hence "chocolate."

Other drinks were brewed by mixing dried and ground unripe grains or fermented masa with water. They were used mostly as medicine.

Fermented corn drinks are generally known as "chicha." A kind of beer, sold as "sandecho," was still made in Mexico until this century. The kernels were sprouted, ground and mixed with water and left to ferment.

Our traditional bourbon or American whisky is obtained by distilling such a mixture of fermented corn. In making the commercial product, sugar is added to the fermenting mash to increase the alcohol content and various chemical additives find their way into this "fire water."

Among other ways of using corn as food we find the following:

Piki. This is the traditional "bread" of the Hopi Indians. It consists of paper-thin, crisp sheets of blue corn that have been cooked on a hot stone. The technique takes years to master since the liquid batter is applied to the stone with the fingertips, and just the right amount must be spread at just the right speed in order to leave a thin layer that doesn't burn.

Cornmeal. One of the most popular ways of eating corn in the United States, cornmeal is especially prized in the South. It is made into such things as corn bread, muffins and fritters. In parts of Europe (mostly Italy and Savoy), cornmeal is cooked into a mush called "polenta" ("gaudes" in Eastern France), which used to be a staple for certain populations, replacing a millet mush dating back to the Neolithic era.

Hominy. White corn is cooked in lye water, thoroughly washed and eaten whole. "Hominy grits" are a coarse white cornmeal.

Unripe ears are roasted or steamed. They are commonly sold on the streets in Mexican and Central American towns, as well as in such other parts of the world as Egypt or India.

The hybrid known as sweet corn (m.a.) is extremely popular in the United States and has recently found its way to Europe as well. The ears are delicious, even raw. They are best when eaten as soon as possible after being picked and simply steamed or baked.

Corn contains proteins, starch (commercially extracted and sold as corn starch), vitamins A and B, niacin and minerals.

Corn germ contains 20 to 30% of an excellent edible oil, which is very rich in vitamin E.

Niacin in corn is found in a bound, unusable form. Cases of pellagra may be observed when the unprepared cereal constitutes a main food source. However, a simple alkaline treatment is sufficient to free this vitamin. This is why in Latin America corn has always traditionally been boiled in lime water.

Before the ears start to form, the tender stem is rich in sugar, especially in warm climates. It can be chewed as such for its pleasant flavor. The ancient Mexicans extracted its sweet juice and let it ferment to obtain "pulque de tlaolle" ("tlaolli" is corn), or they boiled it down to a syrup ("ohuatlnecutli"). The latter was commonly sold in markets before the Spanish conquest. Sugar can be obtained by prolonged boiling.

Up until this century, sweet and tender corn stems were still sold for chewing like sugar-cane stems. They are less fibrous than the latter.

American Indians used to sometimes eat the young and tender husks enveloping the ears.

Corn stigmata contain oil, sugars, saponins, minerals, tannins, allantoine and various other substances.

They are diuretic, cholagogue and sedative of the urinary tract.

The styles of certain tropical forms are said to contain alkaloids and to have been used by Indians as a narcotic.

Zizania   (C-H 4)   Wild Rice
Greek and Latin name of darnel (*Lolium temulentum*).
E. & C. N.Am., introduced in N.W. U.S.

The long, dark grains of *Z. aquatica* have an exquisite taste. They were frequently used as food by Indians, who often used to roast them to enhance their flavor.

Wild rice is commercialized in the United States and Europe and commands high prices. However, its harvesting is regulated; in most cases, Indians still gather it traditionally by shaking the ripe spikes over their canoes with their paddles so that the grains fall to the bottom of the boats.

In China due to a parasitic mold the thickened bases of the culm of a similar species are eaten as a vegetable. The young shoots are eaten as well, and the plant is sometimes cultivated.

Endangered species: *Z. texana* – Tex.

Zizaniopsis miliacea   (C 4)   Water Millet, Southern Wild Rice
See "Zizania," the preceding genus; from the Greek "opsis," alike.
E. & C. N.Am.

The rhizomes have reportedly been used as food.
The grains are edible.

SPARGANIACEAE

Sparganium (C 3) Burweed
From the Greek "sparganion," a swaddling band: referring to the long narrow leaves.
Throughout.

The tuberous <u>rootstock</u> and the bulbous <u>base of the stems</u> of *S. eurycarpum* – almost throughout – are edible.

TYPHACEAE

Typha (B 1) Cattail
Greek and Latin name of the plant from "typhê," "typha."
Throughout.

The starchy core of the fleshy <u>rhizomes</u> is edible raw or cooked after the spongy outer part is removed. A sweet juice, which could possibly be boiled down into syrup, can be extracted from it.

By drying, grinding and sifting, it yields a flour with a pleasant taste. It is rich in proteins and contains 55% carbohydrates.

It is considered best to dig up the rhizomes from late fall to early spring when they are filled with starchy reserves and the aerial parts are dead. However, the water in which they grow is extremely cold at this time of year.

The very <u>young shoots</u> are white, tender, crisp, juicy and have a nutty flavor. They are excellent to eat raw and have occasionally been pickled.

The <u>base of the leaves</u> has the same quality before the plant starts to bloom. The leaves, which tightly overlap each other, must be cut just above the rhizome and the green outer ones removed, uncovering a second sheath of leaves with a tender, white base, which can be cut off and eaten raw. The process is repeated until all the leaves have yielded a few inches of a delicate texture and flavor, reminiscent of palm hearts. Instead of cutting the leaves, it is also possible to pull off the inner ones, the base of which is white and tender.

The <u>unripe inflorescences</u> can be steamed or roasted and eaten from their "cob," just like corn. The flowers themselves can be detached with a knife from the axis of the inflorescence and eaten raw or cooked. It is best to use the female flowers, which are grouped into a voluminous inflorescence just below the thinner male inflorescence.

The <u>male flowers</u> yield great quantities of a yellow <u>pollen</u> that can be gathered and eaten mixed with other food. With a little bit of honey, for instance, it makes a delicious dessert.

In some parts of the world, especially in Southeast Asia, cattail pollen is added to cereal flour for making breads and cakes. Because the pollen is water repellent, it is difficult to use by itself. However, it can be simply sprinkled over salads and various dishes.

Generally, flower pollen is an excellent food, rich in complete proteins, sugars, vitamins A, B, C and E and many minerals. It also contains enzymes and various other substances.

It helps to tonify, detoxicate and balance the body.

Cattail <u>seeds</u> are edible, but they are very small and covered with down. To eliminate the down, Indians placed the seeds along with glowing embers in a bag and shook it until the down was burnt, parching the seeds at the same time.

The seeds contain about 20% of a drying, edible oil.

The following species have been used as a food on our continent: *T. angustifolia*, *domingensis* and *latifolia*.

Others are eaten in various parts of the world.

MUSACEAE

Musa x paradisiaca   (A 5)   Banana

After Antonius Musa, physician for the Roman emperor Augustus.

This species originated long ago in cultivation from Asiatic parents and is now grown for its fruits throughout the Tropics of both hemispheres. It persists on abandoned homesites in S. Fla. & Mex.

The <u>fruits</u> of var. *sapientum* (= *M. sapientum*) are usually eaten raw as such. They are also made into fruit salads, smoothies ("licuados" in Mexico), cakes, banana bread and many other foods. They are sundried (Ecuador is one of the main exporting countries for dried bananas), sliced and fried into banana chips, fermented into wine and vinegar and made into liquors (crème de bananes).

Ripe bananas are rich in sugars (25%) and contain proteins (4%), vitamins A, B, C and E and minerals.

They are very nutritious and have a balancing effect upon the nervous system.

Unripe bananas contain less sugar but more starch and tannin.

The fruits of var. *normalis*, known as plantains (from the Spanish "platano," banana), are eaten as vegetables. They are boiled, roasted or fried, dried and ground into a nutritious flour, or torrefied and used as a coffee substitute. They are frequently eaten in Central and South America and are a staple in Equatorial Africa.

The bitter flowers and the central young shoot (terminal leaf bud) of this variety are eaten after cooking, especially in Asia.

In India, a salt substitute is made by burning the petioles, leaves and skin of the fruits. The ashes are added to curries.

Roots, shoots and fruits of numerous local species are used as food throughout the Tropics of both hemispheres. Several of them are cultivated. Some are also planted for ornament in North America.

"Manila hemp" is derived from the fibers of the petioles of a species native to the Pacific Islands (*M. textilis*). The plant is grown for making ropes and paper pulp.

CANNACEAE

Canna (B 4)
Greek name of reeds used for weaving mats made into fences.
S.E. U.S., Mex.
Several tropical American species and hybrids are planted for ornament.
Some of the arrowroot-producing *Canna* spp. are grown for ornament in N. Am., including *C. indica*, Indian shot, which escapes from cultivation in S. Fla. & Mexico.

The tuberous rootstock of *C. flaccida* was eaten cooked by Indians. It must be gathered before the plant blooms as it later becomes fibrous.

Starch can be obtained by crushing or grating the tubers and washing them in water over or in a container so the starch settles to the bottom. When the water is clear, it is carefully poured off and the starch is generally dried and ground.

In tropical America, several species (such as *Canna edulis*) are grown for the starch found in their rootstock, known as "arrowroot." Arrowroot is also produced from *Maranta* spp., or "toloman" in the West Indies. The starch is very nutritious and digestible. Made into mush for babies and invalids, arrowroot is used for thickening sauces and soups.

Young shoots and leaves of certain species have been used as food after cooking.

MARANTACEAE

Maranta arundinacea (C 5) Arrowroot
Etymology unknown.
Originally from tropical America, the plant is grown for the starch in its root ("arrowroot"). It is occasionally found as an escape in Mex.

The tuberous rootstock is edible cooked after the unpalatable outer skin has been removed. The raw root is acrid and rubefacient. It was used as a remedy for wounds caused by poisoned arrows, hence the name "arrowroot."
The starch can be obtained by the method described above (see *Canna* spp.). It is used in pastries and biscuits, as baby food or food for invalids.
A Brazilian species is planted for ornament.

Thalia (C 4)
After Johann Thal (1542–1583), German naturalist.
S.E. U.S. & Mex.

The rootstock of *T. geniculata*, swamp lily – S. Fla., Mex. – can be eaten after cooking. The inner part turns pink upon boiling. A starch similar to arrowroot (see *Canna* and *Maranta* spp.) can be extracted.
The young leaves are said to be edible.
The root of a South American species is used locally as food.

ARECACEAE (PALMAE)

This family is of immense economic importance, probably second only to the Poaceae (Graminae). It yields edible fruits (dates), terminal buds (palm cabbage) and oils (palm oil), as well as various nonedible products such as waxes, fibers and building materials. Many palm trees are grown as ornamentals.

Brahea dulcis (B 5)   Palma Dulce
After Tycho Brahe (1546–1601), Danish astronomer.
Mex.

The yellow <u>fruit</u> is sweet and edible.
That of a Central American species yields an oil resembling coconut oil.

Coccothrinax argentata (D 5)   Silver Thatch Palm
From the Greek "kokkos," seed, and "thrinax," three-pointed pitchfork.
S. Fla.

The small <u>terminal bud</u> is edible, but gathering it kills the tree, which is not worthwhile.
The <u>fruit</u> (up to 1 cm in diameter) can be eaten raw, but its thick pulp is unpalatable.
Another species is sometimes planted for ornament.

Cocos nucifera (A 5)   Coconut
Etymology unknown.
The exact origin of this tree is not precisely known; it is thought to be somewhere between the Indian and the South Pacific oceans. Coconut trees are now found along the tropical shores of both hemispheres; they are widely cultivated for their fruits.
The tree is both cultivated and naturalized in Fla. & Mex. Several species are grown for ornament in S. Fl., S. Calif. & Mex.

Coconuts are a staple in many tropical regions. They are the main food of certain Islanders living in the Pacific Ocean.
The green <u>fruit</u> contains a refreshing "water" secreted by the plant, slightly acid and rich in vitamin C.
A transparent jelly can be scraped off the inside of the shell with a spoon. It progressively hardens and turns white. This coconut "meat" is eaten by itself or grated, dried and used as a flavoring in pastries and candies. After grating, it can be pressed to yield coconut "milk," an important ingredient in Southeast Asian and Polynesian cooking, as well as for making heavenly smoothies.

The milk contains protein (4%) and fat (25%). The fat can be gathered by letting the milk set overnight: the fat separates and floats to the surface, where it can easily be skimmed off like cream. Coconut milk and cream, mostly manufactured in Southeast Asia, are sold commercially in North America and in Europe.

Coconut oil is obtained by drying the meat in the sun and pressing it. The oil is solid below a temperature of 74°F as it is rich in saturated fatty acids. Coconut oil is widely used for cooking, mostly in the Tropics where the tree grows, but also in western countries after deodorizing and packaging. It is frequently used in the production of margarine.

Sun-dried coconut meat, known as "coprah," is an important commercial product of many South Pacific islands and of India as well.

A traditional method of extracting the oil in Polynesia was to place fresh gratings, mixed with odoriferous plants, in a container left in the hot sun. After a while, the oil was obtained by squeezing the mass. Then the oilcake itself was often fermented in salt water and used as food.

Besides protein and fat, coconut meat contains B-complex vitamins and minerals. It is remarkably low in sodium.

The spongy pulp found inside a sprouting coconut is eaten raw as a delicacy. It has a pleasant, sweet flavor.

A sweet sap flows from several slashes made on the tips of the flower buds or by cutting them off. This sap can be drunk fresh, boiled down to syrup and sugar (named "jaggery" in India), fermented into wine ("toddy") and vinegar and distilled into a strong alcohol known as "arrack" or "fenny."

The terminal leaf bud is eaten raw, cooked or occasionally pickled.

A beverage is reportedly prepared from the roots of the tree.

The brown husk is a local commercial source of very strong but rough fibers widely used in making carpets and rugs which are commonly sold in North America and in Europe.

The fruits of a few other species are used as food in South America.

Erythes (B 5)   Hesper Palm
After one of the Hesperides, daughter of Evening.
Mex.
E. armata, blue hesper palm – Baja – is sometimes planted for ornament.

Its fruits are edible.

The terminal bud and fruits of *E. edulis* – Mex. – are edible.

Phoenix dactylifera   (B 5)   Date Palm
Greek and Latin name of the tree.

Originally from N. Africa & S.W. Asia, the date palm is cultivated commercially for its fruits in S. Calif. (mostly around Indio in the Imperial Valley). It is also grown for ornament in S. Fla., where the tree is naturalized.

The date palm has been known and highly esteemed since Antiquity. The fruits are still a staple for the populations of the African and Arabian deserts. More than 200 varieties are known.

The fruits of some varieties are extremely fleshy and sweet and often sticky. They are usually eaten as such, fresh or dried, and are probably the best natural candies that can be found in the world. Those of other varieties are dry and can be ground into a meal. They are generally used as animal feed. Date kernels are put to the same use after crushing and softening with boiling water.

Dates contain sugars (often over 50%), proteins (2%), vitamins A, B and C, provitamin D and minerals.

They are very nutritious, tonic and expectorant.

The terminal bud of the tree is sometimes used as food ("palm cabbage"), which kills the tree.

The sweet sap is drunk, either fresh or fermented into palm wine, which can be distilled to yield alcohol.

The fruits of other species are used as food in Africa and Asia.

Rhapidophyllum histrix   (B 4)
From the Greek "rhapis, rhapidos," needle, and "phyllon," leaf.
Ga. & Fla.

This palm is sometimes planted for ornament.

The brownish fruit is sweet and edible.

Roystonea elata (H 5)   Florida Royal Palm
Etymology unknown.
S. Fla.

The terminal bud and the fruits are edible. But the Florida Royal Palm is endangered, and the terminal bud of the wild plants should never be used as food.

The Cuban Royal Palm (*R. regia*) is grown for ornament in Florida and Mexico. The bud is edible.

Sabal (B 4)   Cabbage Palm, Palmetto
Etymology unknown.
S.E. U.S., Mex.
S. minor – S.E. U.S. – is sometimes planted for ornament.

The terminal bud ("cabbage") of this species as well as that of *S. palmetto* is edible raw, but removing it by chopping it off with a machete will kill the tree.

The pith of the upper trunk can also be eaten. It contains a sweet sap and the tree has reportedly been tapped for it.

Ashes of the wood can be used as a salt substitute.

The fruit has a sweet but peculiar taste and is edible raw. It can be cooked into a syrup or dried and ground into meal.

Serenoa repens (B 4)   Saw Palmetto
Etymology unknown.
S.E. U.S.

The terminal bud is edible raw. Its flavor is delicate.

The fruits, juicy, bluish-black drupes up to 2 cm long, can be eaten, but they have a strong taste.

They are used medicinally as a diuretic, expectorant and tonic.

Juice extracted from the pulp of the fruits has been mixed with carbonated water and commercialized in Florida.

The seeds have reportedly been used as food as well.

Washingtonia (C 4)   Fan Palm
After George Washington (1732–1799).
S. Calif., Ariz., Son. & Baja. Naturalized in S. Fla.
W. filifera, California fan palm – S. Calif., W. Ariz., Baja – and *sonorae* (= *robusta*), Mexican fan palm – Son., Baja – are planted for ornament. The former species is naturalized in S. Fla.

The terminal bud of *W. filifera* (m.a.) has reportedly been used as food.
The fruits of both species are edible. Those of *W. filifera* (m.a.) are black and of small size, with a thin, sweet pulp. Their seeds were ground into meal by Cahuila Indians.

ARACEAE

Most members of this family (sweet flag is an exception) contain sharp crystals of calcium oxalate, named "raphides," which are mechanically extremely irritating to the skin, especially to mucous membranes. The plants can be dangerous if ingested without preparation: the throat swells up, impeding respiration and causing intense pain and possibly death. If the juice of these plants comes into contact with the eyes, serious inflammations can follow.

However, heating generally destroys these crystals and certain plants in this family can be eaten safely after prolonged cooking. In some cases, thorough drying works best. Several *Araceae* are an important food in various parts of the world. Taro (*Colocasia esculenta*), for instance, was a staple food for various populations in Southeast Asia and some islands of the Pacific, while tannia (*Xanthosoma sagittifolium*) is still a common vegetable in the West Indies.

Acorus calamus (B 3)   Sweet Flag
Greek name of a plant with an aromatic root, "akoros."
Almost throughout, also in the Old World.
Sweet flag is occasionally grown as an ornamental water plant. It was formerly cultivated – mostly in Eur. – because of its aromatic rhizome.

The rhizome has a tangerine-like odor and has been used as a condiment. It was candied for making confectionery. It was also used for flavoring beer and alcoholic drinks such as gin and for preparing aromatic vinegar. It was chewed as a breath freshener and for its medicinal properties and was sold for this purpose in Eastern cities (Boston, among others) in the 19th century. It was used in perfumery as well.

Sweet flag contains an essential oil (rich in asarone, a substance with antibiotic properties, but also somewhat toxic), minerals, tannin, starch, a glucoside (acorine) and an alkaloid (calamine).

It is stimulant, stomachic, carminative, diuretic, diaphoretic and emmenagogue.

However, large doses can be toxic.

The rhizome has been used as an insecticide.

The tender inner part of the <u>young shoots</u> is edible raw.

Acorus calamus

Arisaema (C–F 4)   Jack-in-the-Pulpit
From the Greek "aris," name of a Mediterranean plant of this family, and "haema," blood: alluding to the reddish leaves of certain species.
E. N.Am.
Our native *A. triphyllum* (= *A. quinatum*) is occasionally planted for ornament, along with an Asian species.

The starchy <u>root</u> of *A. triphyllum* (m.a.) has been used as food after processing. It must be sliced thinly and dried for two to three months or roasted. It can then be eaten as such or ground into a nutritious and palatable flour. Boiling is usually not sufficient to remove the acridity of the root.

The <u>berries</u>, toxic in the raw stage, were reportedly boiled and eaten with game by Indians.

<u>Roots</u> and <u>leaves</u> of several species are used as food in East Asia.

Calla palustris (E–F 4)   Water Arum
Name of a plant in Pliny.
N.E. & N.C. N.Am. A monotypic genus.
It is occasionally grown as an ornamental water plant.

In Scandinavia, where water arum is also native, the <u>roots</u> were sometimes used as food. They were dried, ground, boiled in water and left for a few days, then dried and ground again. The resulting meal was mixed with other kinds of flours, including that of fir cambium (*Abies alba*, Pinaceae), and baked. The roots were also simply dried, ground and heated until their acrid principles were removed.

Indians dried and ground the berries into a nutritious but unpalatable flour. The seeds themselves were used similarly.

The berries are toxic, due to their high saponin content. They can cause nervous, digestive and cardiac disorders.

Colocasia esculenta (C–F 5)   Taro
(= *C. antiquorum*, = *Caladium esculentum*)
Latin name of the plant in Pliny.
Originally from tropical Asia, taro is cultivated throughout tropical regions for its esculent root and for ornament; it is occasionally found persisting on abandoned sites in S. Fla. & Mex.

Taro was traditionally the staple food of numerous populations in Polynesia and Southeast Asia. The fleshy root contains, like the rest of the plant, crystals of calcium oxalate, but it becomes edible after thorough cooking. Its taste is very pleasant: it can be boiled, steamed, fried or roasted.

In Hawaii, more than 300 varieties with various colors, tastes and calcium oxalate content were in cultivation. The root was cooked in a fire pit ("imu"), pounded with a stone into a paste, mixed with water, kneaded for a long time and left to ferment slightly. The end product, known as "poi," was the main food of the Hawaiians. It keeps for quite a long time, even in the hot and humid tropical climate, but turns sour by fermenting. This particular taste is not unpleasant, however, and sour poi was much relished by certain people.

Taro is also an important vegetable in Southeast Asia, India, the West Indies, tropical America and parts of Africa.

The young leaves, the stems (petioles and peduncles) and the spadix are edible after cooking. They have a pleasant taste.

The roots of a few other species are used as food in tropical Asia and Polynesia.

Lysichiton americanum (C-F 4)   Yellow Skunk Cabbage
From the Greek "lysis," loose, and "chitôn," tunic, covering: referring to
the spathe.
W. N.Am.

The <u>roots</u> were used as food by certain Indians. They were roasted and then
dried and ground into flour.
The <u>young leaves</u> are edible after boiling in several changes of water.
The fresh plant is acrid and has a strong, skunk-like smell.
The yellow skunk cabbage is occasionally grown for ornament in Europe.
The <u>buds</u> of a local species are eaten in Northeast Asia.

Orontium aquaticum (C-F 4)   Golden Club
Ancient Greek name of some water plant.
E. N.Am. A monotypic genus.

The <u>roots</u> were dried and ground into flour by Indians.
The <u>seeds</u> were dried and then boiled in several changes of water until they
became palatable.
The <u>flowers</u> have reportedly been eaten in the same way.

Peltandra (C-F 4)   Arrow Arum
From the Greek "peltê," shield, and "aner, andros," man: alluding to the
shape of the stamens.
E. U.S.

The starchy <u>root</u> of *P. sagittaefolia* – S.E. U.S. – and *virginica* is edible after
long cooking. It can also be dried and ground into flour.
The <u>spadix</u> is edible after cooking.
The <u>berries</u> are good to eat after drying and boiling. They have a sweetish
taste and have occasionally been added to breads, to which they give a pleasant
flavor. Fresh berries are toxic.
Roots, spadices and berries of the two species mentioned above were eaten
by certain Indians.

Symplocarpus foetidus   (C-F 4)   Skunk Cabbage
From the Greek "symplokê," connection, and "karpos," fruit: referring to the compound fruits.
N.E. N.Am.

The <u>root</u> has been eaten after long cooking. It can be dried and ground into flour.

It has been used medicinally as an expectorant, antispasmodic and diuretic, but it can be emetic and slightly narcotic.

The <u>young shoots</u> are edible after boiling in several changes of water. They can also be dried and then cooked in soups or stews. They have a pleasant flavor.

The <u>leaves</u> of a local species are used as food in Northeast Asia.

Xanthosoma hoffmannii   (C-F 5)   American Taro
From the Greek "xanthos," yellow, and "sôma," body.
Introduced from S.Am. into S. Fla.

<u>Young leaves</u> and <u>stems</u> are edible after thorough cooking.

<u>Roots</u> and <u>leaves</u> of various other species are used as food in tropical America and Asia. Some of them are cultivated as vegetables in these regions.

PONTEDERIACEAE

Eichhornia crasipes   (B 2)   Water Hyacinth
After J. A. F. Eichhorn (1779–1856), Prussian minister.
Originally from Brazil, water hyacinth is grown in warm areas as an ornamental. Due to its amazing rate of vegetative reproduction, the plant is one of the most serious aquatic pests in the Tropics, choking hundreds of square miles of waterways; it is naturalized in S. U.S. & Mex.

Young <u>leaves, petioles</u> and <u>inflorescences</u> are edible after cooking. The flowers become somewhat gelatinous.

Eating the plant in the raw stage often causes itching.

Another Brazilian species is planted for ornament in North America.

Monochoria vaginalis (B 2)

(= *Pontederia v.*)

From the Greek "monos," single, and "chorion," membrane.

Originally from S.E. Asia, it is naturalized as a weed in S. U.S. & Mex.

In Asia, the whole plant is eaten raw or cooked.

The root has been used to cure asthma and toothaches, as well as liver and stomach problems.

A few other species are used as food in East Asia.

Pontederia (B 2) Pickerelweed

After Giulio Pontedera (1688–1757), professor of botany in Padua.

E. N.Am.

The young leaves of *P. cordata* have been eaten raw or cooked.

The seeds are edible raw, roasted, boiled or ground into flour.

The plant is sometimes grown as an aquatic ornamental in Europe.

LILIACEAE

This family is an important source of ornamental plants.

It includes very few garden vegetables: the most common one is asparagus.

However, many Liliaceae have edible bulbs, but they should only be gathered in case of emergency: this not only kills the plant, but the results are quite meager since the bulbs are generally very small.

Some of these plants contain toxic alkaloids and glucosides. They can be very dangerous, even lethal, when ingested.

Androstephium (G 4)

From the Greek "aner, andros," man, and "stephanos," crown: referring to the united filaments of the stamens.

S.W. U.S.

The corms of *A. coeruleus* have reportedly been used as food by Indians.

Asparagus (B 3)
Greek and Latin name of the plant.
Throughout. Introduced from Eurasia & S. Africa.
Several S. African species are grown for ornament. They are commonly known as "asparagus fern."
A. officinalis, garden asparagus – from Eurasia – is widely grown as a vegetable; it is naturalized on our continent. The plant has been cultivated since Roman times, around the 3rd century B.C. Several varieties (green, white or purple) are known.

The <u>young shoots</u> are generally eaten after steaming but can also be eaten raw. Naturally green, they are often blanched by gathering soil around the base of the plant and over the shoots.

Asparagus contains vitamins A, B, niacin and rutin, minerals, tannin and asparagin (which gives urine a characteristic smell).

Young shoots and roots are diuretic, depurative and slightly laxative but must not be eaten when the kidneys are inflamed.

The red berries are rich in saponins and can cause digestive troubles and hemolysis.

Their <u>seeds</u> can reportedly be used as a coffee substitute.

The <u>roots</u> of certain tropical Asian species have been used as food.

The <u>shoots</u> of many local species are eaten raw or cooked in Europe, Asia and South Africa.

Asparagus officinalis

Calochortus (C-H 4)   Mariposa Lily
From the Greek "kalos," beautiful, and "chortos," grass: alluding to the showy flowers and the grass-like leaves.
C. & W. N.Am.
A few native species are planted for ornament.

The <u>bulbs</u> were often used as food by Western Indians. They are edible raw but were most often cooked in a fire pit, pressed into cakes and dried in the sun.

They were also dried and ground into a meal. Mormons survived largely on the bulbs of *C. nuttallii*, sego lily – W. N.Am. – during their first years in Utah (it is Utah's state flower).

The bulbs are sweet and nutritious. Those of the following species have been eaten: *C. aureus* – S.W. U.S. –, *elegans* – N.W. U.S. –, *gunnisonii* – Rocky Mountains –, *luteus* – Calif. –, *macrocarpus* – N.W. N.Am. –, *nuttallii* (m.a.), *pulchellus* – Calif. –, *tolmiei* (= *maweanus*) – Calif. to Wash. – and *venustus* – Calif.

Young leaves and seeds are edible as well.

Endangered species: *C. clavatus* subsp. *recurvifolius*, *coeruleus* var. *westonii* – both Calif. –, *greenei* – Ore., Calif. –, *indecorus*, *longebarbatus* var. *peckii* – both Ore. – and *monanthus*, *persistens* and *tiburonensis* – all three Calif.

Camassia (C-G 4) Camas

From a N.W. Indian name of the plant, "quamash" or "camas."
Throughout but mostly W. N.Am.
A few native species are planted for ornament.

The bulbs of *C. leichtlinii* – Calif. to B.C. – and *quamash* (including = *C. esculenta*) – N.W. N.Am. – were an important food for Western Indians. They were cooked in a fire pit, roasted on embers or boiled. They have a sweet, pleasant taste and are very nutritious.

As is the case with most underground parts of plants, it is best to dig up the bulbs from late fall to early spring while they are filled with reserves. However, it is then difficult to identify the plants precisely, and camas bulbs can be confused with those of death camas (*Zigadenus* spp.), which are extremely toxic and can be lethal. Sometimes Indians themselves were deceived by the poisonous bulbs. When the plants are in bloom, they can easily be told apart because *Camassia* spp. have blue flowers (occasionally white) and *Zigadenus* spp. have white flowers: if one gathers only the blue-flowered plants, there is no risk of poisoning.

Chlorogalum (C-F-H 4)   Soap Plant, Amole
From the Greek "chloros," green, and "gala," milk.
Calif., S. Ore., N. Baja.
C. pomeridianum is occasionally planted as an ornamental.

The <u>bulbs</u> of *C. parviflorum* – S.W. Calif. & Baja – and *pomeridianum* (m.a.) were used as food by Indians after long cooking to remove the saponins they contain. Amole bulbs are nutritious and have a pleasant flavor, but the edible part is very sticky and must be removed from the strong fibers embedded in it.

As the name "soap plant" suggests, the bulbs produce lather when mashed and beaten in water. They were used as soap and as fish poison by Indians.

The <u>young shoots</u> are edible cooked.

Endangered species: *C. grandiflorum, purpureum* var. *purpureum* and *reductum* – all Calif.

Clintonia (B 3)   Wood Lily
After De Witt Clinton (1769–1828), governor of New York and naturalist.
N. N.Am. & Mountains.

The young unrolling <u>leaves</u> of *C. borealis* and *umbellata* have a pleasant cucumber taste and are good to eat raw. Older leaves are better cooked or chopped up and mixed with other greens in salads.

Another species is used as food in Northeast Asia.

Disporum (D 4)   Fairy Bells
From the Greek "dis," double, and "spora," seed: referring to the paired ovules.
Throughout.

The <u>berries</u> of the various species are edible, but they must be eaten in moderation only. Those of *D. hookeri* var. *trachyandrum* (= *D. trachyandrum*) – W. N.Am. – yellow to orange in color, were eaten raw by the Blackfoot Indians.

The young <u>leaves</u> of similar species are used as food in Korea and Japan.

Erythronium (B-H 3)   Fawn Lily, Adder Tongue, Trout Lily, Glacier Lily, Dogtooth Violet
From the Greek "erythros," red: the flower of the European species is dark pink and the leaves are dotted with purplish dots.
A few native species are planted for ornament.

The corms of the following species were used as food by Indians: *E. albidum* – C. N.Am. to Pa. (including var. *mesochoreum* – C. U.S) –, *americanum* – E. N.Am. – and *grandiflorum* (including = *parviflorum*) – N.W. N.Am.
They were generally boiled or roasted.
The leaves are edible raw in small amounts or cooked, but each plant has only two leaves, and if both of them are removed, the plant will die. Those of *E. hendersonii* – W. N.Am. – and of other Western species have been eaten.
However, the fresh plant can be emetic when eaten in large quantities. *E. oregonum* – Calif. to B.C. – has been reported to be slightly toxic.
The green, immature seed pods have reportedly been eaten.
In Japan, starch is derived from the rootstock of a local species (*E. japonicum*). Known as "katakuri-ko," it is used in dietetic food, to thicken soups and to make dumplings, fritters or confections.
Another species (*E. dens-canis*) has been used as food in Eurasia.
Endangered species: *E. grandiflorum* (m.a.) subsp. *pusaterii* – Calif. – and *propullan* – Minn.

Fritillaria (C-H 3)   Fritillary, Mission Bells
From the Greek "fritillus," dice box: referring to the shape of the flowers or of the capsules.
Throughout.
Several native and Eurasian species are planted for ornament.

The bulbs of *F. atropurpurea* – W. U.S. –, *lanceolata*, checker lily – W. U.S., Canada – and *pudica* – N.W. N.Am. – were used as food by Northwestern Indians, raw, boiled or dried.
The bulbs are sometimes surrounded by tiny bulblets.
In some species the bulbs are bitter. Those of a European species (*F. meleagris*) contain a very toxic alkaloid (imperialine) and are poisonous. Care should

therefore be taken to properly identify the plants of this genus down to the specific level when they are to be used as food, as other species can also be toxic. At any rate, it would be unreasonable to kill these beautiful plants except in case of emergency.

The bulbs of a few species have been eaten in Eastern Asia, including those of *F. camchatcensis*, Indian rice, black lily – Wash. to Alaska, also in E. Asia.

The <u>unripe seed pods</u> of our species have reportedly been used as food.

Endangered species: *F. adamantina* – Ore. –, *phaeanthera* and *roderickii* – both Calif.

Hemerocallis (B 2–3)   Day Lily
From the Greek "hêmera," day, and "kallos," beauty: the flowers last only one day.
Originally from S. Eur. & Asia, *H. flava* (= *H. lilioasphodelus*) and *fulva* are widely grown for ornament. The former species is occasionally found as an escape from cultivation; the latter is naturalized in E. N.Am. Other Asian species and hybrids are also planted for ornament.

Numerous *Hemerocallis* spp. are used as food in Eastern Asia, including *H. flava* and *fulva* (both m.a.).

The young <u>roots</u> are eaten raw. Older ones must be cooked.

The <u>young shoots</u> are edible raw.

The <u>flower buds</u> are eaten raw or slightly steamed. They are also pickled. They can be made into delicious omelettes.

The expanded <u>flowers</u> are eaten raw, fried or added to soups as an aromatic thickener. They are often dried or preserved in salt, and must then be soaked in water before using. Wilted flowers are added to soups or stews.

Hemerocallis fulva

Hesperocallis undulata (C-H 4)   Desert Lily, Ajo
From the Greek "hesperos," pertaining to the evening, western, and "kallos," beauty.
S.E. Calif., W. Ariz. A monotypic genus.

The large bulbs have been eaten by local Indians, but they often grow 15 to 20 inches (35 to 50 cm) below the surface of the ground and are therefore very hard to dig up.
Early Spanish explorers named the plant "ajo" (garlic).

Hosta (B 4)   Plantain Lily
After N.T. Host (1761–1834), Austrian botanist.
Originally from E. Asia, a few species are grown for ornament, two of which occasionally escape in N.Am., including *H. lancifolia*.

In Eastern Asia, the young leaves of the species mentioned are eaten cooked or preserved in salt.

Leucocrinum montanum (G 4)   Star Lily
From the Greek "leukos," white, and "krinon," lily.
W. N.Am. A monotypic genus.
The plant is sometimes grown for ornament.

The fleshy root was used as food by Crow Indians.
The plant has reportedly poisoned sheep in Northern California.

Lilium (B-H 4)   Lily
Latin name of the plant, from the classical Greek name, "lirion."
Throughout.
Many native, European and Asian species are commonly planted as ornamentals.

The bulbs of the following species were used as food by Indians: *L. canadense* – E. N.Am. –, *columbianum*, Columbia lily – N.W. N.Am. –, *philadelphicum* – almost throughout – and *superbum*, Turk's cap lily – E. N.Am.

They can be eaten raw or cooked and are sweet, with an excellent flavor. But since digging them up kills the plant, they should only be gathered in case of emergency.

In Eastern Asia, especially in China and Japan, lily <u>bulbs</u> have long been a popular food. Several species are grown for this purpose, including *L. bulbiferum*, orange lily – from Eurasia, escaped in Que. & N.Y. – and *tigrinum*, tiger lily – from E. Asia, occasionally escaped in E. N.Am.

The bulbs are generally boiled or dried for later use. They are an important ingredient in the traditional "namono," eaten to celebrate the Japanese New Year. Starch was extracted from the bulbs and used for making steamed cakes ("mochis").

Lily bulbs are emollient and demulcent. When cooked and applied as a poultice, they hasten the ripening of abscesses.

The <u>pollen</u> can be gathered in relatively important amounts and eaten as such or sprinkled over various dishes. It is nutritious and has a pleasant taste.

Lily petals are used to heal wounds (after macerating them in alcohol) and burns (after macerating them in olive oil).

If the flowers are kept in a closed room, especially at night, their penetrating scent can cause headaches.

Endangered species: *L. iridollae* – Ala., Fla. –, *occidentale* – Ore., Calif. – and *pitkinense* – Calif.

Maianthemum (G 3)   False Lily-of-the-Valley
From the Latin "maius," the month of May, and G. "anthemon," flower: the plant blooms in May.
N. N.Am. & Mountains.

The <u>berries</u> of *M. canadense* – N.E. & N.C. N.Am. & Appalachians – have been reported to be edible, but only in small amounts as they are known to be cathartic.

Those of the European species (*M. bifolium*) contain cardiotonic glucosides and saponins. They can cause serious – possibly lethal – nervous and cardiac disorders. It is probably best therefore to avoid using our native species as food.

*Maianthemum
canadense*

Medeola virginiana (C 4)   Indian Cucumber
Commemorating Medea, a sorceress in Greek mythology.
E. N.Am. A monotypic genus.

The <u>root</u> is crisp, juicy and tastes somewhat like cucumber. It is very good to eat raw and can also be pickled. As the common name suggests, the plant was used as food by Indians.

Muscari (C-4)   Grape Hyacinth
From the Arabic "muskarimi," name of the fragrant Muscari (*M. moschatos*), from the Greek "moschos," musky smell.
Originally from Eur. & W. Asia, the plants are grown for ornament and naturalized in E. N.Am.

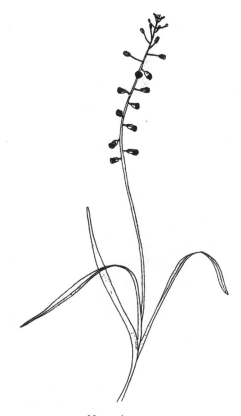

The <u>bulb</u> of *M. racemosum* (= *M. neglectum*) is edible raw and has a sweet, pleasant taste. It has been used as food in the Mediterranean region in spite of its small size.

The <u>flower buds</u> have reportedly been pickled.

The dark blue flowers are fragrant.

After cooking in water, the bitter <u>bulbs</u> of *M. comosum* – occasionally naturalized in N.E. N.Am. – have been highly prized as food in Greece since ancient times. Dioscorides described them as excellent for the stomach. They are not found abundantly in Greece anymore and must be imported there from Morocco.

Muscari comosum

Ornithogalum (C-F 4) Star of Bethlehem
Greek and Latin name of the plant from "or-
nis, ornithos," bird, and "gala," milk: of uncertain application.
Originally from Eurasia and N. Africa, the
plants are grown for ornament and naturalized
in E. N.Am. A few S. African species are also
cultivated as ornamentals.

The bulbs of ***O. umbellatum*** have been eaten
after cooking in Europe, Asia and Northern
Africa. But they are bitter and toxic raw. They
have reportedly poisoned children and livestock
in Europe.
The young shoots of a Eurasian species (*O.
pyrenaicum*) are used locally as food. They were
sold in English markets under the name of
"Bath asparagus."

Ornithogalum umbellatum

Polygonatum (B 4) Solomon's Seal
From the Greek "polys," many, and "gony," knee: referring to the aspect
of the rhizome; same etymology as *Polygonum* spp., *Polygonaceae*.
E. & C. N.Am.

The rootstocks of ***P. biflorum*** (= *P. multiflorum*; including *P. commutatum* in
part) – E. U.S. – and ***canaliculatum*** – C. U.S. – have been used as food by Indians.
But the rhizomes contain saponins and crystals of calcium oxalates, undesirable substances which should be eliminated by long cooking. Indians sometimes dried the rootstock and ground it into a flour.
In Europe, where the plant is native as well, a kind of bread was made from
a mixture of cereal flour and of the purée obtained by boiling the rhizome and
passing it through a food mill to eliminate the fibers. Starch can be extracted by
chopping the rhizome, cooking it in water, filtering it, pouring it into a container
and letting the water rest so that the starch settles to the bottom.

Due to its saponins, the rhizome is toxic and hemolytic in the raw stage. It is used externally as an antiecchymotic. The raphides of calcium oxalate it contains are irritating to the skin, especially to mucous membranes. The rhizome also contains mucilage and tannin.

It is astringent, tonic and, when raw, emetic.

When gathering Solomon's Seal roots, care must be taken not to confuse them with those of mayapple (*Podophyllum peltatum*, Berberidaceae), which are toxic. Both plants often grow together and their rootstocks can be hard to differentiate. Those of Solomon's Seal are whiter and bear characteristic scars ("seals")

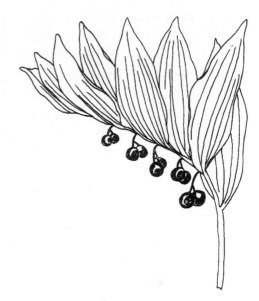

Polygonatum biflorum

at the points of attachment of previous years' stems.

The young shoots of our native species were cooked and eaten by Indians.

The fruits are toxic. They are rich in saponin and, when raw, can cause digestive and cardiac disorders, as well as hypoglycemia and hemolysis. They are also irritating.

Rhizomes and young shoots of various species are used as food in East Asia. The rootstocks are often soaked overnight or cooked in several changes of water to remove their acridity.

In Japan, the flower buds and flowers are eaten after blanching and rinsing in cold water to dispel their bitterness.

Smilacina (D 3)   False Solomon's Seal
(= *Vagnera* spp.)
Diminutive of "smilax," Greek name of various plants and botanical name of greenbriar and sarsaparilla.
Almost throughout.

S. racemosa and *stellata* were used as food by Indians.

The <u>roots</u> are bitter, and in order to render them edible, they must be boiled in several changes of water. It has even been suggested to soak them overnight in lye to dispel their bitterness, then to wash them thoroughly and boil them to remove all the lye. They can also be pickled.

The <u>young shoots</u> are edible after cooking.

The fresh <u>berries</u> have a sweet, aromatic taste, somewhat reminiscent of molasses, but they are purgative and cathartic if ingested in large amounts. It is preferable to cook them.

The <u>shoots</u> of a Northeast Asian species are used as food in Korea.

Streptopus (D 3)   Twisted Stalk
From the Greek "streptos," twisted, and "pous," foot: referring to the aspect of the pedicel.
N. N.Am. & Mountains.

<u>Young shoots</u> and <u>berries</u> of *S. amplexifolius* were cooked and eaten by Indians.

The raw berries are potentially toxic. Their saponins can cause digestive troubles and hemolysis.

Trillium (D-H 3)   Trillium, Wake Robin
From the Latin "trilix," with a triple cloth: the plant has three verticillate leaves and its flower parts come in threes.
Throughout.
Several native species are grown for ornament, including *T. grandiflorum* – N.E. N.Am. & Appalachians.

The <u>young leaves</u> of *T. grandiflorum* (m.a.) and *ovatum* – Calif. to B.C. & Mont. – have been eaten after cooking. They are said to be edible raw before the flowers appear, after which they become bitter and must be boiled. The leaves of other species are probably edible as well, but all *Trilium* spp. should be left alone as they are not very common.

The roots are strongly emetic. Those of *T. pendulum*, birthroot – C. & W. U.S. – have been used medicinally for their astringent, emmenagogue, expectorant and tonic properties. Some Western Indians were said to use them as an aid in childbirth.

T. erectum, red trillium -- N.E. N.Am. & Appalachians – is said to contain hormone-like substances.

The berries of our native *Trillium* spp. have at times been reported to be emetic. However, the fruits of several local species are eaten with impunity in Northeastern Asia.

Endangered species: *T. persistens* – S.C., Ga. – and *pusillum* var. *virginianum* – Va., Md., N.C.

Uvularia   (B 4)   Bellwort

From the Latin "uvula," the soft palate: far-fetched allusion to the pendent flowers.

E. N.Am.

The roots of *U. perfoliata* and *sessiliflora* have been used as food after cooking. Those of the latter species were reportedly used in making root beer-like drinks.

The young shoots are edible raw or cooked. Those of *U. grandiflora* can be eaten as well.

The leaves and the flowers of *U. sessiliflora* (m.a.) were used as cooked vegetable by Cherokee Indians.

Xerophyllum   (E 4)   Bear Grass, Turkey Beard

From the Greek "xeros," dry, and "phyllon," leaf: referring to the foliage.

W. N.Am. & C.E. U.S.

The fibrous root of *X. tenax* -- N.W. N.Am. – was used as food by Indians after roasting or boiling. But it is not very pleasant to eat.

Indians used to make clothing and decorate baskets with the long, thin leaves.

AMARYLLIDACEAE

Aletris (E 4)   Stargrass, Colic Root
Greek name of a female slave who ground grain: alluding to the apparent mealiness of the flower.
E. N.Am.

The bulbous roots of *A. farinosa*, although very bitter, have been used as food after thorough cooking.

Allium (B-H 2–3)   Onion, Garlic and so on
Latin name of the plant.
Throughout. Both native and species introduced from Eurasia.
Some Eurasian species are grown for ornament. Others cultivated in almost every vegetable garden for their bulbs or their leaves are used as condiments or greens. Among these, the following three occasionally escape from cultivation:

A. cepa, onion: Probably derived from a C. Asian species (*A. ischaninii*). It is sometimes adventive in E. N.Am. The plant has been in cultivation for over 3,000 years in Egypt and China, and its bulb is now commonly used in cooking throughout the world. Many varieties are known, some of which are sweet, not pungent and good to eat raw. Size, shape and color are extremely variable.

Onions are used as a condiment or as a vegetable (baked, in soup or as "purée soubise," for instance). Small white ones are pickled. The bulbs are also dehydrated and mixed with salt to make onion salt or blended in various seasonings.

Most people find it hard to digest raw onions.

Besides a tear-producing essential oil, the bulb contains sugars, vitamins A, B and C, minerals, organic acids and enzymes.

It is diuretic, stimulant, expectorant, antiseptic, hypotensive, antispasmodic, vermifuge, and it reduces glycemia. The juice expressed from the bulb is used medicinally as well.

Onion is applied externally as an antiseptic when raw and cooked as an emollient to hasten the ripening of abscesses and boils.

The strong odor of the bulb repels insects.

The young <u>leaves</u> can be eaten raw like green onions (*A. fistulosum*, cultivated in N.Am.).

A. sativum, garlic: Probably derived from a C. Asian species (*A. longicuspis*). It occasionally escapes from cultivation in N.Am. Garlic has been cultivated since Antiquity and was highly esteemed by the ancient Egyptians, Hebrews, Greeks and Romans. Many varieties are known.

The <u>bulbs</u> have a very strong, well-known odor. Garlic is indispensable in Mediterranean and Latin American cooking where people relish its aromatic and pungent flavor, while it is generally disliked in Northern Europe and Anglo-Saxon countries. However, in the past few years the trend has been changing and garlic is becoming increasingly popular.

The bulblets are used fresh or dried and ground into garlic powder. They can also be pickled.

Garlic contains an essential oil rich in vitamins A and B, enzymes and antibiotic substances. The bulbs also contain vitamin C, minerals and starch.

Garlic is tonic, stimulant, stomachic, carminative, antiseptic, vermifuge, hypotensive, diuretic, expectorant, antispasmodic and more. Whole books have been written exalting its beneficial properties.

But high doses are irritating: it can burn the mucous membranes and cause digestive and urinary troubles. Garlic oil, extracted from the bulbs by distillation, is dangerously caustic.

Garlic is used externally as an antiseptic and vulnerary and also to remove corns and warts.

Its strong odor repels insects.

The young green <u>leaves</u> are edible raw or cooked.

At the top of its stem the plant produces small bulblets (used for propagation) and a few flowers. These aerial bulblets can be used like those of the underground bulb.

A. schoenoprasum var. **schoenoprasum**, chives: Originally from Eurasia. It escapes from cultivation in N.Am.

The cylindrical, hollow <u>leaves</u> are used fresh as an herb. They are finely chopped, but never cooked, to preserve their delicate flavor. Chives are an important ingredient in French

*Allium
schoenoprasum*

cooking: as part of "fines herbes" (like chervil, tarragon, sorrel and parsley), they are added to salads, sauces, dressings and omelettes.

Composition and medicinal properties of the plant are similar to those of onion (see *A. cepa*).

A. schoenoprasum var. *sibiricum* is native to N. N.Am. In N.E. Asia, where the plant is also native, the leaves and bulbs are used as a condiment or a vegetable. The small bulbs are sometimes pickled.

Bulbs and/or leaves of numerous wild species were used as food by Indians and settlers. They can be used raw as a condiment or cooked as a vegetable. They were often roasted on embers. The generally small bulbs can also be pickled or stored for later use.

All wild garlics and onions (like the cultivated species mentioned above) are easily recognized by their characteristic odor due to an essential oil formed by the action of a ferment on a glucoside. The essential oil content of the plants, which determines the strength of their smell and flavor, varies according to each species.

Wild garlics and onions have medicinal properties similar to those of their cultivated counterparts (see *A. cepa* and *sativum*), only less pronounced. They are mostly diuretic, stomachic and hypotensive. But when eaten raw in too large amounts, they can irritate the digestive and urinary tracts.

The bulbs of the following native species have been used as food: *A. bisceptrum* – W. U.S. –, *bolanderi* – N. Calif., S.W. Ore. –, *canadense*, wild onion – E. & C. N.Am. –, *cernuum*, nodding wild onion – N. N.Am. & Mountains –, *geyeri* – W. U.S. & B.C. –, *mutabile* – S.E. U.S. –, *nuttallii* – C. U.S. –, *sabulicola* – W. U.S. –, *stellatum* – N.C. U.S. (to Okla.), Can. – , *textile* (= *reticulatum*) – C. & W. U.S., Can. –, *tricoccum*, ramps, wild leek – N.E. N.Am. & Appalachians –, *unifolium* – Calif. – and *validum* – W. N.Am.

The large, flat and fleshy leaves of *A. tricoccum* (m.a.) are picked with the bulbs in the springtime and eaten raw or in omelettes. Ramps are still com-

Allium tricoccum

monly used as a wild vegetable in Appalachia. They have a strong flavor, which tends to dissipate during cooking.

The leaves of other species are edible, but they are thin and generally tough. They are best chopped raw when young and used as a condiment.

The bulbs, leaves and bulblets produced at the top of the stems of *A. oleraceum* and *vineale*, field garlic – naturalized from Eur. – have been used as a condiment.

The bulblets produced in the umbels of *A. canadense* (m.a.) can also be eaten.

Basically all *Allium* spp. are edible. Bulbs and leaves of many species are eaten in Europe, Asia and North Africa. Several of these are cultivated as condiments or vegetables.

The milk of cows grazing in pastures where wild garlics and onions grow in large quantities may acquire an unpleasant flavor, due to the volatile oils inhaled by the animal; it is not even necessary for the cow to actually eat the plant.

Endangered species: *A. aaseae* – Idaho –, *dictuon* – Wash. –, *hickmanii* – Calif. – and *passeyi* – Utah.

Bloomeria (C-H 4)   Golden Stars
After H. G. Bloome, early San Francisco botanist.
Calif.

B. crocea (= *B. aurea*) is sometimes planted for ornament.
The corms were eaten by California Indians.
Endangered species: *B. humilis*.

Brodiaea (C-H 4)
(= *Dichelostemma*, *Calliprora*, *Hesperoscordum*, *Hookera* and *Triteleia* spp.)
After James J. Brodie, Scotch cryptogamic botanist.
W. N.Am.
Some native species are planted for ornament.

The small corms are sweet, somewhat mucilaginous, and edible raw or cooked. Especially in California, they were an important food for Indians, who steamed them in a fire pit or roasted them on embers.

The following species have been used as food: *B. coronaria* – Calif. to B.C. –, *douglasii* – N.W. N.Am. –, *elegans* – harvest brodiaea – Calif., Ore. –, *hyacinthina* – Calif. to B.C. & Idaho –, *laxa* – Calif., S. Ore. –, *lutea* (= *ixioides*), golden brodiaea – Calif. –, *peduncularis* – Calif. –, *pulchella* (= *capi- tata*) – Calif., S. Ore., Baja – and *volubilis*, snake lily, twining brodiaea – C. Calif.

The young, tender shoots can be eaten raw or cooked.

Endangered species: *B. coronaria* (m.a.) var. *rosea, filifolia, orcuttii* and *pallida* – all Calif.

Zephyranthes   (G 4)

From the Greek "zephyros," zephyr, west wind, and "anthos," flower.
S. U.S., Mex.
Some native species are planted as ornamentals under the name "zephyr lily."

The bulbs of *Z. atamasco*, Atamasco lily – S.E. U.S. – were reportedly eaten by the Creek Indians after cooking.

They are believed, however, to be toxic when raw and to produce the horse disease known as "staggers" in the Southeastern states.

IRIDACEAE

Iris   (E-H 3)   Iris, Flag

Greek name of an undetermined plant (possibly in this genus) from "iris," rainbow, and the name of the messenger of the Olympian gods.
Throughout. Both native and species introduced from Eurasia.
Several native (including *I. cristata*, crested iris – S.E. U.S), European and Asian species, as well as hybrids, are planted as ornamentals.

I. germanica (including var. *florentina* = *I. florentina*), orris – exact origin un- known, probably a hybrid –, *pallida* – from Italy and former Yugoslavia – and *pseudoacorus*, yellow flag – from Eurasia – are naturalized on our continent.

The dried rootstock of *I. germanica* (especially of var. *florentina*) and *pallida* (both m.a.), known as "orris root," has a delicate violet fragrance and is often used in perfumery as a fixative. Its aromatic properties have been known since Antiquity. The rhizome was occasionally used as a condiment and chewed as a breath freshener.

Orris root contains an essential oil, starch (50%), mucilage, tannin and a glucoside.

It is expectorant and diuretic. High doses can be emetic.

If the fresh rhizome is applied to a wound, it may cause fever and diarrhea.

I. germanica (m.a.) is the oldest of all cultivated irises.

The rootstocks of most *Iris* spp. are extremely acrid due to a resinous substance called "irisin." They are rubefacient, vesicant, emetic and purgative. They also contain a glucoside and, if ingested in large amounts, are toxic. Some people contract dermatitis from handling iris rhizomes.

However, the rootstock of *I. cristata* (m.a.) has occasionally been chewed or used as a spice; it has a sweetish taste at first, which is soon replaced by a burning sensation.

The starchy rhizomes of several species are eaten in Eastern Asia, and in some cases, the plants are cultivated on their account.

I. setosa – Alaska, also N.E. Asia – is grown in Japan for its edible rhizome under the name "hiôgi-ayame."

The seeds of *I. pseudoacorus* (m.a.) and *setosa* (m.a.) have been used as a coffee substitute after thorough roasting.

The rhizome of *I. pseudoacorus* (m.a.) is very irritating.

Iris leaves were often used as a source of fibers by Indians: the two outermost fibers of each leaf were spun into a very fine, strong, highly esteemed twine.

Endangered species: *I. tenax* var. *klamathensis* – Calif. – and *tenuis* – Ore.

Tigridia   (C 4)   Tiger Flower
From the Greek and Latin "tigris," tiger: petals and sepals are spotted.
Mex.

T. pavonia, cacomite, is sometimes grown for ornament.

The starchy rootstock of this species has long been used as food, and the plant has been cultivated for this since the time of the Aztecs. The rootstock is still eaten by certain Mexican tribes, generally after roasting or boiling. It is nutritious.

AGAVACEAE

In the following genera, the <u>flower stalk</u> is edible, but it must be kept in mind that its removal kills the plant.

Agave (B-C-H 4)   Agave, Century Plant, Maguey
From the Greek "agauos," admirable, marvelous, and from the early Spanish name given to the plant "arbol de maravillas."
S. U.S., Mex.
A few native species are grown for ornament in warm regions. The most commonly planted ornamental agave is *A. americana* – Mex. This species, along with several others (especially *A. atrovirens* – Mex.), is often cultivated in Mex. under the name "maguey," for making "pulque," tequila, and a sort of candy (see below).

The following species have been used as food: *A. americana* (m.a.), *atrovirens* (m.a.), *cantala* – Mex. –, *chrysantha* – Ariz., N.W. Mex. –, *complicata, crassipina* – both Mex. –, *deserti* – S. Calif., Ariz., Baja –, *palmeri* – Ariz., N.M., N. Mex. –, *parryi* – S.W. U.S., Mex. –, *scabra* (= *wislizeni*) – Tex., Mex. – and *utahensis* – S.W. U.S.

Agaves held an extremely important place in the economy of the ancient Mexicans and of the Indians of our Southwestern deserts. In Mexico, they have been in cultivation since the time of the Aztecs.

Agaves vary in size from quite small to giant (with leaves up to 7 or 8 feet long). If the latter are the most productive, the small species were not necessarily used as well.

Just before the flower stalks appear, the plant is dug up and all the leaves are chopped off at their base, leaving a cylindrical, white and pulpy <u>trunk</u>. This "crown" (or caudex) is cooked in a fire pit for several days if a large number of plants are prepared at the same time. It becomes brown, juicy and soft, and acquires a pleasant sweet taste, reminiscent of molasses. The flesh must be eaten off the fibers which are embedded in it.

Agave sp.

This cooked crown is still sold as candy in Mexican markets. Cut into slices and dried, it keeps for years.

This preparation is said to be antiscorbutic.

In Northern Mexico and Southwestern United States, cooked agave crowns were the main food of certain Indian tribes which traveled seasonally to gather wild agaves. They cooked a large quantity, feasted on all they could eat for several days and brought the rest back home for later use. Numerous agave roasting pits can be seen in Southwestern deserts. Even now, a small quantity of this traditional food is prepared by the Papagos.

A sweet juice can be expressed from the cooked crown. It was formerly boiled down into a syrup and sold in Mexican markets. Its principal use today is in the production of "mezcal." The cooked crown is mashed, mixed with water, left to ferment and then distilled. In older days, an adobe still was used for this purpose. Mezcal contains 50 to 55% alcohol. "Tequila" is a mezcal originally produced in the area around the town bearing that name in Central Mexico.

Mezcal is also the name of the roasted crown used as food. A pleasant drink can be made by dissolving pieces of mezcal in water and straining.

The tender parts of the young <u>leaf bud</u> at the top of the crown were also eaten after cooking.

The <u>leaves</u> contain acrid substances and saponins. They are rubefacient and vesicant. But they were occasionally cooked, chopped and their pulp was eaten off the fibers.

The unexpanded <u>flower stalk</u> (before the flowers begin to develop) is tender. It was cooked in a fire pit and pressed into cakes which were dried and stored. It has a pleasant sweet taste after cooking.

<u>Flower buds</u> and <u>flowers</u> were considered a delicate vegetable. They were generally boiled and often dried for later use.

<u>Nectar</u> was gathered from the flowers of certain species, such as *A. shawii* – Calif.

Agave <u>seeds</u> were ground into flour.

In the central plateau region of Mexico, the most important agave product is "pulque," a milky and mucilaginous fermented drink with a particular taste.

Just before the flower stalk starts to shoot, when the plant has accumulated the largest amount of food reserves, the bud is removed and a cavity is hollowed out in its place. A sweet liquid called "agua miel" (honey water) exudes from the cavity walls and is collected every day – traditionally with a gourd pierced at both ends named "acocote."

This juice readily ferments and in a day and a half yields the sweet pulque. After a few more days of fermentation, it becomes somewhat sour, having acquired its characteristic smell and flavor. At this stage it contains 3 to 5% alcohol.

The fresh juice is diuretic, emmenagogue and laxative. Pulque is stimulating and nutritious. It was formerly the staple beverage of Mexico.

The large-sized *A. atrovirens* (m.a.) is the main source of pulque today, but other species have been used. The plants are tapped when about 14 years old. More than a gallon per day can be gathered from each one for a period of four to five months, after which the plant dies.

Roots and leaves of *Agave* spp. contain saponins and were used as soap.

Mexicans and Southwestern Indians formerly used the leaves like tiles as a roof cover, as containers and as a source of fibers. The terminal spine of the leaf with fibers attached to it was used as a needle and thread. Fiber production is the most important commercial use of *Agave* spp. nowadays: certain species, especially sisal (*A. sisalana* – from Yucatan), are cultivated for this purpose on a large scale in tropical regions of the world. Outer fibers yield rope and paper pulp, while the inner ones can be made into cloth.

Agaves had still other uses. They were the source of a black pigment after the leaves were smoked. They were often planted in Mexico as a protective hedge.

A. lechuguilla – Tex., N.M. & N. Mex., occasionally planted for ornament – is known to be toxic. It contains both a photodynamic agent, causing the plant to be dangerous to animals exposed to sunlight after grazing on it, and a nephrotoxin. Sheep and goats have occasionally been poisoned.

A characteristic feature of most, but not all, agaves is the fact that they bloom only once in their life – when they are from five to twenty years old or more – and then die.

Endangered species: *A. arizonica, mckelveyana, schottii* var. *treleasei* and *toumeyana* var. *bella* – all Ariz.

Dasylirion (C 4) Sotol
From the Greek "dasys," hairy, tufted, and "leirion," lily.
Ariz. to Tex., Mex.

The crown (caudex) with the base of the leaves and the unexpanded flower stem in the bud stage were eaten by Indians after cooking in fire pits, as described for *Agave* spp. Plants of both genera were often prepared together.

Both the cooked crowns and the sap obtained from the bud are rich in sugar and were often fermented into a drink known as "sotol," which can be distilled to increase the alcohol content.

The following species have been used as food and beverage: *D. acrostichum*, *longissimum* – both Mex. –, *texanum* – Tex. – and *wheeleri* – Ariz. to W. Tex., Mex.

Nolina (C-H 4)   Bear Grass, Sacahuista
(including some *Dasylirion* spp.)
After C. P. Nolin, joint author of an agricultural essay in 1755.
Ariz. to Tex., Mex.

The crown (caudex) and the unexpanded flower stalk of *N. microcarpa* were cooked and eaten by local Indians in the same way as *Agave* spp.

The seeds have also been used as food.

N. texana – Tex. – is known to be toxic. Sheep and goats grazing on the plant may develop a disease with symptoms similar to those caused by *Agave lechuguilla* (see above).

Endangered species: *N. atopocarpa, brittoniana* – both Fla. – and *interrata* – Calif.

Yucca (B 4)   Yucca, Spanish Bayonet
Haitian name for *Manihot* spp..
S. U.S., Mex.
Several native species are planted as ornamentals, including the
following: *Y. baccata*, datil, banana yucca – S.W. U.S. –, *brevifolia*
(= *aborescens*), Joshua tree – S. Nev., N.W. Ariz., S.E. Calif. –, *filamentosa*,
Adam's needle – Md. to Ga. –, *glauca*, bear grass – C. & W. U.S. –,
gloriosa – S.E. U.S. – and *whipplei*, Our Lord's candle – Calif., N.
Baja.

Many *Yucca* spp. were used as food by Indians.

The flower stalk is edible before the inflorescence starts to develop. It was chopped and boiled or cooked in a fire pit. The tough rind is quite easy to remove after cooking. The stalk is naturally more tender while still young.

Flower buds and flowers may be added raw to salads, but only in moderation, as they tend to irritate the throat. They can be eaten with impunity after cooking, and were commonly roasted or boiled by Indians. They have a pleasant taste. The flowers were often dried and ground into a meal. A yucca flower soup in a thin tomato broth is sold in Guatemalan markets.

Several species bear fleshy fruits which are edible raw when ripe. Yucca fruits are very rich in sugar; their palatability depends on the species. Indians ate them fresh or dried and ground them, kneading them into cakes which were sundried. They also roasted them, boiled them down into a paste which could be dried or mashed them up, mixing them with water and letting them ferment into a drink. Yucca fruits can also be made into pies or breads.

Yuccas with fleshy fruits – botanically, berries, up to 5 inches (10 cm) or more – are collectively known as "datil."

The following species produce edible berries which were used as food by Indians: *Y. aloifolia* (= *Y. elephantipes*) – Mex. – (the fruit is rather bitter), *arizonica* – S. Ariz., N. Mex. –, *baccata* (m.a.) (it has probably the best fruit of all yuccas and was used extensively by Indians), *glauca* (m.a.), *macrocarpa* – Ariz. to Tex. –, *schidigera* (= *mohavensis*) – S. Calif., Nev., Ariz., Baja –, *schottii* – Ariz., N.M., N. Mex. –, *thornberryi* – S. Ariz. –, *treculeana* – S. Tex., Mex. – and *valida*.

The fruits of most other species are dry capsules, but they can be eaten raw or cooked when unripe and still tender. They are mucilaginous and have a pleasant taste.

The seeds of *Y. brevifolia, macrocarpa, whipplei* (all m.a.) and possibly other species were ground and eaten as mush by Indians.

The leaf base of certain yuccas is fleshy enough to be edible after cooking.

Flower stalks, buds, flowers and unripe capsules of several of the species previously described as bearing edible, fleshy fruits (berries) were also eaten by Indians. In addition, the following yuccas have been used as food: *Y. australis* – Mex. – and *brevifolia, filamentosa,* and *whipplei* (all m.a.).

The roots of *Y. gloriosa* (m.a.) have reportedly been used by Indians for making a kind of bread, but this statement is doubtful as yucca roots are very rich in saponin. They were commonly used as soap and shampoo by Indians under the name "amole." A piece of root is chopped up and mashed in a mortar with a small quantity of water until suds form. The mixture is then filtered and thoroughly worked through the hair, which it leaves glossy and clean after rinsing.

The leaves were a source of fibers used for making ropes, mats, sandals, bags and clothing. The terminal thorn, with its fibers attached, makes a convenient needle and thread.

The smallest of the semi-aerial roots of the Joshua tree (m.a.) are red and were used by Indians in basket making.

Yucca seeds are the unique food of the larvae of a small moth which gathers the pollen into a mass and pushes it onto the stigma, thus pollinating the flowers.

SMILACACEAE

Smilax (B 2-3)   Greenbrier, Greenbriar, Catbrier, Carrion Flower
Greek name of a Mediterranean species.
Throughout.

The fleshy <u>roots</u> of the following species were used as food by Indians: *S. auriculata* – Va. to Fla. & La. –, *beyrichii* – S.E. U.S. –, *bona-nox* – S.E. U.S., Mex. –, *glauca* – E. U.S. –, *hispida* (= *pseudo-china*, = *tamnoides*) – E. & C. U.S. –, *laurifolia* – E. U.S. – and *rotundifolia* – E. N.Am.

The young, tender roots were eaten after boiling or roasting.

Starch was frequently extracted from older roots. They were chopped up, pounded, mixed with water and strained over a container. After a while the starch settled to the bottom. It was gathered by carefully pouring off the water and was then dried and ground into flour.

Greenbrier starch is reddish in color. A small amount of it mixed with hot water produces a jelly to which honey can be added to improve the taste. If more water is used, the mixture makes a pleasant drink.

The starch can also be used as a soup thickener or mixed with cereal flour and made into cakes and breads.

The roots themselves served to make the original root beer. A piece of the fresh root boiled in water yields a reddish tea.

Greenbrier roots were called "contichatie" (red flour root) by Florida Indians, for whom it was an important food item.

The <u>young shoots</u> of most of our species are edible raw or cooked. They generally have a pleasant, mild taste somewhat reminiscent of asparagus; sometimes they have a slightly acid flavor. But in some cases the shoots are bitter and require cooking, possibly in a change of water.

The <u>fruits</u> of *S. herbacea*, carrion flower – E. & C. N.Am. – and *havanensis* – Fla., W.I. – have been eaten raw. They are sweet and quite pleasant, with a date-like flavor. Those of *S. bona-nox* (m.a.) have a rubbery texture and can be chewed like gum.

It must be noted that the berries of the European species (*S. aspera*) are toxic because of their saponin content.

<u>Roots</u>, <u>shoots</u> and <u>berries</u> of various species are used as food in Asia. In Japan, the shoots are often cooked and mixed with crushed nuts or seeds.

The roots of a few tropical American species are the source of "sarsaparilla," used medicinally as a depurative, diuretic and tonic and commercially to produce foaming in soft drinks and beer.

They contain an essential oil, starch, a resin and saponins.

DIOSCOREACEAE

Dioscorea (C 4) Yam
Commemorating Dioscorides, Greek naturalist and physician of the 1st century.
E. U.S., Mex. Both native and species introduced from Asia.
A tropical species is sometimes grown as a house plant in the U.S.
D. batatas, Chinese yam, cinnamon vine – originally from China – is often planted for ornament and for the cinnamon-like odor of its white blossoms; it is naturalized on our continent, especially in S.E. U.S.

The small, white, starchy, tuberous <u>roots</u> of this plant are very good to eat after cooking. In Japan, they are grated, beaten until viscous and poured over rice, making a dish known as "tororo imo." The grated root is also added to soups or eaten with vinegar, fish or eggs.

The shoots are said to be purgative.

D. bulbifera, air yam, air potato – originally from tropical Asia – is one of the few true yams cultivated for food in the United States, especially in the Southeast. (Varieties of sweet potatoes (*Ipomea batatas*, Convolvulaceae) with moist flesh are often called "yams" in North America, although they actually belong to a very different family.) The air yam is naturalized in Southern Florida and Mexico.

The plant produces both aerial and subterranean tuber-like roots. In some varieties, the roots are devoid of all bitterness, while in others, they are bitter and even considered to be toxic, especially the ones growing in the ground. These bitter roots are nonetheless used as food in various parts of the Tropics; the bitterness is removed by soaking the grated roots in lye water or by mixing them with water. They must subsequently be thoroughly washed and cooked.

The slender, tuberous rootstock of our native *D. villosa*, wild yam – E. U.S. – has been said to be edible.

It is used medicinally as a diuretic, diaphoretic and antispasmodic. High doses may be emetic.

The roots of innumerable species are used as food in the Tropics of both hemispheres, especially in Africa, Southeast Asia and Polynesia. They are a staple in Fiji and other Pacific islands.

ORCHIDACEAE

With 700 genera and 20,000 species, this is the largest family of flowering plants, although it is by far outnumbered by other families in terms of individual plants as most orchids are rare. It is especially abundant in the Tropics where orchids are generally epiphytes with large, showy flowers. In our regions, however, they are small terrestrial plants, usually with rather small, sometimes even inconspicuous, flowers (except for lady's slippers, *Cypripedium* spp.).

Many tropical species are cultivated in greenhouses for their flowers.

As for foodstuffs, this family yields vanilla, the well-known flavoring, and salep, a starch obtained from the tubers of some Mediterranean orchids, which is made into drinks and food for babies and invalids.

Although the rootstock of several of our species is edible, eating orchids or picking them for any other reason must definitely be discouraged because they are very rare plants.

Aplectrum hyemale (G 4) Putty Root
From the Greek "a," without, and "plectron," spur: alluding to the shape of the flowers.
N.E. & N.C. N.Am. A monotypic genus.

The <u>corm</u> has reportedly been eaten after cooking.

Calypso bulbosa (H 4) Deer Orchid, Fairy Slipper
After the mythological nymph Calypso.
N. N.Am. & Mountains. A monotypic genus.

The corm-like <u>root</u> has been used as food by certain Indians.

Goodyera (G 3) Rattlesnake Plantain
After John Goodyer (1592–1664), British botanist.
N. N.Am. & Mountains.

It has been reported that the sticky substance exuding from the <u>scape</u> of *G. oblongifolia* (= *G. menziesii*, = *Peramium decipiens*) – N. N.Am. & W. Mountains – was used like chewing gum.

All of our species are covered with glandular hairs on the scape, bracts, sepals and ovaries.

Habenaria (D 3) Bog Orchid, Rein Orchid
From the Greek "habenula," a narrow strap: alluding to the strap-shaped lip of some of the species.
Throughout.

The <u>roots</u> of *H. dilatata* and *sparsiflora* have occasionally been eaten. Those of local species are used as food in Southeastern Asia.

Vanilla (C 5)   Vanilla
From the Spanish "bainilla," small pod: referring to the fruit.
S. Fla., E. Mex.
V. planifolia (= *V. fragrans*) – S. Fla., E. Mex. & tropical Am. – is cultivated
in tropical regions of both hemispheres (mostly in Reunion, Seychelles,
Madagascar, Tahiti and Java) for its <u>fruits</u>, the source of commercial
vanilla. Green to begin with, the long pods are dried and fermented
through an exacting process to yield the well-known black vanilla
"beans."
Vanilla was cultivated by Indians before European settlers came to America. Outside the native range of the plant, it is necessary to pollinate the
flowers by hand because of the absence of a local insect which is their exclusive pollinator under natural conditions.
The wild plant yields a smaller and less aromatic pod, known in Latin
America as "baynilla cimarona."

Vanilla is indispensable for flavoring ice cream, confectionery, chocolate,
desserts, liqueurs (crème de vanille), tobacco and other unusual things. Either
the beans themselves or the alcohol in which they have been macerated (vanilla
extract) are employed for this purpose. Unfortunately, in many cases natural
vanilla flavoring is much more expensive.

The fermented pods are covered with a crystalline efflorescence (technically
known as "givre," which means "frost" in French) containing vanillin, which
gives vanilla its particular fragrance. Vanillin is also found in raw sugar. It is soluble in alcohol, boiling water, oil and ether.

Besides vanillin, the pods contain a fixed oil (11%), a resin (2%), sugar, oxalate of lime and vanillic acid (odorless).

The fruits of several other species are used for flavoring food in tropical
America and Southeastern Asia. Some are commercialized and used as a source
of vanillin.

Glossary of Botanical and Medical Terms 🐝

List of Abbreviations

n.: noun
adj.: adjective
v.: verb
*: see this word in the glossary

ABORTIVE (n., adj.): interrupting pregnancy, causing the premature expulsion of a fetus.

ACETIC FERMENTATION*: transformation of an alcoholic liquid into vinegar, containing acetic acid (CH_3–COOH), caused by bacteria (*Mycoderma aceti*). This fermentation occurs only in the presence of oxygen.

ACETYLCHOLINE (n.): acetic ester* of choline*: $(CH_3)_3$ N(OH)–CH_2-CH_2-O-CO-CH_3.

ACHENE (n.): dry, indehiscent* fruit, in which the seed is attached to the inner wall only at the seed stalk.

ACRID (adj.): pungent and irritating.

ADVENTIVE (adj.): introduced,* but not yet fully naturalized.*

ALCOHOLIC FERMENTATION*: transformation of glucose* ($C_6H_{12}O_6$) into ethyl alcohol (CH_3–CH_2–OH), caused by yeasts. Carbon dioxide (CO_2) is liberated in the process. This fermentation occurs only in the absence of oxygen.

ALDEHYDE (n.): organic compound formed by the oxidation (removal of hydrogen atoms) of an alcohol, characterized by a -CHO group.

ALKALINE (adj.): having the properties of an alkali, a substance able to accept a proton.

ALLANTOIN (n.): one of the products of the oxidation of uric acid ($C_4H_6N_4O_3$).

535

ALTERATIVE (n.): a medicine that alters the processes of nutrition and excretion, restoring the normal body functions.

ALUM (n.): sulfate of potassium and aluminum ($A_1 K (SO_4)_2-1_2H_2O$).

AMINO ACID (n.): any organic compound containing both an amino group ($n.H_2$) and a carboxylic group (COOH). In particular, a compound of the form $R-CNH_2-COOH$, found as a component of the protein* molecule.

   Nine amino acids are called "essential amino acids" since the body cannot synthesize them; they must thus be provided by food. These essential amino acids are: cystine, isoleucine, leucine, lysine, methionine, phenylalalnine, threonine, tryptophane and valine.

ANALEPTIC (n., adj.): restoring strength and health.

ANALGESIC (n., adj.): soothing or relieving pain.

ANAPHRODISIAC (n., adj.): reducing sexual desire.

ANGIOSPERM (n.): plant bearing its ovules* within an enclosed pistil cell (ovary).

ANNUAL (n., adj.): of only one season's growth from seed to maturity and death.

ANODYNE: see ANALGESIC.

ANTHELMINTIC (n., adj.): expelling worms.

ANTHER (n.): the pollen-bearing part of a stamen, generally found at the top of a filament.

ANTHESIS (n.): the time of opening of a flower.

ANTIALLERGIC (n., adj.): helping to suppress allergies (pathological reactions to specific substances in amounts that do not affect most people).

ANTI-ANEMIC (n., adj.): fighting anemia. Anemia is a pathological deficiency in the oxygen-carrying material of the blood.

ANTIBIOTIC (n., adj.): inhibiting the growth of or destroying certain micro-organisms.

ANTICOAGULANT (n., adj.): preventing blood clotting.

ANTIECCHYMOTIC (n., adj.): helping to dissolve ecchymosis (effusions of blood into subcutaneous tissues, causing bluish spots or bruises on the skin).

ANTI-EPILEPTIC (n., adj.): useful in cases of epilepsy (nervous system disease characterized by loss of consciousness and convulsions).

ANTIGALACTIC (n., adj.): reducing or stopping the secretion of milk.

ANTIHYPERTENSIVE (n., adj.): lowering blood pressure.

ANTILITHIASIC (n., adj.): helping to dissolve "stones," concretions forming in various organs.

ANTIPHLOGISTIC (n., adj.): reducing inflammation (localized heat, redness, swelling and pain as a result of irritation, injury or infection).

ANTIPUTREFACTIVE (n., adj.): preventing putrefaction (organic decomposition, decay).

ANTISCORBUTIC (n., adj.): preventing or fighting scurvy, a disease due to a lack of vitamin C, characterized by spongy and bleeding gums, bleeding under the skin and extreme weakness.

ANTISEPTIC (n., adj.): destroying the microorganisms which cause disease or putrefaction.

ANTISPASMODIC (n., adj.): counteracting or curing spasms (sudden, involuntary muscular contractions).

ANTISUDORAL (n., adj.): diminishing perspiration.

ANTITUSSIVE (n., adj.): soothing coughs.

ANTIVENOMOUS (adj.): allaying the detrimental effects of the venom of snakes and other animals.

ANTIVITAMIN (n.): a substance which prevents a vitamin from playing its part in bodily reactions.

APERITIF (n.): an alcoholic beverage taken before a meal.

APERITIVE (n., adj.): stimulating the appetite.

APPETIZER (n.): a food or drink served before a meal to stimulate the appetite.

APHRODISIAC (n., adj.): arousing or exciting sexual desire or potency.

ARIL (n.): a fleshy appendage growing at or near the point of attachment of a seed.

AROMATHERAPY (n.): treatment of diseases by using the essential oils extracted from plants.

AROMATIC (adj.): having a pleasant, often spicy fragrance.

ARTHRITIS (n.): inflammation of a joint.

ASPARAGIN (n.): substance found in various plants as a NH_2 reserve/spartic acid monoamine $(n.H_2$–CO–CH_2–CH$(n.H_2)$–COOH).

ASTRINGENT (n., adj.): contracting organic tissues and reducing discharges.

AWN (n.): a stiff, bristle-like appendage.

BACTERICIDAL (adj.), BACTERICIDE (n.): destroying bacteria.

BALLAST (n.): in our case, any heavy material, such as rocks or soil, placed in the hold of a ship to enhance stability.

BALSAMIC (adj.): having an aromatic odor reminiscent of balsam, a resinous substance with healing and soothing properties, exuding from various trees.

BARK (n.): the tough external covering of a woody perennial* stem or root, exterior to the cork cambium.*

BECHIC (n., adj.): see ANTITUSSIVE.

BERRY (n.): a soft, fleshy fruit in which the numerous small seeds are disseminated throughout the pulp.

BETAIN (n.): a substance found in various plants, formed by oxidation (loss of hydrogen) of choline* ($C_5H_{11}NO_2$).

BIENNIAL (n., adj.): of two seasons' growth, from seed to maturity and death, typically blooming and fruiting during the second season.

BLANCH (v.): (1) to boil in water for less than a minute in order to tenderize, to remove acridity or bitterness. (2) to render parts of a plant white by piling dirt around the young shoots (such as asparagus, endive, etc.) so that their texture becomes more tender and their taste less pronounced.

BLOOD PURIFIER (n.): see DEPURATIVE.

BOLT (v.): to partially sift a flour in order to remove some of the bran.

BRACT (n.): a more or less modified or reduced leaf subtending the flowers in an inflorescence.*

BRINE (n.): water containing large amounts of a salt, especially of sodium chloride (n.aCl).

BUD (n.): an undeveloped or rudimentary stem, branch or unexpanded flower.

BULB (n.): a globular, dormant bud,* usually subterranean, in which the leaves are thickened with reserve food material. Mostly found within the Monocotyledonae.

BULBLET (n.): small bulb* borne singly or clustered, either subterranean or aerial (then associated with the flowers or the leaves).

BUTYRIC ACID (n.): oily substance with an unpleasant and very tenacious smell, found primarily in butter and in sweat (C_3H_7–COOH).

CACTIFORM (adj.): resembling a cactus in appearance.

CALMATIVE (n., adj.): see SEDATIVE.

CALTROP (n.): a several-pointed iron ball used for maiming horses in medieval wars.

CALYX (n.): the outer envelope of a flower, formed by the sepals.*

CAMBIUM (n.): cellular tissue in which annual growth of wood and bark occurs. This is the living part of the trunk of a tree.

CANE (n.): in our case, a slender, flexible stem, from the bushes in the genus *Rubus* (Rosaceae), springing directly from the base of the plant.

CAPSULE (n.): a dry, dehiscent* fruit composed of more than one carpel,* opening at maturity by valves or teeth.

CARBOHYDRATE (n.): any organic compound containing carbon, hydrogen and oxygen, having the general formula $Cx(H_2O)y$. Among carbohydrates are found the various sugars, starches and cellulose.

CARDIOACTIVE (adj.): having an action upon the heart.

CARDIOTONIC (n., adj.): stimulating the heart.

CARDIOTOXIC GLUCOSIDE*: specific substance able to disturb the normal functioning of the heart even in moderate doses. Very small quantities are often used medicinally to treat heart problems.

CARDIOVASCULAR (adj.): relating to the heart and the blood vessels.

CARMINATIVE (n., adj.): expelling gas from the intestine.

CAROTENE (n.): an orange-yellow to red hydrocarbon (organic compound containing only carbon and hydrogen), occurring in many plants and converted to vitamin A in the animal liver (C_4OH_{56}).

CARPEL (n.): an enrolled seed-bearing leaf, the female organ of the flower, composed of the ovary,* the style* and the stigma.*

CARUNCLE (n.): excrescence at or near the hilum* of certain seeds.

CARUNCULAR (adj.): pertaining to a caruncle.

CARYOPSIS (n.): dry, indehiscent* fruit, in which the seed is completely attached to the inner wall.

CATHARTIC (n., adj.): strongly purgative.*

CATKIN (n.): hanging spike of small, petal-less, unisexual (either male or female) flowers, densely clustered along the axis of the inflorescence.* Characteristic of a few families of trees and shrubs. Also called "ament."

CAUDEX (n.): the persistent base of an otherwise annual herbaceous stem.

CAUSTIC (adj.): able to burn, corrode.

CEREAL (n.): an edible grain, most generally but not always, of a plant in the Poaceae (Graminae).

CHAPPARAL (n.): shrubby vegetation-type characteristic of Mediterranean climates (dry summers, relatively wet winters) as in California.

CHLOROPHYLL (n.): green pigment unique to plants, found mostly in the leaves. Chlorophyll is essential in photosynthesis (the transformation of carbon dioxide and water into carbohydrates and oxygen by plants, using light energy). The molecular structure of chlorophyll is close to that of hemoglobin,* with an atom of magnesium in chlorophyll replacing the atom of iron in hemoglobin.

CHOLAGOGUE (n., adj.): promoting the flow of bile.

CHOLERETIC (n., adj.): increasing the secretion of bile.

CHOLINE (n.): substance necessary to the liver in order to use lipids,* (CH_2-OH-CH_2-N(CH_3)$_3$ OH).

CIRCUMPOLAR (adj.): occurring in cold regions of the Northern hemisphere — North America, Europe and Asia.

CITRIC ACID (n.): organic acid, frequently found in plants, especially in fruits of the genus *Citrus* (Rutaceae).

COAGULANT (adj.): inducing clotting of the blood.

CONDIMENT (n.): aromatic substance used for enhancing the flavor of food.

CONJUNCTIVITIS (n.): inflammation of the conjunctiva (mucous membrane lining the inner surface of the eyelid and the exposed surface of the eyeball).

CORM (n.): short, thick underground stem, bulb-like but solid.

CORONA (n.): any appendage standing, in the flower, between the petals and the stamens.

CORRICIDE (n., adj.): helpful in removing corns (local thickenings and indurations of the skin, as on the toes).

CORTEX (n.): a layer of tissue in roots and stems lying between the epidermis and the vascular tissue.

COSMOPOLITAN (adj.): found in all parts of the world.

COUMARIN (n.): substance having a characteristic, pleasant smell (somewhat reminiscent of vanilla), found in the form of glucosides* in various plants such as tonka bean, sweet clover and woodruff ($C_9H_6O_2$).

COUMAROU (n.): the Guyanese name of *Coumarouna odorata* (Fabaceae), the source of tonka beans, used as a fixative* in perfumery.

CROWN (n.): the part of a plant just above the surface of the ground, formed by the lower portion of the basal leaves and of the stem.

CULM (n.): the hollow, jointed stem of grasses and sedges.

CULTIVAR (n.): a cultivated variety of a given plant species.

CYANOGENETIC GLUCOSIDE*: any of a definite group of substances able to release hydrocyanic acid* by hydrolysis.

DECOCTION (n.): (1) action of boiling various plant parts in water for a given amount of time. (2) the resulting preparation. This process is used for extracting mineral salts, bitter principles and active substances contained in roots, bark and stems, sometimes in leaves, and which cannot be obtained by infusion.*

DEFOLIANTS (n.): toxic chemical substances provoking the death of trees and other plants by causing their leaves to fall off. Defoliants are used to destroy broad-leaved trees competing with conifers in commercial forests. Some of these chemicals, such as 2-4 D and 2-4-5 T (used during the Vietnam war to defoliate the jungle) are known to produce miscarriages and malformations of the fetus. Numerous cases have been documented in Western North America where drinking water has been contaminated with defoliants.

DEHISCENT (adj.): splitting open at maturity to liberate its contents, as in the case of a fruit.

DEMULCENT (n., adj.): soothing, allaying irritation, particularly of a mucous membrane, thanks to a mucilaginous* texture.

DEPRESSANT (n. adj.): diminishing functional activity.

DEPURATIVE (n., adj.): cleansing, purifying the human organism.

DERMATITIS (n.): inflammation of the skin.

DETERGENT (n.): an agent used for cleansing wounds and ulcers, thus helping them to heal.

DETERSIVE (adj.): adjective corresponding to detergent.*

DETOXICANT (n., adj.): eliminating toxins from the organism.

DIAPHORETIC (n., adj.): producing perspiration.

DICOTYLEDON (n.): a flowering plant having an embryo with two equal seed-leaves or cotyledons.

DIGESTIVE (n., adj.): aiding digestion.

DIGITATE (adj.): compound, with the divisions spreading from the top of the support, like the fingers of the hand.

DISINFECTANT (n., adj.): preventing or fighting infection (invasion of a part of the body by pathogenic* micro-organisms).

DISTILLATION (n.): process by which a liquid is vaporized under the action of heat and its vapors condensed so that its different components can be separated. This is used for obtaining essential oils or to concentrate alcohol and flavors.

DIURETIC (n., adj.): increasing the flow of urine.

DRASTIC (n., adj.): violently effective. In particular, a powerful purgative,* stronger than a cathartic,* irritating the mucous membrane* lining the intestines.

DRUPE (n.): a fleshy or pulpy fruit with a hard pit or "kernel" (the inner portion of the ripened ovary which has become woody).

DRUPLET (n.): a small drupe.

DRYING OIL (n.): an oil which dries rapidly and leaves a thin, resinous film. Drying oils such as linseed oil are often used for making paints.

EAR (n.): the seed-bearing spike* of a cereal* plant, such as corn or wheat.

ECOLOGY (n.): study of the interactions between living organisms and their natural environment.

ECOTYPE (n.): subdivision of a species, related to particular environmental conditions, but not to a given geographical area.

EDEMA (n.): excessive accumulation of serous (serum-like) fluid in the tissues.

EFFLORESCENCE (n.): a hydrated salt assuming a powdery appearance, due to spontaneous loss of water. This occurs when the aqueous tension of the hydrate is greater than the partial pressure of the water vapor in the air.

EMBRYO (n.): the undeveloped, dormant plantlet within the seed.

EMETIC (n., adj.): causing vomiting.

EMMENAGOGUE (n., adj.): stimulating and regulating menstrual flow.

EMOLLIENT (n., adj.): said of an agent used externally to soften tissues.

ENDEMIC (n., adj.): native to and restricted to a small area.

ENDOCRINIAN (n., adj.): related to the endocrine glands (any of the ductless glands such as the thyroid or adrenal, the secretions of which pass directly into the bloodstream from the cells of the gland).

ENDOSPERM (n.): the reserve food-storage tissue of many seeds, external to the embryo.

ENERGIZING (adj.): giving energy (the ability to work).

ENFLEURAGE (n.): extraction of delicate perfumes by placing flowers in contact with a solid fat such as purified lard.

ENZYME (n.): any of numerous proteins produced by living organisms, functioning as a biocatalyst (a substance able to cause or increase the speed of certain chemical reactions taking place in living organisms, without being modified itself).

EPIPHYTE (n.): an "air plant," growing on another plant (generally a tree), but not parasitic* upon it. Epiphytes are common in dense, wet tropical forests.

EPIPHYTIC (adj.): adjective corresponding to epiphyte.*

ESCAPE (n.): a cultivated plant which is able to reproduce, without human's help, for a certain time in an area where it is not native, but which is not fully naturalized.*

ESCULENT (adj.): edible.

ESSENTIAL OIL: volatile, odoriferous oil contained in aromatic plants. These oils are complex mixtures of various principles. Essential oils are obtained by distillation,* rarely by pressure (from the rinds of *Citrus* fruits, for example) or by enfleurage.* They are generally liquid, may be colored or colorless, soluble in alcohol but not in water.

ESTABLISHED (to become): term used to designate the fact that a plant is able to reproduce itself from generation to generation while becoming naturalized.*

ESTER (n.): substance resulting from the action of an acid upon an alcohol, with the elimination of a molecule of water.

ESTROGEN (n.): any of several steroid hormones produced chiefly by the ovary, allowing fertility in female mammals.

EXCITANT (n., adj.): stimulating the nervous system.

EXPECTORANT (n., adj.): promoting the discharge of mucus from the respiratory passages.

EXPRESS (v.): to press out, as in making juice.

FACULTATIVE SELENIUM ABSORBER: a plant able to concentrate dangerous amounts of selenium from soils rich in this element. These plants are harmless when growing on other soils.

FASCICLED ROOTS: root system made up of numerous roots of similar size growing in all directions; the opposite of "taproot."*

FATTY ACIDS: any of a large group of organic acids having the general formula CnH_{2n+1}-COOH. They are termed "fatty" due to their physical character (water repellent, oily consistency and so on). Lipids* are made of fatty acids. Unsaturated fatty acids (linoleic, linolenic and arachidonic acids) are necessary for the human organism to function properly and are known collectively as "vitamin F."

FEBRIFUGE (n., adj.): reducing fever.

FERMENTATION (n.): chemical splitting of complex organic compounds into relatively simple substances, occurring when certain organic matters are placed in contact with specific agents under determined conditions. Alcoholic* fermentation is the most common type.

FIXATIVE (n.): substance used in perfumery for fixing odors.

FIXED OIL: a fat which is liquid at room temperature. Fixed oils are extracted from seeds and fruits or rarely from the roots of certain plants. There are animal oils as well. As opposed to essential oils, fixed oils are not volatile and have little smell, or at least cannot be considered aromatic. These oils are soluble in alcohol but not in water.

FLAVONOIDS (n.): substances derived from cyclic hydrocarbons and analogous to phenol (C_6H_5OH), a yellow substance derived from benzene (C_6H_6). The name comes from the Latin "flavus," yellow.

FLOWER HEAD: the flower-bearing top of a stem.

FORMIC ACID: a colorless, caustic acid, (H-COOH).

FROND (n.): the leaf of ferns, palms and some other plants. In the case of ferns, it often bears fructifications.

FRUCTIFICATION (n.): the reproductive organs of a plant, especially of ferns.

FRUIT (n.): mature ovary* bearing one or several seeds, with all the other remaining floral parts. In common language, the word "fruit" is generally used to designate the sweet and fleshy production of certain plants succeeding the flower. This use often coincides with the botanical definition, but corn "kernels," wheat "berries," sunflower or cumin "seeds," green beans, eggplants, zucchinis and such are actually fruits. On the other hand, strawberries, raspberries, rosehips, figs, pineapples and such are not true fruits.

FUSIFORM (adj.): spindle-shaped.

GALACTAGOGUE (n., adj.): stimulating the production of milk.

GALL (n.): a swelling of plant tissues, often on leaves, usually due to insect parasites, fungi or bacteria.

GALLIC ACID: organic acid contained in the tannin of oak galls* and in various other plants. It is used for tanning hides, and was formerly used in photography.

GASTRIC (adj.): pertaining to the stomach.

GASTROENTERITIS (n.): inflammation of the stomach and of the intestines.

GASTROINTESTINAL (adj.): pertaining to the stomach and to the intestines.

GENUS (n.): group of species* having certain characters in common. Plural: GENERA.

GLANDULAR (adj.): covered with small glands (organs of secretion).

GLOCHID (n.): tiny hooked barbs on certain cacti (*Opuntia* spp.).

GLUCIDE (n.): see CARBOHYDRATE.

GLUCOSE (n.): the most common simple sugar* ($C_6H_{12}O_6$) produced by photosynthesis in all green plants. Glucose has a sweet taste. It ferments readily to yield alcohol if diluted in water to a proper concentration.

GLUCOSIDE (n.): substance in which a heterogeneous, nonglucidic part (genine) is linked to one or several sugars.*

GLUME (n.): a chaff-like empty bract* at the base of the spikelet of grasses and sedges.

GLYCEMIA (n.): level of sugar in the blood.

GOUT (n.): a disturbance of the uric acid metabolism occurring predominantly in males and marked by very painful attacks of arthritis.*

GRAIN (n.): dry fruit* of small size, in particular, caryopsis* of the Poaceae (Graminae).

GYMNOSPERM (n.): plant bearing naked ovules,* without an ovary.

HALLUCINOGEN (n.), HALLUCINOGENIC (adj.): inducing hallucinations.

HALOPHYTE (n.), HALOPHYTIC (adj.): growing in a saline or alkaline habitat, "salt-loving."

HEMOGLOBIN (n.): the coloring matter of red blood cells, an iron-containing protein* serving as an oxygen carrier.

HEMOLYSIS (n.): breaking up of the wall of red blood cells, thus freeing hemoglobin* and preventing the transportation of oxygen.

HEMOLYTIC (n., adj.): causing hemolysis.

HEMOSTATIC (n., adj.): stopping bleeding.

HEPATIC (adj.): pertaining to the liver.

HEPATOTOXIC (n., adj.): toxic to the liver.

HERB (n.): (1) a plant with no persistent woody stem above the ground. (2) an often aromatic plant used as seasoning or in medicine.

HERBACEOUS PLANT (n.): see HERB (1).

HILUM (n.): the scar or point of attachment of a seed.

HISTAMINE (n.): a white crystalline compound found in most animal and some plant tissues. It plays a part in such allergies as urticaria and asthma (n.=CH-NH-CH=C-CH$_2$-CH$_2$-NH$_2$).

HORMONE (n.): a chemical substance produced by an endocrine* gland which, passing into the bloodstream and reaching a functionally associated organ, is capable of exciting the latter to activity.

HORTICULTURAL VARIETY: an artificial variety* of a species* obtained through cultivation and selection.

HYBRID (n.): the natural or artificial offspring of genetically dissimilar parents, as that of plants of different species* or varieties;* rarely of different genera.*

HYDROCYANIC ACID: the first term in the series of nitriles* (HCN). This acid is very toxic: it inhibits certain respiratory ferments and can cause death by asphyxiation. But if present only in small quantities, it is easily eliminated thanks to the amino acids in the body.

HYDROLYSIS (n.): decomposition of a chemical compound by reaction with water.

HYDROLYZED (adj.): having been submitted to hydrolysis.

HYPERACIDITY (n.): excessive acidity.

HYPERTENSION (n.): abnormally high arterial blood pressure.

HYPERTENSOR (n.), HYPERTENSIVE (adj.): causing hypertension.

HYPERTHYROIDISM (n.): abnormal condition caused by an excessive functional activity of the thyroid gland.

HYPNOTIC (n., adj.): inducing sleep.

HYPOTENSOR (n.), HYPOTENSIVE (adj.): lowering blood pressure.

INDEHISCENT (adj.): said of a fruit that does not split open at maturity; persistently closed.

INDIGENOUS (adj.): native to an area.

INFERIOR OVARY: an ovary* which is united with the calyx.*

INFLORESCENCE (n.): a flower cluster.

INFUSION (n.): (1) action of pouring almost boiling water over plants and steeping for a few minutes. (2) the resulting brew. Infusions are employed when most of the volatile substances contained in the flowers and leaves are to be preserved, or when fewer minerals and bitter principles as would be extracted by decoction* are to be used.

INNER BARK: see CAMBIUM.

INSECTICIDE (n.): a substance used to kill insects.

INSULIN (n.): a pancreatic hormone that regulates carbohydrate metabolism (physical and chemical processes involved in the maintenance of life) by controlling the blood glucose level.

INTRODUCED (adj.): brought from another part of the world.

INULIN (n.): carbohydrate polymeric* of fructose, mostly found in the Asteraceae ($C_6H_{10}O_5$). This sugar is easily assimilated, even by diabetics.

INVERTED SUGAR: saccharose* partially hydrolyzed* into glucose* and levulose.*

INVOLUCRAL (adj.): referring to the involucre.*

INVOLUCRE (n.): a circle of bracts surrounding a single flower or more often a flower cluster, as in the heads of the Asteraceae or the umbels* of the Apiaceae.

IRRITANT (n., adj.): producing irritation (inflammation and uncomfortable sensations).

ISOMER (n.): a compound having the same percentage composition and molecular weight as another compound, but differing in chemical or physical properties.

LACRYMOGEN (adj.): producing tears.

LACTIC FERMENTATION: transformation of milk sugar, lactose ($C_{12}H_{22}O_{11}$), into lactic acid (CH_3-CHOH-COOH). This fermentation occurs only in the absence of oxygen. Sauerkraut, yogurt, kefir and so on are produced by lactic fermentation.

LANCEOLATE (adj.): shaped like a lance head, several times longer than wide, broadest above the base and tapering to both ends.

LATEX (n.): the milky, viscous sap of certain trees and herbaceous plants.

LAXATIVE (n., adj.): causing evacuation of the bowel contents; mildly purgative.*

LEAF (n.): a usually green, flattened plant structure attached to a stem and functioning as a principal organ of photosynthesis (formation by the plant of carbohydrates and oxygen from carbon dioxide and water, using light energy).

LEAFLET (n.): a single division of a compound leaf.

LECITHIN (n.): a phosphorized substance occurring in various animal and plant tissues, such as egg yolk, fish roe and soybeans ($C_{44}N_{90}NPO_9$).

LEES (pl. n): dregs, the sediment of a liquid.

LEGUME (n.): (1) a plant in the Fabaceae (Leguminosae). (2) the pod or seed of such a plant, especially when used as food.

LEUCORRHEA (n.): a whitish discharge from the vagina, either mucous (normal) or mucopurulent (sign of internal infection).

LEVULOSE (n.): levogyre glucose (deviating to the left the polarization plane of light).

LINEAR (adj.): long and narrow with almost parallel sides, such as blades of grasses.

LIPID (n.): substance containing fatty acids in the form of esters* or amides (organic compounds obtained by dehydration of ammoniacal salts); a fat or an oil. Lipids are classified according to the molecule linked to the fatty acids. They are soluble in organic solvents, but not in water.

LITHIASIS (n.): the formation of stones in the body.

MACERATION (n.): (1) action of steeping plant parts in cold or lukewarm water, usually for several hours. (2) the resulting brew. Macerations are used to extract only the most soluble and volatile substances contained in plants. They generally have a light, pleasant, nonbitter taste.

MACHETE (n.): a large, broad-bladed knife used especially for cutting vegetation.

MACROBIOTIC (adj.): literally "pertaining to the great life." The macrobiotic system is based on the understanding of the universal laws governing all phenomena. A particular diet is one of the manifestations of this philosophy.

MALIC ACID: organic acid frequently found in fruits, especially before they are totally ripe (COOH-CH_2-CHOH-COOH).

MATURATIVE (n., adj.): hastening the ripening (formation of pus) in boils and abscesses.

MELLIFEROUS (adj.): secreting a nectar gathered by bees for making honey.

MENTHOL (n.): a white crystalline compound with a refreshing fragrance, found in oil of peppermint and used in perfumes, as a mild anesthesic and as a flavoring ($C_{10}H_{19}OH$).

MONOCOTYLEDON (n.): a plant having an embryo with one conspicuous seed-leaf or cotyledon.

MONOTYPIC GENUS (n.): genus* with only one species.*

MORDANT (n.): substance with which a textile fiber or a cloth is impregnated before being dyed so that the color of the dye will be fast.

MUCILAGE (n.): vegetable substance that swells in contact with water, taking on a viscous consistency and thus acquiring adhesive and demulcent* properties.

MUCILAGINOUS (adj.): having the nature of a mucilage,* viscous.

MUCOUS MEMBRANE: a very thin membrane lining all bodily channels that come in contact with the air. Their glands secrete mucus.

MYDRIATIC (n., adj.): causing the dilation of the pupil.

NARCOTIC (n., adj.): inducing drowsiness, sleep or insensibility. Narcotics become addictive with prolonged use.

NATURALIZED (adj.): said of an introduced* plant which has become established in the wild, reproducing itself naturally from generation to generation.

NEPHROTOXIN (n.): a substance toxic to the kidneys.

NERVINE (n.): a substance that calms nervous excitement.

NITRATE (n.): a salt or ester of nitric acid (HNO_3): (R-NO_3).

NITRE (also NITER) (n.): a white, gray or colorless mineral of potassium nitrate, also named saltpeter (KNO_3); used in making gunpowder.

NITRILE (n.): a compound of nitrogen with a trivalent radical (R-CN).

NITRITE (n.): a salt or ester of nitrous acid (HNO_2): ($R-NO_2$).

NODE (n.): the joint of a stem at which leaves are normally inserted.

NODULE (n.): a small, knotlike protuberance, especially in the roots of certain Fabaceae where they contain nitrogen-fixing bacteria.

NUT (n.): a hard-shelled, indehiscent* fruit, one-seeded by abortion of one or several ovules.*

NUTRITIOUS (n.): aiding growth and development when used in suitable quantities; nourishing.

OFFICINAL (adj.): plant or preparation formerly for sale by pharmacists; listed in a pharmacopoeia (reference book containing a list of drugs with directions for their use).

OIL (n.): a slippery, viscous substance, liquid at room temperature, soluble in various organic solvents, but not in water. See ESSENTIAL OIL and FIXED OIL.

OIL CAKE (n.): the residue left after pressing out the oil of seeds, fruits and such.

OINTMENT (n.): a soft mixture of fat and medicinal substances to be used externally, also called "unguent." See POULTICE.

OPERCULE (n.): a lip or cap; the upper portion of certain capsules.

ORGANIC (adj.): of or derived from living organisms.

OVARY (n.): an ovule*-bearing modified leaf, part of the pistil of a flower, ripening into a fruit.*

OVULE (n.): a minute plant structure that after fertilization becomes a seed.*

OXALATE (n.): a salt of oxalic acid.*

OXALIC ACID (n.): a crystalline organic acid, toxic in high doses, found in various plants ($C_2H_2O_4$-$2H_2O$). Combined with calcium salts, oxalic acid yields calcium oxalate, a strongly irritant substance. It can cause gastroenteritis* and inhibits the intestinal absorption of calcium.

OXIDATION (n.): (1) the combination of a substance with oxygen. (2) a reaction in which the atoms in an element lose electrons.

OXYTOCIC (n., adj.): promoting uterine contractions and hastening childbirth.

PANICLE (n.): a loose, irregularly compound inflorescence in which each flower is borne on a pedicel.*

PAPPUS (n.): the modified calyx* of Asteraceae forming a crown having various characters such as bristles, hairs, scales, teeth at the summit of the achene.*

PARASITE (n.): an often harmful organism living on and deriving its subsistence from another living organism.

PARASITIC (adj.): adjective corresponding to parasite.*

PARASITICIDE (n.): a substance that destroys parasites.*

PARBOIL (v.): to boil in water for a brief period to remove bitterness, toxic substances and so on.

PATHOGENIC (adj.): capable of causing disease.

PEAT (n.): partially carbonized moss or other vegetable matter found in bogs and occasionally used as fuel.

PECTIN (n.): mucilaginous, colloidal (insoluble in water where it becomes dispersed in the form of tiny particles) substances of high molecular weight, found in certain ripe fruits such as apples, quince and so on. Pectin is used for jelling various foods, drugs and cosmetics.

PECTORAL (n., adj.): in our case beneficial for chest afflictions.

PEDICEL (n.): a small stem bearing a flower in an inflorescence.*

PEDUNCLE (n.): a small stem bearing an inflorescence or a solitary flower.

PELTATE (adj.): (of a leaf) shield or umbrella-shaped, the petiole* being attached to the surface of the leaf, inside the margin.

PEMMICAN (n.): a high-energy food made by Indians, prepared by pounding a mixture of dried fat meat and various berries into a paste.

PEPSIN (n.): a digestive enzyme found in gastric* juice.

PERENNIAL (n., adj.): said of a plant having a life span of more than two years.

PERIANTH (n.): the floral envelope; commonly used for flowers in which there is no clear distinction between petals* and sepals,* as in the Liliaceae.

PERICARP (n.): the ripened walls of the ovary* which has become a fruit.

PERISTALSIS (n.): wavelike muscular contractions that push the content of the intestines forward throughout the intestinal canal.

PETAL (n.): a modified leaf, often attractively colored. The union of the petals forms the corolla, the inner part of the floral envelope, placed between the calyx* and the reproductive organs of the flower.

PETIOLE (n.): narrowed part of a leaf, connecting the stem and the leaf surface; a leaf stalk.

PHOTODYNAMIC (adj.): becoming active under the influence of light.

PHOTOSENSITIZATION (n.): the fact of becoming sensitive to sunlight, accompanied by the development of dermatitis,* due to prolonged exposure to the sun after ingesting photodynamic substances.

PHYTOHEMAGGLUTININ (n.): a vegetable substance able to agglutinate red blood cells.

PHYTOTHERAPY (n.): the art of healing with plants.

PILL STORE (n.): "health food store" selling mainly vitamins, food supplements and other drugs, as well as prepackaged and often processed foods.

PIÑOLE (n.): (name of Spanish origin) a mixture of seeds from different plants, generally parched, then ground and made into a mush by North American Indians.

PLEURISY (n.): inflammation of the membranes enclosing the lungs.

POD (n.): a dry, dehiscent* fruit.

POLLEN (n.): a powder produced in the anthers* of a flower, made up of tiny grains containing the male element necessary to ensure fertilization. Pollen is an excellent food, rich in complete proteins, carbohydrates, vitamins (A, B, C, E), minerals, enzymes and other substances. It helps to tonify, detoxicate and balance the human organism.

POLLINATION (n.): the act of fertilizing a flower by transporting pollen to the stigma* of a pistil.

POLLINATOR (n.): an animal, generally an insect in our regions, that commonly ensures the pollination* of flowers.

POLYMER (n.): any of numerous natural or synthetic compounds, usually of high molecular weight, consisting of repeated linked units, each a relatively light and simple molecule.

POLYMORPHOUS (adj.): of variable shape.

POLYUNSATURATED (adj.): pertaining to long-chained carbon compounds, especially fats, having many unsaturated bonds. See FATTY ACIDS.

POULTICE (n.): a moist, soft mass of various adhesive substances (such as meal and clay), mixed or not with medicinal plant parts, and applied externally to warm, soothe or stimulate an aching or inflamed part of the body.

PROPOLIS (n.): a resinous, balsamic* substance gathered by bees on certain trees (especially poplars), which they use to insulate the hive and as a disinfectant.

PROTEIN (n.): any of a group of complex organic compounds containing amino acids* as their basic structural units, as well as nonprotidic substances. Term generally used as a synonym of protid.*

PROTEIN (COMPLETE): a protein containing the nine essential amino acids* indispensable to the human organism in a balanced ratio.

PROTID (n.): large-size molecule containing nitrogen that occurs in all living matter and is essential for the growth and repair of animal tissues. Protids include amino acids, peptids (condensation of several amino acid molecules) and proteins.*

PROVITAMIN A (n.): a precursor of vitamin A. See CAROTENE. Vitamin A probably does not occur in plants, but it is found in animals after transformation by the liver of the provitamin A in plants.

PSYCHOACTIVE (adj.): having an action on mental processes.

PUNGENT (adj.): having a hot, biting taste or smell.

PURGATIVE (n., adj.): causing evacuation of the bowels. A purgative has a more vigorous action than a laxative.*

QUININE (n.): a white, bitter alkaloid from the bark of *Cinchona* spp., used to fight malaria ($C_{20}H_{24}N_2O_{23}H_2O$).

RAPHIDE (n.): a needle-shaped crystal, often found in bundles in the tissues of some plants, like the Araceae.

RAY FLOWER (n.): the strap-shaped marginal florets (small flowers, usually in dense clusters) of many Asteraceae.

RECEPTACLE (n.): the expanded tip of a stem bearing the organs of a flower or the assembled florets (small flowers) of a head (dense cluster of sessile* flowers).

REFRIGERANT (n., adj.): having cooling properties.

RENAL (adj.): pertaining to the kidneys.

RESIN (n.): a viscous, flammable substance, usually with a strong balsamic* smell, found in various plants. Resin is not soluble in water.

REVULSIVE (n., adj.): causing a local irritation meant to stop an existing congestive state in another part of the body by drawing blood out of this zone.

RHEUMATISM (n.): any of several pathological conditions of the muscles, tendons, joints or bones, characterized by pain, inflammation and disability.

RHIZOME (n.): horizontal, subterranean stem, usually rooting at the nodes.*

ROOT (n.): a part of a plant bearing neither leaves nor reproductive organs and functioning mainly as an organ of absorption, food storage or mechanical support.

ROSETTE (n.): a cluster of closely assembled radiating leaves appearing to rise from the ground.

RUBEFACIENT (n., adj.): a local irritant,* producing redness of the skin.

SACCHAROSE (n.): a carbohydrate* often found in plants, which yields glucose* and levulose* by hydrolysis* ($C_{12}H_{22}O_{11}$). White cane or beet sugar is almost pure saccharose. It is also found in large amounts in maple syrup.

SALICYLIC ACID: a white crystalline acid, found as an ester* in various plants ($C_7H_6O_3$). It is used for making aspirin and colorings and as an analgesic.*

SALVE (n.): a medicinal ointment.*

SAMARA (n.): an indehiscent* winged fruit.

SAPONIN or SAPONOSIDE (n.): a glucoside* with foaming properties found in various plants. Saponin acts upon the permeability of membranes. High doses cause hemolysis* and are toxic. Several saponins are known. Some are digestive and depurative in small amounts.

SCAPE (n.): a leafless peduncle* arising from the ground and bearing one or more flowers at the top.

SCIATICA (n.): chronic nerve pain in the area of the hip or thigh.

SEDATIVE (n., adj.): having a soothing, calming or tranquilizing effect.

SEED (n.): a fertilized, ripened ovule* containing an embryo capable of developing into a new plant.

SELENIUM (n.): a nonmetallic element which certain plants can accumulate in relatively large amounts, symbol: Se. Plants containing significant quantities of selenium can cause cattle poisoning.

SEPAL (n.): one of the modified leaves forming the calyx.*

SEPTUM (n.): a partition.

SESSILE (adj.): without a stalk of any kind.

SHRUB (n.): a woody perennial, usually producing several stems from a common base (unlike a tree in this respect).

SIALAGOGUE (n., adj.): increasing the flow of saliva.

SICCATIVE (adj.): said of a drying oil.*

SILICLE (n.): a silique* less than twice as long as wide.

SILIQUE (n.): a dry, dehiscent* fruit, opening by two valves and more than twice as long as wide. Siliques and silicles are the characteristic fruits of Crucifers (Brassicaceae).

SOPORIFIC (adj.): producing sleep.

SORUS (pl. SORI) (n.): a group of spore cases found on the fertile fronds* of ferns.

SPADIX (n.): a spike* with a thick, fleshy axis, as in the Araceae.

SPATHE (n.): a large, leaf-like often colored bract surrounding the inflorescence, as in the Araceae.

SPECIES (n.): a group of individuals having similar characters and capable of interbreeding, transmitting the same characters to their offspring, whereas members of different species cannot usually interbreed or produce hybrids.*

SPIKE (n.): a flower cluster of many sessile* flowers closely arranged along an unbranched, elongated axis.

SPIKELET (n.): a small or secondary spike*; the unit of the inflorescences of grasses and sedges.

STAMEN (n.): one of the anther-bearing organs of a flower.

STAMINATE (adj.): said of a male flower bearing only stamens (having no ovary).

STARCH (n.): a carbohydrate found chiefly in the seeds, fruits, tubers and roots of plants $(C_6H_{10}O_5)n$. Starch is an important food reserve for plants and a source of energy for animals. It is commonly extracted from corn, potatoes and other plants in the form of a white, tasteless powder.

STIGMA (n.): the terminal portion of the pistil, modified for the reception and germination of the pollen.*

STIMULANT (n., adj.): increasing or quickening the functional processes taking place in the body.

STOLON (n.): a slender modified stem running along the ground and rooting at intervals.

STOMACHIC (n., adj.): strengthening or stimulating the stomach; promoting appetite and aiding digestion.

STYLE (n.): the usually slender portion of the pistil connecting stigma* and ovary.*

SUGAR (n.): any of a class of water-soluble crystalline carbohydrates* having a characteristically sweet taste. The most commonly used sugar is saccharose.*

SYCONIUM (n.): a collective fleshy false fruit, in which the ovaries are borne upon an enlarged hollow receptacle, as in the fig.

SYMBIOTIC (adj.): related to symbiosis: the close association between two different organisms that enables them to live with reciprocal advantages.

SYRUP (n.): a thick, sweet, sticky liquid, such as a concentrated sugar solution or the boiled sap of certain plants, maple in particular.

TANNIN (n.): any of various polymers* of the general formula $(C_{14}H_{10}O_9)n$ found in many plants. Tannins are strongly astringent* and precipitate albumin. They are used for tanning hides, as a mordant* in dyeing, as a counterpoison of alkaloids,* among other things.

TAPROOT (n.): a thick primary root, growing vertically in the ground, such as in the carrot.

TARTRIC ACID: organic acid found in various plants (COOH-CHOH-CHOH-COOH).

TAXONOMY (n.): the science of the laws of classification of organisms in categories, based upon common characteristics. Taxonomy is an effort to reflect evolution.

TENDRIL (n.): a thread-like, coiling modified leaf or stem by which a climbing plant clings to a support.

TENIFUGE or TENIAFUGE (n., adj.): expelling tapeworms.

THRESH (v.): to beat out grain from a plant, using a flail.

TONIC (n., adj.): invigorating specific organs or the entire system.

TORREFY (v.): to roast a seed, root and so on in order to enhance its flavor.

TUBER (n.): a swollen part of a commonly underground stem, having numerous buds from which new plants sprout.

TUBEROUS (adj.): tuber-like.

TYPE SPECIES: the species* upon which the genus* to which it belongs has been based.

ULCER (n.): an open sore on the skin or on an internal mucous surface of the body.

UMBEL (n.): an inflorescence in which the peduncles* or pedicels* of a cluster radiate from a common point at the top of the scape.*

UNGUENT (n.): see OINTMENT.

URTICATING (adj.): causing a burning sensation by contact with the skin, as in the case of nettles (*Urtica* spp.).

USDA: United States Department of Agriculture.

VANILLIN (n.): the fragrant active principle of vanilla ($C_8H_8O_3$).

VARIETY (n.): a subdivision of a species*; a group of similar individuals with particular characteristics but digressing insufficiently from other members of the species to entitle them to a specific rank.

VASCULAR (adj.): in our case, said of plants containing vessels organized for the circulation of the sap in their tissues.

VASOCONSTRICTOR (n.): a substance producing constriction of blood vessels, thus raising blood pressure.

VASODILATOR (n.): a substance producing dilatation of blood vessels, thus lowering blood pressure.

VERJUICE (n.): the expressed juice of unripe fruit, especially that of grapes. Verjuice is very acid and was formerly much used instead of vinegar.

VERMIFUGE (n., adj.): expelling worms.

VERTICILLATE (adj.): arranged in whorls, with three or more leaves or branches at a node.*

VESICANT (n., adj.): causing blisters.

VITAMIN (n.): any of various organic substances, of relatively complex structure, indispensable in very small amounts to the proper growth and functioning of the organism. The lack of specific vitamins produces characteristic diseases. The body must therefore be regularly furnished with these vitamins through food intake.

VULNERARY (n., adj.): healing wounds.

WAIF (n.): "stray" plant, introduced here and there out of its normal range but unable to establish itself and soon disappearing.

WEED (n.): "a plant, the uses of which are unknown," to paraphrase R. W. Emerson, or have been forgotten; a plant growing where humans would not like it to be and competing with cultivated plants; often a plant habituated to living with humans for centuries. Many "weeds" were formerly cultivated as vegetables.

WINNOW (v.): to fan grain free of chaff (husks).

YEAST (n.): (1) any of various unicellular fungi capable of fermenting carbohydrates. (2) a commercial preparation containing yeast cells, used as a leavening agent and in brewing beer. *Saccharomyces cerevisiae* is known as brewer's yeast. Rich in proteins, fats, carbohydrates, in vitamins B, D and E and in minerals, it is therefore commonly used as a food supplement. Certain pleasant-tasting strains make a good condiment.

Bibliography

Angier, Bradford. *Free for the Eating.* Harrisburg, Pa.: Stackpole, 1966.

——————. *More Free for the Eating Wild Foods.* Harrisburg, Pa.: Stackpole, 1969.

——————. *Feasting Free on Wild Edibles.* Harrisburg, Pa.: Stackpole, 1969.

——————. *Field Guide to Edible Wild Plants.* Harrisburg, Pa.: Stackpole, 1974.

Balls, Edward K. *Early Uses of California Plants.* Berkeley: University of California Press, 1970.

Beatty, Bill. *Bill and Bev Beatty's Wild Plant Cookbook.* Happy Camp, Calif.: Naturegraph, 1987.

Beedell, Suzanne. *Pick, Cook and Brew Food from the Hedgerow.* St. Albans, England: Mayflower, 1975.

Benoliel, Doug. *Northwest Foraging Guide to Edible Plants of Pacific Northwest.* Lynnwood, Wash.: Signpost, 1974.

Berglund, Berndt, & C. E. Bolsby. *The Edible Wild: A Complete Cookbook and Guide to the Edible Wild Plants in Canada and North America.* Toronto: Modern Canadian Library, 1974.

Black, Marmelade. *It's the Berries.* Seattle: Hancock House, 1977.

Blankinship, J. W. "Native Economic Plants of Montana." *Bulletin of the Montana Agric. Experim. Station,* 56 (1909): 1–38.

Boxer, Arabella. *Nature's Harvest.* Chicago: Henry Regnery Co., 1974.

Brackett, Babette, & Maryann Lash. *The Wild Gourmet: A Forager's Cookbook.* Boston: David R. Godine Publ., 1975.

Brill, Steven. *Shoots and Greens of Early Spring in Eastern North America*. Published by the author, Jamaica, N.Y., n.d.

——————, & Evelyn Dean. *Identifying and Harvesting Edible and Medicinal Plants in Wild (and Not So Wild) Places*. New York: Hearst Books, 1994.

Brown, Tom. *Tom Brown's Guide to Wild Edible and Medicinal Plants*. New York: Berkley Books, 1985.

Brugge, D. "Navajo Use of Agave." *Kiva* 31, no. 2 (1965): 88–98.

Burgess, R. L. "Utilization of Desert Plants by Native People. Contribution committee on desert and arid zone research." *Bulletin of the American Association for the Advancement of Science*, 8 (1966): 6–21.

Burlage, Henry M. *Index of Plants of Texas with Reputed Medicinal and Poisonous Properties*. Austin, Tex.: n.p., 1968.

Burns, Ken. "Cooking with Wild Foods." *East-West Journal*. Boston: n.p., 1982.

Cameron, T. *The Wild Foods of Great Britain*. Chalmington, England: Prism Press, 1977.

Ceres. *Free for All: Weeds and Wild Plants as Source of Food*. N.p.: Thorsons, 1977.

Chase, Myron. *Field Guide to Edible and Useful Wild Plants of North America*. N.p.: Red Wing, 1965.

Cheatham, Scooter, & Marshall C. Johnston. *The Useful Wild Plants of Texas, the Southeastern and Southwestern United States, the Southern Plains and Northern Mexico*, vol. 1. Austin, Tex.: Useful Wild Plants, Inc., 1995.

Chesnut, V. K. *Plants Used by the Indians of Mendocino County, California*. Fort Bragg, Calif.: Mendocino County Hist. Society, 1974.

Christensen, Alma. *For Soul and Kitchen: Wild Food Cookbook*. Pine River, Minn.: published by the author, 1993.

Churchill, James E. "Food Without Farming." *Mother Earth News*, July, 1972.

Clarke, Charlotte Bringle. *Edible and Useful Plants of California*. Berkeley: University of California Press, 1977.

Coffey, Timothy. *The History and Folklore of North American Wildflowers*. Boston: Houghton Mifflin, 1993.

Cogle, Jeanette. *A Field Guide to the Common and Interesting Plants of Baja California*. La Jolla, Calif.: Natural History Pub. Co., 1975.

Cohen, Russ. "'Shooting' for Your Supper: How to Develop Intimate Relationships with Wild Plants by Eating Them." *Massachusetts Wildlife*, Spring 1995.

Coon, Nelson. *Using Wild and Wayside Plants*. New York: Dover, 1980.

Cooper, Marion R. *Poisonous Plants in Britain and Their Effects on Animals and Man*. Ministry of Agriculture, Fisheries and Food, Reference Book 161. London: Her Majesty's Stationery Office, 1984.

Cox, Kathryn. *Pocket Guide to Wild Edible and Medicinal Plants*. Laporte, Colo.: Motherlove Herbal, 1996.

Cronquist, Arthur. *The Evolution and Classification of Flowering Plants*. Boston: Houghton Mifflin, 1968.

——————. *An Integrated System of Classification of Flowering Plants*. New York: Columbia University Press, 1981.

Crowhurst, Adrienne. *The Weed Cookbook*. New York: Lancer Books, 1972.

——————. *The Flower Cookbook*. New York: Lancet Books, n.d.

Dall, W. H. "Useful Indigenous Alaskan Plants." *Report of the Department of Agriculture*. Washington, D.C.: USDA, 1868, pp. 172–89.

Densmore, Frances. *How Indians Use Wild Plants for Food, Medicine and Lore*. New York: Dover, 1974.

Derby, Blanche Cybele. *My Wild Friends: Free Food from Field and Forest*. Northampton, Mass.: White Star Press, 1997.

Dore, William G. *Wild Rice*. Ottawa: Queen's Printer, 1969.

Douglas, James Sholto. *Alternative Foods: A World Guide to Lesser-Known Edible Plants*. London: Pelham Books, 1978.

Duke, James A. *Handbook of Edible Weeds*. Boca Raton, Fla.: CRC Press, 1992.

——————. *Handbook of Phytochemical Constituents of GRAS Herbs and Other Economic Plants*. Boca Raton, Fla.: CRC Press, 1992.

Ebeling, Walter. *Handbook of Indian Food and Fibers of Arid America*. Berkeley: University of California Press, 1986.

Eley, Geoffrey. *Wild Fruit and Nuts*. Yorkshire, England: EP Publishing, 1976.

Elias, Thomas S., & Peter A. Dykeman. *Field Guide to North American Edible Wild Plants*. Outdoor Life Books, New York: Van Nostrand Reinhold Co., 1982.

Elliott, Doug. *Wild Roots: A Forager's Guide to the Edible and Medicinal Roots, Tubers, Corms and Rhizomes of North America*. Rochester, Vt.: Healing Arts Press, 1995.

Ellis, Carlyle. "Wild Vegetables of the Desert Indians." *Primitive Man*, no. 3 (1941): 9–10.

Environmentarian newsletter (monthly magazine). Edited by Linda Runyon. Newport Beach, Calif.: Wild Foods Co., Inc., 1988–1995.

Fernald, M., & A. C. Kinsey. *Edible Wild Plants of Eastern North America*, revised by R. C. Rollins. New York: Harper & Row, 1958.

Firth, Grace. *A Natural Year.* New York: Simon & Schuster, 1972.

Forey, Pamela, & Cecilia Fitzsimmons. *Edible Plants*, N.p.: Atlantis Publications, 1990.

Freethy, Ron. *From Agar to Zenry, a Book of Plant Uses, Names and Folklore.* Ramsbury, England: Crowood Press, 1985.

Freitus, Joe. *160 Edible Plants Commonly Found in the U.S. and Canada.* Boston: Stone Wall Press, 1975.

————. *Wild Preserves, Illustrated Recipes for Over 100 Natural Jams and Jellies.* Boston: Stone Wall Press, 1977.

Furlong, Marjorie, & Virginia Dill. *Wild Edible Fruits and Berries.* Healdsburg, Calif.: Naturegraph, 1974.

Gaertner. *Harvest Without Planting: Eating and Nibbling Off the Land.* Published by the author, Chalk River, Ontario, 1967.

Gail, Peter A. *The Dandelion Celebration: A Guide to Unexpected Cuisine.* Cleveland: Goosefoot Acres Press, 1994.

Garrett, Blanche Pownall. *A Taste of the Wild.* Toronto: Lorimer, 1975.

Gearing, Catherine. *Field Guide to Wilderness Living.* N.p.: Southern Publishers Assoc., 1973.

George, Jean Craighead. *The Wild, Wild Cookbook: A Guide for Young Wild-Food Foragers.* New York: Thomas Y. Crowell, 1982.

————. *Acorn Pancakes, Dandelion Salad and 38 Other Recipes.* New York: Harper-Collins, 1995.

Gibbons, Euell. *Stalking the Wild Asparagus.* New York: McKay, 1962.

————. *Stalking the Blue-Eyed Scallop.* New York: McKay, 1964.

————. *Stalking the Healthful Herbs.* New York: McKay, 1966.

————. *Stalking the Good Life.* New York: McKay, 1971.

————. *Handbook of Edible Wild Plants.* N.p.: Donning Press, 1979.

Gillespie. *Compilation of the Edible Plants of West Virginia.* New York: Scholar's Library, 1959.

Gray, Patience. *Honey from a Weed: Feasting and Fasting in Tuscany, Catalogna, the Cyclades and Apulia*. London: Papermac, 1987.

Hall, Allan. *The Wild Food Trailguide*. New York: Holt, Rinehart & Winston, 1976.

Hamel, Paul B., & Marie U. Chiltoskey. *Cherokee Plants and Their Uses: A 400-Year History*. Sylva, N.C.: Herald Publishing Company, 1975.

Hardin, J. W. *Human Poisoning from Native and Cultivated Plants*. Durham, N.C.: Duke University Press, 1969.

Harrington, Harold D. *Edible Plants of the Rocky Mountains*. Albuquerque: University of New Mexico Press, 1967.

—————. *Western Edible Plants*. Albuquerque: University of New Mexico Press, 1972.

Harris, Ben C. *Eat the Weeds*. New Canaan, Conn.: Keats Publishing, Inc., 1995.

Hatfield, Audrey W. *Pleasures of Wild Plants*. London: Museum Press, 1966.

—————. *How to Enjoy Your Weeds*. N.p.: Muller, 1974.

Hedrick, U. P. *Sturtevant's Edible Plants of the World*. New York: Dover, 1972.

Heller, Christine. "Wild Edible and Poisonous Plants of Alaska." *University of Alaska Extension Bulletin*, no. 40 (1958).

Hicks, Sam. *Desert Plants and People*. San Antonio, Tex.: Naylor Co., 1968.

Hill, Jason. *Wild Foods of Britain*. London: Adam & Charles Black, 1944.

Hitchcock, Susan Tyler, & G. B. McIntosh. *Gather Ye Wild Things: A Forager's Year*. Charlottesville: University Press of Virginia, 1995.

Hough, W. "The Pulque of Mexico." *Proceeds of the U.S. National Museum*, no. 33 (1908): 577–92.

Hutchens, Alma R. *Indian Herbalogy of North America*. Windsor, Ontario: Merco Publishers, 1969.

Hvass, Else. *Plants That Feed and Serve Us*. London: Blandford, 1973.

James, W. R. *Know Your Poisonous Plants*. Healdsburg, Calif.: Naturegraph, 1973.

Jason, Dan. *Your Own Food: A Forager's Guide*. Vancouver, B.C.: Intermedia, 1979.

————— & Nancy. *Some Useful Wild Plants*. Vancouver, B.C.: Talonbooks, 1975.

Johnson. *The Useful Plants of Great Britain*. London: n.p., 1862.

Jones, V. H. "The Bark of Bittersweet as an Emergency Food." In *Michigan Archaeological Bulletin* 11 (3–4): 170–80.

Kavash, Barrie. *Native Harvests, Recipes and Botanicals of American Indians*. New York: Random House, 1979.

——————. *Guide to Northeastern Wild Edibles*. Surrey, B.C.: Hancock House, 1994.

Kinghorn, Douglas. *Toxic Plants*. New York: Columbia University Press, 1979.

Kingsbury, John M. *Poisonous Plants of the United States and Canada*. Englewood Cliffs, N.J.: Prentice Hall, 1964.

——————. *Deadly Harvest: A Guide to Common Poisonous Plants*. New York: Holt, Rinehart & Winston, 1965.

Kirk, Donald. *Wild Edible Plants of the Western United States*. Happy Camp, Calif.: Naturegraph, 1975.

Kluger, Marilyn. *The Wild Flavor*. Los Angeles: Jeremy P. Tarcher Co., 1984.

Kunkel, Günther. *Plants for Human Consumption*. Koenigstein, Denmark: Koeltz Sientific Books, 1984.

Lanner, Ronald. *The Pinion Pine: A Natural and Cultural History*. Reno: University of Nevada Press, 1981.

Launert, Edmund. *Edible and Medicinal Plants of Britain and Northern Europe*. Hamlyn, England: Country Life Books, 1984.

Lee, Deborah. *Exploring Nature's Uncultivated Garden*. Tacoma Park, Md.: Havelin Communications, 1989.

Loewenfeld, C., P. Bach, & P. Bosanquet. *Britain's Wild Larder*. Newton Abbot, England: David & Charles, n.d.

Lucas, J. M. *Indian Harvest, Wild Food Plants of North America*. Philadelphia: Lippincott, 1945.

Lust, John. *The Herb Book*. New York: Bantam Books, 1974.

Lyle, Katie Letcher. *The Foraging Gourmet*. New York: Lyons and Burford, 1997.

Lyle Kalças, Evelyn. *Food from the Fields: Edible Wild Plants of Egean Turkey*. Izmir: Birlik Matbaasi, 1974.

Lynas, L. *Medicinal and Food Plants of the North American Indian*. Bronx, N.Y.: New York Botanical Garden, 1972.

Mabey, Richard. *Food for Free: A Guide to the Edible Wild Plants of Britain*. London: Collins, 1972.

——————. *Plants with a Purpose: A Guide to the Everyday Uses of Wild Plants*. Glasgow: Fontana/Collins, 1979.

Manning, D., & D. & N. Jason. *Some Useful Wild Plants*. Vancouver, B.C.: Talon Books, n.d.

Maurice, H. A. "Some Wild Food Plants of the Indians." *Quarterly Bulletin of the Archaeological Society of Virginia* 4, no. 3 (1960), 8–10.

McPherson, Alan & Sue. *Wild Food Plants of Indiana and Adjacent States*. Bloomington, Ind.: Indiana University Press, 1977.

Medsger, Oliver Perry. *Edible Wild Plants*. New York: Macmillan, 1972.

Mellinger, Marie. *Roadside Rambles*. N.p.: n.d.

Menzies, Rob. *The Herbal Dinner: A Renaissance of Cooking*. Millbrae, Calif.: Celestial Arts, 1977.

Meuninck, Jim. *The Basic Essentials of Edible Wild Plants and Useful Herbs*. Merrillville, Ind.: ICS Books, 1988.

Michael, Pamela. *A Country Harvest: An Illustrated Guide to Herbs and Wild Plants*. London: Peerage Books, 1986.

Miller, Ann. *Wild Foods Delights*. Published by the author, Baldwinsville, N.Y., n.d.

Mohney, Russ. *Why Wild Edibles? The Joys of Finding, Fixing and Tasting*. Seattle: Pacific Search, 1972.

Morton, Julia F. "Principal Wild Food Plants of the United States Excluding Alaska and Hawaii." *Economic Botany* 17, no. 4 (1963): 319–20.

————. *Wild Plants for Survival in S. Florida*. Miami, Fla.: Hurricane House, 1968.

Muenscher, Walter Conrad. *Poisonous Plants of the United States*. New York: Macmillan, 1962.

Murphey, Edith Van Allen. *Indian Uses of Native Plants*. Ukiah, Calif.: Mendocino Co. Historical Society, 1987.

Nabhan, Gary Paul. *Gathering the Desert*. Tucson: University of Arizona Press, 1985.

Naegele, Thomas. *Edible and Medicinal Plants of the Great Lakes*. Davidsburg, Mich.: Wilderness Books, 1996.

National Research Council. *Amaranth: Modern Prospects for an Ancient Crop*. Emmaus, Pa.: Rodale Press, 1985.

Nequakewa, E. "Some Hopi Recipes for the Preparation of Wild Plant Foods." *Plateau*, no. 18 (1943): 18–20.

Newberry, John S. "Food and Fiber Plants of North American Indians." *Popular Science Monthly*, no. 32 (1887): 31–46.

Niethammer, Carolyn. *American Indian Food and Lore*. New York: Collier-McMillan, n.d.

North, Pamela. *Poisonous Plants and Fungi in Colour*. Poole, Dorset, England: Blandford Press, 1967.

Nuttall, Z. "The Gardens of Ancient Mexico." *Annual Report of the Smithsonian Institution* (1923): 453–64.

Nyerges, Christopher. *Guide to Wild Foods: In the Footsteps of Our Ancestors*. Los Angeles: Survival News Service, 1995.

Nyerges, Dolores. *Why Eat Wild Food?* Los Angeles: School of Self-Reliance, 1995.

O'Ceirin, Cyril & Kit. *Wild and Free: 100 Recipes and Folklore of Nature's Harvest*. Dublin: O'Brien Press, 1978.

Oswald, F. *The Ranger's Guide to Useful Plants of the Eastern Wilds*. Boston: Christopher, 1964.

Pammel, L. H. *A Manual of Poisonous Plants*. Cedar Rapids, Iowa: Torch Press, 1911.

Parke, G. *Going Wild in the Kitchen*. New York: McKay, 1965.

Paterson, Wilma. *A Country Cup: Old and New Recipes for Drinks of All Kinds Made from Wild Plants and Herbs*. London: Pelham Books, 1980.

Peterson, Lee. *A Field Guide to Edible Wild Plants of Eastern and Central North America*. Boston: Houghton Mifflin, 1978.

Phillips, Roger. *Wild Food: A Unique Photographic Guide to Finding, Cooking and Eating Wild Plants, Mushrooms and Seaweeds*. London: Pan Books, 1983.

Plant Deck. *Edible and Poisonous Plants of the Eastern States*. Lake Oswego, Ore.: Plant Deck, Inc., n.d.

——————. *Edible and Poisonous Plants of the Western States*. Lake Oswego, Ore.: Plant Deck, Inc., n.d.

Porsild, A. E. "Edible Plants of the Arctic." *Arctic* 6, no. 1: 15–34.

Roos-Collins, Marget. *Wild Greens of the Bay Area*. Berkeley, Calif.: Heyday Publishers, 1990.

Ross Russell, Helen. *Foraging for Dinner*. N.p.: Thomas Nelson Inc., 1975.

Runyon, Linda. *A Survival Acre*. Published by the author, Indian Lake, N.Y., 1982.

——————. *Wild Cards*. Published by the author, Indian Lake, N.Y., 1986.

——————. *Wild Foods Nutritional Wheel*. Phoenix, Ariz.: Wild Foods Company, 1997.

—————. *Backyard Wild Food Recipes*. Phoenix: Professional Scribe, 1997.

Saunders, Charles Francis. *Edible and Useful Wild Plants of the United States and Canada*. New York: Dover Publications, 1976.

Schofield, Janice J. *Discovering Wild Plants: Alaska, Western Canada and Pacific Northwest*. Anchorage: Alaska Northwest Books, 1989.

Scoones, Ian, Mary Melnyk, & Jules Pretty. *The Hidden Harvest: Wild Foods and Agricultural Systems, a Literature Review*. London: Sustainable Agriculture Program, 1992.

Seymour, John. *Complete Book of Self-Sufficiency*. N.p.: Faber, 1978.

Silverman, Maida. *A City Herbal*. Woodstock, N.Y.: Ash Tree Publishing, 1997.

Soothill, Eric. *Nature's Wild Harvest*. Poole, Dorset, England: Blandford Press, 1983.

Squier, Tom. *Living Off the Land*. N.p.: n.d.

Stewart, A. M., & L. Kronoff. *Eating from the Wild*. New York: Ballantine, 1975.

Sweet, Muriel. *Common Edible and Useful Plants of the West*. Happy Camp, Calif.: Naturegraph Publishers, 1976.

Szczawinski, Adam F. *Edible Garden Weeds of Canada*. Ottawa: National Museums of Canada, 1978.

—————. *Wild Coffee and Tea Substitutes of Canada*. Ottawa: National Museums of Canada, 1978.

—————. *Wild Fruits and Nuts of Canada*. Ottawa: National Museums of Canada, 1979.

—————. *Edible Wild Greens of Canada*. Ottawa: National Museums of Canada, 1980.

————— & G. A. Hardy. *Guide to Common Edible Plants of British Columbia*. Victoria, B.C.: Provincial Museum Handbook, no. 20, n.d.

Tampion, John. *Dangerous Plants*. London: David & Charles, Newton Abbot, 1977.

Tanaka, Tyôzaburô. *Tanaka's Cyclopedia of the Edible Plants of the World*, edited by Sasuke Nakao. Tokyo: Keigaku, 1976.

Tatum, Billy Joe. *Billy Joe Tatum's Wild Foods Cookbook and Field Guide*, edited by Helen Witty. New York: Workman Publishing Co., 1976.

Taylor, Sharon, & Joan Elk. *Eat the Weeds at Your Feet: An Edible Plant Guide of Sonoma County*. Citrus Heights, Calif.: Rose of Sharon Press, 1994.

Thompson, Steven & Mary. *Wild Food Plants of the Sierras*. Berkeley, Calif.: Dragtooth Press, 1972.

Tokin, Jack. *A Taste of the Wild*. N.p.: Hallmark Editions, 1974.

Tonikel, John. *Edible Wild Plants of Pennsylvania and New York*. Elgin, Pa.: Allegheny Press, 1973.

Tull, Delena. *A Practical Guide to Edible and Useful Plants*. Austin: Texas Monthly Press, 1987.

Turner, Nancy. *Food Plants of British Columbia Indians*: Vol. 1, *Coastal Peoples*, Vol. 2, *Interior Peoples B.C.* Victoria, B.C.: Provincial Museum Handbooks, 1978.

——————. *Thompson Ethnobotany, Knowledge and Usage of Plants by the Thompson Indians of British Columbia*. Victoria, B.C.: Royal B.C. Museum, 1990.

——————. *Food Plants of Coastal First Peoples*. Victoria, B.C.: Royal B.C. Museum, 1995.

—————— & Harriot V. Kuhnlein. *Traditional Plant Foods of Canadian Indigenous Peoples: Nutrition, Botany and Use*. N.p.: Gordon & Breech, 1991.

—————— & Adam F. Szczawinski. *Common Poisonous Plants and Mushrooms*. Portland, Ore.: Timber Press (Dioscorides), 1995.

Underhill, J. E. *Wild Berries of the Pacific Northwest*. Seattle: Hancock House, 1974.

Uphof, J. C.Th. *Dictionary of Economic Plants*. Lehre, Germany: J. Cramer, 1968.

Urghart, Judy. *Food from the Wild*. London: Penny Pinchers, David & Charles, 1978.

Usher, Georges. *A Dictionary of Plants Used by Man*. London: Constable, 1976.

Von Reis Altschul, Siri. *Drugs and Foods from Little-Known Plants*. Cambridge, Mass.: Harvard University Press, 1973.

—————— & Frank J. Lipp. *New Plant Sources for Drugs and Foods*. Cambridge, Mass.: Harvard University Press, 1982.

Waugh, F. W. "Iroquois Food and Food Preparation." *Anthropological Series*, Memoir 86, no. 12. Ottawa: Canada Dept. of Mines and Geological Survey, 1916.

Weiner, Michael A. *Earth Medicine, Earth Food: Plant Remedies, Drugs & Natural Foods of the North American Indian*. New York: Collier Books, 1980.

Wigginton, Eliot, et al. *Foxfire 2: Ghost Stories, Spring Wild Plant Foods, Spinning and Weaving, Etc.* Garden City, N.Y.: Anchor Books, 1973.

——————, et al. *Foxfire 3: Animal Care, Banjos and Dulcimers, Summer and Fall Wild Plant Foods, Etc.* New York: Anchor Books, 1975.

Wild Foods Forum (monthly magazine). Edited by Vickie Shufer. Virginia Beach, Va., 1989–1998.

Williams, Kim. *Eating Wild Plants*. Missoula, Mont.: Mountain Press Publishing Co., 1984.

Williamson, Darcy. *The Rocky Mountains Wild Foods Cookbook*. Caldwell, Idaho: Caxton Printers, Ltd., 1995.

Wilson, T. "The Use of Wild Plants as Food by the Indian." *Ottawa Nat.*, no. 30 (1916): 17–21.

Wittock, M. A. & G. L. "Food Plants of the Indians." *Journal of the N.Y. Botanical Garden*, no. 43 (1942): 53–71.

Wood, Edelene. *A Taste of the Wild*. Elgin, Pa.: Allegheny Press, 1990.

Yanowsky, Elias. *Food Plants of the North American Indians*. Washington, D.C.: USDA Miscellaneous Publications, 1936.

Young, Kay. *Wild Seasons: Gathering and Cooking Wild Plants of the Great Plains*. Lincoln: University of Nebraska Press, 1993.

Plant Index 🌿

Afterword

I would like to tell you briefly the story of this book. It all started about thirty years ago. After living a rather intense city life in Paris, playing more music than I could handle, I had to leave in order to stay alive. What saved me was engulfing myself in the endless world of wild edible plants, which I had started exploring as a child with my parents in the French Alps. Then, picking a fragrant mushroom or a juicy wild raspberry was sheer magic. And the magic worked again on me years later.

I had the chance to study plants with an eighty-year-old botanist who was also a poet, writing beautiful sonnets about the flowers of the Vosges Mountains in Eastern France. He gave me a strong base to work from. At the same time I learned the edible uses of plants with an old uncle of mine in Provence (he was also in his eighties and had been a vegetarian for over forty years) with whom I stayed for a while. Then I started experimenting on my own, reading the few books then available, interviewing people who still knew the plants (mostly older people in the country and in the mountains) and cooking "wild dinners" for my friends who were trustful enough to try my strange concoctions.

After spending a year in Corsica, where gathering wild plants for food has long been a tradition, I crossed the ocean and came to America. There I discovered a lot of new plants, who soon became my friends, and I learned about their traditional uses by Indians and early settlers. I had the chance to stay for a while with different Indian tribes in Arizona, California, New Mexico and North Carolina. I also spent a lot of time in the woods with very little in my backpack, finding my food in the plants I gathered. Going back to civilization from time to time, I cooked wild dinners for my friends with the plants I picked, using my background in French cooking to create some rather unusual dishes. I even worked as a cook for a while in Oregon, but freedom was my leitmotiv so it wasn't long before I quit.

I soon started setting up workshops, mostly on the West Coast, teaching people which plants to use and how to fix them. It was a lot of fun and a great way to share. By then I had been taking notes on my experiments for quite a few years, and opportunities to add to them came almost daily. I soon started organizing them into what became the first draft of this book, completing my field notes by studying all the literature I could lay my hands on in libraries and bookstores.

As *The Encyclopedia of Edible Plants of North America* started taking shape, Buzz Erikson, co-owner of Ross-Erikson Publishing Company in Santa Barbara, Calif., offered to publish it. Buzz soon became my friend and offered much valuable advice and support, as my project was definitely an ambitious one. I must admit I was rather unstable at the time, moving throughout the country, from the Sierras to the Appalachians, from Washington state down to Mexico, spending a lot of time attending healing festivals in between my workshops and numerous hikes in forests, deserts and mountains. I was not yet ready to publish the book.

I happened to have the opportunity to go back to Europe, which my girlfriend wanted to discover. She fell in love with France and we decided to stay. I set up workshops there, and people were ready for them. I had pretty much the whole scene to myself, and it soon picked up speed. I was approached by a French publisher who asked me to write an encyclopedia of the edible plants of Europe. The book was soon published in three separate volumes. By then I felt I could finish writing my American encyclopedia, which I did. Unfortunately, my friend Buzz, who had been sick for a while, died while I concentrated on my European endeavors.

I published more books in France and Switzerland in French and German; to date, sixteen have come out. I developed my "wild gastronomy" workshops and a "soft" concept of survival trips, bought a large chunk of land in the mountains of Southern France and started working at the National Museum of Natural History in Paris, where I received my Ph.D. in paleoethnobotany and was encouraged to continue my studies by some of the most renowned scientists in France.

Not only scientists, but also French chefs started showing an interest in wild plants. Several of them read my books or even joined the organization I created to promote wild foods. I was in demand in France, Switzerland, Germany as well as in the United States to show top-rated cooks which plants to use and how. I found lots of pleasure in this work. Using wild plants, chef Michel Bras in Laguiole was awarded two stars Michelin, and Marc Veyrat, who was to become a very close friend, received three stars, the highest distinction given by the world-famous guide. He was also elected French chef of the year in 1995. In New York, I connected with chef Jean-Georges Vongerichten by taking him on an herb walk in Central Park. In his words: "There are only so many different fishes I can find, but the world of wild edible plants is endless." He was granted four stars by *The New York Times* for the new restaurant he opened on Columbus Circle where his menus include wild plants.

During one of my visits to New York, I had the chance to meet Norman Goldfind of Keats Publishing Co. in New Canaan, Conn., to whom I sent a synopsis of this encyclopedia. After seeing the manuscript, he immediately agreed to publish it. I will always be grateful to him for ensuring publication of this book, some twenty-five years after I started writing it.

My travels continue. One of my next projects is an encyclopedia of the edible plants of the world, which I want to illustrate with my own pictures. I still give many lectures and seminars in various countries, write articles and enjoy working with chefs. At the same time, I raise my two young children, who love to eat wild plants, with my wife on a farm in Switzerland. It's a good life.

I do hope you enjoy this book. If you have any information on wild edible plants, any criticism or suggestion, if you want to know about the workshops I lead in North America, Europe or elsewhere around the world or simply want to get in touch, please contact me. Your input will be most valuable and will help update and improve this book.

François Couplan
CH-1692 Massonnens
Switzerland
Phone + fax: 011.41.26.653.1978

Or c/o my publisher:
Keats Publishing Co.
27 Pine St. (P.O. Box 876)
New Canaan, CT 06840-0876

About the Author ❧

François Couplan, ethnobotanist (Ph.D., Docteur ès-Sciences), was born in Paris in 1950. He has been teaching the uses of plants since 1975 in the United States and Europe. To his scientific training he adds a deep personal experience of living with nature, which he has explored on all continents.

François Couplan lived in the United States for ten years beginning in 1974 and traveled extensively across the North American continent where he spent time with different Indian tribes. Couplan started giving seminars on wild edible plants in 1975 on the West and East Coasts.

He is a successful writer in Europe, with seventeen books published to date in French and German, including *The Encyclopedia of the Edible Plants of Europe* in three volumes. He also writes regular columns in major French and Swiss nature and health magazines. In addition, he is a professional photographer and illustrates most of his books and articles.

François Couplan is currently working on the diet of our Paleolithic forebears at the National Museum of Natural History in Paris (Institut de Paléontologie Humaine), which expands on his Ph.D. thesis. He also works with several top chefs in France, Germany and the United States to help them incorporate wild plants into their menus.

Nowadays, François Couplan spends much of his time in Paris, in the south of France and on a farm in Switzerland when he is not traveling somewhere in Africa, Central America or Southeastern Asia looking for new plants and new people to learn from.